MARK BAUER

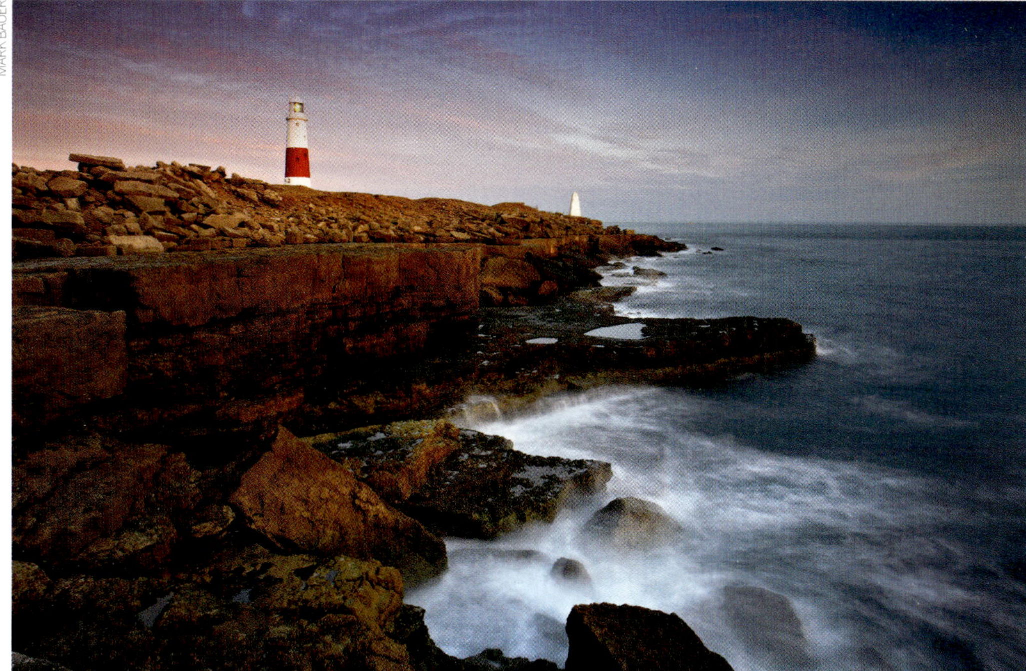

Welcome...

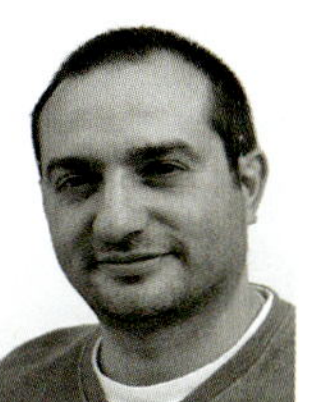

"Heading out to the great outdoors to capture stunning images is a passion shared by millions of photographers from novices through to enthusiasts and professionals. Heading to a location, where we wait prepared for that fleeting moment where all the elements come together to bless us with an incredible scene, is what draws so many of us to landscape photography. Of course when that moment arrives, you need to know what to do to ensure you capture the scene to its maximum potential. *The Essential Guide to Landscape Photography* provides all the information, advice and inspiration that you need to take great landscape images. This guide is packed with expert guidance from some of the UK's most successful and popular outdoor photographers. Our emphasis is on in-camera techniques, in other words, how to develop your creative eye and master your digital SLR, but we also cover the key Photoshop techniques and tools you need to add that final touch of class to your images. We hope this guide helps you improve how you compose a scene so you can shoot landscape images like a pro. All the best!"

DANIEL LEZANO, EDITOR

Meet our landscape experts

All our experts are regular contributors to *Digital SLR Photography* magazine. For expert advice and inspiration to help you improve your photo skills, pick up the latest issue, available on the second Tuesday of every month. For further information, visit: www.digitalslrphoto.com

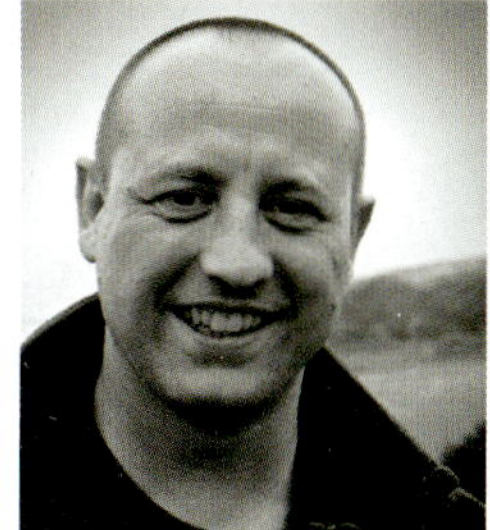

MARK BAUER

Former teacher Mark is now one of the UK's leading landscape photographers and an expert on Dorset's Jurassic coastline and the New Forest.

www.markbauerphotography.com

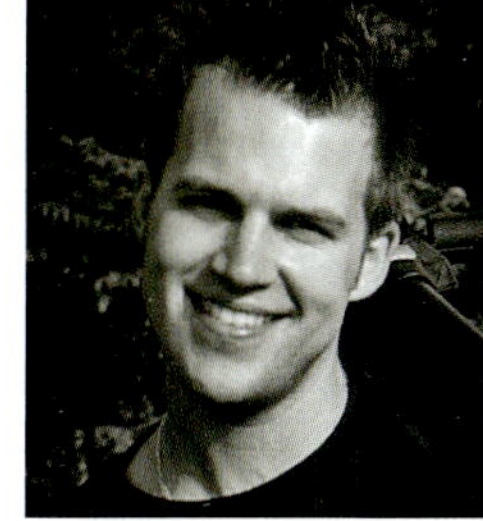

ROSS HODDINOTT

Ross is an award-winning photographer with many years of experience capturing the diverse beauty of the Britain's landscapes and wildlife.

www.rosshoddinott.co.uk

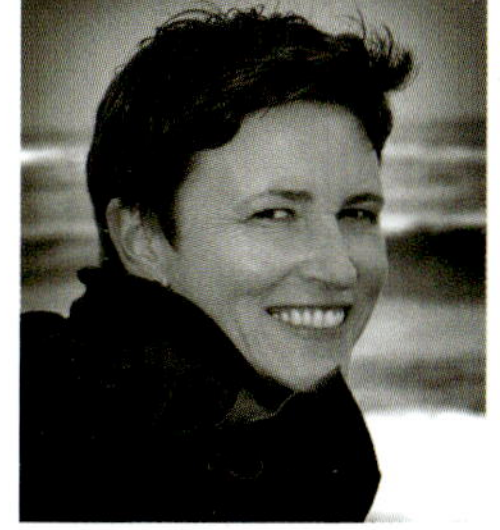

HELEN DIXON

Helen is living the dream, having given up a full-time job to become a professional landscape photographer. She is one of the UK's brightest talents.

www.helendixonphotography.co.uk

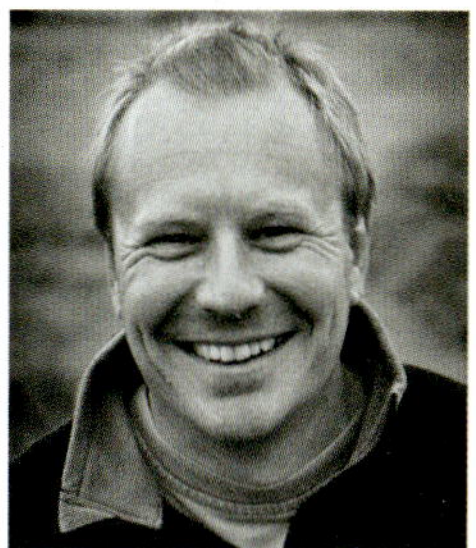

LEE FROST

A pro for two decades, Lee Frost's one of the best-known names in the UK photography business, with 20 books to his name and worldwide image sales.

www.leefrost.co.uk

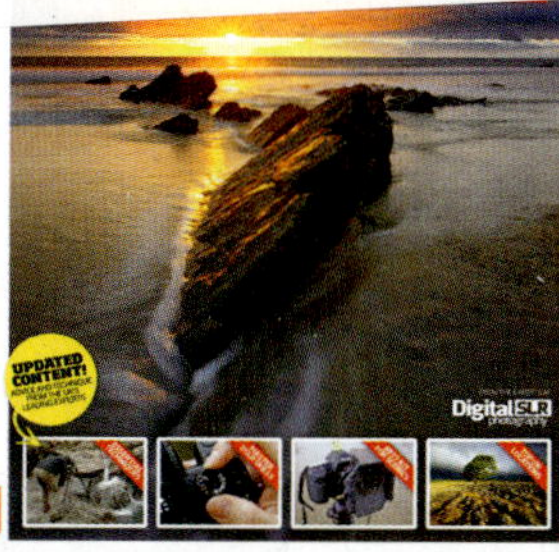

EN DIXON

The Essential Guide to Landscape Photography

Produced by *Digital SLR Photography* at:
6 Swan Court, Cygnet Park,
Peterborough, Cambs PE7 8GX
Phone: 01733 567401. Fax 01733 352650
Email: enquiries@digitalslrphoto.com
Online: www.digitalslrphoto.com

Editorial

To contact editorial phone: 01733 567401

Editor **Daniel Lezano**
daniel_lezano@dennis.co.uk

Art Editor **Luke Marsh**
luke_marsh@dennis.co.uk

Editorial Co-ordinator **Jo Lezano**
jo_lezano@dennis.co.uk

Editorial contributors:
Ross Armstrong, Mark Bauer, Adam Burton, Helen Dixon, Lee Frost, Matty Graham, Ross Hoddinott, Joanna Marsh, John Patrick & Caroline Wilkinson

Advertising & Production

To contact advertising phone: 01733 293913
Display & Classifield Sales: 0207 907 6651

Advertising Director **Natasha Blatcher**
natasha_blatcher@dennis.co.uk

Advertising Sales **Guy Scott-Wilson**
guy_scott-wilson@dennis.co.uk

Production Controller **Dan Stark**
dan_stark@dennis.co.uk

Publishing & Marketing

NICKY BAKER DIGITAL PRODUCTION MANAGER
DHARMESH MISTRY BOOKAZINE MANAGER
ROBIN RYAN PRODUCTION DIRECTOR
JULIAN LLOYD-EVANS MD OF ADVERTISING
MARTIN BELSON NEWSTRADE DIRECTOR
BRETT REYNOLDS CHIEF OPERATING OFFICER
IAN LEGGETT GROUP FINANCE DIRECTOR
JAMES TYE CHIEF EXECUTIVE
FELIX DENNIS CHAIRMAN

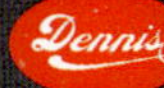

The Essential Guide to Landscape Photography ISBN
Printed by Benham Goodhead Print (BGP)

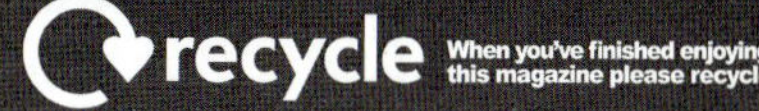

THE ESSENTIAL GUIDE TO LANDSCAPE PHOTOGRAPHY

CONTENTS

007 Introduction to landscapes
Be prepared to learn and exploit the fundamentals of landscape photography

008 Composition
We reveal the key techniques you'll need to master to take perfectly-exposed landscapes
014 EXPERT TUTORIAL: USING LEAD-IN LINES
016 EXPERT TUTORIAL: FOREGROUND INTEREST

019 Exposure
Master these simple techniques and your handling of light levels will be right every time
024 EXPERT TUTORIAL: APERTURE-PRIORITY
026 EXPERT TUTORIAL: SHUTTER SPEEDS
028 PHOTOSHOP TUTORIAL: RAW FILES

031 Sharpness
The best techniques for super-sharp scenes
032 EXPERT TUTORIAL: HYPERFOCAL FOCUSING
034 EXPERT TUTORIAL: FOCUS FOR SHARPNESS
038 EXPERT TUTORIAL: SHAKE-FREE IMAGES

040 Lighting
Predict and exploit the best lighting
046 EXPERT TUTORIAL: TIME OF DAY
048 EXPERT TUTORIAL: MAGIC HOUR & SUNSETS
050 EXPERT TUTORIAL: MISTY MORNINGS
052 EXPERT TUTORIAL: TWILIGHT SEASCAPES
054 EXPERT TUTORIAL: STAR TRAILS

057 Filters
Use filters to improve and enhance your shots
062 EXPERT TUTORIAL: USING AN ND GRAD
064 PHOTOSHOP TUTORIAL: DIGITAL FILTER

066 Water in landscapes
Why water works so well in landscapes
070 EXPERT TUTORIAL: SHOOT MOVING WATER

073 Colour
Learn the relationship on colour in scenes.
076 EXPERT TUTORIAL: VASELINE A SCENE
078 EXPERT TUTORIAL: WHITE BALANCE
080 EXPERT TUTORIAL: BLACK & WHITE
082 PHOTOSHOP TUTORIAL: B&W CONVERSION

086 Expert Gems: Seasons
Brilliant ideas to keep you busy all year round.
096 PHOTOSHOP TUTORIAL: SEASONAL COLOUR

099 Landscape gear
The best equipment for outdoor photography
100 IDEAL KITS FOR *YOUR* REQUIREMENTS
106 WIDE-ANGLE LENSES
110 EXPERT TUTORIAL: WIDE-ANGLE LENSES
112 EXPERT TUTORIAL: TELEPHOTOS
114 CHOOSING THE RIGHT TRIPOD
116 CHOOSING THE RIGHT BAG
119 LANDSCAPE ACCESSORIES

123 UK location guide
40 great UK locations for you to explore!

154 Perfect exposures
Cut out and use our free grey card!

156 PAGES OF EXPERT LANDSCAPE ADVICE

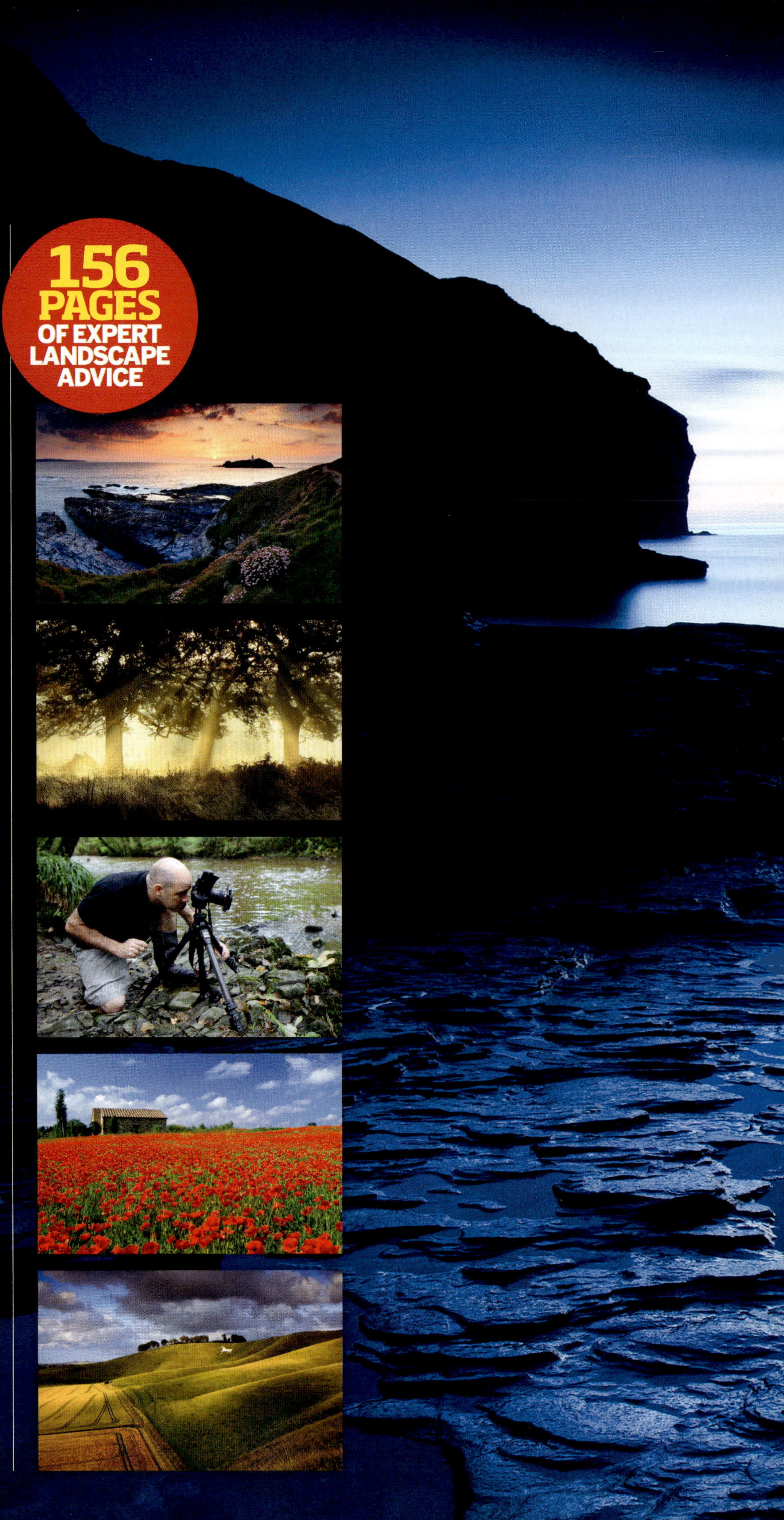

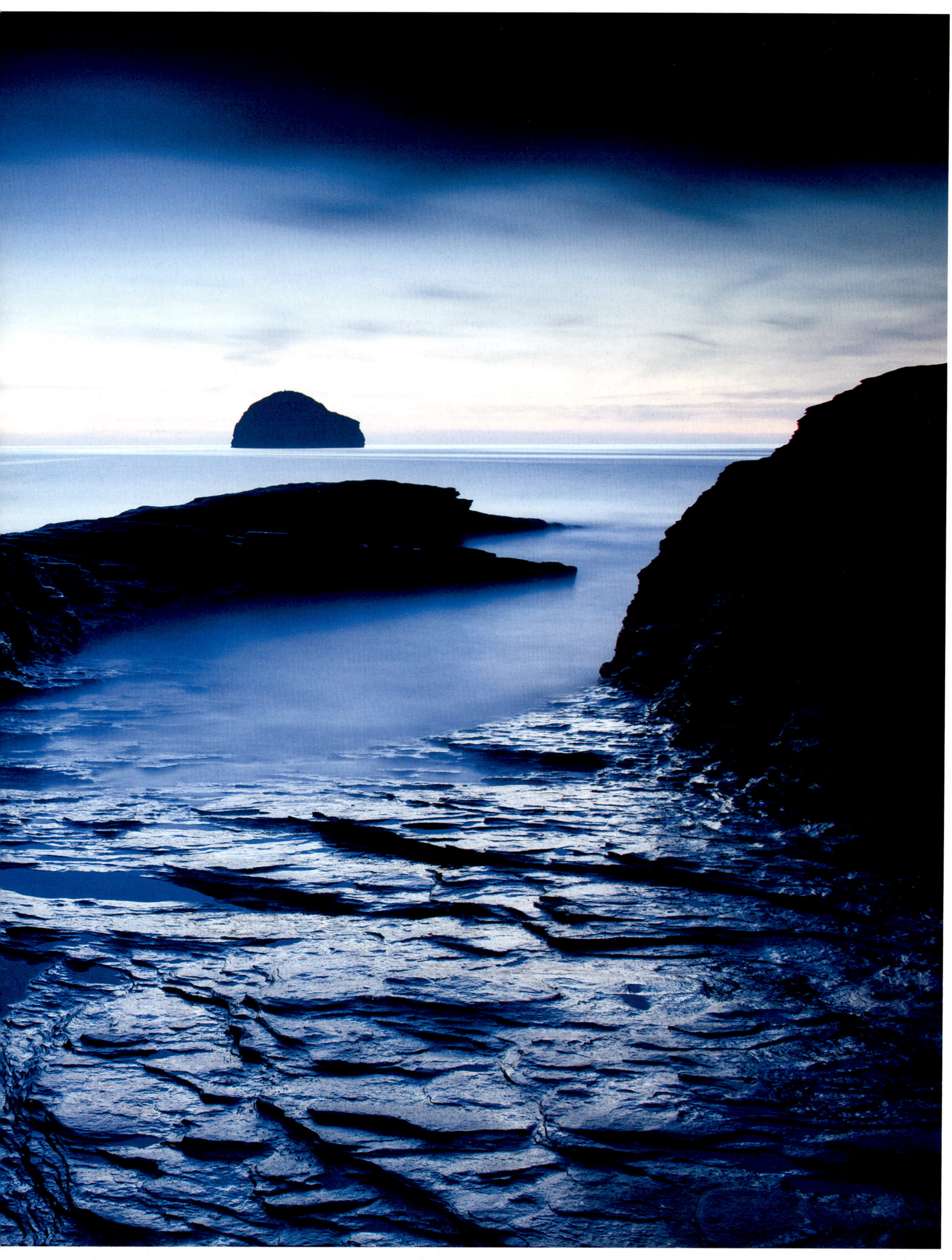

ROSS HODDINOTT

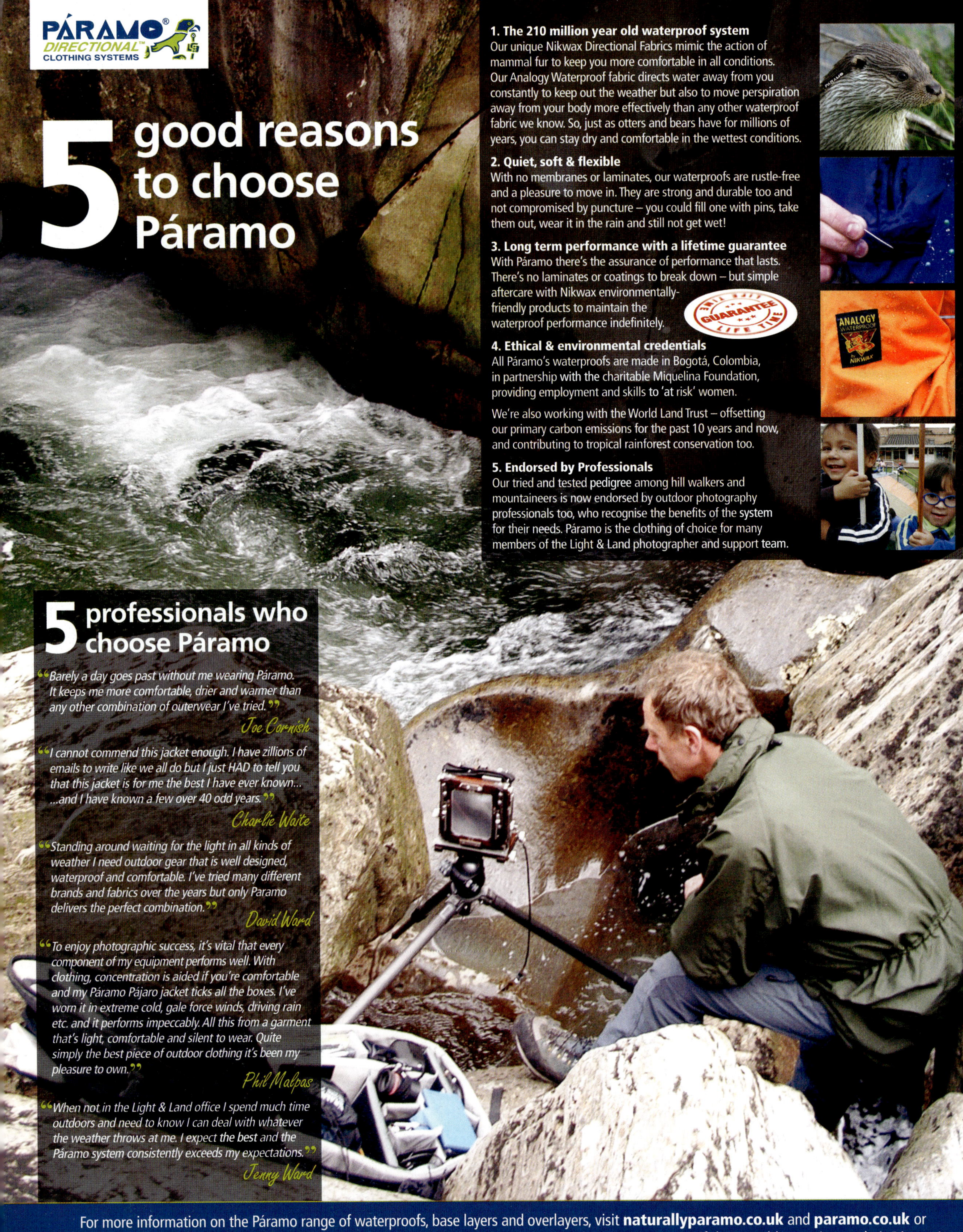
PÁRAMO® DIRECTIONAL™ CLOTHING SYSTEMS
5 good reasons to choose Páramo
1. The 210 million year old waterproof system
Our unique Nikwax Directional Fabrics mimic the action of mammal fur to keep you more comfortable in all conditions. Our Analogy Waterproof fabric directs water away from you constantly to keep out the weather but also to move perspiration away from your body more effectively than any other waterproof fabric we know. So, just as otters and bears have for millions of years, you can stay dry and comfortable in the wettest conditions.
2. Quiet, soft & flexible
With no membranes or laminates, our waterproofs are rustle-free and a pleasure to move in. They are strong and durable too and not compromised by puncture – you could fill one with pins, take them out, wear it in the rain and still not get wet!
3. Long term performance with a lifetime guarantee
With Páramo there's the assurance of performance that lasts. There's no laminates or coatings to break down – but simple aftercare with Nikwax environmentally-friendly products to maintain the waterproof performance indefinitely.
GUARANTEE LIFE TIME
ANALOGY WATERPROOF NIKWAX
4. Ethical & environmental credentials
All Páramo's waterproofs are made in Bogotá, Colombia, in partnership with the charitable Miquelina Foundation, providing employment and skills to 'at risk' women.
We're also working with the World Land Trust – offsetting our primary carbon emissions for the past 10 years and now, and contributing to tropical rainforest conservation too.
5. Endorsed by Professionals
Our tried and tested pedigree among hill walkers and mountaineers is now endorsed by outdoor photography professionals too, who recognise the benefits of the system for their needs. Páramo is the clothing of choice for many members of the Light & Land photographer and support team.
5 professionals who choose Páramo
"Barely a day goes past without me wearing Páramo. It keeps me more comfortable, drier and warmer than any other combination of outerwear I've tried."
Joe Cornish
"I cannot commend this jacket enough. I have zillions of emails to write like we all do but I just HAD to tell you that this jacket is for me the best I have ever known... ...and I have known a few over 40 odd years."
Charlie Waite
"Standing around waiting for the light in all kinds of weather I need outdoor gear that is well designed, waterproof and comfortable. I've tried many different brands and fabrics over the years but only Paramo delivers the perfect combination."
David Ward
"To enjoy photographic success, it's vital that every component of my equipment performs well. With clothing, concentration is aided if you're comfortable and my Páramo Pájaro jacket ticks all the boxes. I've worn it in extreme cold, gale force winds, driving rain etc. and it performs impeccably. All this from a garment that's light, comfortable and silent to wear. Quite simply the best piece of outdoor clothing it's been my pleasure to own."
Phil Malpas
"When not in the Light & Land office I spend much time outdoors and need to know I can deal with whatever the weather throws at me. I expect the best and the Páramo system consistently exceeds my expectations."
Jenny Ward
For more information on the Páramo range of waterproofs, base layers and overlayers, visit naturallyparamo.co.uk and paramo.co.uk or telephone 01892 786444 for our latest catalogues. And if you still need convincing, ask a Páramo wearer if they would ever give up their Páramo!

THE BASICS

CAPTURE STUNNING LANDSCAPES – we all want to be able to do it. Fantastic landscapes inspire more photographers than any other type of image and on the face of it, well, it should be easy to do. Find an awesome vista and point your digital SLR at it, press the shutter and that should do the trick. This simple approach will probably bag you a decent snap, but often the image you capture will not do justice to the glorious scene in front of you. We've all been a little bit disappointed by a photo that doesn't quite live up to our great expectations. The difference between a decent snap and a stunning image is often down to a few versatile ideas, some easily-learned expert knowledge, the right equipment choice and careful planning. This inspirational guide will provide you with an excellent grasp of these fundamentals and help you transform your shots from the ordinary into something very special indeed.

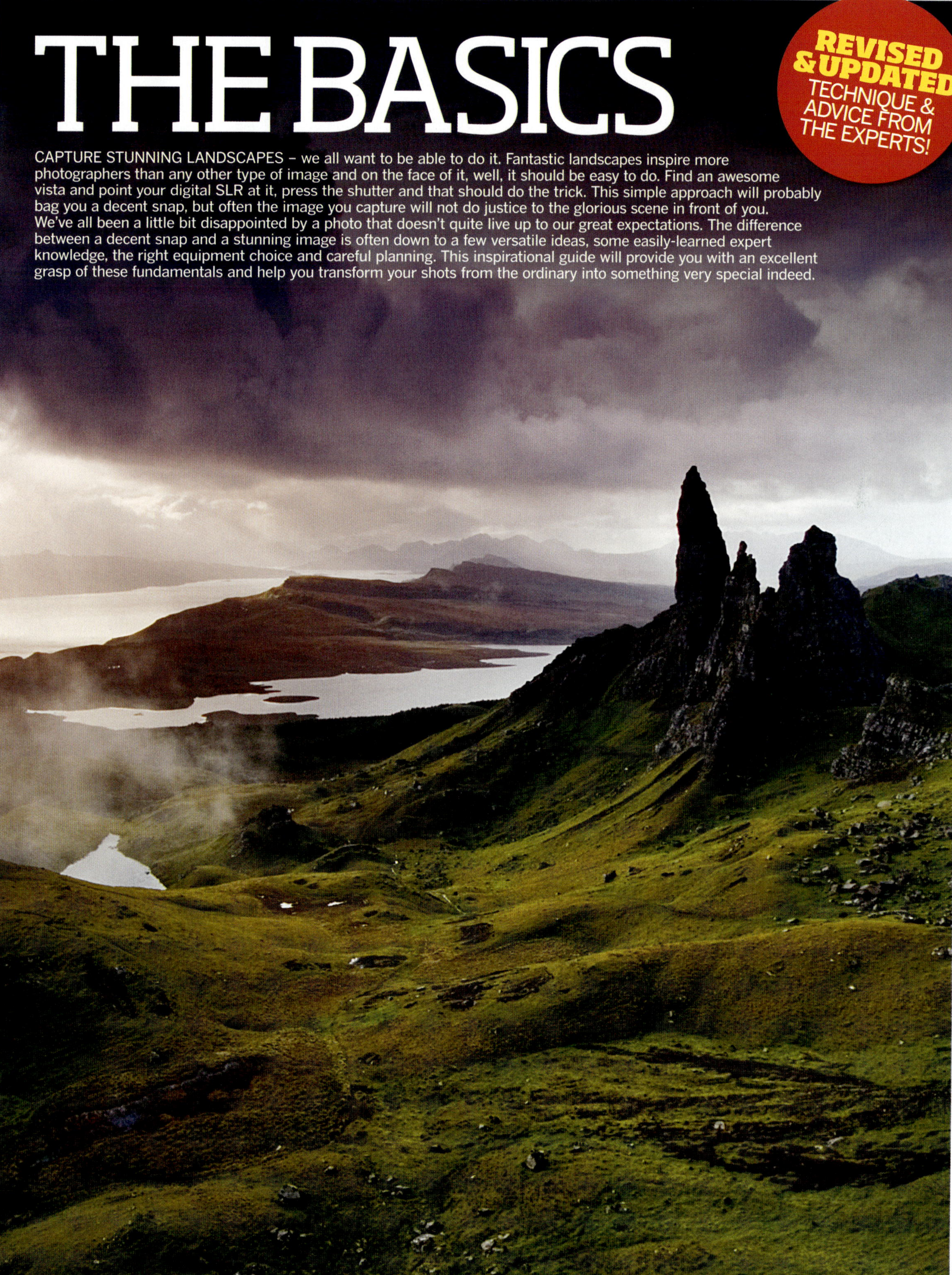

ADAM BURTON

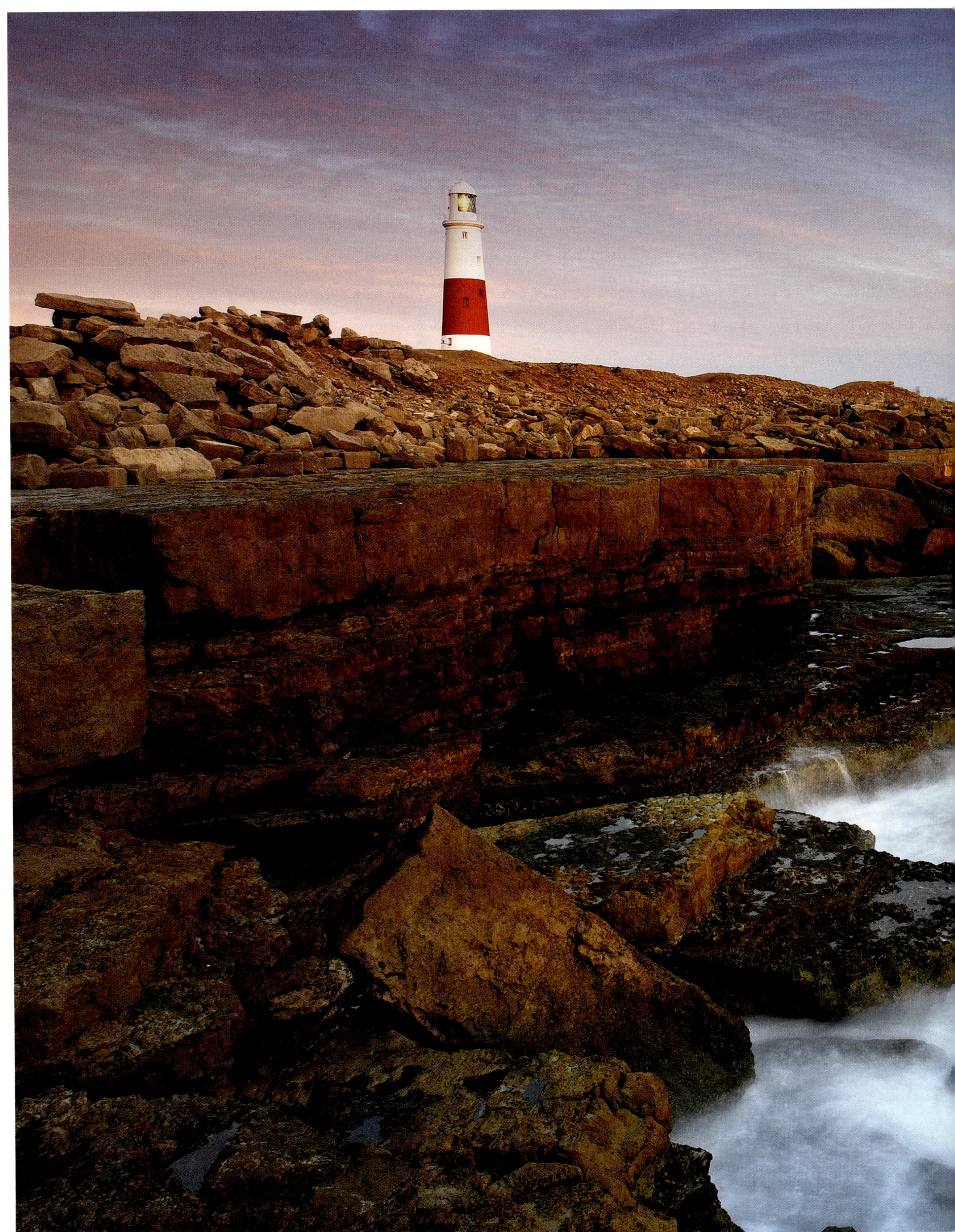

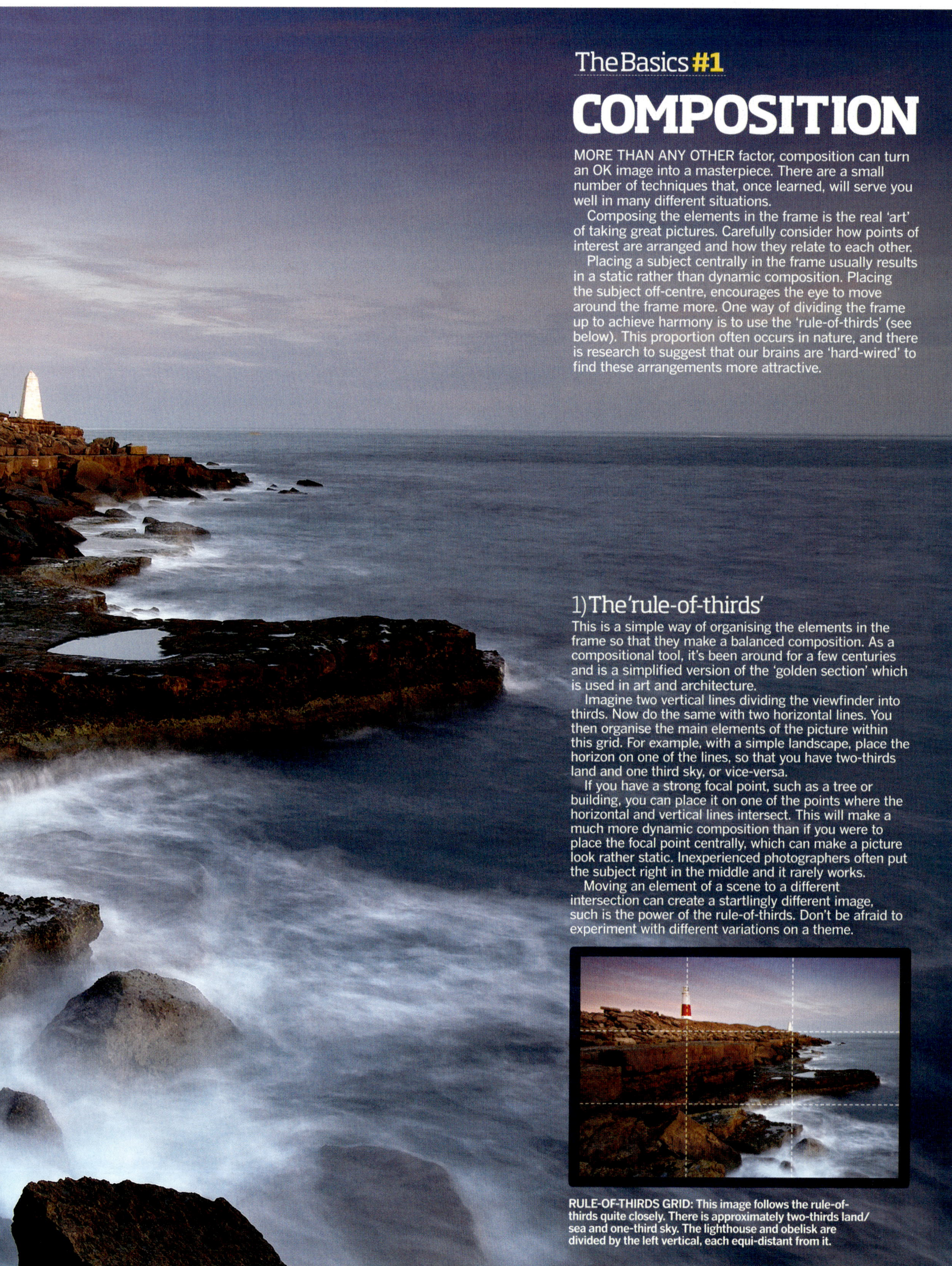

MARK BAUER

The Basics #1

COMPOSITION

MORE THAN ANY OTHER factor, composition can turn an OK image into a masterpiece. There are a small number of techniques that, once learned, will serve you well in many different situations.

Composing the elements in the frame is the real 'art' of taking great pictures. Carefully consider how points of interest are arranged and how they relate to each other.

Placing a subject centrally in the frame usually results in a static rather than dynamic composition. Placing the subject off-centre, encourages the eye to move around the frame more. One way of dividing the frame up to achieve harmony is to use the 'rule-of-thirds' (see below). This proportion often occurs in nature, and there is research to suggest that our brains are 'hard-wired' to find these arrangements more attractive.

1) The 'rule-of-thirds'

This is a simple way of organising the elements in the frame so that they make a balanced composition. As a compositional tool, it's been around for a few centuries and is a simplified version of the 'golden section' which is used in art and architecture.

Imagine two vertical lines dividing the viewfinder into thirds. Now do the same with two horizontal lines. You then organise the main elements of the picture within this grid. For example, with a simple landscape, place the horizon on one of the lines, so that you have two-thirds land and one third sky, or vice-versa.

If you have a strong focal point, such as a tree or building, you can place it on one of the points where the horizontal and vertical lines intersect. This will make a much more dynamic composition than if you were to place the focal point centrally, which can make a picture look rather static. Inexperienced photographers often put the subject right in the middle and it rarely works.

Moving an element of a scene to a different intersection can create a startlingly different image, such is the power of the rule-of-thirds. Don't be afraid to experiment with different variations on a theme.

RULE-OF-THIRDS GRID: This image follows the rule-of-thirds quite closely. There is approximately two-thirds land/sea and one-third sky. The lighthouse and obelisk are divided by the left vertical, each equi-distant from it.

2) Foreground interest

You see, the problem is, the world is three-dimensional and a photograph is two-dimensional. One of the main reasons that landscape images fail is that they don't convey the sense of depth that our eyes see. Fortunately, there are a few compositional tricks that we can employ to get round this rather frustrating little problem.

A very effective way to create depth in a photograph is to include a strong foreground, often in conjunction with a wide-angle lens. Emphasising the foreground in this way will add depth to the picture by creating an 'entry-point' for the eye, pulling the viewer into the scene and giving the picture a sense of distance and scale.

Wide-angle lenses help this technique because they stretch perspective, exaggerating the elements close to the lens and opening up the view beyond the foreground.

But be careful, this can result in the middle distance looking empty and lacking in interest so the trick is to shoot from a lower viewpoint. This compresses the middle distance, so that there isn't too much empty space in the composition. You'll also need to use a small aperture and focus carefully to maximise depth-of-field, keeping foreground and distant objects in focus (we'll explain how to do this later).

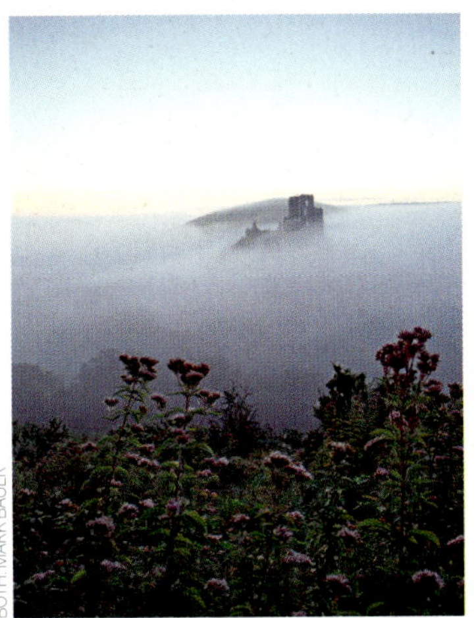

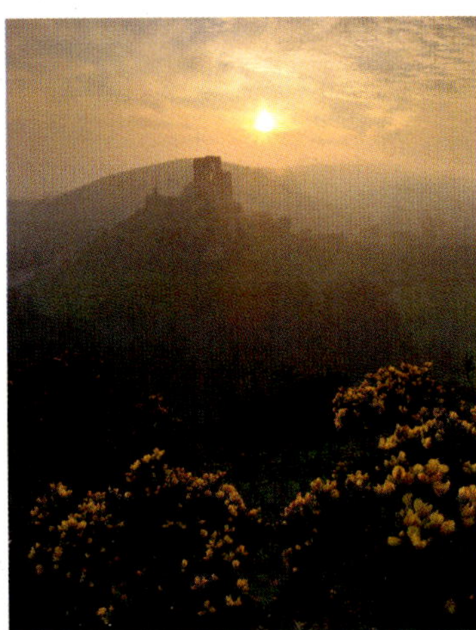

BOTH MARK BAUER

GETTING IT RIGHT: The cow parsley and gorse both make an attractive foreground to lead the eye into the scene and provide suitable frames for the view beyond. A wide-angle lens and a small aperture of f/22 provides plenty of depth-of-field.

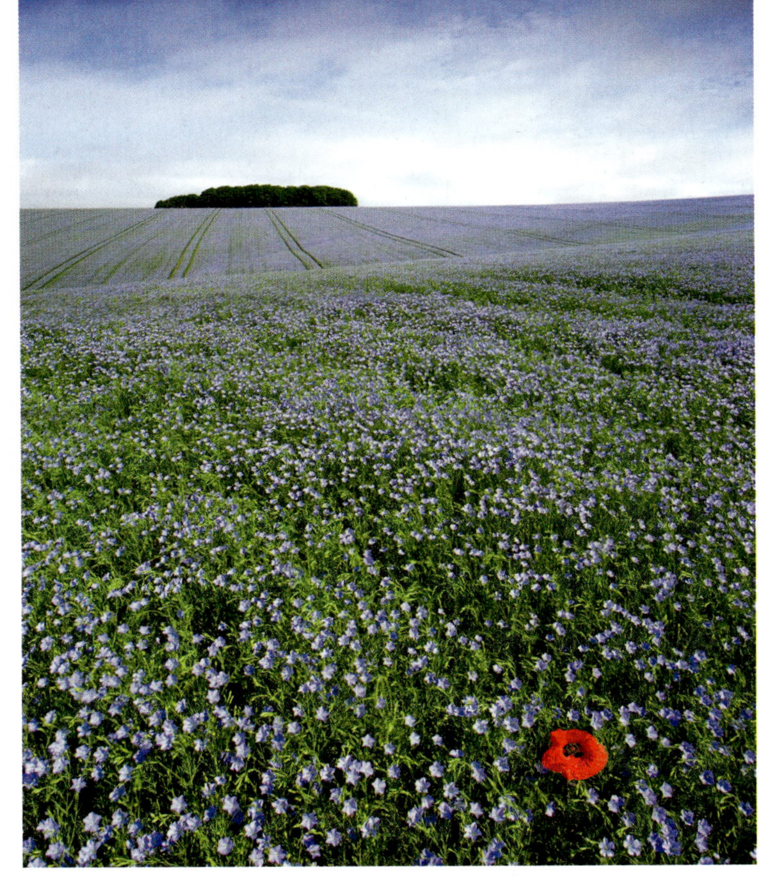

HELEN DIXON

BIG FOREGROUND OR SMALL DETAIL: It's not always necessary to have a 'big' foreground; colour, texture and patterns can all provide attractive foreground interest. The delicate carpet of flowers is as effective as the strong shapes of rocks, opposite.

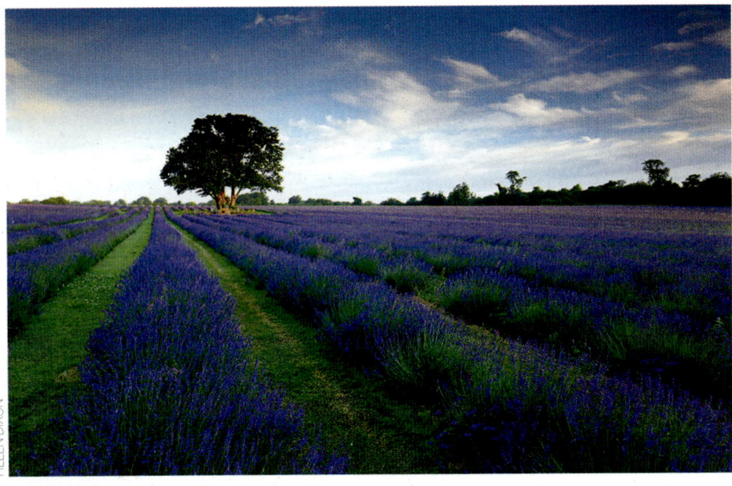

HELEN DIXON

3) Lead-in lines

Lines represent depth in a picture and can be used to lead your eye into the picture and guide it around the scene.

Lines are everywhere: man-made, such as roads, paths and hedgerows, or natural, such as rivers or the coastline – all will add dynamism to your photographs. Lines don't have to be real, they can be 'implied' like the patterns created by waves over a longish exposure, or objects pointing into the frame. Lots of things can bring linear energy into your work.

Straight, converging lines are very dynamic and can give a lot of impact to a picture, but there is always the danger that the eye follows the lines into and then very quickly out of the frame again. Pictures with only converging lines might have immediate impact, but can still be unsatisfying. It's a good idea to try and place some object of interest within the frame – a figure or a tree, for example – to give the eye something to settle on within the scene.

Lines that curve gently in an 'S' shape lack the immediate impact of straight, converging lines, but can result in a more satisfying image. They can lead the eye gently through the whole picture, allowing the viewer to take in other elements within the composition.

4) Layers and planes

Another in-camera technique that can be used to add depth to an image is to create a 'layered' effect. Layers in an image can be created by having a series of overlapping shapes (see right) or by strong side-lighting, creating alternative bands of light and shade that can give the effect of a 'layering of light'.

This kind of technique works particularly well with longer lenses that have the effect of compressing perspective and 'stacking' overlapping forms. Each layer, or plane, appears thinner and closer to the next, exaggerating the effect. Just remember longer lenses will produce less depth-of-field so you'll need to use smaller apertures, such as f/16, if elements are in the foreground or near middle distance.

This shot was taken at dawn near Lyme Regis using a 70-200mm zoom at around 100mm. The longer focal length compresses the distances between the layers and the strong, directional light helps emphasise the layers – the early morning mists add bags of atmosphere.

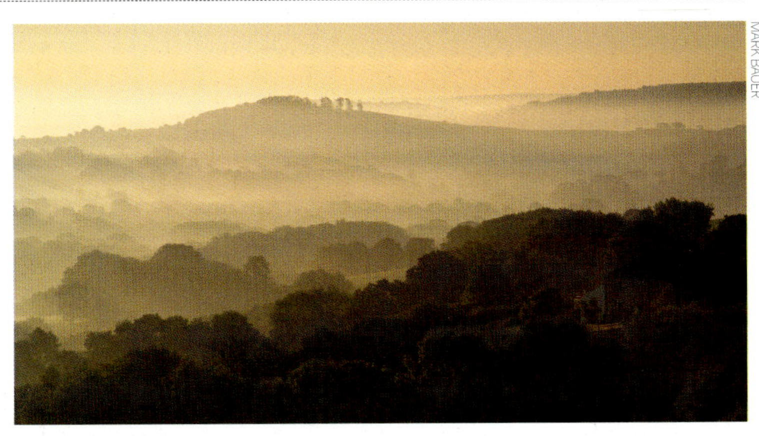

MARK BAUER

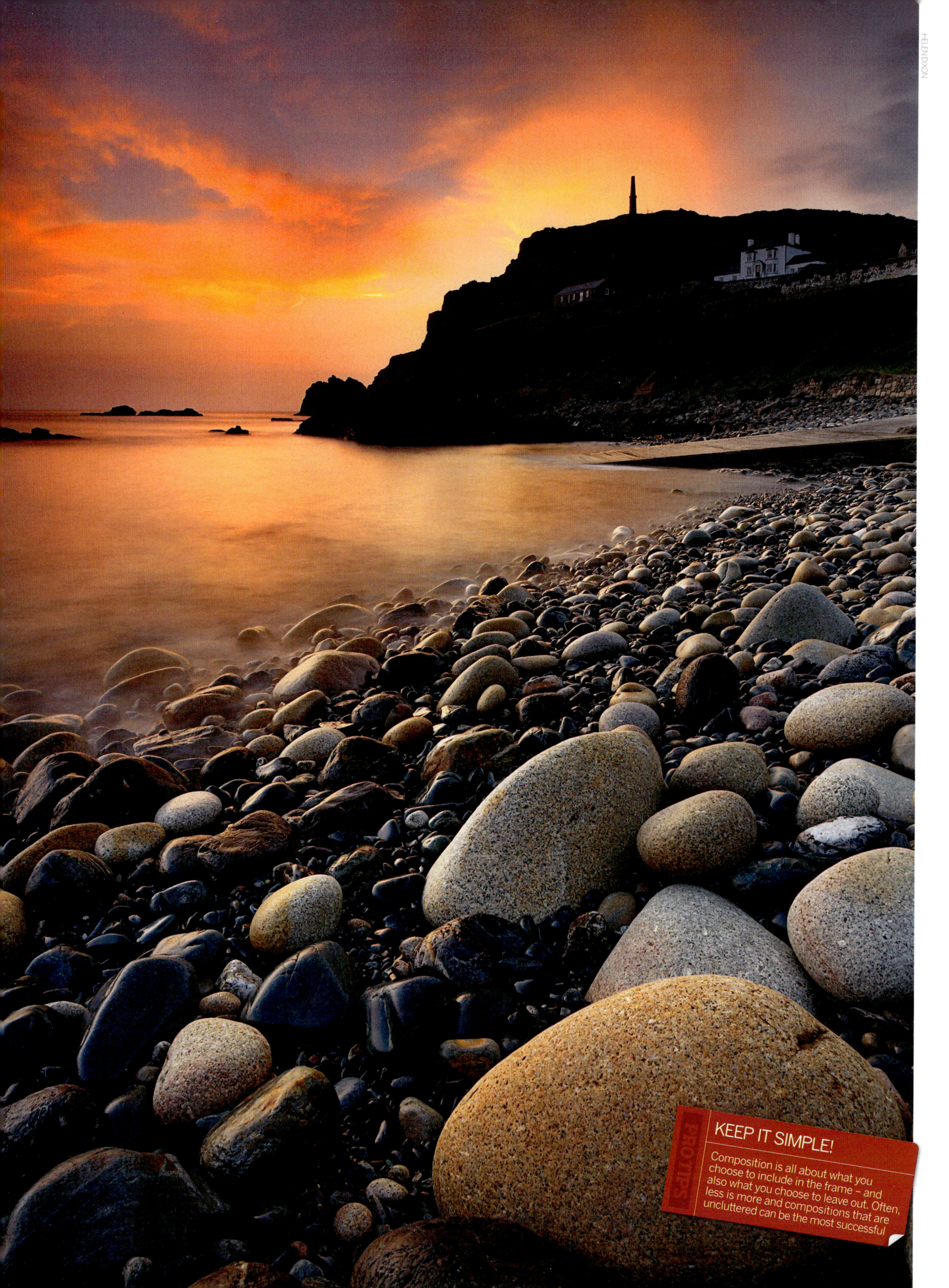
HELEN DIXON
PRO TIPS
KEEP IT SIMPLE!
Composition is all about what you choose to include in the frame – and also what you choose to leave out. Often, less is more and compositions that are uncluttered can be the most successful

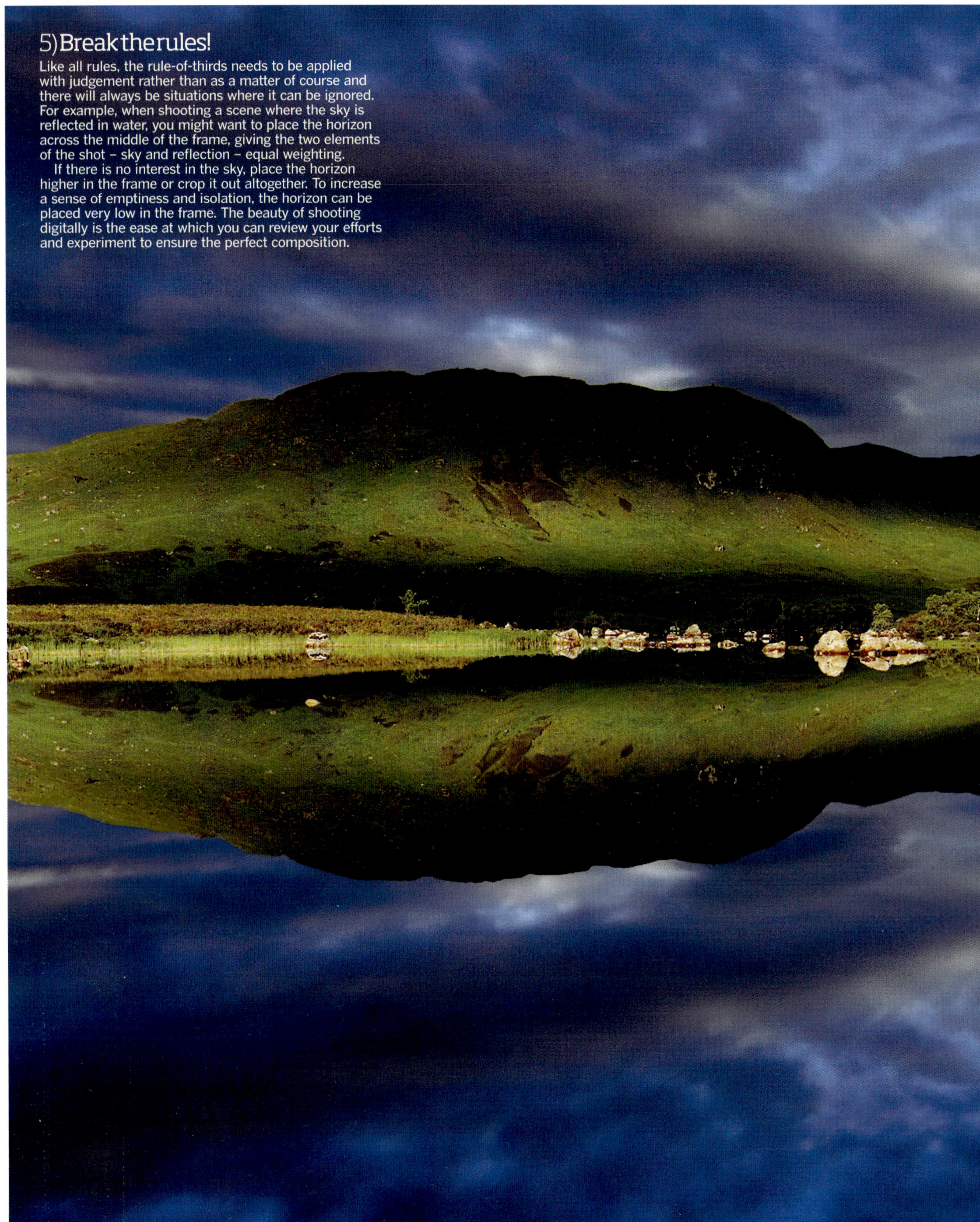

5) Break the rules!

Like all rules, the rule-of-thirds needs to be applied with judgement rather than as a matter of course and there will always be situations where it can be ignored. For example, when shooting a scene where the sky is reflected in water, you might want to place the horizon across the middle of the frame, giving the two elements of the shot – sky and reflection – equal weighting.

If there is no interest in the sky, place the horizon higher in the frame or crop it out altogether. To increase a sense of emptiness and isolation, the horizon can be placed very low in the frame. The beauty of shooting digitally is the ease at which you can review your efforts and experiment to ensure the perfect composition.

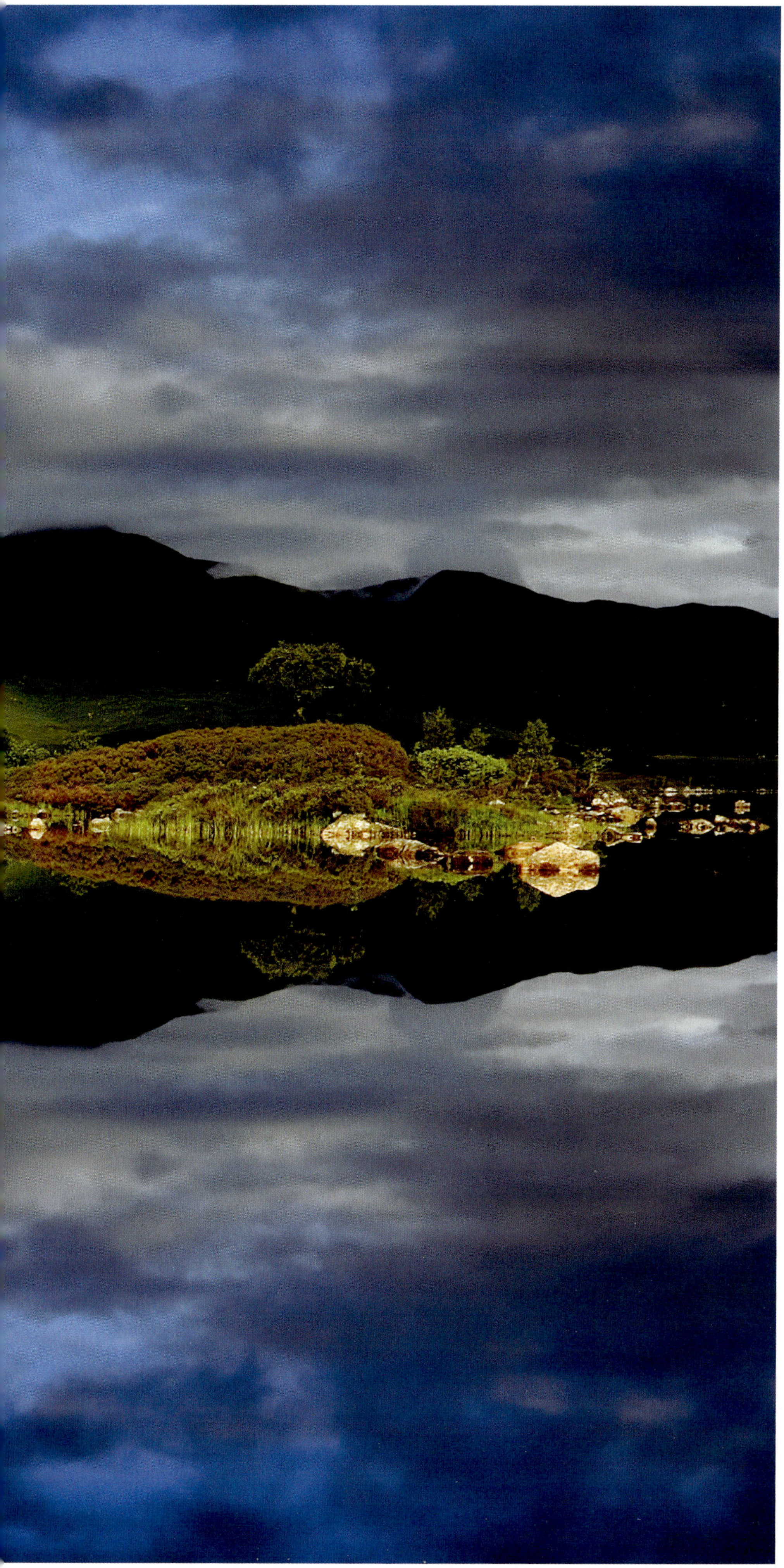

RICHARD JOHNSON

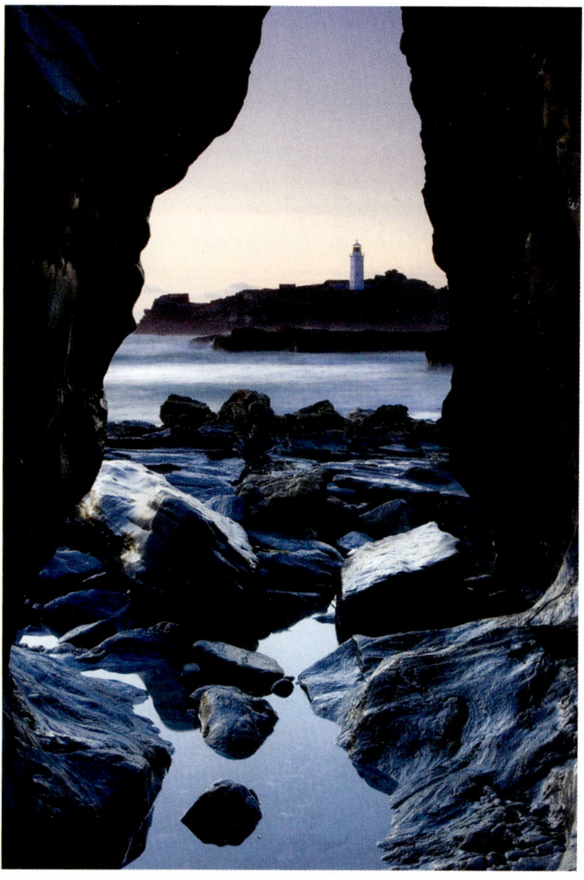

IAN WOOLCOCK

6) Find natural frames

A popular compositional 'trick' is to use something to frame the view beyond, such as an archway, doorway, window or the overhanging branches of trees.

Try using frost-covered plants and gateposts to create a 'natural' frame for the main subject of your shot. Use the 'frame' to lead the viewer's eye into the shot for some truly eye-catching results.

Control the amount of sharp focus carefully. Very out-of-focus framing leaves help keep attention on the main subject, slightly soft leaves might look like a mistake.

Use this idea with care as it can often be detrimental to the scene and can suggest to the viewer that the view beyond the natural frame is even more spectacular.

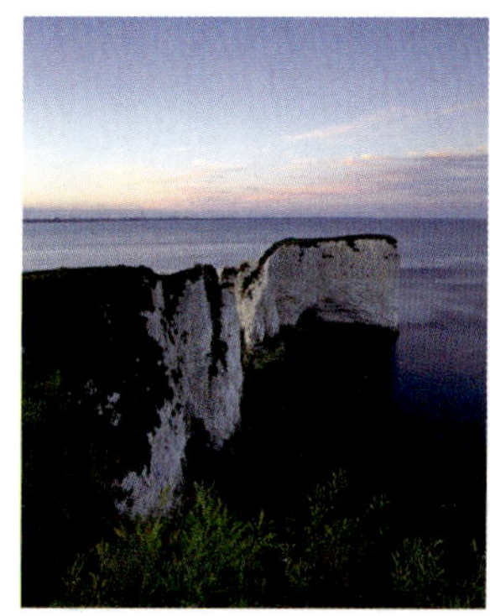

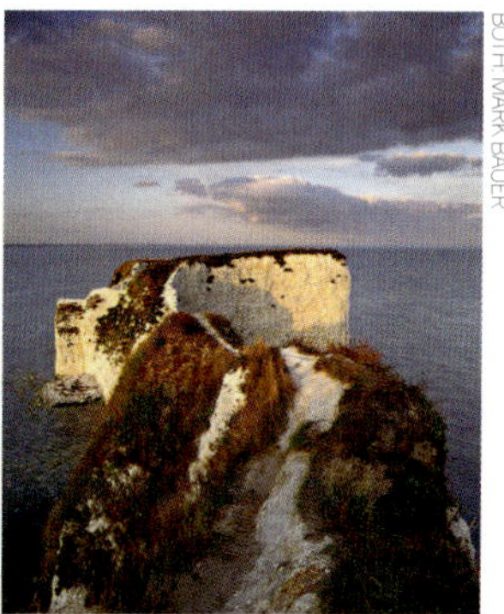

BOTH: MARK BAUER

7) Experiment with viewpoints

Finding the right viewpoint is key to successful landscape composition. Rather than shooting everything from head height, experiment with high and low viewpoints.

Higher viewpoints have the effect of opening up the planes in the image and is useful with standard and telephoto lenses. When photographing well-known landmarks, it's tempting to use the established viewpoints, but spend time looking for a fresh view, as it's much more satisfying to capture something original.

While there's nothing wrong with the first picture, it's the 'standard' view of Old Harry Rocks in Dorset. Without having to move very far, however, a less photographed and more dramatic viewpoint has been found.

EXPERT TUTORIAL

How to compose a scene

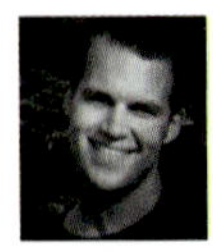

WITH ROSS HODDINOTT Beautiful scenery and good light are still no guarantee that a photographer will take a great landscape image. While they might both be essential ingredients to great scenic shots, you, the photographer, still need to have the vision and ability to create a strong image. When shooting landscapes, you'll have ample time to consider, arrange and fine-tune how you frame the scene.

Composition is the art of arranging the elements of a scene in such a way that they are visually pleasing. It is an ability that becomes instinctive the more you take photographs, so don't worry if this is a skill that doesn't come to you naturally – just keep practising and you will improve over time. By using two relatively simple guidelines, based around the rule-of-thirds and lead-in lines, you will see an immediate improvement in your landscapes.

The rule-of-thirds requires that you imagine the frame is split into nine equal parts by two horizontal and two vertical lines. It's a technique I use for the majority of my scenics. A horizon that cuts centrally through an image normally weakens a shot, but a landscape composed of one-third sky and two-thirds foreground, or two-thirds sky and one-third foreground, looks far more dynamic.

Another useful 'rule' is to use some sort of lead-in line within your composition. A lead-in line uses the natural perspective of receding or converging lines to create foreground interest. The technique works well in tandem with the rule-of-thirds, so try combining the two wherever possible.

Powerful compositions often have strong lines passing through them, as they help to lead the viewer's eye through the scene to the point in the distance where the line diminishes – the 'vanishing point'. All types of subject can be used: a road, path, bridge, walkway, river, ploughed field, crop lines or fence. By using such an object in the foreground, leading into the picture, you can transform an otherwise ordinary looking view. Often a lead in-line that stretches diagonally works best, but don't overlook positioning your lead-in lines centrally, as this can also create striking results.

I spent an evening on Dartmoor photographing the moors. Though the evening light was warm, the view looked quite ordinary, but I knew that a nearby dry stone wall would create more interest. A vertical format worked best, with the wall leading from the bottom of the frame to the distant view. I tried taking a few shots looking directly down its length, then changed my position so that the wall led from one corner into the distance. I composed the shot with one-third sky, two-thirds foreground, and, with my camera set to aperture-priority mode, I selected a small aperture of f/22 to ensure back-to-front sharpness thanks to lots of depth-of-field.

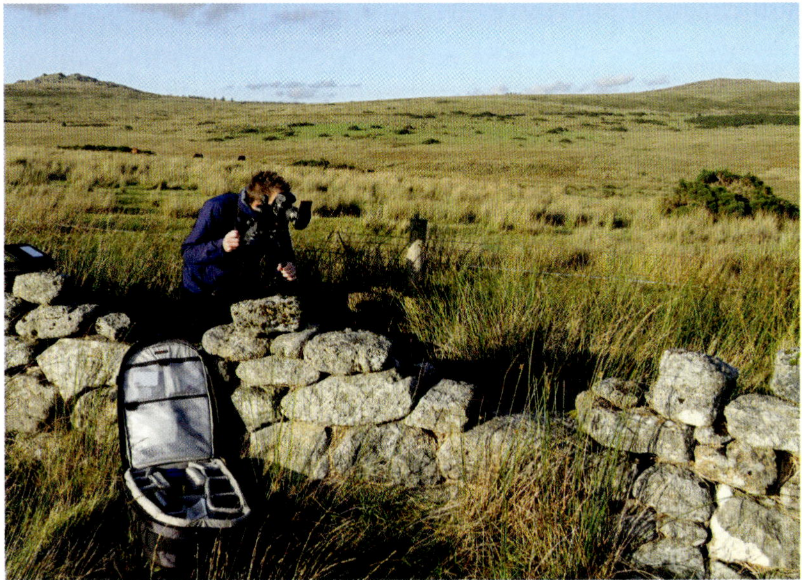

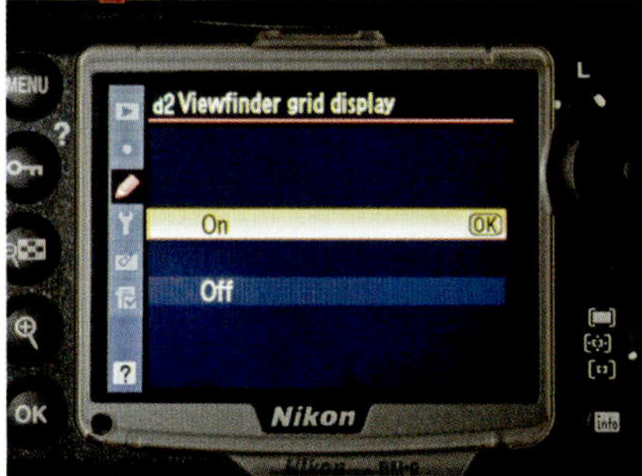

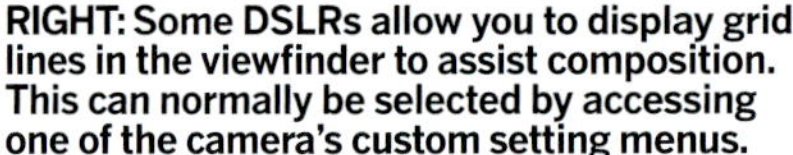

RIGHT: Some DSLRs allow you to display grid lines in the viewfinder to assist composition. This can normally be selected by accessing one of the camera's custom setting menus.

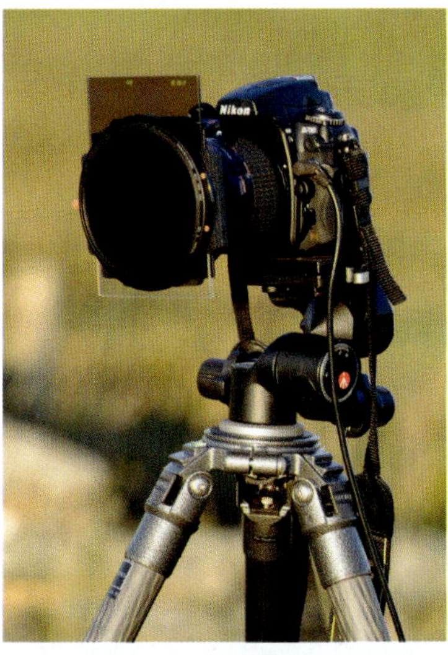

ABOVE: I used a Nikon D700 with a Nikkor 24-85mm zoom, set to f/22, on a Gitzo tripod. I fired the shutter with a remote release. I also used a Lee Filter system using a polarising filter and 0.6ND graduate filters together.

DON'T PANIC!

Positioning the horizon

Though it may seem natural to place the horizon in the centre of the image, more often than not, it will produce disappointing results. In this instance, composing the shot to be only one-third sky, as opposed to half, gives greater emphasis to the foreground and creates a better balance overall. However, there isn't a set rule to follow and you should base your composition on the merits of each scene. For instance, if the sky had been more interesting, such as on a stormy day, I may well have considered giving it more emphasis in the frame.

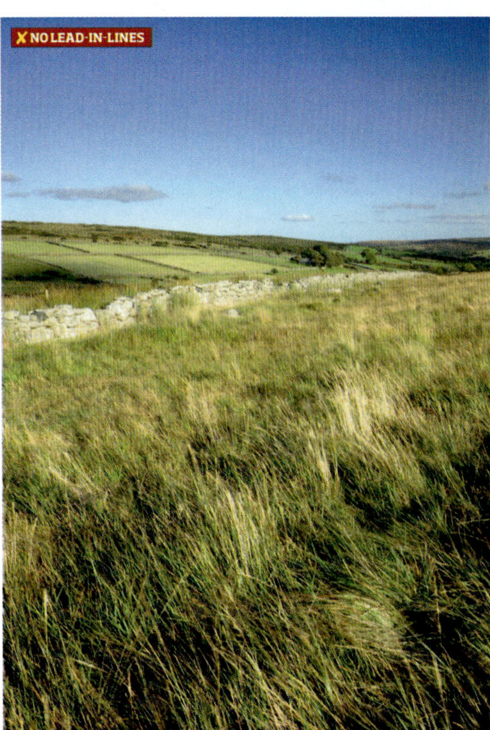

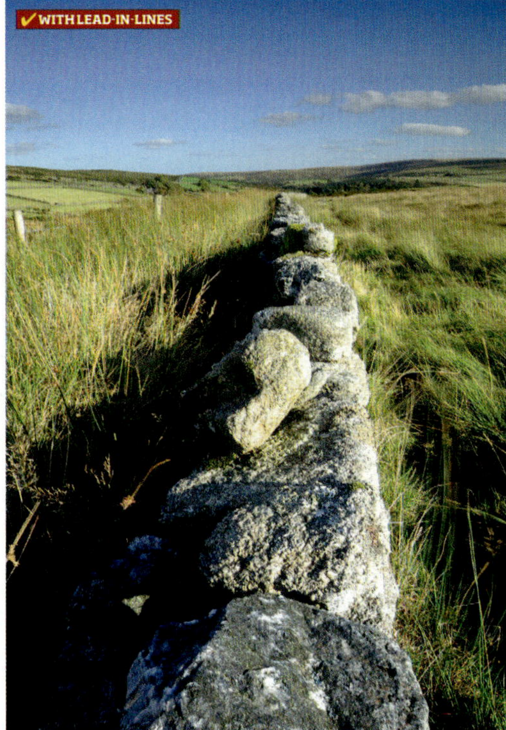

ABOVE: Without a lead-in line, or any foreground interest, this scene lacks impact and depth. I moved closer to the wall to use it as a lead-in-line and took this shot looking down its length. This leads your eye into the picture and towards the horizon, but there is still too much empty, wasted space either side of the wall.

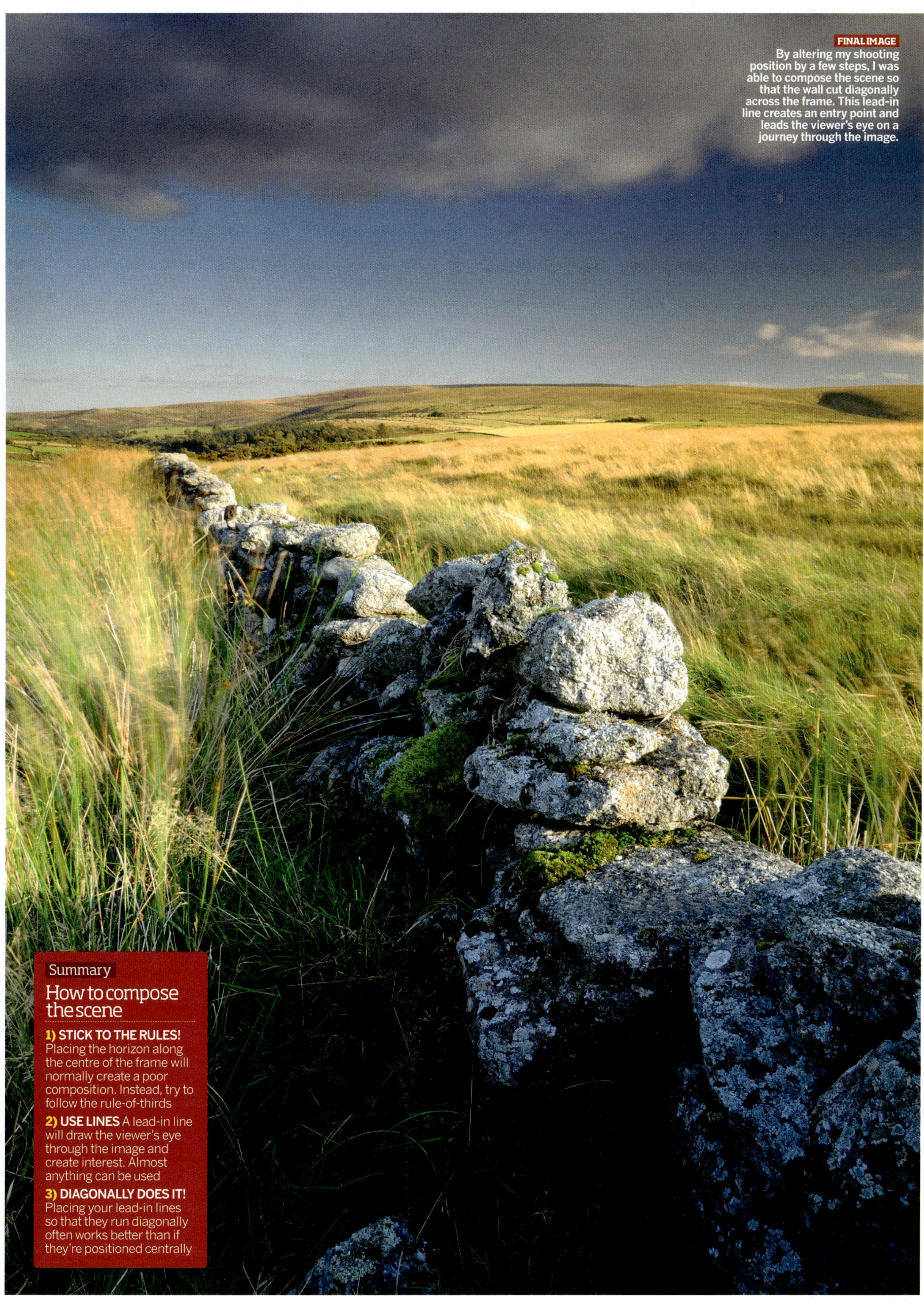

FINAL IMAGE
By altering my shooting position by a few steps, I was able to compose the scene so that the wall cut diagonally across the frame. This lead-in line creates an entry point and leads the viewer's eye on a journey through the image.

Summary

How to compose the scene

1) STICK TO THE RULES! Placing the horizon along the centre of the frame will normally create a poor composition. Instead, try to follow the rule-of-thirds

2) USE LINES A lead-in line will draw the viewer's eye through the image and create interest. Almost anything can be used

3) DIAGONALLY DOES IT! Placing your lead-in lines so that they run diagonally often works better than if they're positioned centrally

EXPERT TUTORIAL

Using foreground interest

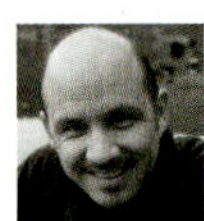

WITH ADAM BURTON Because I'm hooked on wide-angle photography, big foregrounds are a constant feature in my landscape images. When selected carefully and photographed well, a good foreground will bring a landscape shot to life and maximise its impact. Photographs with detailed foregrounds can give the viewer a sense of 'being there', instantly drawing their attention and gaze into the image. I should point out that I don't go out primarily searching for foregrounds. The most important thing is always the main subject in your image, but for me, the foreground comes in a close second. So whenever I head out to take landscapes, I look for a location that has a lot of potential shooting opportunities. On arrival, I'll scout around the area, looking for the most appealing subject and the best angle to shoot it from. Once I have chosen the area in which I want to shoot, I begin to search around for foreground interest.

There are no rules as to what qualifies as good foreground interest but, as always, there are a few points to consider. Only you can be the judge of what you want to focus on and, obviously, this is also determined by which objects are close at hand. But it is important to pay careful attention to which objects you include, rather than just shooting the first thing you stumble across. As I favour landscapes, I almost always look for natural elements to make a foreground – rocks, flowers and water being the usual suspects. These, I know, will fit into the bigger picture that I am composing, whereas a man-made object could look unbalanced.

Once you've decided what to include as foreground, consider how to compose your shot to give the strongest possible result. Ideally, the foreground leads the eye into the main subject, but if composed wrongly, can become a distraction. One mistake many photographers make is to always shoot at eye-level; if you are including low-level rocks and shooting from a standing position, your resulting image will lack impact. Try moving lower and closer to your desired foreground, and your image will spring to life! Having said that, be careful not to move too low and close or you risk unbalancing your image by making the foreground more dominant than your background. For this same reason, try and keep your subject matter clean and simple – a fantastic background will be lost behind a cluttered or messy foreground! Finally, it's important to use a small aperture and focus a third of the way into the scene to provide a good depth-of-field. By following these simple measures, you can greatly improve the composition of your landscape images.

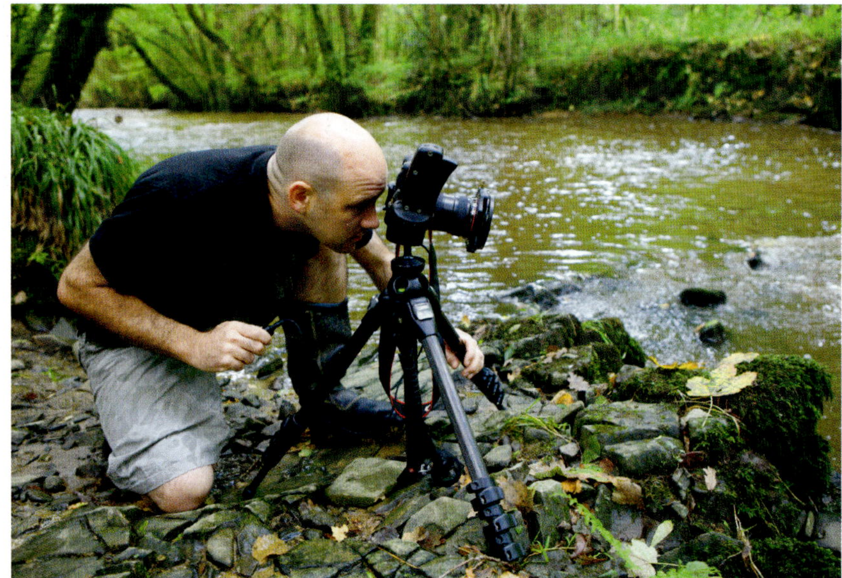

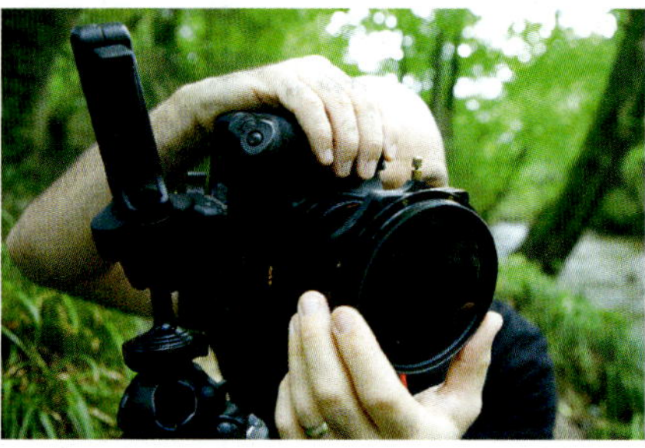

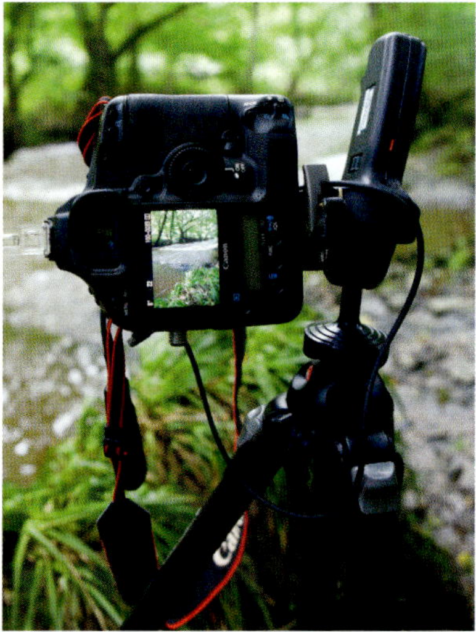

TOP: While your natural instinct may be to extend your tripod and shoot from a standing position, it's worth trying low viewpoints too.

ABOVE & RIGHT: Using a tripod really helps with landscape photography. I adjusted the height until I was happy with the composition and used a polariser to improve the colours. By reviewing my shots on the LCD monitor, I was able to check the exposure and depth-of-field to ensure I got the best possible result.

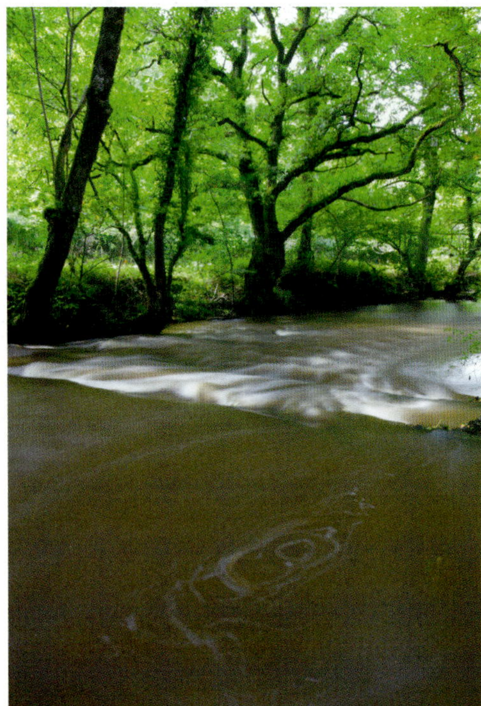

NO FOREGROUND INTEREST Without a foreground, the image lacks impact and can look dull and uninteresting. While water can make an attractive subject, its muddy colour in this shot lacks appeal.

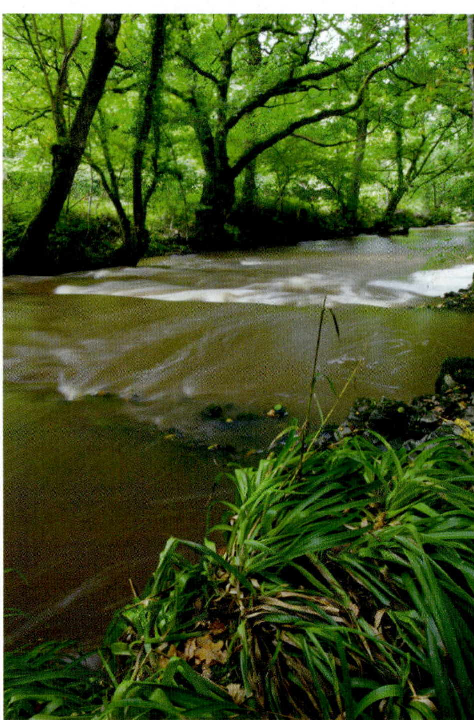

WITH FOREGROUND By including a foreground, the image immediately looks more balanced and eye-catching. However, don't just settle on the first thing you find. This plant is quite unattractive.

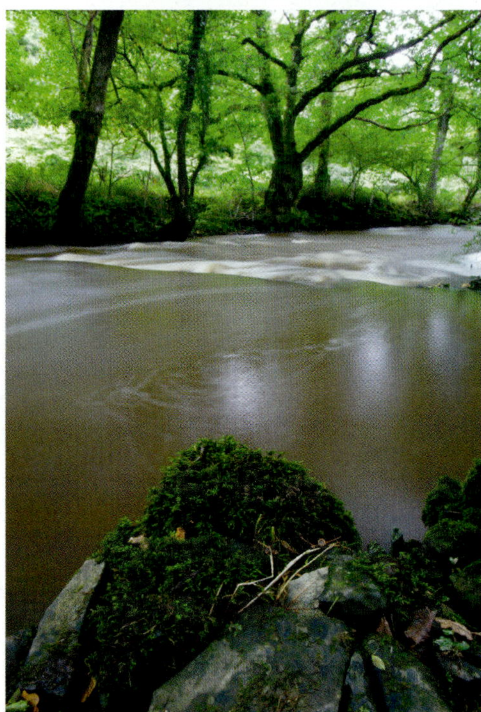

LOW VIEWPOINT Composing from a low viewpoint helps to pick out details in this mossy rock. It is simple, uncluttered and provides a satisfactory foreground; but it still lacks something special...

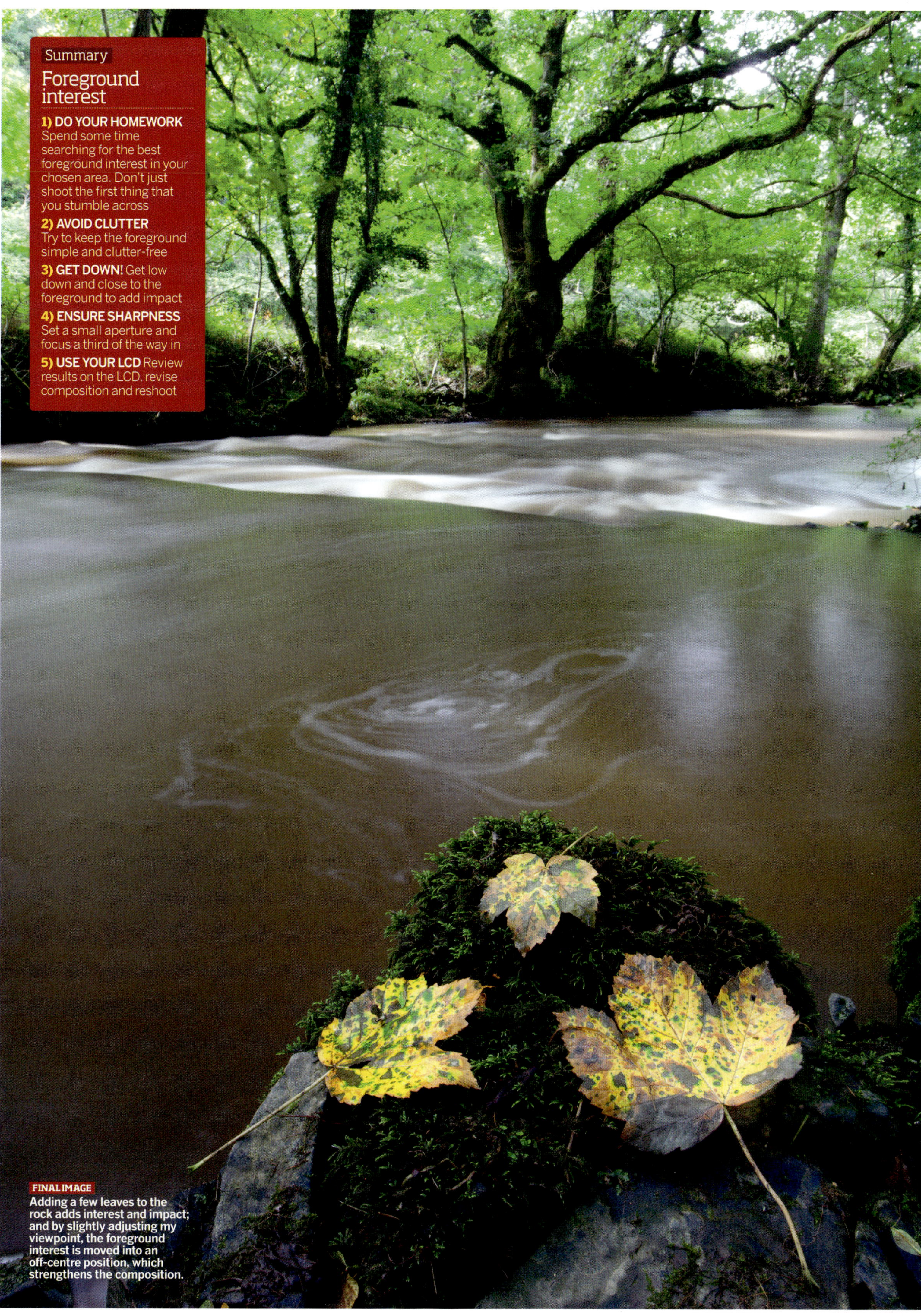

Summary

Foreground interest

1) DO YOUR HOMEWORK Spend some time searching for the best foreground interest in your chosen area. Don't just shoot the first thing that you stumble across

2) AVOID CLUTTER Try to keep the foreground simple and clutter-free

3) GET DOWN! Get low down and close to the foreground to add impact

4) ENSURE SHARPNESS Set a small aperture and focus a third of the way in

5) USE YOUR LCD Review results on the LCD, revise composition and reshoot

FINAL IMAGE
Adding a few leaves to the rock adds interest and impact; and by slightly adjusting my viewpoint, the foreground interest is moved into an off-centre position, which strengthens the composition.

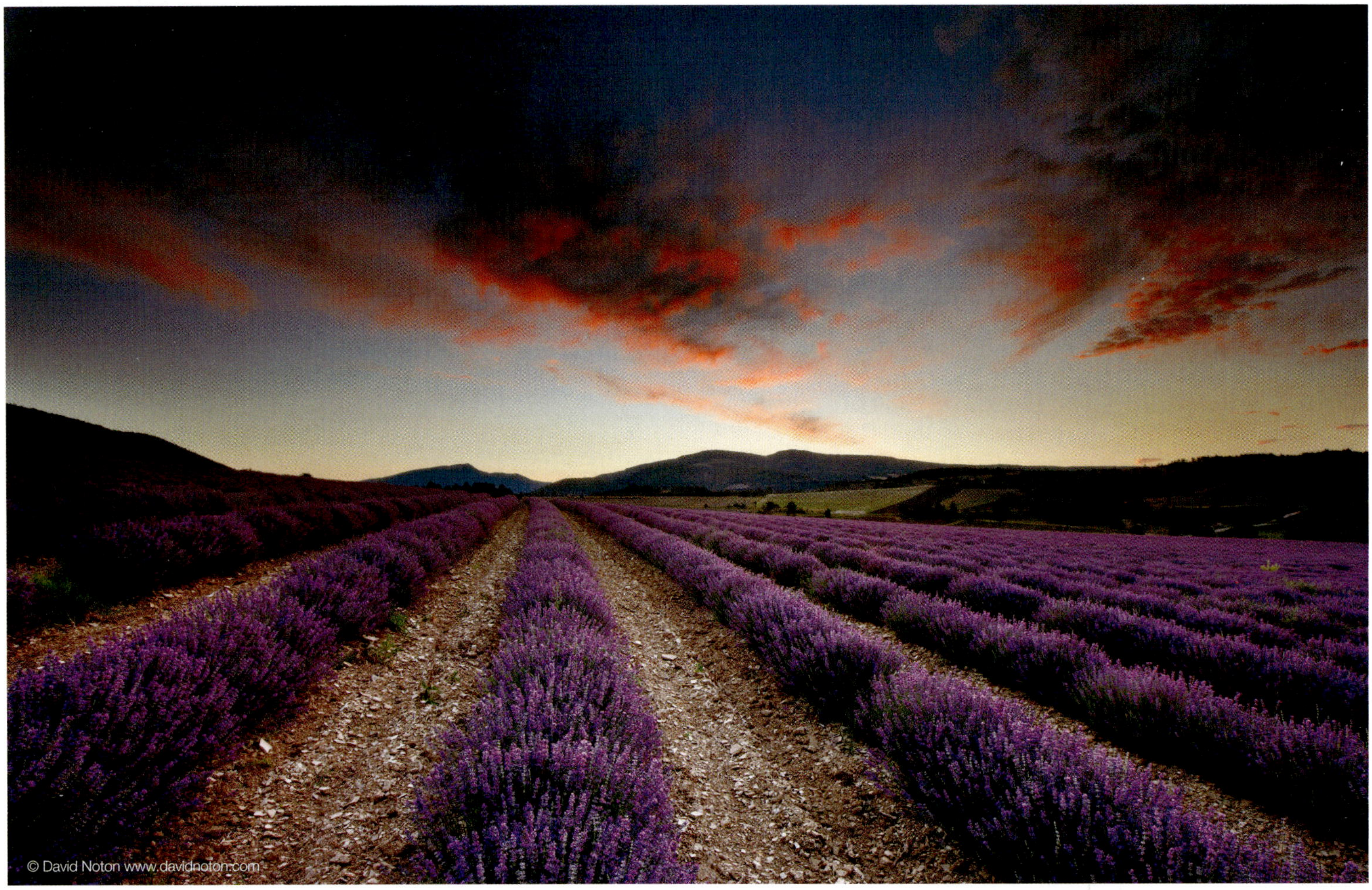

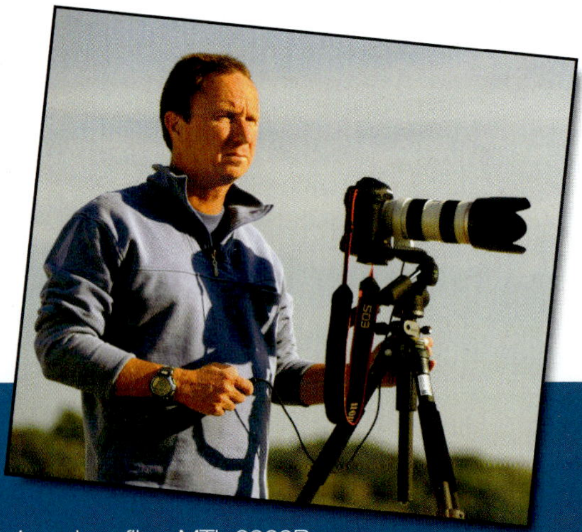

The Basics #2

PERFECT EXPOSURES

DIGITAL SLRs HAVE EXTREMELY ACCURATE, multi-zone metering systems, with a histogram function to help us check accurate exposure, so getting it right has never been easier. However, for more creative control, you need to take things into your own hands.

The basic problem is that as we gaze at a beautiful landscape our eyes adjust constantly to register detail in the highlights and the shadows. Our pupils open and close according to the level of light and our optic nerve has impressive range and latitude. Our cameras, despite their impressive technical specifications, make exposures within fairly limited parameters – the aperture and shutter speed combination will be chosen for the level of light in the scene. A perfectly-exposed sky results in gloomy shadows; detail in the shadows results in a burned-out sky. We need to help our camera to expose the right part of the scene, or find the right balance. The following expert techniques will help you capture perfect exposures by knowing what types of scenes causes problems and what action you'll need to take.

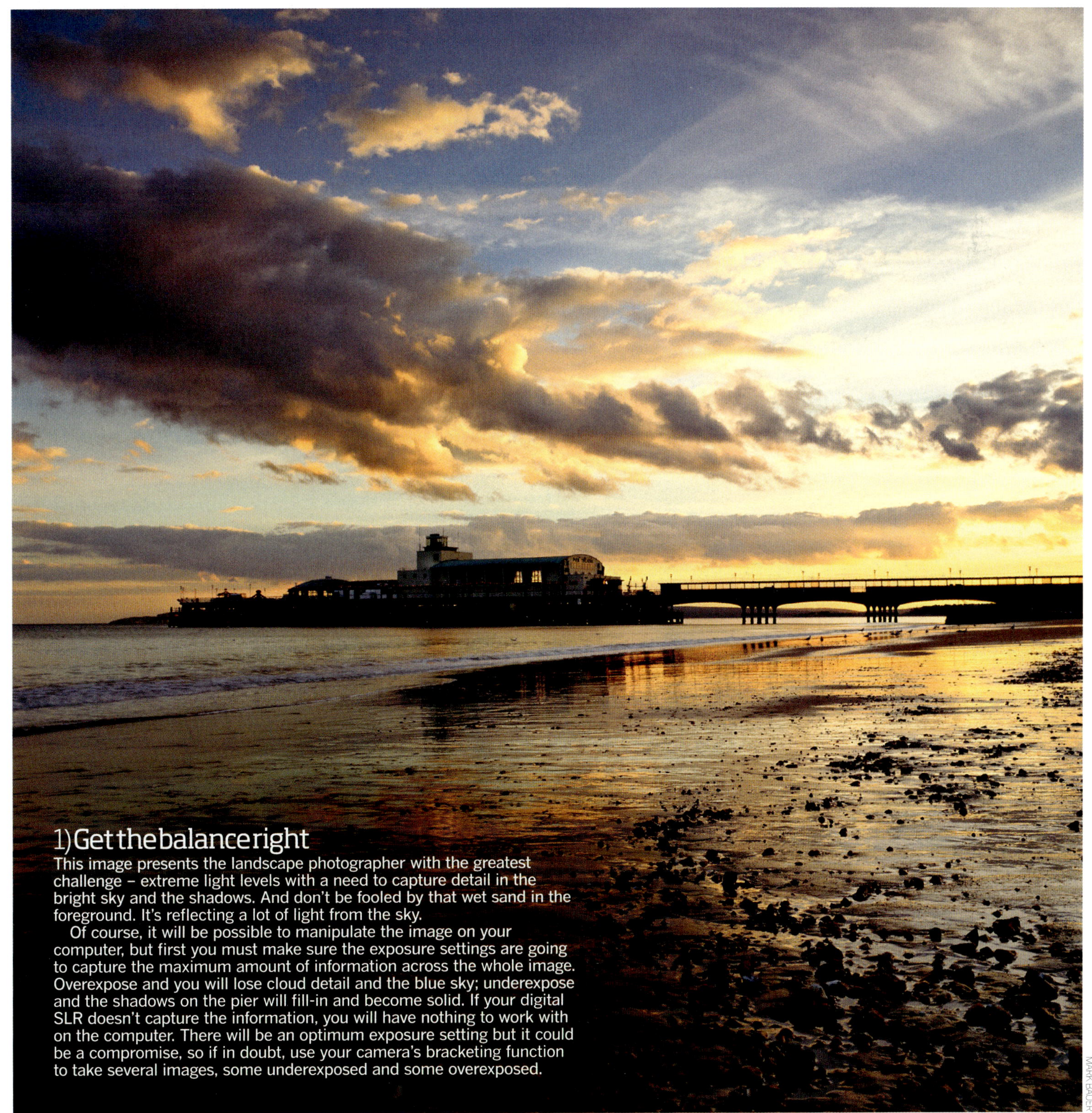

1) Get the balance right

This image presents the landscape photographer with the greatest challenge – extreme light levels with a need to capture detail in the bright sky and the shadows. And don't be fooled by that wet sand in the foreground. It's reflecting a lot of light from the sky.

Of course, it will be possible to manipulate the image on your computer, but first you must make sure the exposure settings are going to capture the maximum amount of information across the whole image. Overexpose and you will lose cloud detail and the blue sky; underexpose and the shadows on the pier will fill-in and become solid. If your digital SLR doesn't capture the information, you will have nothing to work with on the computer. There will be an optimum exposure setting but it could be a compromise, so if in doubt, use your camera's bracketing function to take several images, some underexposed and some overexposed.

MARK BAUER

2) Getting the right exposure

Mark Bauer was looking for a 'different' view of Corfe Castle in Dorset, so he sauntered along to the graveyard in the village. Having found a composition based around one of the crosses, the next problem was sorting out the exposure. Mark explains, step-by-step, how he tackled the challenge:

1) "This is what the camera's multi-zone meter came up with, without the aid of any filtration. The scene is very contrasty, and the camera has struggled to capture all the tonal information."

2) "Spot meter readings from the base of the cross and the sky revealed a difference in brightness of about 4½ stops. Setting an exposure for the land, I fitted a 0.9ND grad filter (three stops) and pulled it down below the level of the horizon, to the edge of the darkest shadow area at the bottom of the frame. I used a soft grad, so that it wouldn't cut into the cross. But there is loss of detail in the brighter parts of the sky so I reduced exposure by two-thirds of a stop and reshot."

3) "The result is 'exposed to the right' (see over the page) as far as possible without clipping the highlights – the histogram shows there are still dark tones, but also plenty of information in the top section, and crucially, no 'clipped' shadows."

4) "A straight conversion of the Raw file looks dull, the picture lacks contrast. For the final version, I've brought the exposure down slightly and added more contrast, especially in the shadows, to recreate the drama of the original scene. I've also tweaked the white balance to add warmth and increased saturation too."

5) "For comparison purposes, I also took a shot underexposed by one stop. This leaves the shadows muddy and lacking in detail, which is very apparent in the crop."

PRO TIPS

MID-TONE METERING

Metering systems in digital SLRs are calibrated to an 18% grey mid-tone. Basing exposure readings on a mid-tone, such as grass, provides a good starting point for accurate exposures

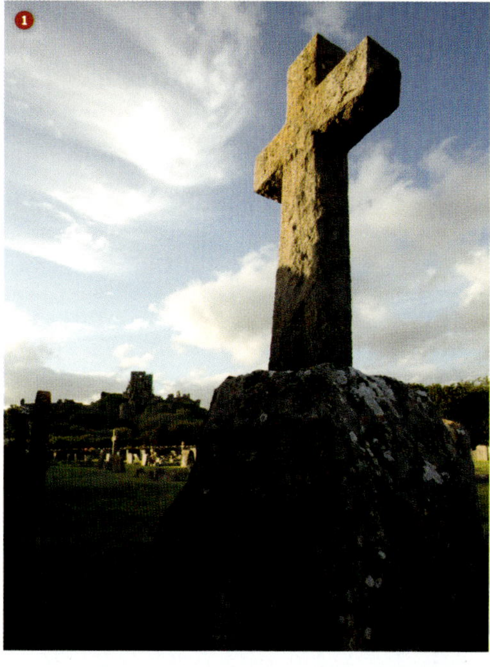

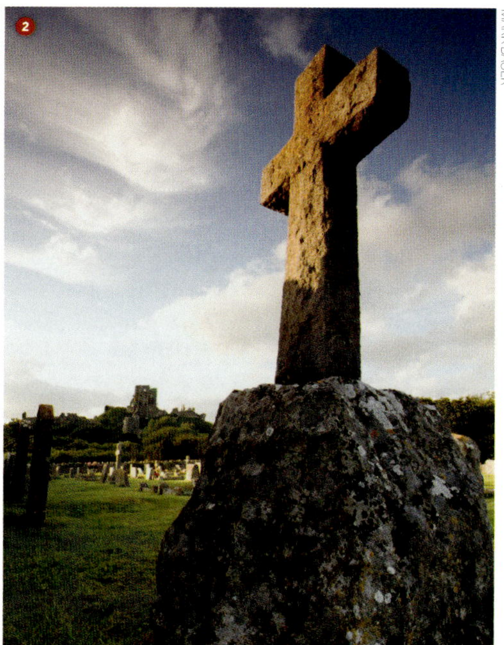

MARK BAUER

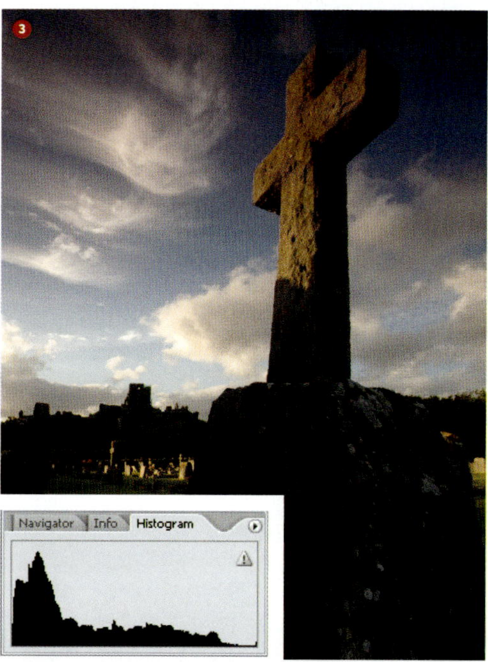

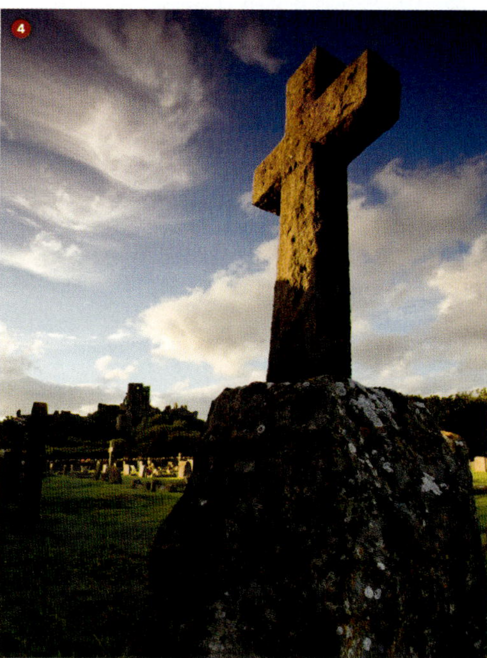

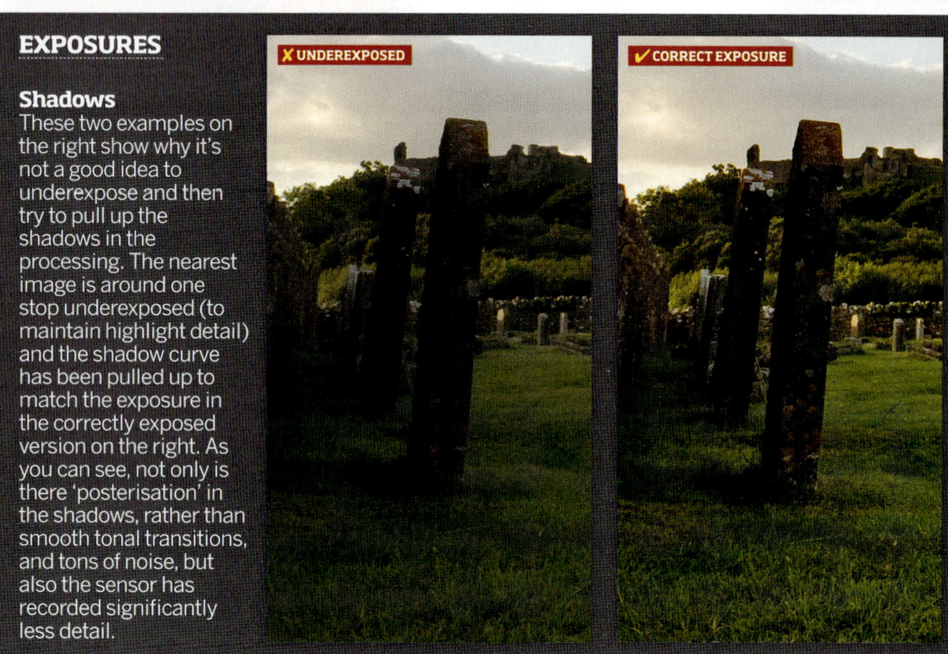

EXPOSURES

Shadows
These two examples on the right show why it's not a good idea to underexpose and then try to pull up the shadows in the processing. The nearest image is around one stop underexposed (to maintain highlight detail) and the shadow curve has been pulled up to match the exposure in the correctly exposed version on the right. As you can see, not only is there 'posterisation' in the shadows, rather than smooth tonal transitions, and tons of noise, but also the sensor has recorded significantly less detail.

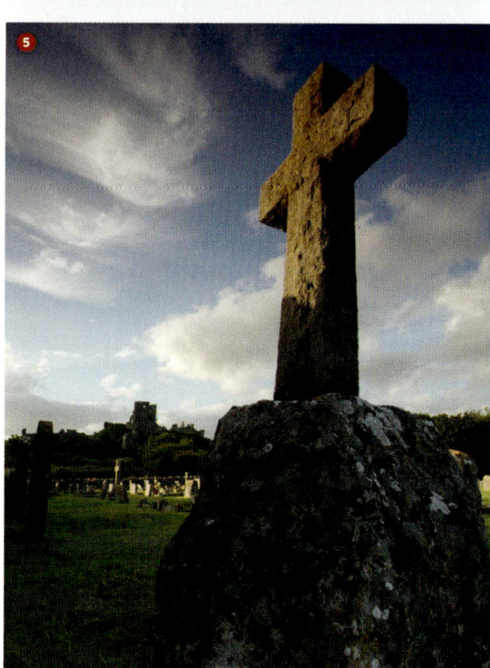

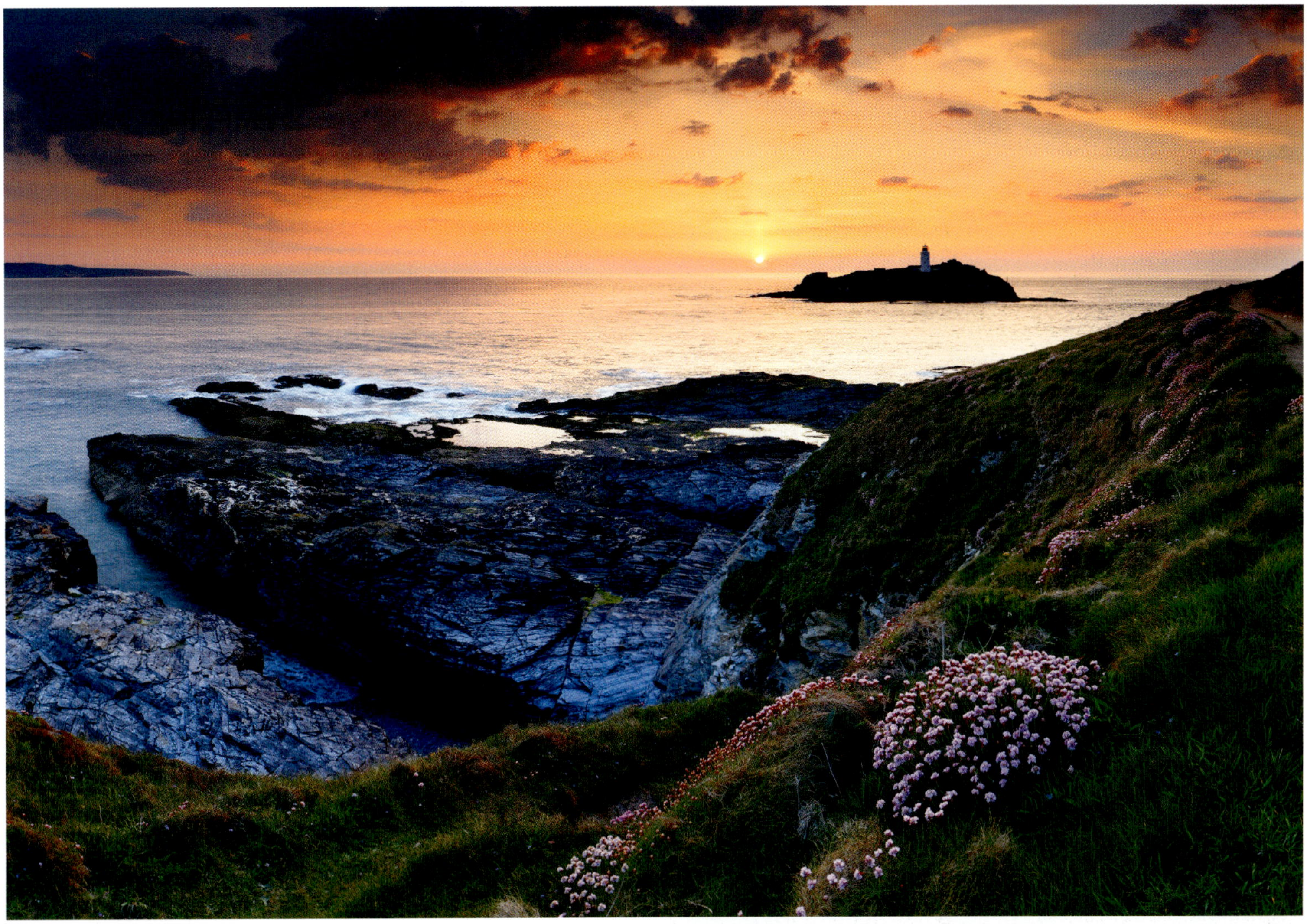

HELEN DIXON

3) Exposure for coastal landscapes

Achieving the correct exposure in coastal shots can be a bit trickier than for inland landscapes, as there are several things that can fool the camera's meter: bright highlights on water or bright white foamy waves can lead to underexposure. On the other hand, if you have chosen a large, dark rock for your foreground, this could cause the camera to overexpose. So you need to keep an eye out for any large areas of particularly bright or dark tones and apply exposure compensation accordingly. It is good practice to check the histogram after each shot and be prepared to re-shoot if necessary.

There can also be a huge range of contrast within any one scene, with bright skies, dark rocks, and bright highlights on water. Neutral Density (ND) graduate filters are essential, and depending on the conditions and the brightness of the sky and sea relative to your foreground, you may need to pull the grad down very low in the frame. This could even be below the horizon, to the top of your foreground. If you don't, you might end up with a correctly-exposed sky and foreground with a band of over-bright water in the middle of the picture. So when metering the scene to choose the strength and placement of the filter, remember to take readings from the foreground, sky and sea.

LONG EXPOSURES

Exposing to capture movement

One of the great things about taking photos by the sea is the opportunities it gives for capturing the movement of waves and adding atmosphere. In low light, with the lens stopped down to extend depth-of-field, long exposures are a necessity. They may range from several seconds to minutes, depending on lighting conditions. As waves wash around rocks or up and down the shore while the shutter is open, they will record as a romantic, mysterious mist. To capture the drama of waves breaking on the shore, speeds of ¼sec or slower works well.

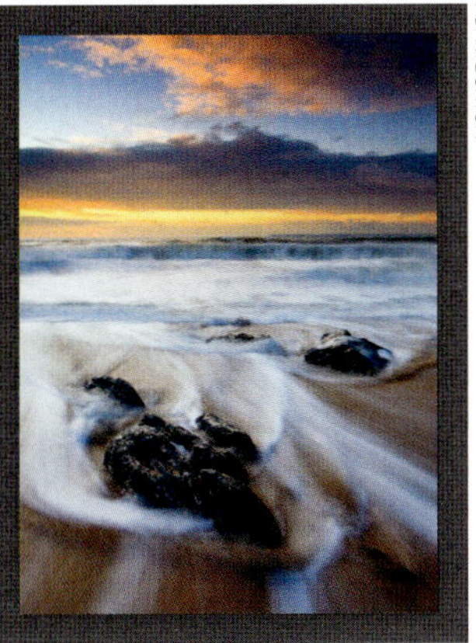

ADAM BURTON

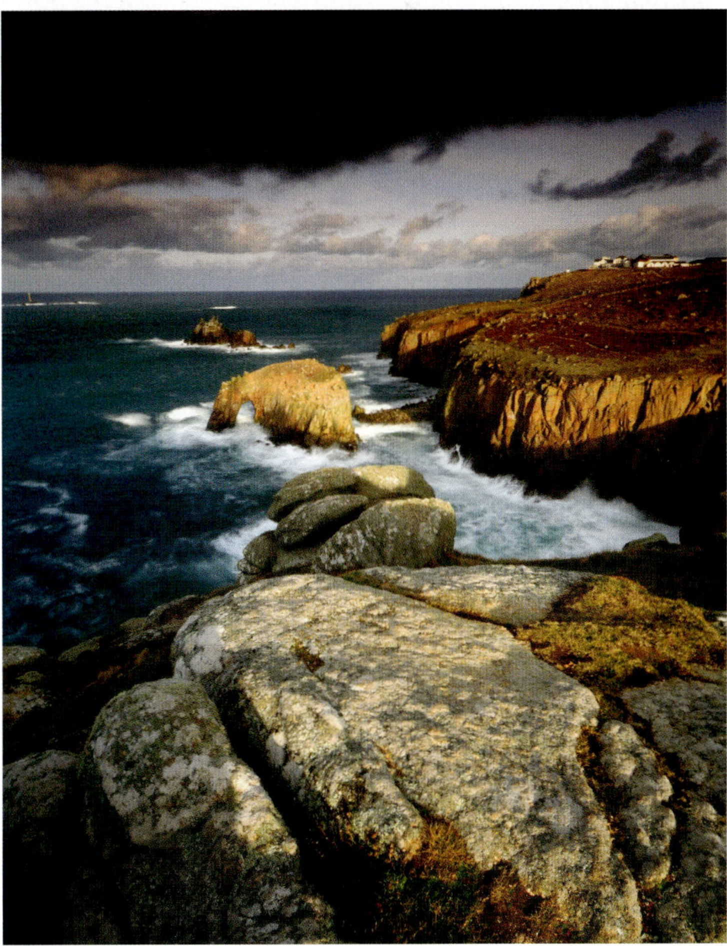

ROSS HODDINOTT

4) Histograms: An aid to checking exposure

THE BASICS In basic terms, a histogram is a two-dimensional graph, often resembling a range of mountain peaks, that represents an image's tonal extent. Whilst, at first glance, histograms might appear quite complex and confusing, they are actually very simple to read. They are an essential aid for digital SLR photographers striving to achieve consistently correct exposures in-camera and are a more accurate method of assessing exposure than looking at images you've taken on the LCD monitor. Therefore, if you are not already in the habit of regularly reviewing your images' histogram, it is time you did so. With the help of this guide, you will soon feel confident assessing histograms.

WHAT IS A HISTOGRAM? A histogram is a visual representation of an image's tonal range. The horizontal axis indicates the picture's extent from pure black (0, far left) to pure white (225, far right). The vertical axis shows how many pixels have that particular value. Looking at an image's histogram, you can tell whether the picture is made up of predominantly light, dark or mid-tones.

Although its appearance is also dictated by the colour and tone of the subject, a histogram with a large number of pixels (or a sharp peak) grouped at either edge is an indication of poor exposure. For example, a histogram with a large number of black pixels (grouped to the left) often signifies underexposure – subject detail will be obscured in the shadow areas. A large number of pixels grouped to the right of the histogram normally indicates an image which is overexposed. The image's highlights will burn out (or 'clip') and this detail is irretrievable. A graph with a narrow peak in the middle and no (or few) black or white pixels indicates an image lacking contrast.

SO WHAT SHOULD A HISTOGRAM LOOK LIKE? This is a tricky one to answer. Despite what some people may say, there is no such thing as the 'perfect histogram'. It simply tells us how a picture is exposed, allowing photographers to decide whether – and how – to adjust exposure settings. Therefore, a histogram of a light scene will be very different to one with predominantly black tones or one with a mix of both. However, generally speaking, a histogram should show a good spread of tones across the horizontal axis, with the majority of pixels positioned near to the middle, (100, mid-point). Normally, it is desirable to avoid peaks to the right-hand side of the graph, as this is usually an indication of 'burnt out' (overexposed) highlights, resulting in lost detail.

When assessing a histogram, it is important to consider the brightness of the subject itself. For example, a scene or subject boasting a large percentage of light or dark tones – like snow or a silhouette – will naturally have an affect on the overall look of the resulting graph. Therefore, whilst it is possible to make recommendations, it is impossible to generalise about what is and isn't a good histogram. Whist an even spread of pixels throughout the greyscale is often considered desirable, you will also need to use your own knowledge gained through experience.

HOW DO I CHECK A PICTURE'S HISTOGRAM? Most digital SLRs allow you to view the histogram on the LCD monitor during playback. To do this, press the playback button to view the image and then cycle through the additional photo info screens until the histogram is displayed. It's worth making this your default setting, so that you can quickly access the histogram and assess exposure immediately after taking the picture when required.

If the histogram indicates underexposure, apply positive exposure compensation. If pixels are grouped to the right hand side and the image appears overexposed, dial in negative compensation. Using the histogram is a far more reliable method of assessing exposure than looking at images on the LCD screen, particularly when trying to view images outdoors in bright light when the light reflecting from the LCD can prove deceptive.

DON'T PANIC!

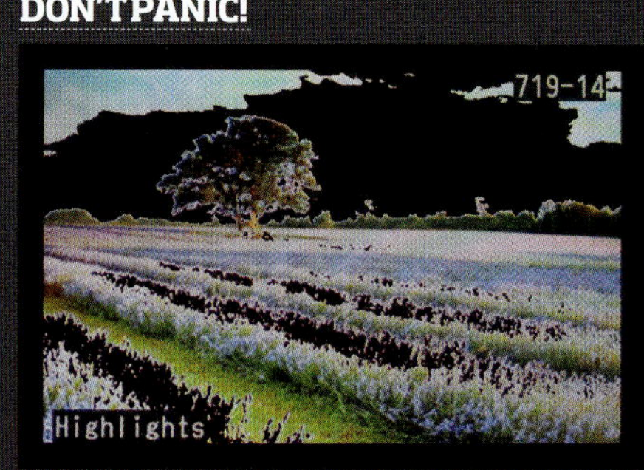

Exposure warnings

The majority of DSLRs are designed with a playback function known as the 'highlights screen'. Whilst histograms provide a graphic illustration of an image's tonal extent, helping you assess exposure overall, the highlights screen – or highlights alert – is aimed specifically at helping photographers to avoid highlights burning out. White or very light subjects in direct sunlight are especially prone to this. A histogram with a sharp peak to the far right will normally indicate that an image is suffering from areas of overexposure. However, the highlights alert actually identifies the pixels that exceed the value for pure white (255). Pixels that do so are not given a value, meaning they cannot be processed and are effectively discarded – having no detail or information recorded. When the image is replayed on the camera's LCD monitor, the pixels falling outside the camera's dynamic range flash or blink – providing a quick and graphic illustration of where picture detail is 'burned out' and devoid of detail. To rectify this, set negative exposure compensation so that the next image is recorded darker.

A digital camera's highlights alert is not always switched on by default. Therefore, consult your user's manual and switch it on when you feel this type of exposure warning would prove useful. Normally this is done via the camera's Playback Menu.

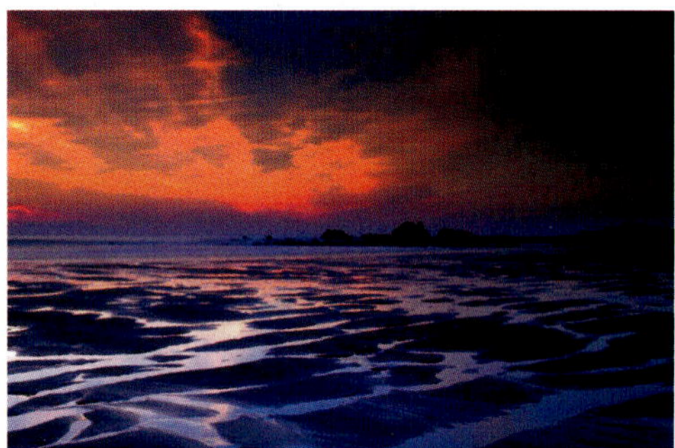

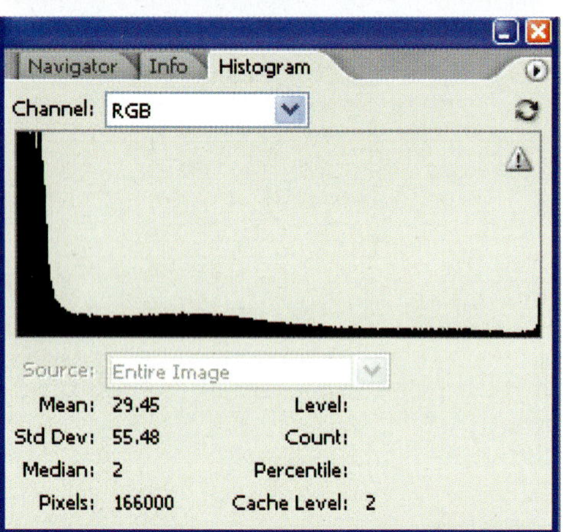

PEAKS TO THE LEFT The histogram is skewed to the left, as the dark backdrop means many of the pixels are in shadow areas, but the image is well exposed.

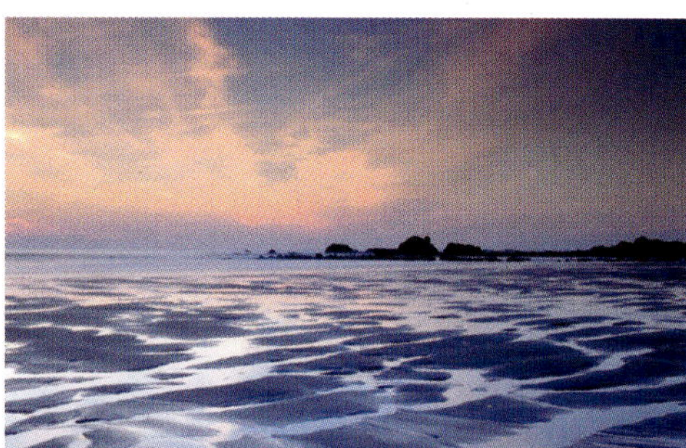

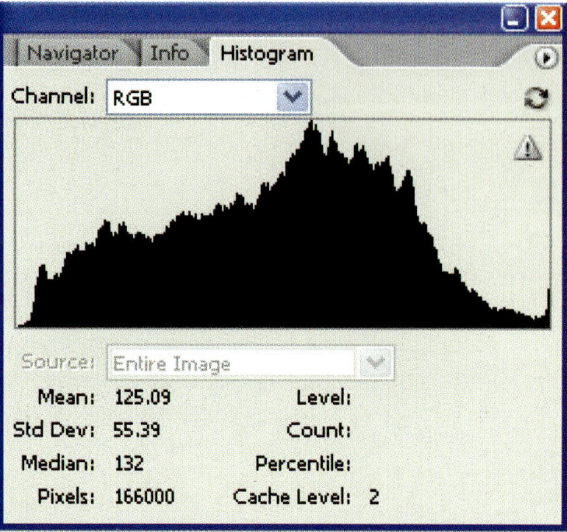

PERFECT EXPOSURE A typical landscape scene gives a so-called 'perfect histogram' as it has a good spread of tones and peaks through the mid-tones.

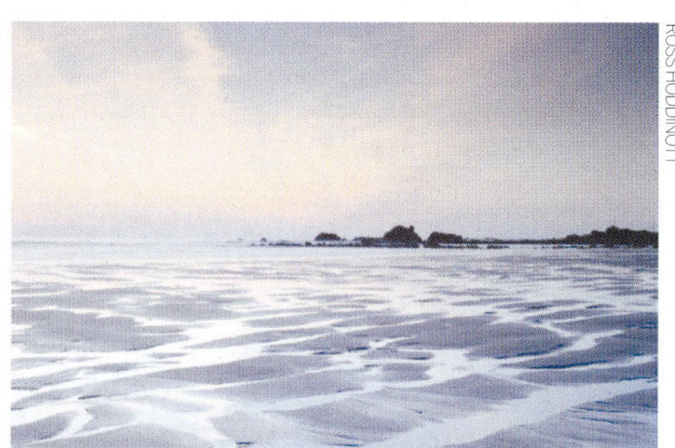

ROSS HODDINOTT

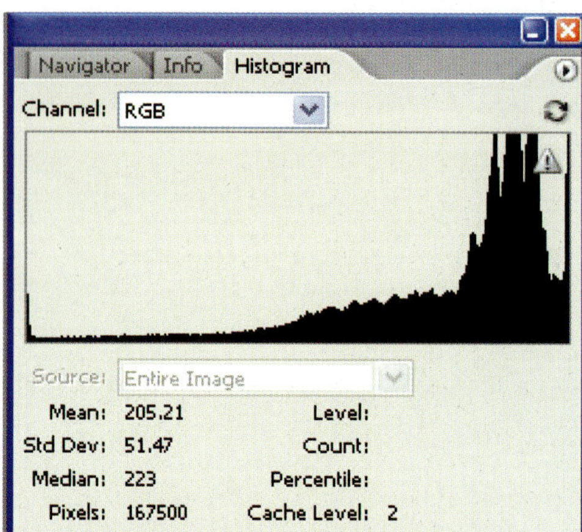

PEAKS TO THE RIGHT A well-exposed shot of an overly-light scene gives a histogram skewed to the right, much like that of an overexposed image.

PRO TIPS

COLOUR HISTOGRAMS

Some DSLRs allow you the option to view separate histograms for the red, green and blue channels. You're better off ignoring this option and using the standard greyscale histogram option

5) Expose to the right

'Exposing to the right' is fast becoming a widely-accepted approach to help maximise image quality – although it only applies if you shoot in Raw. With this technique you effectively push exposure settings as close to overexposure as possible without actually clipping the highlights. The result is a histogram with the majority of pixels grouped to the right of mid point – hence the name 'expose to the right'. So, when you're confident you understand exposures well enough, give this technique a try and try pushing the exposure as far to the right of the histogram as you can, without clipping the highlights. The image will probably look a little light once in the Raw converter, but this is easily corrected with the brightness and contrast controls and will give much better results than trying to lighten a darker image.

CCD and CMOS sensors count light in a linear fashion. Most digital SLRs record a 12-bit image capable of recording 4,096 tonal values over six stops. But the tonal values are not spread evenly across the six stops, each stop records half the light of the previous one. So, half of the levels are devoted to the brightest stop (2,048), half of the remainder (1,024 levels) are devoted to the next stop and so on. As a result, the last and darkest of the six stops, only boasts 64 levels. This might seem confusing but, simply, if you do not properly use the right side of the histogram, which represents the majority of tonal values, you are wasting up to half the available encoding levels. So if you deliberately underexpose to ensure detail is retained in the highlights – a common practise among many digital photographers – you are potentially losing a large percentage of the data that can be captured.

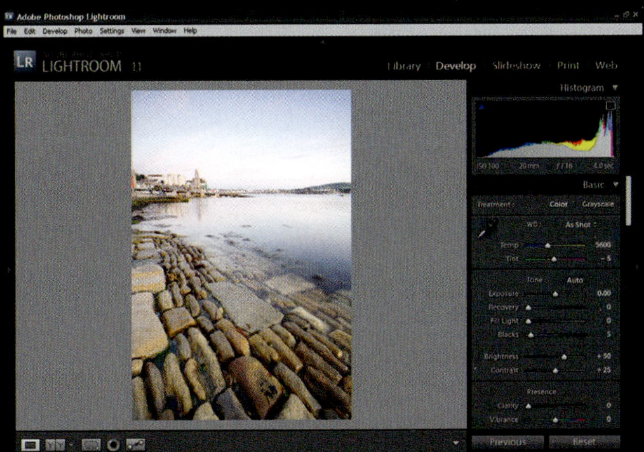

MAIN IMAGE & INSET: Exposure to the right of the histogram will capture maximum detail and minimum noise. Once in the Raw converter the image will look too light and washed out so use the brightness and contrast controls to adjust the image's appearance.

MARK BAUER

Aperture-priority is the mode for you!

So what is it that makes the aperture-priority mode more useful than any of the other exposure modes when shooting landscapes. Read on, and all will be revealed

APERTURE-PRIORITY GETS ITS NAME because it allows you to decide which aperture (f/number) you want to use to take a photograph, while the camera automatically sets a shutter speed, based on light levels, to achieve the correct exposure. In other words, it lets you prioritise the aperture selection, and it chooses the shutter speed accordingly.

As the lens aperture is the most influential factor over the depth-of-field (the zone of sharp focus) in a photograph, aperture-priority mode is the most practical choice of shooting mode if you are photographing a subject or situation in which control over depth-of-field is important.

Landscape photography is the best example. Generally, when shooting landscapes, you'll want to make sure your depth-of-field is broad enough to record the whole scene in sharp focus, from the immediate foreground to infinity, which means that you'll need to set a small aperture, such as f/11. Aperture-priority mode lets you do that easily, because you have to actively set the required aperture.

When shooting portraits, the opposite tends to apply – you want shallow depth-of-field, so that your subject is recorded in sharp focus but the background is thrown out of focus. That means making sure you take the picture at a wide aperture such as f/4 or f/2.8, which again is easy when shooting in aperture-priority mode because it's you and not the camera who decides which aperture to use.

That said, you can still control which aperture is set using other exposure modes, but it just requires a slightly different (and longer) way of working. In shutter-priority (S or Tv) mode, for example, all you need to do is change the shutter speed until the camera sets the aperture you want. Similarly, in program mode, you can use the program shift function to change the aperture and shutter combination that the camera has set until you get the right aperture.

Where aperture-priority triumphs over these alternative modes is that once you've set a particularly aperture, the camera won't change it, even if light levels change. Instead, the shutter speed adjusts to maintain the correct exposure. This wouldn't be the case if you set the camera to shutter-priority mode – if light levels change, your DSLR automatically adjusts the aperture to maintain correct exposure, giving the shutter speed priority, so your control over the depth-of-field is diminished. Similarly, in program mode, the camera would change the aperture/shutter speed combination in response to changing light.

Aperture-priority is also a handy mode to set for general use, when you're just wandering around, shooting anything that takes your fancy, whether it's architecture, details, abstracts or candids. Depth-of-field requirements will vary depending on the shot – one minute you need lots of it, the next, as little as possible – but this can be quickly altered with the flick of the camera's input dial, and the viewfinder display will keep you fully informed of exactly which aperture (and corresponding shutter speed) you're using.

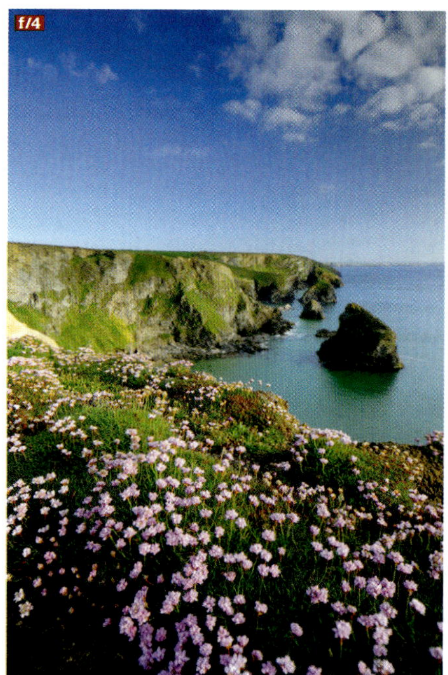

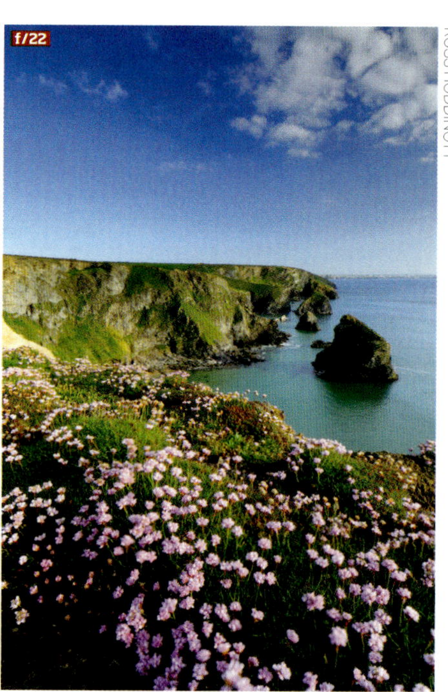

ROSS HODDINOTT

THE EFFECT OF APERTURES With depth-of-field having such an effect on the final image, it's no surprise that many experienced photographers rate aperture-priority as their favourite mode. These two shots show how different apertures can produce very different results.

Setting aperture-priority on your DSLR

Choosing aperture-priority mode is simple – all you need to do is turn your exposure dial (or in some cases push the exposure mode button) and select A or Av. Your DSLR will then be set to aperture-priority mode and all you need to do is rotate the small adjustment dial (found either on the handgrip or on the top-right corner of the rear of your camera) to change your aperture. If you lightly depress the shutter button to activate the exposure system, you can keep a check on the shutter speed the camera has selected.

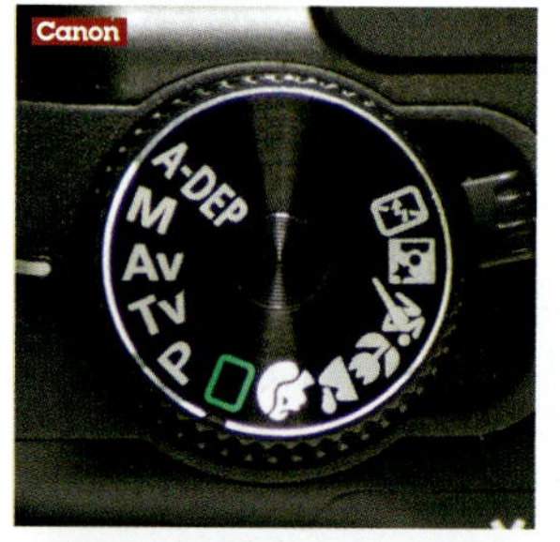

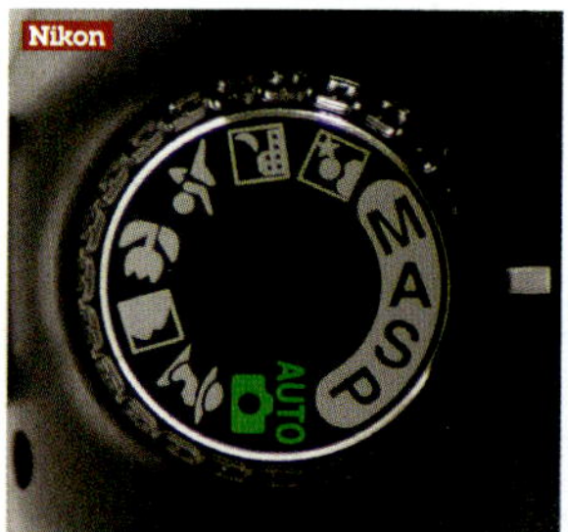

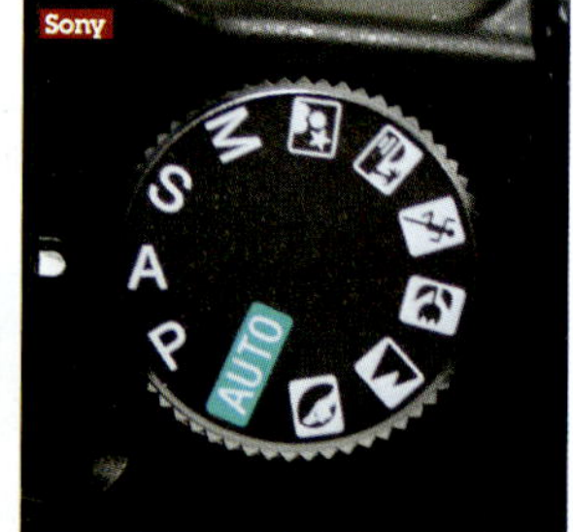

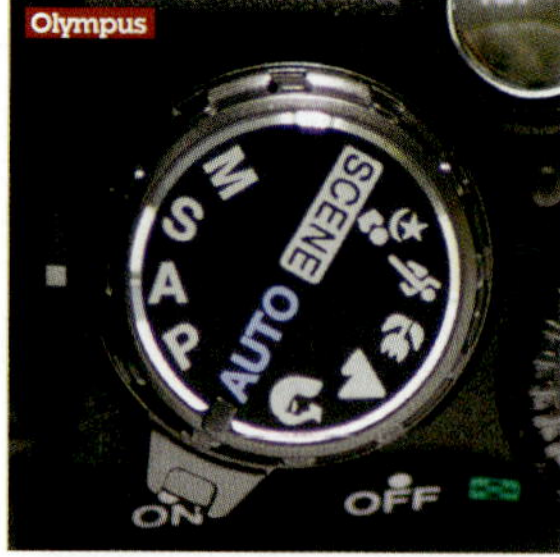

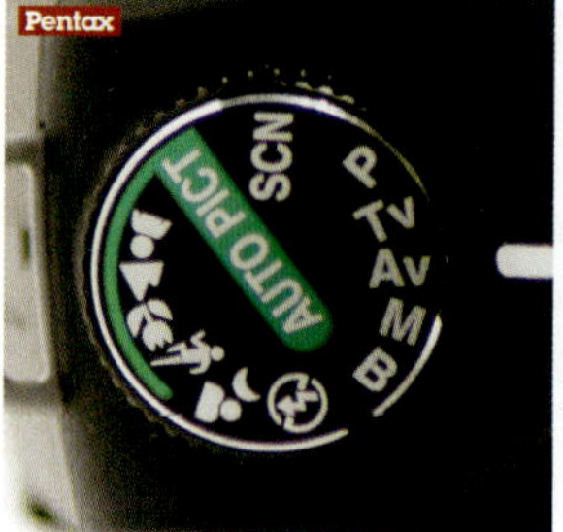

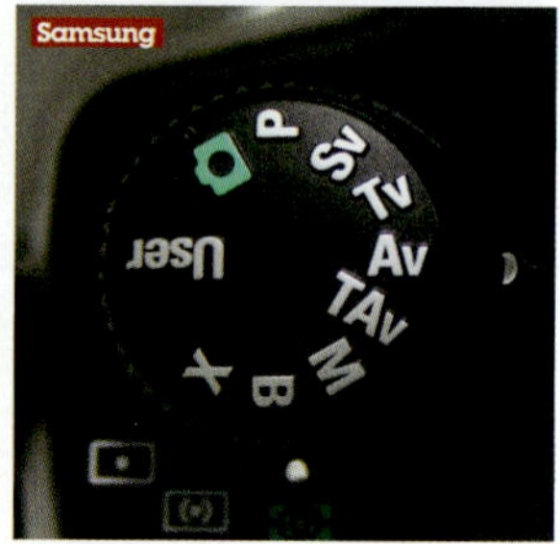

How other exposure modes work

We've already established that in aperture-priority mode, you set the desired aperture and the camera sets the accompanying shutter speed to give the correct exposure. Here's a quick rundown of how the other modes work.

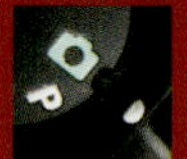

Full-auto Mode

The camera sets the shutter speed and aperture to achieve correct exposure and you can't change the combination to use a specific aperture or shutter speed.

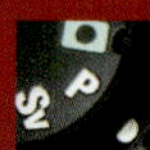

Program Mode

Program works in a similar way to full auto, but you can usually alter the aperture/shutter speed combination if you need to use a specific aperture or shutter speed.

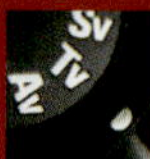

Shutter Priority

You set a shutter speed and your DSLR sets the appropriate aperture. If light levels change, the same shutter speed is used and the aperture changed.

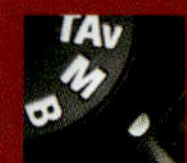

Metered Manual

You manually set both the aperture and shutter speed independently of each other, so neither changes unless you adjust them, even if light levels fall or rise.

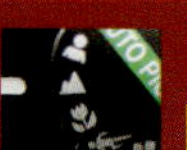

Subject Modes

These program modes are tailored to suit a specific subject, with various camera functions like the AF, flash and exposure systems set accordingly.

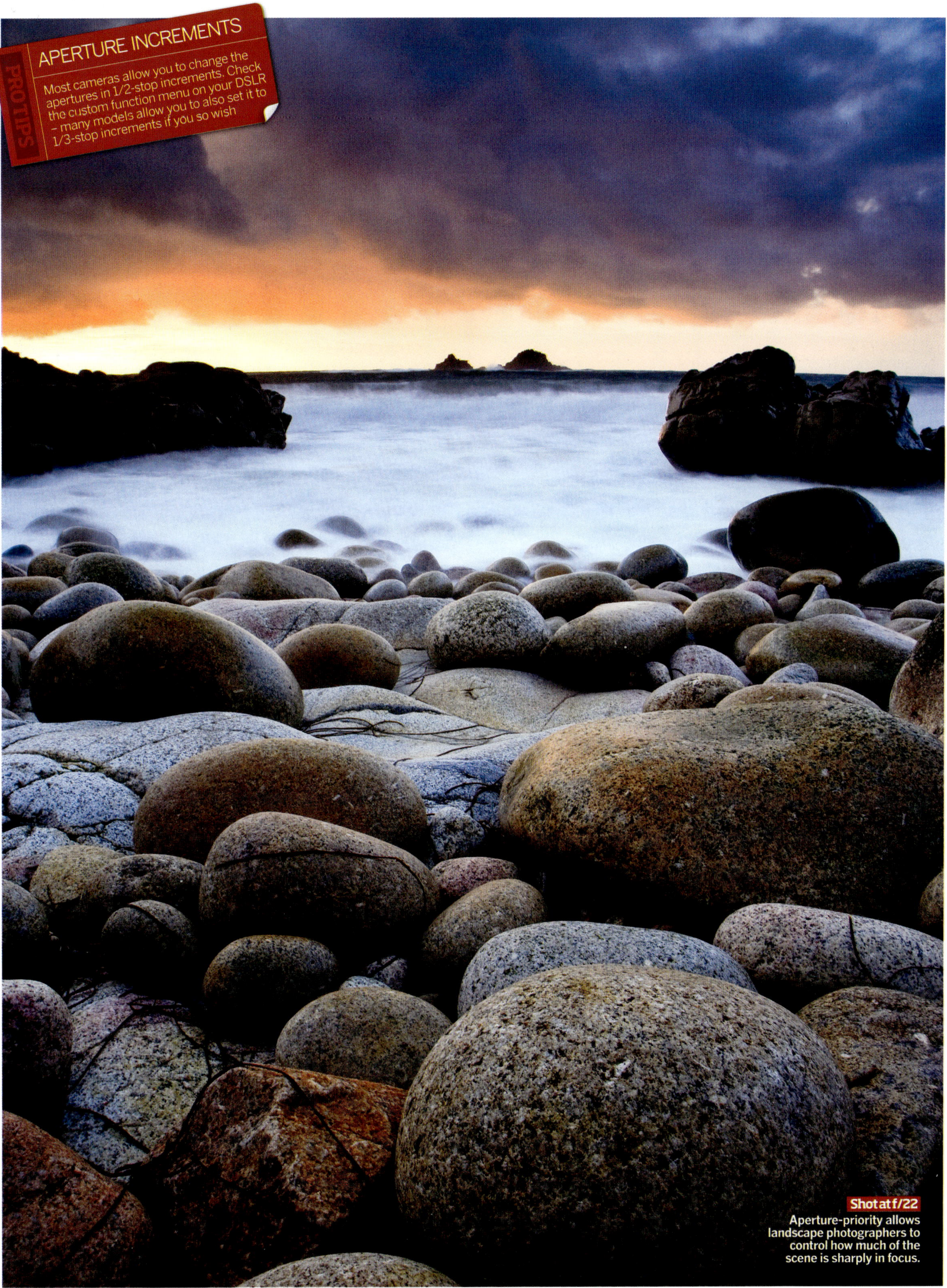

PROTIPS
APERTURE INCREMENTS
Most cameras allow you to change the apertures in 1/2-stop increments. Check the custom function menu on your DSLR – many models allow you to also set it to 1/3-stop increments if you so wish

MARK BAUER

Shot at f/22
Aperture-priority allows landscape photographers to control how much of the scene is sharply in focus.

EXPERT TUTORIAL

Shutter speeds & landscapes

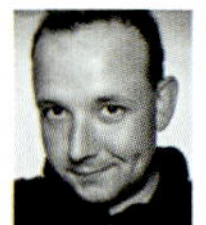

WITH ROSS ARMSTRONG Landscape photographers understandably give priority to apertures, but in some situations, shutter speed is just as important, as it can be used to capture the effect of movement within a scene. Because you want to maintain sharpness in landscape images by maximising depth-of-field, you can really make shutter speeds work for you as the smaller apertures you'll require also mean slower shutter speeds. This is easily done by setting your camera to shutter-priority (Tv or S) on the mode dial. This ensures you get the right exposure as you set the shutter speed for the desired length of time, while your DSLR adjusts the aperture accordingly. So why choose the shutter speed rather than the aperture? Well, setting the slower speed means anything moving when you fire the shutter, such as flowing water or foliage blowing in the wind, is captured as a soft blur, while anything static, like a fence or rock, remains sharp and in focus. The effect of setting a long exposure is to give images extra depth and dimension whilst illustrating a real sense of movement. The result is usually closer to how you remember the scene, rather than a lifeless image of grass with every blade in focus.

But remember, even digital SLRs can be fooled. Be careful not to overexpose an image when shooting, for example, a field of golden sweeping grass in the evening sun. As you lower the shutter speed, the camera's chosen aperture will eventually flash, indicating that the image will be overexposed. You can, of course, check the image and the histogram on the LCD monitor for blown-out highlights.

For even slower shutter speeds and the chance to lift your landscape photography to another level, use filters. A polariser will cut out reflections and darken blue skies to give clouds that 'wow' factor, as well as reduce the amount of light reaching your sensor by two stops at the same time. You can further enhance movement and blur by using a Neutral Density filter, which is a neutral grey filter that doesn't affect colour balance but has the effect of reducing the amount of light passing through it, allowing you to select slower shutter speeds as a result.

For optimum results shoot at dawn and dusk and always use a tripod. Shoot on darker, cloudy days, and let nature work for you – less light means you'll get slower shutter speeds. On windy days, hang your camera bag from the tripod to keep your outfit stable. A helpful hint is to use a remote release/self-timer and mirror lock-up to avoid contact with the camera during the exposure to gain the maximum effect. Wait for the wind, open the shutter and whatever happens, don't get blown away!

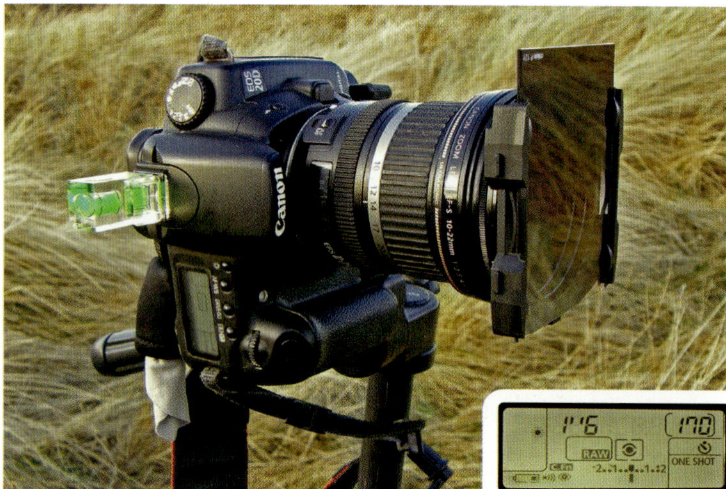

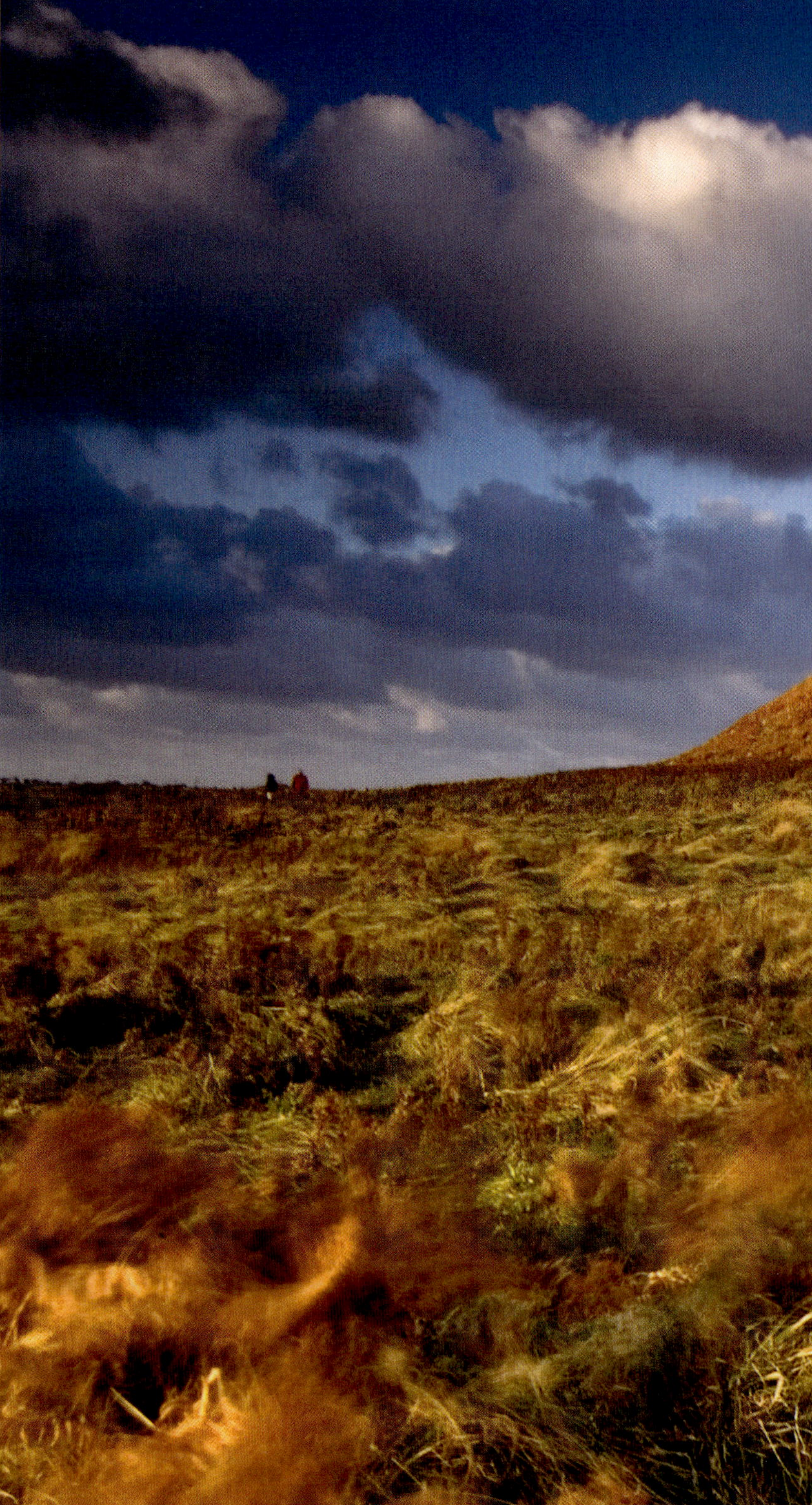

ABOVE, POLARISER AND ND GRAD: "I used a polariser combined with an ND grad filter to hold back the bright sky and ensure a well balanced, long exposure. Shooting in Raw, I used the self-timer and an exposure of 1.6 seconds."

SHUTTER SPEED COMPARISON: "For this series, the lens (10-22mm set to 13mm) was focused on the long Marram grass in the foreground. The only thing I changed was the shutter speeds in a sequence from 1/50sec to 1.6sec. Note how the movement of the grass in the breeze becomes increasingly blurry as the shutter speed is slowed. My favourite image from the sequence is the longest exposure, which captures the movement in the Marram grass exactly like I remember it, in the low, winter sunshine."

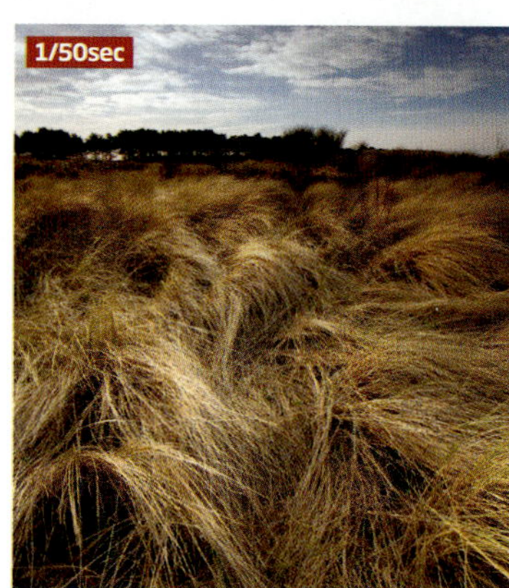

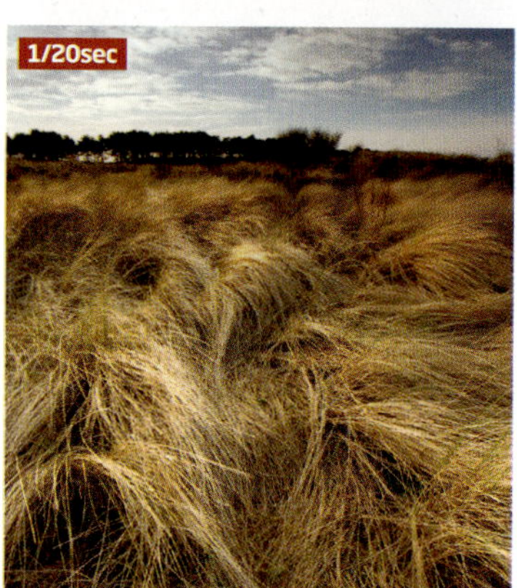

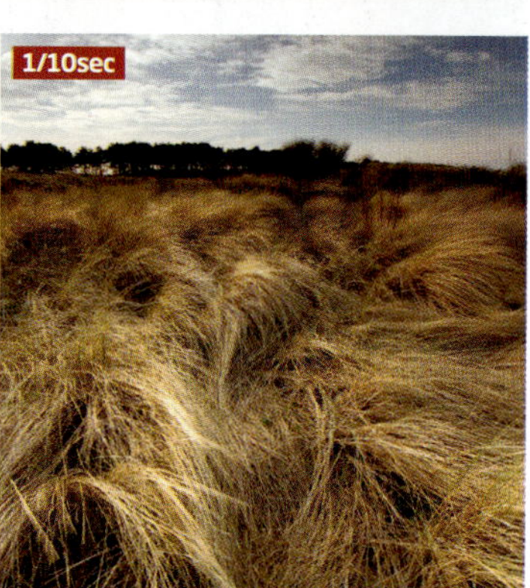

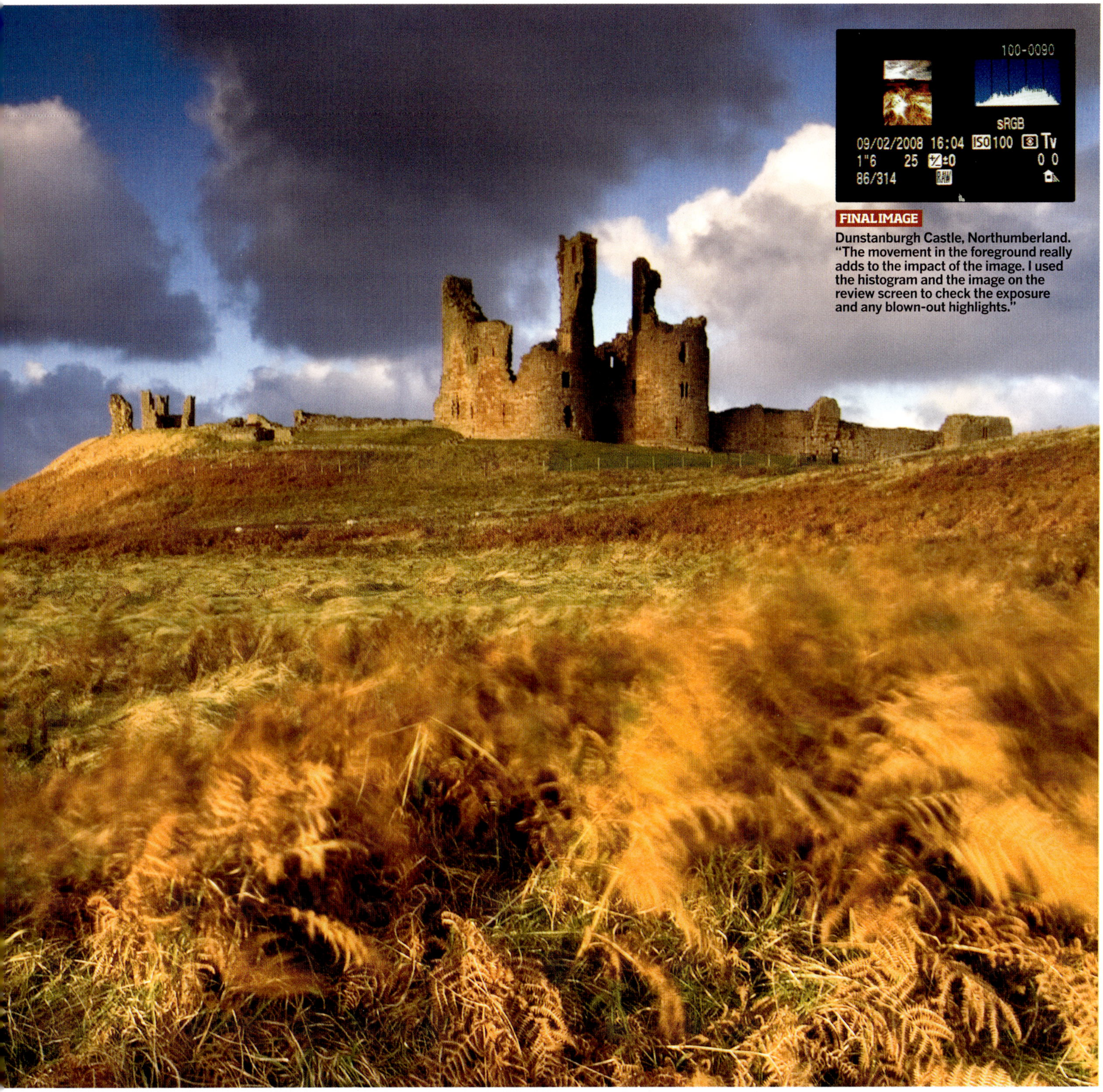

FINAL IMAGE

Dunstanburgh Castle, Northumberland. "The movement in the foreground really adds to the impact of the image. I used the histogram and the image on the review screen to check the exposure and any blown-out highlights."

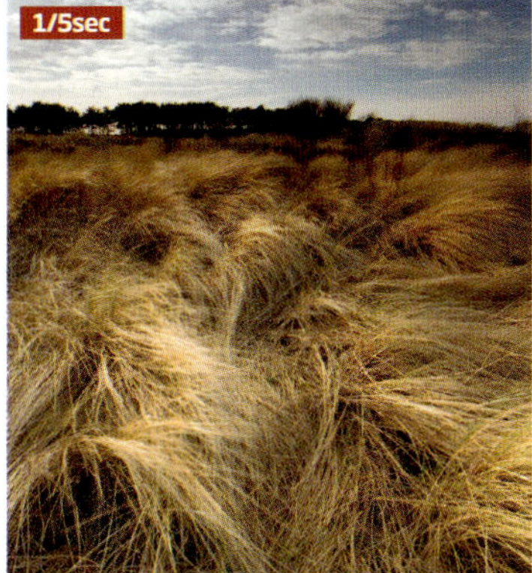

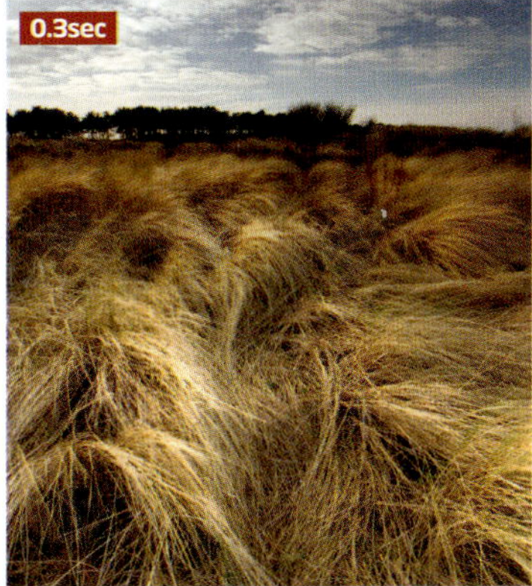

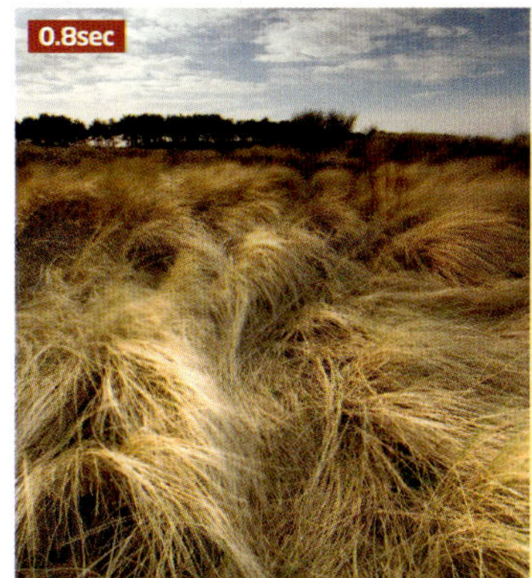

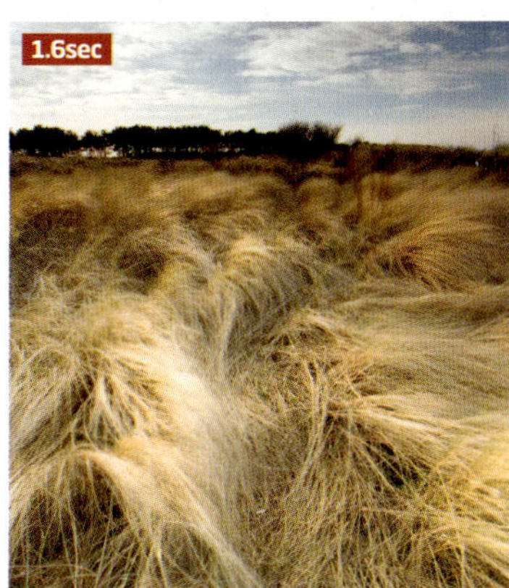

Combining Raw files

WITH LUKE MARSH Setting your DSLR to shoot in Raw means you're able to recover hidden detail from areas of the scene that are overexposed, such as bright sky. Photoshop expert Luke Marsh shows how to use the Photoshop Elements Raw converter to create two different images at different exposure levels exposures from the same Raw file and then recombine them for the perfect result. Techniques used in this easy-to-follow step-by-step tutorial include exposure adjustment, layer creation and editing, level adjustment, sharpness control using the High Pass filter, opacity effects and colour adjustment. This technique is especially satisfying as you are only working with image data captured in the original single exposure. Elements 4.0 was used here, but more recent versions are suitable too.

ORIGINAL IMAGE

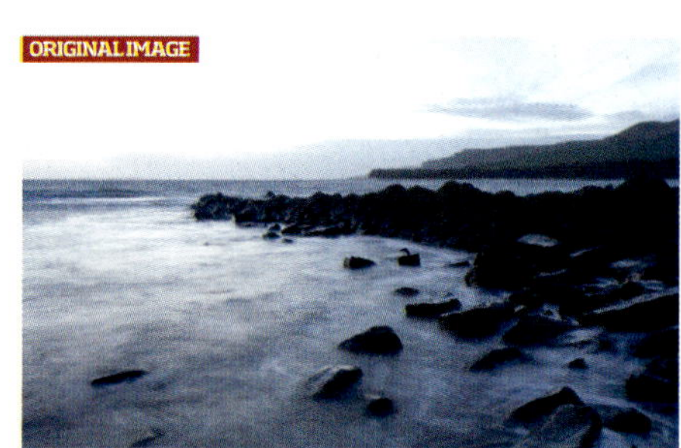

1

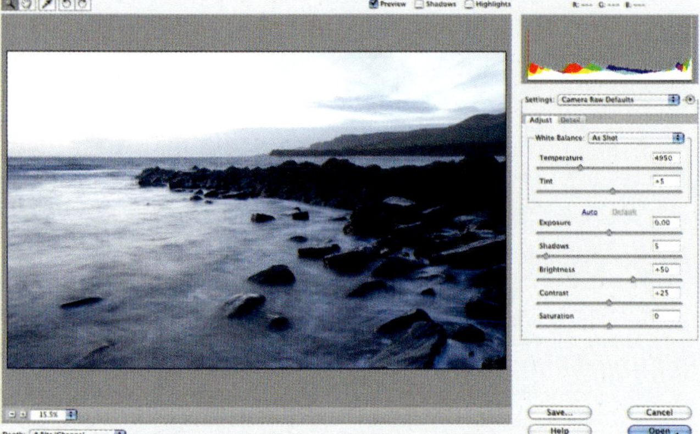

If you've never used the Elements Raw converter before, the first thing you'll notice on opening files is the image opens in the Raw control window (above). For the first step, I simply click **Open**, leaving the settings as they are, then go **File>Save As** and create a Photoshop file (.psd) as we are going to be working with layers.

2

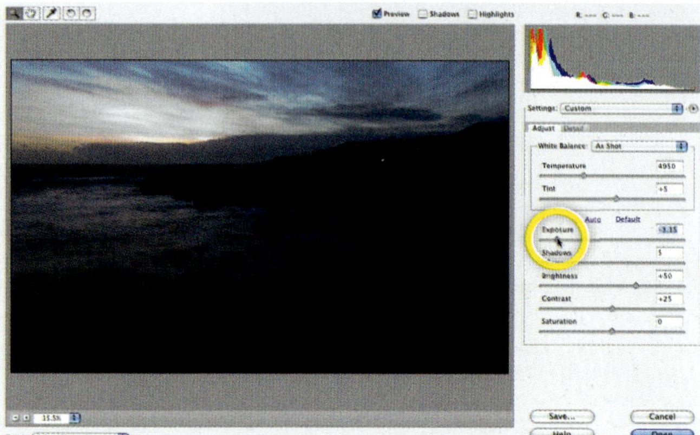

I reopen the original Raw file, and again the Raw control window appears with the image. This time, I use the **Exposure** control (circled) and move the slider left, to underexpose the image, pulling back the detail from the sky area hidden on the original image. Happy with the results, I click **Open** to take the image into Elements.

3

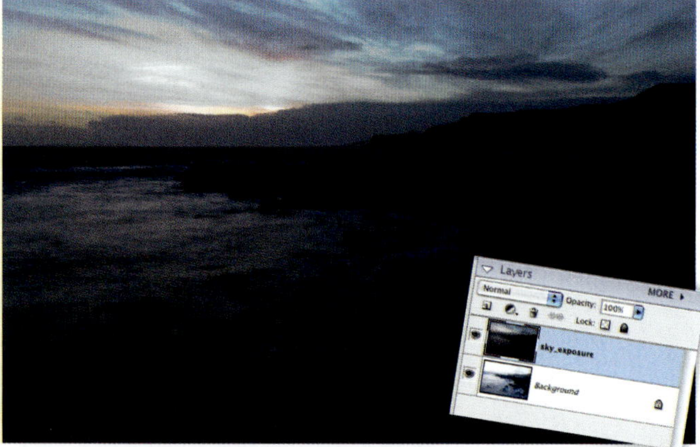

I now have two files open. One contains the original exposure and the other is the new underexposed image. With the underexposed file active, I go **Select>All** then **Edit>Copy** placing the image into the pasteboard memory. Now I can close this file and use **Edit>Paste** to place this image into a new layer on the original file.

4

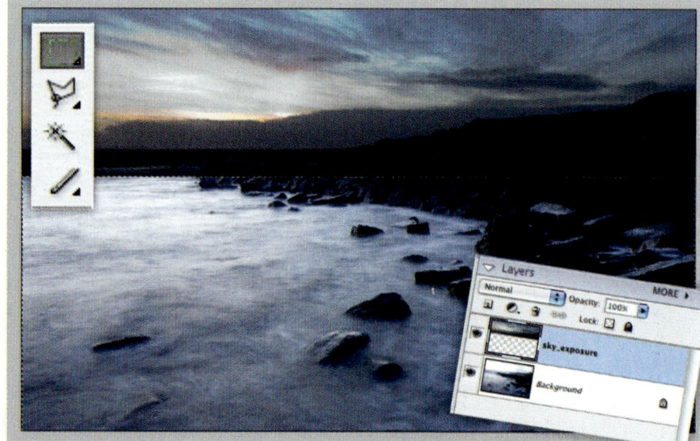

With the two exposures in place I want to combine the correctly-exposed foreground with the newly-exposed sky. With the sky layer active and using the **Rectangular Marquee** I select a large area of foreground, just short of the horizon, and use **Edit>Delete** to remove the area noting the effect in the layer palette preview (inset).

5

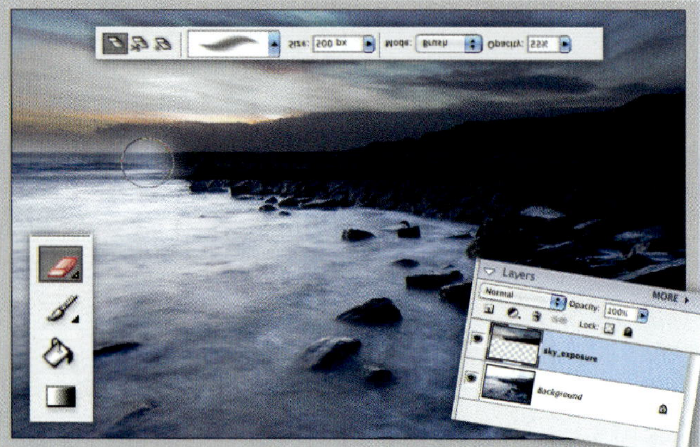

Now it's time to tidy up the horizon, so with the **Eraser** tool set to a medium-sized, soft-edged brush at an Opacity of 55%, I gradually erase areas of the newly-exposed layer, revealing the original horizon exposure. The slight feathering effect between the two layers creates a misty effect which further enhances the image's mood.

6

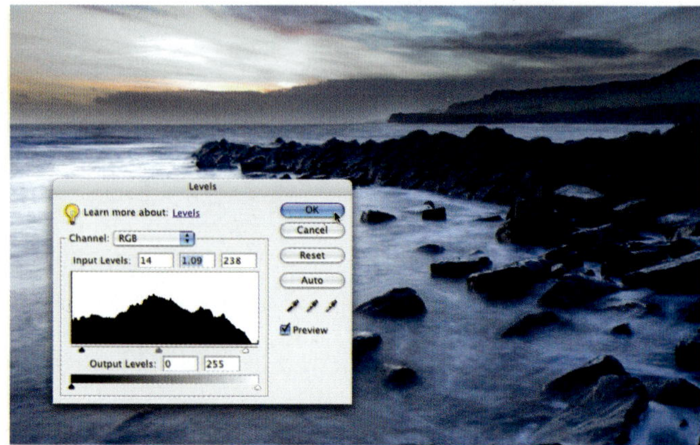

The initial layer work is complete, so to save my work so far, I go **Layer>Flatten Image** then **File>Save As** to create a new file. With both layers merged, it's time for some overall enhancement, so I go **Enhance>Adjust Lighting>Levels** to lighten up the image and improve the definition. I click **OK** to apply the changes.

FINAL IMAGE

STORMY SKIES AHEAD!
It's clear to see the benefits of shooting your images in Raw, as it's possible to rescue more detail than if you'd captured the scene as a JPEG.

7

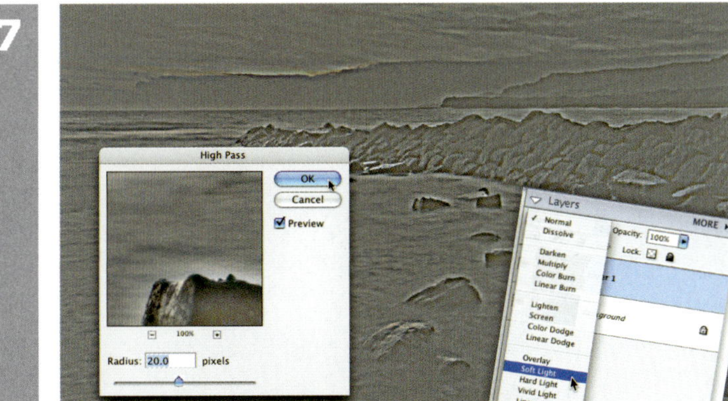

The **High Pass** filter is a far more forgiving way to enhance detail than sharpening. To use it, I first go to **Layer> Duplicate Layer** to preserve the original image. Then I go to **Filter>Other>High Pass,** adjusting the **Radius** to around **20 pixels** before clicking **OK**. I change the **Blend Mode** in the layer palette to **Soft Light**.

8

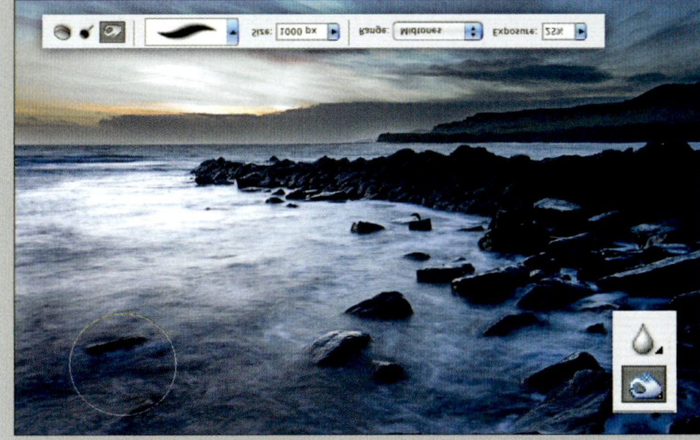

Use **Layer>Flatten Image** again, saving a copy if required. Now, using the **Burn** tool (inset right) with a large soft-edged brush and the **Opacity** at approximately 25%, I darken the exposure of specific areas, which helps to improve the depth of the image. I focus on the edges of the frame and build the effect up gradually.

9

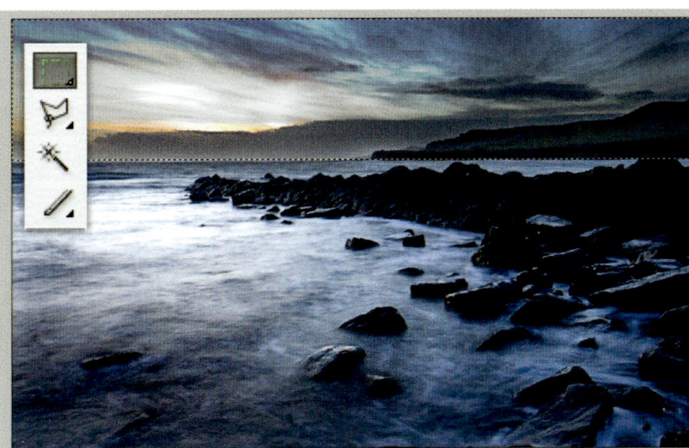

The image is predominately blue in hue and I'd quite like to inject a different tone to the sky area. Using the **Rectangular Marquee** tool**,** I select the area above the horizon and **Select>Feather,** entering an amount of 50 pixels to soften the selection, then I go **Edit>Copy** then **Edit>Paste,** placing the selection into a new layer.

10

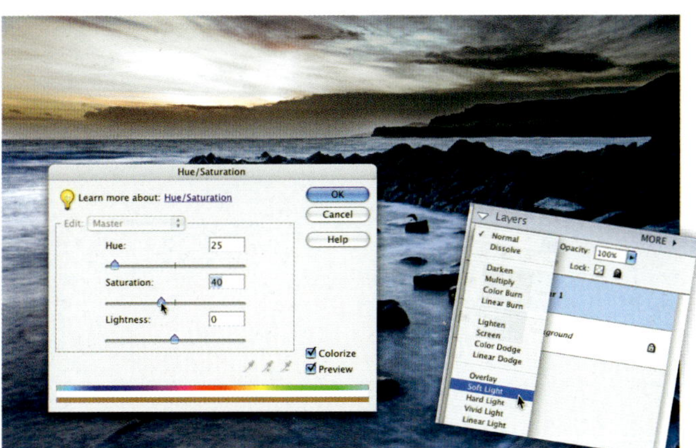

Change the **Blend Mode** of the new layer to **Soft Light**, and then go to **Enhance>Adjust Colour>Adjust Hue/Saturation**. In the window, I start by clicking the **Colorize** box and immediately see the effect in the preview. Finally, I adjust the **Hue** and **Saturation** sliders until I am happy with the colour, and click **OK**.

CALUMET

Calumet Photographic has been serving the needs of professional and serious photographers since 1939. We have gained the trust of our customers by providing them with highly dependable products at affordable prices, a philosophy reflected in Calumet's ever-growing branded product range.

Calumet Tripods

From highly portable, lightweight tripods to mid-size and heavy-duty models for extra stability with longer lenses, Calumet's tripod range provides a wide choice of models for all applications and budgets.

Calumet 7100 lightweight tripod kit

Supplied with a 3-way pan & tilt head with quick release, this is the perfect travelling companion for those shooting with a digital or 35mm SLR in the field.

Max height: 146.7cm/57.7"
Min height: 22.9cm/9"
Folded length: 54cm/21.3"
Max load: 5kg/11lb

Calumet 7300 tripod kit

Support your camera in the field or in the studio with this compact, yet sturdy tripod and 3-way pan & tilt head.

Max height: 171.5cm/67.5"
Min height: 27.3cm/10.8"
Folded length: 62.2cm/24.5"
Max load: 5kg/11lbb

Calumet 7500 tripod

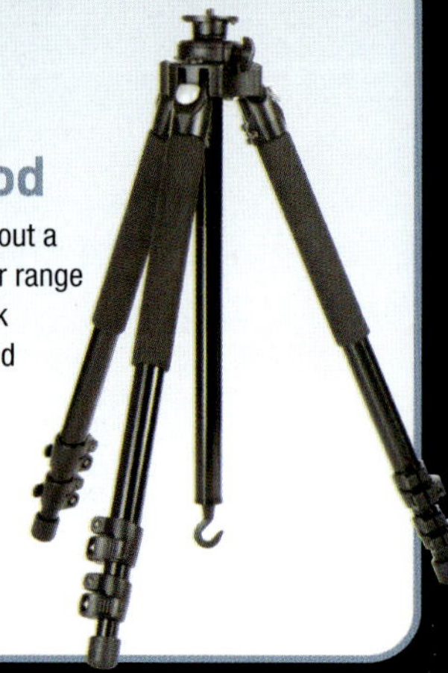

This mid-sized tripod is supplied without a head, allowing you to choose from our range of pan & tilt, ball & socket and joystick heads. The CK7500 has been designed for use with cameras up to medium format in the field and in the studio.

Max height: 173.3cm/69"
Min height: 24.4cm/9.6"
Folded length: 63.5cm/25"
Max load: 5.9kg/13lb

Calumet Monopods

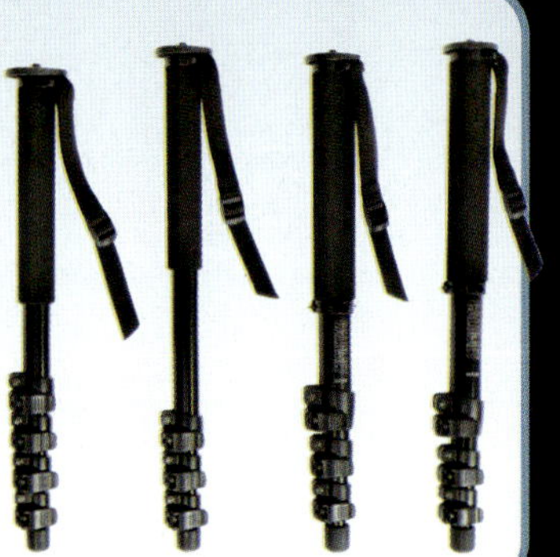

Whether you're shooting landscapes, sports or wildlife, often nothing can beat the convenience of a monopod for dependable camera support. Our compact, lightweight monopods can handle an impressive load capacity for their weight and can be stored just about anywhere when collapsed.

Supplied in a range of 4 & 5-section models in both aluminium or carbon fibre, Calumet monopods are available to support cameras up to 13.6kg/30lb in weight at heights of up to 186cm/73" (model quoted is CK8105 5-section carbon fibre).

NEW Calumet Gimbal Head

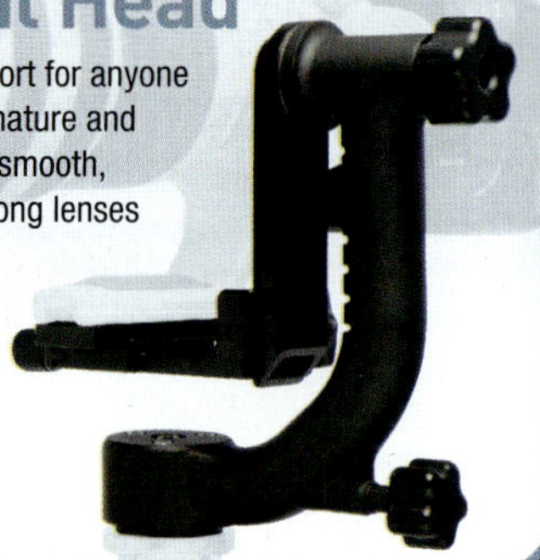

This is the simplest, smartest, and most versatile support for anyone shooting long-lens photography, including landscape, nature and sports photographers. The Gimbal head provides fluid-smooth, virtually weightless, pan and tilt movements for most long lenses that will not only improve your performance and image quality, but will also minimize accidental damage to your expensive equipment. Suitable for use with Calumet CK7800 or similar tripods only.

Calumet Backpacks

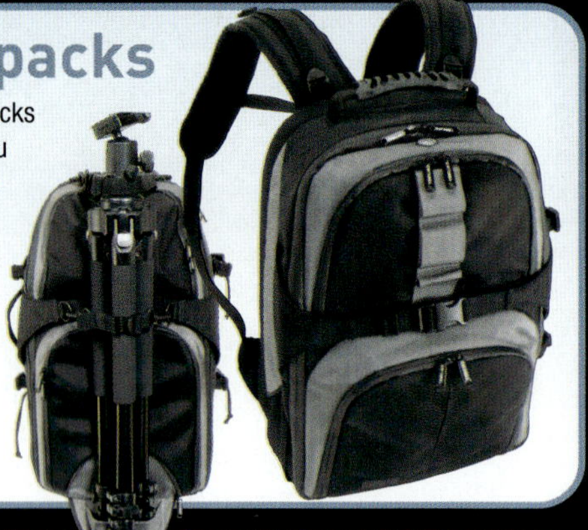

These tough and travel-friendly backpacks combine the comfort and protection you require when transporting your camera gear and laptop on lengthy photographic treks.

RM2180
Calumet BP935 Small Backpack
RM2184
Calumet BP1500 Large Backpack

Calumet Watertight Cases

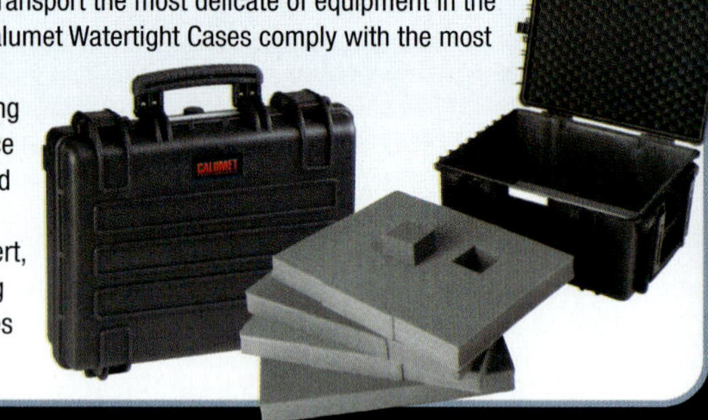

Designed to safely store and transport the most delicate of equipment in the most severe environments, Calumet Watertight Cases comply with the most rigorous of testing standards. Their thick plastic/resin housing provides exceptional resistance to impact, corrosion, water and dust. Includes a watertight Neoprene seal, dice-foam insert, pressure valve, with self-oiling wheels and retractable handles on selected models.

Calumet Filters

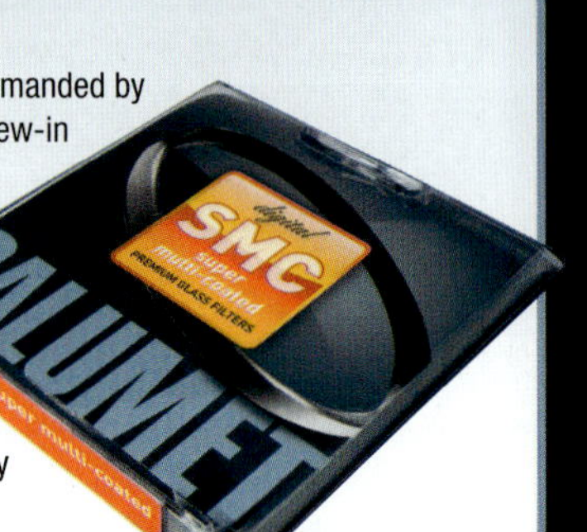

Manufactured in Germany to the highest standards demanded by busy professional photographers, Calumet's latest screw-in camera filters are available in two ranges:

Multi-coated filters – available in UV/P, circular polariser, ND, colour correction and colour effects in sizes from 49-82mm.

Digital Super Multi-coated filters – slim-profile mounted for use with wider angle lenses and available in UV/P and circular polariser only in sizes from 49-82mm

ProSpec Memory Cards **Exclusive to Calumet**

ProSpec memory cards are cards that you can really count on. Available in CompactFlash (CF) UDMA 420x speed and SDHC 150x speed, ProSpec cards can be used for both digital stills and video capture in operating temperatures from tropical to sub-zero!

ProSpec 8Gb UDMA CF Card 420x	CM6271
ProSpec 16Gb UDMA CF Card 420x	CM6277
ProSpec 32Gb UDMA CF Card 420x	CM6281
ProSpec 64Gb UDMA CF Card 420x	CM6291
ProSpec 4Gb SDHC card 150x	CM6442
ProSpec 8Gb SDHC card 150x	CM6454
ProSpec 16Gb SDHC card 150x	CM6458
ProSpec 32Gb SDHC card 150x	CM6464

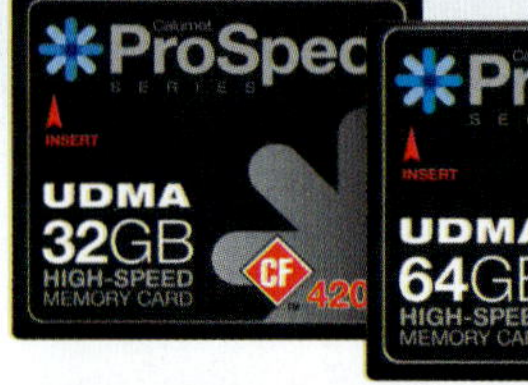

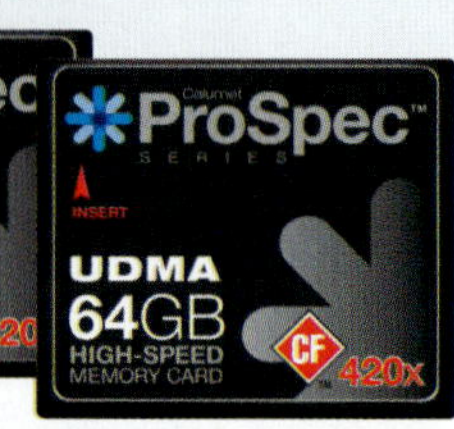

for latest prices check online, in-store or call

www.calumetphoto.co.uk

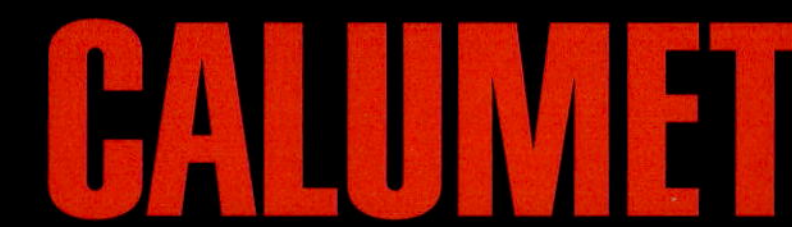

The Basics #3

SHARPNESS

LET'S IMAGINE YOU'VE JUST FOCUSED on an object that is five metres away. How sharp will something be at six metres? Or even five-and-a-half metres? The answer is governed by depth-of-field – the distance either side of the point of focus that is deemed to be acceptably in focus. As long as you control the aperture that you are shooting at, then you are in control of depth-of-field, and you can use it creatively. There will be occasions when you don't want much of it at all, and you'll get that effect by shooting with a large aperture like f/4. However, for most of the time that you're shooting landscapes you'll want to maximise depth-of-field to get as much of a scene in focus as possible. .

Foreground detail is important and has to be in focus, but so does the rest of the scene. This means using small apertures to get good sharpness either side of the focus point. But just consider this last phrase for a moment, and then think about where you might focus when shooting a landscape. Many novice landscape photographers are happy focusing at infinity when shooting a landscape, but don't forget that depth-of-field extends either side of the point of focus. In fact the area of depth-of-field extends one-third in front of the focused point and two-thirds behind, in other words, you get more depth-of-field behind the subject than in front of it. Obviously there is no benefit to having acceptable sharpness extending beyond infinity, but what you can do is pull the point of focus back towards you, so it's the end of the depth-of-field zone that is at infinity instead. This way you'll get more of the scene sharp. This technique is called hyperfocal focusing, and has been used by professional landscape photographers for decades. The optimum point of focus for any particular scene relies on the choice of aperture setting and the focal length of the lens you use – and changes for full-frame and cropped sensor DSLRs! There are calculators and pocket reference tables you can stash in your camera bag, or you can use a dependable rule-of-thumb that suggests you aim a third of the way into the picture with your lens set to a small aperture. We'll be covering both focusing techniques, as well as providing you with other expert advice to ensure you maximise image sharpness. This includes revealing why using the smallest aperture won't necessarily produce the sharpest results, even though it gives the most depth-of-field!

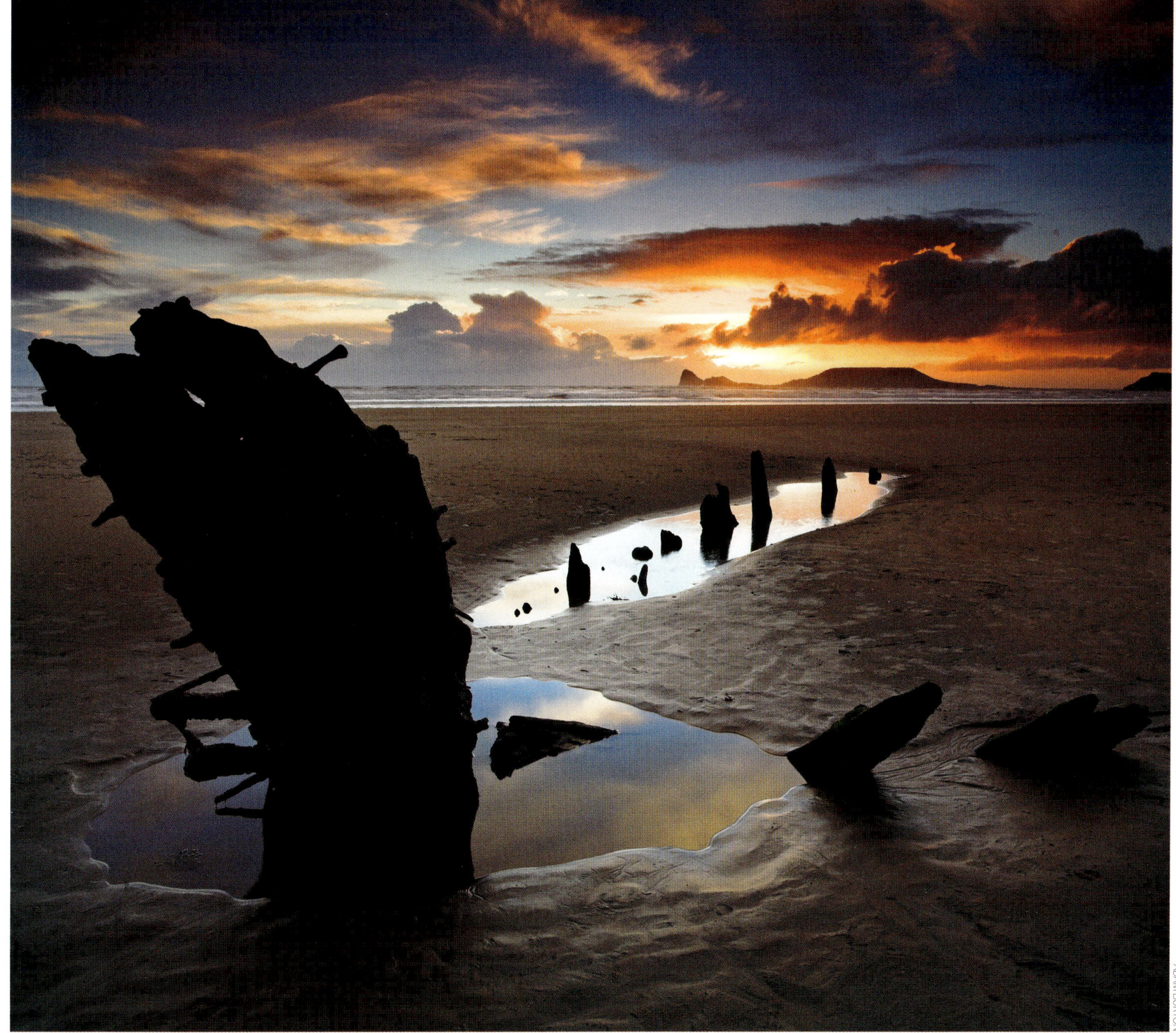

ADAM BURTON

Focusing with the hyperfocal distance

Landscape specialist Lee Frost explains how to use the hyperfocal focusing distance and aperture-priority for super-sharp scenics

ONE OF THE FUNDAMENTALS of successful landscape photography is being able to control and assess depth-of-field to ensure that the image is sharp from front-to-back.

Aperture-priority mode helps you to achieve this, not only by forcing you to think about which aperture to set, but also by making sure that once it is set, that aperture won't change if light levels fluctuate or you put filters on the lens. If the exposure has to be adjusted when shooting in aperture-priority mode, the camera does it by changing the shutter speed, so the aperture remains constant. This is vitally important because achieving extensive depth-of-field is not just about aperture selection, but also focusing distance, and a careful balancing act between the two is required to ensure the best possible results. You could take every picture at f/22 with the lens set to infinity and most wide-angle shots would be sharp from front to back. Unfortunately, this simple approach won't always work – so you're not going to get the best results. Wide-angles and zooms tend to give their worst optical performance when at minimum aperture and their best around f/11, so ideally you should shoot as close to f/11 as you can to achieve optimum optical quality, and focus the lens at a distance that maximises depth-of-field at that aperture. Over the page, Helen Dixon provides a simple focusing method along these lines that yields excellent results.

My favourite technique is based around something known as hyperfocal focusing, which involves focusing on a point known as the hyperfocal distance, where depth-of-field is maximised for the aperture in use. Lenses used to feature a hyperfocal distance scale on the barrel but virtually none do today. There is an equation for calculating hyperfocal distance for any lens and aperture, so in true *Blue Peter* fashion, I did just that and created a hyperfocal distance chart, which you can copy and refer to when you're on location. The distances in feet (ft) represent the hyperfocal distances for each focal length and aperture. If you focus your lens on that distance and set the corresponding aperture, depth-of-field will extend from half the hyperfocal distance to infinity. So, if you're using an APS-C-sized sensor, shooting at 24mm and f/11, focus on a point 9ft away and depth-of-field will extend from 4.5ft (half the hyperfocal distance) to infinity – which is more than enough depth-of-field in most situations.

Aperture-priority and multi-zone metering

Before finally 'going digital' back in the spring of 2008, I'd spent 20 years shooting with film cameras that had no internal metering, so I used a handheld spot meter to determine correct exposure – which then had to be manually set on the camera. Thankfully, those days are long gone. Digital SLRs have fantastic integral metering systems that are capable of producing perfectly exposed images in all but the most demanding situations, so I can't see the point in making my life more complicated than it needs to be. These days my digital SLR is set to aperture-priority mode and multi-zone metering and generally stays that way. Combined with the feedback provided by the camera's preview image and the image histogram, I've got all I need to ensure I get perfect exposures in any shooting situation. The same applies to you.

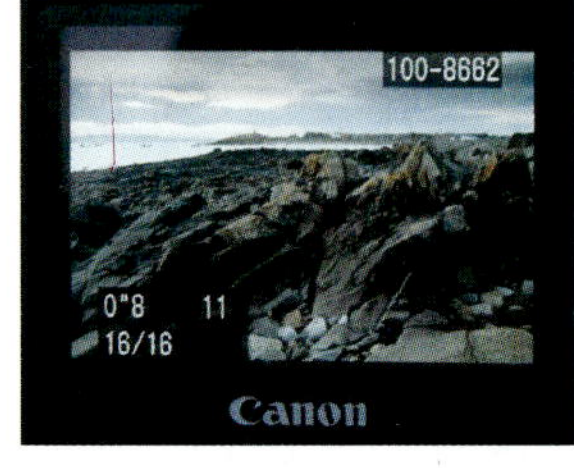

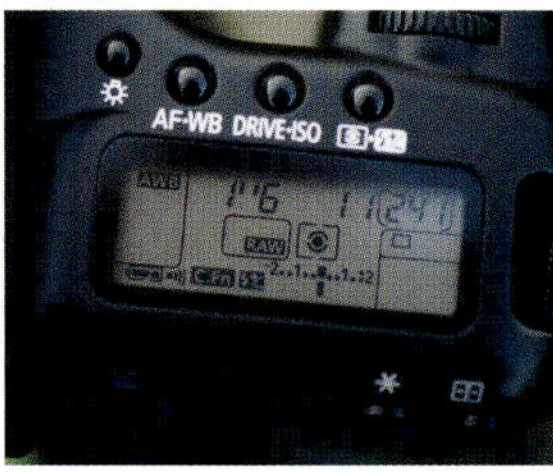

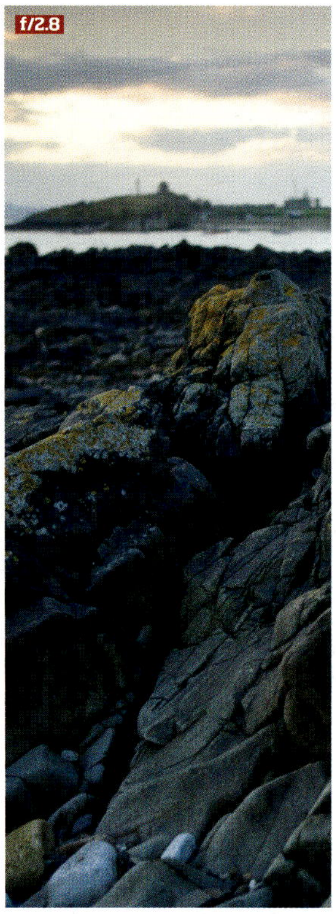

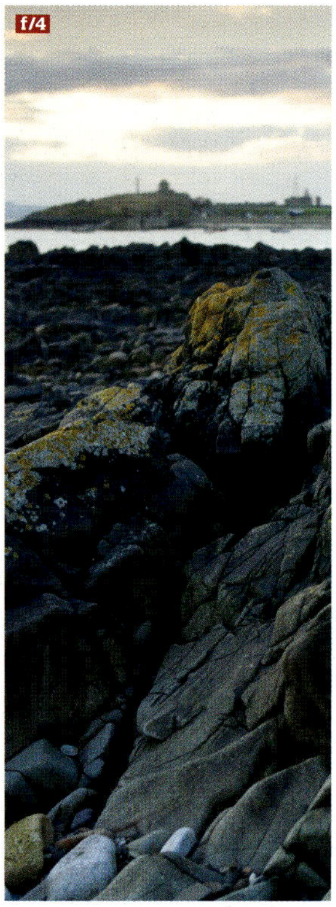

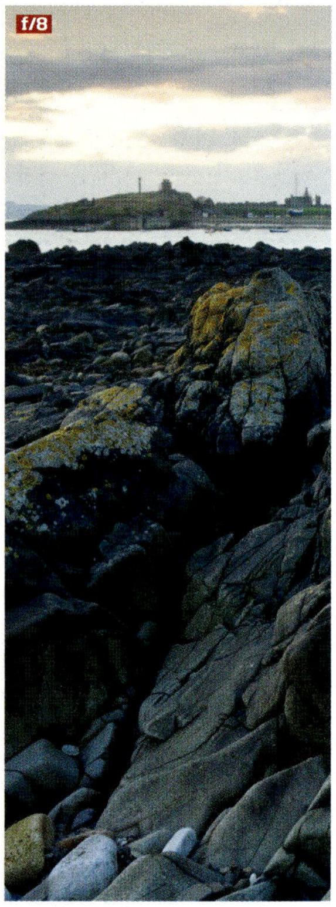

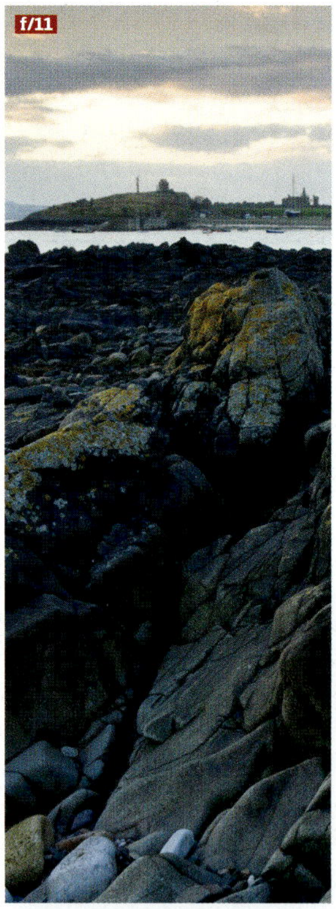

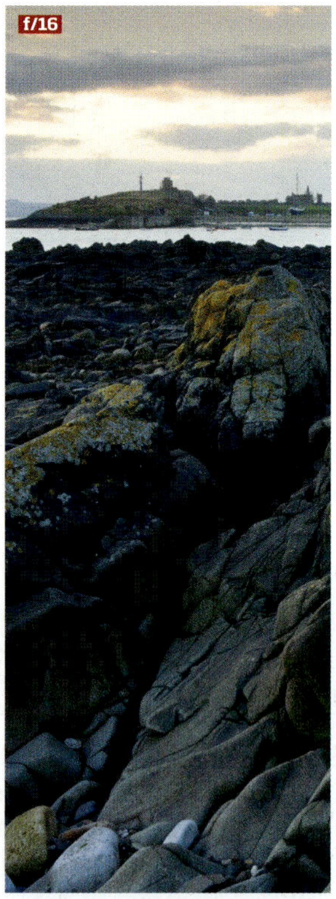

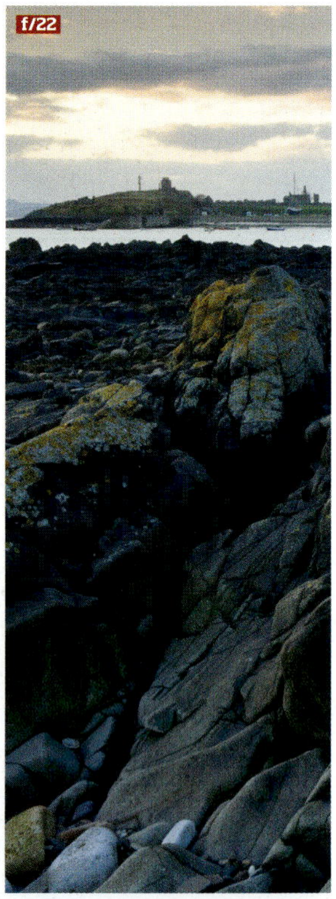

f/2.8 | f/4 | f/8 | f/11 | f/16 | f/22

Hyperfocal distance: APS-C sensors

Focal length	12mm	15mm	17mm	20mm	24mm	28mm	35mm	50mm	70mm	100mm	135mm
Aperture f/8	3.2ft	5ft	6.4ft	8.9ft	12.6ft	17ft	27ft	55ft	105ft	218ft	395ft
f/11	2.3ft	3.5ft	4.5ft	6.2ft	9ft	12ft	19ft	39ft	75ft	155ft	280ft
f/16	1.7ft	2.5ft	3.3ft	4.4ft	6.4ft	8.6ft	14.5ft	27ft	54ft	110ft	198ft
f/22	1.2ft	0.9ft	2.3ft	3.2ft	4.5ft	6ft	9.5ft	19.2ft	38ft	77ft	140ft

Hyperfocal distance: Full-frame sensors

Focal length	16mm	20mm	24mm	28mm	35mm	50mm	70mm	100mm	135mm
Aperture f/8	3.8ft	5.6ft	8.0ft	11ft	17ft	35ft	68ft	138ft	250ft
f/11	2.6ft	3.9ft	5.8ft	7.8ft	12ft	25ft	48ft	98ft	178ft
f/16	1.9ft	2.9ft	4.0ft	5.5ft	8.5ft	17.5ft	34ft	70ft	125ft
f/22	0.4ft	2.0ft	2.9ft	3.9ft	6ft	12.5ft	24ft	49ft	89ft

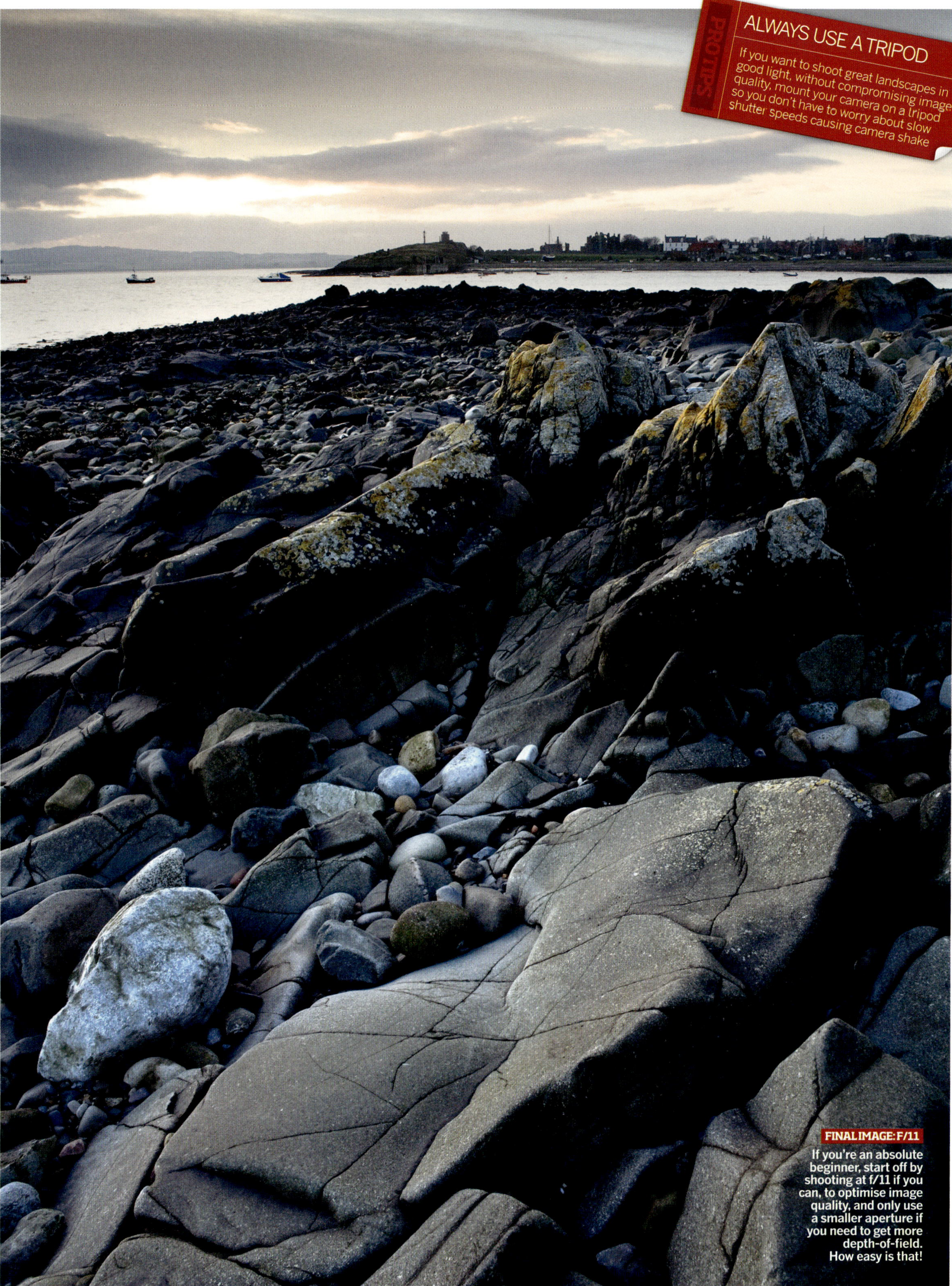

PRO TIPS

ALWAYS USE A TRIPOD

If you want to shoot great landscapes in good light, without compromising image quality, mount your camera on a tripod so you don't have to worry about slow shutter speeds causing camera shake

FINAL IMAGE: F/11

If you're an absolute beginner, start off by shooting at f/11 if you can, to optimise image quality, and only use a smaller aperture if you need to get more depth-of-field. How easy is that!

EXPERT TUTORIAL

Focus a third of the way into the scene for sharp results!

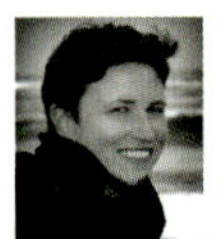

WITH HELEN DIXON The normal practice for beginners shooting landscapes is to place their DSLR on a tripod, focus on infinity and set a very small aperture to give enough depth-of-field to keep most or all of the scene in focus. It's a tried and tested method that works well, but can be improved upon by fine-tuning focusing technique and the choice of aperture.

Looking at focusing first, when you focus on 'infinity', i.e. on the distance, the depth-of-field will extend a third of the way in front of the focusing point and two-thirds behind. So while part of the foreground is sharp, the area closest to you may well be out of focus. Also, you'll have wasted two-thirds of the available depth-of-field, which stretches beyond infinity. Instead, by focusing part of the way into the frame, you can maximise depth-of-field so that it covers the foreground and the distance.

The optimum distance at which you should focus is termed the hyperfocal distance and there are various elaborate ways of calculating it. The simplest method for focusing by far (and one that works 99% of the time) is to focus one third of the way into the scene. By doing this, and setting a small aperture, you're ensuring that the depth-of-field in front of the focusing point covers most, if not all, of the foreground, while the area behind is kept sharp by the other two-thirds of the depth-of-field. If you want to be as precise with your focusing as possible, use the table on the previous page.

With the focusing technique taken care of, we'll move onto your choice of aperture. While setting the smallest aperture (e.g. f/32) gives the most depth-of-field, it doesn't necessarily give the sharpest results. That's due to two main reasons: most lenses are optically designed to give the sharpest results at apertures of around f/8 to f/13, while at smaller apertures the effects of diffraction softens the image, thus negating any benefits provided by depth-of-field. The optimum aperture to use varies from lens to lens so the only way to discover for yourself is through trial and error, shooting at different apertures and comparing the sharpness on your LCD monitor or ideally at home on you computer, where you can magnify images for close scrutiny.

For the sharpest possible results, using the hyperfocal distance method explained by Lee Frost on the previous pages is best. Of course, you must make sure that you set your camera up on a tripod, to reduce the risk of camera shake. But this process can be time-consuming and for most people, my technique is ideal. The images shown here were shot using a fairly dominant foreground to emphasise the effect of changing the focusing distance. The aperture was f/13 for all three images.

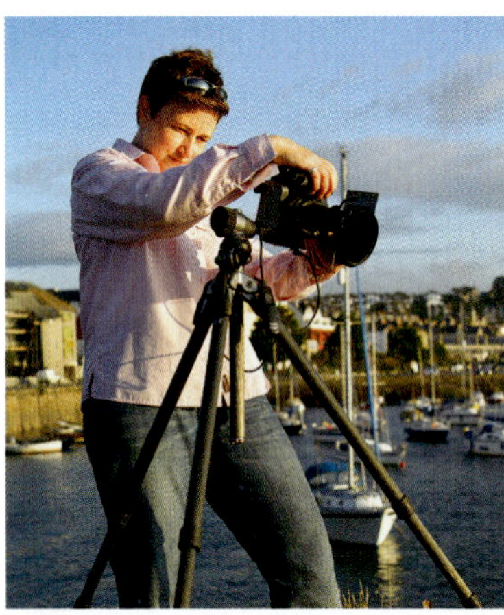

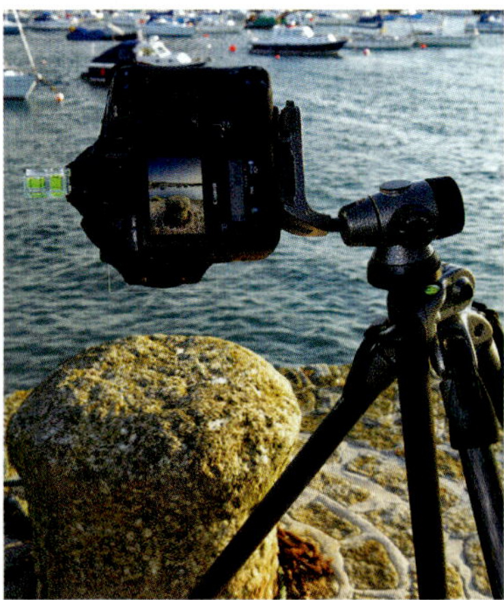

TAKING THE SHOTS: Helen sets up a tripod, essential for preventing blurred shots caused by shake, then uses Live View to check the depth-of-field of the shot on her LCD monitor while selecting the aperture. After taking the shot, she can then check the image's sharpness on the LCD screen by magnifying different parts of the frame.

DON'T PANIC!

Blurry viewfinder

When using the hyperfocal distance method, you'll notice that the viewfinder image looks unsharp when you've focused a third of the way into the frame. This is because your lens is always set to the widest aperture to provide a bright viewfinder image – depth-of-field will be minimal. Use the depth-of-field preview button or take a shot at your chosen aperture and you'll see that the image really has far more depth-of-field, because the lens has closed down for the exposure.

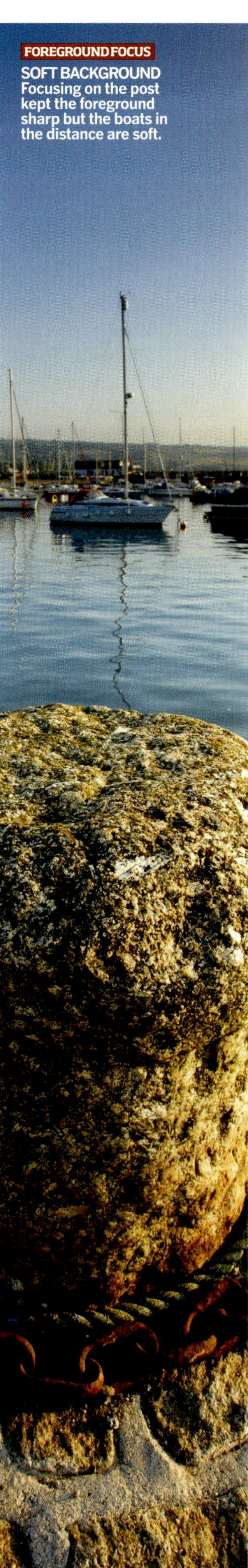

FOREGROUND FOCUS

SOFT BACKGROUND
Focusing on the post kept the foreground sharp but the boats in the distance are soft.

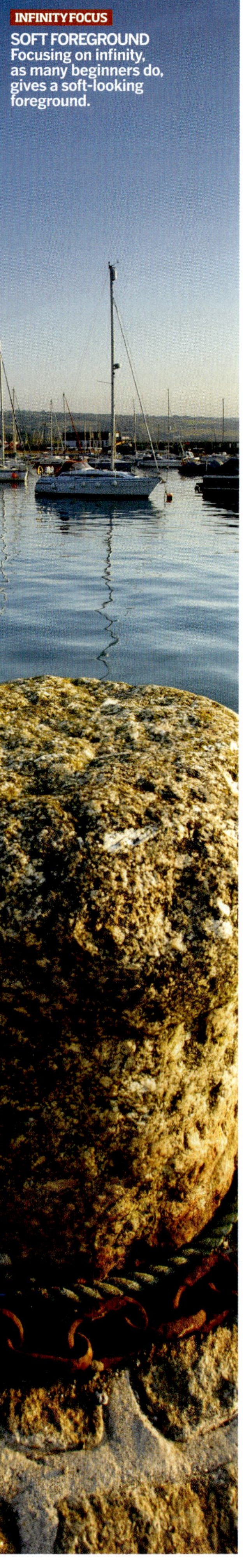

INFINITY FOCUS

SOFT FOREGROUND
Focusing on infinity, as many beginners do, gives a soft-looking foreground.

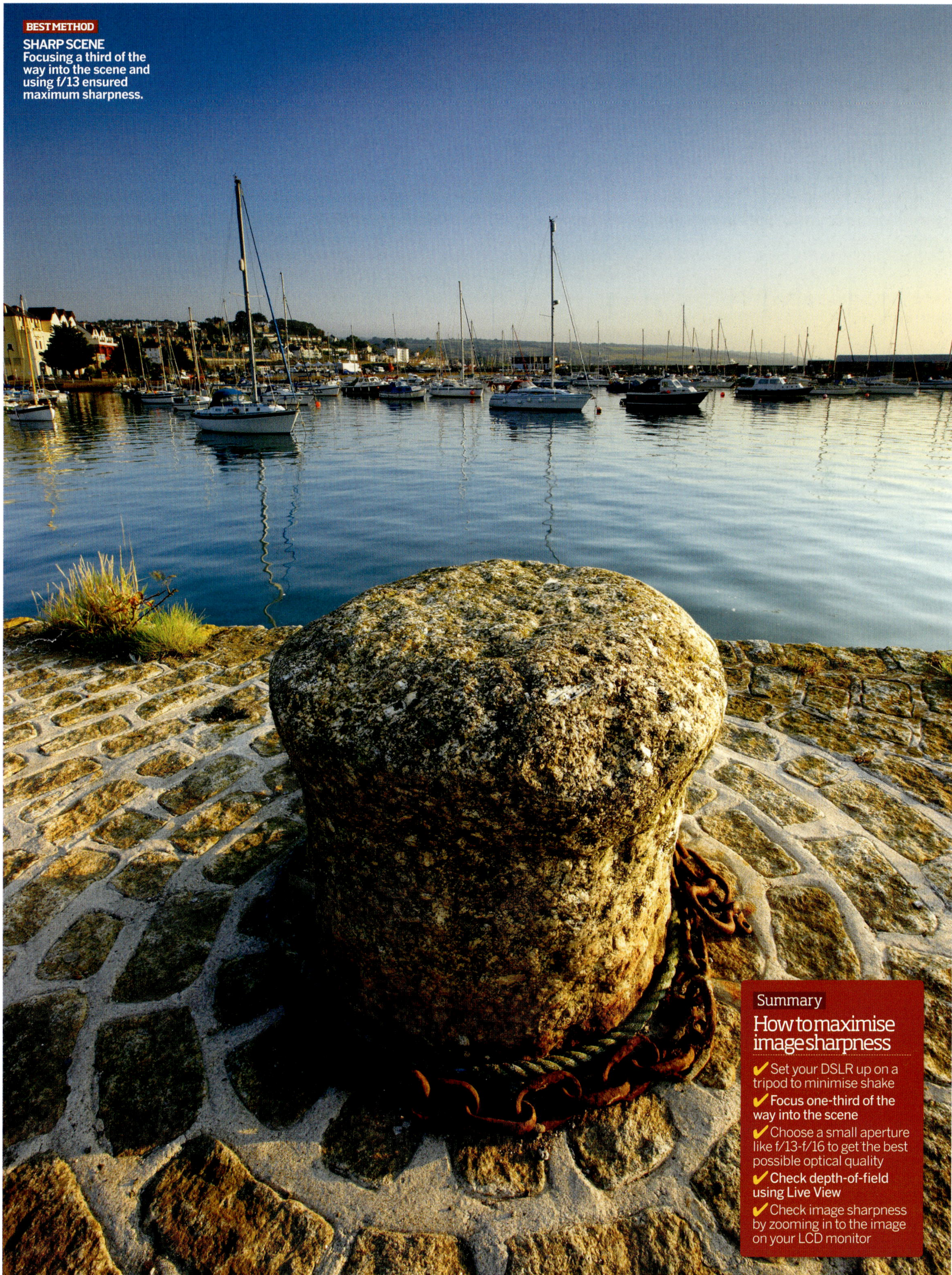

BEST METHOD

SHARP SCENE Focusing a third of the way into the scene and using f/13 ensured maximum sharpness.

Summary

How to maximise image sharpness

- ✔ Set your DSLR up on a tripod to minimise shake
- ✔ **Focus one-third of the way into the scene**
- ✔ Choose a small aperture like f/13-f/16 to get the best possible optical quality
- ✔ **Check depth-of-field using Live View**
- ✔ Check image sharpness by zooming in to the image on your LCD monitor

The effects of diffraction

The more you close the aperture down, the greater the depth-of-field, so the usual advice given for sharp results is to use very small apertures, such as f/16 and f/22. However, stopping down too far can actually be detrimental to image sharpness and this is due to an optical effect called 'diffraction'.

The simple explanation of diffraction is that when light passes through the aperture of a lens, the edges of the hole disperse the light waves. As the aperture is stopped down, the amount of diffracted light becomes a larger percentage of the total amount of light being recorded and the image becomes noticeably less sharp, meaning less detail is resolved on the image.

APS-C and full-frame sensors are affected slightly differently, and certain lenses will be more prone to diffraction than others. But in general, with an APS-C-sized sensor, you'll start to notice the effects of diffraction if you stop down beyond f/11 and with a full-frame camera, once you go beyond f/16.

Of course, you can use apertures smaller than that and decide between overall sharpness and depth-of-field relevant to the amount of fine detail you think it's necessary to record in any one particular image. That said, it's worth remembering that a 17mm lens on an APS-C-sized sensor will give you a depth-of-field from 2¼ feet to infinity when set to the hyperfocal distance at f/11 – enough for most situations.

To illustrate the effects of diffraction at different apertures, we've shown a series of pictures at f/8, f/11, f/16 and f/22 – focusing and overall exposure remained constant – the only change was the lens aperture. The pictures were all processed using the same software and settings when post-processing. More sharpening than usual has been used to make the effects more obvious.

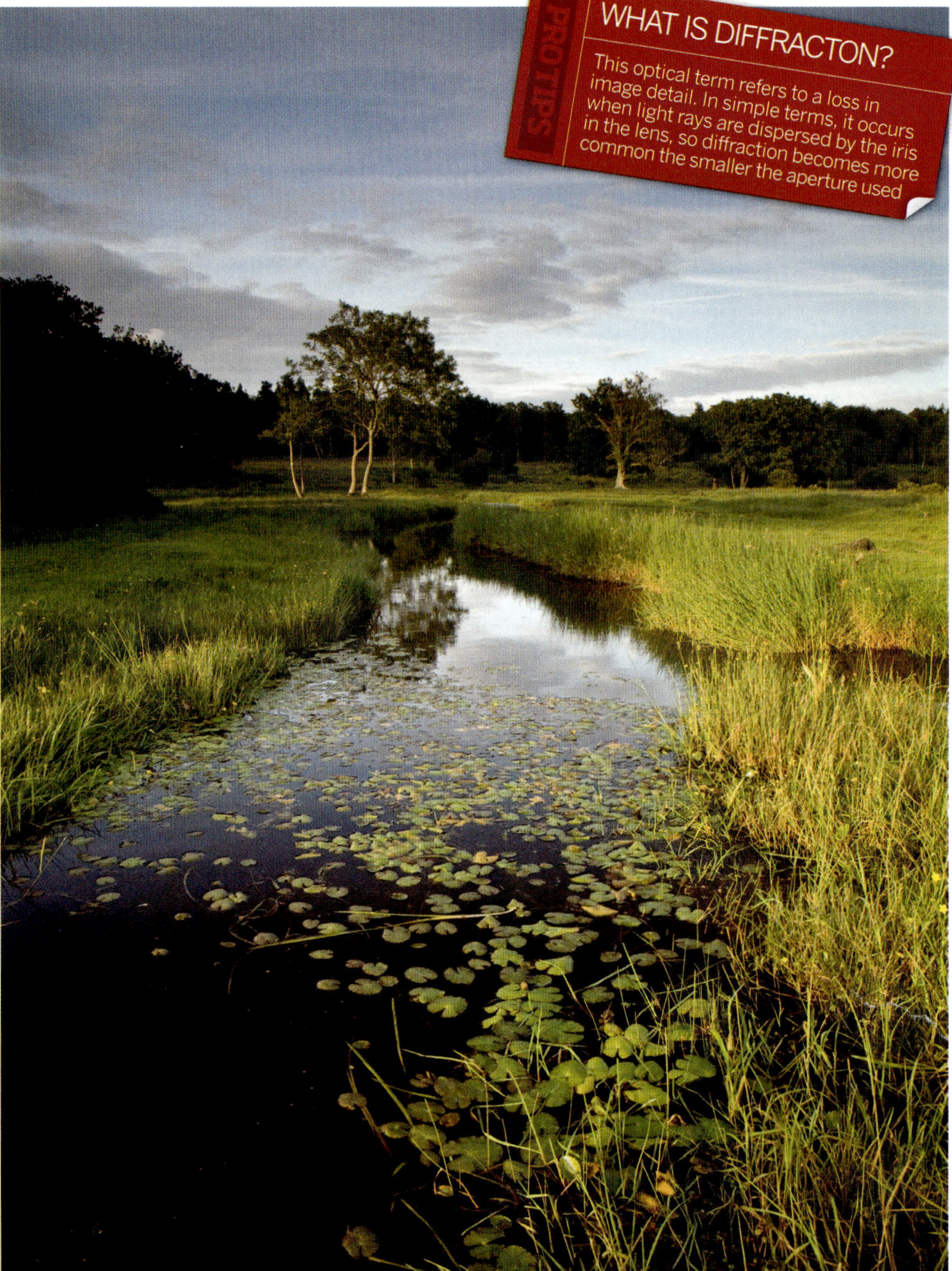

PRO TIPS

WHAT IS DIFFRACTON?

This optical term refers to a loss in image detail. In simple terms, it occurs when light rays are dispersed by the iris in the lens, so diffraction becomes more common the smaller the aperture used

MARK BAUER

EFFECTS OF DIFFRACTION: This image shows the full frame. The box shows the cropped section used to illustrate the effect of diffraction. It was taken with a Canon EOS 20D and 17-40mm lens.

COMPARISON RESULTS: The results may not be so obvious in magazine reproduction, but are very clear in large prints. At f/8, everything looks pretty sharp, with good detail in the background foliage. Things still look good at f/11, but once stopped down further than this, instead of becoming sharper as depth-of-field increases, the image becomes noticeably less sharp and detailed. This is crucial in landscape photography, especially when making large prints, and it is this 'mushy' looking foliage that spoils digital landscapes for many photographers.

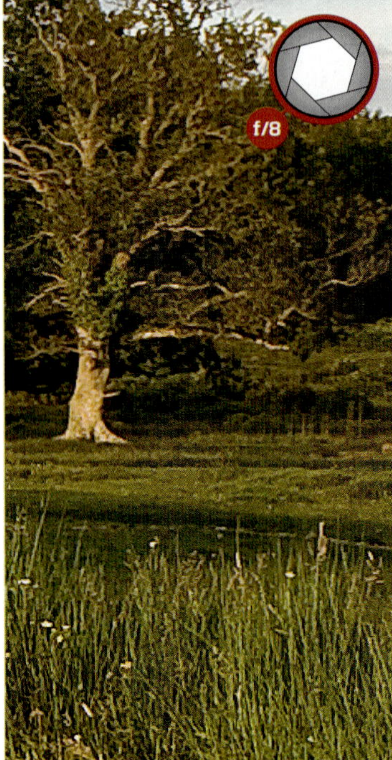

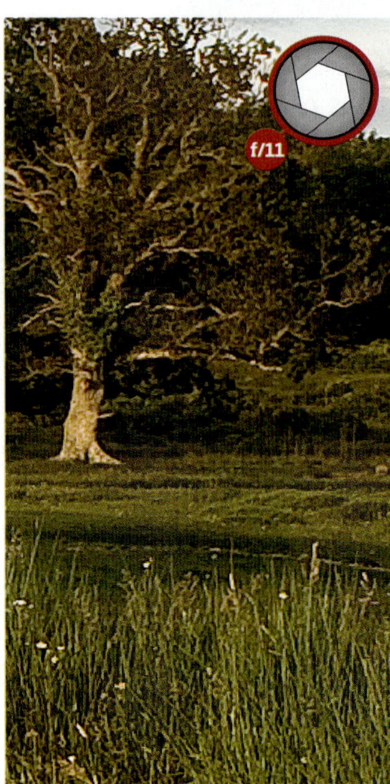

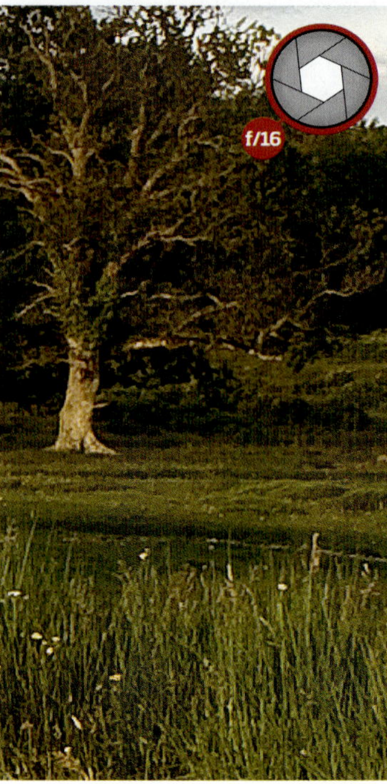

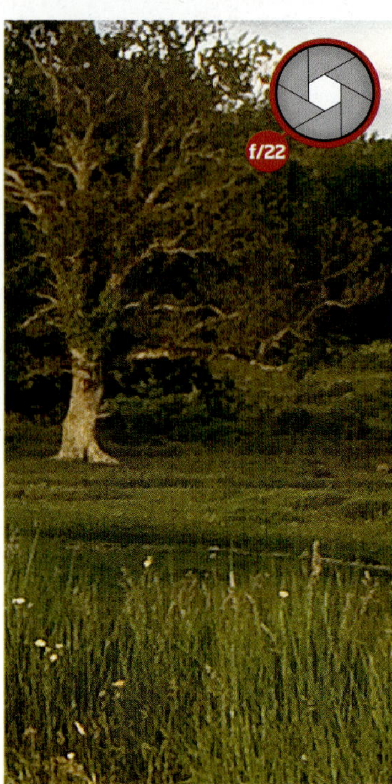

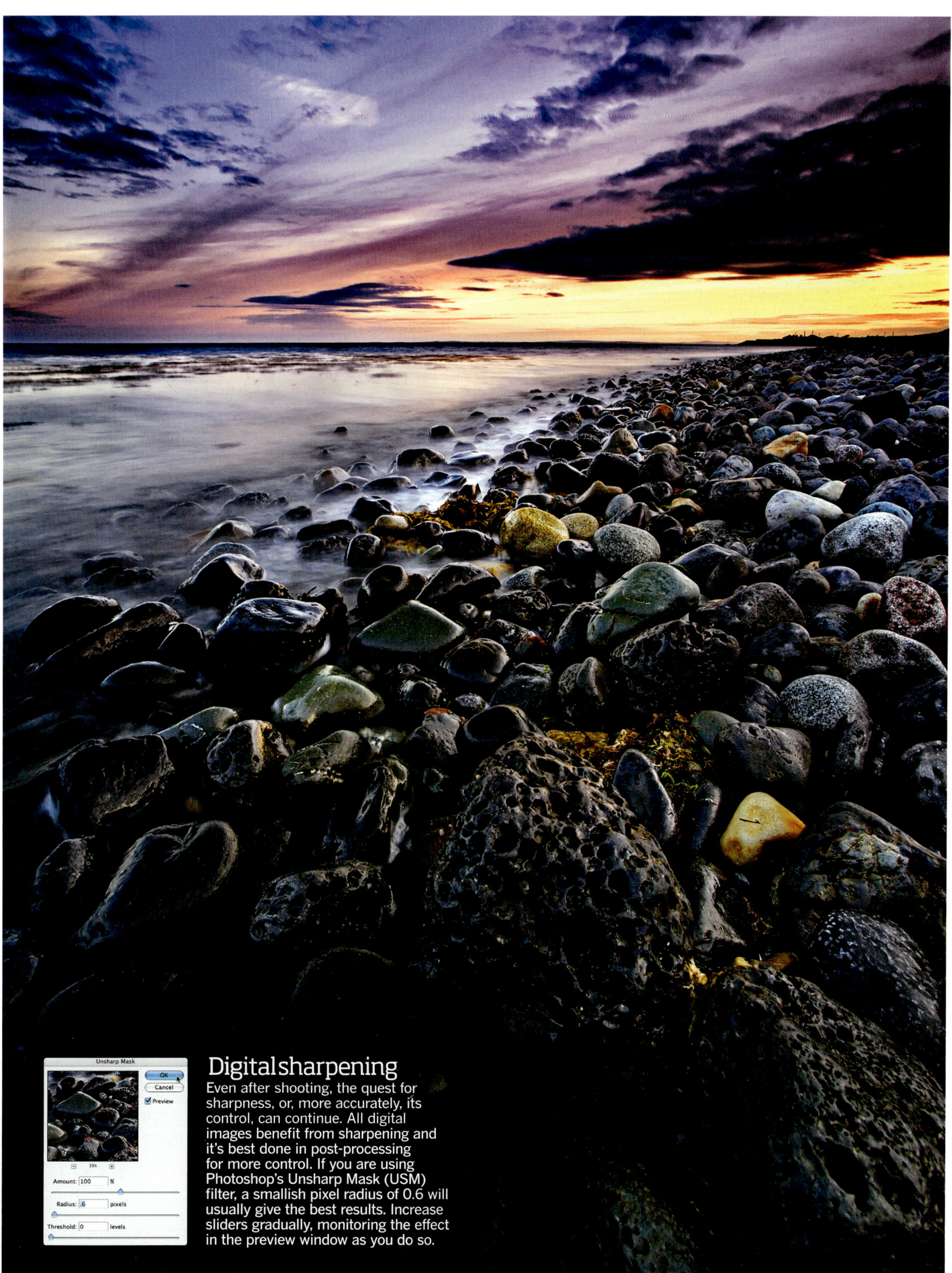

GARY McPARLAND

Digital sharpening

Even after shooting, the quest for sharpness, or, more accurately, its control, can continue. All digital images benefit from sharpening and it's best done in post-processing for more control. If you are using Photoshop's Unsharp Mask (USM) filter, a smallish pixel radius of 0.6 will usually give the best results. Increase sliders gradually, monitoring the effect in the preview window as you do so.

Shake-free landscapes

Landscape photographer Ross Hoddinott shows how using a tripod and mirror lock-up is well worth the effort

THERE'S ALWAYS A RISK OF CAMERA SHAKE spoiling landscape shots. Setting a small aperture for lots of depth-of-field, along with a low ISO rating for the best possible image quality, means that shutter speeds are always likely to be slow, even in bright conditions. This is why a tripod is seen as essential for this type of photography, but even then, there is always the risk of shake. Let's see how using a remote release or a self-timer can help you to reduce the risk of blur, and how seeking out your camera's mirror lock-up facility can lead to sharper results too.

Essential kit for shake-free results

A sturdy tripod is an essential accessory and the right one will last you for years. But just how do you pick the right one? It's all about compromise: you want something solid, but not so heavy that you always leave it at home. Turn to page 114 for a selection of tripods at various price points that are all ideal for landscape photography. You should also look at investing in a remote release, an inexpensive accessory that offers an alternative to using the self-timer for contact-free firing of the shutter.

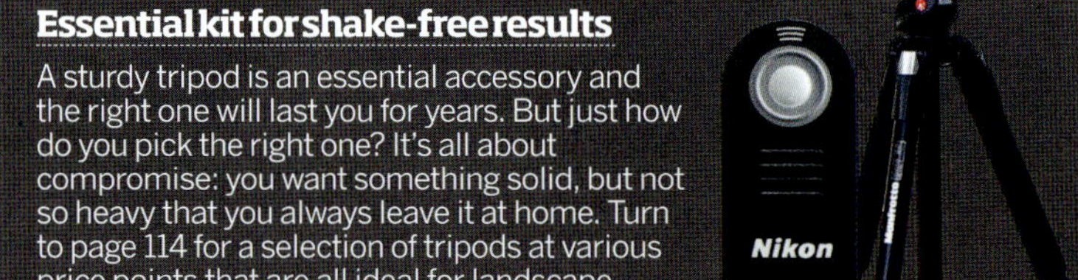

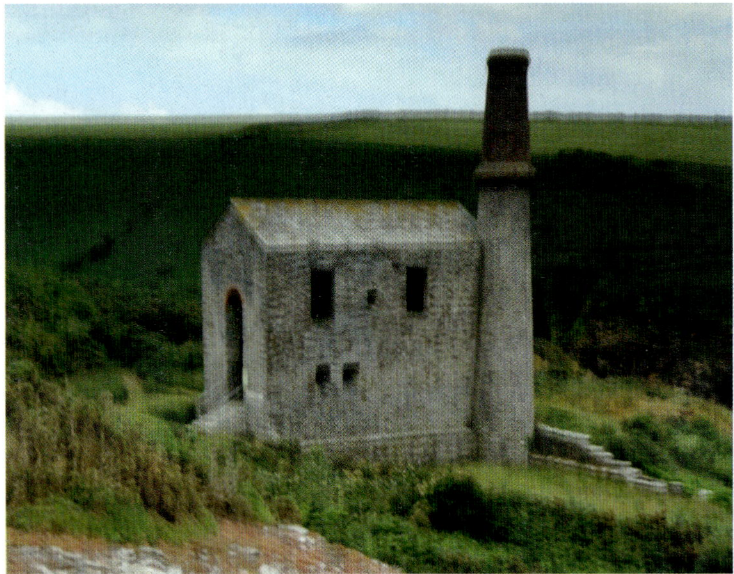

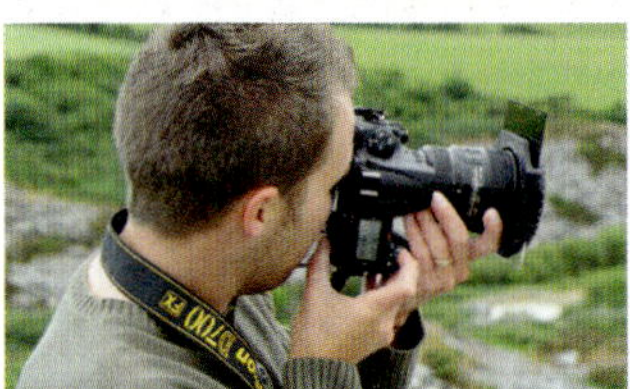

Handheld At 1/15sec at f/22, it's not surprising that handholding the camera resulted in a lot of shake that has blurred the image. I need a small aperture though, to maintain front-to-back sharpness. I could raise the ISO rating to compensate, but I prefer to use a tripod instead to preserve picture quality.

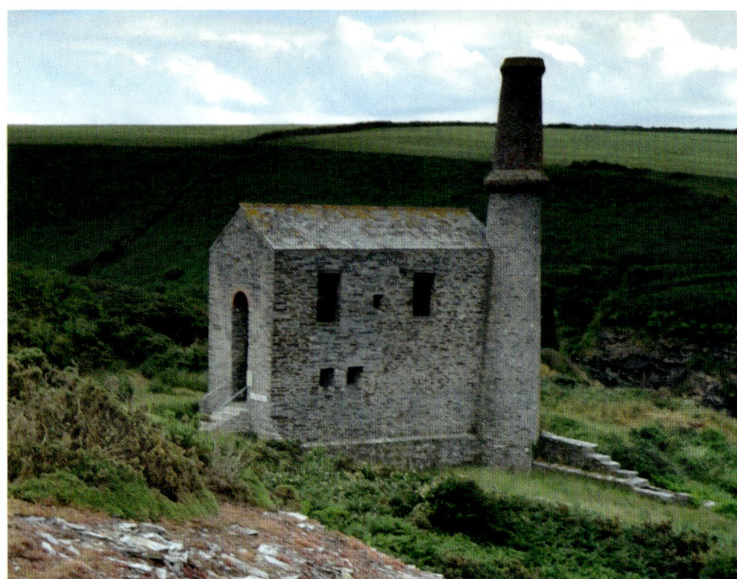

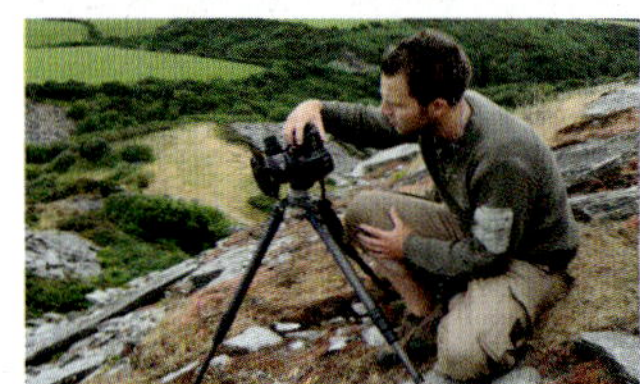

Tripod Putting the camera on a tripod has made a huge difference to image sharpness, but zooming on fine detail reveals that there is still some blur present. This is probably because I'm wobbling the camera very slightly as I press the shutter release. I need a way of tripping the shutter without touching it.

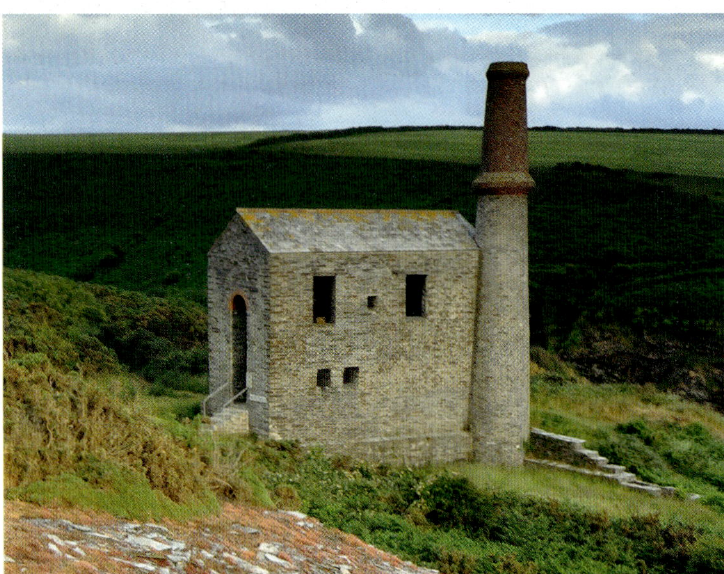

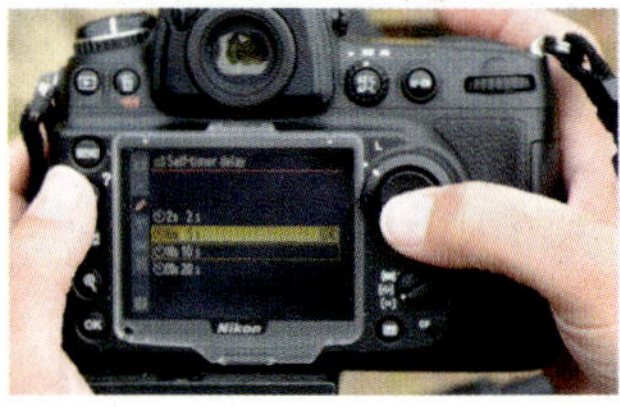

Tripod & self-timer An easy way to avoid moving your camera while it's on a tripod is to fire it with the built-in self-timer. This way you can touch the camera, but any movement will have subsided by the time the shutter fires. Many DSLRs give you the option of setting the self-timer delays at two or ten seconds.

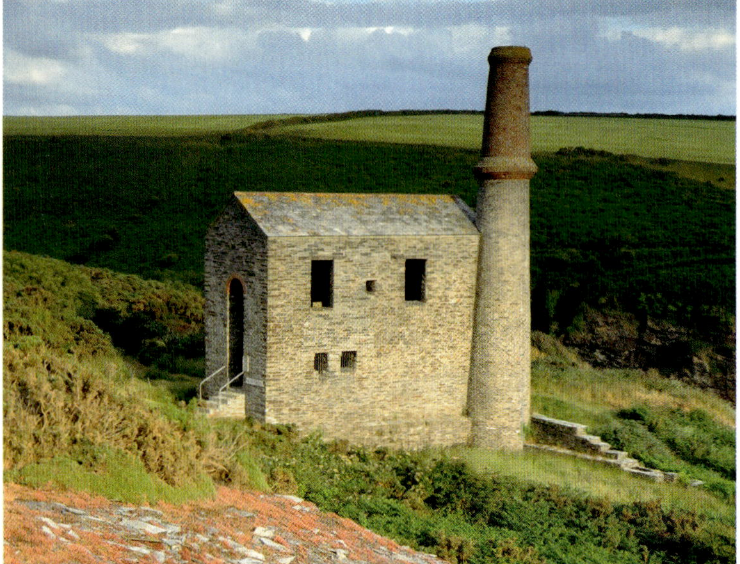

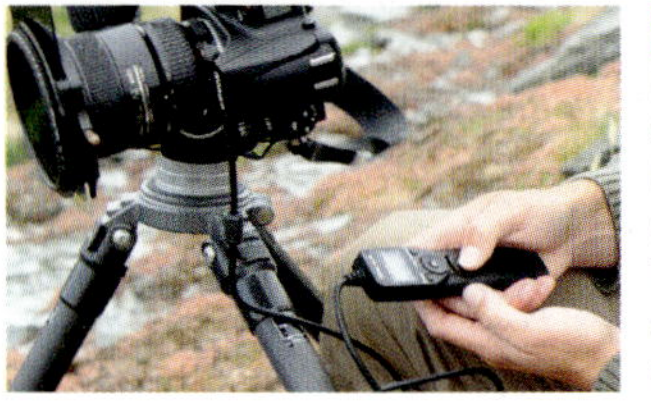

Tripod & remote Better still is a remote release. This will also lets you trip the shutter without wobbling the camera but, because there is no delay involved, you can be more precise with your timing. This can be very useful if you have rapidly changing lighting conditions, as I did when shooting this location.

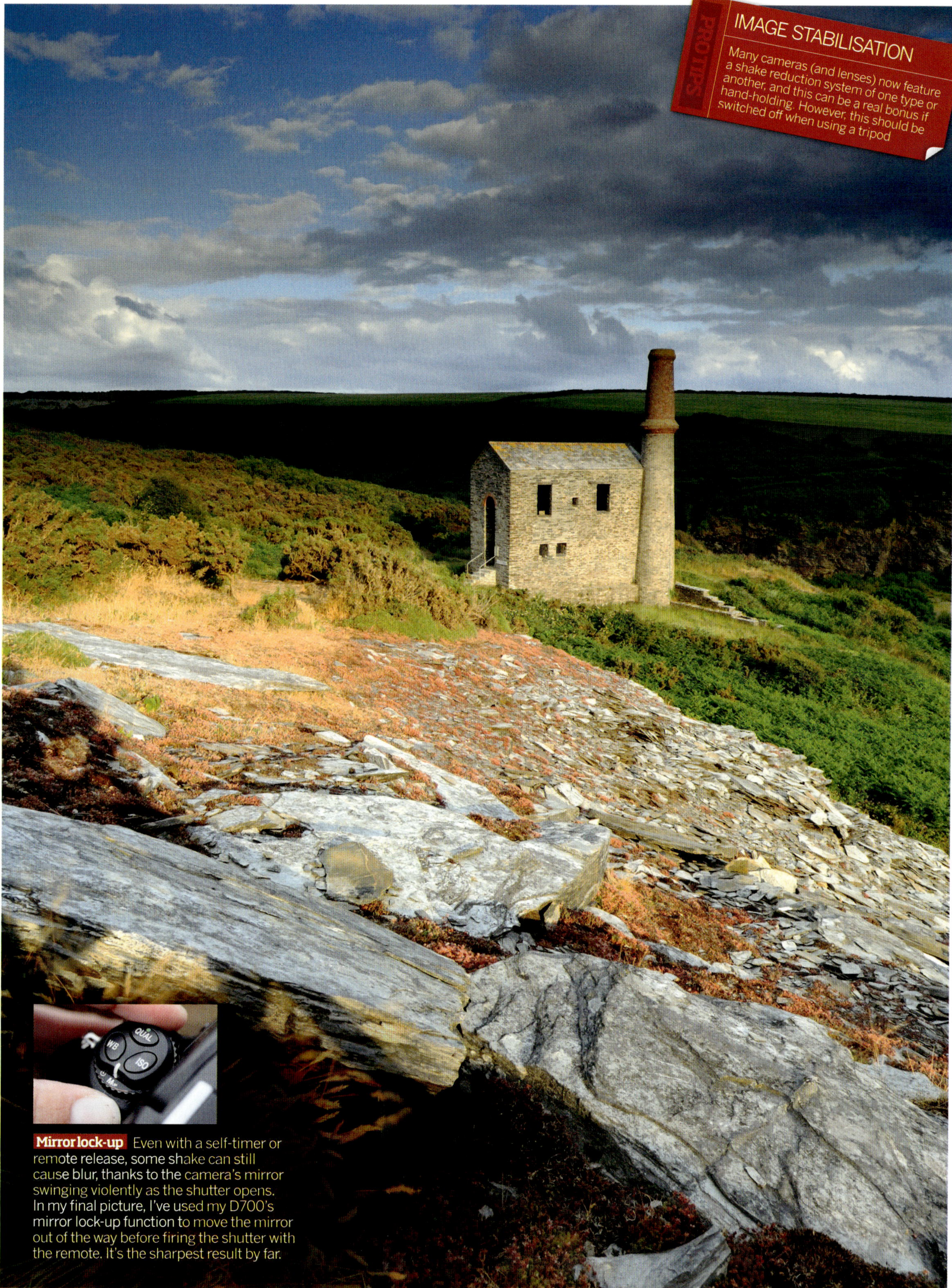

PRO TIPS

IMAGE STABILISATION

Many cameras (and lenses) now feature a shake reduction system of one type or another, and this can be a real bonus if hand-holding. However, this should be switched off when using a tripod

Mirror lock-up Even with a self-timer or remote release, some shake can still cause blur, thanks to the camera's mirror swinging violently as the shutter opens. In my final picture, I've used my D700's mirror lock-up function to move the mirror out of the way before firing the shutter with the remote. It's the sharpest result by far.

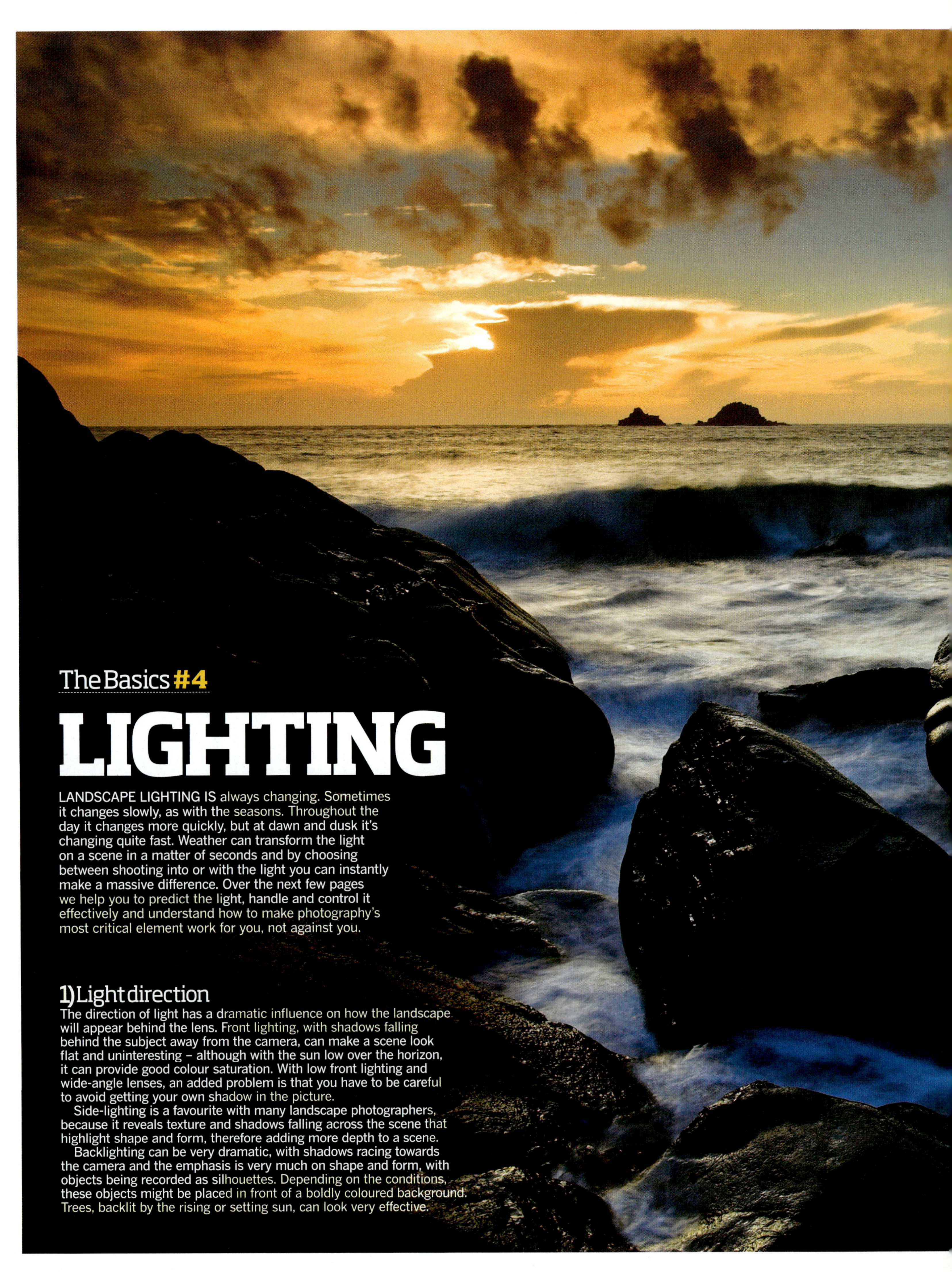

The Basics #4

LIGHTING

LANDSCAPE LIGHTING IS always changing. Sometimes it changes slowly, as with the seasons. Throughout the day it changes more quickly, but at dawn and dusk it's changing quite fast. Weather can transform the light on a scene in a matter of seconds and by choosing between shooting into or with the light you can instantly make a massive difference. Over the next few pages we help you to predict the light, handle and control it effectively and understand how to make photography's most critical element work for you, not against you.

1) Light direction

The direction of light has a dramatic influence on how the landscape will appear behind the lens. Front lighting, with shadows falling behind the subject away from the camera, can make a scene look flat and uninteresting – although with the sun low over the horizon, it can provide good colour saturation. With low front lighting and wide-angle lenses, an added problem is that you have to be careful to avoid getting your own shadow in the picture.

Side-lighting is a favourite with many landscape photographers, because it reveals texture and shadows falling across the scene that highlight shape and form, therefore adding more depth to a scene.

Backlighting can be very dramatic, with shadows racing towards the camera and the emphasis is very much on shape and form, with objects being recorded as silhouettes. Depending on the conditions, these objects might be placed in front of a boldly coloured background. Trees, backlit by the rising or setting sun, can look very effective.

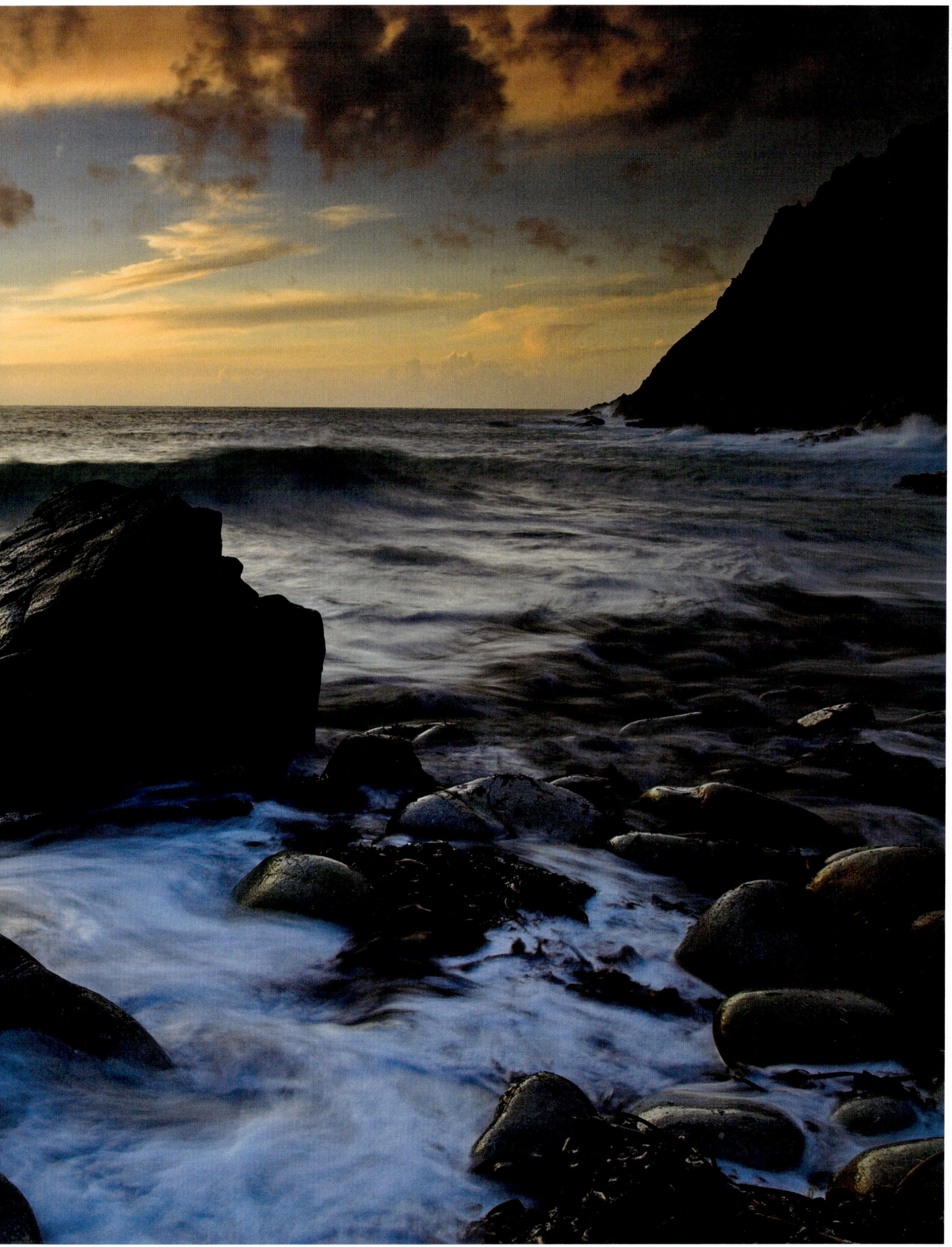

ADAM BURTON

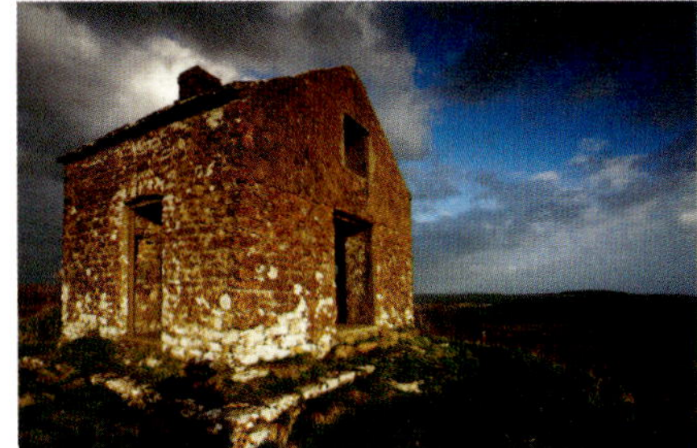

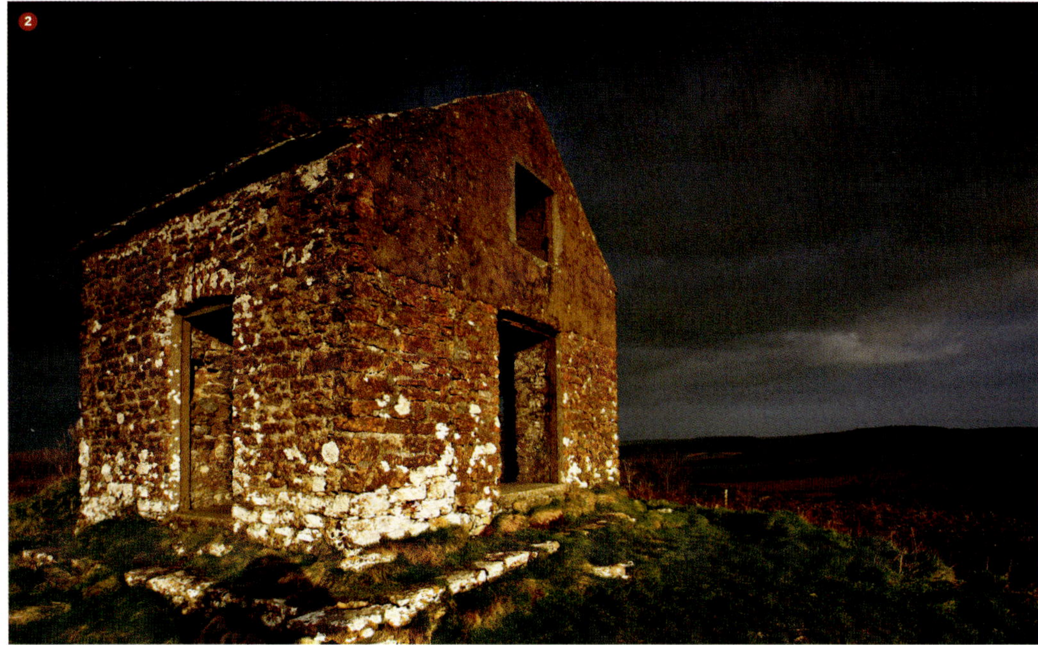

2) Weather and light

In theory, there's no such thing as good or bad weather in landscape photography – good images can be produced in any conditions. Of course, certain conditions will produce more dramatic shots and the trick is learning how to recognise and anticipate them.

If you're planning a sunset or sunrise shoot, don't cancel it if there's cloud cover. If there's a break on the horizon, there's a possibility that the clouds will be lit from below when the sun is very low, giving a very dramatic sky.

Sunshine and showers can be stunning in the moments when the rain stops and the sun breaks through, with foreground objects spot-lit against a dark, brooding sky. These moments are fleeting, however, and don't last for long, so you need to have your camera prepared beforehand.

If the weather is bad – grey, overcast and raining – there are still shots to be made. In these conditions head for woodland: the diffused, less contrasty lighting suits this type of location. Surprisingly, using a polariser can really enhance a picture, by cutting out the reflections and glare from wet foliage as well as saturating the colours.

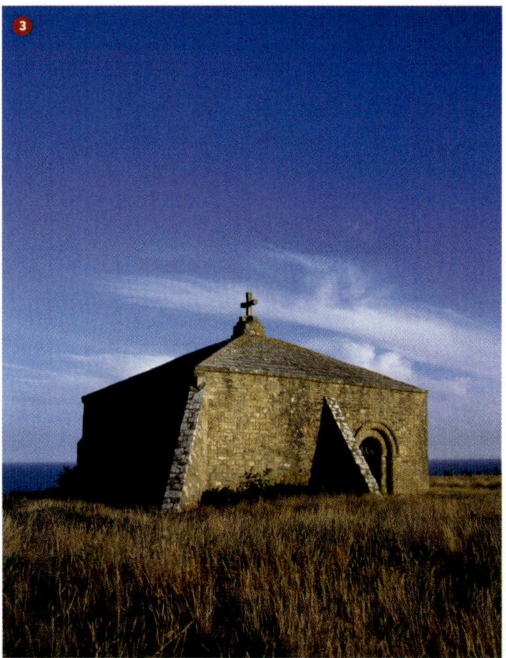

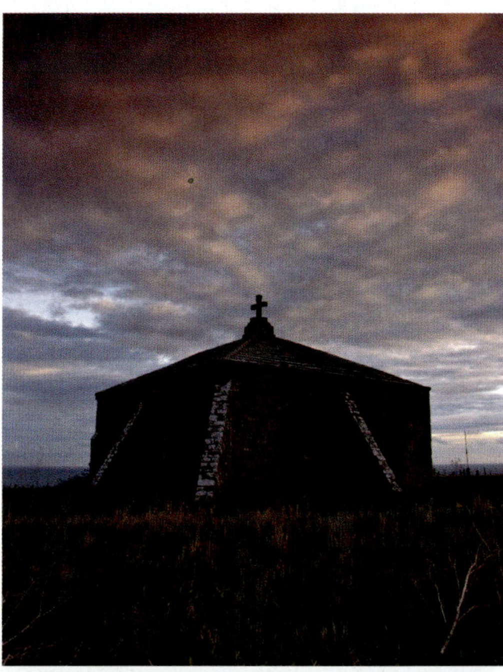

3) Capture the right mood for the scene

Shoot in lighting conditions that will enhance the natural mood of your subject. For example, some scenes are naturally more tranquil and will look best in the corresponding soft light of dawn and with pastel colours. Others have a naturally brooding atmosphere and demand dramatic, theatrical and directional lighting. And the best light might be months away.

Look at the pictures of the Norman Chapel at St Aldhelm's Head in Dorset on the right. The chapel has a brooding presence, which, as can be seen from these pictures, is best suited to low light and heavy skies.

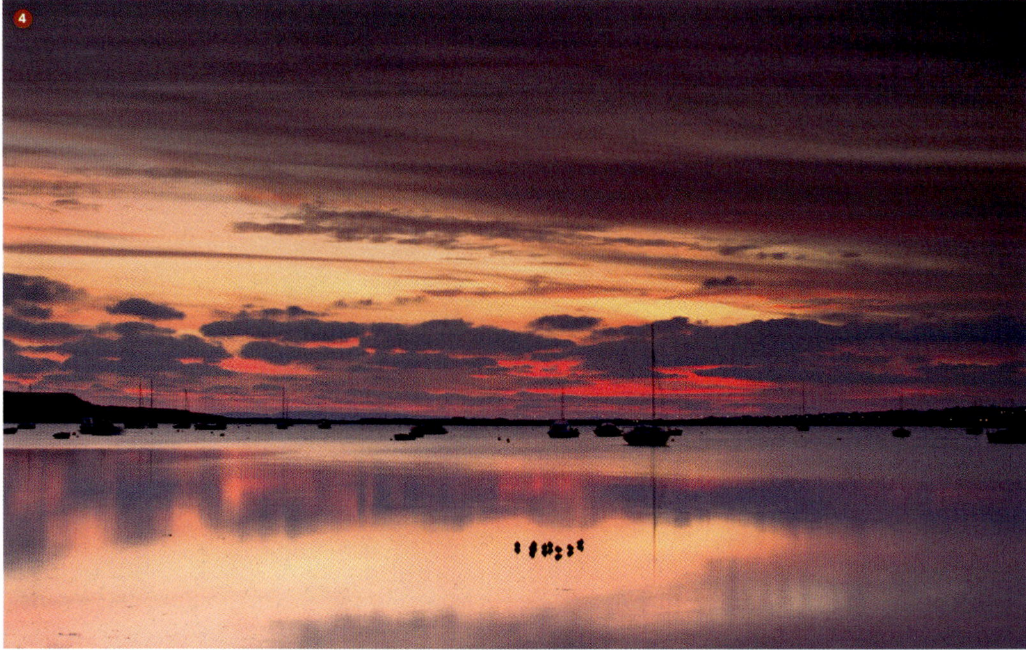

4) Enhance low light with reflections

Pre-dawn and twilight are very moody times for landscape photography, but the land itself can be almost completely in shadow, with very little detail.

Near water you can include reflections as a foreground, which will help to balance the shot and throw more drama and impact into your image. The more still the conditions the more mirror-like a surface.

With the sun yet to appear above the horizon, the wonderful colours in the sky can be used to add colour and impact into the foreground. The slight breeze of this scene in Mudeford (right) had to drop before the water was still enough to provide this perfectly clear reflection.

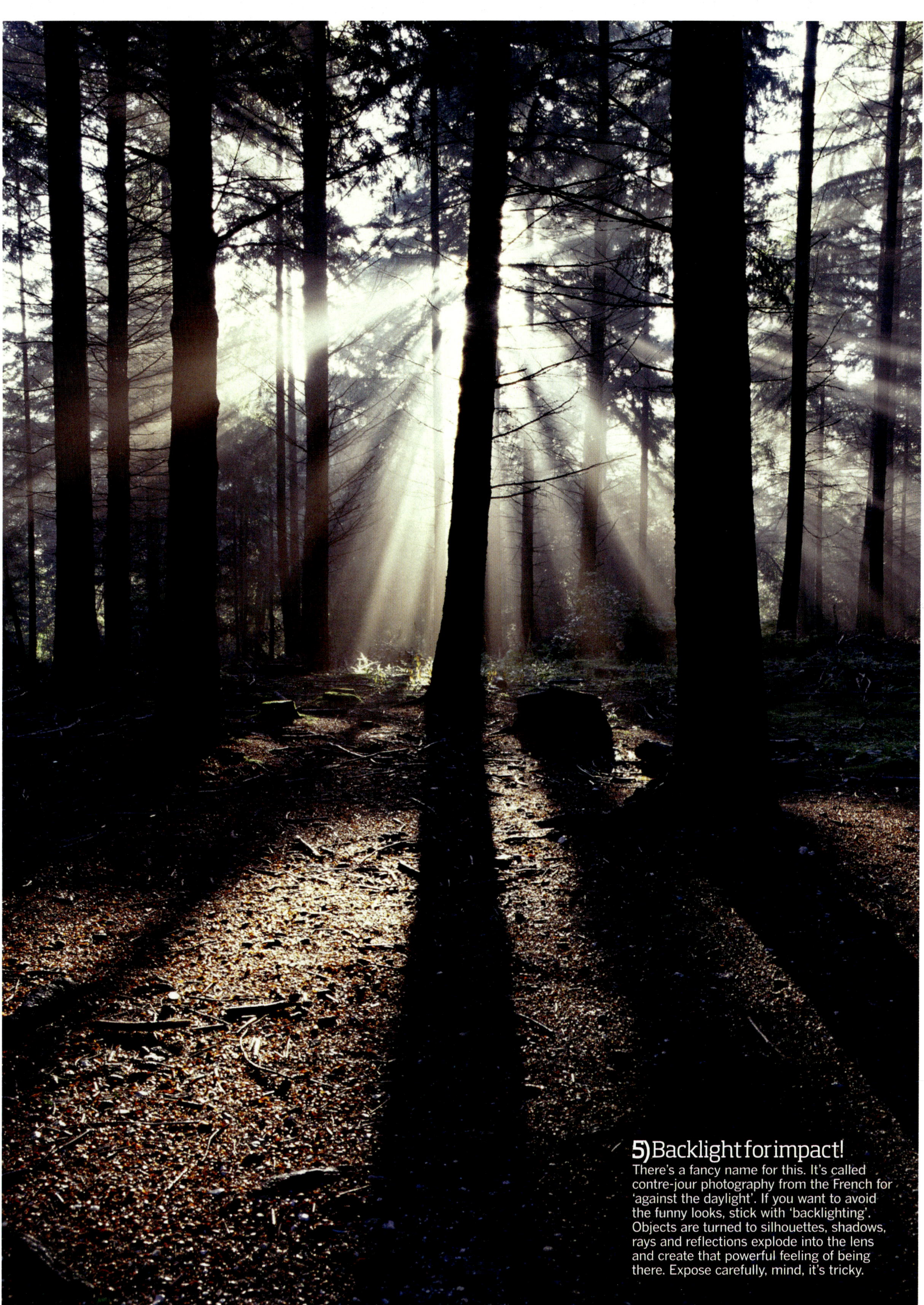

ALL IMAGES: MARK BAUER

5) Backlight for impact!

There's a fancy name for this. It's called contre-jour photography from the French for 'against the daylight'. If you want to avoid the funny looks, stick with 'backlighting'. Objects are turned to silhouettes, shadows, rays and reflections explode into the lens and create that powerful feeling of being there. Expose carefully, mind, it's tricky.

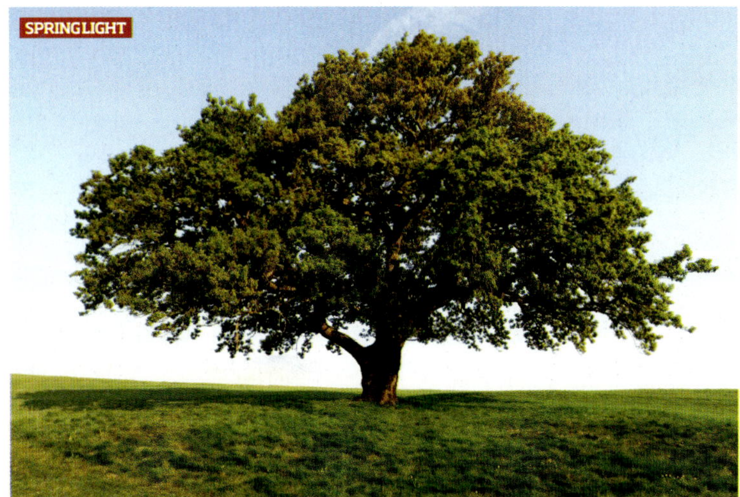

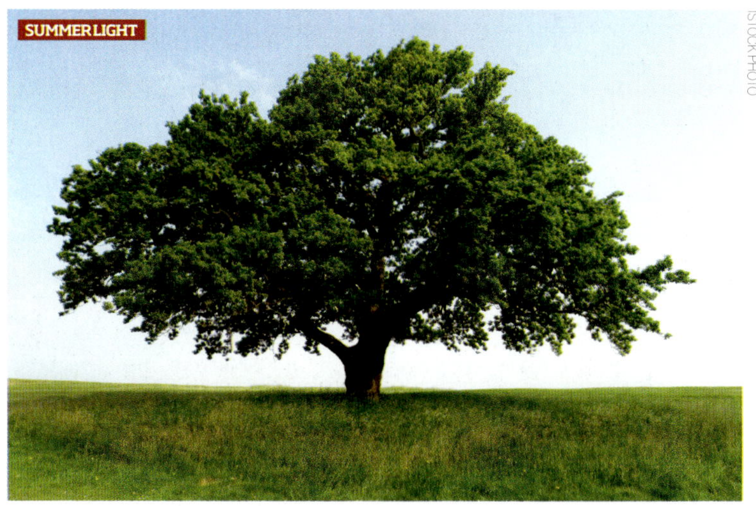

ISTOCKPHOTO

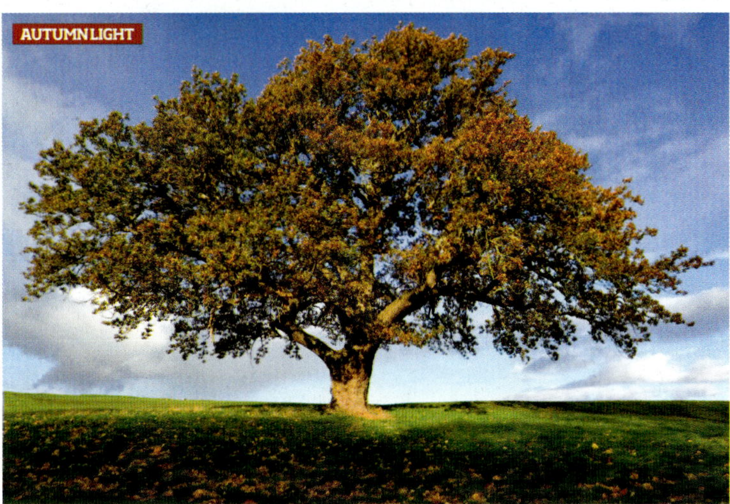

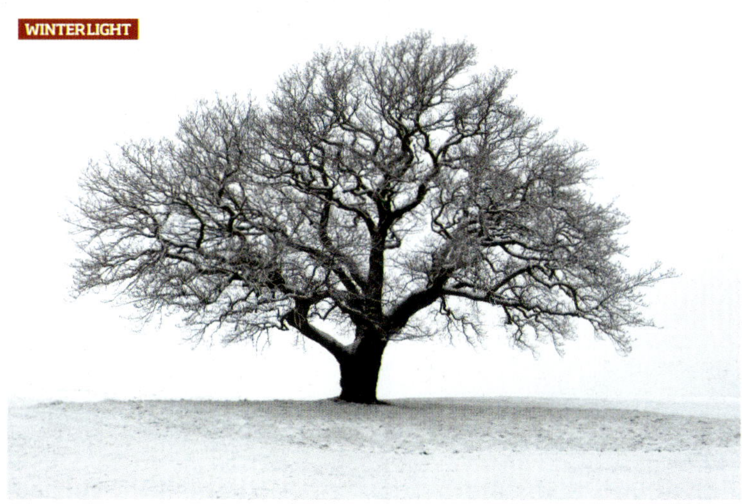

6) Seasonal light

In winter the landscape is more exposed and the low sun casts long shadows throughout the day. The air has less dust, giving the light clarity. Clear, cold nights lead to frosty mornings with pastel skies.

The light in summer is often less favourable for landscape photography, with the high sun creating harsh light for a large part of the day, with more dust and heat haze meaning the light is generally less clear.

In early spring and late autumn, the light and clarity are better than in summer and it's possible to shoot for most of the day. The weather is changeable, which can create moody and dramatic photo opportunities. In late spring and early autumn, after a cool night, mist can often form at dawn as the land begins to warm up.

BE READY TO GO: **A covering of snow might only last a few hours, even at high altitude. It's a good idea to have a bag packed and ready to go when the weather forecast mentions the white stuff. Time saved not having to hunt for your filters or a charged battery might make the difference between a shot like this (below) and a later one with slushy footprints all over it.**

KIT WATCH!

Keep comparisons in camera

Digital SLRs make seasonal comparisons like the set of four, above, much easier. When you revisit a location every three months, carry the previous images on the memory card to help you to recreate the exact distance and crop.

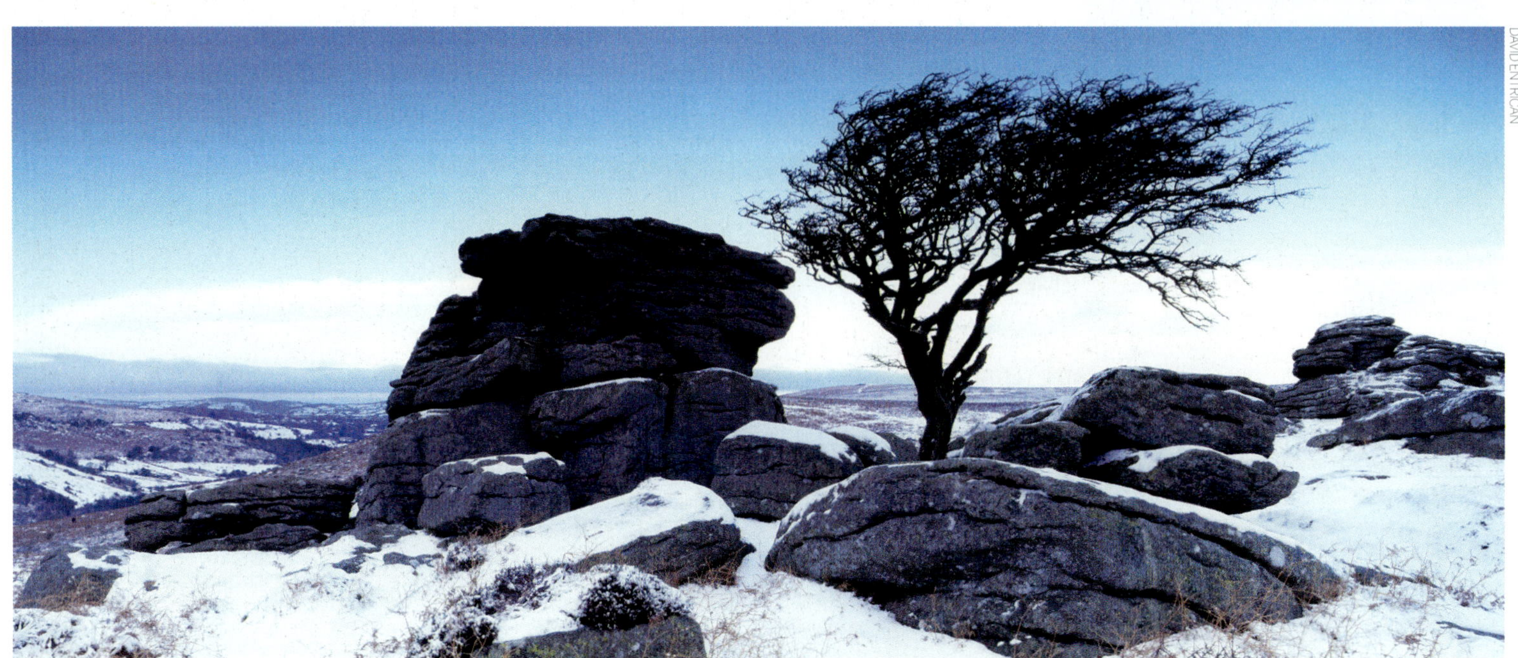

DAVID ENTRICAN

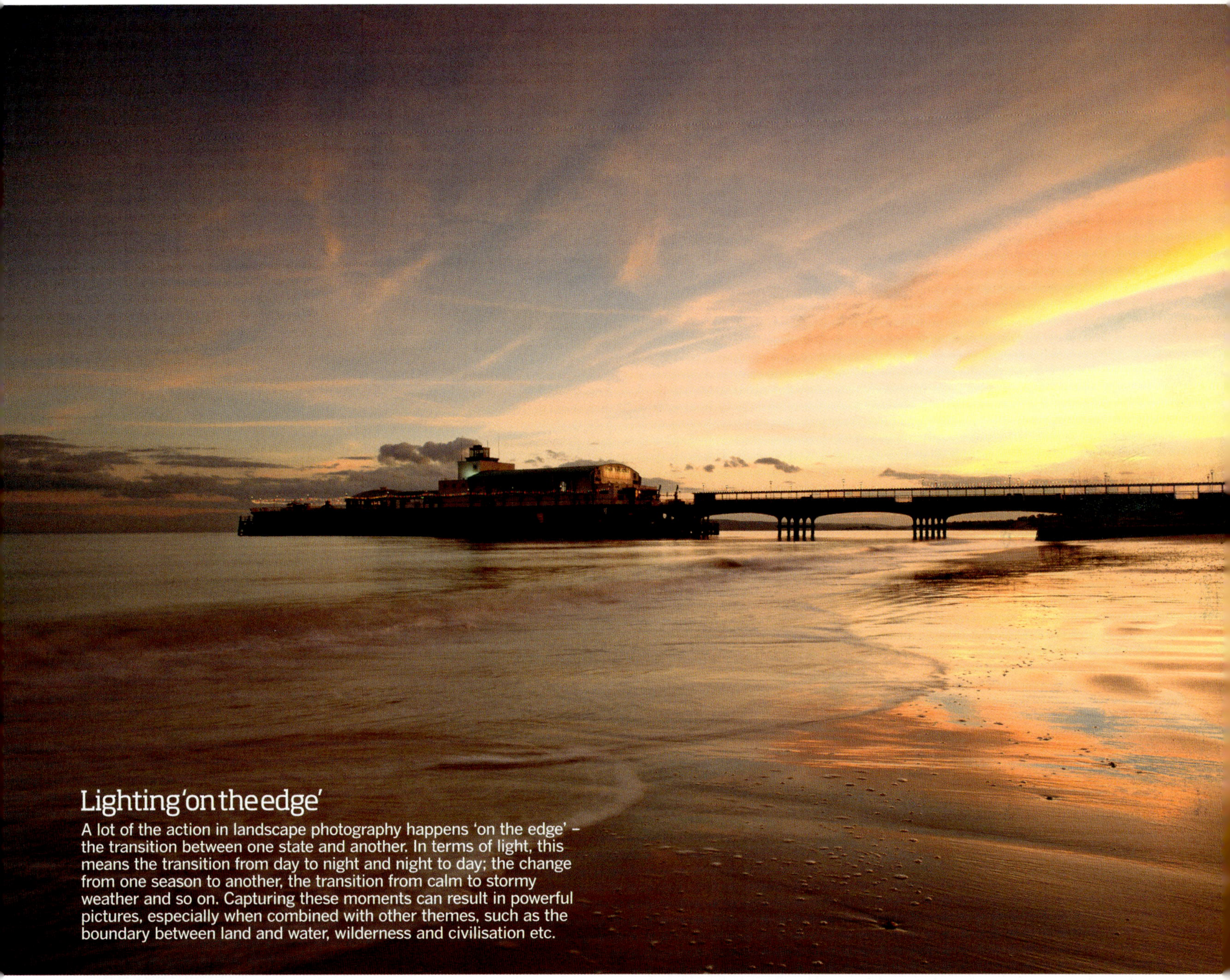

Lighting 'on the edge'

A lot of the action in landscape photography happens 'on the edge' – the transition between one state and another. In terms of light, this means the transition from day to night and night to day; the change from one season to another, the transition from calm to stormy weather and so on. Capturing these moments can result in powerful pictures, especially when combined with other themes, such as the boundary between land and water, wilderness and civilisation etc.

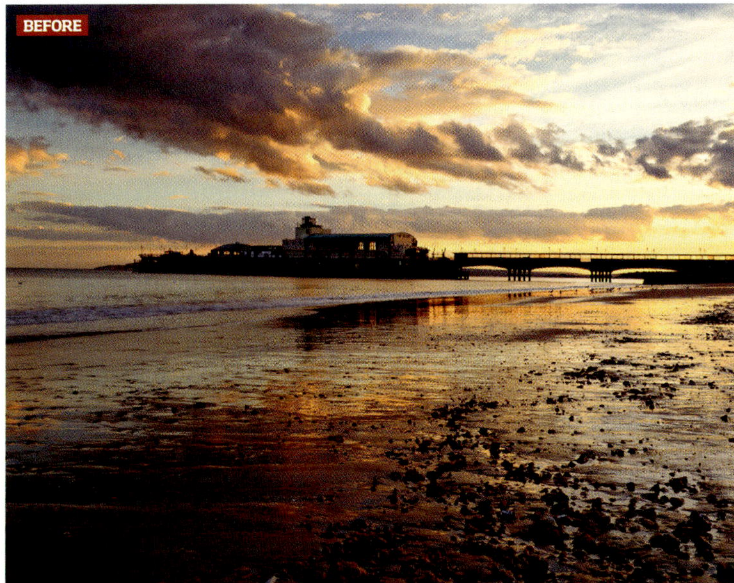

Several 'edge' themes come together here: the interval between one storm passing and another arriving, the edge of land and water and the transition between night and day.

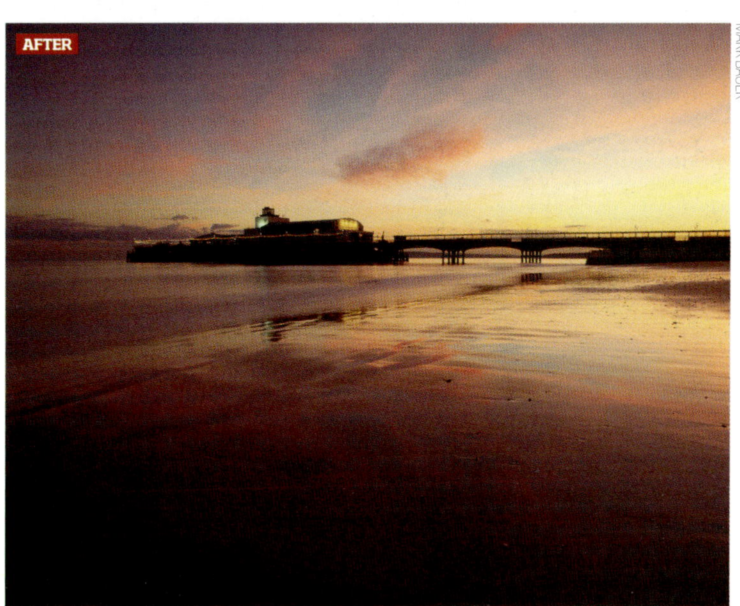

MARK BAUER

In the first shot (left), the storm is still clearing as the sun is setting and in the second (above) there was a fantastic afterglow before the next storm rolled in.

EXPERT TUTORIAL

Light and the time of day

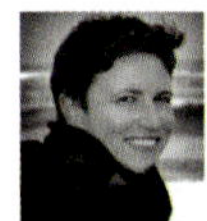

TIME OF DAY is one of the key factors that influences the mood of a landscape image. The low sun in the mornings and evenings can add warmth and colour to a scene, but it's equally important to know how different seasons and certain weather conditions can provide particular types of lighting.

Remember that some locations work better at certain times of the year – the position of sunrise and sunset varies throughout the year, so research your location first.

Arrive early and learn to pre-visualise and spot the potential in a scene. This is a key ingredient to capturing great landscape images, as it gives you time to find the best composition before the most photogenic light of the day arrives, so you can prepare without having to rush.

This location at Botallack in Cornwall looks its best in the evening light, especially in August when the high sun during the day can make it look a bit boring. In the sequence shown here, I arrived at late afternoon, anticipating attractive evening light. I found my spot and took a frame at 5pm to use as a comparison shot for my time of day sequence. As you can see, the light is harsh and the scene appears 'flat' and colourless.

At 6pm, it's improved a little – a break in the cloud meant that the blue sky was reflected in the sea, adding to the colour intensity. I had to wait over 2½ hours for the perfect light – the sun broke through the clouds, bathing my view in a beautiful warm light for all of ten minutes, before the clouds merged again.

The sun had set but I hadn't finished yet, as the twilight was still to come. At this time, there is no directional light and the scene now takes on a new dimension – a more surreal, calming quality. This is all down to the light, or should I say lack of light. Shooting the scene at this time of day means a longer exposure, and this creates a calming effect. The sea appears smooth, the colours are cooler and more subtle and there is a kind of harmony between the two.

Successful landscape photography is as much a state of mind as a technical skill. Patience and dedication are as important as the right camera, lenses and tripod. It felt good knowing that it was worth the wait, and it really does prove that although patience is a virtue, you should always give yourself plenty of time to find a good viewpoint. Waiting is the name of the game, as light can be very fickle and difficult to predict – you can never know how it will turn out.

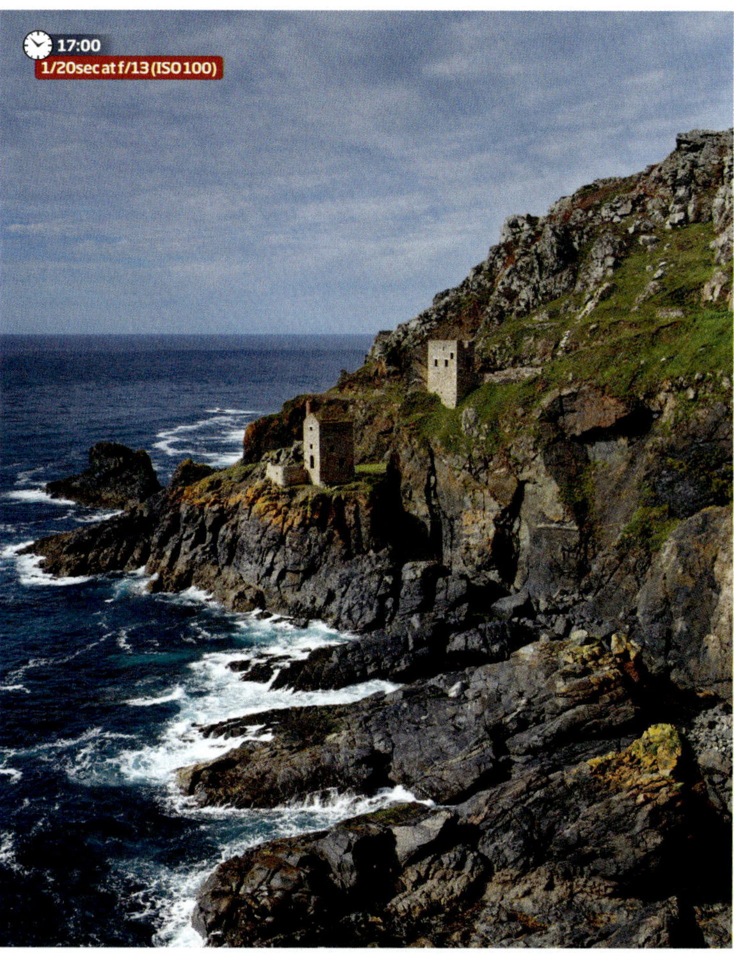

This was a test shot to check composition. I rarely shoot during the time of day when the sun is so high in the sky, but it allows us to see how light improves later.

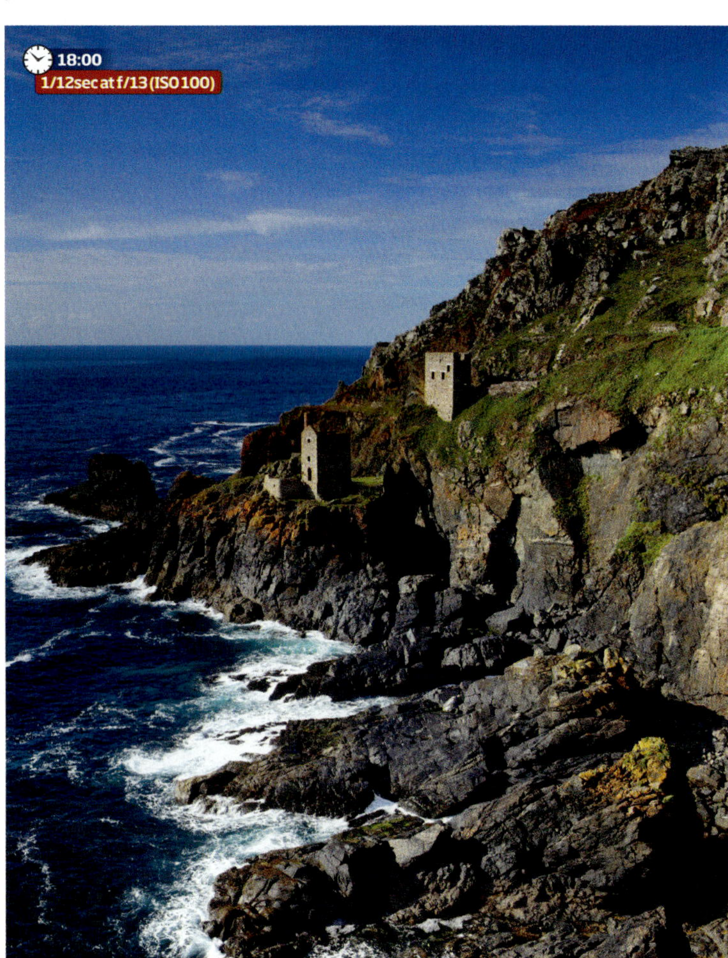

The second in the series shows a difference, the scene has more colour and because it was taken at a later time, the light is already starting to get better.

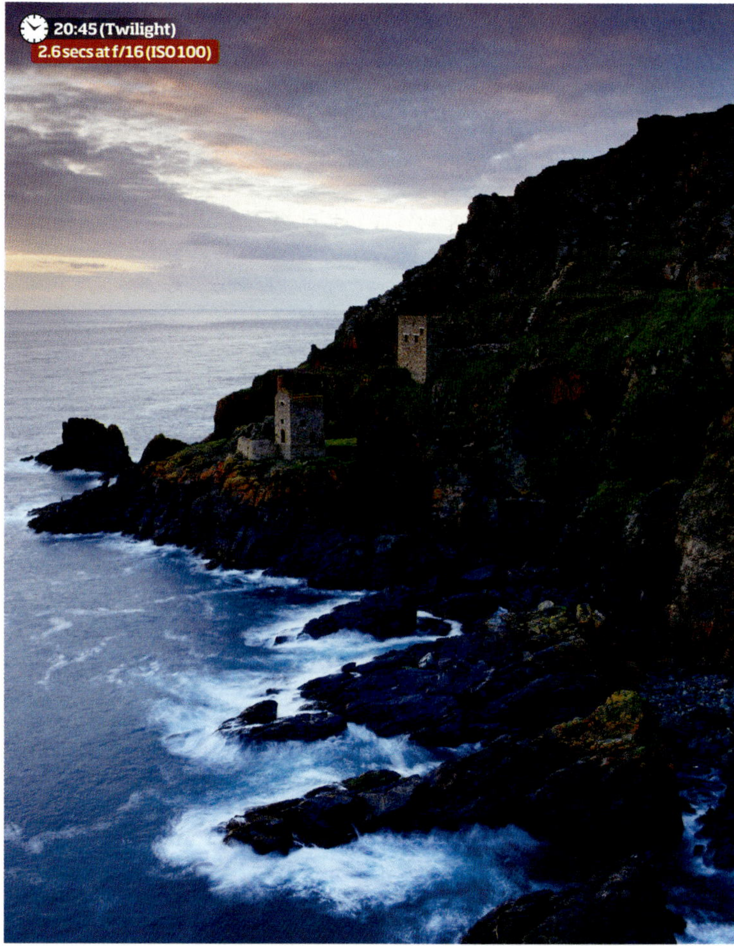

This was the last shot of the day and shows how the twilight can make even the roughest of seas seem calm. The longer the exposure, the calmer it looks.

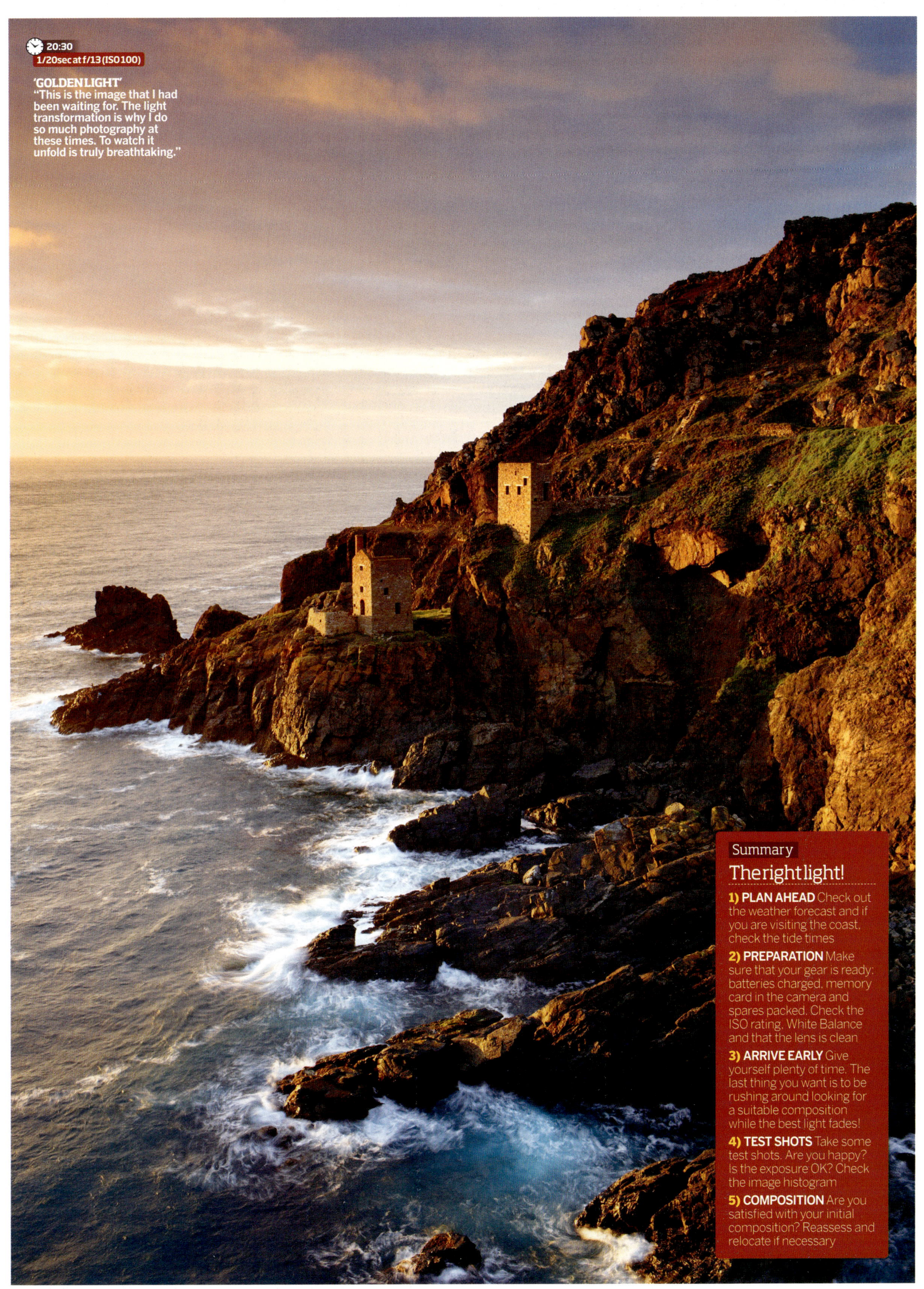

20:30
1/20sec at f/13 (ISO 100)

'GOLDEN LIGHT'
"This is the image that I had been waiting for. The light transformation is why I do so much photography at these times. To watch it unfold is truly breathtaking."

Summary

The right light!

1) **PLAN AHEAD** Check out the weather forecast and if you are visiting the coast, check the tide times

2) **PREPARATION** Make sure that your gear is ready: batteries charged, memory card in the camera and spares packed. Check the ISO rating, White Balance and that the lens is clean

3) **ARRIVE EARLY** Give yourself plenty of time. The last thing you want is to be rushing around looking for a suitable composition while the best light fades!

4) **TEST SHOTS** Take some test shots. Are you happy? Is the exposure OK? Check the image histogram

5) **COMPOSITION** Are you satisfied with your initial composition? Reassess and relocate if necessary

EXPERT TUTORIAL

Get up early for 'magic hour' lighting

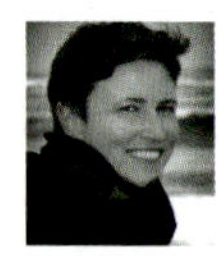

WITH HELEN DIXON Waking a couple of hours before sunrise, which is often in the middle of the night, is not most people's idea of fun. But if you're prepared to make the effort, you will almost always reap the rewards. To do it right, planning is essential. Check the weather forecast and the sunrise times on the internet. Remember to check the tide times if you are travelling to the sea – a low tide is usually the best time to visit. If the light fails to materialise, you can always do beach close-ups.

I try to be on location at least half an hour before the sun rises – if not earlier – because it's often before the sun appears that the real magic happens. This also gives me time to set up the camera and to find the best viewpoint. Don't just look for clear days, it's better to have cloud around as this creates wonderful colours in the sky as the cloud reflects the light of the sun. Try to pre-visit and research your location before the day of the shoot. I use Ordnance Survey maps for detailed information on rights of way and parking. Look for appealing places where there will be opportunities for shots that include foreground interest.

Mist mainly develops during a cold night and it will only linger for a short time during the morning or until the heat of the sun burns it away. Something to bear in mind is that during misty conditions, your camera's metering system will often underexpose the scene, resulting in a dull, lifeless landscape. To compensate for this, alter the exposure by +½ or +1 stop as this helps bring the scene to life. Check the histogram on the camera's LCD monitor to make sure you haven't overexposed the scene.

The use of Neutral Density graduate filters is pretty much standard in landscape photography. They help to control the brightest part of the image, which is usually the sky. Early in the day, there is a noticeable difference between the light in the sky and the light on the land.

Be aware of lens flare if the sun is included in the frame. To help eliminate this make sure that your filters and lens optics are spotlessly clean. I rarely use a warm-up filter. A disadvantage with these filters is that it will make any green foliage appear a yellow-brown colour. Instead I set my camera's White Balance to cloudy or shade to help warm the scene. Try to avoid using the Auto White Balance (AWB) setting as you are sure to cool down the light, unless of course this is the effect you want.

There are a number of reasons why I personally prefer dawn light over sunset. I like to capture atmosphere in my shots if I can, and early morning is the best time to do this as you are more likely to have a misty or frosty start to the day. The light is often diffused and softer at this time, but it's more of a challenge to include the sun in the shot during the morning than in the evening, because at sunset the pollution levels have risen throughout the day, which helps to diffuse the brightness slightly. Another great advantage of early morning is that it's so peaceful, I rarely see another soul. The world belongs to me – it's so satisfying to watch the day unfold and witness the magical light of dawn.

Once the sun has risen and become too strong to photograph, turn away to the side or even put your back to the sun, but be careful not to cast a shadow in the foreground.

It's now time to start using the warm light illuminating the land. Light is never static but continually changes – it's the main ingredient that allows us to create something beautiful.

KIT WATCH!

Helen's magic hour kit

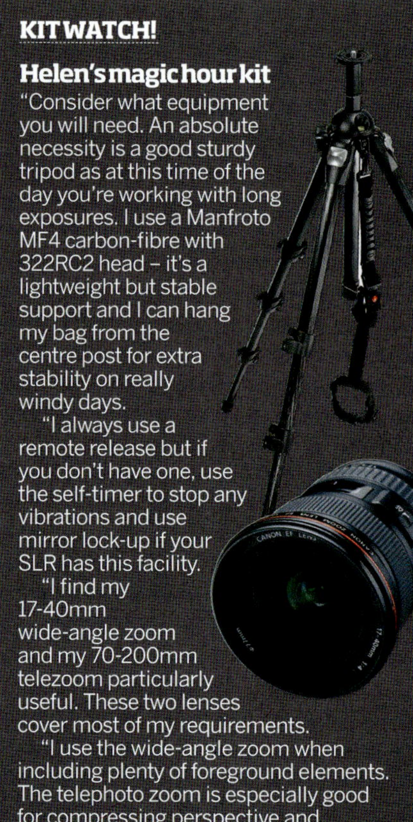

"Consider what equipment you will need. An absolute necessity is a good sturdy tripod as at this time of the day you're working with long exposures. I use a Manfroto MF4 carbon-fibre with 322RC2 head – it's a lightweight but stable support and I can hang my bag from the centre post for extra stability on really windy days.

"I always use a remote release but if you don't have one, use the self-timer to stop any vibrations and use mirror lock-up if your SLR has this facility.

"I find my 17-40mm wide-angle zoom and my 70-200mm telezoom particularly useful. These two lenses cover most of my requirements.

"I use the wide-angle zoom when including plenty of foreground elements. The telephoto zoom is especially good for compressing perspective and creating layers on misty mornings."

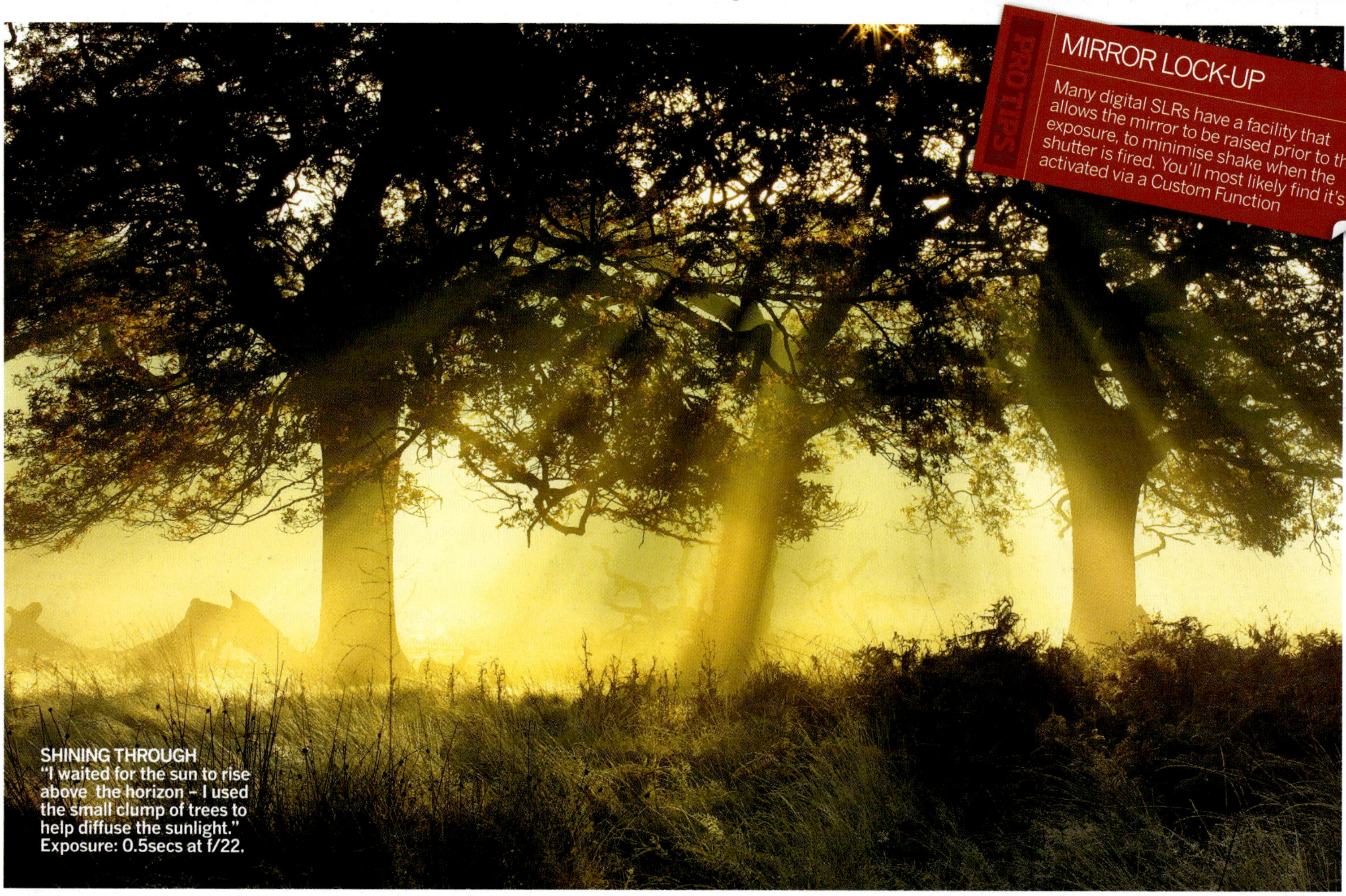

PRO TIPS

MIRROR LOCK-UP

Many digital SLRs have a facility that allows the mirror to be raised prior to the exposure, to minimise shake when the shutter is fired. You'll most likely find it's activated via a Custom Function

SHINING THROUGH
"I waited for the sun to rise above the horizon – I used the small clump of trees to help diffuse the sunlight."
Exposure: 0.5secs at f/22.

EXPERT TUTORIAL

Stay out late and shoot stunning sunsets

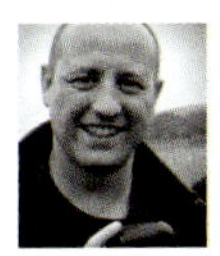

WITH MARK BAUER Although it's possible to take landscape photographs at most times of the day, there are two times when most landscapers agree the light will give the best results – the first and last hours of the day. What makes these times of day special is that the low sun casts long shadows and helps to pick out the features of the landscape. If you're out pre-dawn or post-sunset, you can also see some spectacular skies as the clouds are lit from below.

The light is quite similar at these two times of day, and whether you prefer one or the other often depends on which direction of light will best suit your chosen subject. So, for example, the south coast in winter will look best at the end of the day rather than the start. Having said that, the light in the final hour of the day tends to be warmer, and as the sun sets, the landscape is often bathed in a golden glow. And, of course, the nice thing about sunset compared to sunrise is that you don't have to force yourself out of bed at a ridiculous hour to make the most of it. Let's be honest, not everyone has the will-power and enthusiasm for sunrises as Helen Dixon (see previous page)!

Almost any type of landscape looks good in the magic hour, but some features really benefit, such as stone buildings or rocky cliffs. When the low sun warms everything up and picks out the texture of rock and stone, scenes that might look dull at any other time of day can be lifted out of the ordinary.

Water is also an excellent subject at this time, because if you have an interesting sky, you can double the impact by using reflections. Moving water can sparkle like diamonds or be made to blur during long exposures. Again, the amount and type of light falling on it will determine the result.

The direction of the light can have a strong influence on the mood of pictures taken at the beginning or end of the day. Front lighting can look flat, as the direction of the shadows doesn't help to pick out the details of the landscape.

With the sun to one side, shadows help create depth in the picture and reveal form and texture. Side-lighting is best if you want to use a polariser to saturate colours, as it will have its strongest effect if the camera is at a 90° angle to the sun. Backlighting can be very dramatic, but exposure is difficult to control and you will have to be careful to avoid flare as light falls directly onto your filters or the front element of your lens.

So, with weather being notoriously unpredictable, how can you tell if the magic hour will live up to your expectations? Looking at weather forecasts is a good idea. The Met Office's website (www.metoffice.gov.uk) is reliable and you can get a fairly detailed forecast for specific regions. Remember that the longer the range of the forecast, the less reliable it will be. Checking the forecast online the night before a dawn shoot gives you the best guide to what to expect.

If you drive to your location, listen to local radio stations in the car, rather than national ones and keeping an eye on what's happening in the sky can tell you a lot.

For sunsets you'll need to look to the west, as this is where the sun will be at magic hour. Most of our weather fronts come from the west too, so by keeping an eye in that direction, it's possible to see if cloud is likely to break up or thicken.

Being aware of wind direction, the points of the compass and weather patterns will help enormously and you will eventually start to recognise the signs of a magic moment.

KIT WATCH!

Mark Bauer's magic hour kit

"Wide-angle lenses are the most popular for landscape work, but longer lenses can also be useful for picking out the kind of patterns and textures that the magic hour can reveal.

"A polarising filter will help you make the most of side lighting by improving overall saturation, but is especially effective when used with blue skies.

"A sturdy tripod is another essential. If you're shooting in the period after sunset, light levels will be low and hand-holding will be out of the question. But it's good practice to use a tripod whatever the lighting conditions – it will slow you down, it makes you think and it enables you to make small but often vital changes to composition.

"Neutral density graduate filters are essential, especially if clouds are lit from below and there is no direct light on the land. ND grads help control contrast."

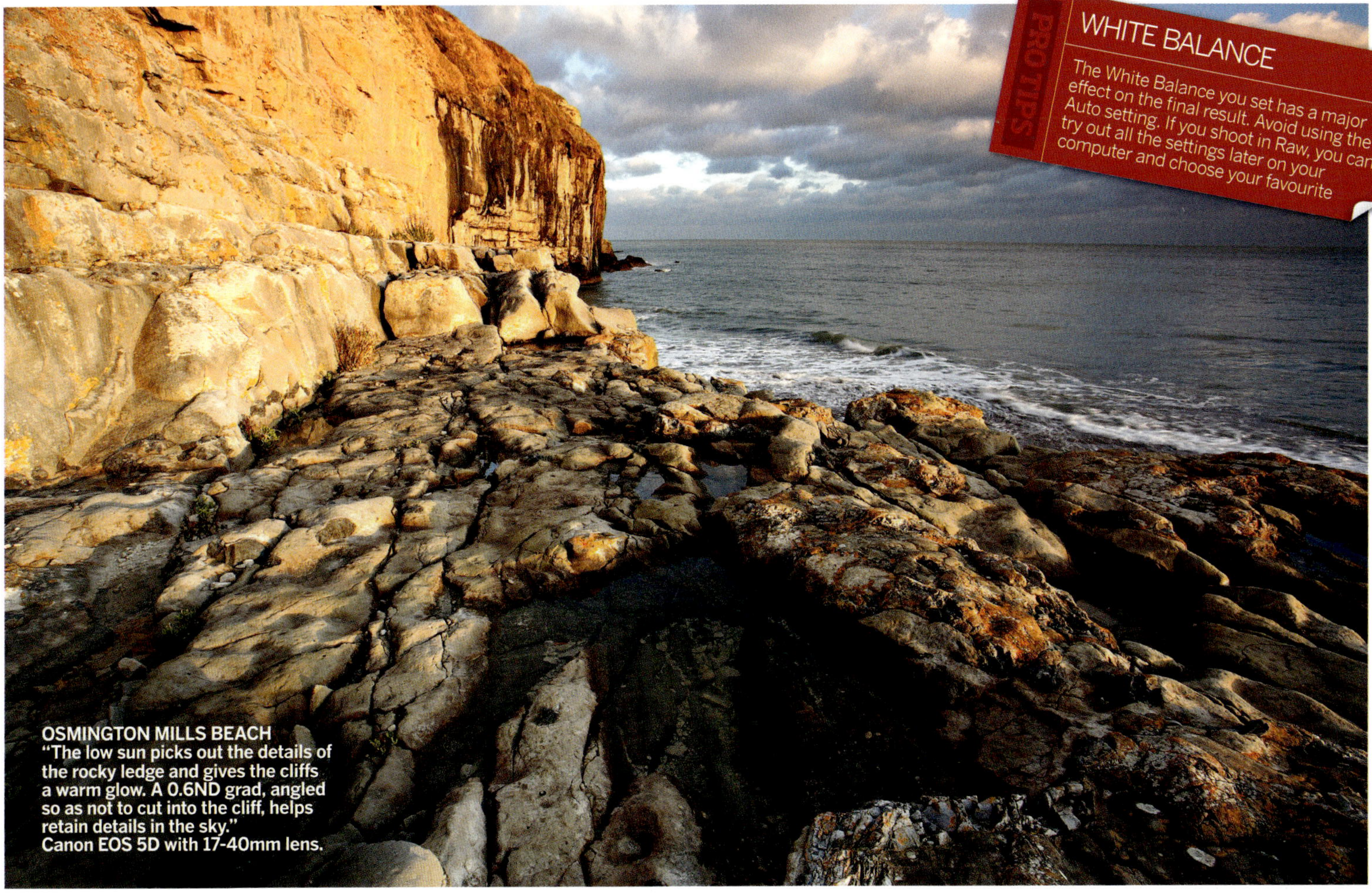

PRO TIPS

WHITE BALANCE

The White Balance you set has a major effect on the final result. Avoid using the Auto setting. If you shoot in Raw, you can try out all the settings later on your computer and choose your favourite

OSMINGTON MILLS BEACH
"The low sun picks out the details of the rocky ledge and gives the cliffs a warm glow. A 0.6ND grad, angled so as not to cut into the cliff, helps retain details in the sky."
Canon EOS 5D with 17-40mm lens.

EXPERT TUTORIAL

Shoot a misty morning

True landscape fanatics don't believe in 'lie-ins'! Get up early for a mist opportunity rather than a missed one!

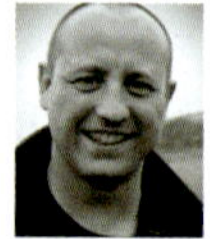

WITH MARK BAUER Late winter/early spring is excellent for shooting atmospheric landscapes, especially if you're prepared to get up early. As one season slips into another, it often brings interesting weather with it. At this time of year, misty mornings are common, often combined with a touch of frost. Foggy scenes convey a sense of romance and mystery, and add an element that can lift otherwise bland scenes out of the ordinary. With careful planning, it's possible to capture dramatic, atmospheric scenics.

How to meter to perfection every time

Mist and fog tend to fool the camera into underexposure, so be prepared to add at least a stop over the metered reading using exposure compensation. If shooting Raw, you'll record the maximum amount of tonal information by exposing 'to the right' (pushing the exposure as far into the highlights as you can without actually 'clipping' the highlights.) You'll need to do some work in the Raw converter on exposure, brightness and contrast, but the end result will be a better image.

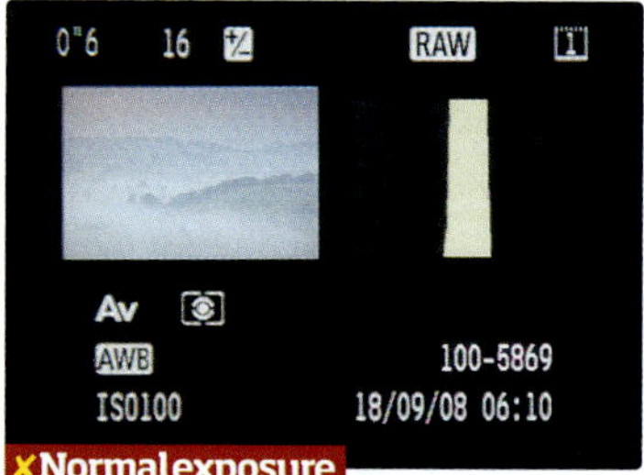

✗ Normal exposure
The meter will assume that whatever it's reading from is a mid-tone, and underexpose the mist so that it records as grey rather than white.

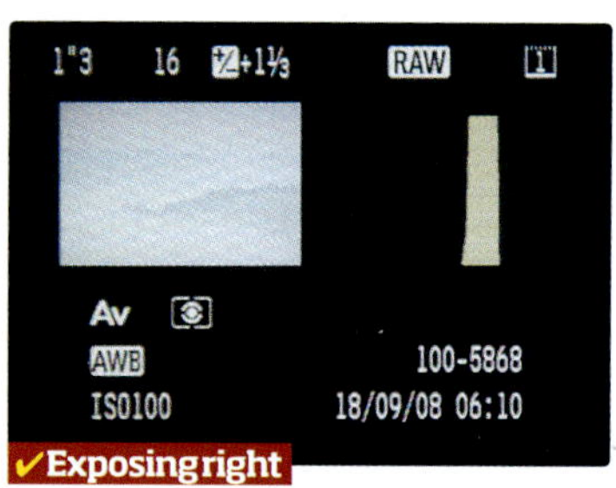

✓ Exposing right
Around +1 stop compensation would be enough to keep the mist looking white. I've added a little more, following the 'expose to the right' theory.

KIT WATCH!

Ideal kit for mist

Using a tripod is good practice for shooting landscapes, but essential if you're heading out for pre-dawn misty pictures, as exposures can be long. A medium telezoom is probably the most useful lens – a long-ish focal length compresses perspective and enhances the misty effect. A set of Neutral Density graduated filters will be necessary in pre-dawn shots, as the sky will be much brighter than the land, which has no direct light falling on it.

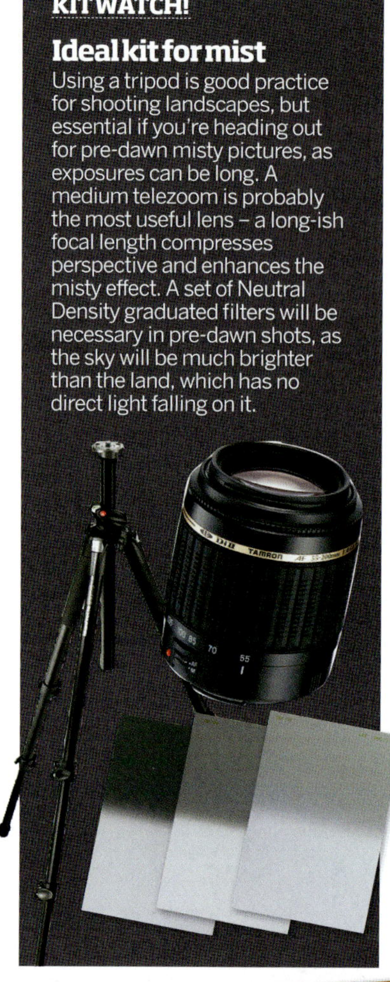

PRO TIPS

MIST OR FOG?

What's the difference between mist and fog? We're happy to provide the clearest of answers – they're basically the same! The only difference is one of density – if visibility is less than 1,000m, it's fog!

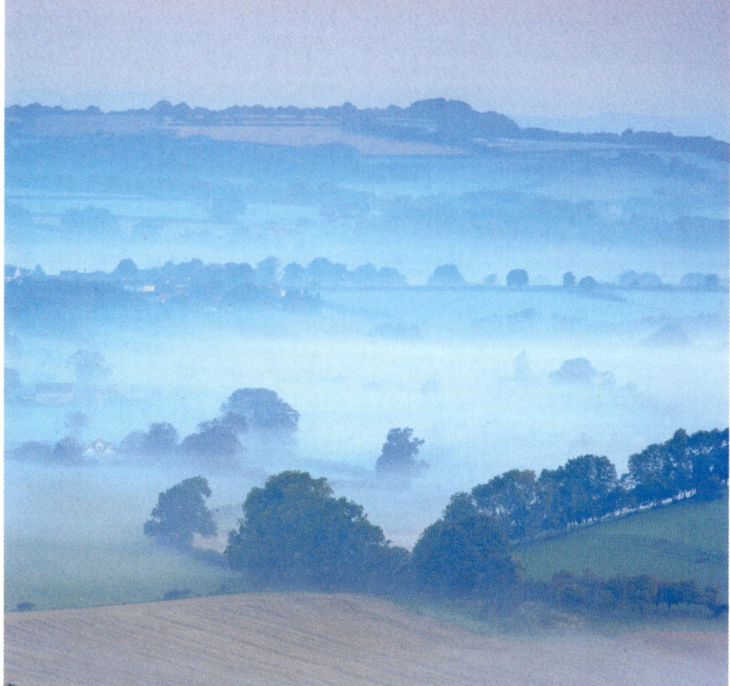

1 choose your day At this time of year, fog and mist are formed when mild, moist air passes over cold ground – the lower layers of the air get cooled down rapidly to the temperature at which fog or mist forms. Keep an eye on the forecast and look out for cold, clear nights with a light south-westerly wind, as this gives a high chance of mist or fog. Even if the conditions seem right, however, an atmospheric sunrise isn't guaranteed – often, for example, you can get a thick fog rather than mist – so persistence is important. Be prepared to make multiple visits to your favourite locations.

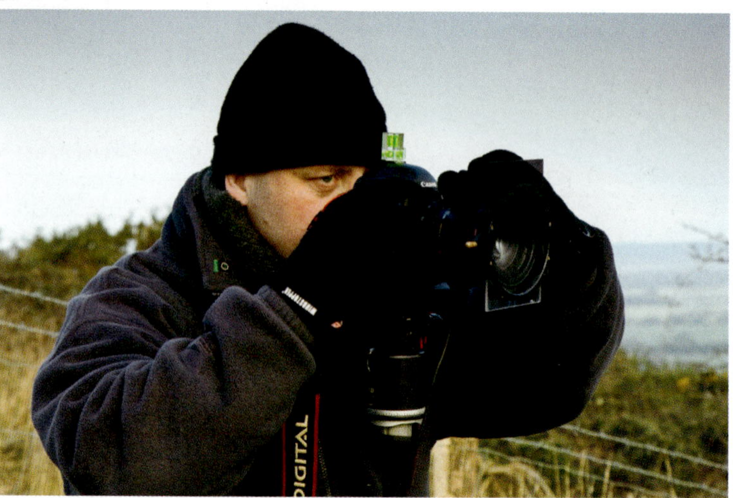

2 Be well prepared Mist often forms at the bottom of valleys, where the ground is colder, so the hills above a valley are good place to be, as this enables you to shoot from above a layer of mist, with hills rising out of it. Being near water also helps, as this helps to cool any air moving over it. Research suitable locations well in advance and arrive a good half an hour before sunrise, as the pre-dawn light can be magical. For this shoot, I set up overlooking the west Wiltshire Downs, with mist lying at the bottom of the hills. Also, be sure to wrap up warm – gloves, a hat and a thick fleece are essential!

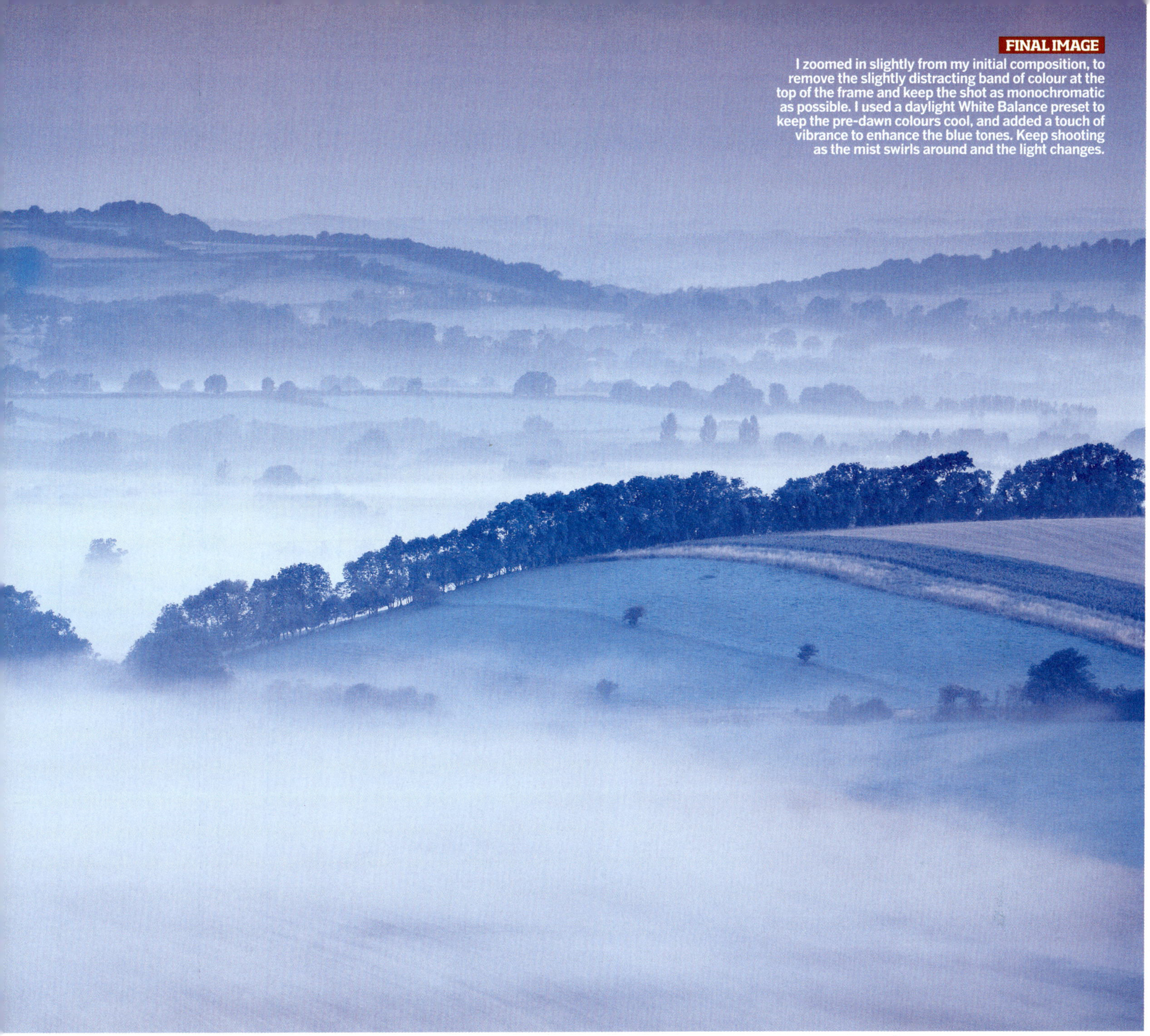

FINAL IMAGE

I zoomed in slightly from my initial composition, to remove the slightly distracting band of colour at the top of the frame and keep the shot as monochromatic as possible. I used a daylight White Balance preset to keep the pre-dawn colours cool, and added a touch of vibrance to enhance the blue tones. Keep shooting as the mist swirls around and the light changes.

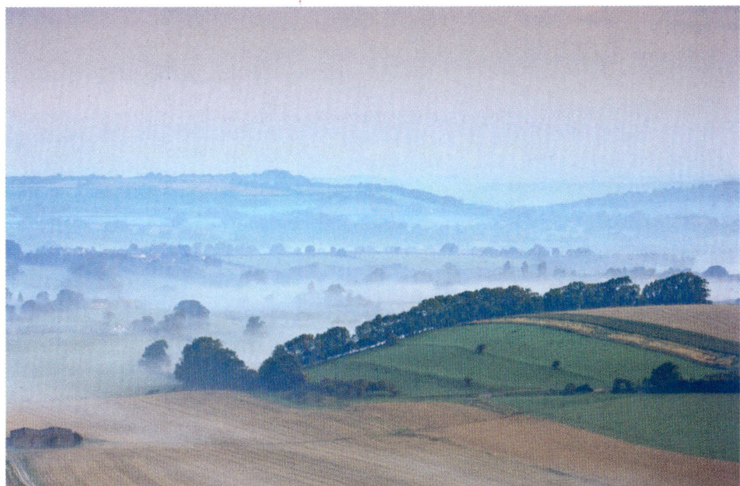

3 **CHECK YOUR composition** You need to look for strong, bold shapes, as mist hides shapes and dilutes colours, making a scene monochrome. I like to look for overlapping and interlocking shapes that help add a sense of depth to the scene. Backlit scenes can also work well, as the shapes of hills are silhouetted in the mist. Flare isn't too much of a problem with backlit shots, as the mist diffuses the sunlight. For this shot, I selected a hill rising out of the mist as the main focal point, and arranged it according to the rule-of-thirds. Behind the foreground hill, the layering effect leads the eye into the backdrop.

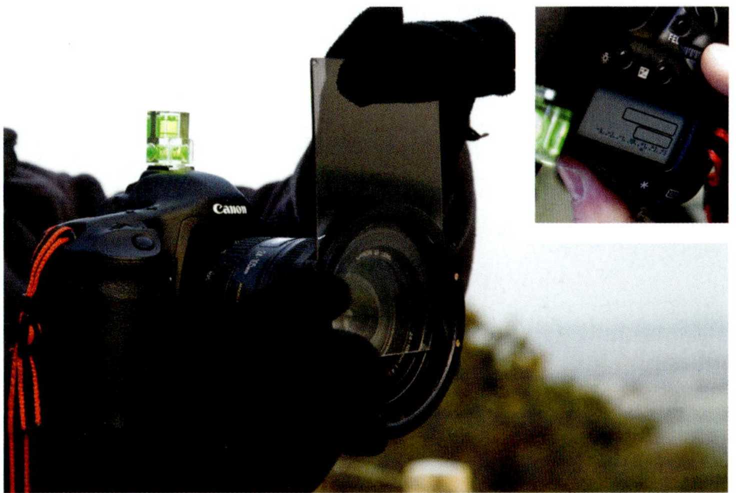

4 **exposure & filtration** Mist can fool the meter into underexposure, so as a starting point, set +1 stop exposure compensation. Meter from the land and the sky to check the difference in brightness, to see if you need a graduated filter and, if so, which strength. Take care not to over-filter the scene (e.g. if there's a four-stop difference in brightness, use a three-stop grad so that the sky remains a little lighter than the land and therefore looks natural). For these shots, I used a one-stop soft grad as, although there wasn't a huge range of contrast, I felt that the sky needed a little bit of help to add interest.

EXPERT TUTORIAL

Evenings by the coast

As well as rising early, landscape enthusiasts tend to stay out until the twilight hours to capture mood and drama

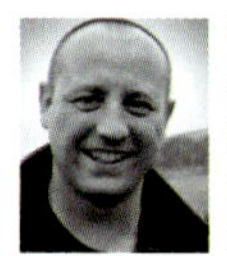

WITH MARK BAUER Seascapes are a hard subject to resist photographing, especially during a sunset when you can get beautiful blue and purple hues from the sky and silky water from a long exposure. When planning your shoot, remember that location and composition are important elements to determine the success of a seascape image. I try to pick places where there are rocks, so the bold shapes and jagged edges contrast with the softness of the water. Leave plenty of space around the static objects too, to allow you to capture movement in the water. I try to shoot low-light seascapes with an incoming tide, so that the waves wash up around the foreground, adding brighter tones. If you shoot when the tide is falling, you could end up with rocks being rendered as dark masses in the foreground because there is not enough light to show their wet, shiny surfaces. Getting the timing right for individual waves is important too; time the exposure so that there is water movement in the frame for at least some of the time the shutter is open.

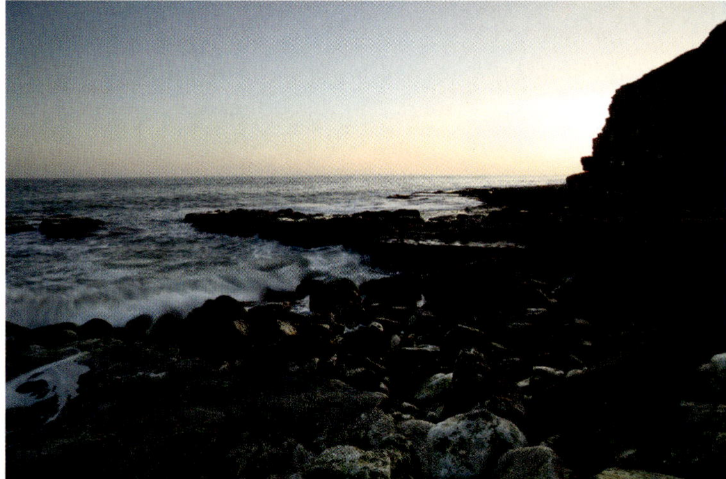

1 This isolated cove on the Purbeck coast is ideal for low-light seascapes, with its jagged, rocky ledges and boulders on the foreshore. However, with the sun only just below the horizon, the light is still a little harsh, and the tide is too far out and would be too far away in the frame.

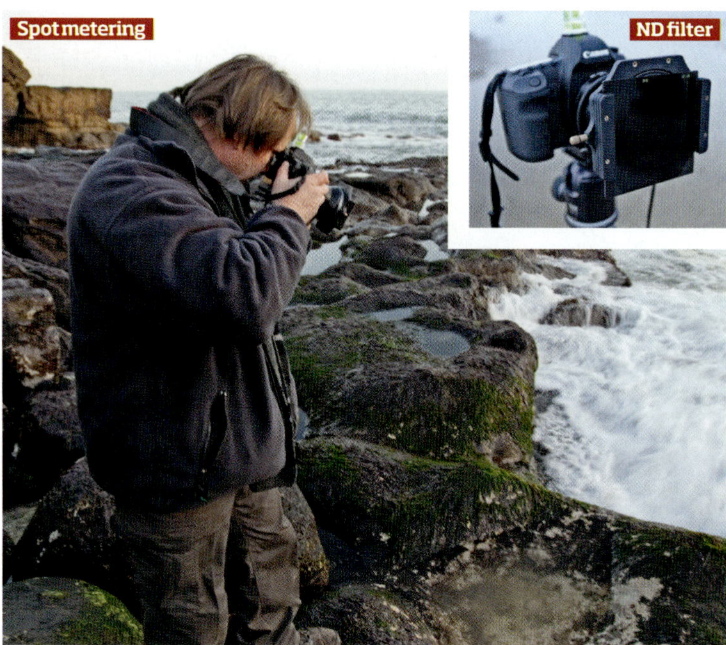

Spot metering

ND filter

2 Spot meter readings from the foreground and the sky tells me that there is a five-stop difference in brightness between them. A three-stop ND grad brings it all within the camera's sensor range. Waiting a few minutes means the waves are now washing up onto the foreground.

KIT WATCH!

Protect your gear

Protect your equipment with a rain cover. You can improvise by using a freezer bag, or there are several which are commercially available. I favour the Optech Rainsleeve – they're cheap, do the job well and you can see all your camera settings properly, which isn't true of some of the more pricey alternatives.

TECHNIQUE WATCH!

Calculating exposure

Most DSLRs allow you to set a maximum exposure time of 30 seconds. You could raise the ISO to stick within this limit but, to get the best image quality, stick to ISO 100 and switch to the Bulb setting, which allows you to keep the shutter open for as long as you want. To calculate how long that should be, in aperture-priority mode, increase the ISO until you get a meter reading. Then work out what the equivalent exposure is at ISO 100, switch to Bulb and take the shot. For example, if at ISO 400 the correct exposure is 30 seconds, the equivalent at ISO 100 is two minutes. At dusk, light levels drop so keep checking and adjust accordingly.

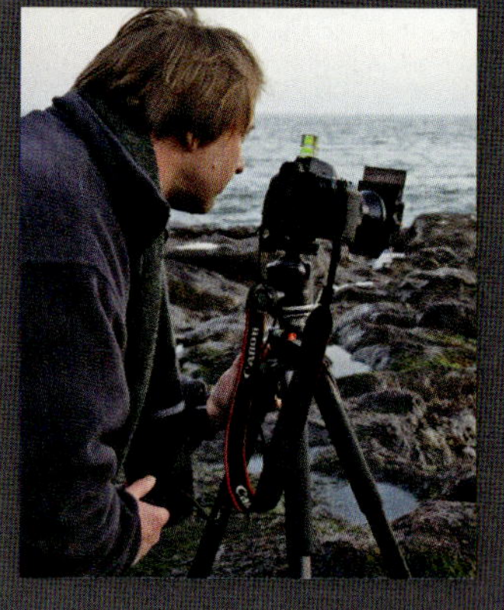

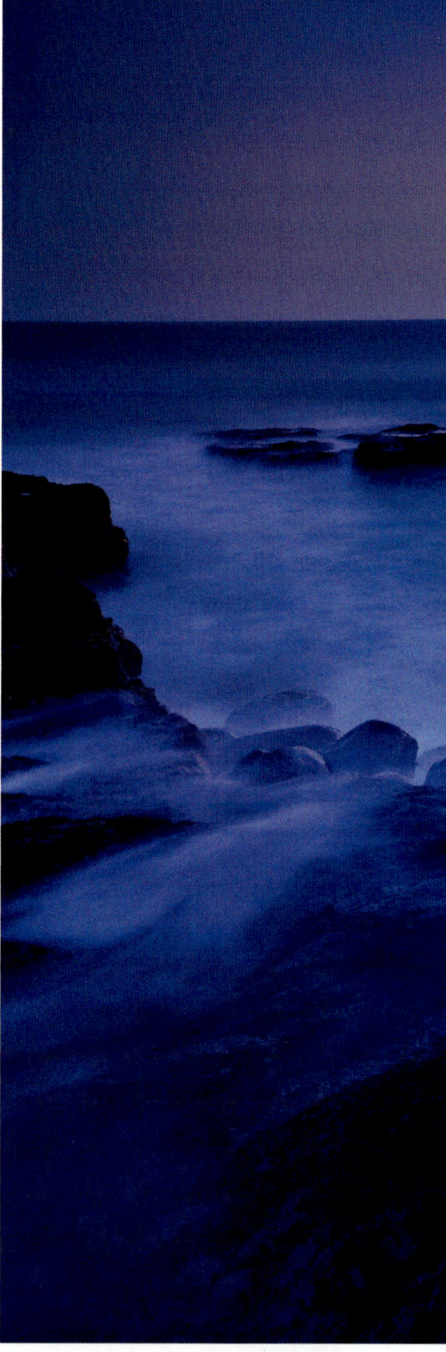

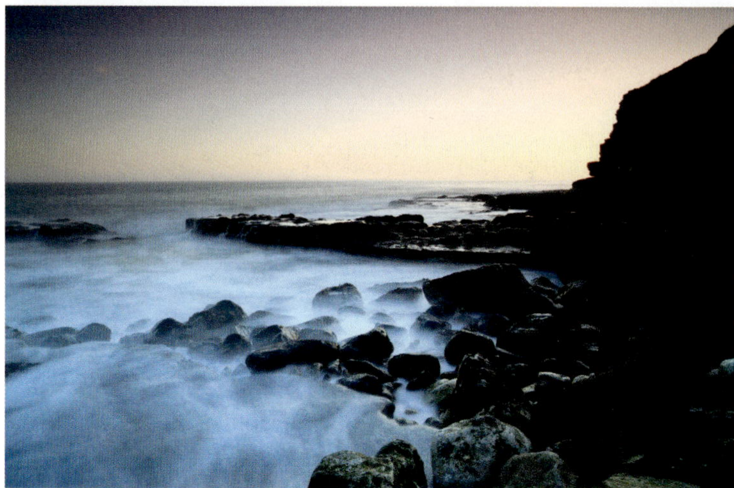

3 Even with the waves intruding into the foreground area, there are still too many dark tones, especially to the right of the frame, so I tweak the composition, moving the camera's view to the left. Now it's just a case of waiting for the light to drop further and the right waves to come in.

FINAL IMAGE
This has the same beautiful hues and tones as the previous shot, but just a little more water adding interest to the foreground and the right side of the picture.

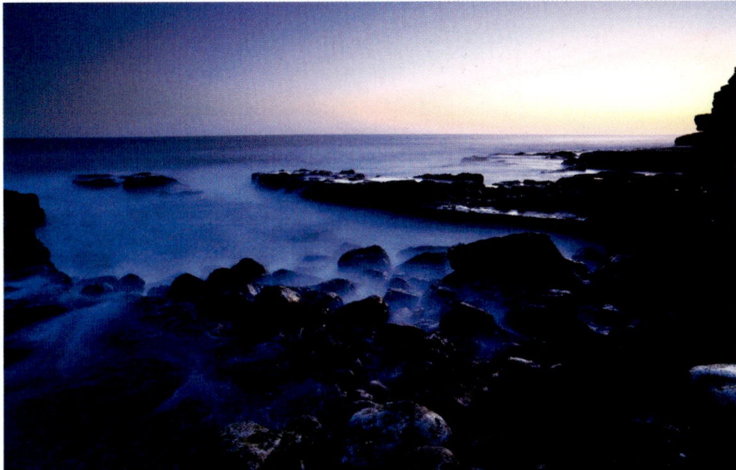

4 The low light levels produce a lovely blue-purple in the sky and the sea. This one's almost there but just needs a little more water washing up on the right-hand side of the picture, to break up the dark tones and help to balance out the foreground interest.

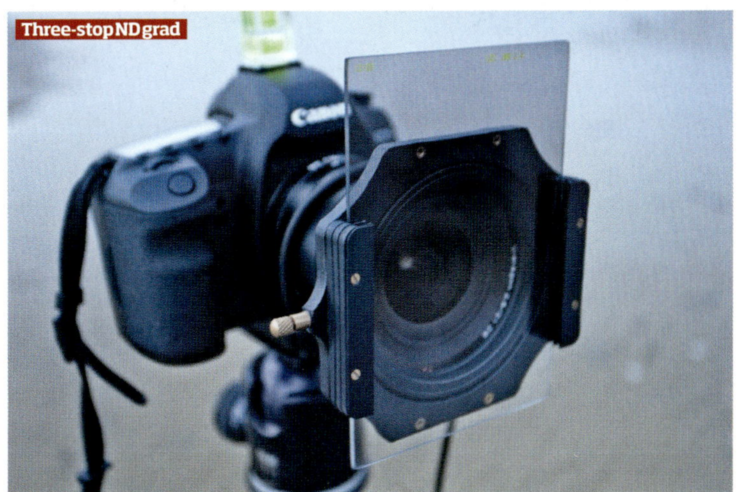

5 The incoming tide forces a change of position. By this time, the light is low enough to allow a 45 second exposure (ISO 100 and f/16) without having to use an ND filter. A three-stop grad is still necessary because there is no direct light falling onto the land or sea, but the sky is lit from below.

EXPERT TUTORIAL

Shooting star trails

If you're in a remote location, take advantage of clear night skies by aiming high and trying to capture star trails

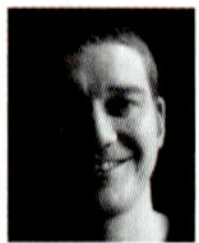

WITH JOHN PATRICK Star trails are rewarding subjects that can add an element of magic to a landscape shot, revealing the scene in a way that isn't visible to the eye. They allow you to extend the day's potential shooting time, and to get out with your camera – especially if you work through the week and can't get outdoors during the daylight hours in winter. If there's any 'secret' to the technique, it's getting the exposure right, but that's simple when shooting digitally...

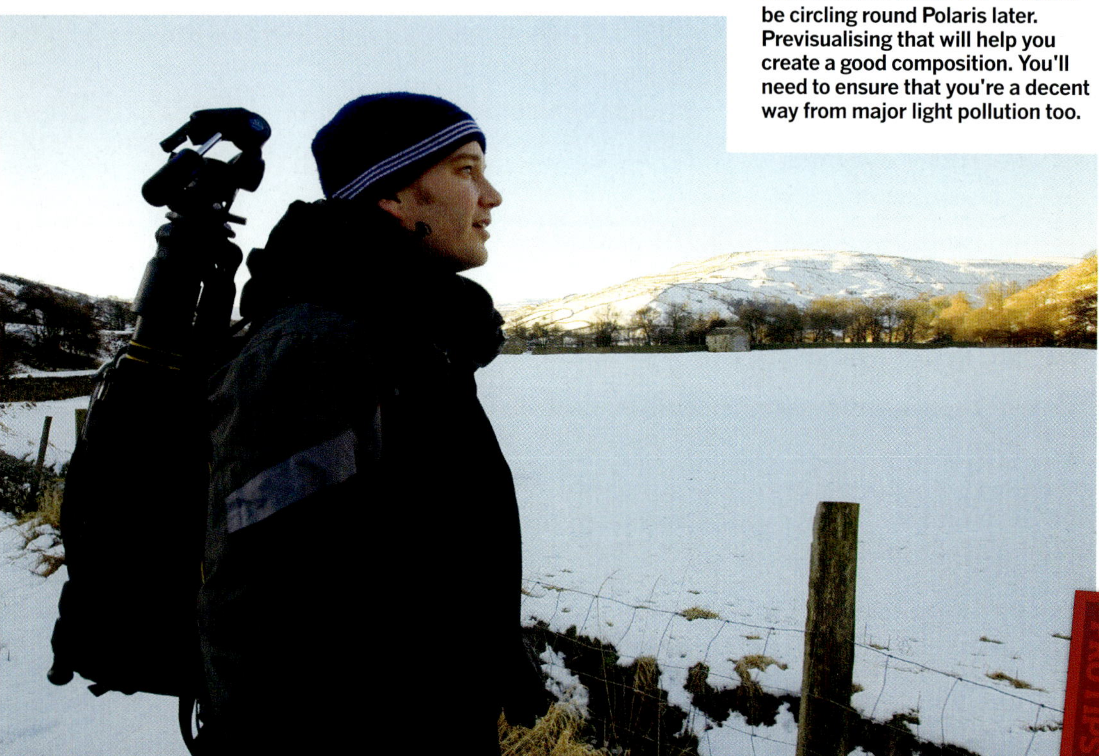

1 FIND THE LOCATION If you can, it helps to find your location in advance, in the daylight hours. Mid-day is a good time to do this for a couple of reasons. One is that it's often dead-time in the landscape photographer's day when the light is too harsh for shooting. The other is that, with the sun to the south, shadows will point north towards where the stars will be circling round Polaris later. Previsualising that will help you create a good composition. You'll need to ensure that you're a decent way from major light pollution too.

KIT WATCH!

Manfrotto 055ProB Tripod

You'll need to keep the shutter open for the long exposure and the best way to do that is to use a remote release with a lock to hold the shutter open. This helps avoid inadvertently knocking or moving the camera. A sturdy tripod is important too and a wide-angle lens is handy as it helps you get plenty of sky in the shot. Other than that, star trails don't need any particularly specialist kit. Don't forget plenty of warm clothing though. Even if you're used to being out in cold weather, standing around for half an hour or more in the dark in sub-zero temperatures can bring a whole new level of chilliness, so pack a few extra layers to keep you comfortable.

PRO TIPS

GET AWAY FROM THE CITY

The glow from urban areas is known as light pollution and can be seen from miles away on a clear night. This might not be obvious to the naked eye but will show up clearly on a long exposure

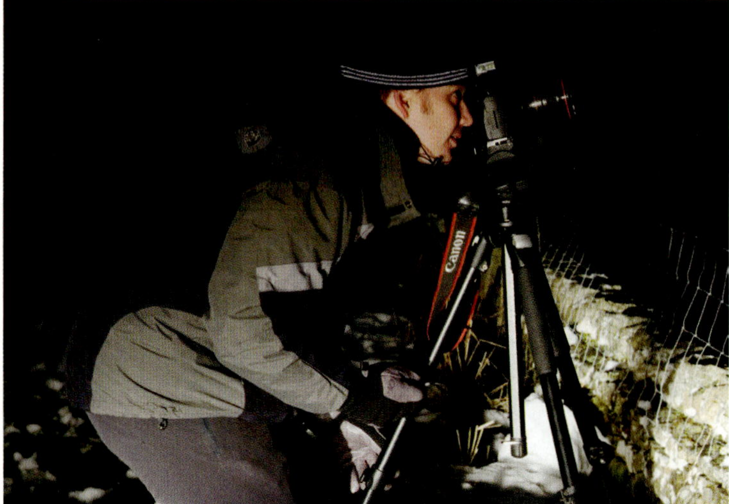

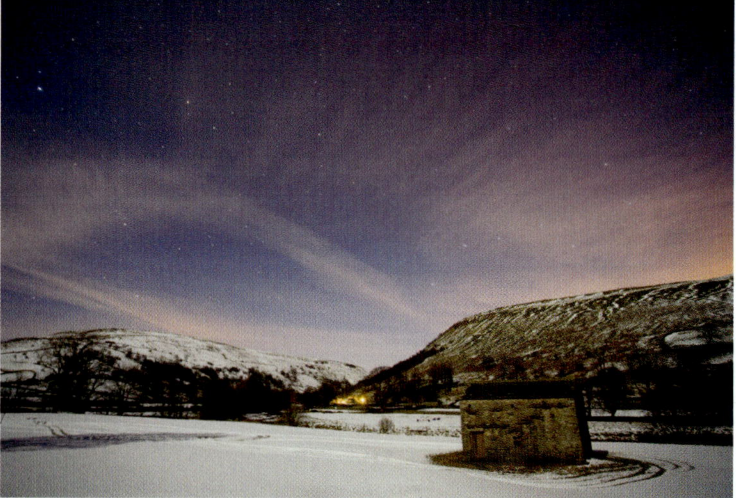

2 SETTING UP Pick your night (a night with a half-moon is a good choice if possible) and set up the camera on the tripod. If it's too dark to see properly through the viewfinder, you can take a few shots with a high ISO and wide aperture, gradually making adjustments to fine-tune the composition. Autofocus is unlikely to work in very low light, so you'll need to focus manually – either by using the distance scale or by placing a torch somewhere in the scene to focus on.

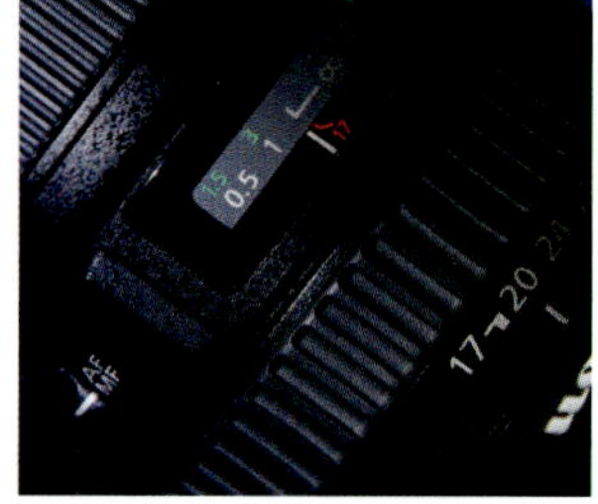

3 METER THE SCENE You can meter the scene before taking the final shot by taking test shots at a high ISO and wide aperture. I'm using ISO 1600 and f/4 here. Set the camera to manual and start with an exposure time of around 20 seconds. Take a shot and check the histogram, then simply alter the exposure time and re-take test shots until the histogram looks correct. After a bit of experimentation I find that one stop underexposed works best.

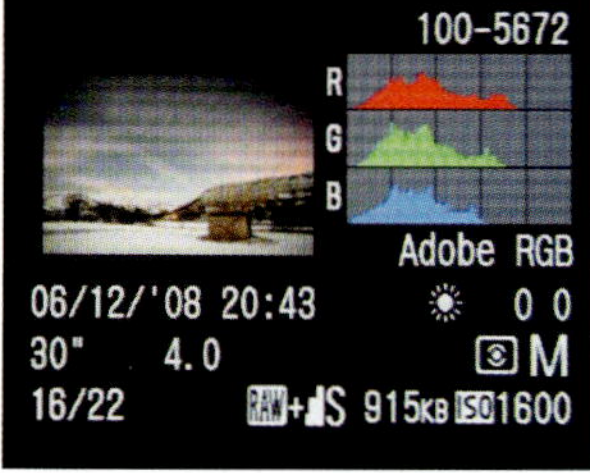

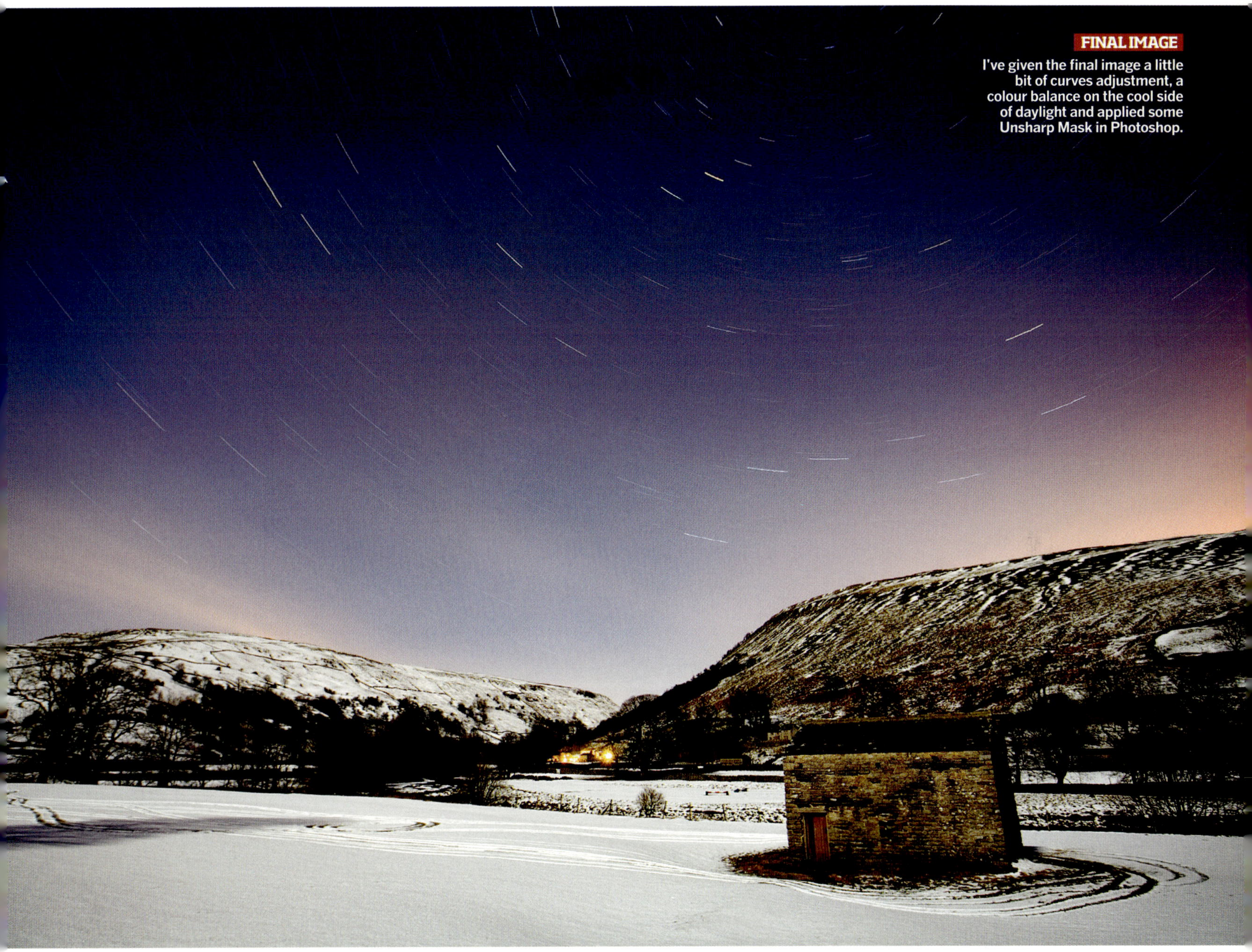

FINAL IMAGE

I've given the final image a little bit of curves adjustment, a colour balance on the cool side of daylight and applied some Unsharp Mask in Photoshop.

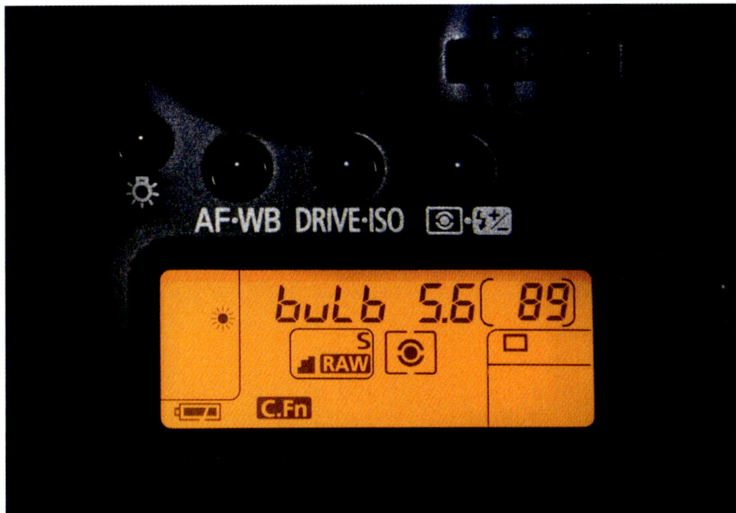

4 SETTINGS FOR THE FINAL SHOT When you're happy with the exposure, set the camera to 'Bulb'. Select ISO 100 and set a wide aperture. I tend to use f/5.6. Now you can use the exposure time from step 3 to work out the time needed for the final shot, compensating for the change in ISO and aperture by increasing the time. For instance, if you needed a 30 second exposure in step 3: 30secs x 2 (for a one-stop change from f/4 to f/5.6) x 16 (for the change from ISO 1600 to ISO 100) gives a 16-minute exposure.

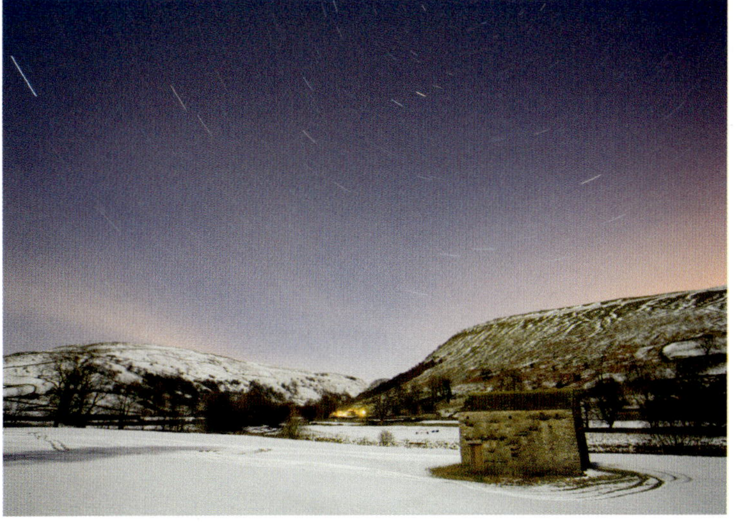

5 TAKE THE SHOT Turn all lights out, note the time and lock the shutter open with the remote release. Get out some coffee and chocolate, have a break for a while and enjoy staring at the stars. Just don't do what I did and discover at this point that the coffee's back down the road, still in the car!
If you need to put a light on at any point to read the time, be careful not to illuminate the foreground at all, as it will show up in the final shot (unless you're deliberately attempting light painting, but that's another topic).

The Basics #5

LANDSCAPE FILTERS

THE HUMBLE FILTER OFFERS offers arguably more creative possibilities for making the most of your digital SLR than any other accessory. We're all aware that digital SLRs are a great way of capturing wonderful images, but some photographers are still oblivious to how filters can dramatically improve their results.

Take a look at the work of established photographers and you'll see most regularly use filters like polarisers or ND Graduates to capture the best possible results. There is a reason why dedicated landscape photographers spent time and money using filters: they give better results. This section looks at the main filter formats, which types of filters you'll find most useful and explains how you should use them. With image manipulation software such as Adobe Photoshop available, the question of whether or not you need filters any more is a fair one to ask. Our answer is simple: Yes. Read on to find out why.

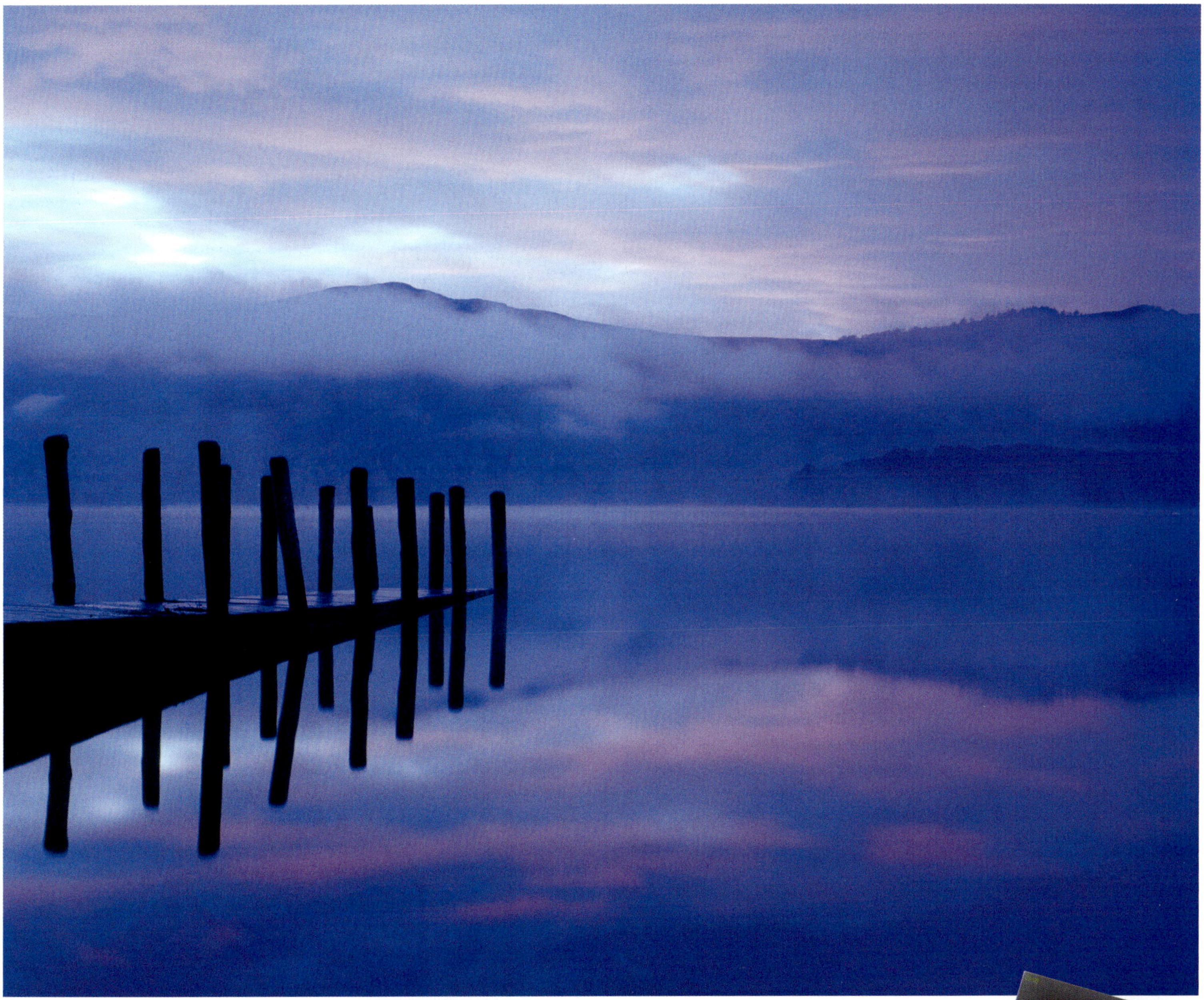

CRAIG ROBERTS

SCREW-IN FILTERS

These attach via the filter thread on the front of most lenses. They offer the advantage of using high quality optical glass, while their small size means they're easy to store and carry around in their protective cases. The disadvantage is that each only fit one diameter of lens, so if your lenses require different filter thread sizes, you'll need extra filters. Using more than one filter together risks vignetting (dark corners on your images).

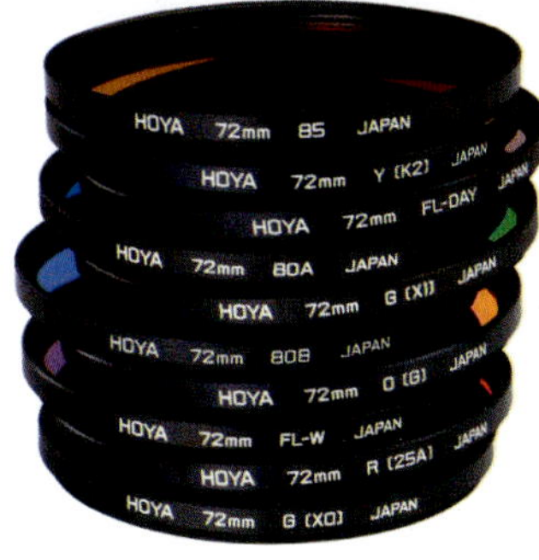

SLOT-IN SYSTEM FILTERS

If you plan to use a number of filters or own several lenses, a slot-in system is more cost-effective. You only need to buy one of each filter type, which is inserted into a holder attached to the lens via an appropriately sized ring. You need a ring for each lens but swap the holder between them. Most slot-in filters are made from a tough resin, which is of high optical quality, but you need to take more care than with glass filters to avoid scratches.

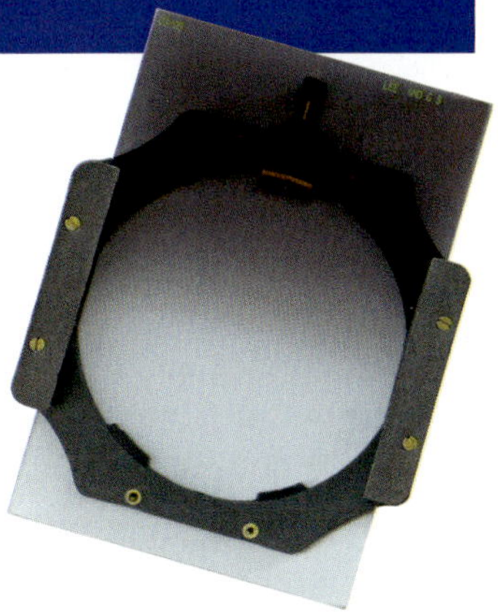

Polarising filters

If you only ever buy one filter, buy a polariser. By simply rotating it in its mount, you can bring your images to life. A polariser is designed to eliminate glare, minimise reflections and enhance saturation.

Polarising filters are best known for their ability to darken blue skies. However, they are equally useful for reducing reflections on non-metallic surfaces (in particular water) and the glare from foliage.

Not only does an enriched, blue sky look appealing as part of a landscape photograph, but a polarised sky can also create an attractive backdrop. Try shooting buildings, people, trees or flowers contrasted against a polarised sky – the results will be bursting with impact.

To understand how polarisers work, it's necessary to get a little technical. Basically, light is transmitted in wavelengths. Light travels in straight lines, vibrating as waves in all directions and at all angles.

When light strikes a surface, a portion of the wavelengths are reflected while others are absorbed. It is the absorbed wavelengths of light that define the colour of the surface it's striking. For example, a red-coloured object will reflect red wavelengths of light whilst absorbing others.

Polarised light is different. It occurs due to the reflection or scattering of light waves and only travels in one direction. It is these wavelengths that create glare and reflection, reducing colour intensity. A polarising filter is designed to block polarised light, thus restoring contrast and saturation.

Polarisers are made from a thin sheet of polarising material, sandwiched between two circular pieces of glass and screwed onto the front of your lens. The front part of the mount can be rotated, affecting the angle of polarisation. As a result, the amount of polarised light passing through the lens can be altered to control the amount of polarisation. Looking through the viewfinder while rotating the filter (or using the LCD monitor with Live View), reflections will come and go and the intensity of colour will strengthen and fade again. Simply stop rotating the filter when you feel the effect is at its best for the scene or subject.

One last thing. A polariser has a two-stop filter factor and, while your camera's automatic metering will allow for this, it's worth bearing in mind how this will affect the range of shutter speeds and apertures you have available. It's worth ensuring you mount your DSLR on a tripod whenever you use a polariser to ensure you avoid the risk of camera shake.

KIT WATCH!

Polariser choice: Linear or circular?

There are two types of polarising filter on the market – Linear and Circular. Only the Circular type will work properly with your digital SLR. Although both varieties are physically circular and similar in appearance, the Linear variety will affect the accuracy of your camera's metering system. This is because digital SLRs polarise some light inside the camera. If this light has already been polarised by a Linear polariser, a false meter reading is given. Circular polarisers are constructed with a wave-retardation plate, allowing the light waves passing through to rotate and appear unpolarised to the camera's metering system. Buy Circular.

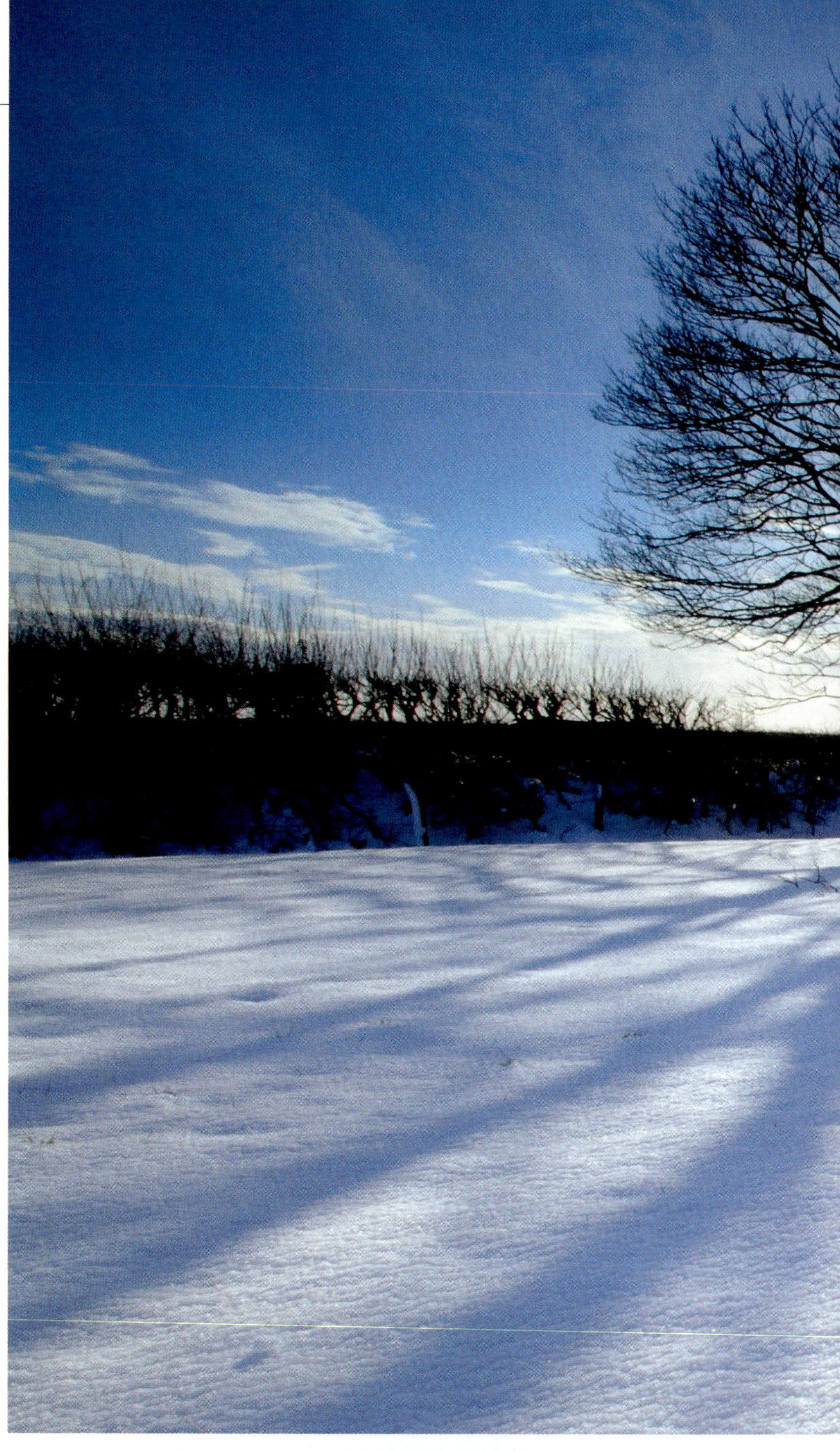

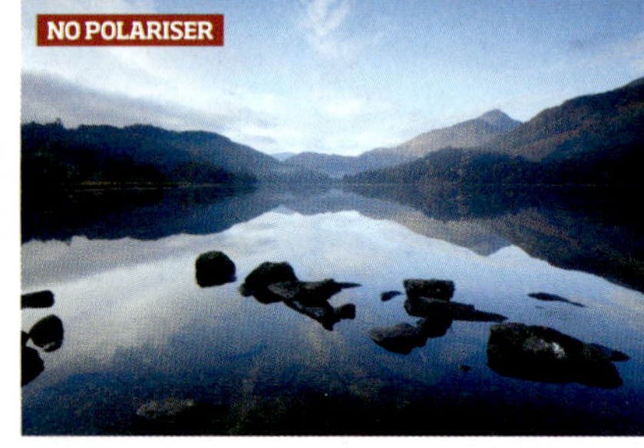

NO POLARISER

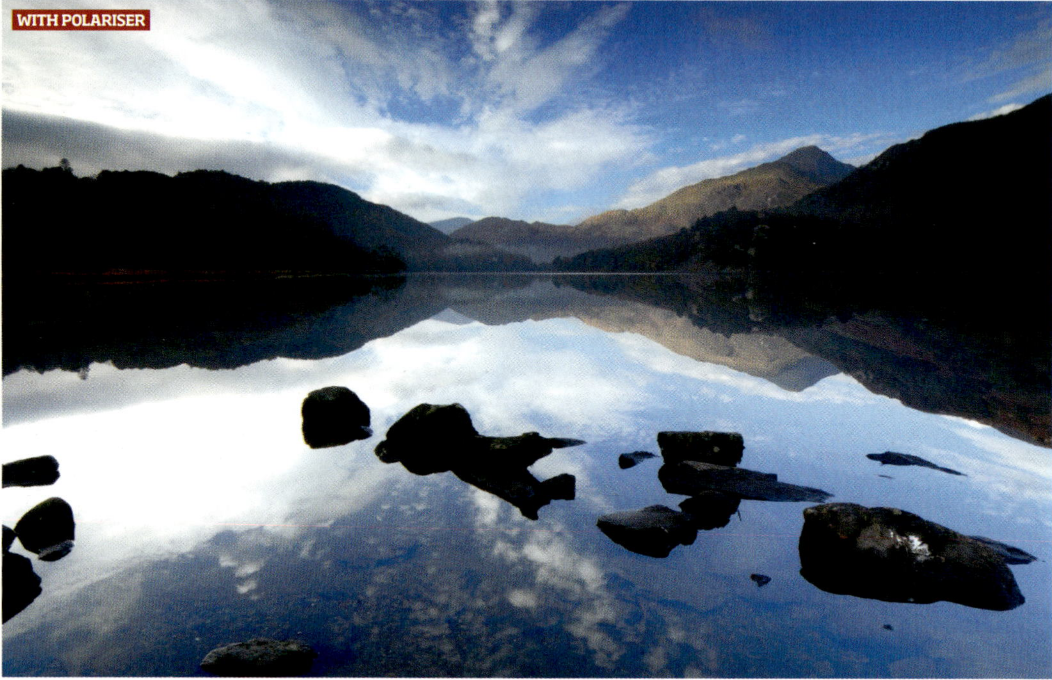

WITH POLARISER

Get the best from reflections

Reflections can either be good or bad. For example, rolling hills or snowy mountain peaks will be enhanced if they're mirrored in the still, reflective surface of water. But the light and glare reflecting from shiny non-metallic surfaces or glass, in a cityscape or on a skyscraper, can be ugly and distracting. A polariser can be used to either emphasise reflections – by reducing surface glare – or eliminate them. However, the strength of the effect will depend on the camera angle in relation to the reflective surface. The maximum effect is at an angle of 30-45°.

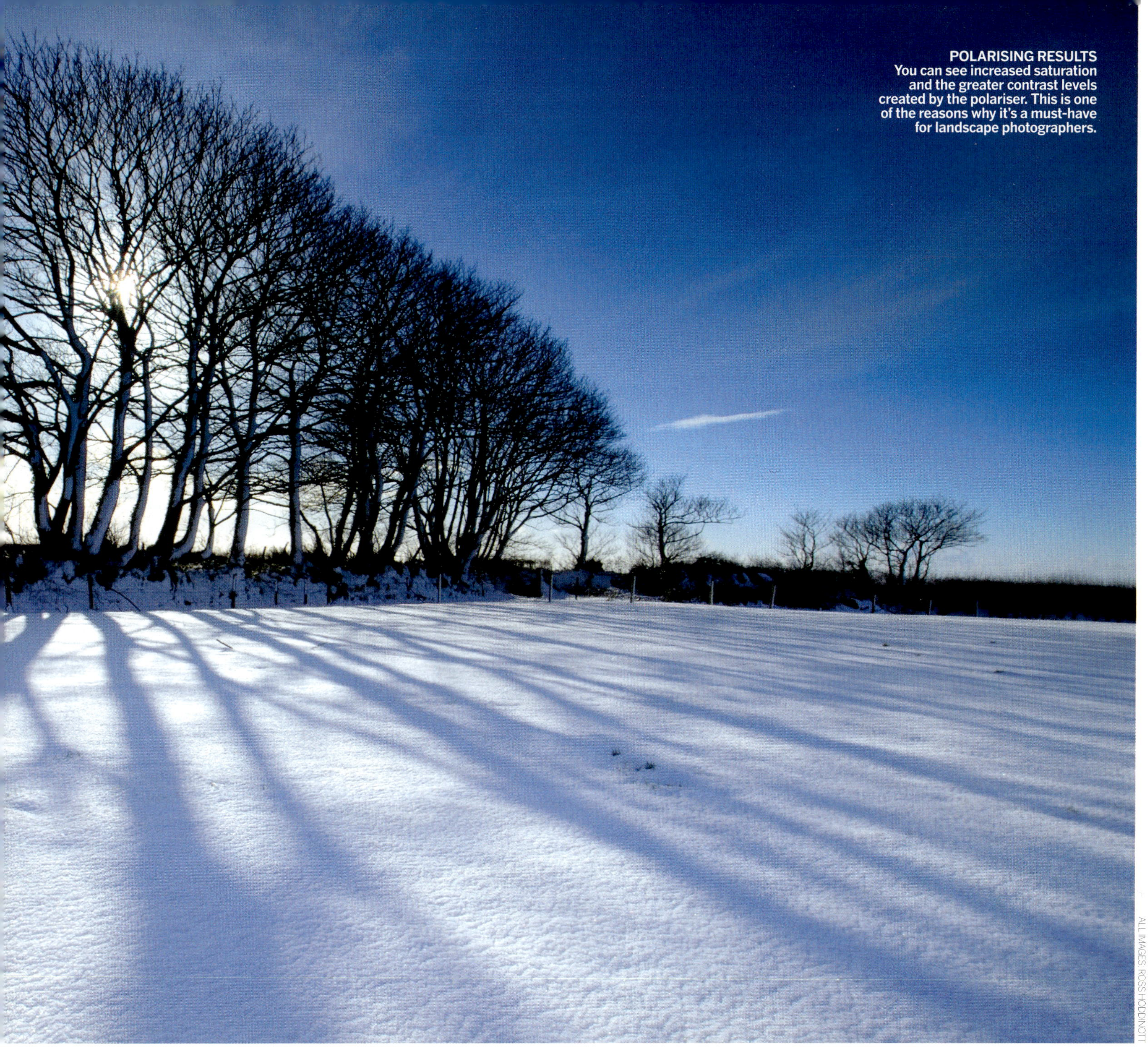

POLARISING RESULTS You can see increased saturation and the greater contrast levels created by the polariser. This is one of the reasons why it's a must-have for landscape photographers.

ALL IMAGES: ROSS HODDINOTT

DON'T PANIC!

Avoiding polarising problems

UNEVEN POLARISATION Natural light polarisation is uneven across the sky; its maximum effect is when facing 90° to the sun and its minimum is at 180°. So when taking pictures at certain angles, you may find that the colour of the sky darkens more noticeably in one area – this region of the sky contains more polarised wavelengths. This effect can look odd and is best avoided. Ultra wide-angle focal lengths (10-14mm) are most prone to this problem. To try and side-step this problem, use a lens with a long focal length lens or adjust your shooting angle. However, if this just isn't practical, you could try positioning a Neutral Density graduate filter at an angle so that it filters the lighter region of the sky. Although this isn't a faultless solution, an ND grad can greatly reduce the effect.

OVER-POLARISATION A deep blue polarised sky may be appealing, but it is possible to overdo the effect. In some situations, a polariser isn't needed at all – or only partial polarisation is required – to produce the best-looking result. If the effect is too great, the sky can appear almost black in colour. This will look unnatural and degrade the aesthetics of the image. So use image playback to check the effect and adjust the rotation of the filter accordingly.

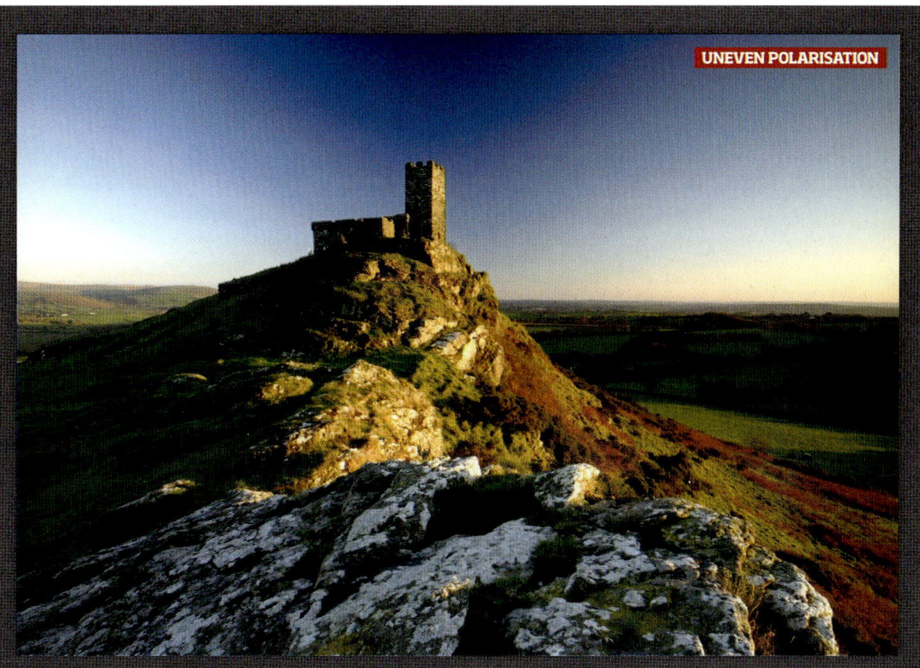
UNEVEN POLARISATION

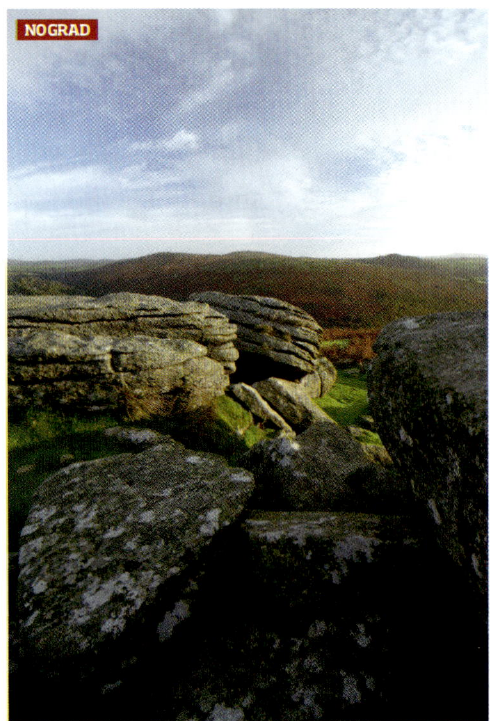

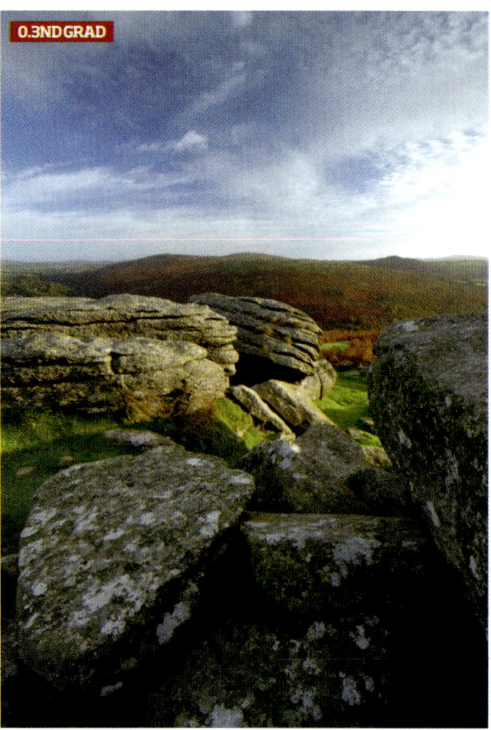

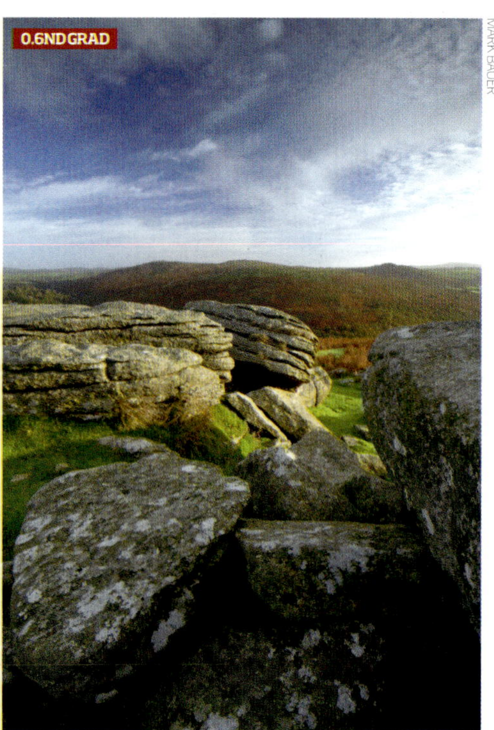

MARK BAUER

Graduated filters (grads)

Grads are half-coated, half-clear, with a transitional zone where the two halves merge. There are two distinct types of grad: Neutral Density (ND) and colour grads. ND graduated filters are designed to darken bright skies and lower contrast levels, whilst the coloured variety are intended to add a splash of colour to otherwise dull, nondescript skies.

ND grads work by absorbing all the colours in the visible spectrum in equal amounts, with no colour cast. This is necessary as the contrast in light between sky and land is often greater than the dynamic range of the sensor – making it impossible to capture a correctly-exposed scene.

They are available individually or in a set of different strengths to suit different conditions. Their strength, or density, is indicated on the filter: 0.3 equals a one-stop exposure reduction, 0.6 a two-stop and 0.9 equates to three stops. ND grads are also available in both hard- and soft-edged transitions.

Soft NDs are designed with a feathered edge, providing a gentle change from the coated portion of the filter to the clear area, whilst a hard ND grad has a more sudden transition. Both types are useful; soft grads are better suited to shooting landscapes with broken horizons as they don't noticeably darken objects like buildings or trees. Hard grads are designed so the full strength of their specified density is spread over a greater proportion of the coated area, allowing you to reduce the brightness of the sky with greater accuracy.

Whilst colour grads are not as useful on a day-to-day basis, they shouldn't be overlooked. To an extent, they also lower contrast, but instead of having the practical role of an ND grad, colour grads are designed for creative effect. There are a wide variety of different colours available, from subtle looking shades of blue, coral and orange, to the artificial look of red, pink and tobacco. Some, such as the wholly-coloured sunset filter, lack a clear area. Instead the whole filter graduates from a strong to weak colour tint.

Colour grads may not be for the purists, but combined with a suitable scene, they can help produce eye-catching results. However, a quick word of warning. They should be used with care and in moderation. Only employ a colour grad when its effect genuinely enhances the image you are about to capture – if you have any doubts, take an unfiltered shot as well. You also need to ensure accurate placement; if you push the filter too far down in the holder, the coated area of the grad will stray over the foreground, ruining the realism of the result.

Neutral Density (ND)?

Neutral Density filters work using a similar principle to a graduated ND. However, unlike a grad, the entire filter is coated.

They are designed to limit the amount of light passing through the lens. Therefore, if after adding the filter the shutter speed is kept the same, a larger aperture must be selected to obtain the correct exposure. You can use this to reduce depth-of-field and control how much of a scene is out of focus.

Alternatively, if the f/stop is maintained, a slower shutter speed must be selected to achieve the right exposure. This can help to blur moving water during longer exposures.

ND filters are available as both slot-in and screw-in types and also in progressive strengths (densities). Whilst they can be employed to compensate for too much light – in situations where you'd like to increase the aperture more than the light or camera capabilities permit – an ND filter is more commonly used by landscape photographers to emphasise movement, especially water.

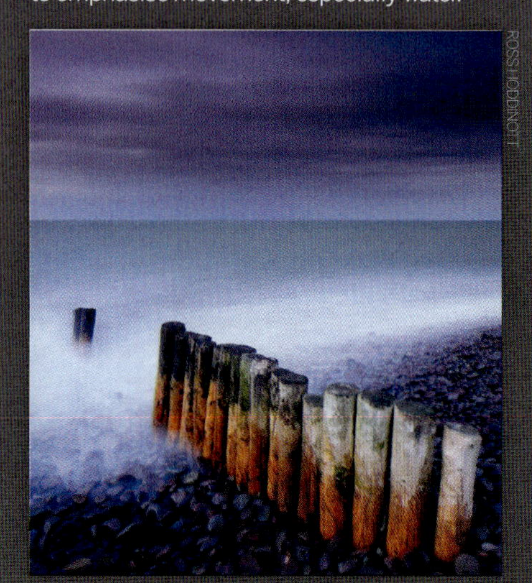

ROSS HODDINOTT

KIT WATCH!

Angle your grad

When using graduated filters, a slot-in filter holder – like the Cokin P system – is virtually essential. Whilst circular, screw-in type graduated filters are available, they are hugely restrictive. This is because, unlike a slot-in filter, the position of the graduation zone cannot be adjusted up or down to suit your composition, greatly limiting your creative possibilities.

Another advantage of using a holder is that, if the scene you are photographing has a sloping horizon, it is possible to adjust the orientation of the holder to match. This will avoid the graduated area of the filter overlapping your foreground, which will either artificially darken or colour part of your scene.

You may also wish to position a grad at an angle to help alleviate uneven polarisation. However, by angling the holder, there is an enhanced risk of vignetting (darkening at the corners of the image) with wide-angle lenses. Therefore, check images through both your viewfinder and via your LCD monitor.

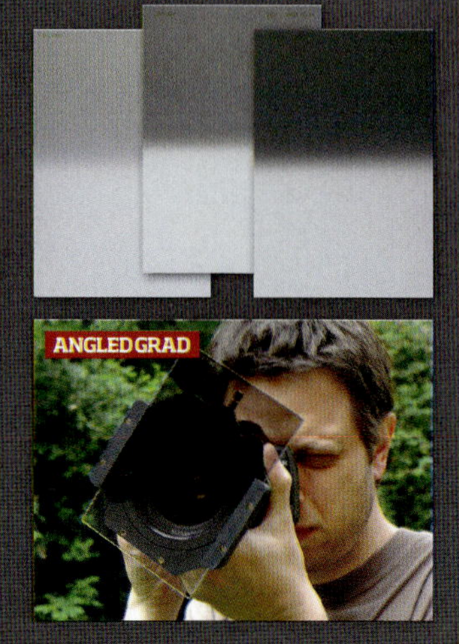

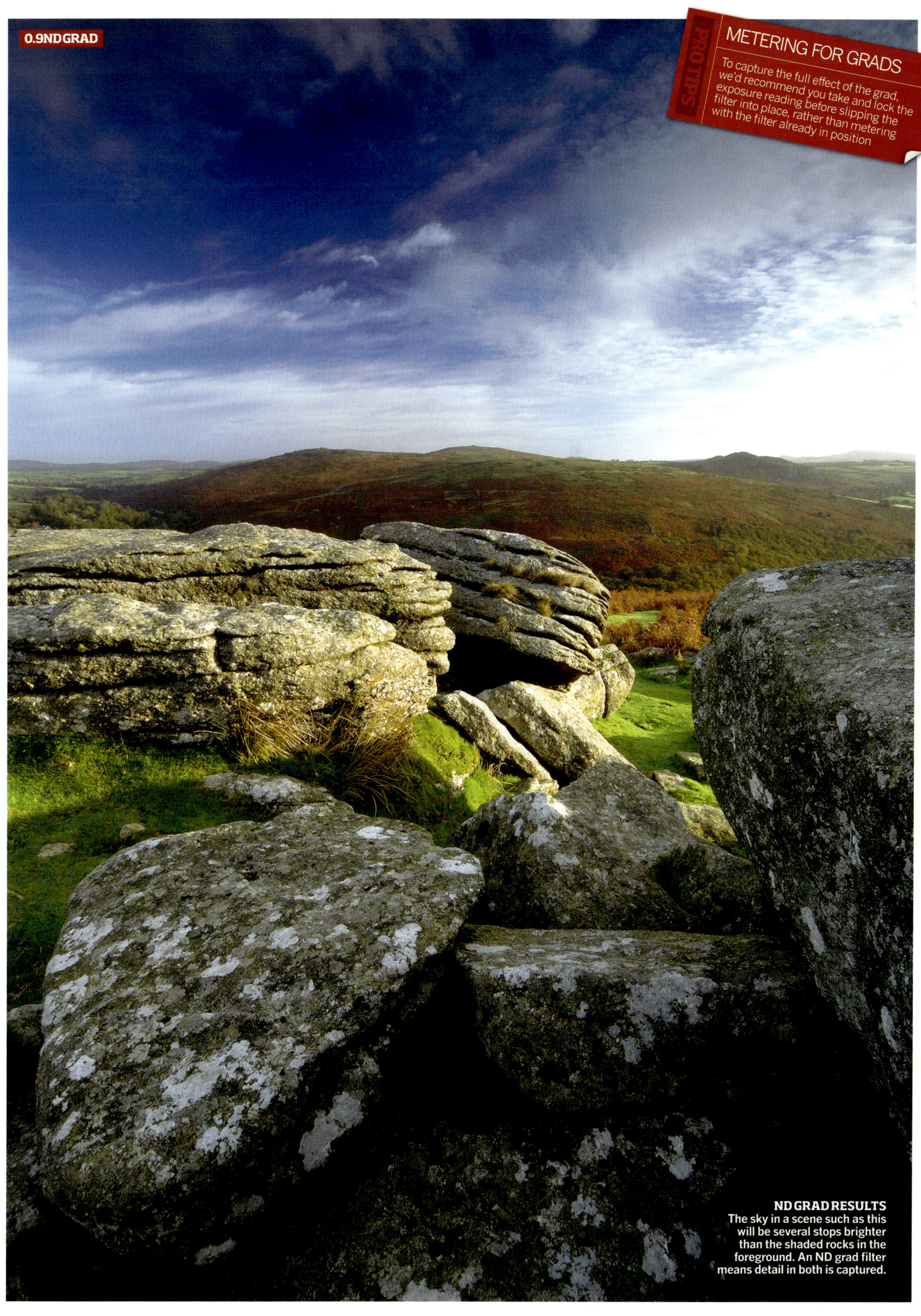

ND GRAD RESULTS
The sky in a scene such as this will be several stops brighter than the shaded rocks in the foreground. An ND grad filter means detail in both is captured.

EXPERT TUTORIAL

ND grads and Photoshop

An ND graduate darkens skies for a more balanced image but post-processing can be necessary in certain scenes

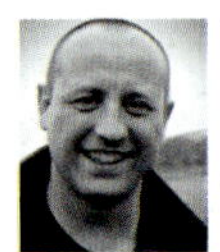

WITH MARK BAUER One of the main technical challenges in landscape photography is controlling the contrast in a scene so that you can accurately record detail in both the land and the sky. Often the sky is a lot brighter than the land, and the contrast in the scene is beyond what the camera's sensor can record, resulting in either a well-exposed sky and underexposed foreground, or the opposite. The usual way around this is to use a Neutral Density (ND) graduated filter. These filters are brilliantly simple – they are dark at the top and clear at the bottom and all you do is position the dark half over the brighter area of the picture, reducing the contrast between the light and dark areas and therefore enabling you to capture detail in both the foreground and the sky. The only problem is that the dividing line between the dark and light areas of an ND grad is a straight line, and not all landscapes have a straight horizon – often the horizon is broken by an object such as a tree, a hill or a building, and the filter can cause an unnatural-looking darkening of the top of these objects. However, help is at hand as, most of the time, post-processing will rescue the shot. Here I explain how to use an ND Grad and remove its effect from specific areas.

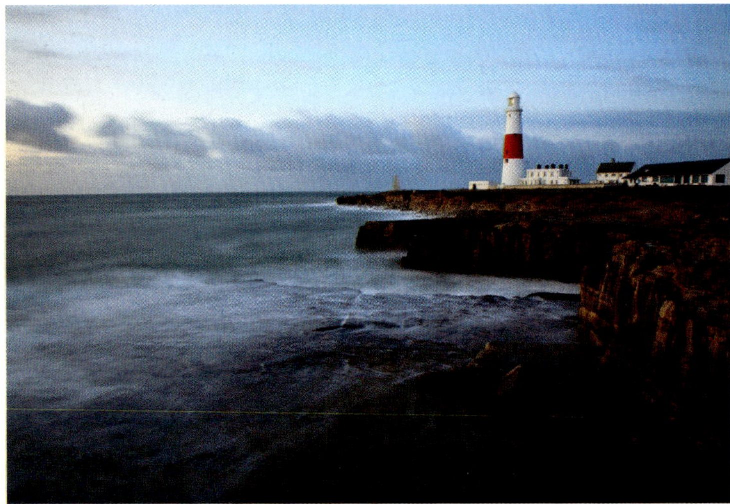

1 Arriving at Portland in Dorset just before dawn, I took a spot meter reading from the foreground rocks and the sky, which revealed a difference in brightness of around four stops. Although this falls within the dynamic range of the sensor, shadow detail has been compromised a little, and lifting this in post-processing could reveal noise in the image.

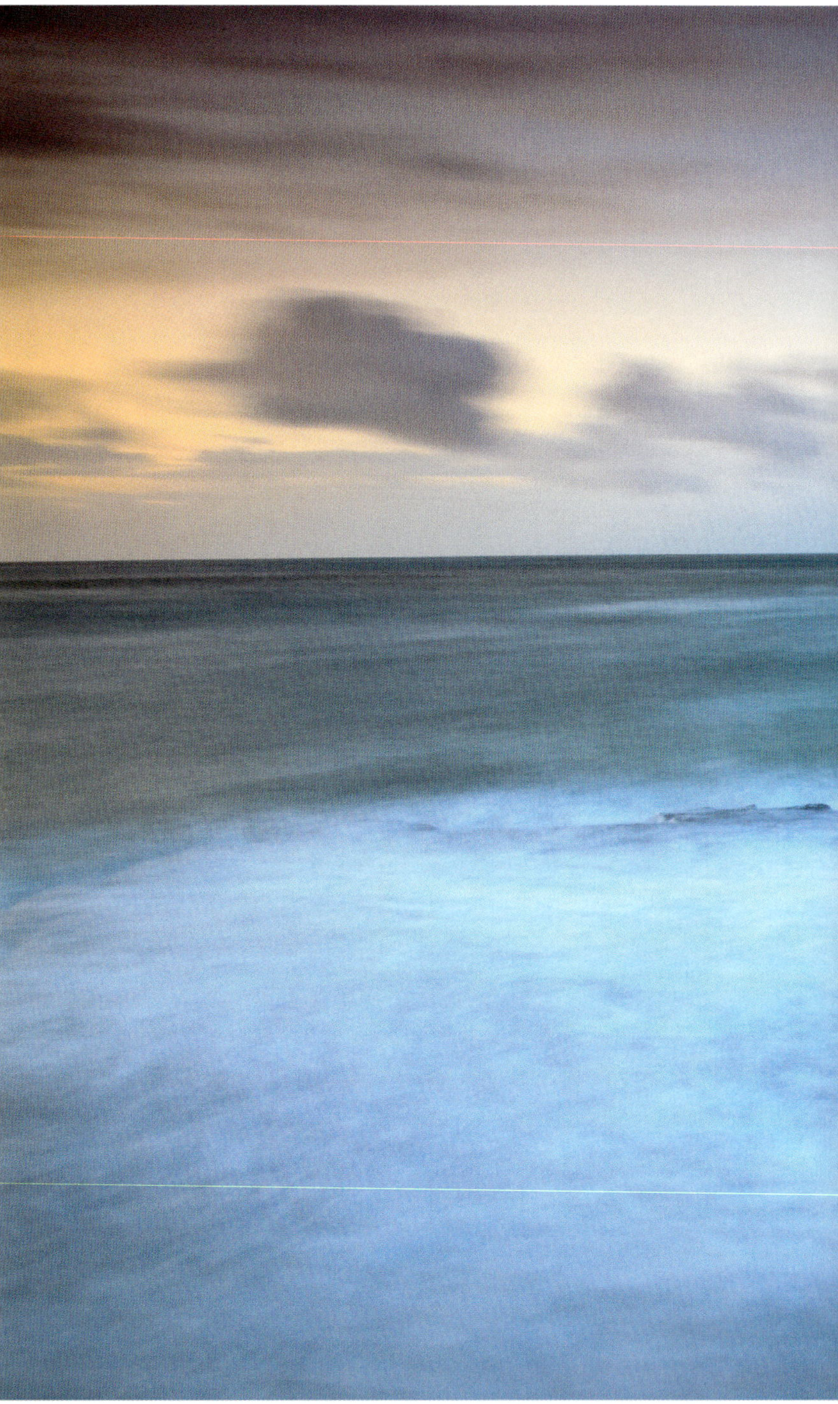

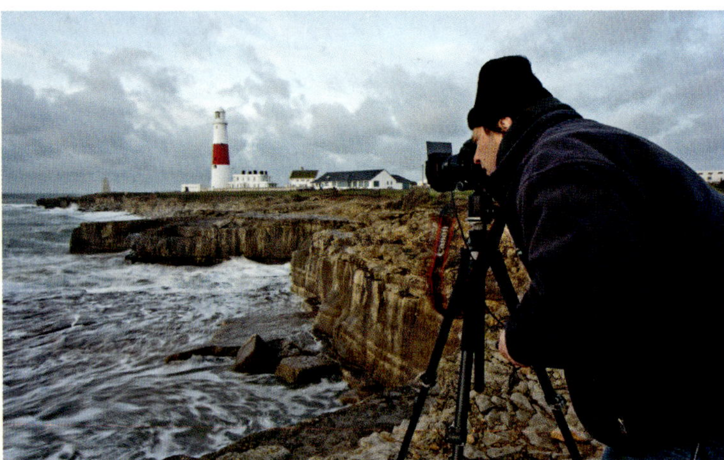

2 With a four-stop difference between the rocks and the sky, I chose a three-stop ND grad filter, as it would leave the sky a little bit lighter than the foreground. The next choice was to use a soft or hard grad (see panel). Soft grads aren't always the best choice for seascapes, as the brightest part of the scene is often across the horizon line, so I decided on a hard grad.

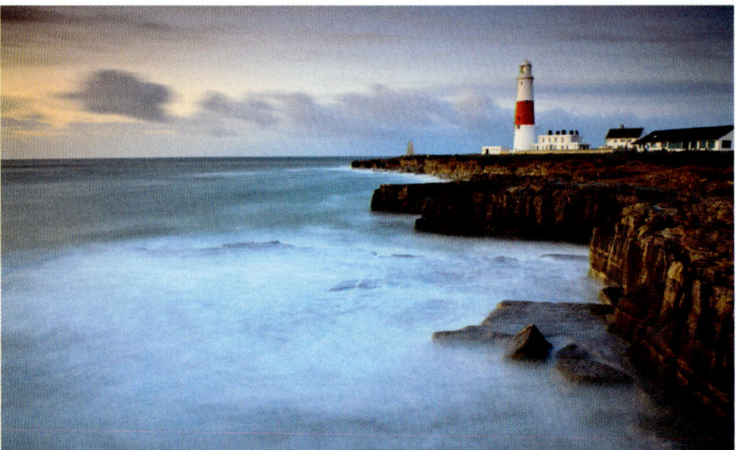

3 Using the hard grad filter has resulted in a much more even exposure, but there is a problem. The top half of the lighthouse, where the filter has cut into it, is a bit too dark. The effect is fairly subtle, but it's definitely there, and doesn't look natural. Fortunately, this common problem can be easily sorted out with a spot of post-processing work.

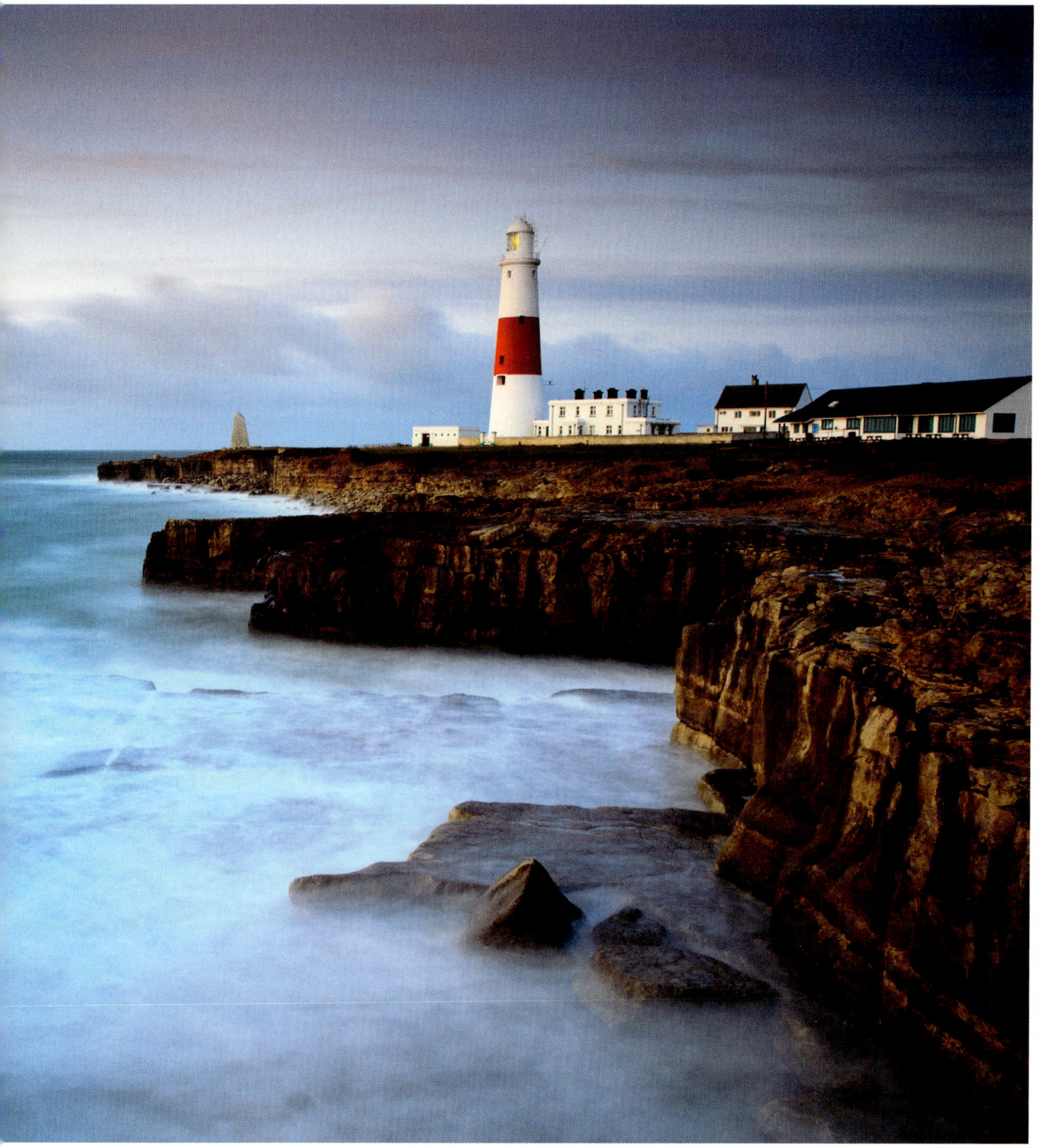

TECHNIQUE WATCH!

Hard and soft grad filters

Neutral density graduated filters come in two varieties: hard and soft. Hard grads have a very obvious and sudden transition from the dark to clear areas, whereas soft grads have a much more gradual transition.

Hard grads are more useful in situations where the horizon line is fairly straight and doesn't have any large objects breaking it. Soft grads on the other hand are a better option when you have an uneven horizon.

Also, opt for a hard grad if you intend to shoot a scene with a straight horizon at sunset or sunrise, as the horizon line will be the brightest part of the scene, and soft grads won't hold back enough light.

So what do you do when you're shooting a scene at sunrise/sunset, which has a large object such as a tree or building breaking the horizon? Here's my way around this.

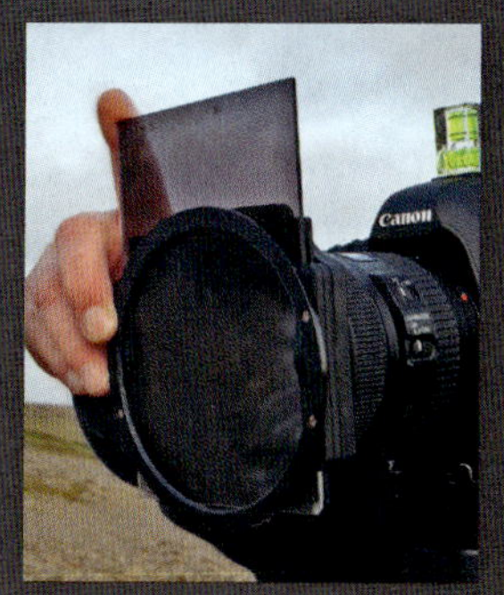

FINAL IMAGE
This is the final result, which exhibits good detail and colour in both the sky and foreground, and a natural-looking lighthouse with no darker section at the top.

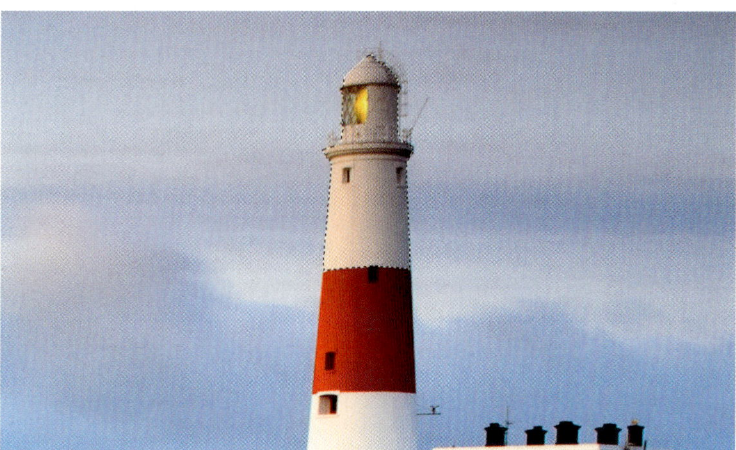

4 Using the Magnetic Lasso Tool in Photoshop, I selected the darker top half of the lighthouse, so that I could work on the problem area without affecting any other part of the image. I decided not to apply any feathering to the selection, as this could leave a 'halo' around the lighthouse once I'd finished lightening the selection.

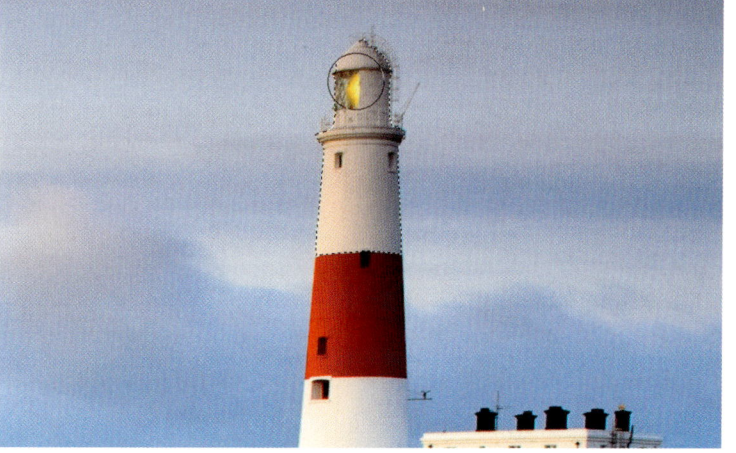

5 There are various ways of lightening or darkening images, such as Curves and Levels, but for this selection I decided to use the Dodge Tool, as I could paint the effect on gradually and build it up in the areas that needed it more. I set the Exposure value to 10%, which enabled me to work gradually on lightening the selection.

Add a digital graduated filter

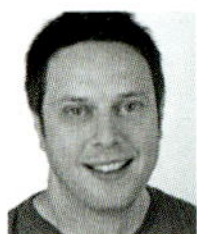

WITH LUKE MARSH Using Photoshop to recreate the effect of a graduate filter allows a variety of effects to be created in minutes. Photoshop expert Luke Marsh explains how to create a stunning graduated effect using adjustment layers, so the effects can be repeated and adjusted until the combination of layers and original image is perfect. In this easy-to-follow step-by-step tutorial, Luke introduces you to Adjustment Layers, Gradient Fill, Gradient Editor, Color Picker, Blending Mode and Photo Filter for mood. Photoshop isn't an alternative to optical filters, it's a complementary skill. Use it to produce images that are not possible on location or when you forgot your grad. Photoshop Elements 4.0 was used here, but more recent versions are suitable too.

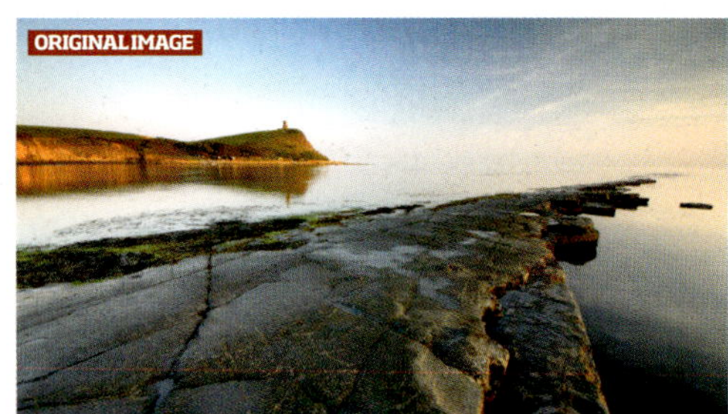

1

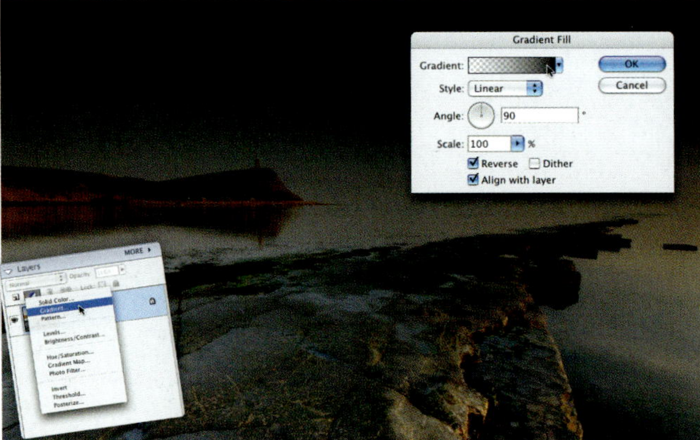

The aim is to create a similar effect to a conventional grad filter, but using a series of digital graduated layers instead. I create my first gradient by clicking the **Create Adjustment Layer** icon ( ), situated at the top of the layers palette, and scrolling to **Gradient** which opens the **Gradient Fill** window.

2

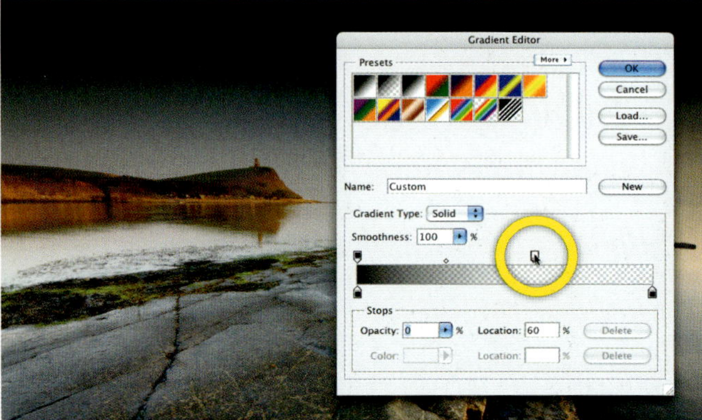

In the **Gradient Fill** window, tick **Reverse** so the gradient runs top to bottom, then click anywhere within the **Gradient** field (situated top) to open the **Gradient Editor** sub-window. The sliders at the top of the visible gradient control opacity, and moving the **White** slider will increase the transparent ratio of the gradient.

3

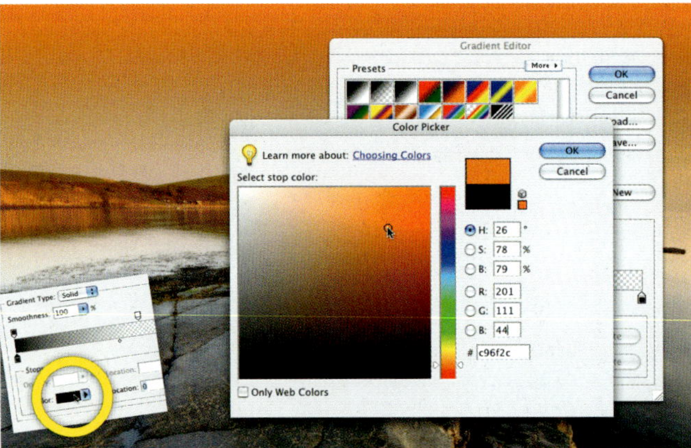

The sliders at the bottom of the gradient control colour, the left representing black. Click the black slider and note that the colour now appears in the field below, clicking here opens the **Color Picker** sub-window. Use the vertical spectrum (centre) and the main window (left) to select the desired colour then click **OK**.

4

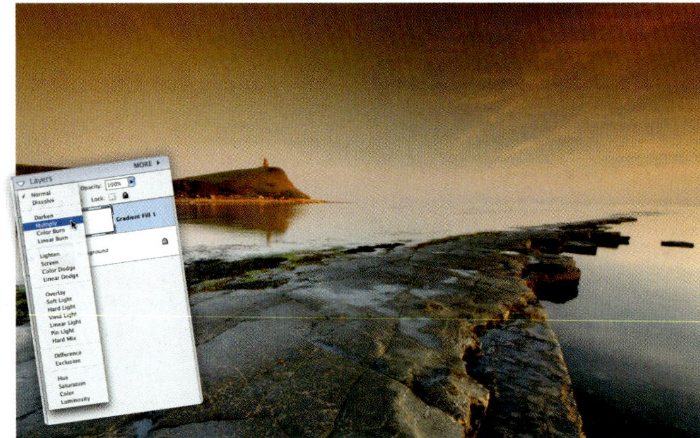

Click **OK** in the subsequent windows to apply the gradient, then choose **Multiply** from the **Blending Mode** menu situated to the top of the layer palette (inset) to create a more natural merging of the gradient to the original image. This **Adjustment Layer Gradient** can be tweaked at any time by selecting it in the layers palette.

5

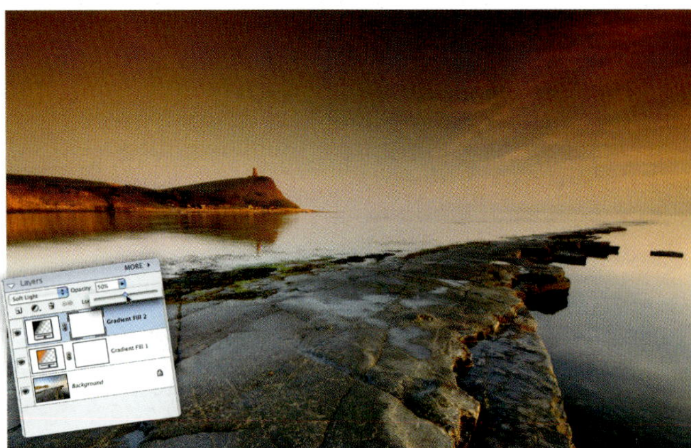

It's quite often necessary to create more than one gradient layer to build up the filter effect. Here, I duplicate steps **1** and **2** creating a gradient that is black to transparent, then, choosing **Soft Light** in the **Blending Mode** menu and reducing the layer **Opacity** (inset) creating a natural darkening effect that can easily be adjusted.

6

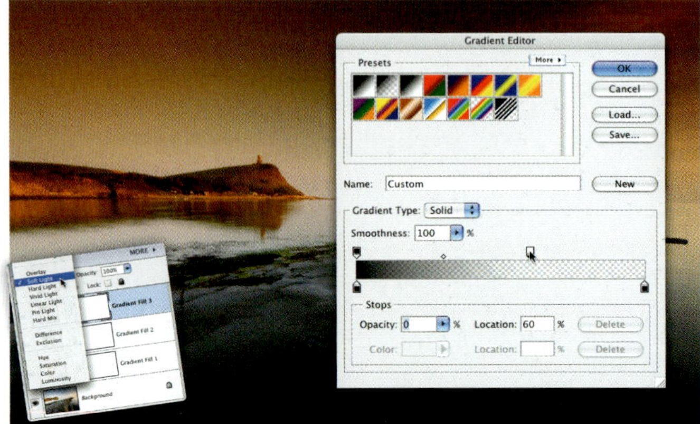

The final gradient layer is going to add a subtle fall-off to the rocks leading out of the image to the bottom of the frame. Again, I repeat steps **1** and **2**, this time leaving the **Reverse** box unticked so the gradient runs from bottom to top. Once again, I set the **Blending Mode** to **Soft Light** and reduced the **Opacity**.

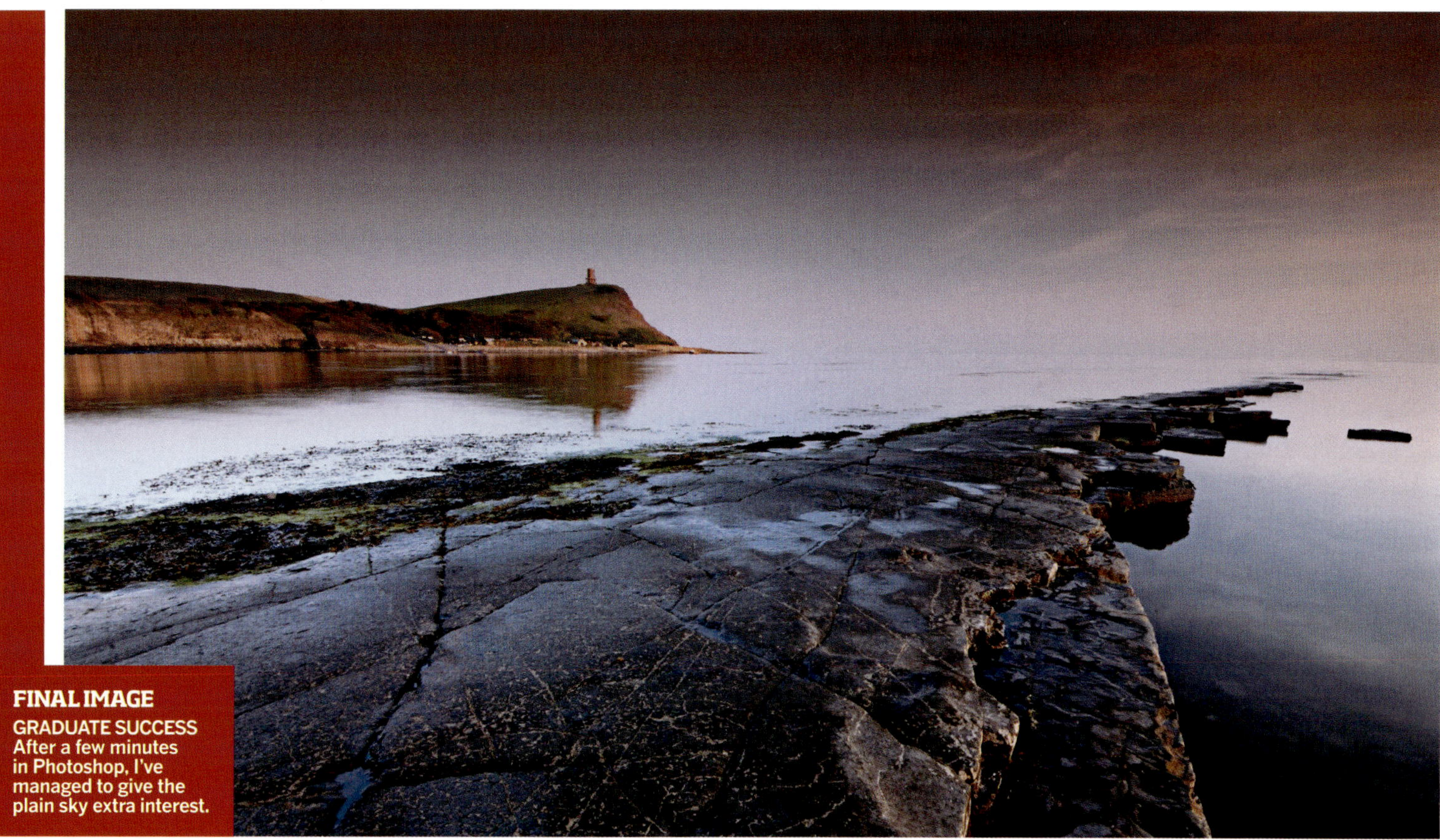

FINAL IMAGE
GRADUATE SUCCESS After a few minutes in Photoshop, I've managed to give the plain sky extra interest.

7 Adding the final touch with Filter > Adjustments > Photo Filter

Photoshop Elements and CS have mood filters that can be used to change the overall tone of your image, much like using a coloured gel or filter on your digital SLR. This handy action, found in the top menu under **Filter>Adjustments>PhotoFilter**, has several preset filters including **Warming**, **Cooling** and **Sepia** or you can choose to manually filter through the **Color Picker**. The intensity of the selected tone can then be adjusted with the **Density** slider to allow for some very subtle effects, giving far greater control than that of an optical lens filters. When you've finished adding a grad effect to an image, it's well worth the time trying some of these out to see if the image can be improved upon further.

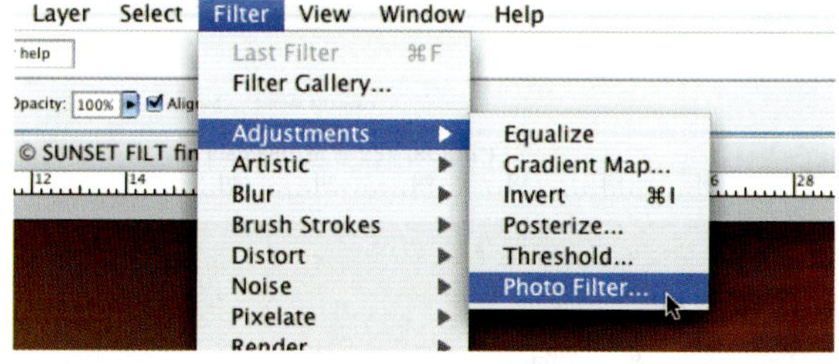

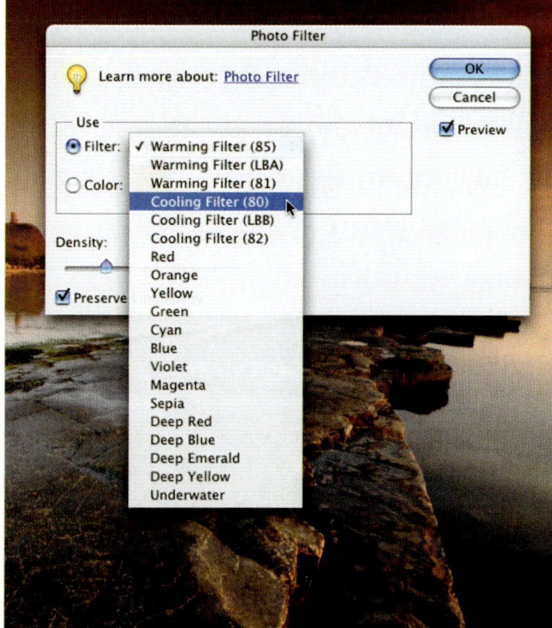

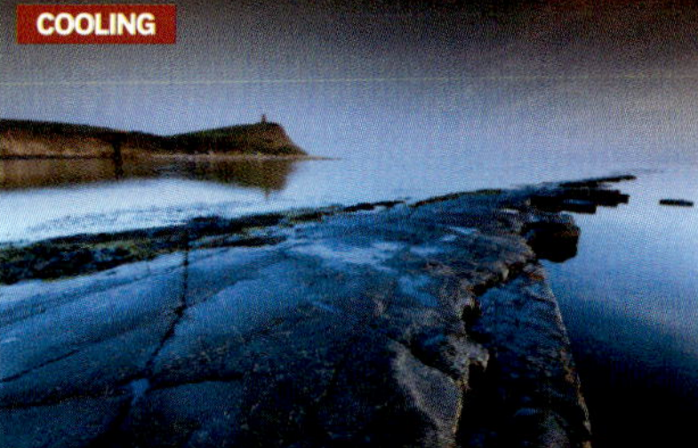

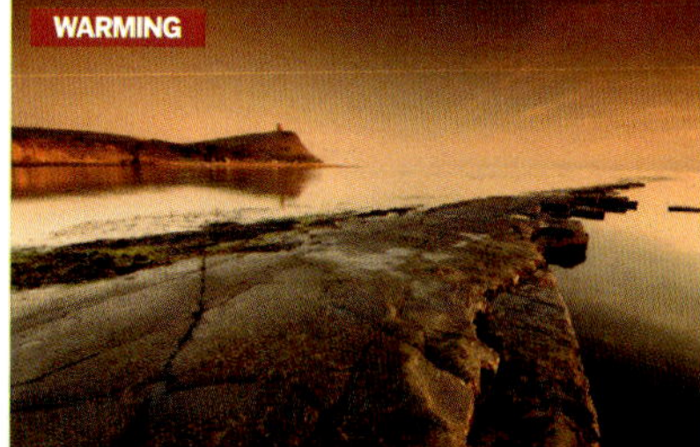

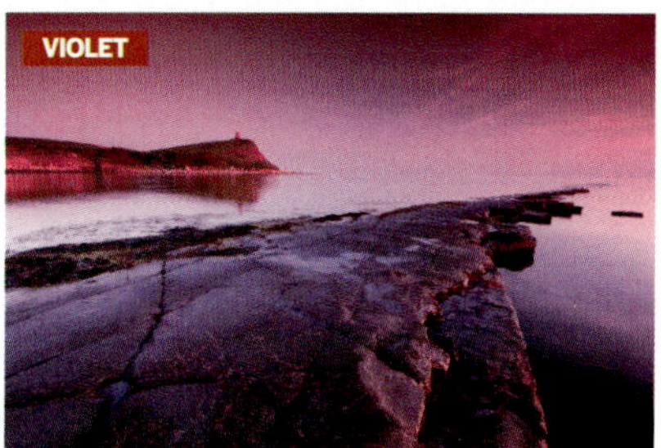

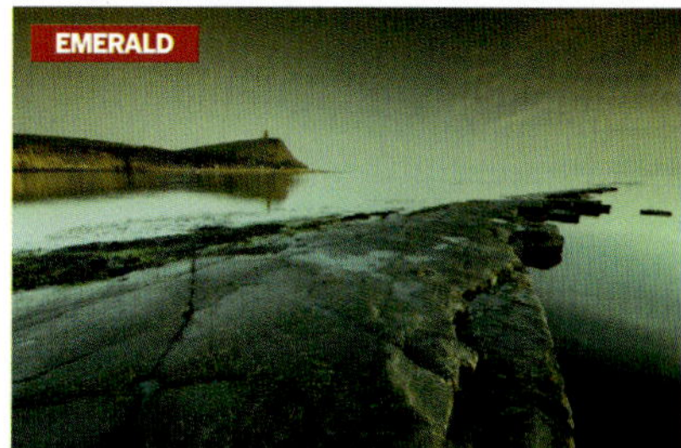

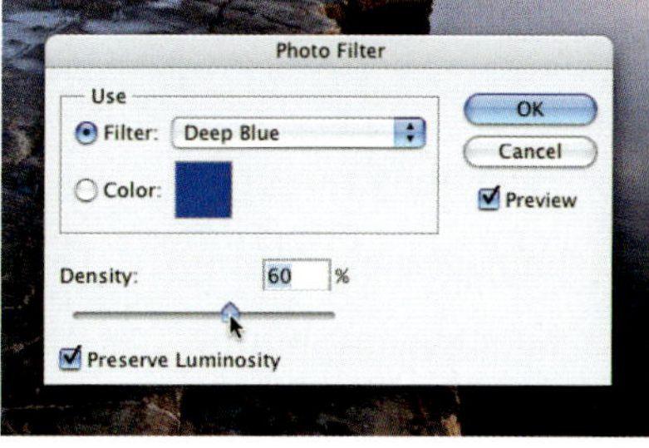

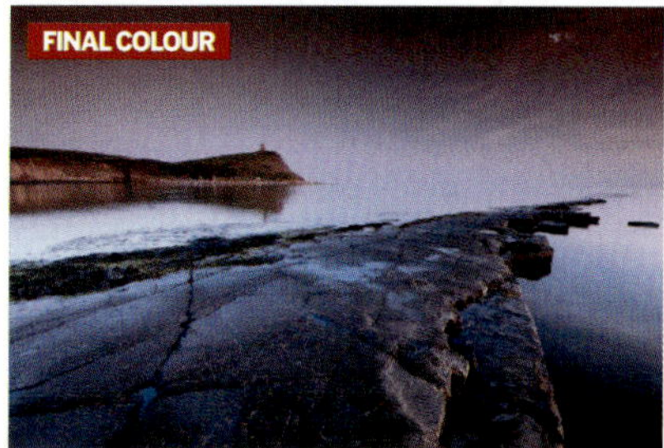

ABOVE: **Choose from a range of preset filters available in the** Photo Filter **function or use the** Color Picker **to customise.**

RIGHT: FINAL COLOUR SELECTION Although happy with the results of my grad filter effect, I found the image could be improved upon further with the use of the Photo Filter **action. After a little experimenting, I began to favour the use of the** Deep Blue **preset filter at about 60%** Density**, making the overall mood of the image slightly cooler, which I think works better with the subject matter.**

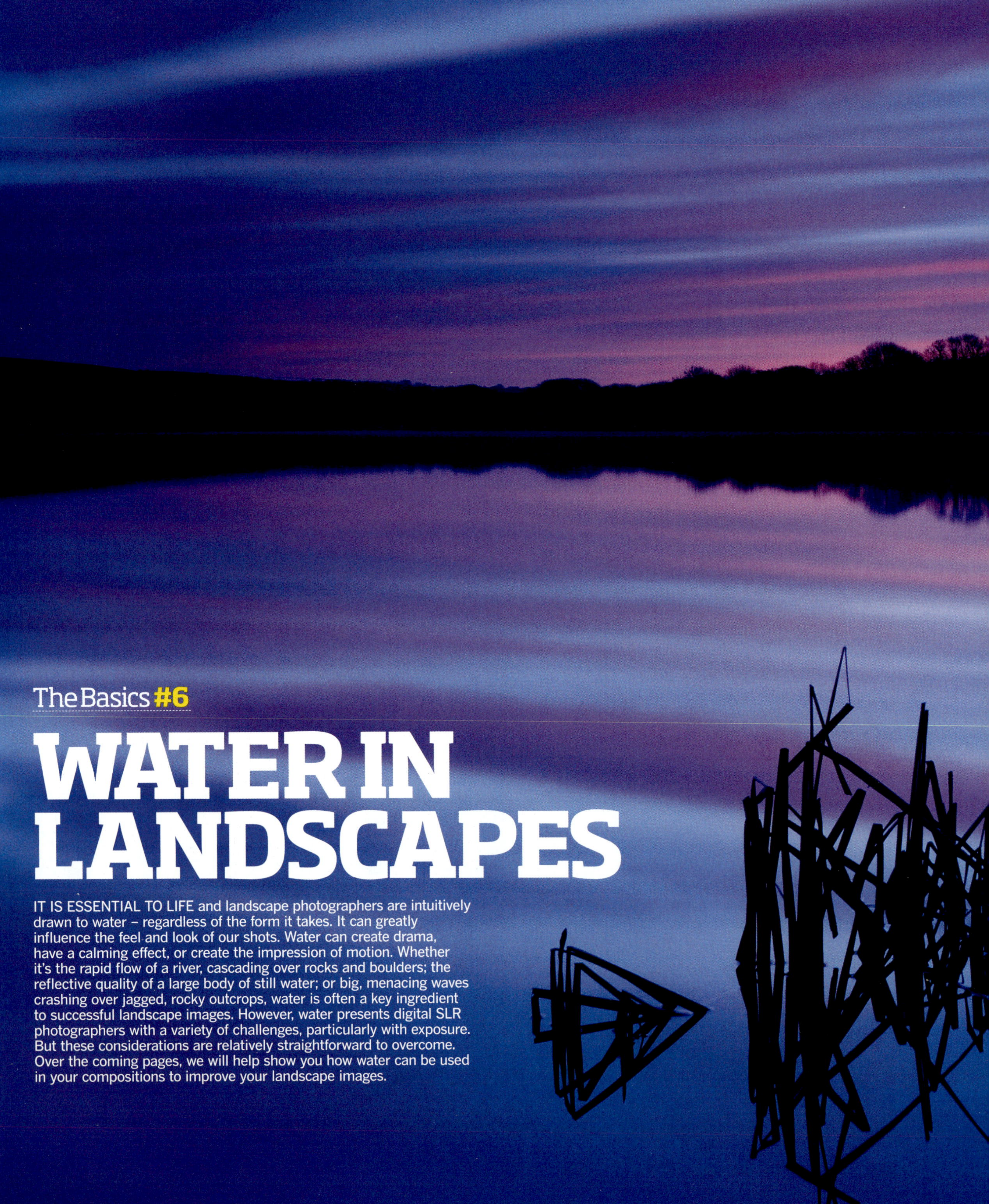

The Basics #6

WATER IN LANDSCAPES

IT IS ESSENTIAL TO LIFE and landscape photographers are intuitively drawn to water – regardless of the form it takes. It can greatly influence the feel and look of our shots. Water can create drama, have a calming effect, or create the impression of motion. Whether it's the rapid flow of a river, cascading over rocks and boulders; the reflective quality of a large body of still water; or big, menacing waves crashing over jagged, rocky outcrops, water is often a key ingredient to successful landscape images. However, water presents digital SLR photographers with a variety of challenges, particularly with exposure. But these considerations are relatively straightforward to overcome. Over the coming pages, we will help show you how water can be used in your compositions to improve your landscape images.

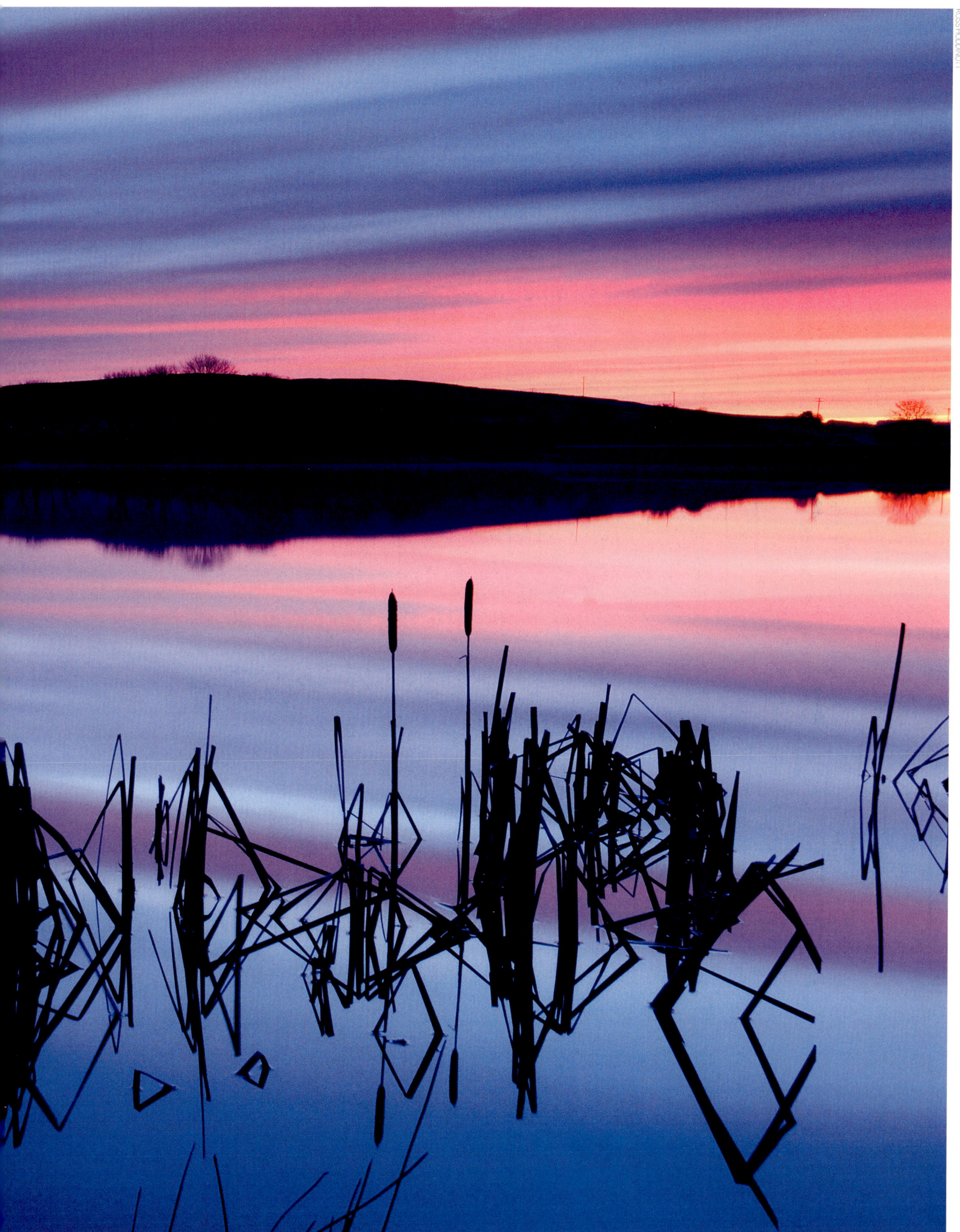

ROSS HODDINOTT

Water and composition

You won't have to travel far to find water. In hilly regions, waterfalls are relatively common, whilst rivers and streams meander through our countryside. In towns and cities, waterways and canals are a common sight and large bodies of water, like lakes, lochs and reservoirs, are dotted around all over the country.

In the UK, you are never that far from the coast and the sea provides photographers with a huge number of opportunities. It creates the perfect backdrop to sandy or rocky bays and rugged cliffs. Whilst the sea is photogenic on calm days, it is at its most dramatic in rough, stormy weather when large, crashing waves bring energy and movement to coastal landscapes. A river, winding its way through your composition, will guide the eye through the image – effectively increasing the photo's depth and interest. Streams and rivers are perfect subjects to create an 'S-curve' or 'lead-in' line. Small puddles can also help composition, creating ideal foreground interest. For example, the shallow pools exposed at low-tide are very photogenic. They will help to add a three-dimensional feel to your pictures if you attach a wide-angle lens and photograph them from nearby to emphasise their curves and reflections.

Water works well when photographed as the main subject. A wide-angle lens, such as an 11-22mm, together with a low viewpoint close to the surface of a river, will create the impression that the water is practically flowing into the camera – but only do this if it's completely safe. To ensure maximum sharpness, ensure sufficient depth-of-field by choosing a small aperture, such as f/13-16, and focus one-third of the way into the scene, using the LCD monitor to check the result.

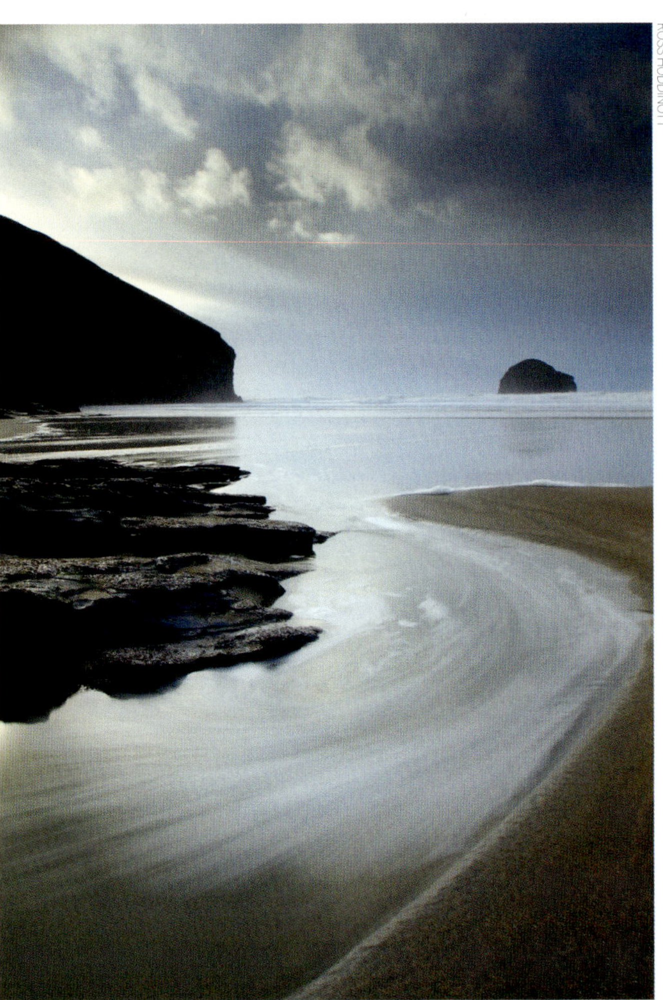

ROSS HODDINOTT

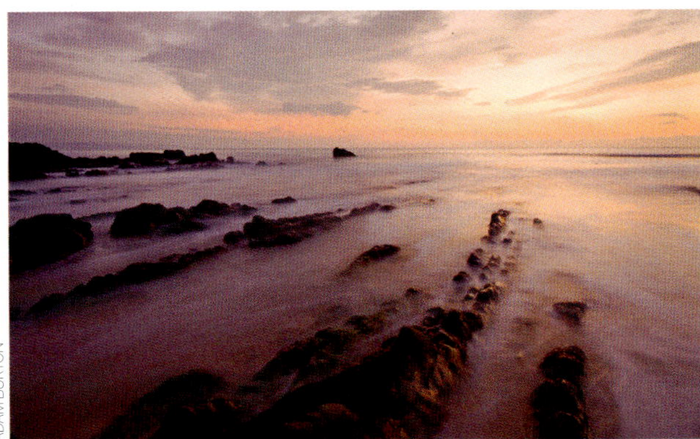

ADAM BURTON

MOTION SLICKNESS
By leaving the shutter open for a long exposure, moving water becomes a mist that is spread across the scene at the average height of the waves and ripples. Flowing bubbles (right) form streaks that follow the stream. The longer the exposure, the less defined the waves become.

Reflections in water

On calm, still days the surface of any body of water will act like a mirror, perfectly reflecting its surroundings and the sky above. Reflections are a favourite subject among landscape photographers, particularly on large bodies of water when strong colours are also evident – during sunrise or sunset, for instance.

Rocks jutting out of the water, tall reeds, a jetty or rowing boats are among the objects that work well as part of a reflected landscape, adding scale and context to the image. The 'rule-of-thirds' states that landscape photographers shouldn't place the horizon centrally in the frame. However, when photographing reflections of a reservoir or loch, a centred horizon will often create a symmetrical result and actually strengthen composition.

Be careful if you are using a polarising filter to saturate colour and deepen blue skies. A polariser can also reduce the intensity of reflections – although to what degree will depend on the camera angle in relation to the reflected surface. In some situations, you may have to decide what is of higher priority – a deep blue sky and saturated colours, but poor reflections; or strong, vivid reflections, but sky and colours that are weaker. A polariser can actually intensify reflections by removing the sheen from the water's surface. Therefore, continue using a polariser, just carefully regulate its effect on the reflections within the scene, by peering through the camera's viewfinder as you rotate the filter in its mount.

If there are distracting ripples on the water, consider using a solid ND filter to lengthen exposure time. A shutter speed exceeding a second will help to eliminate gentle ripples and help maximise the strength of the reflections.

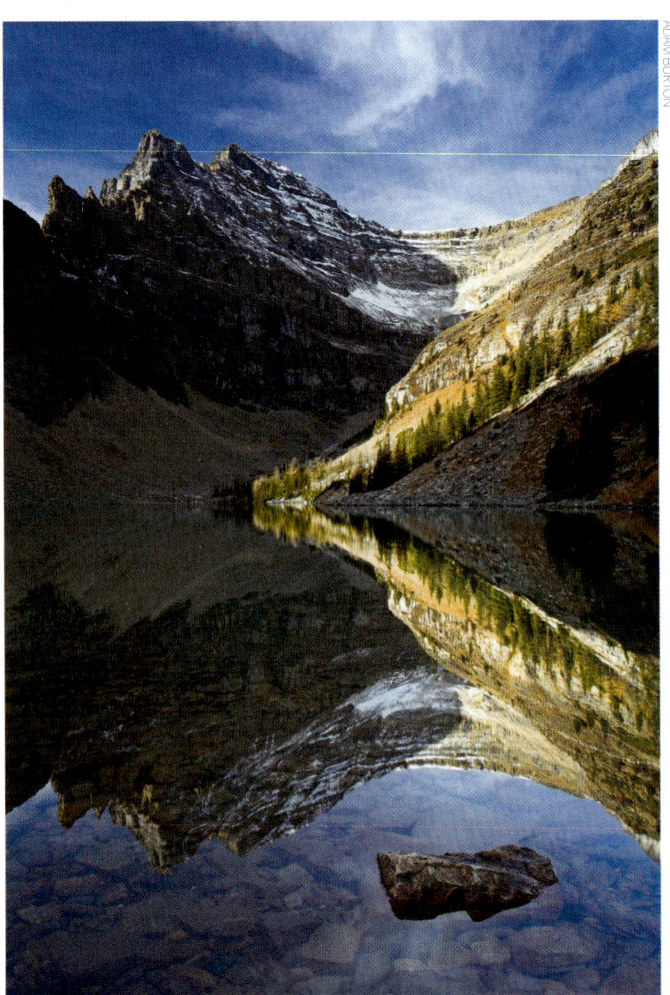

ADAM BURTON

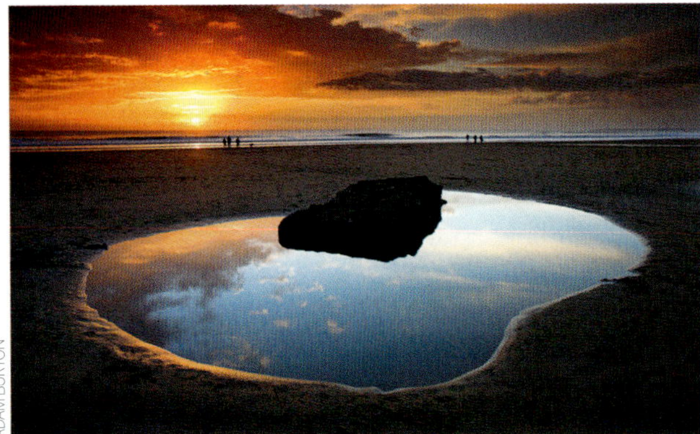

ADAM BURTON

ON REFLECTION
These two images featuring reflections in water show how applying the rule-of-thirds (left) and ignoring it (right) both have their place. As the shot of the mountain lake demonstrates, running the far shoreline across the middle of the frame creates a powerful symmetry. Don't be tempted to skim stones!

Water and exposure

Moving water has a tendency to appear white. As a result, accurate exposure is essential – overexposure will lead to white water being 'burnt out' and devoid of detail. Even if you shoot in Raw, such detail cannot be retrieved during post-processing, which is why it is important to achieve the correct exposure at the time of capture.

Your camera's multi-zone meter can normally be relied upon to achieve the right exposure. However, don't rely on the replayed image on your DSLR's LCD monitor to assess exposure. Instead, view the image's histogram. The graph represents the distribution of tones within the scene. Far left (0) represents pure black; far right (255) pure white; whilst the middle area covers mid-tones. If water is overexposed, this will be indicated by sharp peaks to the far right of the graph.

Most DSLRs also have a 'highlights' screen. This alert causes groups of pixels that have exceeded the sensor's dynamic range to flash as a warning. If water within your landscape is overexposed, apply negative exposure compensation.

Problems occur in very bright daylight – particularly around midday. Brightly lit, frothy white water can prove very intense and there is no simple way to achieve an overall correct exposure in-camera. This is why the softer, less intense light of early morning and evening is better suited to shooting water.

The quality of light on overcast days is also excellent for photographing water, particularly if using a long exposure to blur its movement. So, if it is a dull day, don't stay indoors thinking you can't shoot landscapes, head to your nearest river or coast instead and start shooting!

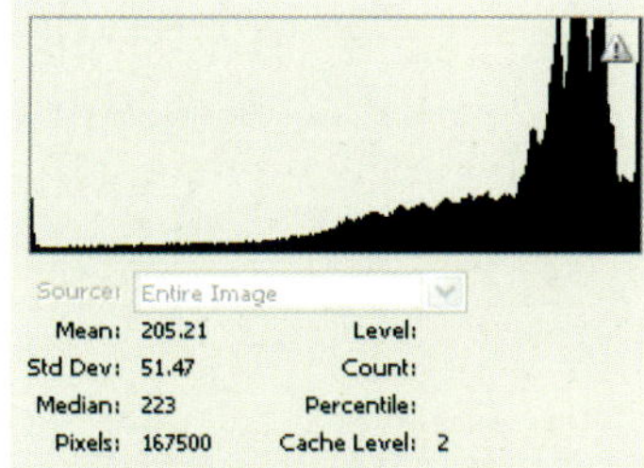

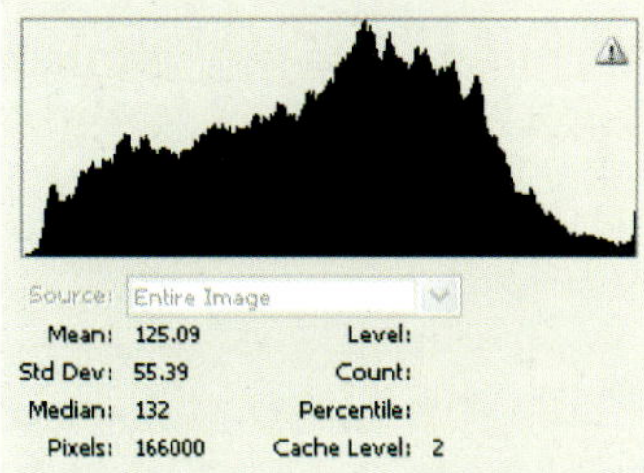

REVIEW YOUR DSLR'S HISTOGRAM
These two histograms show the difference between an overexposed scene and one that has been exposed correctly. The top diagram, showing all the peaks to the far right of the horizontal scale and crashing the top of the vertical scale, indicates 'clipping' or overexposure. The highlights have exceeded the ability of the sensor to retain image information and this data is lost forever. Post-processing in Photoshop will not be able to get it back. Look for a more even spread of peaks in the histogram, without clipping, as shown in the bottom image.

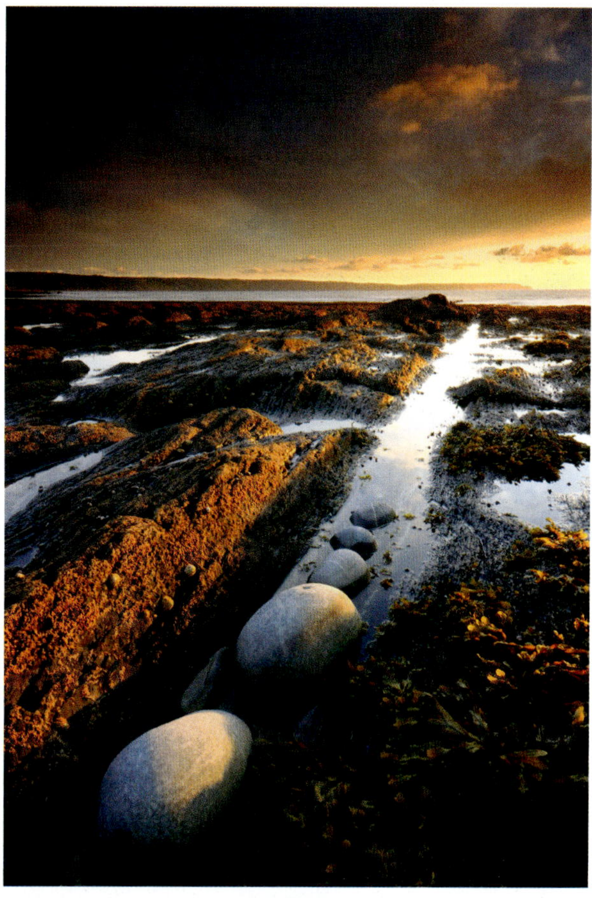

ROSS HODDINOTT

Water movement - freeze or blur?

How best to capture water's motion is a contentious issue. Some photographers like to capture water authentically, freezing its movement using a fast shutter speed. Others prefer to intentionally 'blur' it, in order to create the feeling of motion. Both techniques work well in the right situation. However, it is important to do one or the other – somewhere in between, when the water is neither blurred or sharp, will usually just look messy and unintentional.

If you wish to suspend water movement, you will normally need to employ a shutter speed of 1/500sec or faster – although the exact speed required will depend on the speed of the water.

Landscape photographers normally use a small aperture (large f/number) to achieve a depth-of-field big enough to render both foreground and background detail in sharp focus. As a result, they are often working with relatively slow exposures, especially when light levels are low.

This is one reason why many photographers go to the other extreme, employing a lengthy exposure to blur the water's flow. To many eyes, this 'blurred' effect, creates more pleasing results – adding life and movement to images.

An exposure of ½ second should do the job, but a speed of several seconds is preferable – this is guaranteed to create an attractive silky, white blur. In order to generate a long exposure, employ the lens's minimum aperture (typically f/22) and ensure that the camera's lowest ISO setting is selected. If the resulting shutter speed still isn't sufficiently slow, you will need the help of filtration.

Neutral density (ND) filters are designed to block light entering the camera – basically, they alter the light's brightness, but not its colour. They allow photographers to employ artificially long exposures in order to blur subject movement. They are available in different strengths – commonly 1-, 2- and 3-stop densities – and as both screw- and slot-in types. A two-stop version will normally be sufficient. Your camera's TTL metering will automatically adjust for the density.

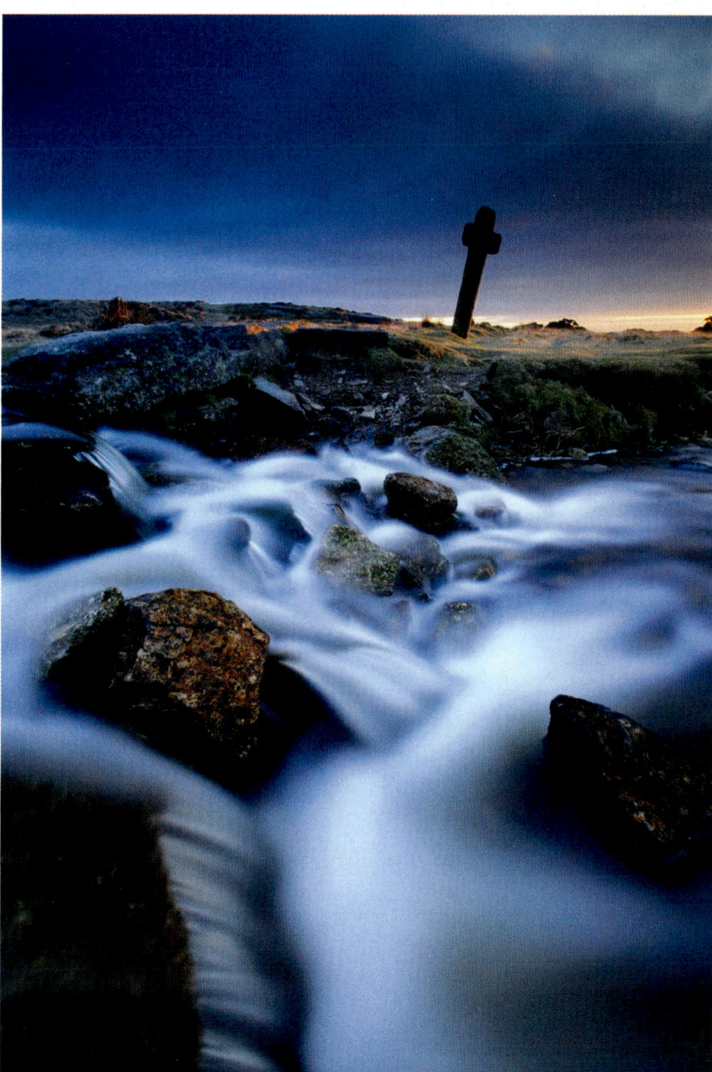

ROSS HODDINOTT

USE AN ND FILTER
Sometimes you might have to reduce the amount of light coming into the lens to force down shutter speeds and create the blur. Neutral Density (ND) filters will do the trick. Polarising filters also reduce the light level by two stops, facilitating slow shutter speeds, but watch out for the effect on reflections.

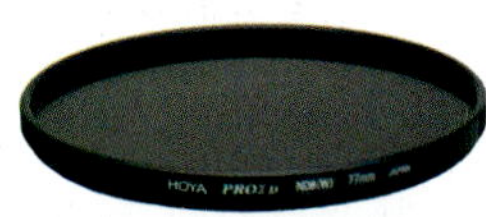

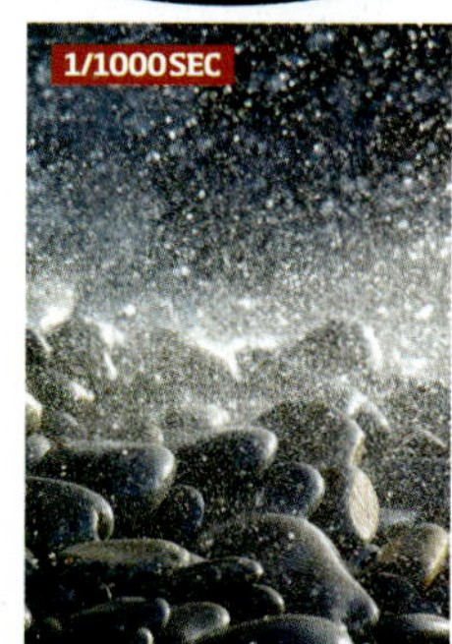

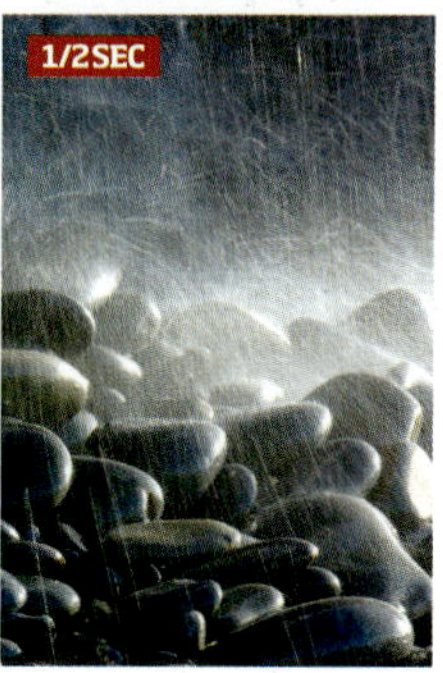

EXPERT TUTORIAL

Shoot moving water

Lee Frost reveals how choosing the correct shutter speed is essential when including running water in landscapes

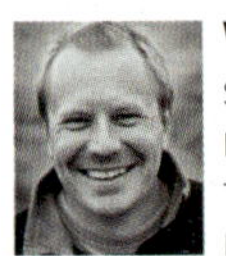

WITH LEE FROST LEE FROST: Although it has become something of a cliché, using a slow shutter speed to record moving water as a graceful, milky blur is an undeniably effective technique, which is why so many photographers, including myself, like to use it. From tumbling mountain streams to bubbling brooks and thundering waterfalls, wherever you find moving water, the same basic approach can be used to capture it and turn an ordinary scene into a creative image that's full of atmosphere. Even better, moving water is best shot on an overcast day with soft light so there are no blinding highlights to contend with, caused by sunlight reflecting on the water. This makes it a perfect subject for those dull, grey days photographers in the UK know so well!

TECHNIQUE WATCH!

Select a slow shutter speed

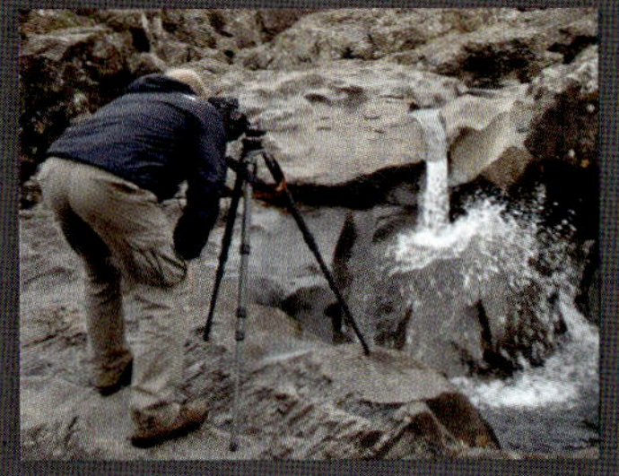

The key to success when shooting moving water is to use a shutter speed that's slow enough to blur the water, so it records with a smooth, milky appearance, but not so slow that areas where the water is more concentrated start to overexpose and burn out. This is a matter of trial and error, but an exposure of one second usually makes a good starting point. The great thing about digital capture is that you can check each shot you take to see how it looks, then shorten or lengthen the exposure time until you get the perfect result.

If tiny areas of water burn out, don't worry – when you download the images and view them as full-size files, chances are those highlight warnings will have disappeared. And if they haven't, it's a simple job to use the Clone Stamp tool in Photoshop to copy and paste water from a different part of the image over the overexposed areas.

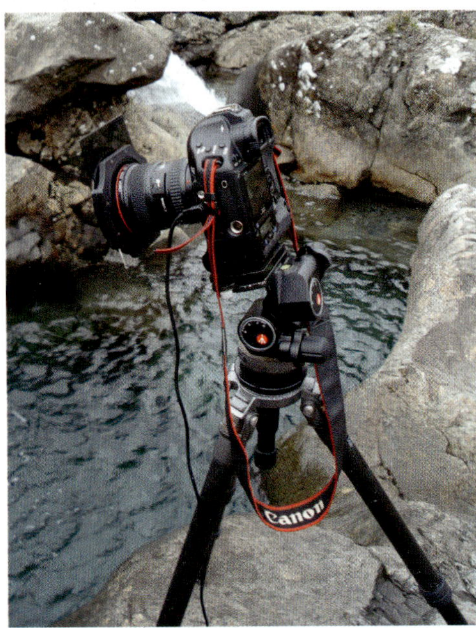

1 Because a slow shutter speed will be used to blur the water movement, always mount your camera on a sturdy tripod to keep it nice and steady. It's also a good idea to attach a remote release so you can trip the shutter without touching the camera, which risks vibrations that could lead to your images being ruined by shake.

2 In dull weather, stopping your lens down to f/16 or f/22 and setting a low ISO may give you a shutter speed slow enough to blur the water. If not, use a Neutral Density (ND) filter to increase the exposure. A polarising filter can also be used to increase the exposure by two stops – so 1/4sec becomes one second, for example.

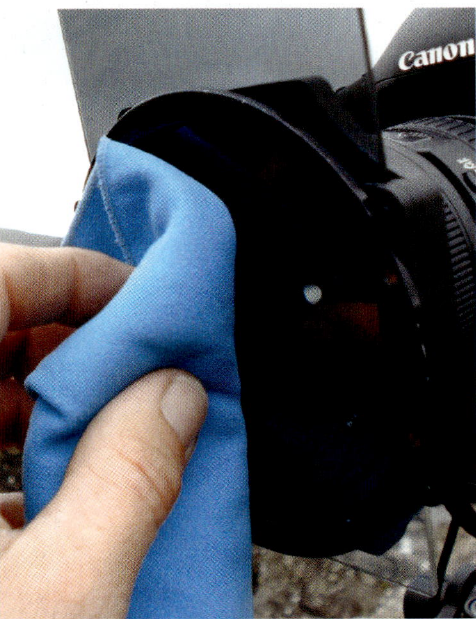

3 Before taking a shot, check the lens or filter for water droplets. If you're shooting close to a waterfall splashes or spray may get on the lens. In this case, drizzle was the culprit. Wipe the water away with a clean microfibre cloth otherwise image quality will suffer. Holding an umbrella over the camera can help in rainy weather.

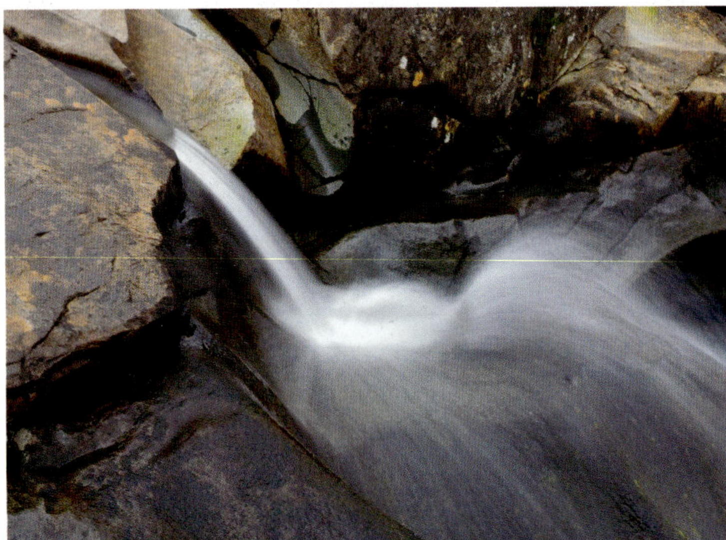

4 Take your first shot and review it. I was initially attracted to this spout of water hitting a rock and cascading in all directions. Shooting side-on proved to be a good angle and a shutter speed of one second offered enough blur. The shot worked, but there were many other options to explore.

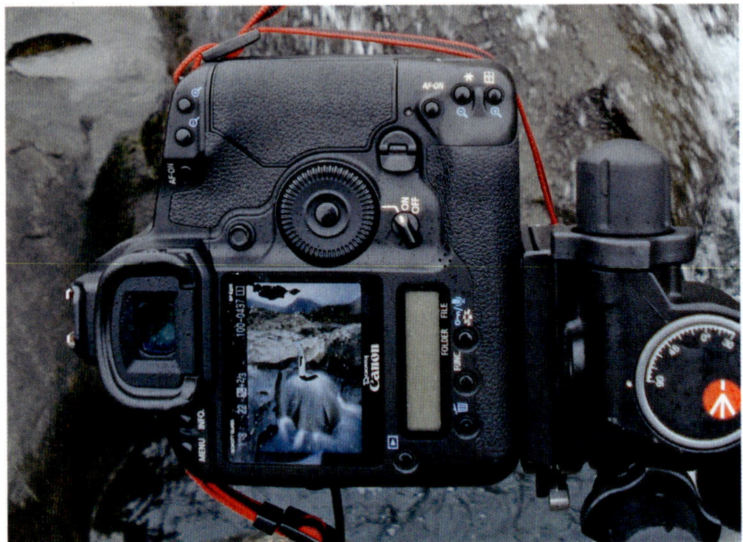

5 I decided to try a wider view, using the water spout in the previous step as foreground interest, carrying the eye up the ravine towards the distant peaks of the Cuillin Ridge. It took a few attempts to get the shutter speed just right so no areas of the moving water were overexposed.

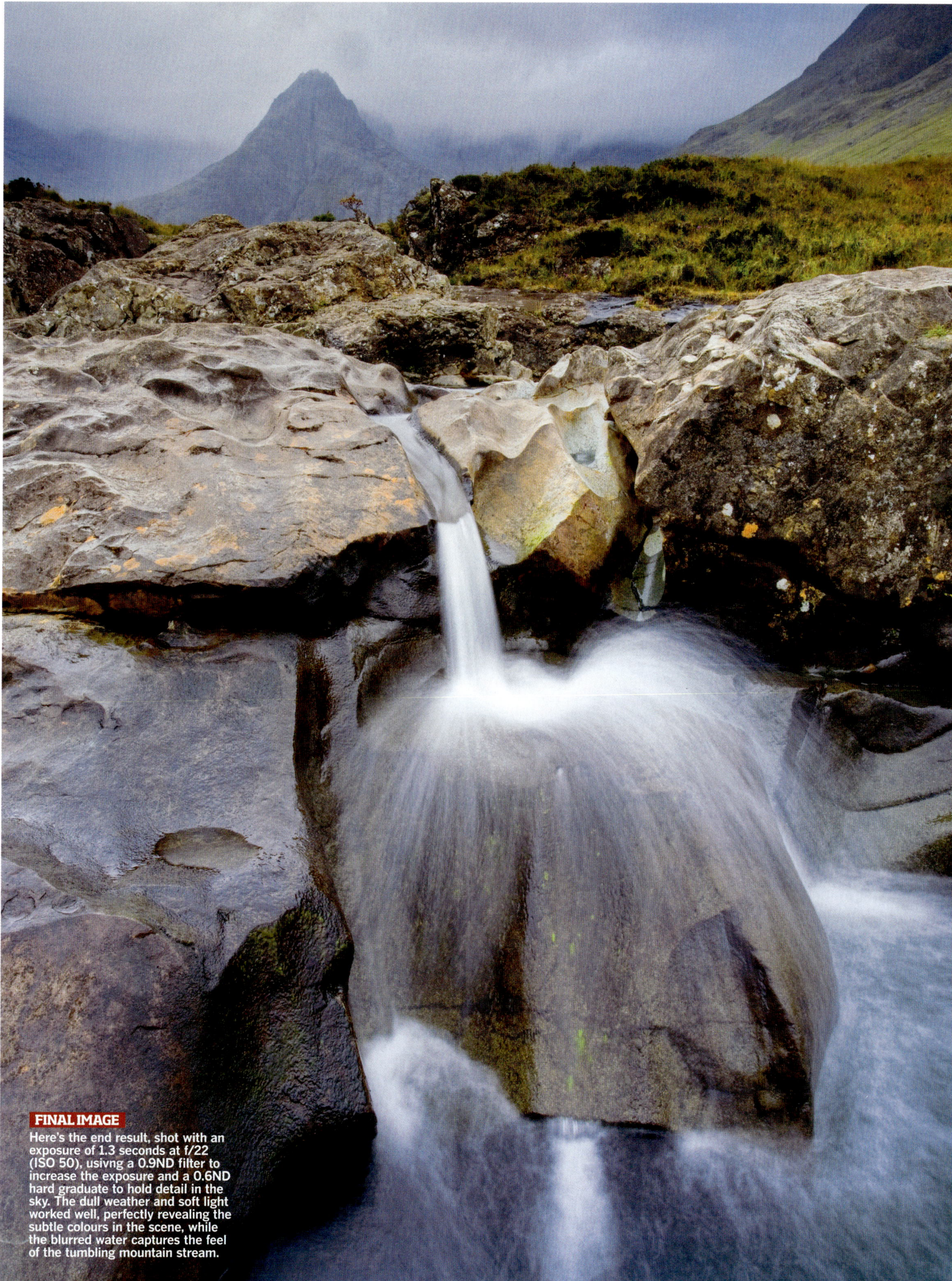

FINAL IMAGE
Here's the end result, shot with an exposure of 1.3 seconds at f/22 (ISO 50), usivng a 0.9ND filter to increase the exposure and a 0.6ND hard graduate to hold detail in the sky. The dull weather and soft light worked well, perfectly revealing the subtle colours in the scene, while the blurred water captures the feel of the tumbling mountain stream.

The Basics **#7**

UNDERSTANDING COLOUR

A LOT OF TIME, energy and thought has been devoted to the study of colour, its practical applications and its psychological effects. Often those applications and effects are linked. It's not an accident that stop signs are red, cool settings on air conditioning are blue or that the environmental movement has adopted the colour green.

Much can be learned about the relationships between colours, too. Colours work together in different ways, with certain combinations creating energy and tension, while others harmonise and create calm. When a colour appears in nature with a greater than normal intensity, the stage is set for great landscape photography. Learning their relationship will reap rewards.

1) Harmony and contrast

There are basically two types of relationship between colours – harmony and contrast. Looking at a colour wheel helps us to understand this. Colours that are next to each other, for example blue and green, are harmonious, while those that are opposite, for example blue and yellow, contrast with each other.

Also, colours that are on the 'warm' side of the wheel harmonise with each other, while all those on the 'cool' side also harmonise. Harmonious colours are more calming to look at, and blues and greens in particular are very tranquil. Contrasting colours are more dramatic and create a tension that can challenge the eye – blue and yellow is a strong contrast.

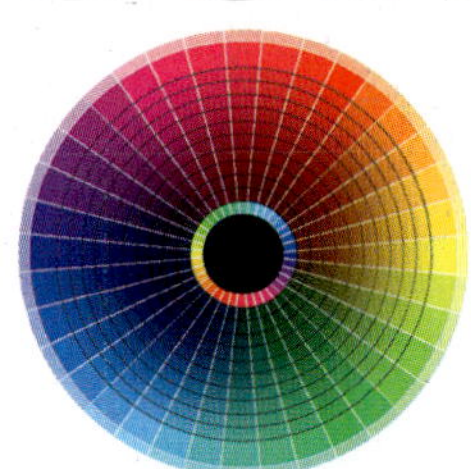

THE COLOUR WHEEL
Contrasting colours such as yellow and blue, or red and green create tension and drama. Colours adjacent to each other are calming.

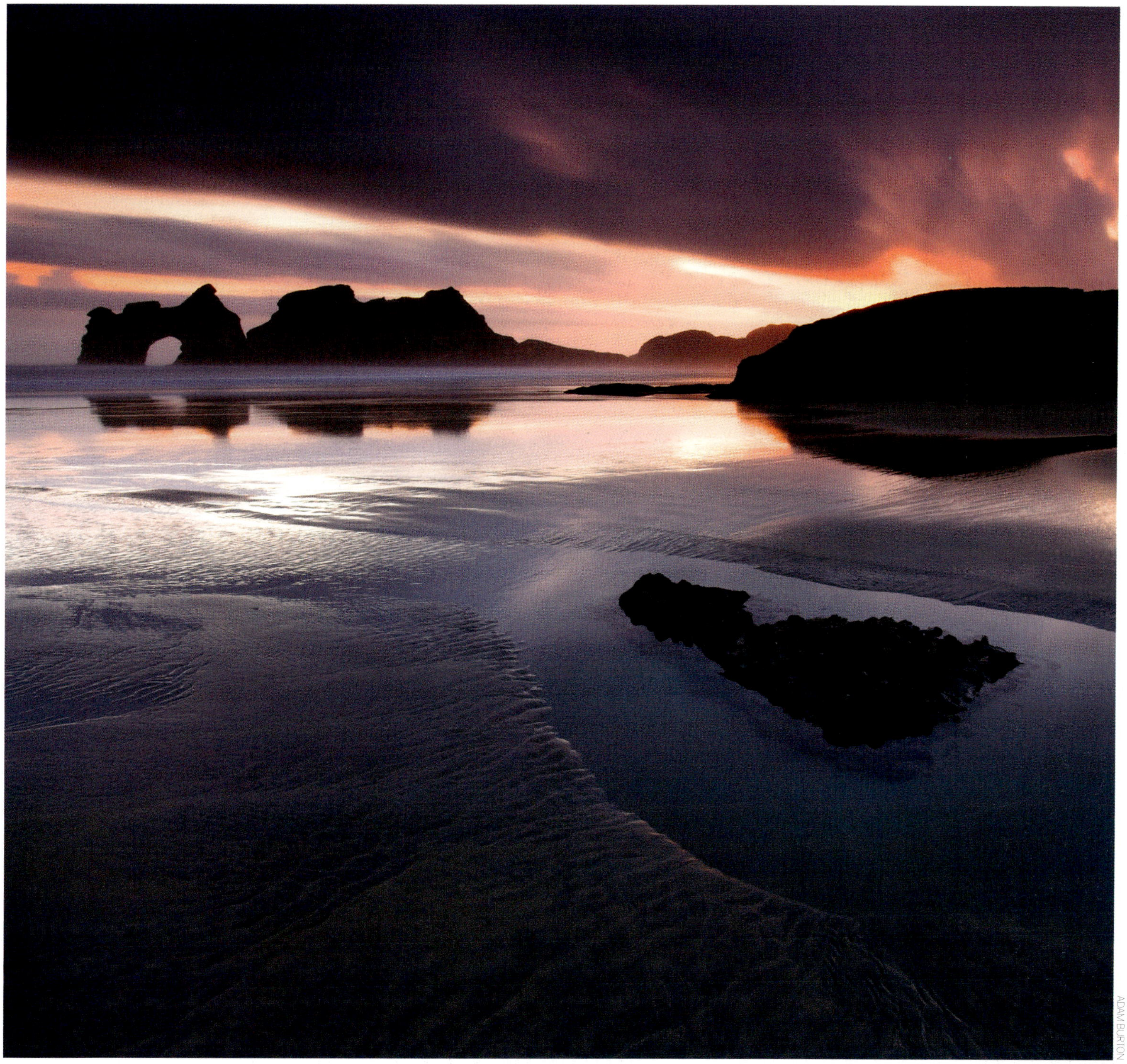

ADAM BURTON

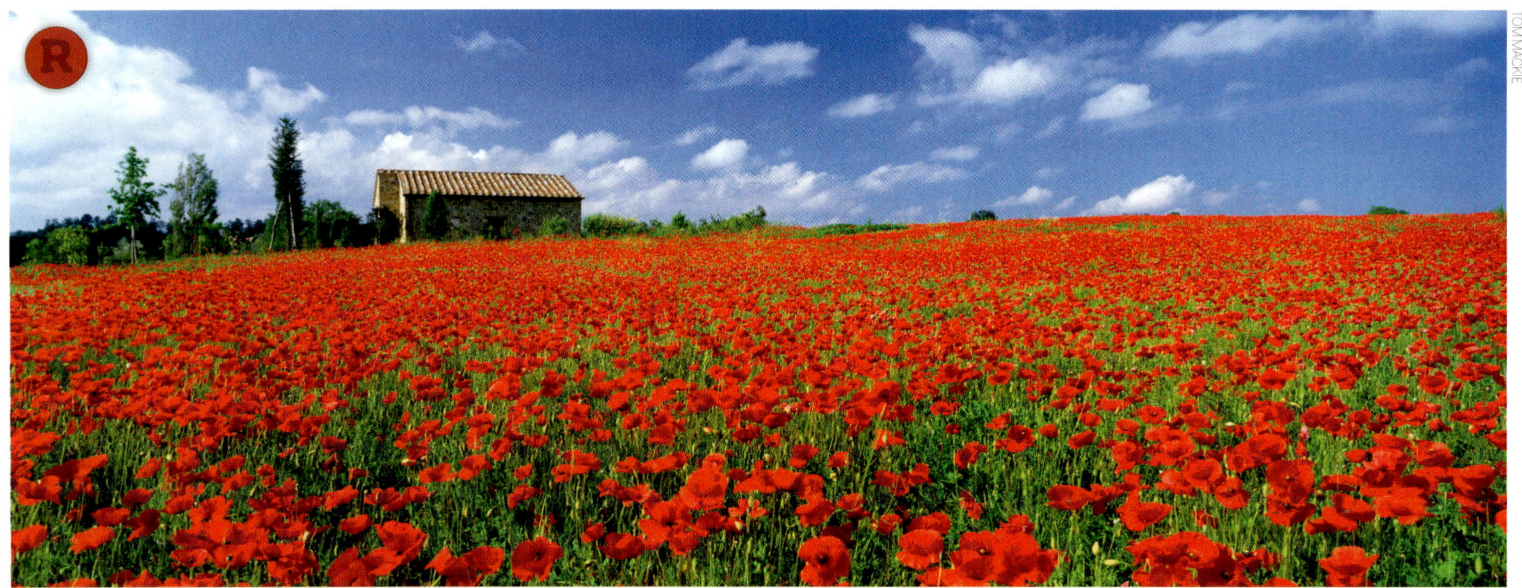

TOM MACKIE

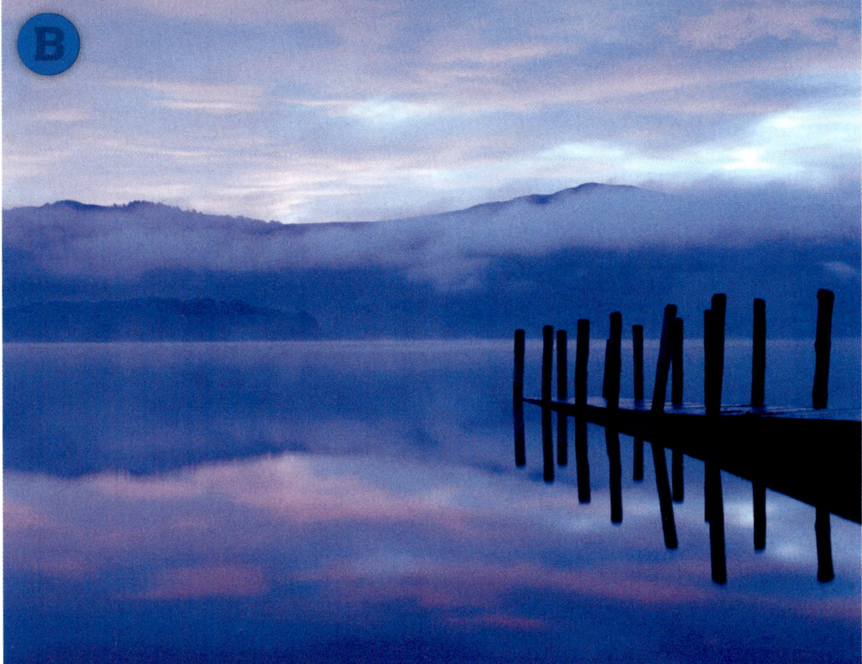

CRAIG ROBERTS

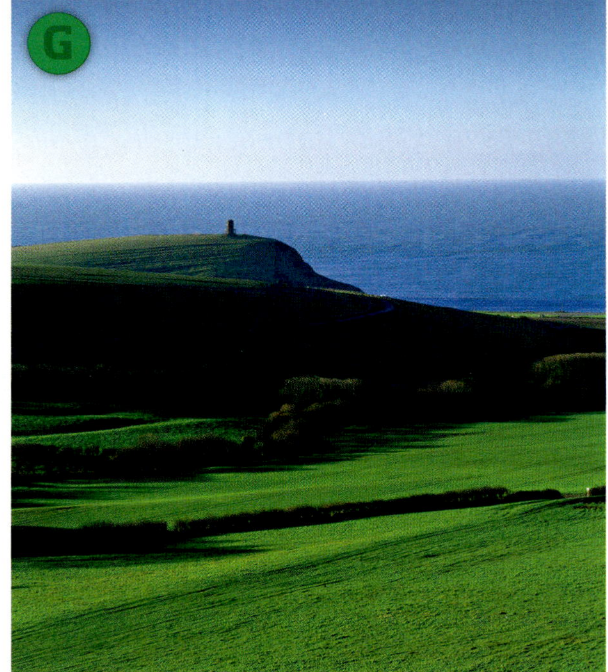

MARK BAUER

2) Colour and emotion

As well as having visual impact, colours can suggest different moods, evoke different emotions and can have symbolic significance related to our culture and background. Think about the effect a dominant colour might have on your image. It might be appropriate to subdue a colour, or emphasise it. Consider colour in the composition, the lighting and through careful use of filtration.

R **RED** is an intense colour, especially when contrasted against a dark background. It is a colour universally used for warning or danger and is hard to ignore. Red is the most powerful and attention-grabbing colour in photography, though it can prove distracting if included small within the landscape, for instance, a distant car, boat or letterbox.

B **BLUE** is a retiring colour, which can be employed to convey restfulness, sadness or tranquility. In photography, it is commonly used to convey coldness, which works especially well when combined with water and wintry scenes. Blue is a very important colour for landscape photographers as a saturated sky creates a flattering backdrop.

G **GREEN** is often used to signify health and life. Obviously, green is the predominant colour of vegetation and therefore it is dominant in many scenic images. Green is easily overwhelmed by bright advancing colours, like red and, generally speaking, has less impact. However, when isolated, green can still create strong, interesting images.

Y **YELLOW** is another bold, advancing colour, often used to represent happiness or brightness. It will add warmth to your image and works particularly well when combined or contrasted with blue. Yellow, along with similarly rich colours, like gold and orange, epitomise autumn. It can prove a good background for still-life images.

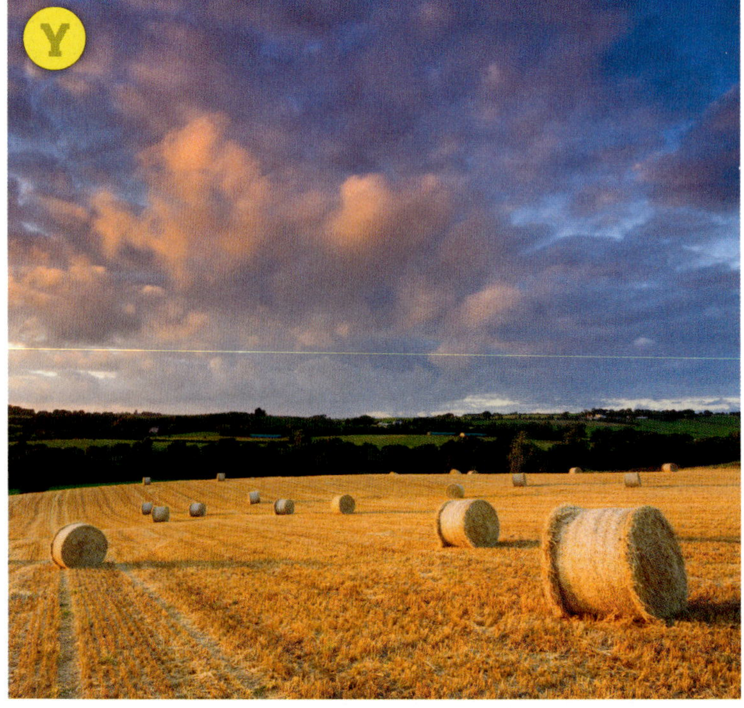

ROSS HODDINOTT

3) Using only one colour

Single colours often give an image a particular mood and it's possible to make successful compositions using just one colour – or shades of one colour.

Certain lighting conditions can create this effect and add atmosphere to a scene. An intensely orange or red sunset will give every neutral colour a strong bias, bathing a scene in a fiery warmth.

Also, strong backlighting can desaturate colours, creating an almost monochromatic effect; while at pre-sunrise and post-sunset, there is no single strong light source and the light is diffused and reflected down from the sky.

The two images on the right are really good examples of monochromatic images. Starting over on the far right you can see how backlighting has drained the colours from this scene, resulting in an image that appears almost devoid of colour.

The pre-dawn light bathing the lake and dead wood in the near right picture is diffused, falling on the scene from virtually the whole sky. It has given the whole scene a fairly cold cast, but the mood is very tranquil. It really suits the cold, wind-free stillness of a winter morning.

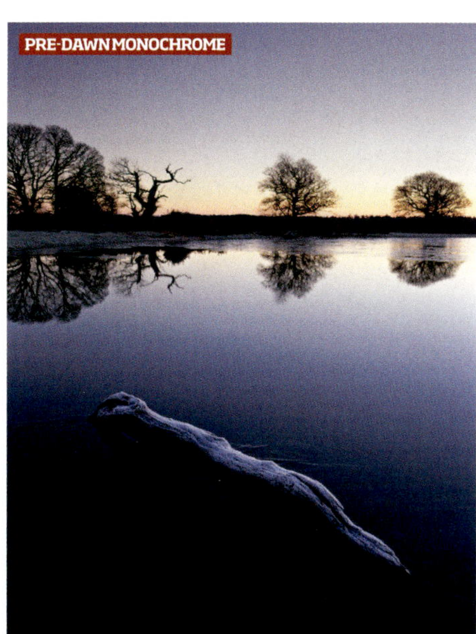
PRE-DAWN MONOCHROME

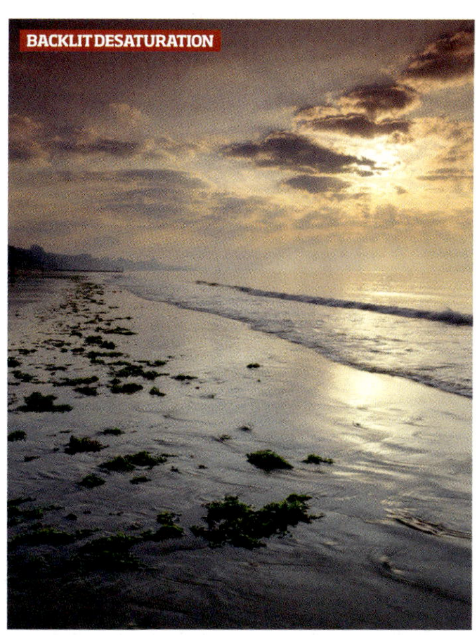
BACKLIT DESATURATION

4) Colour saturation

OK, if were going to be strictly technical about this, the term 'saturation' refers to how pure any given colour is. But over time and in practical terms, saturation has come to mean how intense or strong a colour appears in an image.

Producing saturated images involves more than simply boosting colours in Photoshop – although much can be done that way, with great results – there are plenty of options at the picture-taking stage. Let's consider those first.

The time of day has an impact on colour saturation. Early-morning and late-evening light, with the sun low in the sky and less glare, will produce more intense colours than at other times, as will front lighting rather than side or backlighting.

A polarising filter, by reducing reflections and cutting down on glare, also improves saturation. A polariser has the maximum effect when the camera is at 90° to the sun. Polarisers are simple to use as the effect is clearly visible through the camera's viewfinder – the most obvious one being the increase in saturation of blue skies.

There are couple of things to watch out for. It is possible to 'over-polarise' a scene, resulting in skies appearing almost black, and also, when using wide-angle lenses (wider than 28mm on a full-frame SLR or 17mm on an APS-C-type SLR) the degree of polarisation can be uneven across the frame.

Of course, it's not always desirable to have strong, vibrant, saturated colours. Muted, pastel tones are more subtle, but can be just as effective with the right subject matter, creating an atmosphere of calm and tranquility. Early morning mist will drain colours, and also give a cold, bluish hue to a scene, which you can enhance by tweaking the White Balance either in camera, or later, if you're shooting Raw, at the conversion stage.

Of course, a lot can be done at the processing stage. Experiment with different White Balance settings to try to fine-tune the overall atmosphere and find an overall cast that suits the image best. Over the page, we'll show how varying the White Balance of a Raw file can have give dramatic results.

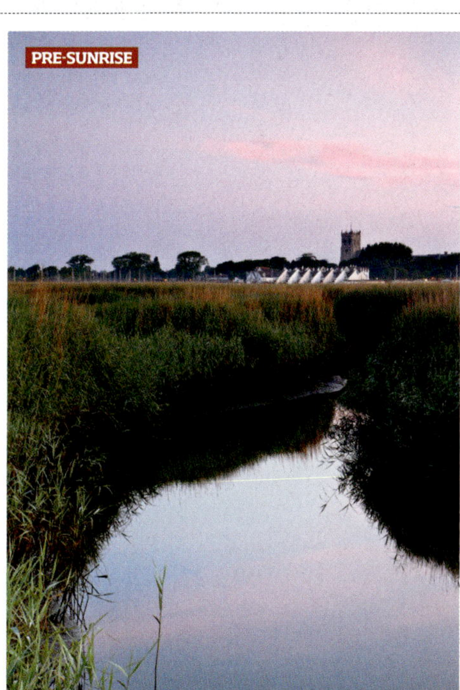
PRE-SUNRISE

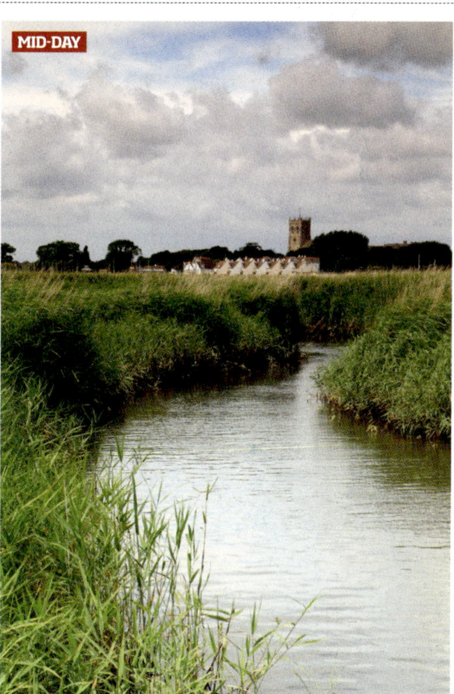
MID-DAY

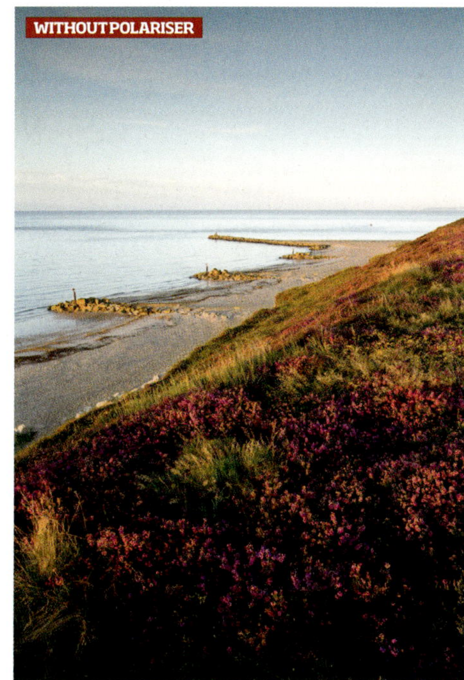
WITHOUT POLARISER

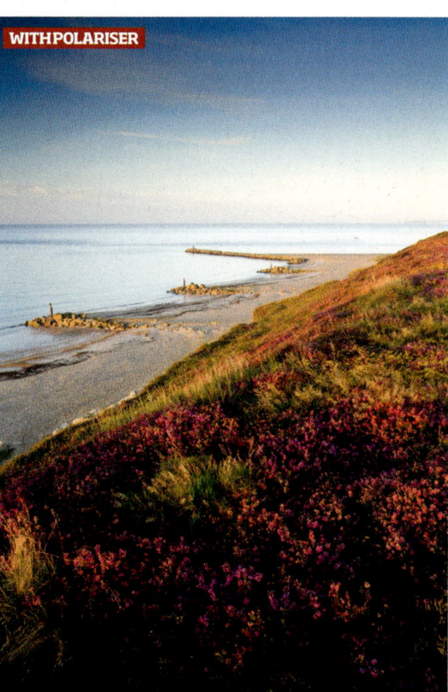
WITH POLARISER

FILTER CHOICE

Types of polariser

There are two types of polariser: circular and linear. This doesn't refer to the physical shape – they're both actually circular – but the way the light is polarised. Make sure you buy a circular polariser for use with your DSLR as linear types interfere with your camera's metering, which can't handle linearly-polarised light.

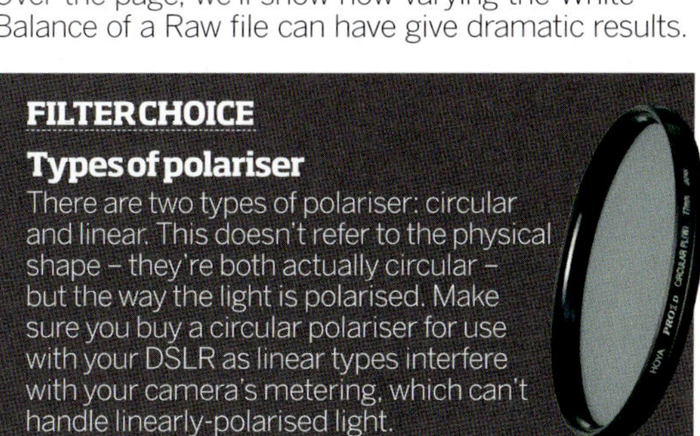

EXPERT TUTORIAL

Blur your vision!

Smearing Vaseline on a filter might not sound sensible, but it can help you capture creative results of colourful scenes

WITH DANIEL LEZANO Photoshop has allowed all sorts of weird and wonderful effects to be applied to images in post-production, but I still prefer to get as close as possible to the final image in-camera. Much of this is because I'm not particularly good with Photoshop to be honest, but mainly because I actually find it fun (as well as occasionally frustrating), to go 'old-school' and use more traditional photographic techniques to give the results I'm looking for. I've recently started experimenting with producing unusual soft-focus effects by smearing Vaseline on a filter. As I discovered, it's very easy to try, so why not give it a go this month and see how you get on.

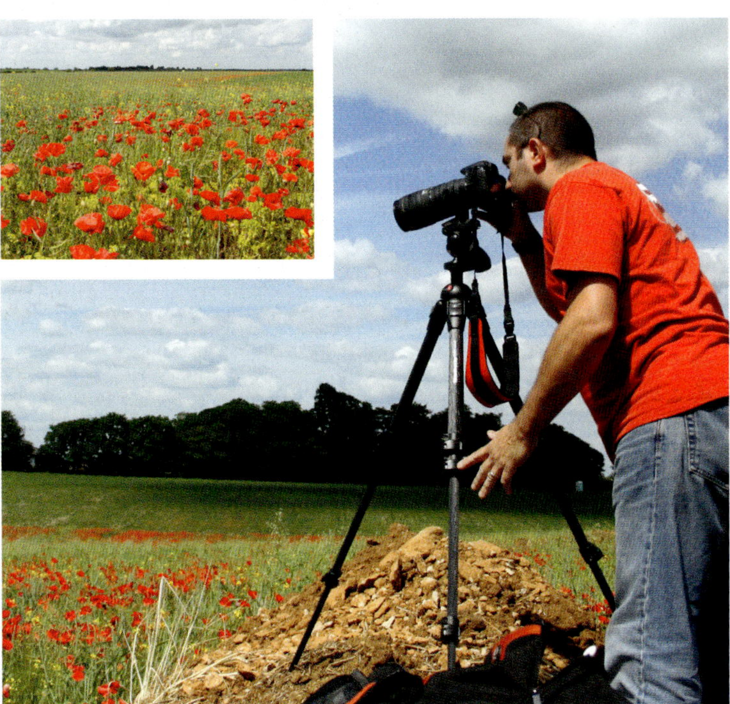

1 The first thing you need to do is to find a suitable scene. Ideally, the location you choose should have some well-defined shapes and areas of strong shadows and bright highlights, such as woodland. However, this colourful field of poppies caught my eye and I hoped to be able to use the Vaseline to create a strong abstract effect based around the bold reds. I mounted my DSLR on a tripod, to ensure images were shake-free, and used Sigma's excellent 70-200mm f/2.8 lens to crop fairly tightly on the poppy field.

KIT WATCH!

Filter, Vaseline & cloth

The minimum of additional kit is required, so it's an affordable technique to try. A tub of Vaseline won't break the bank, but you'll need a UV or skylight filter to screw onto the front of your lens. I cannot over-emphasise how important it is that you apply Vaseline to the filter and not to the front element of your lens, as it could permanently damage the optics. You should also keep a clean lens cloth handy, for wiping away Vaseline when you want to clean the filter and try again, or at the end of your day's shooting. That's about all you need in terms of accessories, with the exception of a tripod, which will keep your camera steady when you're preparing the composition and focusing on the scene.

TECHNIQUE WATCH!

Applying vaseline

As you'll discover, getting a desired effect requires lots of trial and error when it comes to smearing the filter. Start off by applying a thin line of Vaseline across the central part of the filter, and apply further smears until you've covered the whole surface. Take a few shots, rotate the filter so the smears are diagonal and shoot again. Apply thicker smears of Vaseline to create random patterns, and then wipe the filter clean and try again!

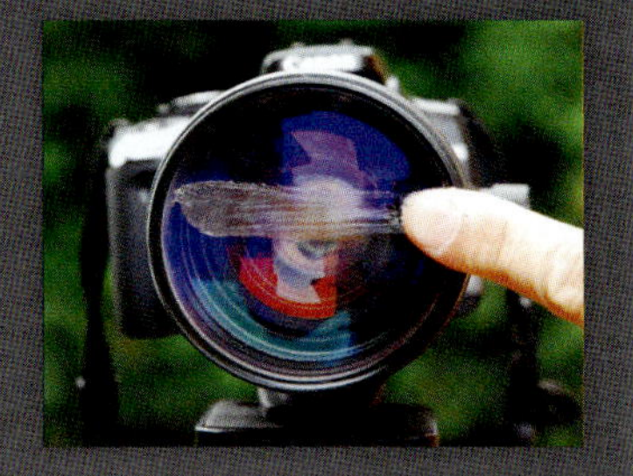

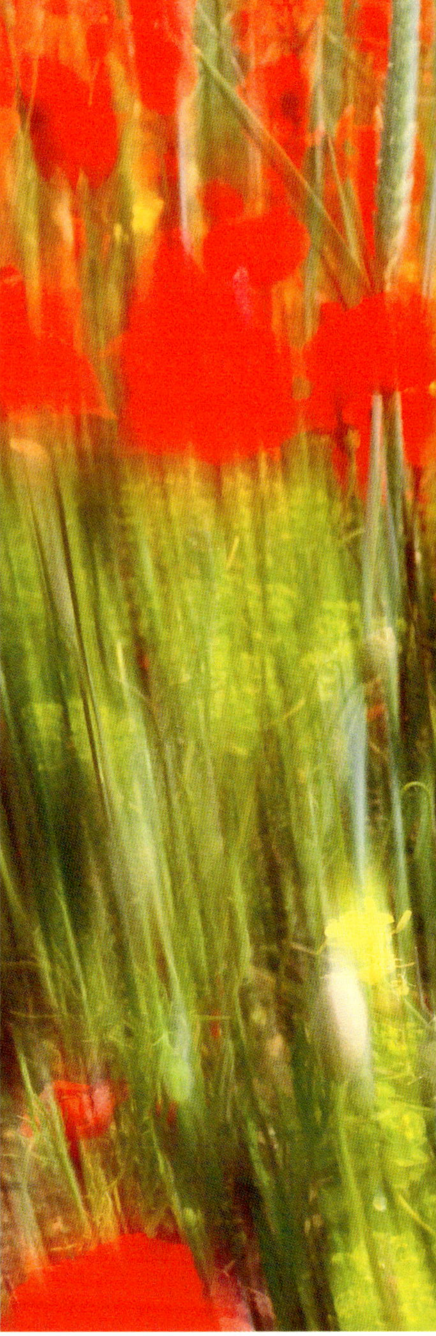

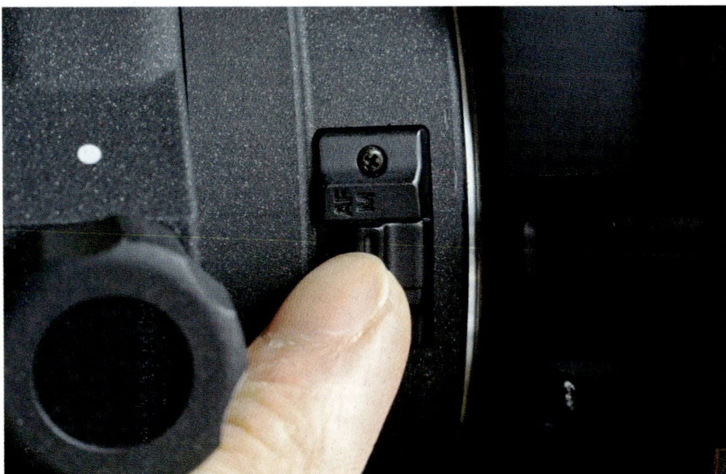

2 With the camera supported on a sturdy tripod, it's important to 'lock' the focus before smearing the filter with Vaseline – the AF system will struggle to focus once it's been applied. To do this, focus on the scene normally and then switch the lens from AF to manual focus, so when you press the shutter button later on, to take a shot, it won't affect the focusing.

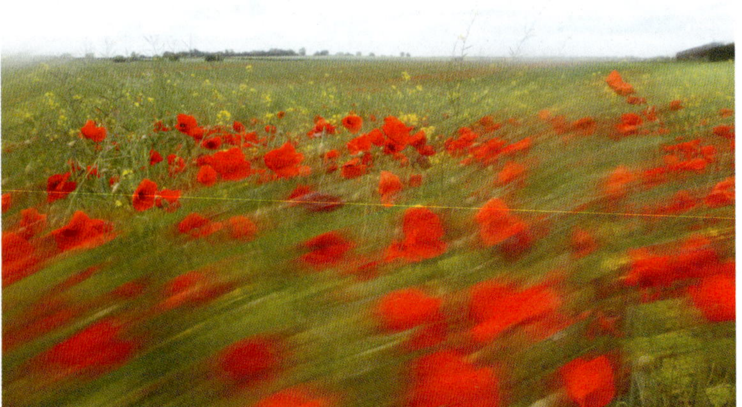

3 With everything prepared, it's time to apply the Vaseline. Rather than scoop big wedges from the tub, gently smear relatively thin lines of Vaseline across the frame. Here, you can see how just a single smear affects the scene. I looked through the viewfinder the whole time I was applying the Vaseline, to see how it was affecting the overall scene.

FINAL IMAGE
My favourite image was one taken towards the end of my session. After refining my composition, angling the camera down towards a smaller area of the field (to make the poppies larger in the frame), I carefully applied very thin smears to the filter.

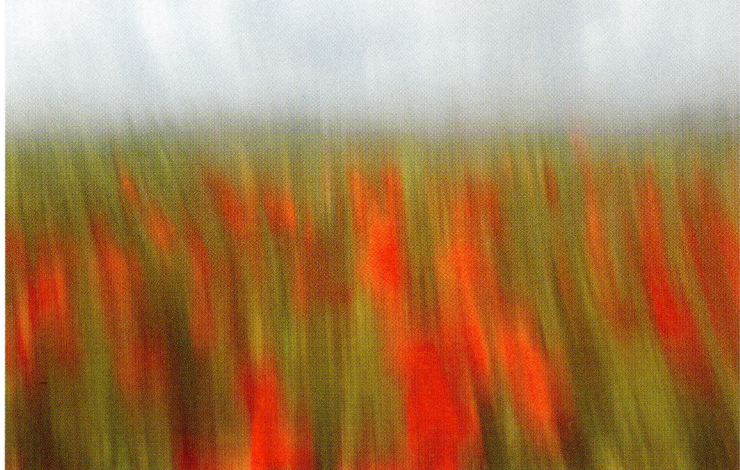

4 Once I'd applied the Vaseline across the filter, I fired off a few frames, choosing a variety of apertures from f/5.6 to f/13, so that I could see how the results varied (in truth, it made little difference). After a few frames, I used my finger to apply more Vaseline, to see if a thicker layer would improve the effect. However, I found that using too much of it led to too soft a result.

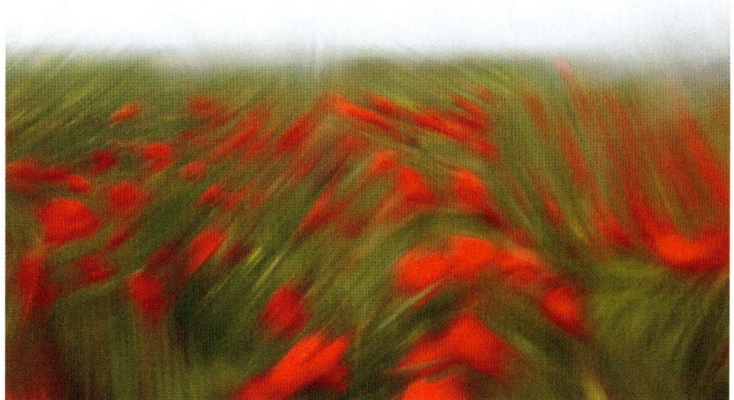

5 As well as horizontal smears, I also rotated the filter so as to make the smears run diagonally and then vertically – this made a big difference to the result. I also tried a variety of smear patterns, such as criss-crossed lines and wavy lines to see what effect it had on the scene. It's worth trying this, as it's impossible to predict what works best.

EXPERT TUTORIAL

Colour temperature and White Balance (WB)

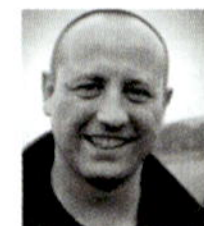

WITH MARK BAUER Different light sources produce different colour casts, basically in terms of how 'warm' or 'cool' the light is and how much green or magenta is present. For example, a household tungsten light bulb will produce a much warmer light than you will find outside on a cloudy day. Fluorescent lighting will have a green colour cast.

The warmth or coolness of a light source is referred to as its 'colour temperature', which is measured in degrees Kelvin (K). The lower the number, the warmer the light – for example, a sunset will have a colour temperature of around 3000K, neutral daylight (noon on a sunny day) is around 5000–5500K, and an overcast sky around 7000–8000K.

Our eyes adapt very quickly and easily to the colour of different light sources and will see a white object as white whether we view it under tungsten light or outside on a cloudy day. To render colour accurately with a digital SLR, however, you will need to set the correct White Balance, which can either be done when taking the picture or when processing the image in your Raw converter. Personally, I'd always recommend shooting in Raw, as it provides a lot more flexibility.

If shooting subjects such as portraits, colour accuracy and correct White Balance is essential, to achieve natural looking skin tones. With landscapes, however, absolute colour accuracy is not always what we strive for – capturing pleasing colours is more what it's all about. So, in the old days of film, landscape photographers would use films like Fuji Velvia for its vibrant colour and use colour correction filters – amber warm-ups and blue cooling filters – to enhance mood and atmosphere rather than produce neutral, accurate colours. For example, a warm-up filter could be used to enhance the already warm light of a sunset. Digital photographers can use different White Balance settings to achieve similar effects.

Enhance mood with WB

For this series of pictures, I took the same Raw file and applied different White Balance settings to find out which one best suited the overall mood of the picture.

1) DAYLIGHT (5500K) The dusk light was cold and blue. There was just a hint of a glow from the sun below the horizon, picked up by the clouds over the distant headland. The daylight WB has rendered the scene well, with cool blue shadows that suit the mood of the image.

2) CLOUDY (6500K) The cloudy setting has warmed things up and added some magenta. This works well for the sky, but for my taste, has failed to enhance the water and shadows. I suspect a lot of people will like it, though.

3) SHADE (7500K) Too warm and magenta, and doesn't reflect the mood of the scene. However, some people will probably like this.

4) FLUORESCENT (3800K) I actually quite like this, as it's true to the mood of the actual scene, though it is a bit over the top and the sky has lost a lot of 'oomph'.

5) CUSTOM WB (4800K) As a compromise, I went back to the daylight WB and cooled things down just a little. I felt that this was a good representation of the mood of the scene, though the sky lacked punch.

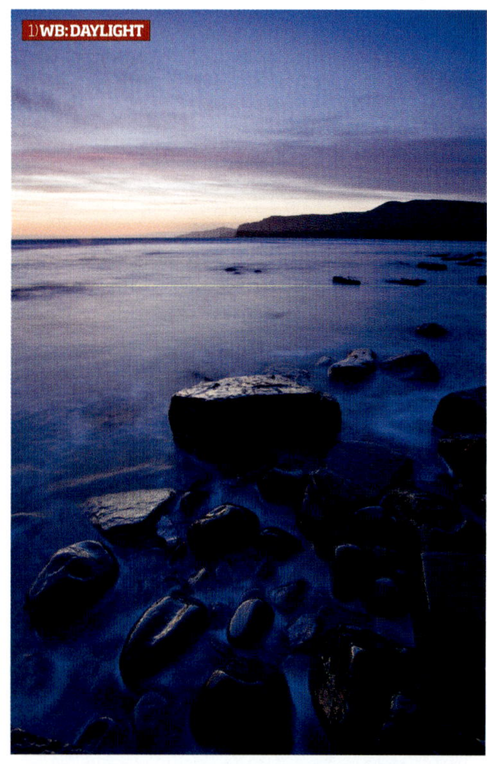
1) WB: DAYLIGHT

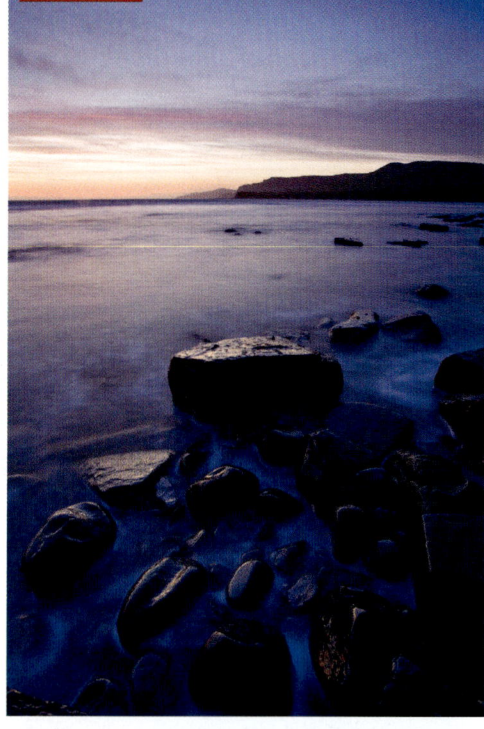
2) WB: CLOUDY

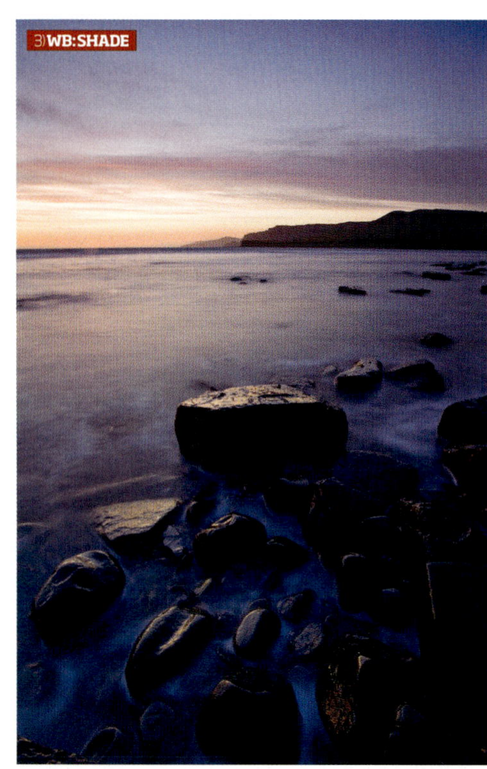
3) WB: SHADE

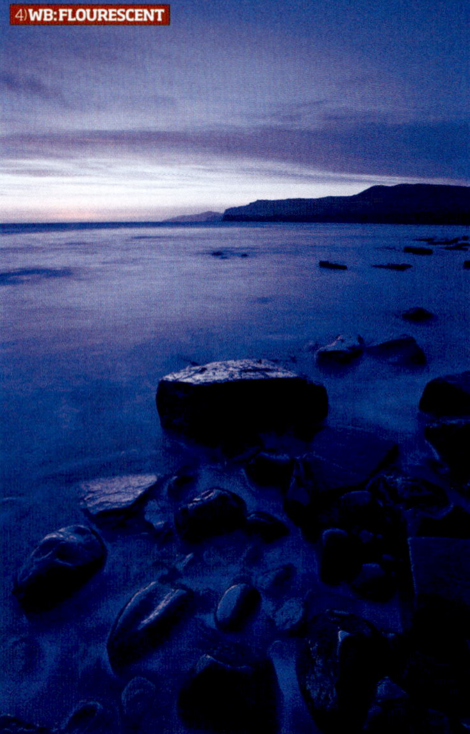
4) WB: FLOURESCENT

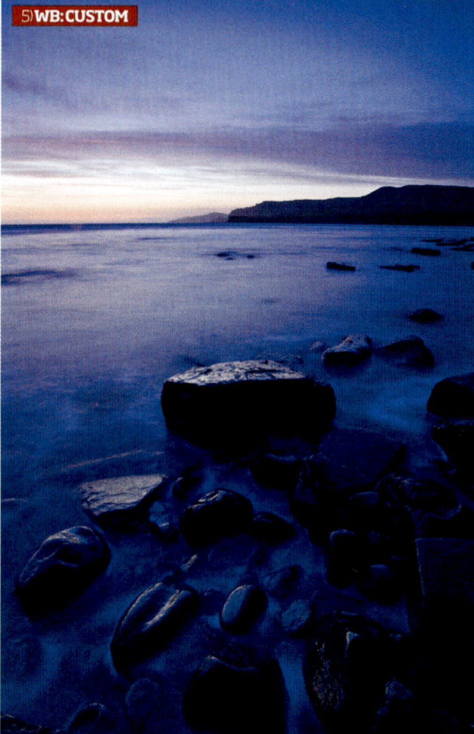
5) WB: CUSTOM

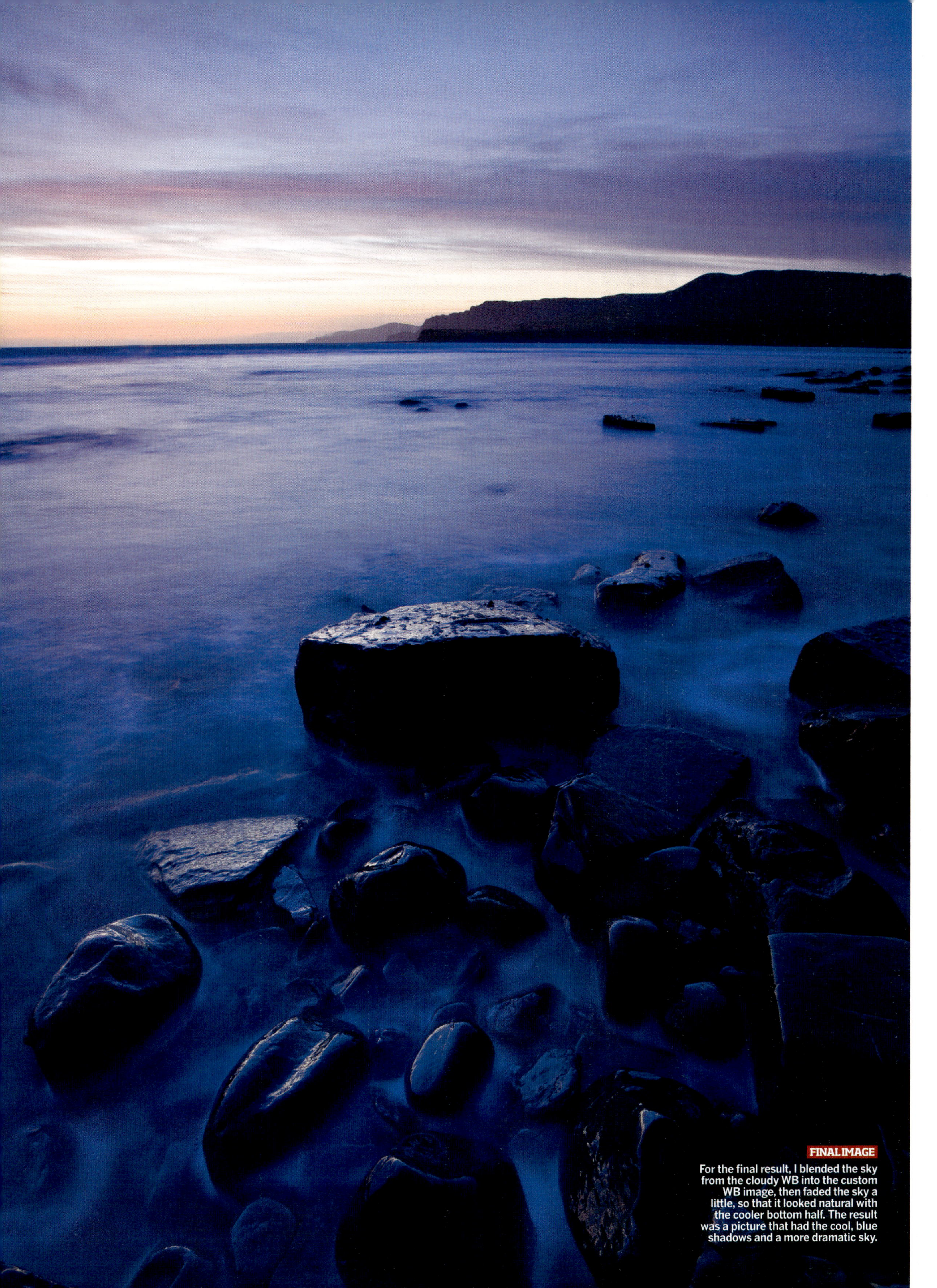

FINAL IMAGE

For the final result, I blended the sky from the cloudy WB into the custom WB image, then faded the sky a little, so that it looked natural with the cooler bottom half. The result was a picture that had the cool, blue shadows and a more dramatic sky.

EXPERT TUTORIAL

Shooting landscapes in black & white

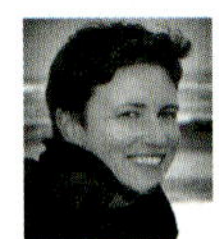

WITH HELEN DIXON I always shoot my landscapes in colour and convert to black & white afterwards (see the feature on converting colour images, over the page). This provides me with the full three channels of information to play with at the Raw processing stage, rather than just one. I do know some people who shoot JPEGs and use the in-camera monochrome setting, often in combination with a red filter to darken greens and blues to give really dark skies, but to get an image with the potential to give the best possible mono results, shoot in colour and convert to black & white on your PC.

You've got to try and visualise a scene in black & white; it's much more challenging than a regular colour landscape. You need a good range of tonal detail, or you will end up with a scene lacking in contrast.

I wouldn't normally shoot an image with a plain blue sky, for example, as you'll just end up with a flat shade of grey. You're looking for an active sky, something with plenty of cloud drama – a scene as a whole that has plenty of shadows and highlights, and separation between foreground and background.

A beach scene, for example, doesn't tend to offer much tonal contrast. You've got the sand and the sea, maybe some cliffs, and the sky; each of which is fairly uniform in tone and texture and can end up looking fairly dull. It's for this reason that I tend to gravitate towards country scenes for my black & white photography, as there's a lot more variation going on in texture and tone.

"Another great thing about shooting black & white is that you don't need the best weather. A dark, brooding sky can add a lot of drama to an image"

I also look for more lead-in lines with monochrome; the composition needs to be that much stronger because of the absence of colour. The viewer's eye is much more focused on other aspects of the shot, such as shape, form, and texture. The viewer's imagination has to work harder. Another great thing about shooting landscapes in black & white is that you don't need the best weather. A dark, brooding sky can add a lot of drama to an image, and you don't need to worry about using ND grad filters either, though I do still make sure to use a polarising filter to enhance the sky.

I don't think enough people dedicate time towards black & white photography anymore. You need to see the image in print, hanging on a wall, to really appreciate it. It seems to have that much more power in exhibition than on-screen. The other advantage is that a black & white image will sit nicely on any interior wall, without the risk of it clashing with the colour. Monochrome imagery really does lend itself to display.

BELOW LEFT: East Head, West Wittering. This type of 'scruffy' location works far better in black & white than it would in colour.

BELOW: St Michael's Mount, Cornwall. Lead-in lines are an important visual aid in my monochrome photography, as typified by the cobbled path in the foreground leading towards the distant mount.

RIGHT: Although the tree provides the foreground interest, the clouds really draw the eye in this monochrome image. The stark and barren landscape with bare and lifeless fields all add to the drama. Noise was added to the sky to keep the graininess going throughout the whole scene.

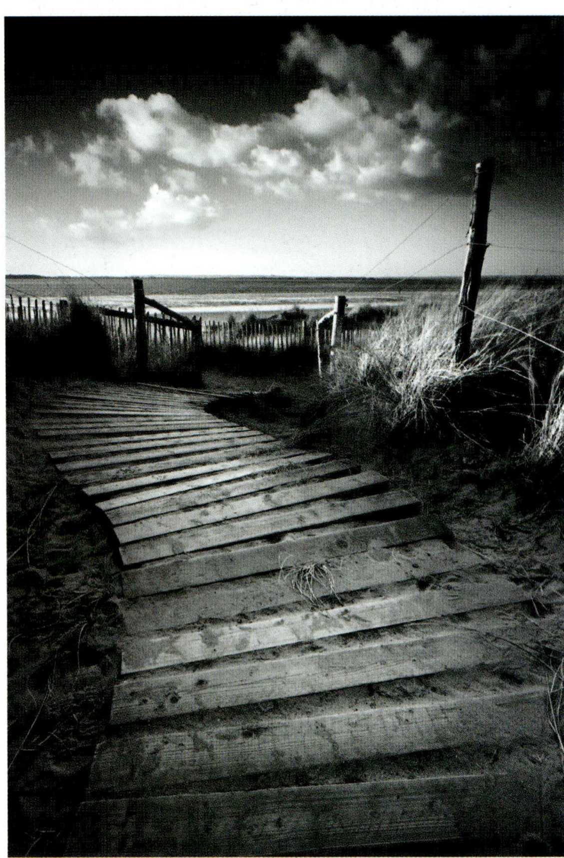

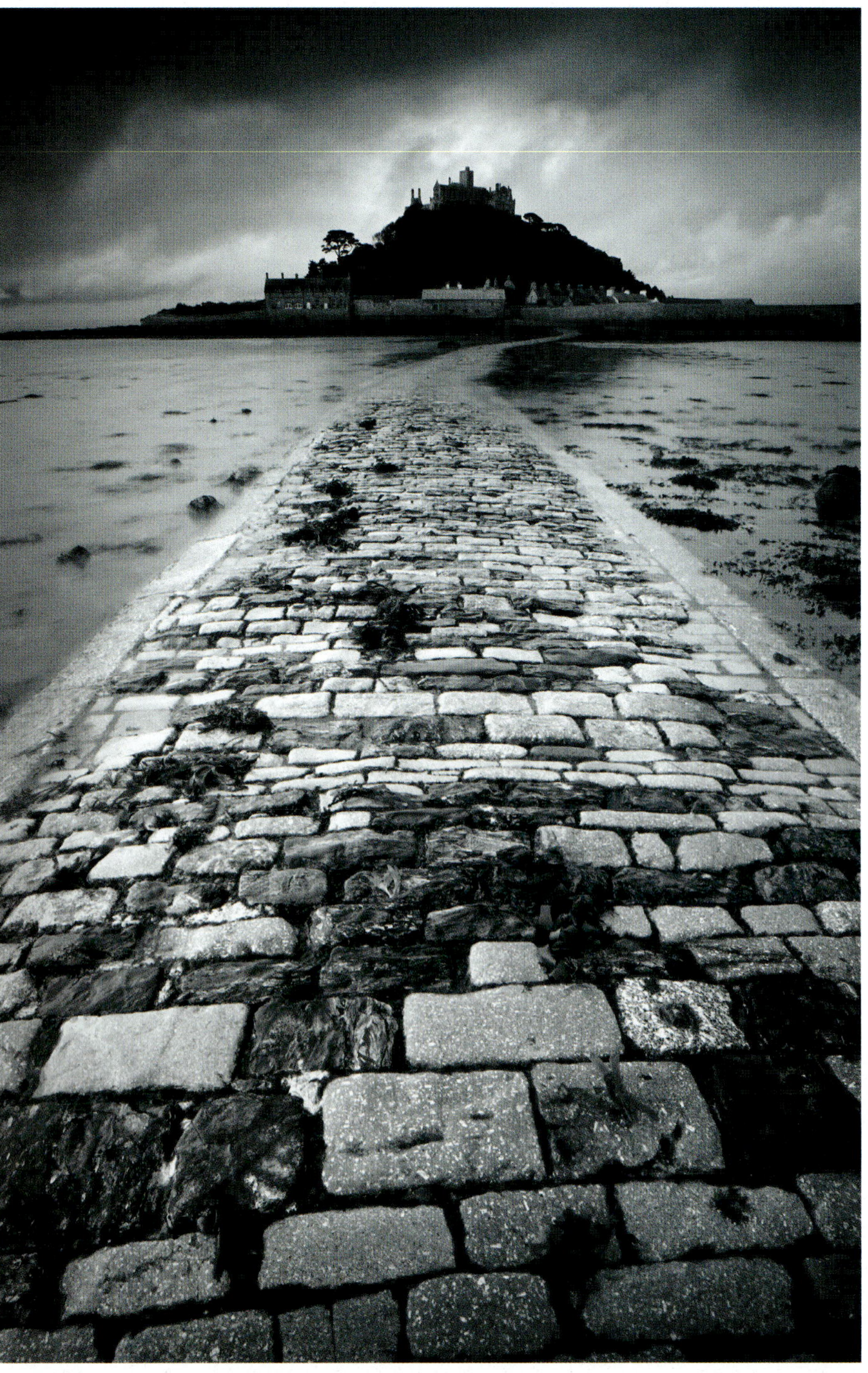

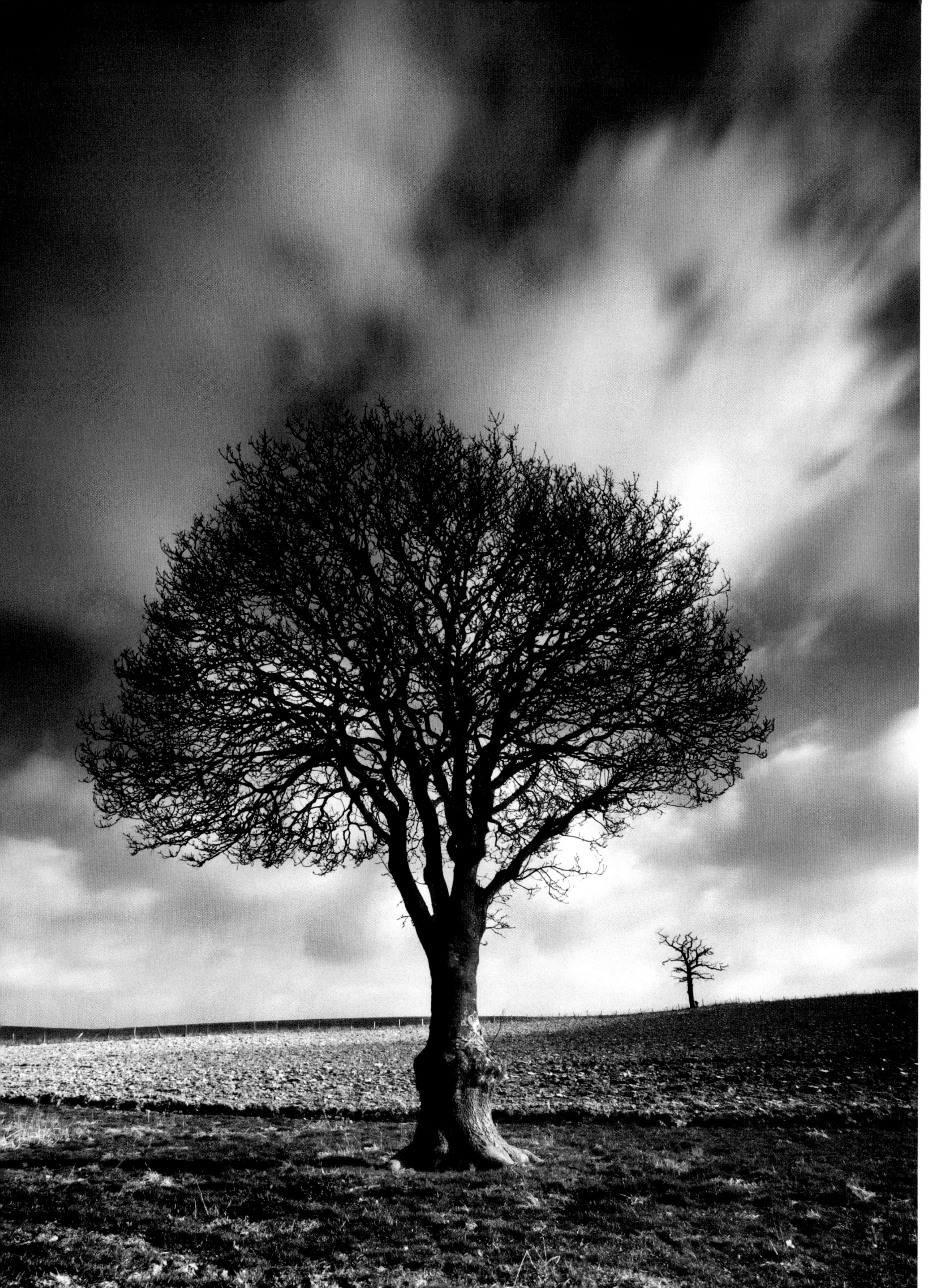

Converting to black & white

One of the wonderful things about digital is that it is easy to convert your colour images to monochrome. There are several ways that you can convert a colour shot into black & white using image manipulation packages like Photoshop. Learning how to convert colour images to black & white is important as you should always shoot in colour, rather than switch your camera to a black & white mode (if it has one). We'd certainly recommend you leave your DSLR set to colour and convert later, rather than set it to its monochrome mode, simply because it's impossible to later convert the monochrome image back to its original colours. With a colour original you have all options covered. Here we cover the four most popular methods to convert colour to black & white and we'd suggest you give each one a try and choose your favourite. In no time at all, you'll be a mono master!

PRO TIPS

ADJUSTABLE LAYERS

Use **Layer>NewAdjustment Layer> Channel Mixer**. It creates a new adjustable layer that can be altered if you change your mind later on. Use this technique for **Curves** and **Levels**, too

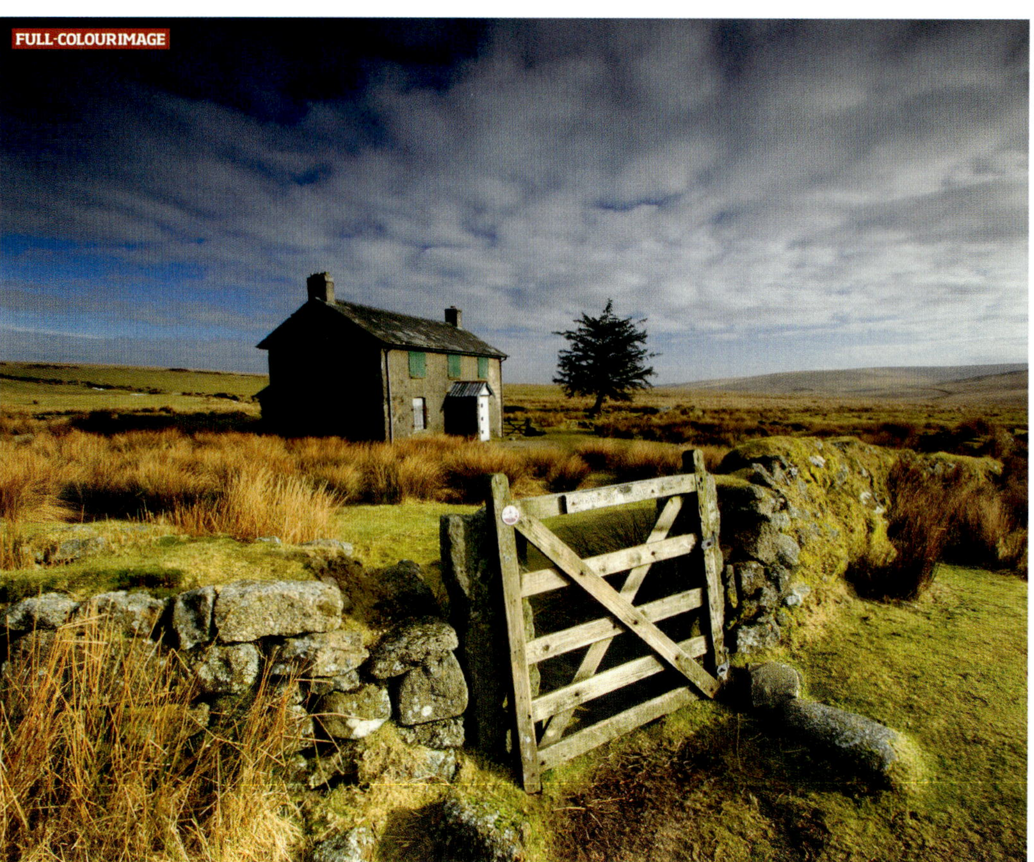

FULL-COLOUR IMAGE

ROSS HODDINOTT

1) Desaturate

This is one of the quickest and easiest routes to convert a colour shot and you've guessed it, the least favourable! Use the shortcut **Cmd/Cntrl+Shift+U** or **Image>Adjust>Desaturate** to remove colour. Alternatively slide the desaturate slider to 0 in the **Hue/Saturation** dialogue box (**Image>Adjustments>Hue/Saturation**).

Looking at the Swatch colour chart, all tones are distinctly muddy – especially yellows, which go more mid-grey than light grey. It can be fine for occasional use but spending a little more time and effort using one of the other methods will yield much better results.

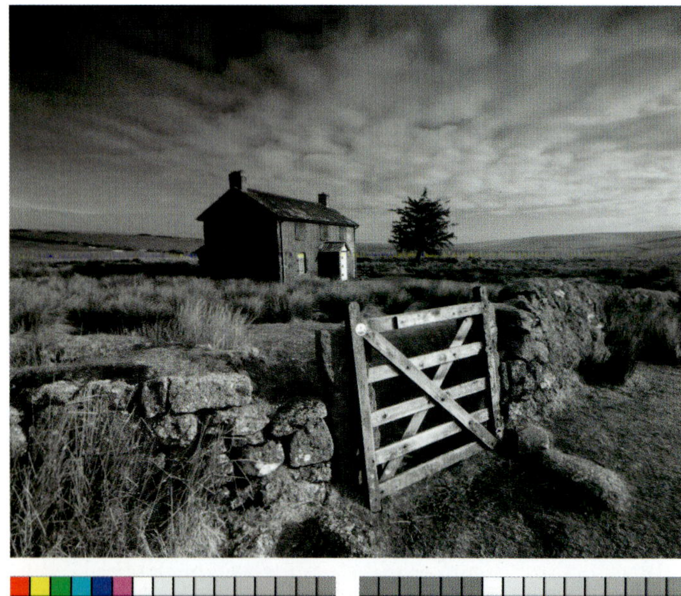

DESATURATION COMPARISON: The Desaturate method is very quick and easy but, as you can see here, it produces a flat b&w image with muddy tones.

2) Greyscale

This is a good starting point for most general shots and we'd recommend using this method most of the time. It's a much better way forward and quickly gives an interesting high contrast black & white image that often needs little extra work doing to it. Go to **Image>Mode>Greyscale** to convert to mono.

You can see that the image looks less muddy and that the blues are a little darker. The tonal separation has created an interesting image. From here you can tweak using **Curves/Levels**, especially if you select areas like skies or backgrounds beforehand.

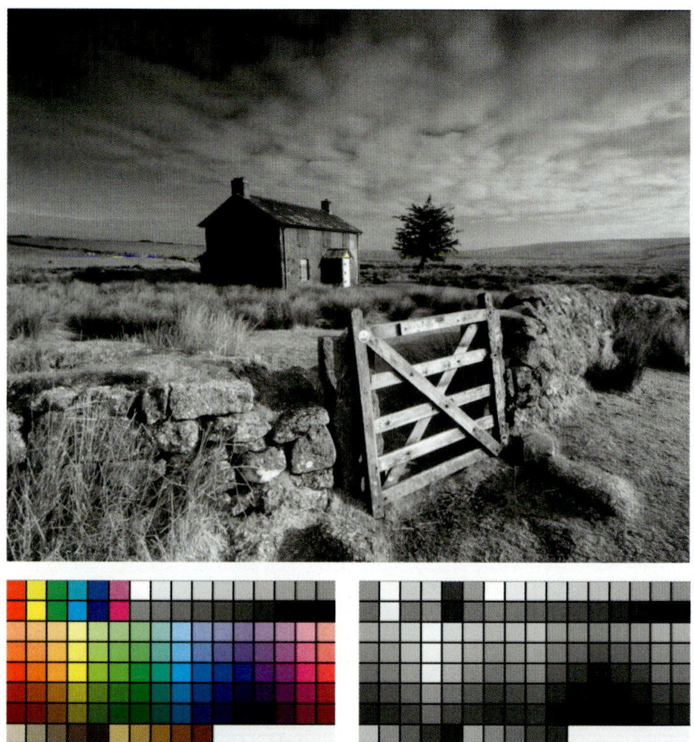

GREYSCALE COMPARISON: Using Greyscale is very easy and usually delivers very good results. Here, there is excellent tonal range and good contrast.

3) RGB channel adjustments

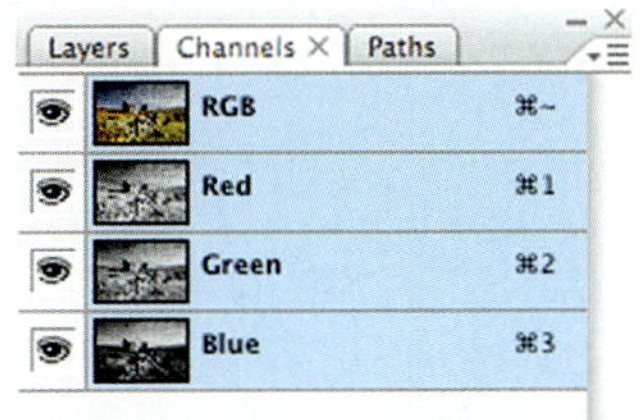

Photoshop uses a Red, Green and Blue channel to create the full spectrum of colours – just like a TV or your camera does.

Open the **Channels** palette and click on one of the colours and it shows the channel in Greyscale. Each one reveals different tones which together create a colour image. This is how colour photography was first created – by shooting on b&w film through consecutive exposures with a red, green and blue filter. You can choose any channel and then go to **Image>Mode>Greyscale** and save it as is. Remember to do a **Save As** and rename the image to preserve the original.

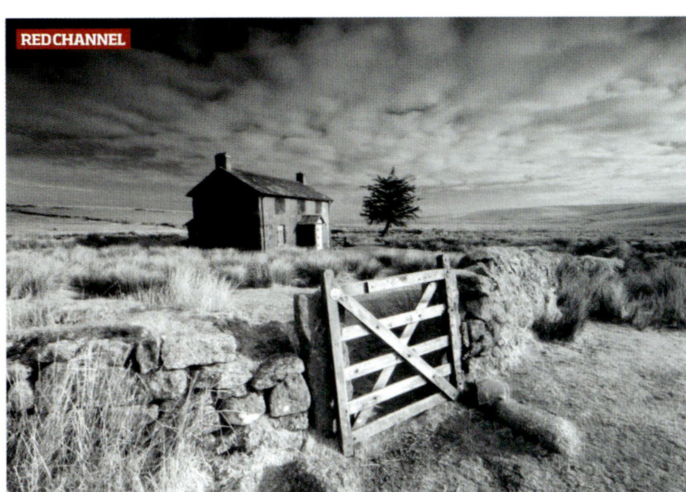

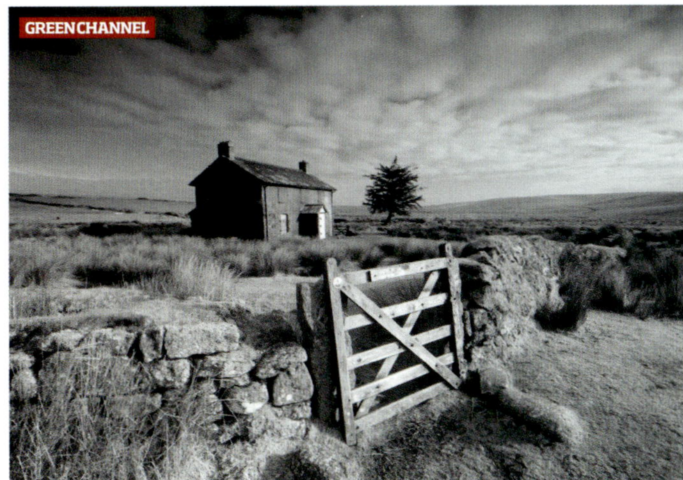

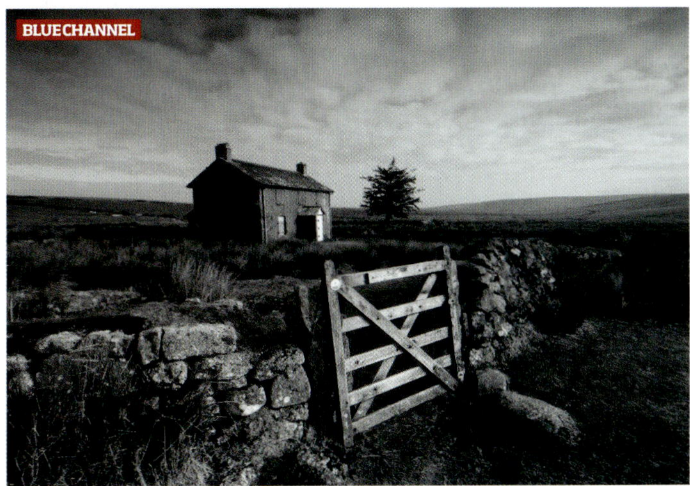

RGB CHANNELS: It's quite amazing to see how the different channels reproduce the various colours. Shoot a test yourself and study the results.

4) Channel Mixer

Channel Mixer is available for Photoshop CS and Paint Shop Pro but not Elements. This is a more complicated version of the previous technique but can yield some very exciting results if you play around with the sliders for a while!

The results are very similar to using a red, green or blue filter in front of your lens and you can mix the sliders to create an orange or yellow filter effect. Go to **Image>Adjust>Channel Mixer** to open the dialogue box. You will have a choice of Red, Green or Blue channels in the **Output Channel** menu. Now tick the **Monochrome** box to convert to mono. The Red channel is a good starting point but check out each before deciding.

You can mix a bit of one channel with another to create new effects. When adjusting the sliders you should aim to keep the combined values of all three sliders to about 100%. For example Red -20%, Green +140% and Blue -20% – some strange effects can be created by ignoring this! The **Constant** slider acts as a general brightness control. Try boosting colours beforehand by increasing saturation using **Hue/Saturation**, this will boost contrast significantly in the black & white version. You can even pick a single colour to boost like Blue from the **Edit** menu if you like.

Levels... ⌘L
Auto Levels ⇧⌘L
Auto Contrast ⌥⇧⌘L
Auto Color ⇧⌘B
Curves... ⌘M
Color Balance... ⌘B
Brightness/Contrast...
Hue/Saturation... ⌘U
Desaturate ⇧⌘U
Match Color...
Replace Color...
Selective Color...
Channel Mixer...
Gradient Map...
Photo Filter...
Shadow/Highlight...
Exposure...
Invert ⌘I
Equalize
Threshold...
Posterize...
Variations...

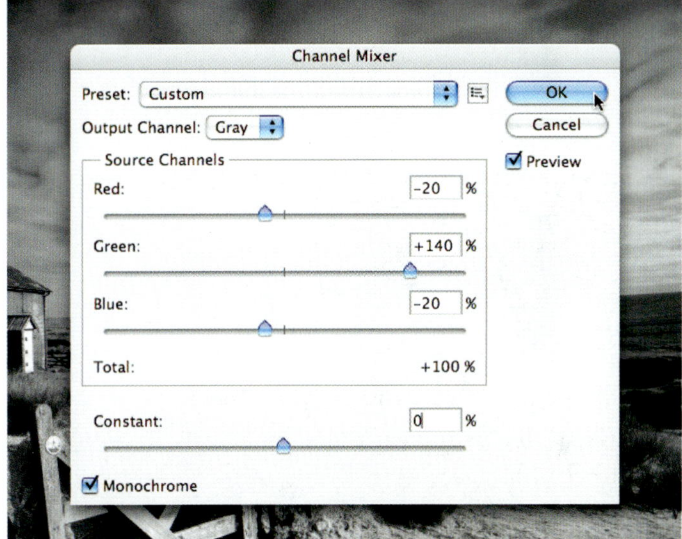

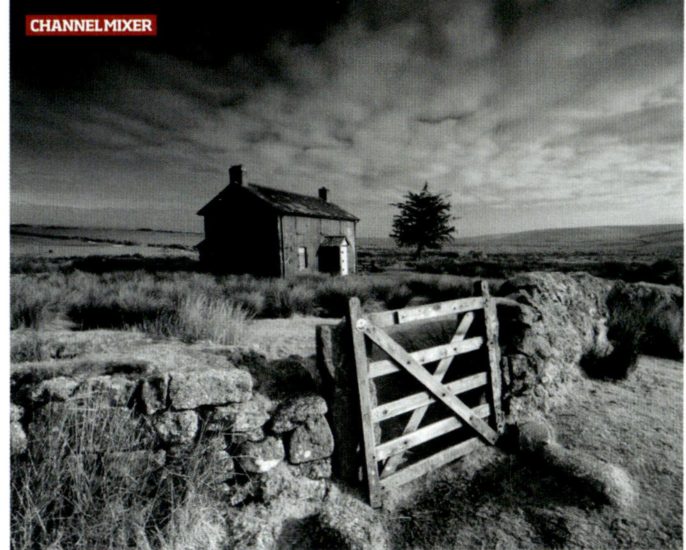

CHANNEL MIXER: The Channel Mixer is the most involved and time-consuming method but your efforts will be rewarded with the best results.

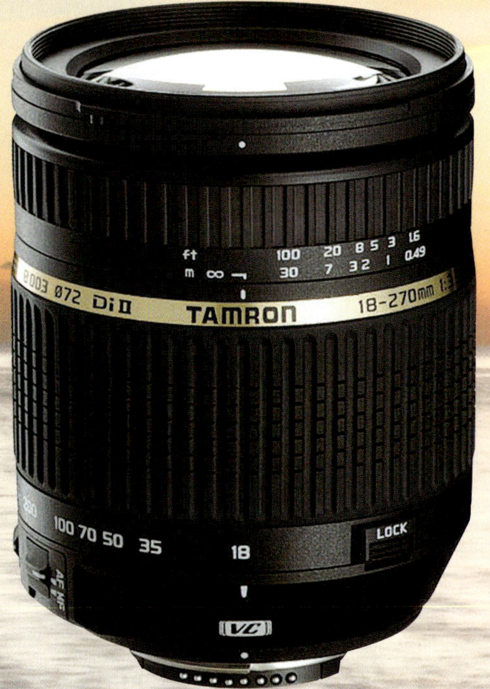

TAMRON 18-270mm f/3.5-6.3 Di II VC LD Aspherical (IF) Macro

SPECIFICATIONS	
Construction:	18 elements in 13 groups
Maximum aperture:	f/3.5-6.3
Mini mum aperture:	f/22
Minimum focus:	49cm
Maximum magnification:	1:3.5
Filter thread:	72mm
Angle of view:	75° 33' to 5° 55'
Diameter x length:	79.6x101mm
Weight:	550g
AF fittings:	Canon EF and Nikon F
Supplied accessory:	Petal-shaped lens hood

Whilst there is no such thing as the perfect 'all-in-one' lens, the Tamron 18-270mm Di II VC Aspherical Macro is surely just about as close as they come. An 'all-in-one' lens is a term used to describe an optic with a versatile zoom range and specification that makes it suited to a wide range of subjects and shooting situations. It is a lens that you will rarely need – or want – to remove from your digital SLR!

The Tamron 18-270mm is the world's first lens to deliver a zoom ratio of 15x. Covering wide-angle to telephoto, its zoom range is equivalent to approximately 28-419mm when attached to a digital SLR with a cropped-type sensor. This lens allows photographers to quickly adapt to the subject or situation, proving the essential difference between success and failure in many instances.

Its versatility is its greatest appeal. At the Tamron's short end, it is possible to shoot wide-angle landscapes, interiors and urban scenes bursting with life and depth. At its long end, photographers can capture telephoto images of distant subjects like wildlife, sports and action. Using the mid focal range of the lens, you can shoot flattering portraits or isolate interesting texture or detail from within the landscape – urban or rural. It also boasts a minimum focusing distance of 0.49m over its entire zoom range – impressively close for a zoom of this power. With a maximum magnification of 1:3.5, it is possible to shoot frame filling close-ups using the Tamron.

Zooming in or out can radically alter your composition or the look and feel of the final image. For example, the short end of the 18-270mm is ideally suited for showing your subject in context with its surroundings, or for creating a feeling of space or solitude. In contrast, its long end is perfect for frame-filling shots, full of energy and life. Thanks to this versatile zoom, you don't have to waste time physically changing lens when you require a longer or shorter focal length – helping ensure you rarely miss a good photo opportunity.

Sharp, shake-free images are essential, but it isn't always practical to carry a support – particularly if you are traveling, or walking long distances. A tripod can also be restrictive, impeding creativity and spontaneity. Shooting handheld is often the only practical option, but camera shake is a risk at slower shutter speeds. Thankfully, the Tamron 18-270mm is equipped with a highly effective Vibration Compensation (VC) mechanism. Its tri-axial anti-shake system helps ensure sharp, handheld images – even at its longest telephoto setting.

Despite its impressive focal range and technology, this lens is compact and lightweight and its handling is intuitive. It zips quickly and quietly into focus when using AF. This is a lens suited to practically any subject or situation. You are sure to be impressed with the quality and versatility of the Tamron 18-270mm.

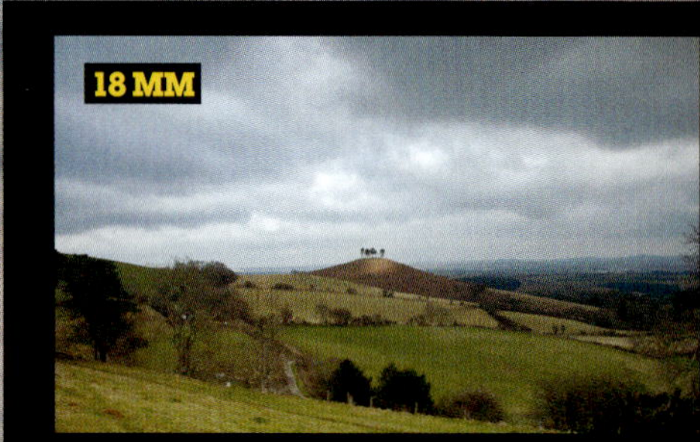
18 MM

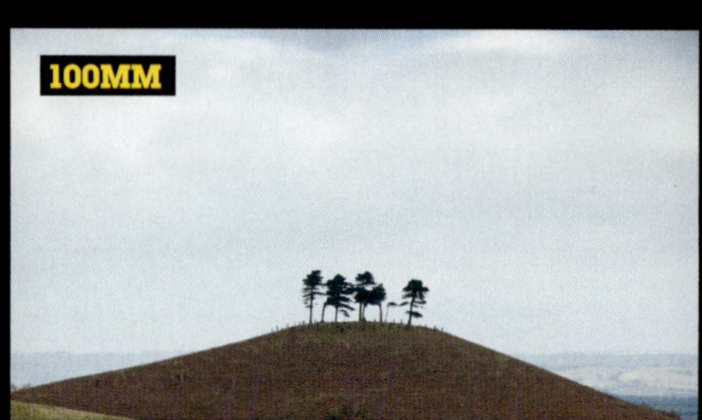
100MM

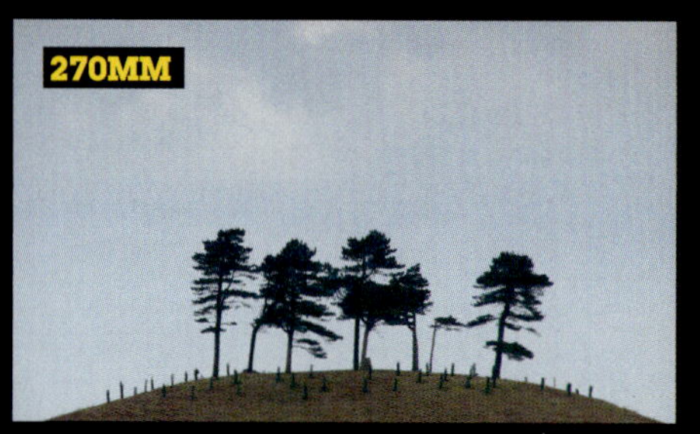
270MM

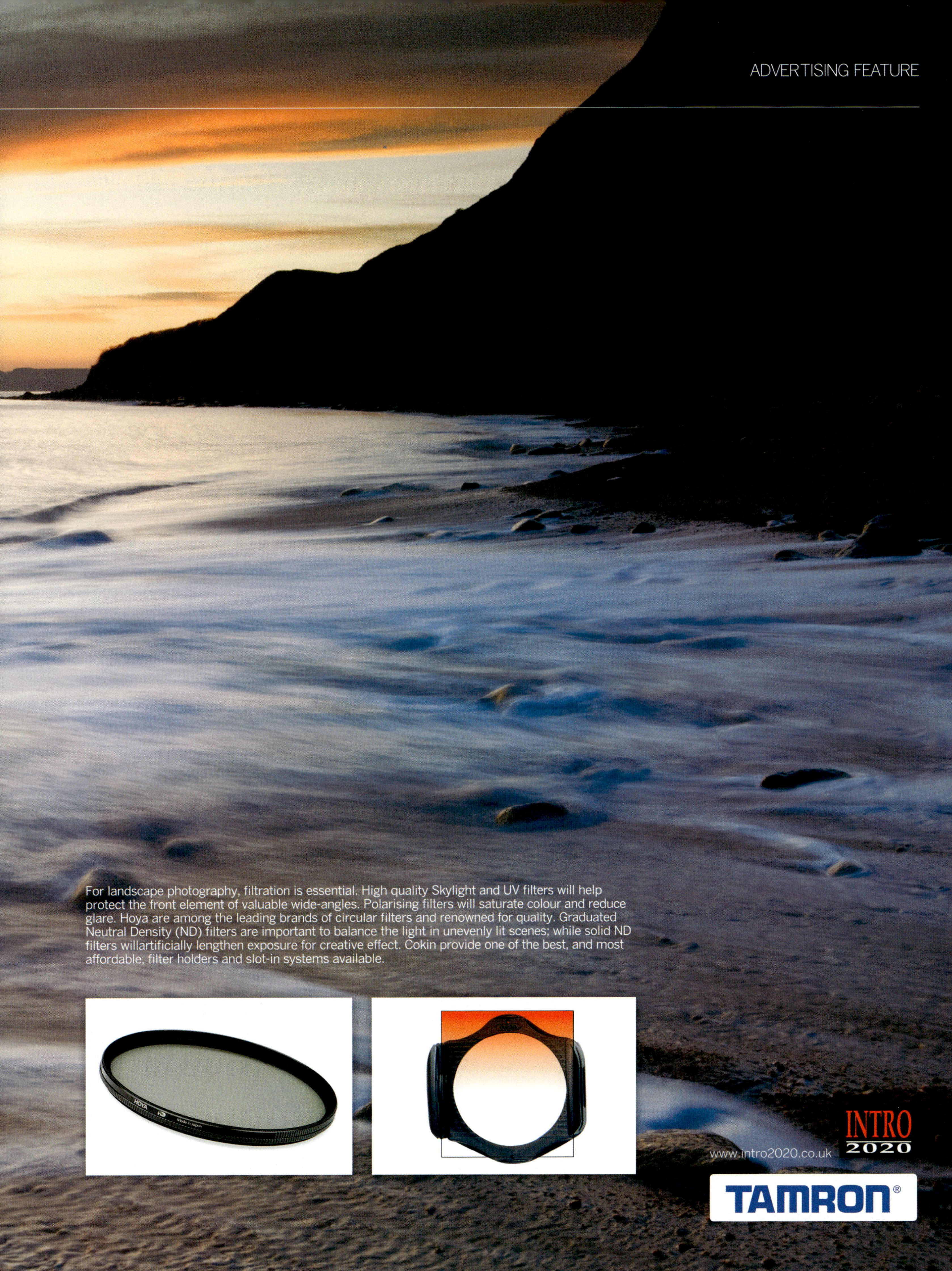
For landscape photography, filtration is essential. High quality Skylight and UV filters will help protect the front element of valuable wide-angles. Polarising filters will saturate colour and reduce glare. Hoya are among the leading brands of circular filters and renowned for quality. Graduated Neutral Density (ND) filters are important to balance the light in unevenly lit scenes; while solid ND filters willartificially lengthen exposure for creative effect. Cokin provide one of the best, and most affordable, filter holders and slot-in systems available.
HOYA
INTRO
2020
www.intro2020.co.uk
TAMRON®

Expert Gems

SEASONAL LANDSCAPES

LANDSCAPES TAKE ON completely different colours and characteristics depending on the season, so make sure to visit your favourite locations at different times of the year.

Winter is many landscape photographers' favourite time of year. The bare trees mean that the texture of the land itself is fully revealed by the low, raking sun that characterises this time of year. The winter air is clear, and the sun is low enough in the sky to make all-day shooting a possibility. Keep an eye on the weather conditions – a heavy frost or, if you're really lucky, a hoar frost, can create a fairy-tale scene. Take care with metering – the light tones and reflective nature of a frosty landscape can fool the camera's meter into underexposure. Snow looks its best under a blue sky, which can be enhanced with a polarising filter.

Spring is characterised by freshness and an abundance of flowers like daffodils, tulips and bluebells. Spring is also the time for showery weather, which experienced landscape photographers love, as the light immediately after a shower passes is often very dramatic, with the sun bursting through and dark, threatening clouds still in the sky.

Summer is the least favourite season for many landscape photographers. For much of the day, the sun is too high in the sky to provide any textural relief on the scene, the land itself is often obscured by dense foliage and there is a lot of dust and haze in the air. However, all is not lost, and there are shots to be found.

Although there is less variety of flowers than in spring, those that are around have plenty of colour – poppies and sunflowers, for example, or the heather that starts to appear at the end of summer; the time when straw and hay bales start appearing in fields. These make great subjects, especially as they have become one of the great symbols of the British summer.

Autumn is a dream season to shoot. The sun is relatively low in the sky for much of the day, so you can be out taking pictures for hours. The colours are fantastic, so fill the frame with autumnal oranges, reds and yellows. In early autumn, a clear sky and a cold night will often result in early morning mist-filled valleys, rivers and lakes as the sun appears. Mist can look effective if you shoot into the sun but take care to avoid underexposure by setting +1 exposure compensation.

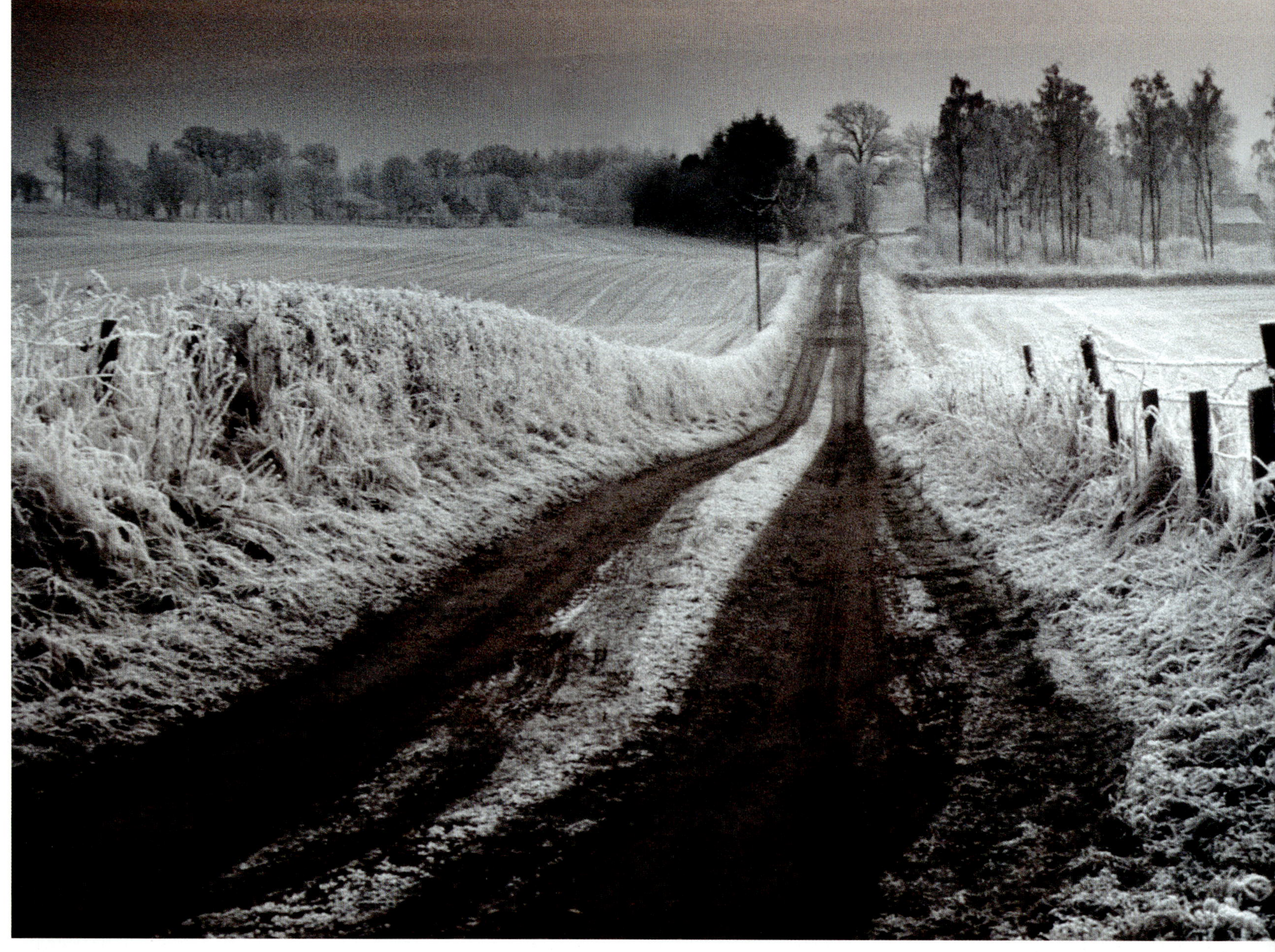

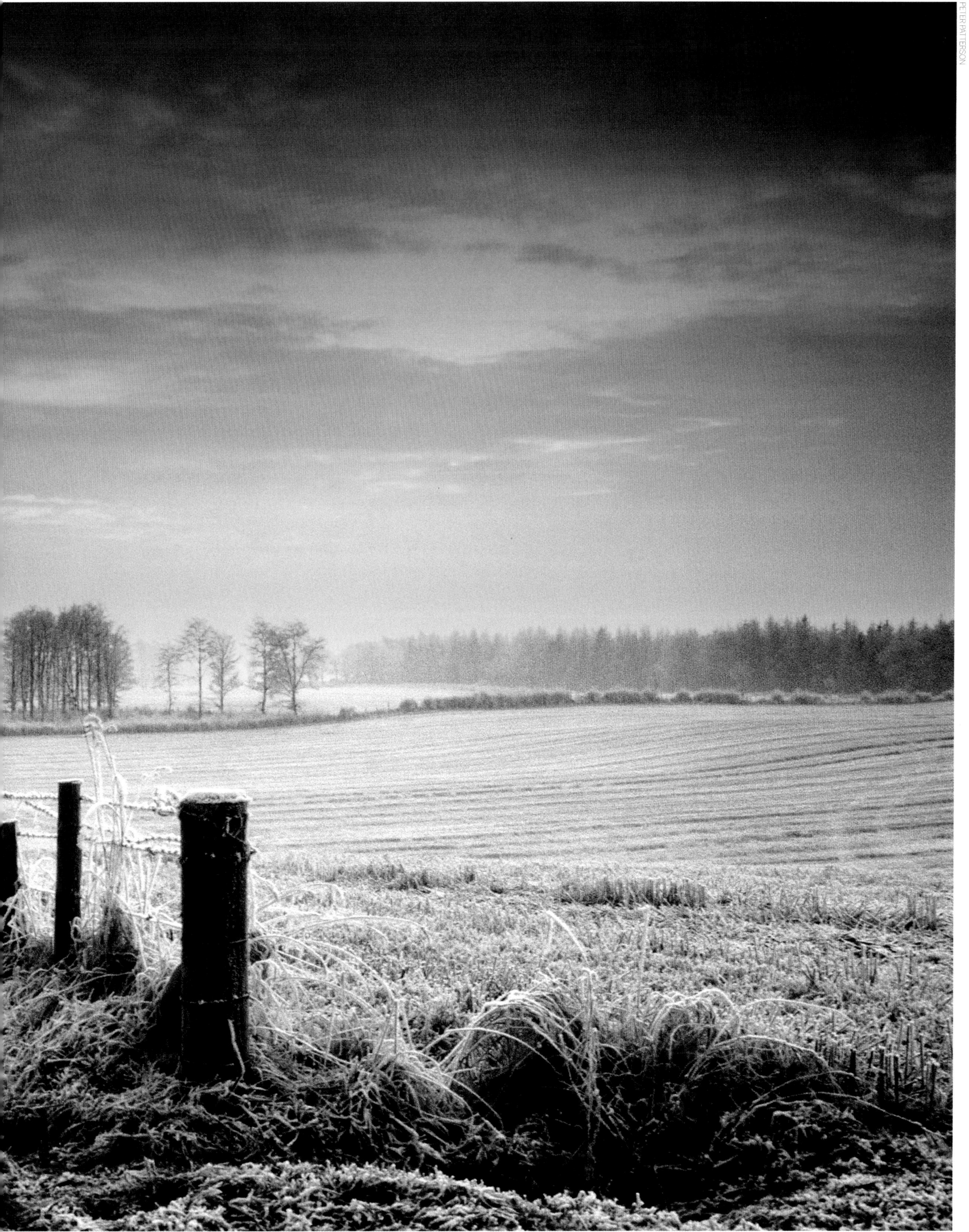

PETER PATTERSON

1) Winter wonderland

A layer of frost adds an instant magical atmosphere to your landscape pictures. You'll find a wide-angle lens will allow you to fill the frame with the magic of a winter wonderland. The cold weather usually brings a clear blue sky, which complements the crisp, frozen landscape and the pastel colours that can be seen in fields and woodland. Go in low and close with a wide-angle lens and remember to include interest in the foreground.

2) Frozen waterfalls

Partially-frozen waterfalls can make stunning abstract shots. Use a long lens to get close to the base of the fall. Most winter water shots are either flowing water or ice, so include both to add some contrast. A long exposure will soften the water, and create a stark division between the static ice and flowing water.

3) Low-lying sun

This kind of image is worth getting up early for. You can capture a similar image at sunset, but you won't have the added appeal of frost. Polarisers perform well on sunny winter days, mainly because the sun remains relatively low in the sky all day long during winter. As well as deepening blue sky it also takes glare off snow. To get the best results, rotate it slowly while looking through the viewfinder. When using wide-angles, take care not to get unevenly polarised skies.

4) Winter sunsets

Although winter light can be harsh, especially in strong sunshine, winter sunsets can be some of the most spectacular of the year. They tend to be very brief, so make sure that you get to your location early, leaving yourself plenty of time to set up and prepare for your shot.

5) A touch of frost

The best time to take winter scenics is without doubt shortly after sunrise when the landscape is covered with a coating of frost. If you're willing to wake up early and head into the great outdoors, you could be blessed with a view like this.

ESSENTIALS

Winter clothing

The best method of staying warm and dry is to wear lightweight layers – thermals, followed by a long-sleeved shirt, a lightweight fleece top, a heavier fleece and finally a decent wind/waterproof jacket. Avoid jeans and instead wear cotton trousers. Hat and gloves are a must and sturdy walking boots to keep your feet warm and dry. In long grass, wear waterproof leggings or gaiters.

See page 121 for more clothing advice

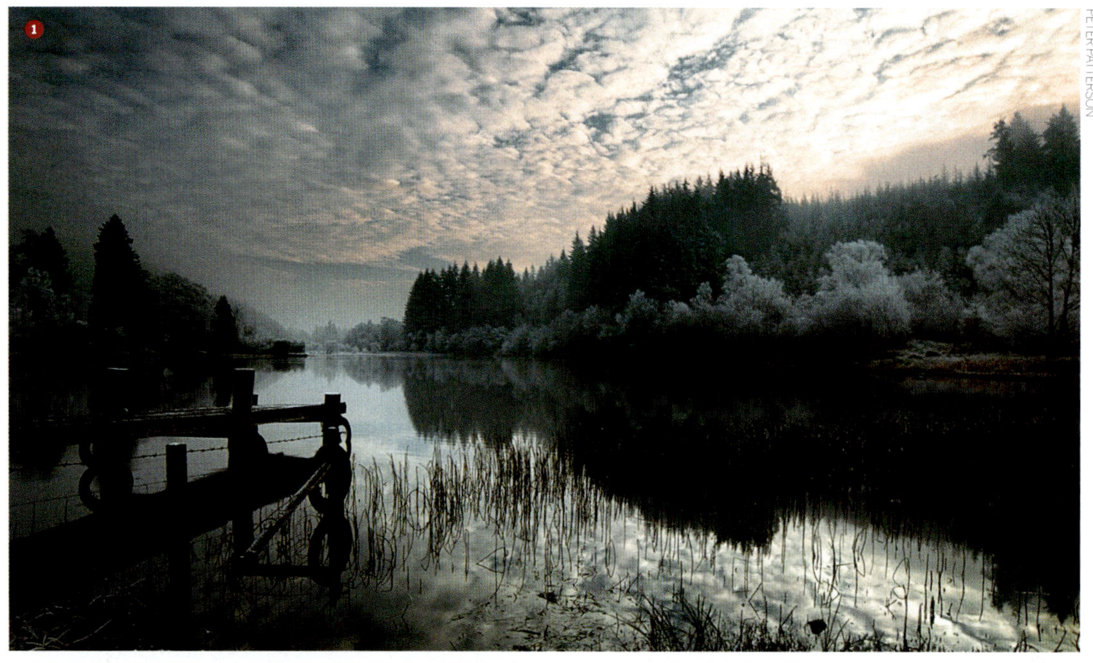
1

PETER PATTERSON

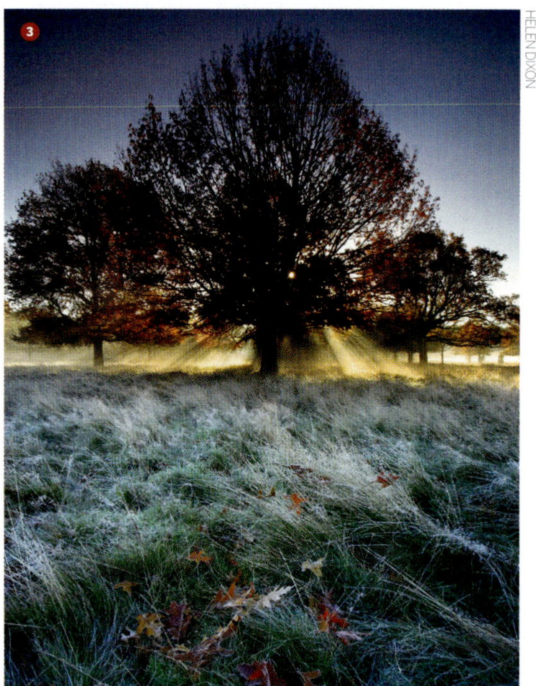
3

HELEN DIXON

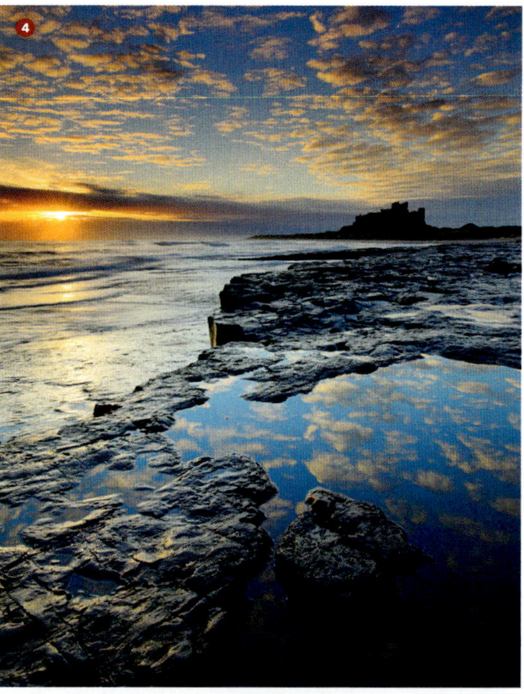
4

ADAM BURTON

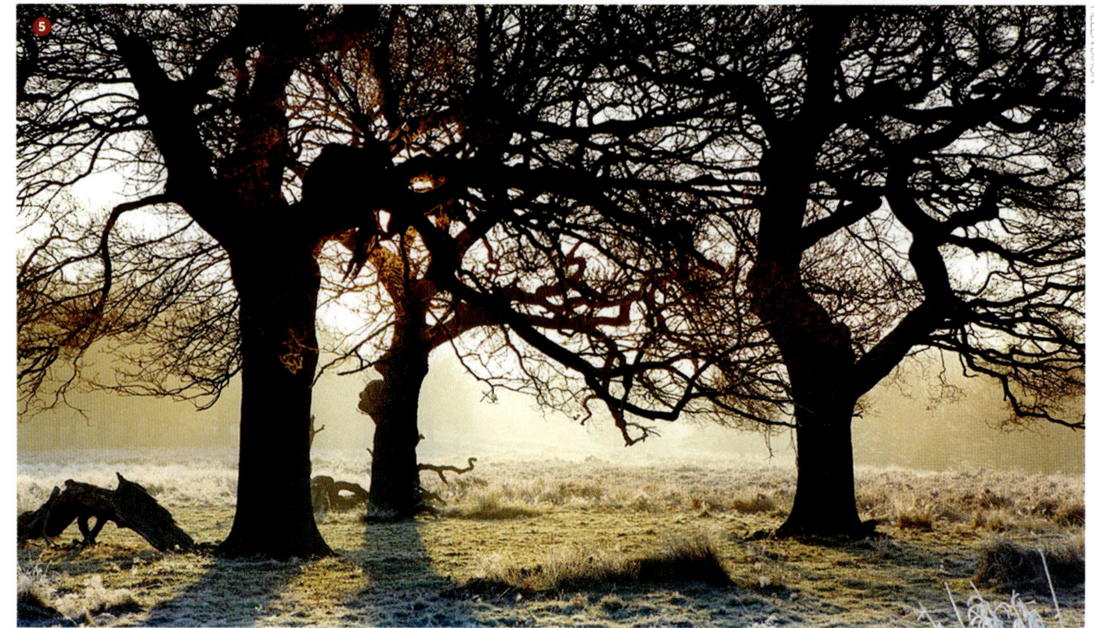
5

HELEN DIXON

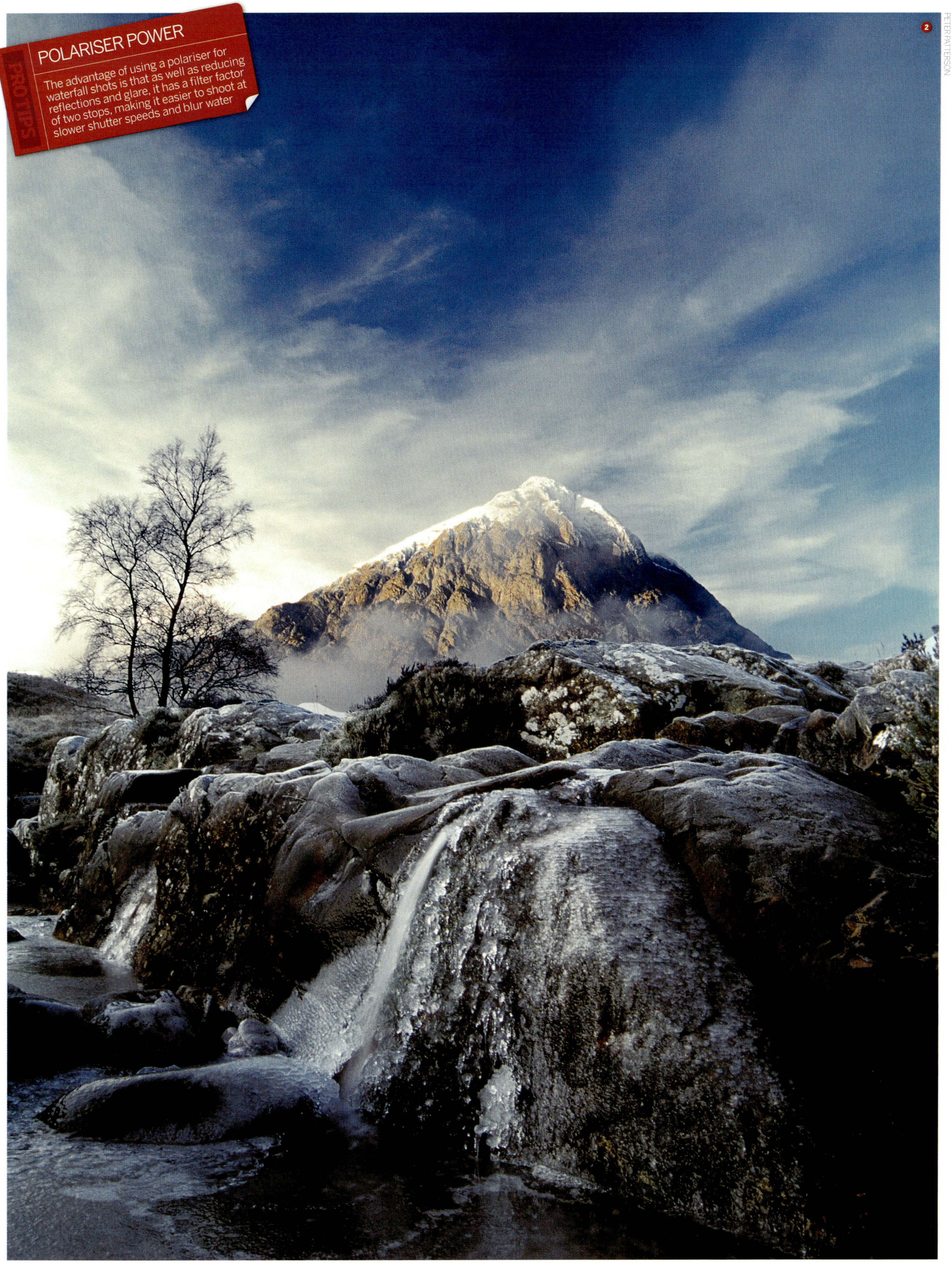

PRO TIPS

POLARISER POWER

The advantage of using a polariser for waterfall shots is that as well as reducing reflections and glare, it has a filter factor of two stops, making it easier to shoot at slower shutter speeds and blur water

2

PETER PATTERSON

1) Spring flowers

Go in low and close with a wide-angle lens to get maximum impact from flowers as foreground interest. Make sure the flowers are in good condition, once petals start to wither and dis-colour, you've missed your chance. Pin-sharp flowers tend to work best, so try to shoot when they are perfectly still. Experiment with moving flowers and slow shutter speeds too, but make the blur effect really obvious.

2) Chasing rainbows

There is no time like spring for shooting rainbows. When you see dark rainclouds hovering above brightly lit landscapes, there's a good chance that you'll also see a rainbow. Bracket your shots to give you the best chance of capturing the bands of colour at their best. You could combine these later in Photoshop to create an image with an extended range, which will allow you a greater degree of control over the details, colours and textures of the final image. Finally, a polarising filter will add contrast to the scene, as well as saturating the colours.

3) Bluebell woods

One of Britain's most popular flowers, bluebells usually flower from early April until the end of May. They are predominantly found in the west of Britain, usually in or around woodland, but can also be found near heath, sea cliffs and even mountain tops.

When you're deep in the woods, shooting with the sun in front of you can create stunning lighting effects, as it allows you to capture the beams of sunlight penetrating the canopy above, projecting rays of light into the image.

4) April showers

Lots of spring showers offers you the chance to capture scenes packed with moody storm clouds, although you will probably find yourself waiting for breaks between the showers. It can be quite tricky to get the exposure right if there is a dark sky with a bright foreground. A weak Neutral Density graduated filter can help even out the exposure across the frame and add mood. We recommend you try a 0.3ND or 0.6ND Graduate filter.

ESSENTIALS

Tripod: Serious landscape photographers don't set out without a tripod. This will help you with composition, to keep the horizon level and to reduce the risk of unwanted shake, which could ruin your shots. They're also useful if you want to try one of our creative techniques.

Polarising filter: Polarising filters are ideal for enhancing detail and saturating colours. For the best results, shoot at 90° to the sun. Make sure you buy a circular and not linear polariser.

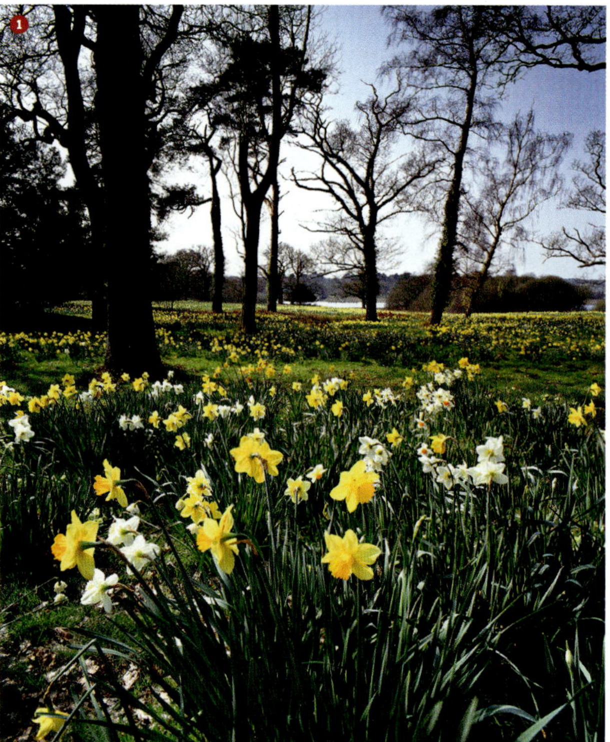

MARK BAUER

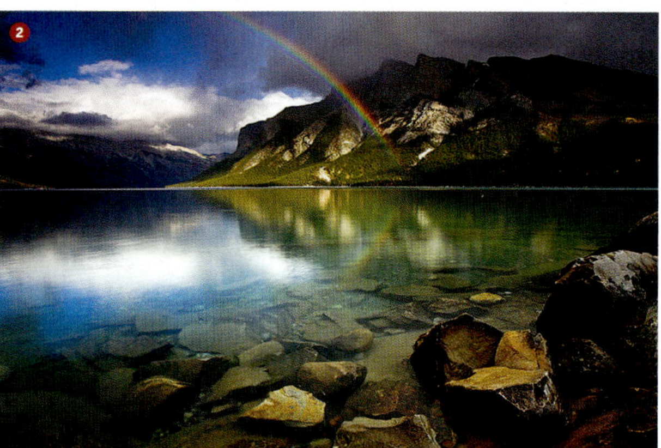

ADAM BURTON

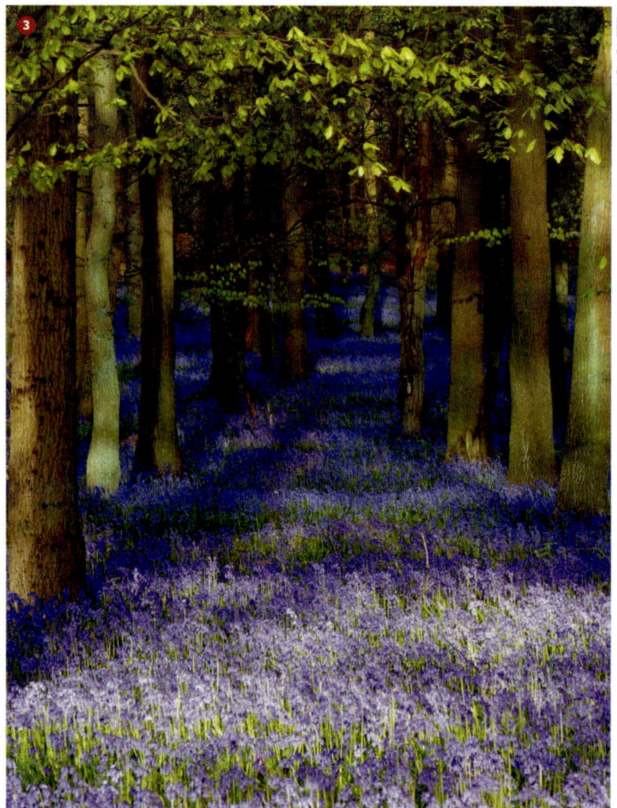

HELEN DIXON

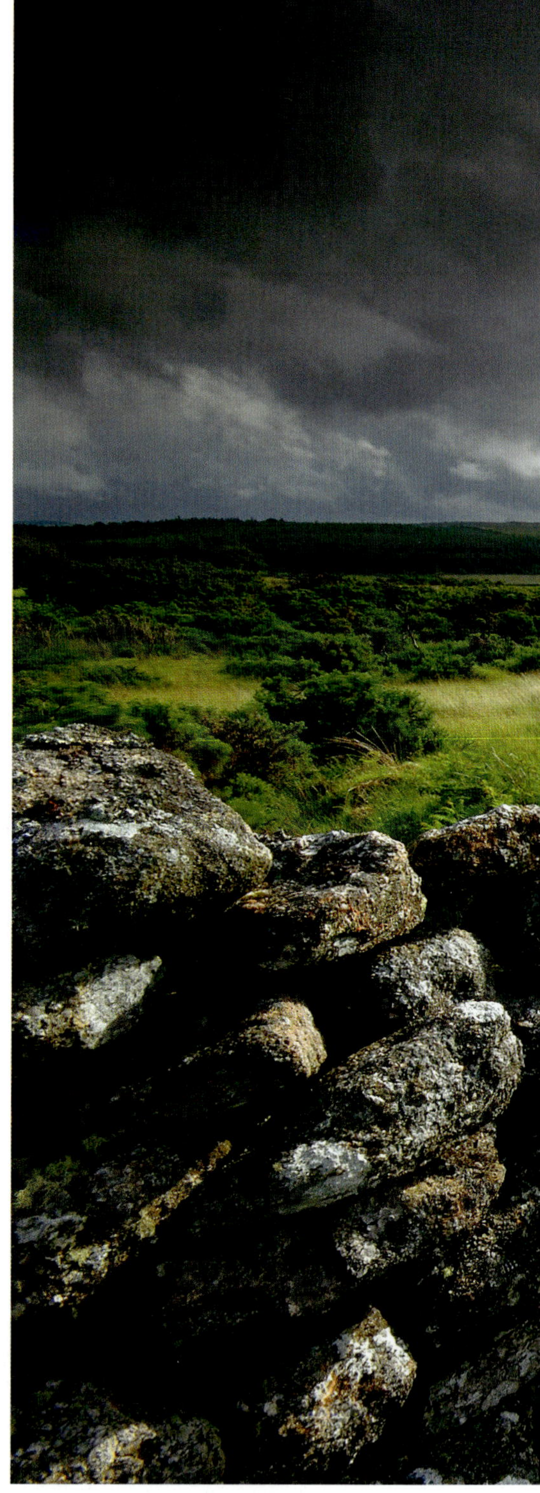

5) In-camera effects

ZOOM BURST With your camera on a tripod, set a low ISO rating (eg ISO 100) and a shutter speed of around 1/6sec. Fire the shutter and during the exposure zoom in from the widest setting. Zoom evenly over the exposure time, to reduce the risk of a jagged zoom burst. Experiment with shutter speeds to vary the results.

MOTION BLUR This technique works really well with bluebells, and the effect is reminiscent of an impressionist watercolour. To achieve this, mount your DSLR on a tripod with a tilt head. Set an exposure of around one to two seconds and a low ISO rating. Use a remote release (or self-timer) to fire the shutter, and smoothly tilt the tripod head down throughout the exposure.

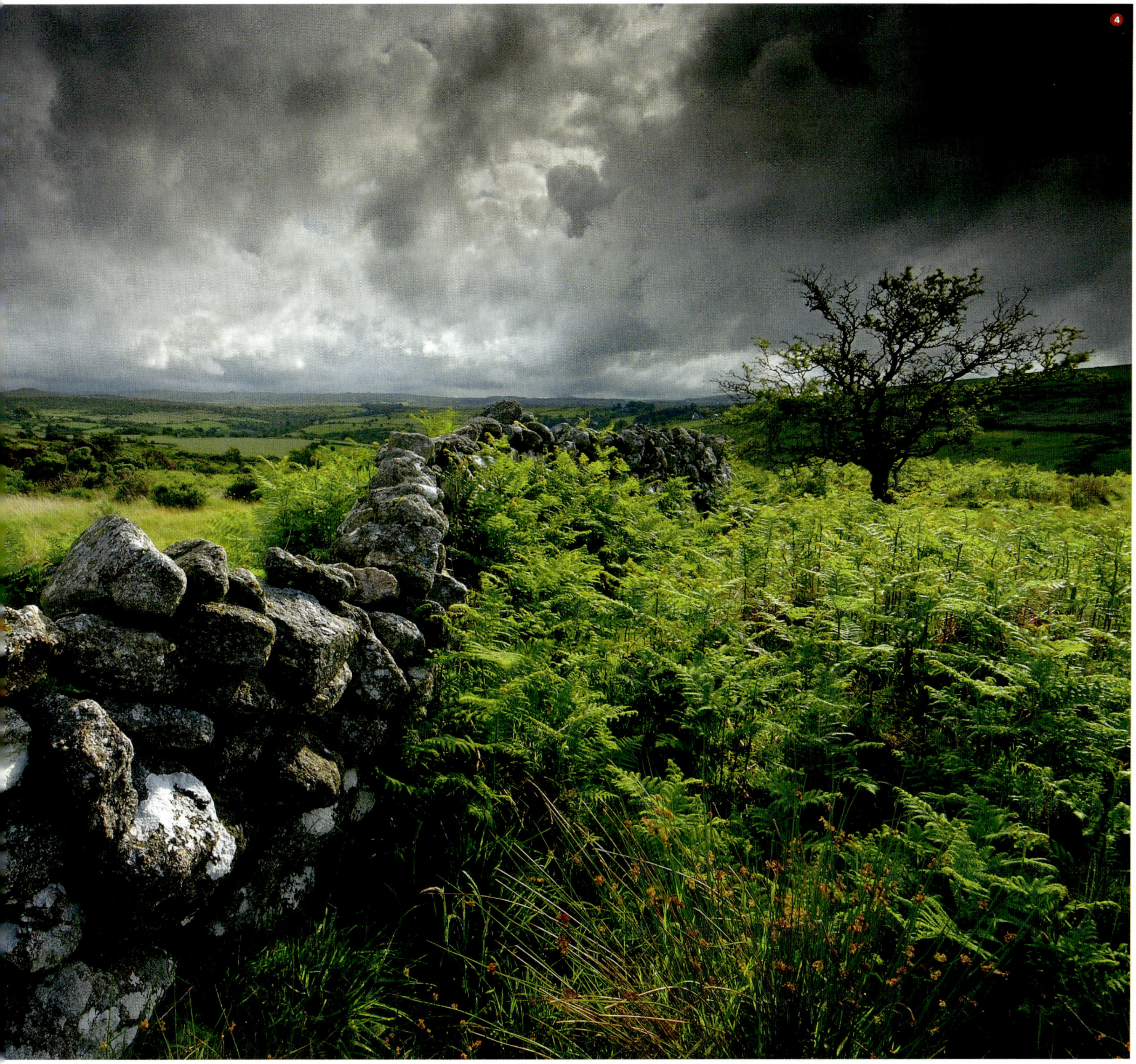

4

ROSS HODDINOTT

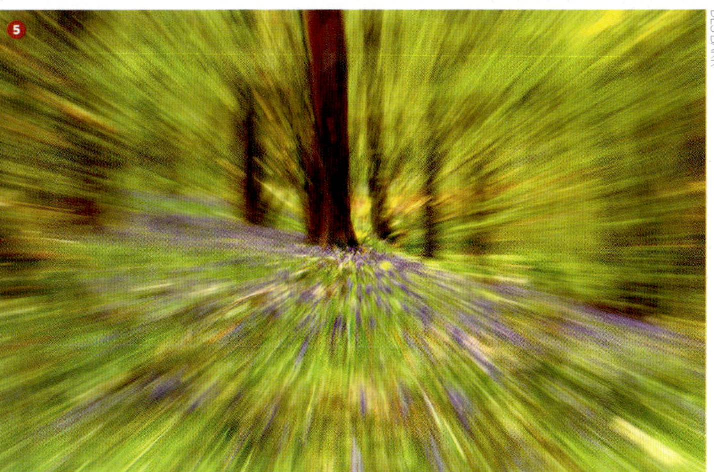

5

DES BARR

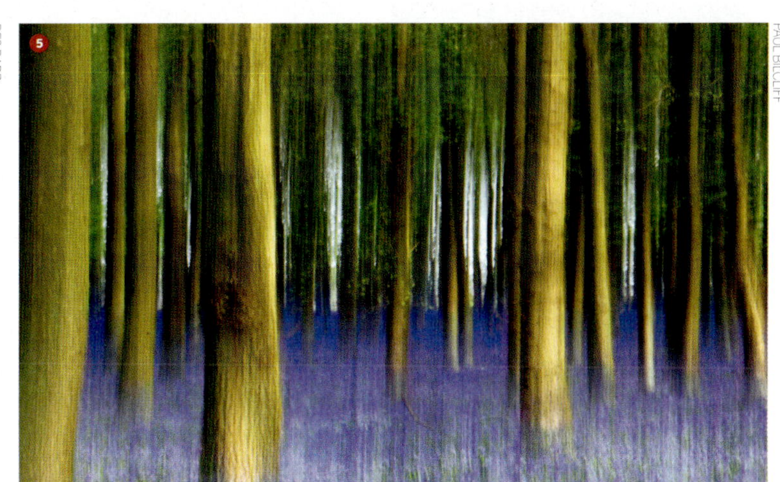

5

PAUL BILCLIFF

1) Blue skies of summer

We've written it before and you'll certainly read it again, nothing deepens a blue sky better than a polariser. But don't overdo it. On a bright day with good light on the foreground, a slightly underexposed (i.e dark) blue sky can pack plenty of punch. Pure blue skies tend to disappear by mid-morning.

2) Seaside sunsets

First of all, if you are visiting the east coast, make that sun*rises*. There are rare coastal areas that loop back on themselves (Hunstanton in Norfolk enjoys sunsets across The Wash) but make sure you head to your location at the right time! Halos around clouds make the very best sunrises and sunsets. Check the exposure via the histogram to ensure you get it right.

3) Evening moods

Evening light stretches very late in summer. The sun hits the horizon at an oblique angle and there is a long afterglow that will produce stunning landscapes long after sunset. Long exposures will capture this soft dreamy time allowing clouds to paint their progress across the sky, emphasising the mood.

4) Fields of dreams

Take a break from the ubiquitous rape fields and their powerful yellow energy and find out what else is growing in the area you're photographing. Lavender fields are appearing across the country, thanks to the plant's essential oils, said to aid sleep. Keep awake to the possibility of trespassing and don't be tempted to pick the flowers. In late summer, shoot wheat fields in morning or evening light.

5) Bold colours

Let's shake you out of your lavender-induced reverie and smack you between the eyes with strong colours at lunchtime. We just mentioned the yellow rape field under clear blue sky cliché, but it's still a great shot. These poppies look stunning, contrasting with the green. This shot can work even when the sun is high and the thin cloud softens the light like a great big studio softbox.

ESSENTIALS

UV or skylight filter: Although we would always recommend fitting a clear filter to your lens to protect the front element, it's during the summer months that these protective filters will make most difference to your photographs. The ultraviolet filter and the skylight filter both help to remove the haze from summer landscapes. Some film photographers used to fit a gentle warm-up filter to deal with the cool blue cast in shadows on sunny days, but digital technology has made this unneccessary.
See page 57 for more filter advice

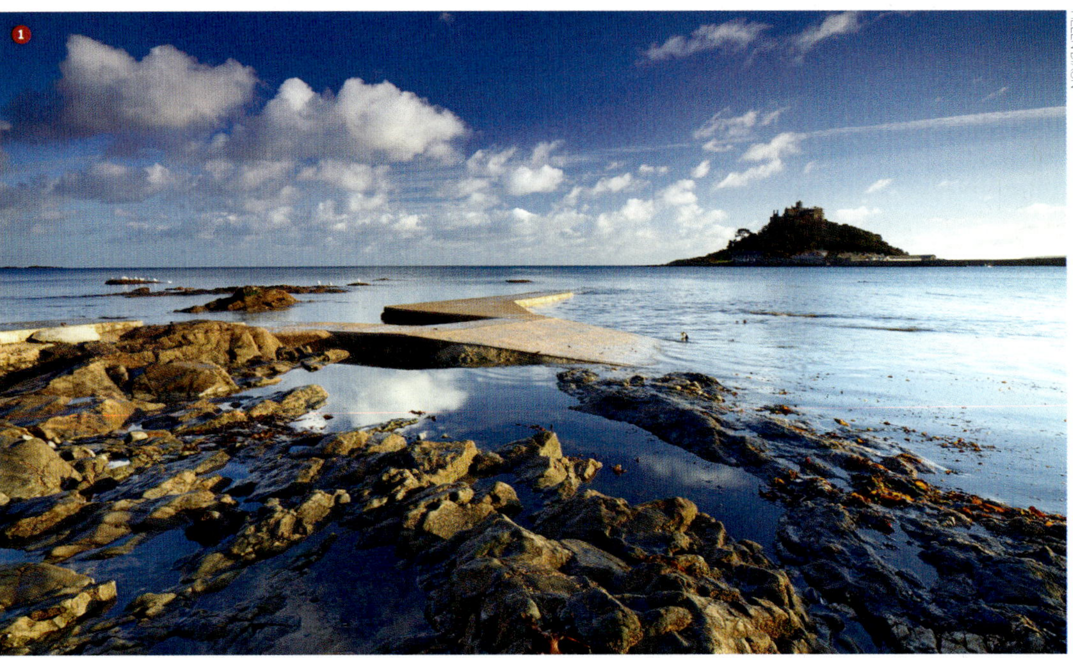
1 HELEN DIXON

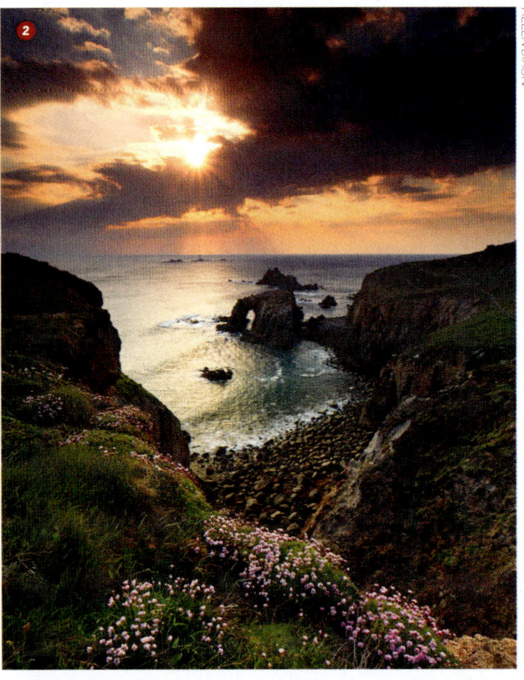
2 HELEN DIXON

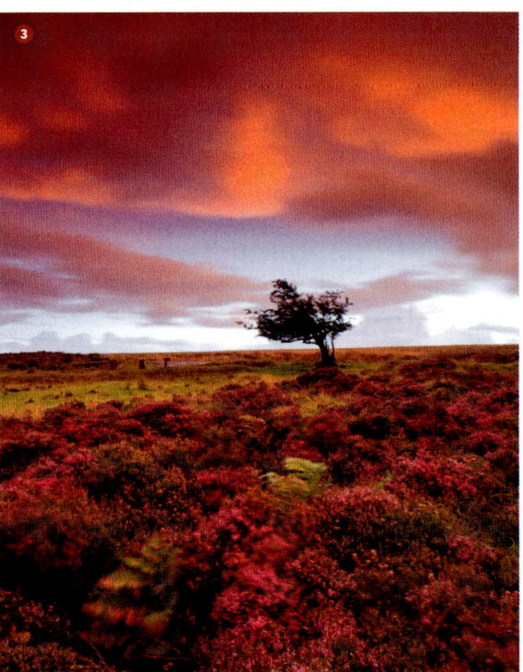
3 ADAM BURTON

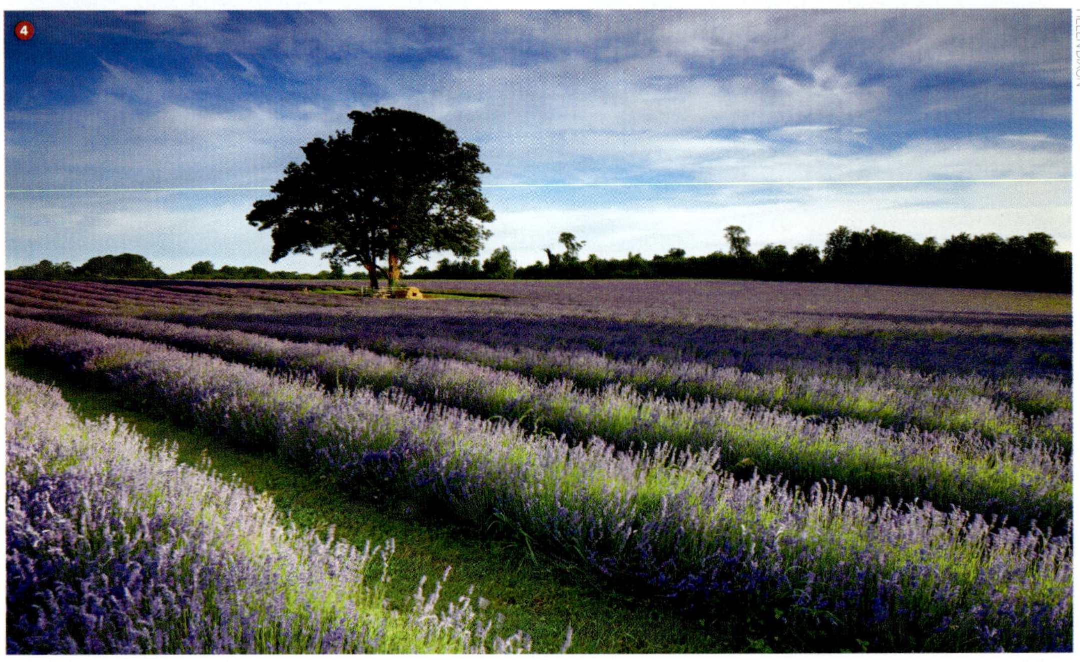
4 HELEN DIXON

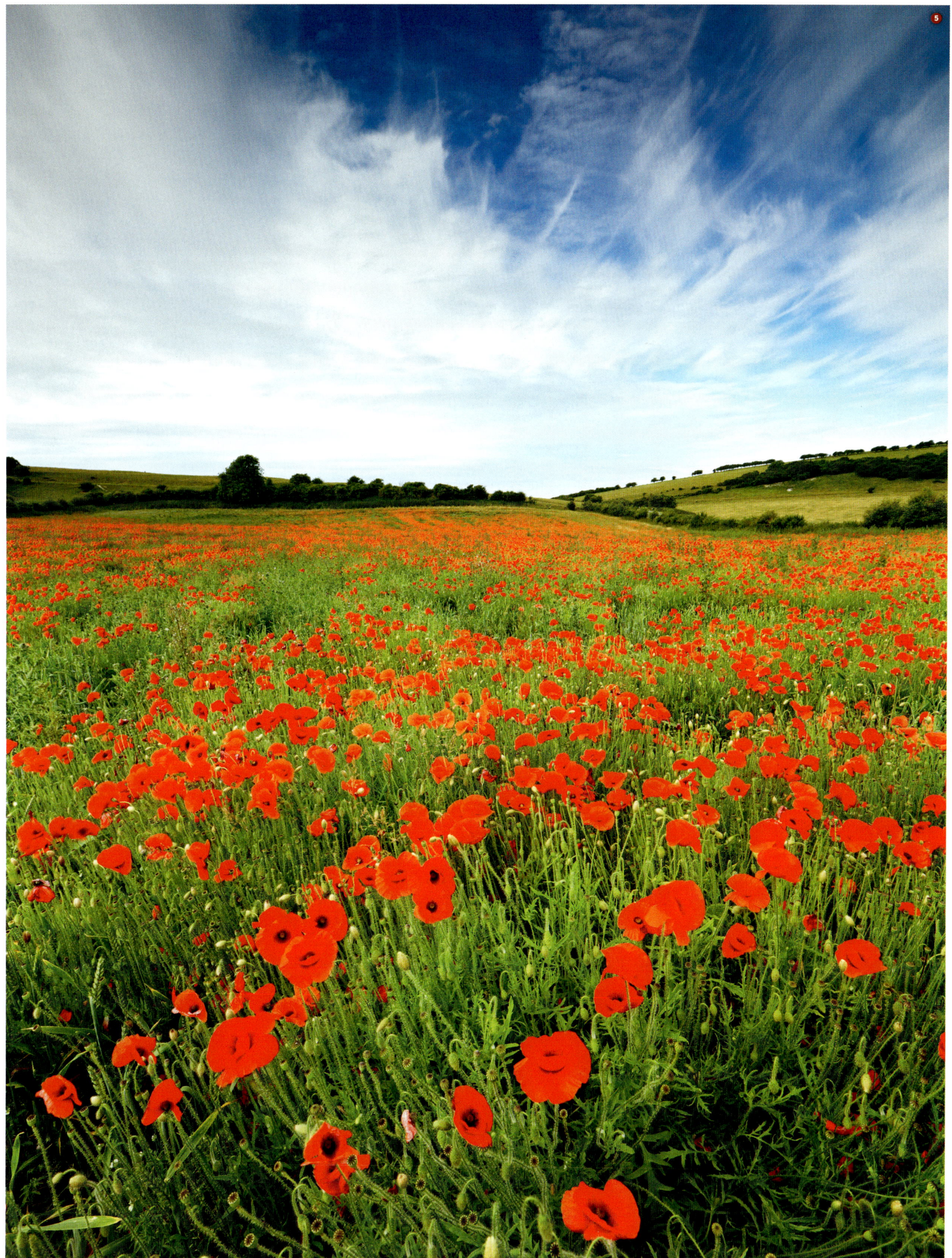

HELEN DIXON

1) Misty mornings

Autumn is a great season for shooting misty scenes, and some areas, such as parts of the New Forest, seem to act as 'mist traps', so head out in the early morning to see what the dawn light reveals. Using the long end of a 24-105mm zoom lens, this composition is based around the overlapping shapes of the hills rising out of the mist. A 0.6ND graduated filter helped keep detail in the sky, and a tripod kept everything steady.

2) Nature's mirror

Use reflections in areas of still water such as ponds and lakes to accentuate the season's golden colours. A beautiful display of colour is emphasised by the late afternoon sunshine in this image, taken beside a small brook in the New Forest. An ND graduate filter was positioned over the upper half of the image, to achieve a balanced exposure over the whole picture. After converting the Raw image to a TIFF file, the picture was tone-mapped using Photomatix software to help bring out some detail in the darker areas of the scene.

3) Blanket of colour

Research areas renowned for autumn colour, such as Westonbirt Arboretum in Gloucestershire, with its spectacular display of Japanese maples. Here you'll find colours ranging from bright golds to deep reds. Revisit locations during the season as colours constantly change. Return late season and take advantage of the opportunity to shoot the fallen leaves creating a carpet of colour on the woodland floor.

4) Isolate a single tree

Admit it, you want to climb this tree, don't you? Its gnarly roots and angle of the trunk and branches provide a perfect lead-in to the scene. The composition takes your eye on a journey that your feet want to follow.

5) Blur water

Only a shutter speed of two seconds or more will blur a woodland stream this much. A long exposure needs a small aperture, giving front-to-back sharpness and the sprinkling of golden leaves adds interest to the moss.

ESSENTIALS

wide-angle zoom: A wide-angle zoom lens, such as the Sigma 10-20mm, will allow you to make the most of the majority of autumnal picture-making opportunities. On this page, only the misty mornings shot was taken with a telephoto. When the wider end of your 'standard' zoom isn't wide enough, autumn is a good time to open up even more.

See page 106 for more lens advice

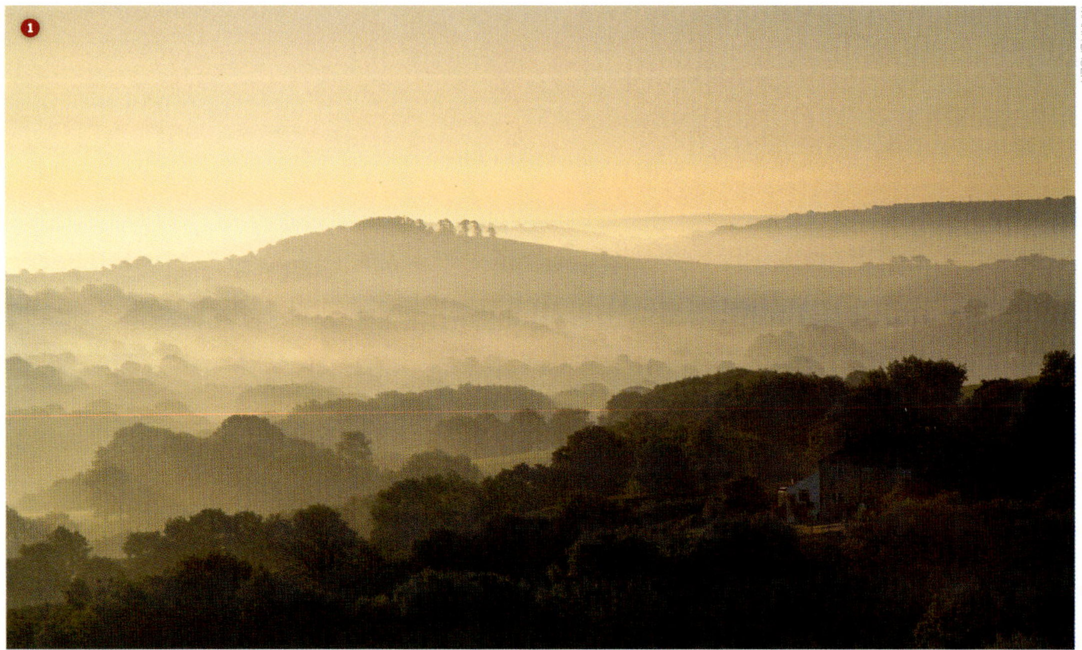

1

MARK BAUER

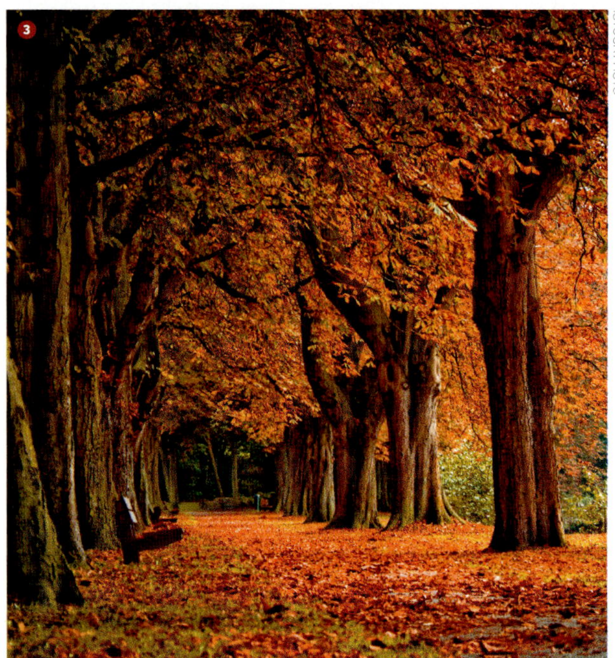

3

ISTOCK PHOTO

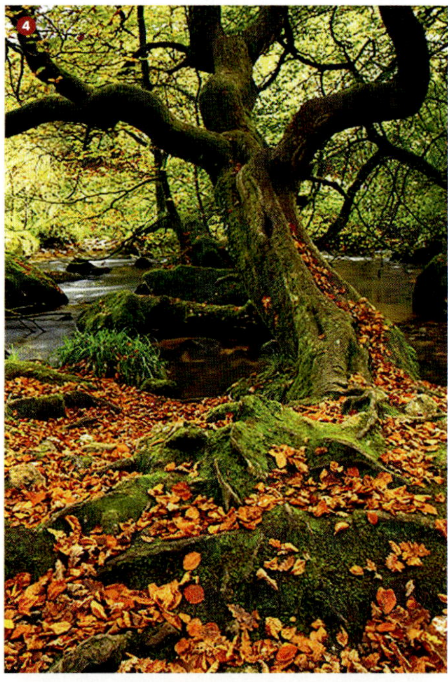

4

HELEN DIXON

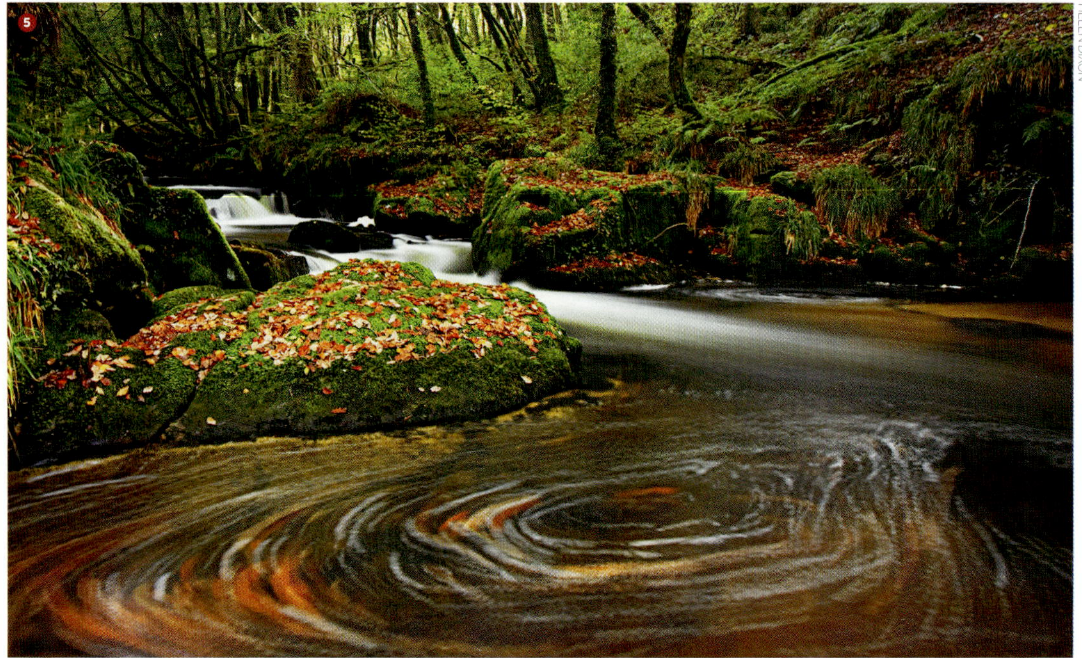

5

HELEN DIXON

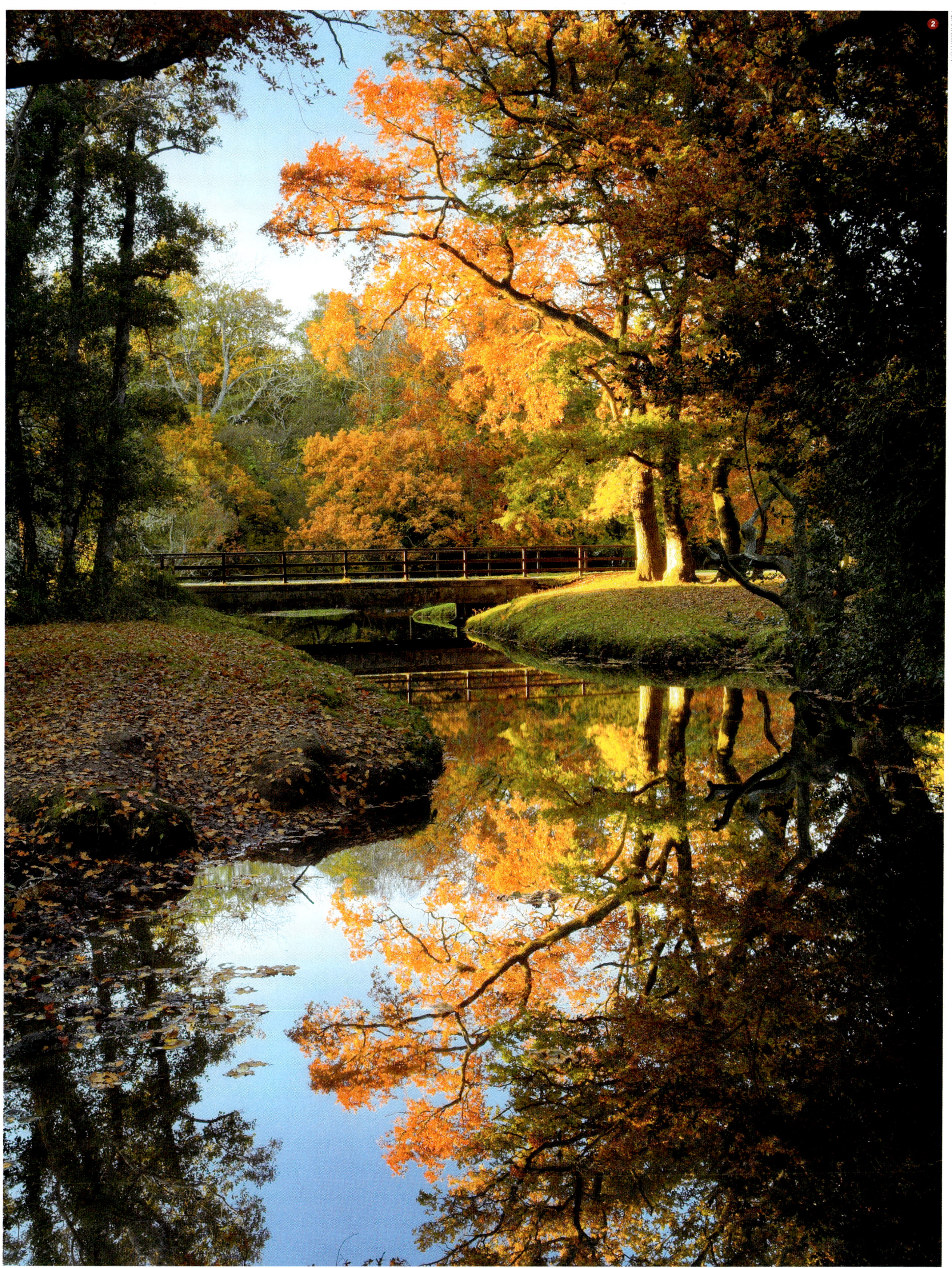

ADAM BURTON

Creating autumnal colour

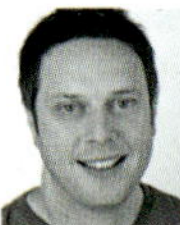

WITH LUKE MARSH In this tutorial we show you how to turn a lush green scene into a misty morning with soft autumnal colour. All from the relative comfort of your desk. There is a hint of diffused light in the original image, around the second curve in the road. This got Luke imagining what the scene might look like with the same bright sunlight but even more mist. Then, using the magic of Photoshop, he made it happen.

In this easy-to-follow, step-by-step tutorial you will learn the value of the Adjustment Layer in post-processing, how to adjust Hue/Saturation and Gradient Fill. Luke will show you how to select a section of the tree trunk and then, using layers, create mist that appears to be in front and behind the tree. Photoshop Elements 4.0 was used here, but more recent versions are suitable too.

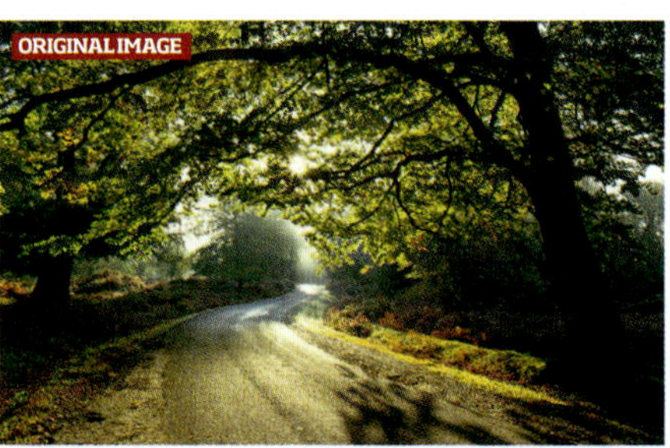

1

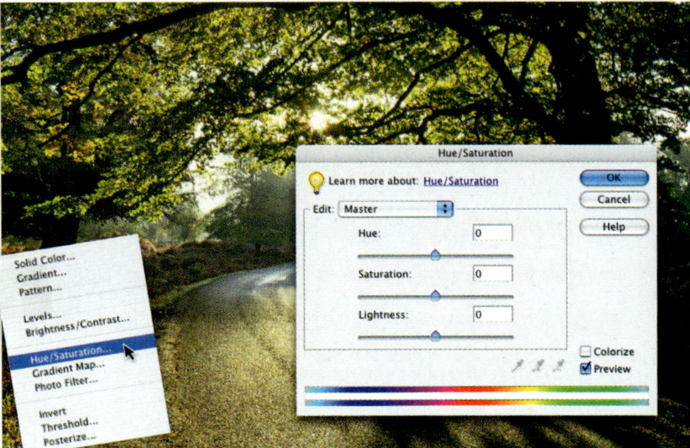

The best way to alter the hue of an image is with Hue/Saturation through the **Adjustment Layers** menu. Adjustment layers are good because they allow you to edit and re-edit your image without actually altering the original. So, go to the **Adjustment Layer** symbol (◐) in the layers palette (inset) and scroll to **Hue/Satuation**.

2

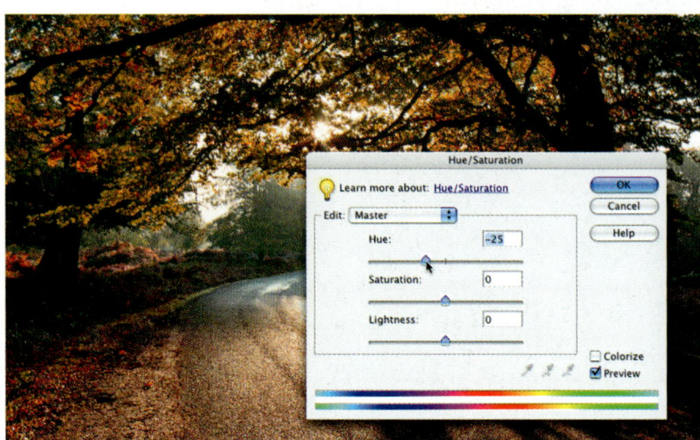

In the Hue/Saturation window I drag the **Hue** slider left (–), changing the hue of the image. I stop when I reach the desired autumnal mood and click **OK**. Because this command affects the entire image, certain areas may look a little odd, such as the road. This is where the **Adjustment Layer** comes in handy.

3

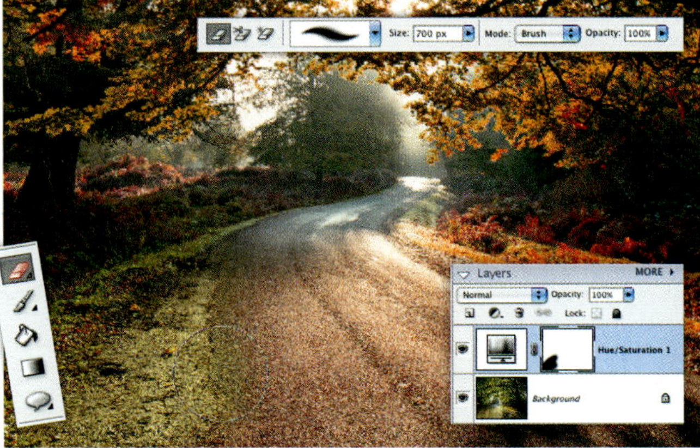

Selecting the **Eraser** tool (inset) with a large soft brush, I begin to 'paint' out the areas of the foreground that look odd due to the change in hue, allowing the original image to be seen from beneath. The thumbnail preview in the **Layers** palette allows me to check my progress, with the erased areas indicated in black (inset).

4

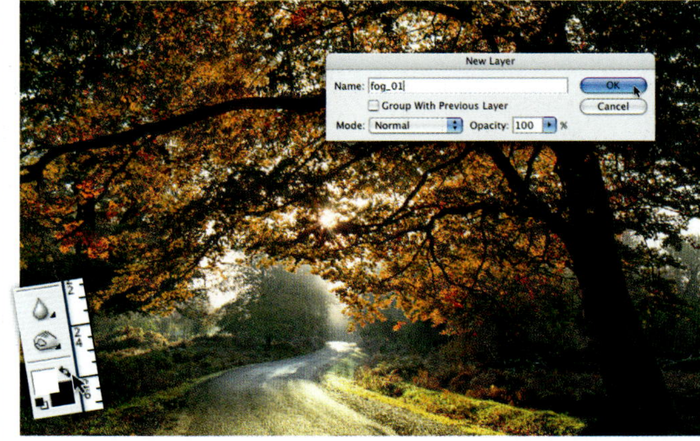

To create the fog effect, I'll use a **Gradient Adjustment Layer**. The gradient will be based on the foreground colour, which by default is black, so to change it to white I click the **Switch Foreground Color** icon at the base of the tool palette (inset). I select **Gradient** through the **Adjustment Layer** (◐) and name it.

5

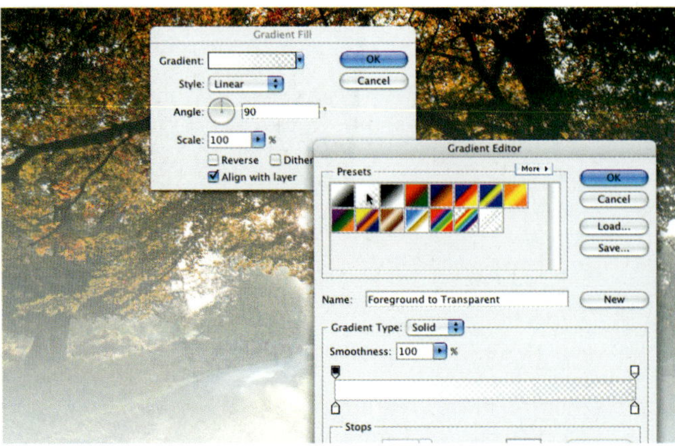

The **Gradient Fill** window appears and the gradient is previewed live on the image. Click in the **Gradient Field** and the **Gradient Editor** opens. You must ensure that **Color to Transparent** is active, the colour being white as set in step four, then click **OK** to close and return to the canvas, complete with gradient.

6

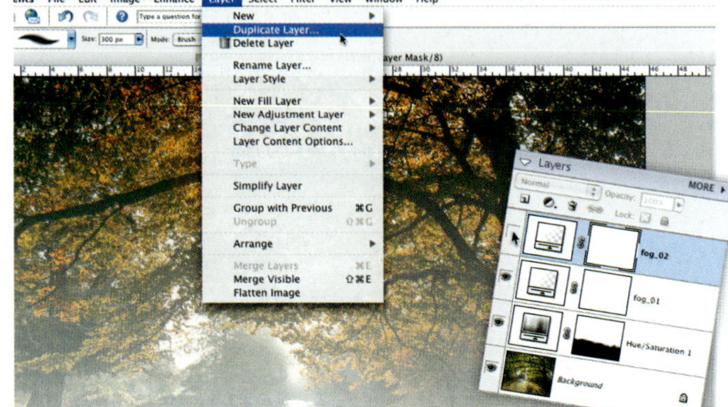

I need another identical gradient to build some depth to the fog effect so I go to **Layer>Duplicate Layer**, naming the new layer accordingly. I won't be using the new layer yet so I want to hide it. To do this I click the **Layer Visibility** icon – note that the eye disappears (inset) to indicate that the layer is no longer visible.

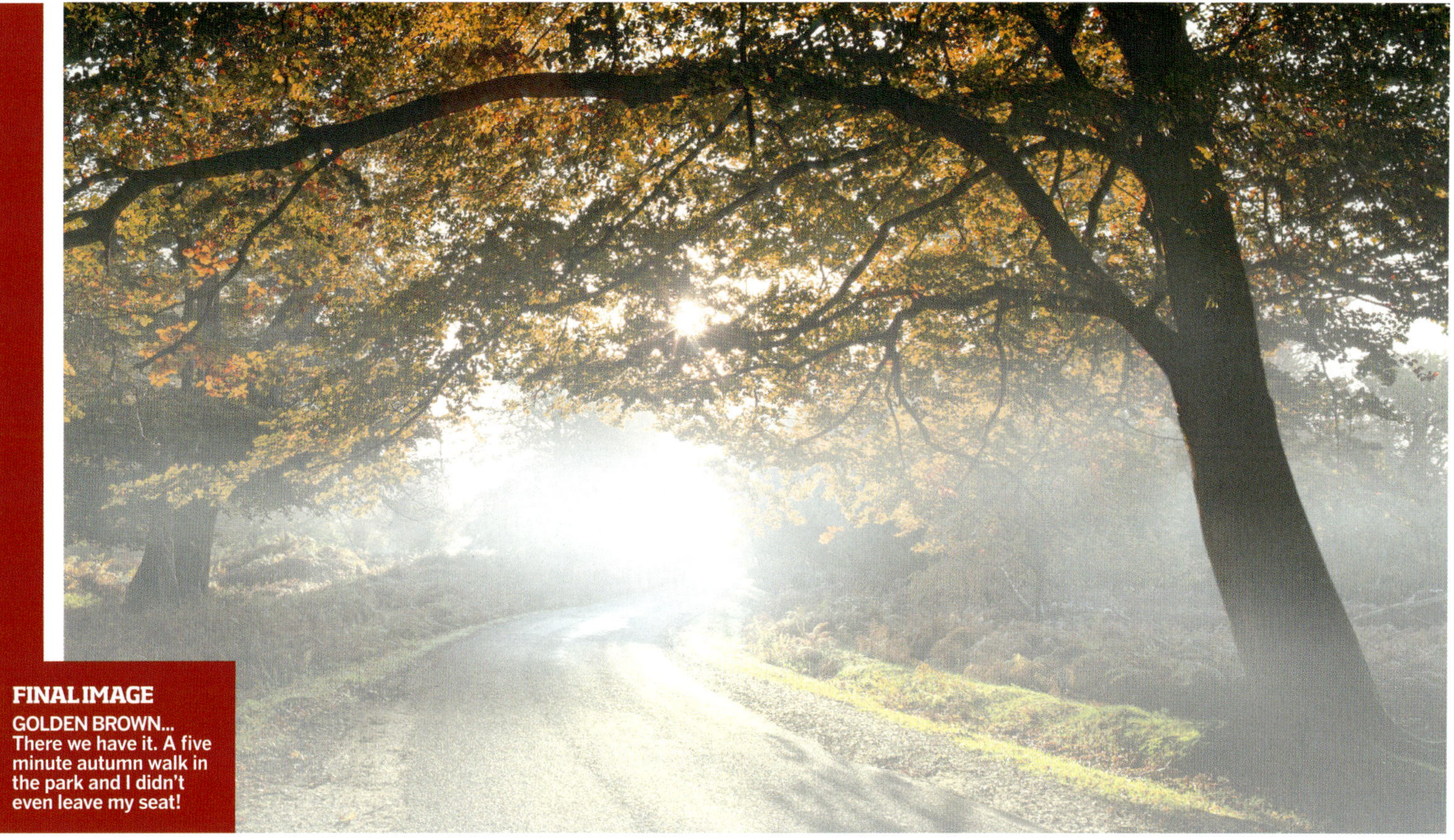

FINAL IMAGE

GOLDEN BROWN... There we have it. A five minute autumn walk in the park and I didn't even leave my seat!

7

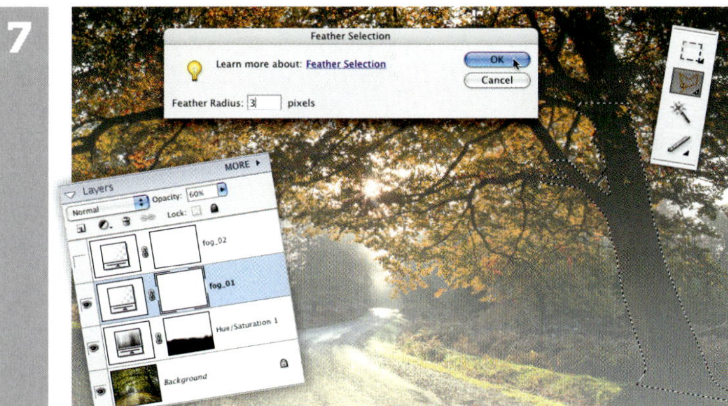

Before moving on I ensure that the original gradient layer I created is active by clicking on its thumbnail in the Layers palette (inset). With the **Polygonal Lasso** selected from the tool palette, I draw an accurate selection around the trunk of the foreground tree using **Select>Feather** at three pixels to soften the selection.

8

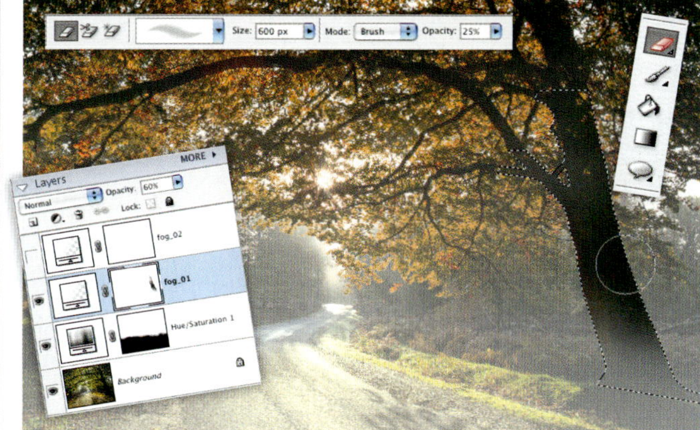

Back to the **Eraser** tool, this time with a smaller soft brush and the **Opacity** to 25%, which allows for a gradual removal and so offers more control. I begin to 'paint' out the 'fog' from the gradient layer, the polygonal selection ensuring only the trunk is affected, giving the illusion that the tree is in front of the layers of fog.

9

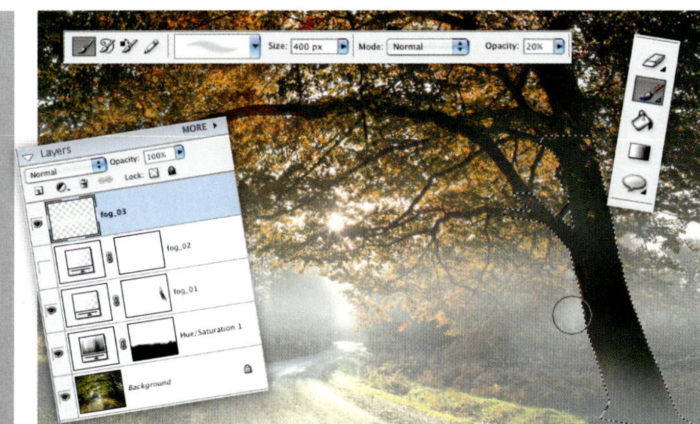

I'm going to use the **Brush** tool to add some depth to the fog behind the tree so I go **Select>Inverse** to select the background. I'll now need a new layer as Adjustment Layers only allow for application of specific tasks, in this case, gradients. I go to **Layer>New Layer** and with the brush set to 20% opacity, I create denser fog areas.

10

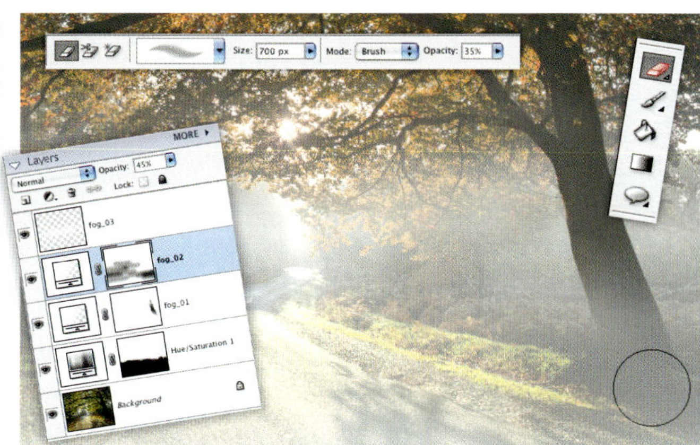

I use **Select>Deselect** to remove the trunk selection, then activate a second gradient in the layers palette, clicking the empty box opposite to make it visible. This gives a denser fog effect, which I tone down by setting the opacity to 45%. Using the **Eraser** with opacity at 35%, I erase creatively to complete the effect.

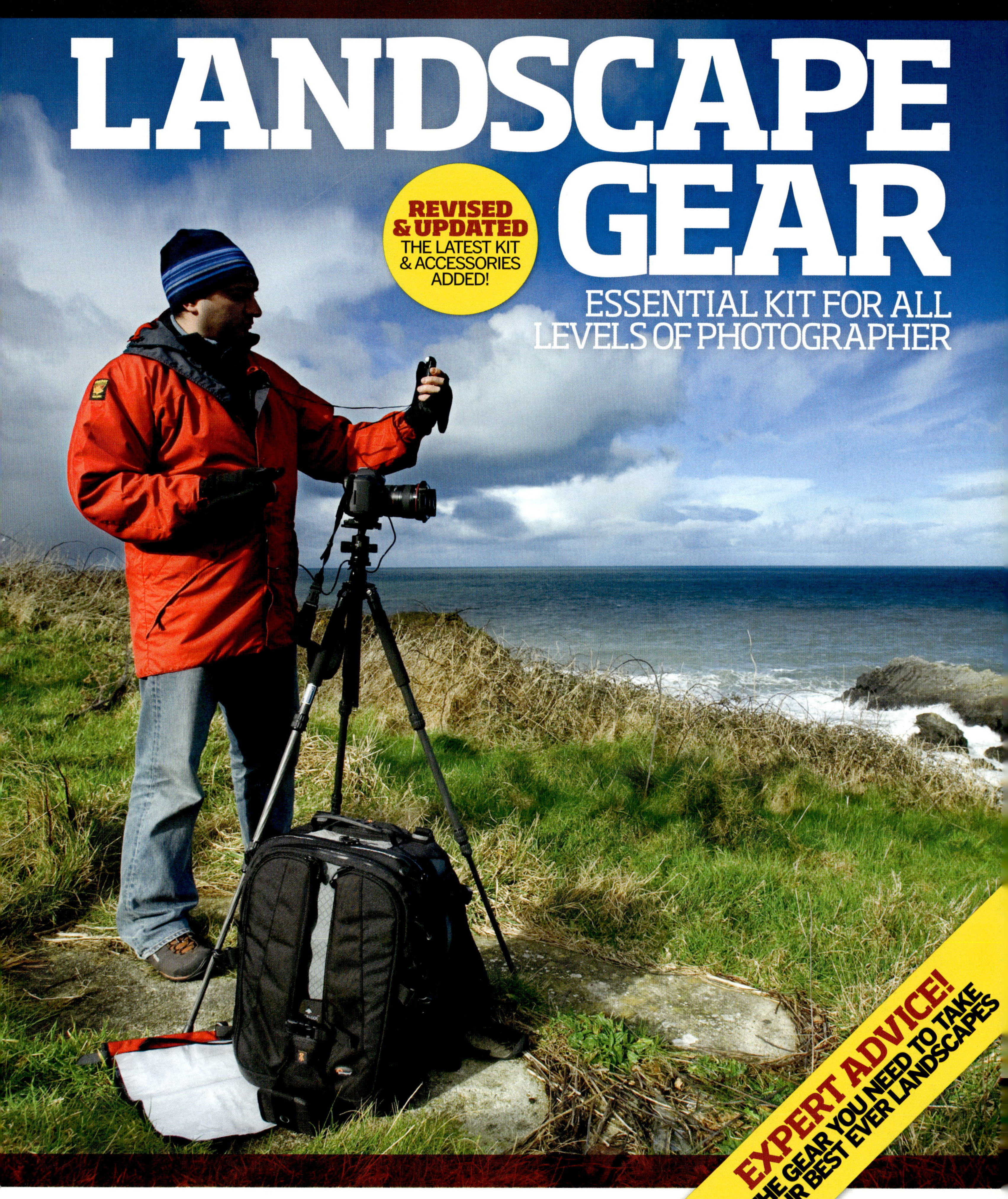
LANDSCAPE GEAR
REVISED & UPDATED
THE LATEST KIT & ACCESSORIES ADDED!
ESSENTIAL KIT FOR ALL LEVELS OF PHOTOGRAPHER
EXPERT ADVICE!
THE GEAR YOU NEED TO TAKE YOUR BEST EVER LANDSCAPES

Gear advice #1

THE NOVICE PHOTOGRAPHER

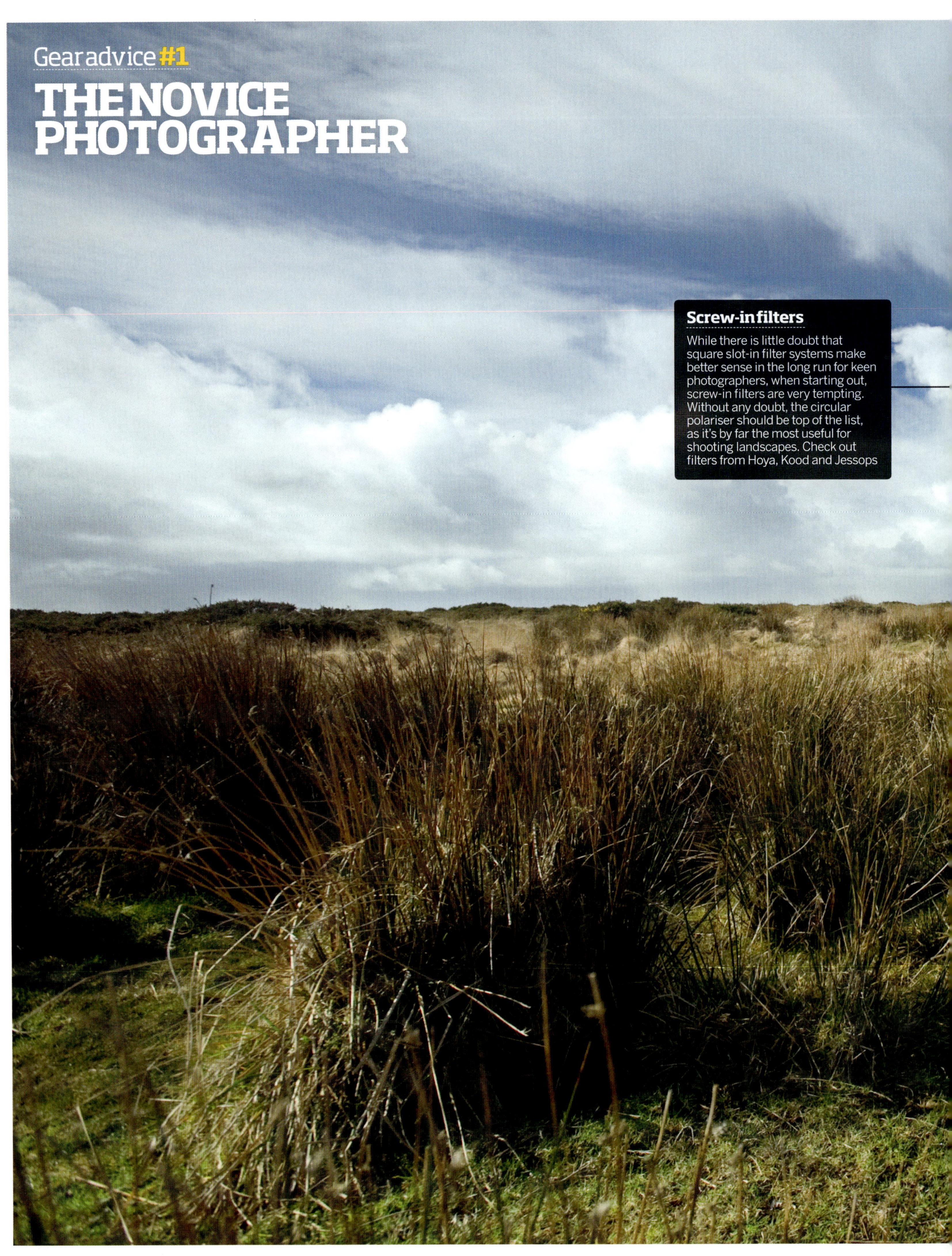

Screw-in filters

While there is little doubt that square slot-in filter systems make better sense in the long run for keen photographers, when starting out, screw-in filters are very tempting. Without any doubt, the circular polariser should be top of the list, as it's by far the most useful for shooting landscapes. Check out filters from Hoya, Kood and Jessops

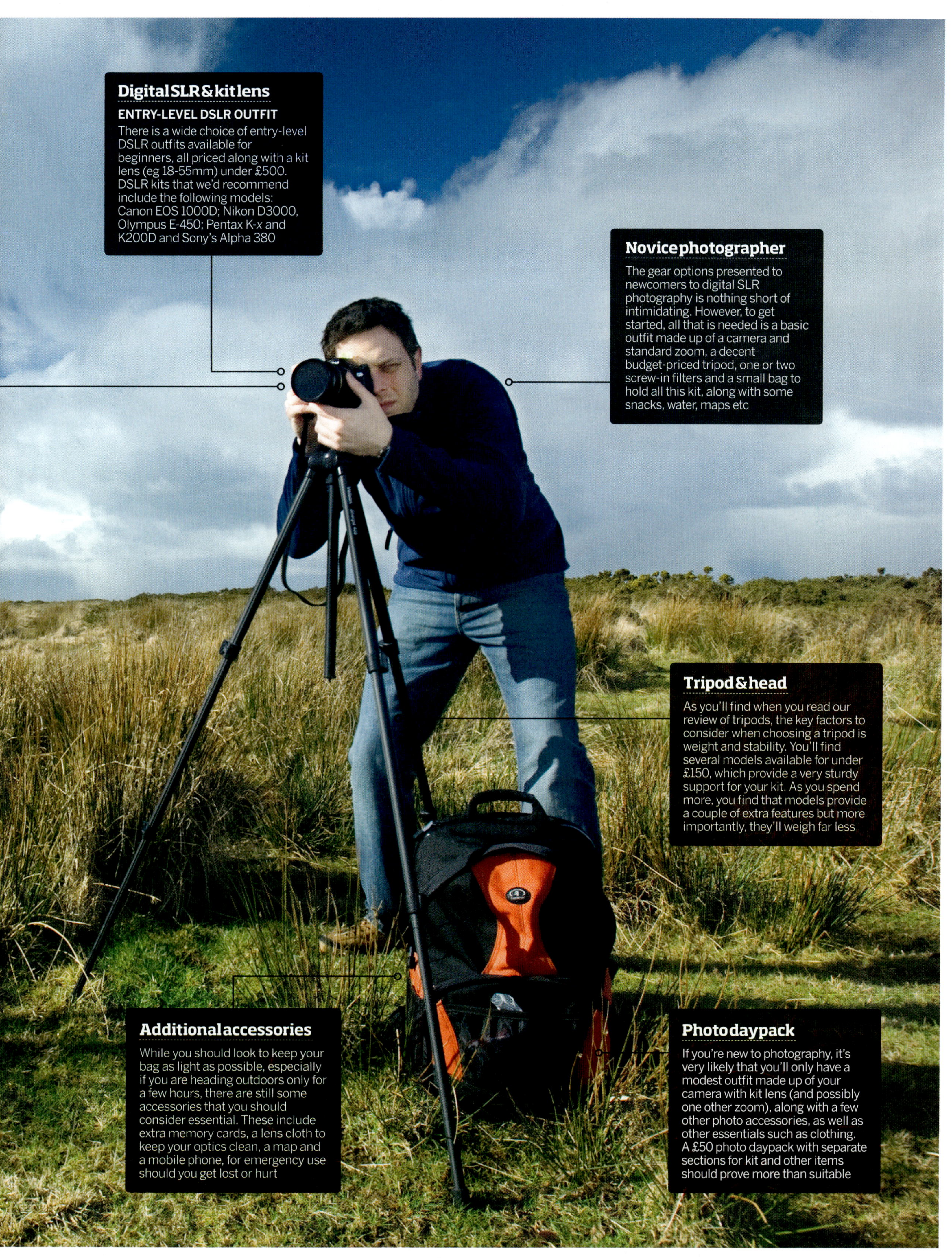
Digital SLR & kit lens
ENTRY-LEVEL DSLR OUTFIT
There is a wide choice of entry-level DSLR outfits available for beginners, all priced along with a kit lens (eg 18-55mm) under £500. DSLR kits that we'd recommend include the following models: Canon EOS 1000D; Nikon D3000, Olympus E-450; Pentax K-x and K200D and Sony's Alpha 380
Novice photographer
The gear options presented to newcomers to digital SLR photography is nothing short of intimidating. However, to get started, all that is needed is a basic outfit made up of a camera and standard zoom, a decent budget-priced tripod, one or two screw-in filters and a small bag to hold all this kit, along with some snacks, water, maps etc
Tripod & head
As you'll find when you read our review of tripods, the key factors to consider when choosing a tripod is weight and stability. You'll find several models available for under £150, which provide a very sturdy support for your kit. As you spend more, you find that models provide a couple of extra features but more importantly, they'll weigh far less
Additional accessories
While you should look to keep your bag as light as possible, especially if you are heading outdoors only for a few hours, there are still some accessories that you should consider essential. These include extra memory cards, a lens cloth to keep your optics clean, a map and a mobile phone, for emergency use should you get lost or hurt
Photo daypack
If you're new to photography, it's very likely that you'll only have a modest outfit made up of your camera with kit lens (and possibly one other zoom), along with a few other photo accessories, as well as other essentials such as clothing. A £50 photo daypack with separate sections for kit and other items should prove more than suitable

Gear advice **#2**

THE ENTHUSIAST PHOTOGRAPHER

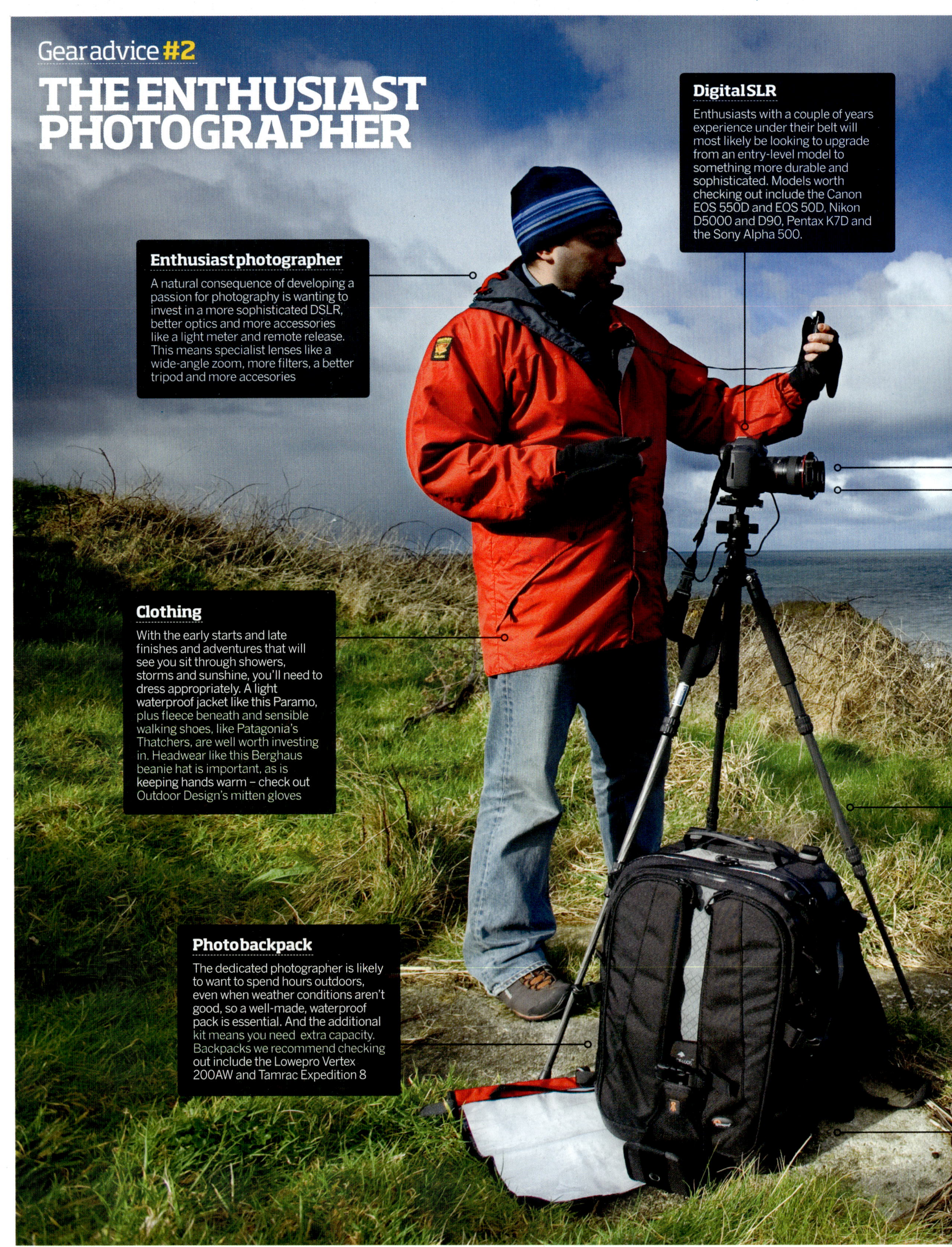

Digital SLR

Enthusiasts with a couple of years experience under their belt will most likely be looking to upgrade from an entry-level model to something more durable and sophisticated. Models worth checking out include the Canon EOS 550D and EOS 50D, Nikon D5000 and D90, Pentax K7D and the Sony Alpha 500.

Enthusiast photographer

A natural consequence of developing a passion for photography is wanting to invest in a more sophisticated DSLR, better optics and more accessories like a light meter and remote release. This means specialist lenses like a wide-angle zoom, more filters, a better tripod and more accesories

Clothing

With the early starts and late finishes and adventures that will see you sit through showers, storms and sunshine, you'll need to dress appropriately. A light waterproof jacket like this Paramo, plus fleece beneath and sensible walking shoes, like Patagonia's Thatchers, are well worth investing in. Headwear like this Berghaus beanie hat is important, as is keeping hands warm – check out Outdoor Design's mitten gloves

Photo backpack

The dedicated photographer is likely to want to spend hours outdoors, even when weather conditions aren't good, so a well-made, waterproof pack is essential. And the additional kit means you need extra capacity. Backpacks we recommend checking out include the Lowepro Vertex 200AW and Tamrac Expedition 8

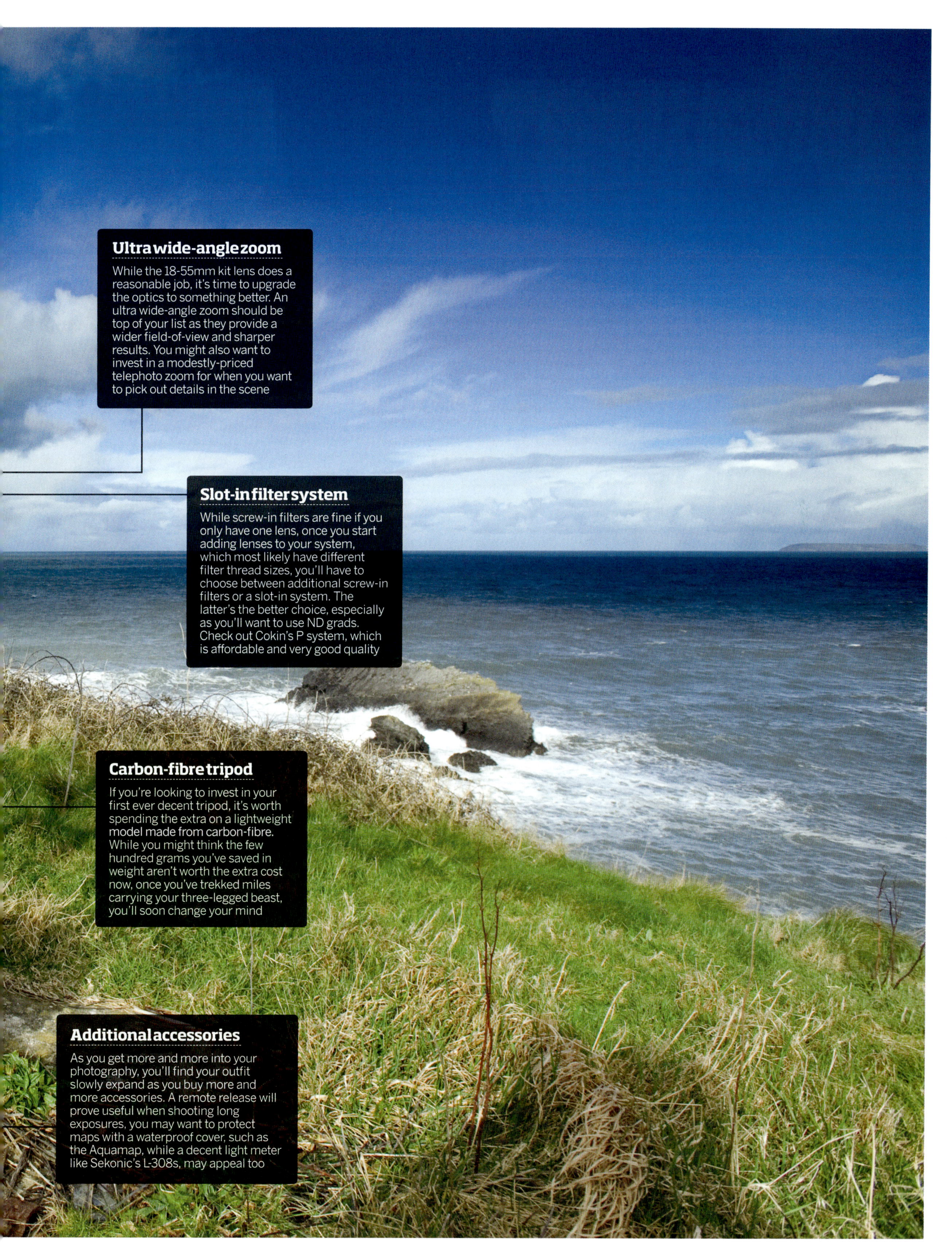
Ultra wide-angle zoom
While the 18-55mm kit lens does a reasonable job, it's time to upgrade the optics to something better. An ultra wide-angle zoom should be top of your list as they provide a wider field-of-view and sharper results. You might also want to invest in a modestly-priced telephoto zoom for when you want to pick out details in the scene
Slot-in filter system
While screw-in filters are fine if you only have one lens, once you start adding lenses to your system, which most likely have different filter thread sizes, you'll have to choose between additional screw-in filters or a slot-in system. The latter's the better choice, especially as you'll want to use ND grads. Check out Cokin's P system, which is affordable and very good quality
Carbon-fibre tripod
If you're looking to invest in your first ever decent tripod, it's worth spending the extra on a lightweight model made from carbon-fibre. While you might think the few hundred grams you've saved in weight aren't worth the extra cost now, once you've trekked miles carrying your three-legged beast, you'll soon change your mind
Additional accessories
As you get more and more into your photography, you'll find your outfit slowly expand as you buy more and more accessories. A remote release will prove useful when shooting long exposures, you may want to protect maps with a waterproof cover, such as the Aquamap, while a decent light meter like Sekonic's L-308s, may appeal too

Gear advice **#3**

THE SEMI-PRO/PRO PHOTOGRAPHER

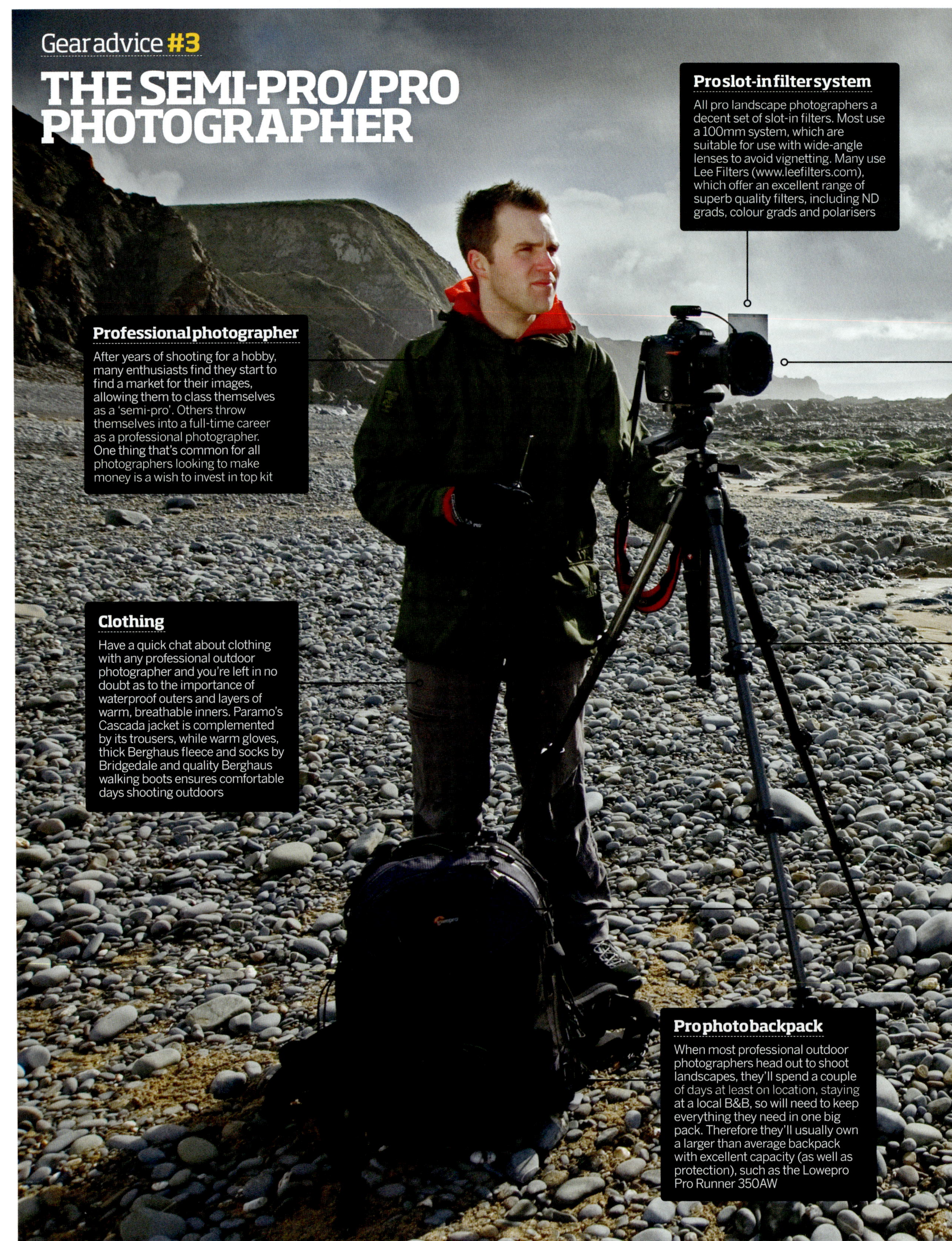

Pro slot-in filter system

All pro landscape photographers a decent set of slot-in filters. Most use a 100mm system, which are suitable for use with wide-angle lenses to avoid vignetting. Many use Lee Filters (www.leefilters.com), which offer an excellent range of superb quality filters, including ND grads, colour grads and polarisers

Professional photographer

After years of shooting for a hobby, many enthusiasts find they start to find a market for their images, allowing them to class themselves as a 'semi-pro'. Others throw themselves into a full-time career as a professional photographer. One thing that's common for all photographers looking to make money is a wish to invest in top kit

Clothing

Have a quick chat about clothing with any professional outdoor photographer and you're left in no doubt as to the importance of waterproof outers and layers of warm, breathable inners. Paramo's Cascada jacket is complemented by its trousers, while warm gloves, thick Berghaus fleece and socks by Bridgedale and quality Berghaus walking boots ensures comfortable days shooting outdoors

Pro photo backpack

When most professional outdoor photographers head out to shoot landscapes, they'll spend a couple of days at least on location, staying at a local B&B, so will need to keep everything they need in one big pack. Therefore they'll usually own a larger than average backpack with excellent capacity (as well as protection), such as the Lowepro Pro Runner 350AW

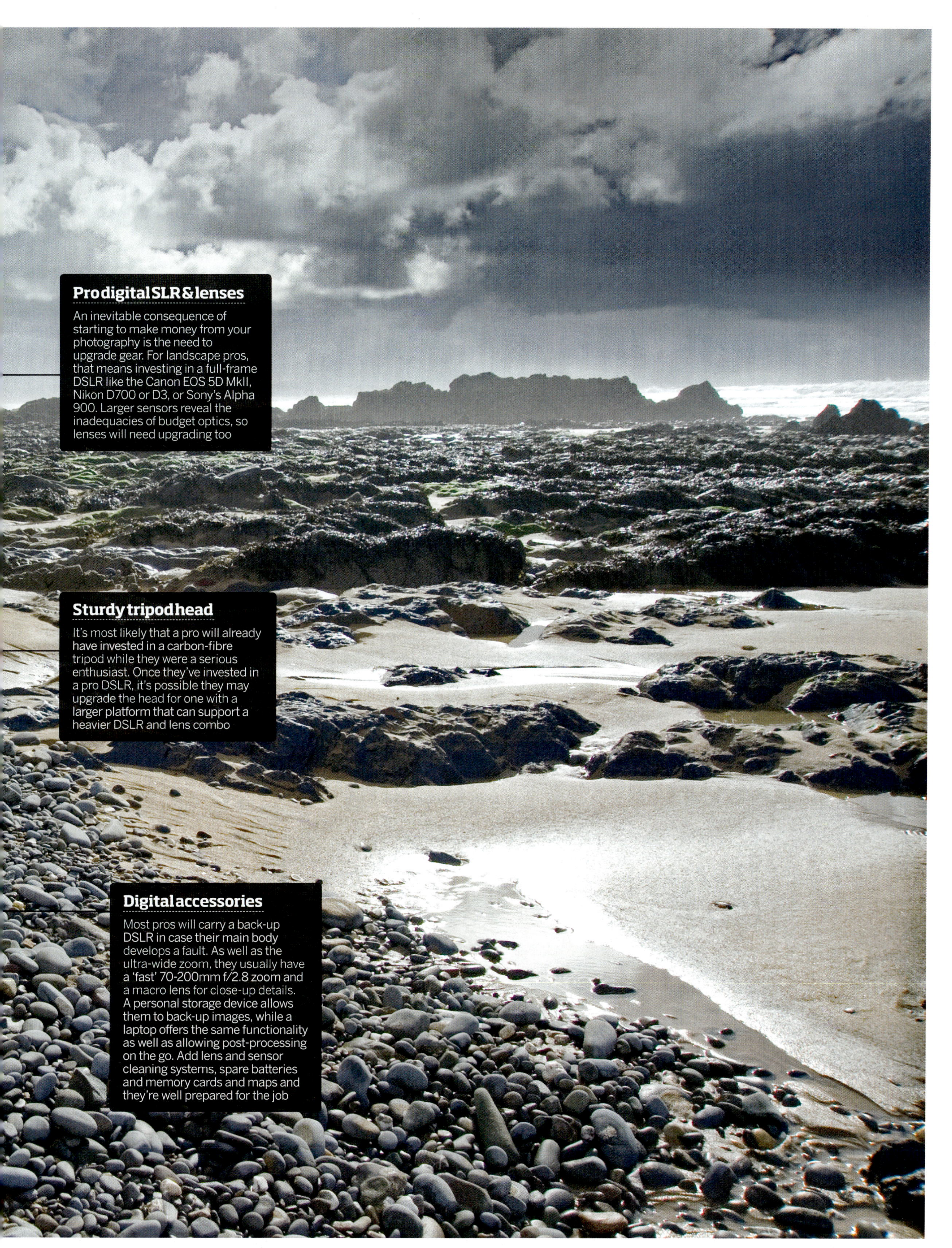

Pro digital SLR & lenses
An inevitable consequence of starting to make money from your photography is the need to upgrade gear. For landscape pros, that means investing in a full-frame DSLR like the Canon EOS 5D MkII, Nikon D700 or D3, or Sony's Alpha 900. Larger sensors reveal the inadequacies of budget optics, so lenses will need upgrading too
Sturdy tripod head
It's most likely that a pro will already have invested in a carbon-fibre tripod while they were a serious enthusiast. Once they've invested in a pro DSLR, it's possible they may upgrade the head for one with a larger platform that can support a heavier DSLR and lens combo
Digital accessories
Most pros will carry a back-up DSLR in case their main body develops a fault. As well as the ultra-wide zoom, they usually have a 'fast' 70-200mm f/2.8 zoom and a macro lens for close-up details. A personal storage device allows them to back-up images, while a laptop offers the same functionality as well as allowing post-processing on the go. Add lens and sensor cleaning systems, spare batteries and memory cards and maps and they're well prepared for the job

Wide-angle lenses

If you're serious about landscape photography, the first addition you should invest in is a decent wide-angle lens. The exaggerated perspective and wide angle-of-view that these lenses gives allows you to fill the frame with your scene and reveal an incredible amount of detail. When you're confronted by a beautiful landscape, there is nothing like a wide-angle lens to ensure the whole scene is recorded, from foreground interest through to distant subjects. Experienced landscape photographers have learned how to use the way that wide-angle lenses stretch perspective to their advantage to give images with strong foreground interest and incredible depth. Another reason why wide-angles are wonderful choices for landscapes is because they have an apparent abundance of depth-of-field, even at mid-aperture settings, to produce images with an excellent amount of sharpness. So, now you're sold on wide-angle lenses, you'll need to decide which type is best for you.

Understanding focal lengths: Wide-angles

The focal length stated on a lens relates to SLRs using 35mm film and full-frame sensors. If your SLR has an APS-C-sized sensor (most have), then you're effectively cropping the image and increasing the focal length of the lens (by 1.5x with Nikon, Pentax and Sony; 1.6x with Canon). The chart below shows popular wide-angles and the change in effective focal length.

Focal length on lens	DSLRs Full-frame	APS-H	APS-C	APS-C (Canon)	Four-Thirds (Olympus)
	1x	**1.3x**	**1.5x**	**1.6x**	**2x**
8mm	8mm	10mm	12mm	13mm	16mm
14mm	14mm	18mm	21mm	22mm	28mm
15mm	15mm	19mm	22mm	23mm	30mm
20mm	20mm	26mm	30mm	32mm	40mm
24mm	24mm	31mm	36mm	38mm	48mm
28mm	28mm	36mm	42mm	45mm	56mm
10-17mm	10-17mm	13-22mm	15-25mm	16-27mm	20-34mm
10-20mm	10-20mm	13-26mm	15-30mm	16-32mm	20-40mm
10-22mm	10-22mm	13-29mm	15-33mm	16-35mm	20-44mm
11-18mm	11-18mm	14-23mm	16-27mm	18-29mm	22-36mm
12-24mm	12-24mm	16-31mm	18-36mm	19-38mm	24-48mm
16-35mm	16-35mm	21-45mm	24-53mm	26-56mm	32-70mm
17-35mm	17-35mm	22-45mm	25-53mm	27-56mm	34-70mm
17-40mm	17-40mm	22-52mm	25-60mm	27-56mm	34-80mm

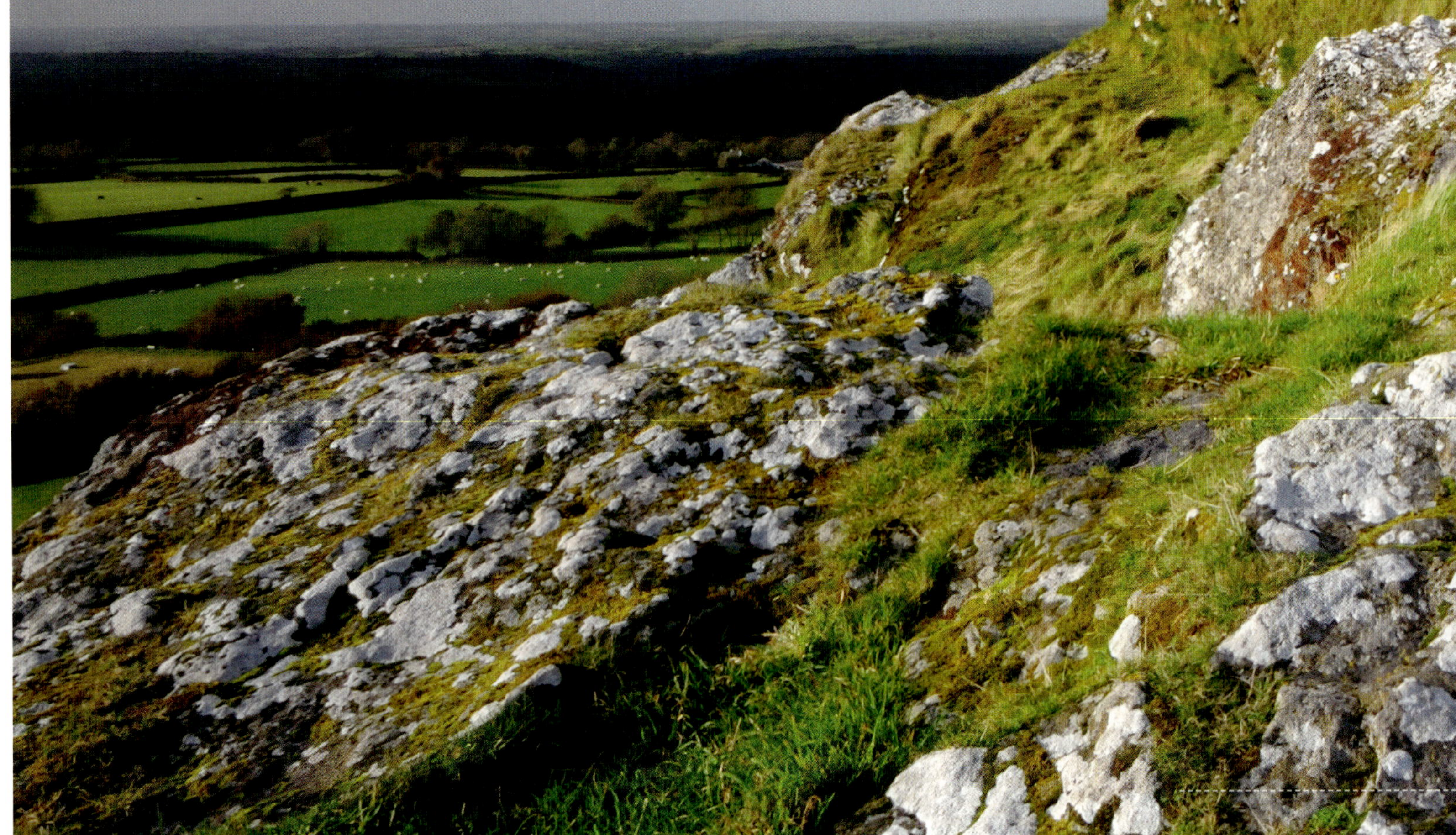

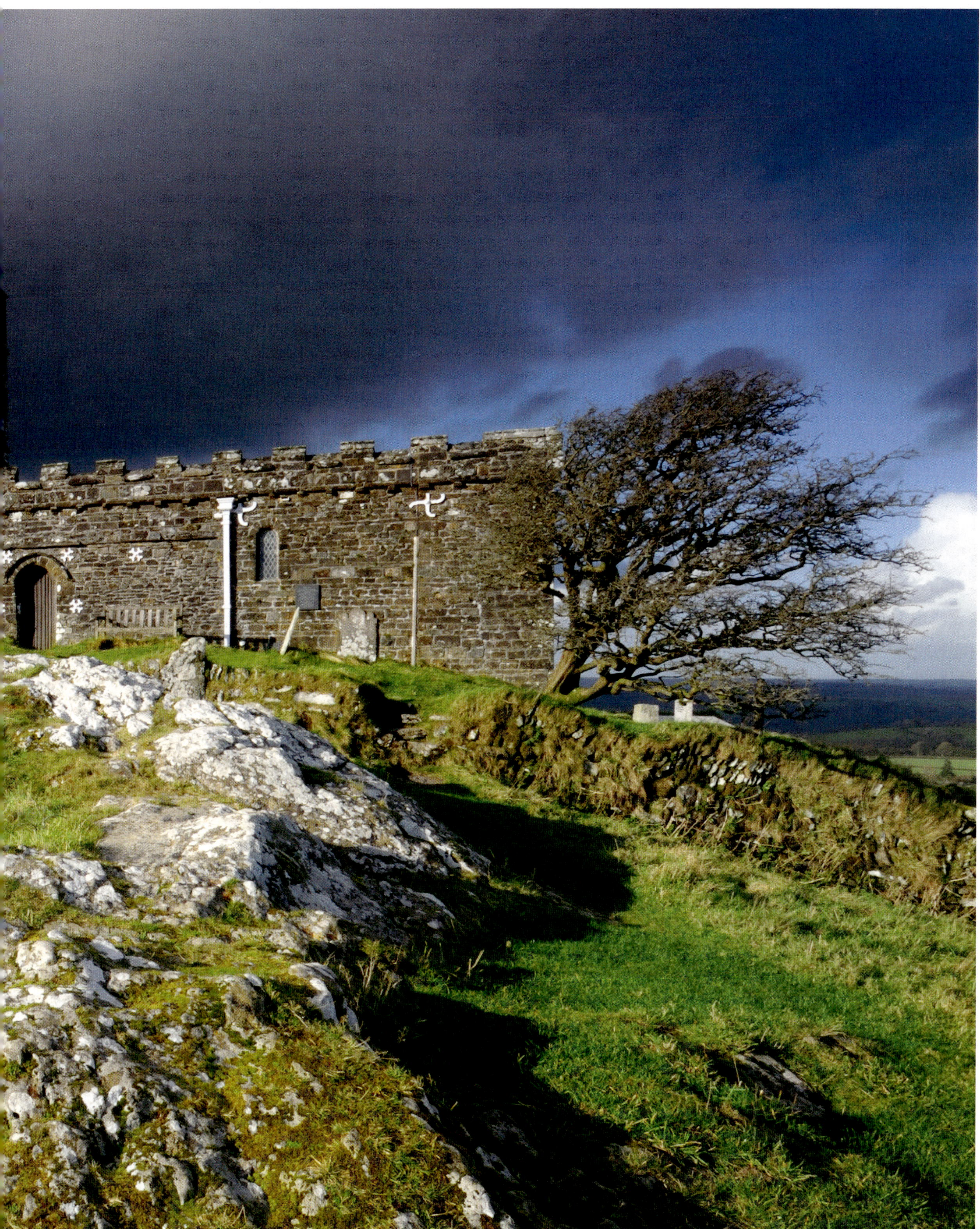

ROSS HODDINOTT

Choosing a wide-angle lens

If your DSLR was supplied with a 'standard zoom' kit lens, such as an 18-55mm, then you'll already have a lens that is capable of shooting decent wide-angle images. However, its capabilities are restricted, as its field-of-view is not wide enough to really make the most of landscape photography, so while it's a good enough choice to get started with, you should add a better wide-angle at your first opportunity. You'll be presented with two main options: a fixed wide-angle lens or a wide-angle zoom. If you want the absolute sharpest possible results, then in theory you want a prime lens, with a 15mm being the best choice if your DSLR has an APS-C sensor, or a 20mm or 24mm if you use a full-frame model. While marque lenses offer the ultimate optical performance, they're very expensive and your choice is very limited. If your DSLR uses the smaller APS-C sized sensor, we'd strongly recommend that you steer clear of fixed lenses and instead go for an ultra wide-angle zoom, as you have far more choice, they're relatively affordable and they deliver excellent quality.

Advances in optical technology saw the development of high-quality ultra-wide zooms in the late '90s and the arrival of DSLRs has seen this group of lenses become increasingly popular. That's no surprise as the range they cover offers incredible versatility in such a small and inexpensive lens. In fact, the ultra wide-angle zoom is arguably one of the best value lenses you could own. There is a variety of focal lengths available, with those around 11-22mm being the most suitable for DSLRs with an APS-C sized sensor. In truth, all cover a very similar range, although there are one or two exceptions to note. The Pentax 10-17mm fish-eye offers a 180° angle-of-view at its widest end, so in a sense you're getting a fish-eye and ultra-wide zoom rolled into one. It's also worth noting that, unlike most ultra-wide zooms, the Sigma 12-24mm can be used on full-frame and APS-C SLRs. Finally, while 16-35mm lenses are popular with film and full-frame DSLR users, the effective focal length of 24-53mm (26-56mm on a Canon) it covers when used with an APS-C sensor is quite limited, so we'd suggest you avoid it.

So which wide-angle lens should you buy? There's little doubt that zooms represent superb value for money and you're spoilt for choice as there aren't any poor performers in this category. Here we recommend our favourite zooms, all of which will deliver great quality results. While primes offer the ultimate in quality, zooms are better value and deliver excellent results. We've stated average street prices at time of publication.

Wide-angle anatomy

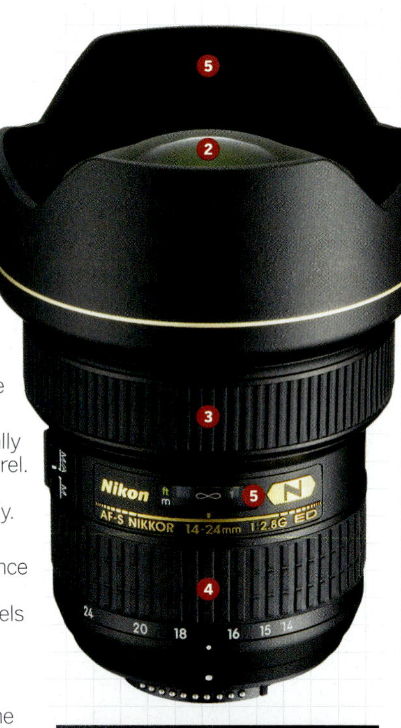

1) PETAL HOOD Ultra wide-angles come supplied with a dedicated hood to avoid vignetting and flare.

2) LARGE, CONCAVE FRONT ELEMENT The front element normally has a prominent curve, leaving it exposed to dust and scratches, so take care to keep it clean.

3) MANUAL FOCUS RING Normally towards the front of the lens and reasonably wide. You'll rarely need to use it, as wide-angle lenses have excellent AF.

4) ZOOM RING These are normally found towards the back of the barrel. Most are wide with a grooved surface to allow you to grip it easily.

5) FOCUS DISTANCE Many lenses have the focus distance scale marked on the barrel, while some of the more upmarket models have a focus distance window.

6) HYPERFOCAL SCALE *(see inset)* This scale allows you to estimate how much of the scene will appear sharp thanks to the depth-of-field created by the choice of aperture that you set.

7) INTERNAL FOCUSING SYSTEM If you're planning to use filters, lenses with an internal focusing system offer the benefit that the front of the lens doesn't rotate when focusing, so you don't have to keep readjusting them.

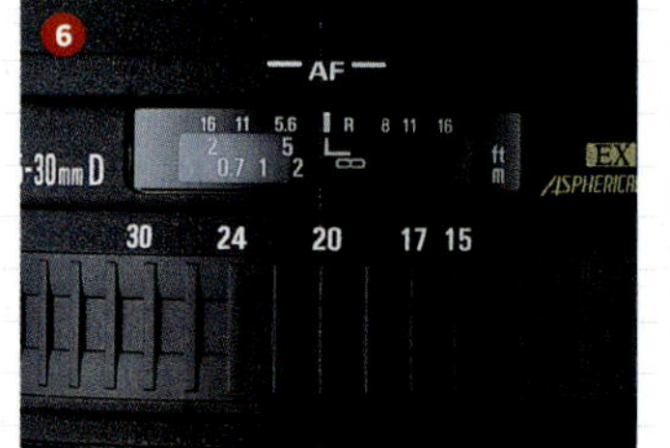

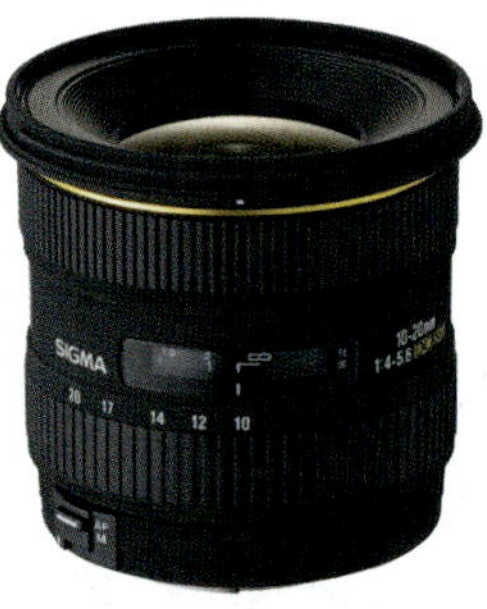

DIGITAL-ONLY LENSES
When you're choosing a lens, check to see if it's for use with film/ full-frame and digital SLRs, or for DSLRs only. Those made for film and digital are usually more expensive; those designed exclusively for DSLRs are optically optimised for digital. Therefore, if you're using a DSLR with the smaller APS-C sensor and never plan to buy a full-frame DSLR, go for for a digital-only lens.

Fixed or zoom lens?

It's the age-old question – why buy a fixed lens with only one focal length when a zoom offers so much more versatility? Well, here's why...

FIXED **('PRIME') WIDE-ANGLE LENS**

✔ Simpler optical design generally means sharper results with better contrast
✔ Fast maximum aperture gives brighter viewfinder and better low-light capabilities
✔ Smaller and more compact than a zoom
✔ Most have a smaller filter thread
✘ **Limited to one focal length**
✘ **Relatively expensive**

WIDE-ANGLE ZOOM LENS

✔ Covers several focal lengths, so you're spoilt for wide-angle versatility
✔ At its wide end, it offers far better coverage than a fixed lens
✔ Most zooms are optically excellent
✔ Lots of flexibility at a very good price
✘ **Not as sharp as a fixed lens, especially towards the edges and corners of the frame**
✘ **Suffers from more distortion**
✘ **Maximum aperture isn't as fast as fixed lens**
✘ **Most have a larger filter thread, so screw-in filters are more expensive**

Zeiss 21mm f/2.8 Distagon

LENS CONSTRUCTION: 16 elements in 13 groups
APERTURE RANGE: f/2.8 to f/22
FILTER THREAD: 82mm
DIMENSIONS: 87x109mm
WEIGHT: 600g
FITTINGS: Canon, Nikon and Pentax
WEBSITE: www.robertwhite.co.uk

This is an almost legendary lens for connoisseurs that has only recently become available in Canon, Nikon and Pentax fittings. It is manual focus only, with a smooth focusing action and it uses a manual aperture ring. The depth-of-field scale is clear and allows for accurate depth-of-field calculations. This is an expensive lens but boasts an exceptional optical performance, resolving an amazing amount of detail. The ultimate choice for quality.

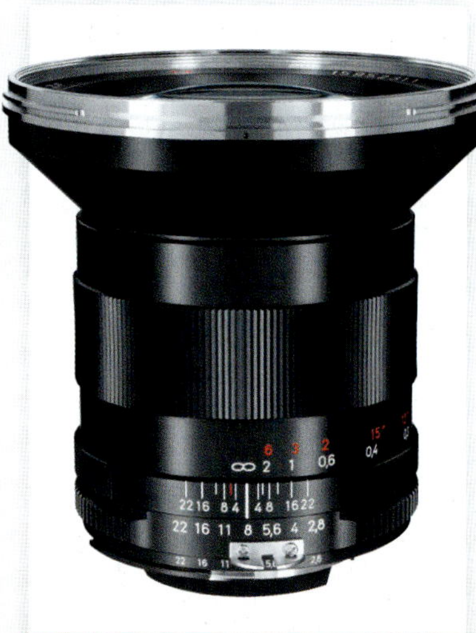

£1,240

Canon 24mm f/1.4L II USM

LENS CONSTRUCTION: 13 elements in ten groups
APERTURE RANGE: f/1.4 to f/22
FILTER THREAD: 77mm
DIMENSIONS: 93.5 x 86.9mm
WEIGHT: 650g
FITTINGS: Canon only
WEBSITE: www.canon.co.uk

This new addition to the Canon range is designed for pro use, as its price tag suggests. As well as offering an extremely fast aperture, it boasts weather and dust seals to protect it from the elements. Optical quality is superb, thanks to the aspherical and UD glass elements, which ensure image sharpness is crisp throughout the frame. A dream lens for those that can afford it, but the Zeiss 21mm f/2.8 Distagon, while manual focus, offers a superior optical performance to the Canon.

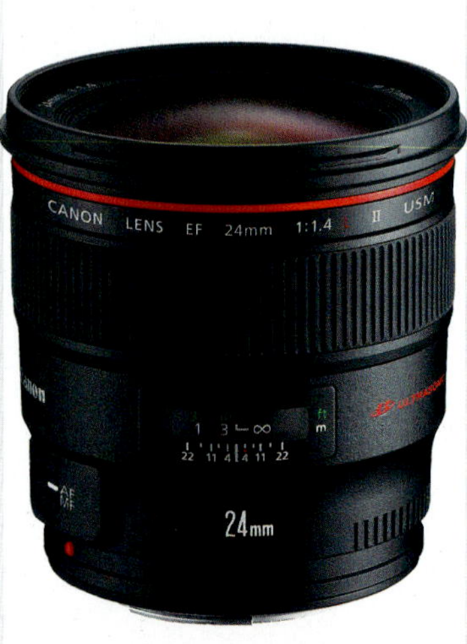

£1,400

Nikon AF-S DX 12-24mm f/4 ED-IF

LENS CONSTRUCTION: 11 elements in seven groups
APERTURE RANGE: f/4 to f/22
FILTER THREAD: 77mm
DIMENSIONS: 82.5 x 90mm
WEIGHT: 485g
FITTINGS: Nikon only
WEBSITE: www.nikon.co.uk

This excellent zoom, for DSLRs with APS-C-sensors only, is compact considering the f/4 maximum aperture. It's partly made of plastic but feels well made. The zoom ring is wide and the focusing ring is adequate with both offering a smooth action. The barrel sports a focusing window and internal focusing. Image quality is very high, delivering very sharp results throughout the range. Chromatic aberration and flare is barely noticeable but slight barrel distortion is evident.

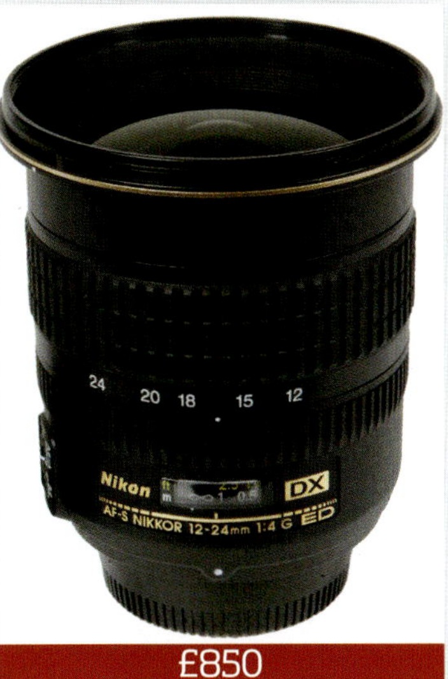

£850

Canon EF 17-40mm f/4L USM

LENS CONSTRUCTION: 12 elements in nine groups
APERTURE RANGE: f/4 to f/22
FILTER THREAD: 77mm
DIMENSIONS: 83.5 x 96.8mm
WEIGHT: 475g
FITTINGS: Canon only
WEBSITE: www.canon.co.uk

The Canon L-series lenses offer higher than normal performance, so this zoom, with its constant f/4 aperture, is one of the most popular optics in the Canon stable. Suitable for use with all EOS models, it's larger than most but robustly built, with great handling and fast AF. Optics are excellent, although with full-frame sensors edge detail becomes a little soft. It's a great lens, although the EF-S 10-22mm is probably a better choice for those with DSLRs boasting an APS-C sensor.

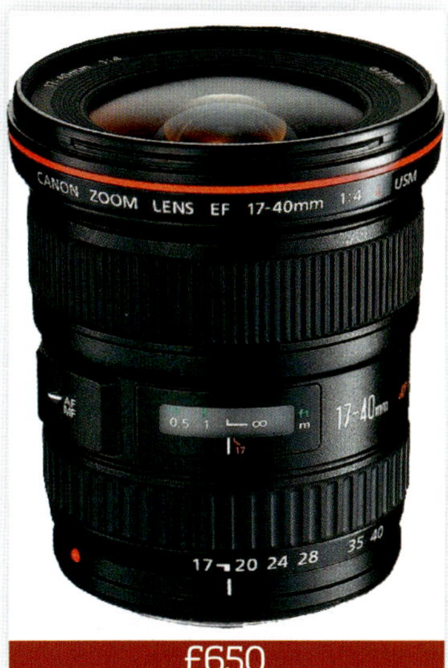

£650

Sigma 10-20mm f/4-5.6 EX DC HSM

LENS CONSTRUCTION: 14 elements in ten groups
APERTURE RANGE: f/1.8 to f/22
FILTER THREAD: 77mm
DIMENSIONS: 83.5 x 81mm
WEIGHT: 470g
FITTINGS: Canon, Nikon, Pentax, Sigma and Sony
WEBSITE: www.sigma-imaging-uk.com

A real favourite with landscape lovers thanks to its compact design and sharp optics. Like all Sigma EX lenses, it's very nicely put together and it feels and looks the part. The barrel sports wide zoom and manual focus rings, both of which have a smooth action. Optics deliver high sharpness and only slight evidence of distortion or aberration. It's a better choice than the newer f/3.5 version.

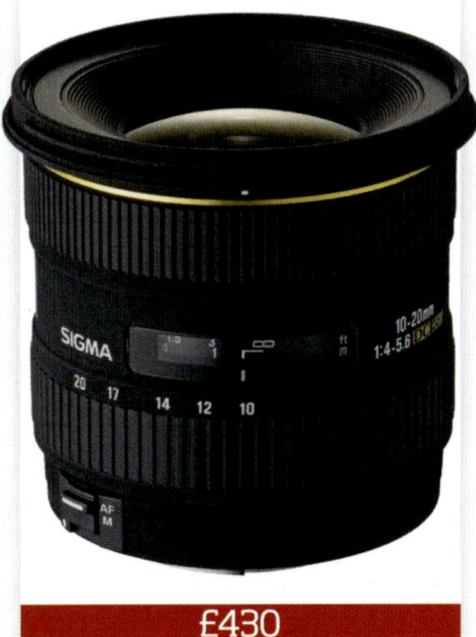

£430

Sigma 12-24mm f/4.5-5.6 EX DG HSM

LENS CONSTRUCTION: 16 elements in 12 groups
APERTURE: f/4.5-5.6 to f/22
FILTER THREAD: Rear gelatin
DIMENSIONS: 87 x 102.5mm
WEIGHT: 600g
FITTINGS: Canon, Nikon, Pentax, Sigma and Sony
WEBSITE: www.sigma-imaging-uk.com

What's particularly impressive about Sigma's 12-24mm zoom is that it's suitable for use with DSLRs with full-frame as well as APS-C sensors. It's larger and wider than average, but very well made with smooth zoom and focusing actions. The barrel features a focus window with hyperfocal scale and an integral petal hood to protect from flare. Optical quality is high with good sharpness and low distortion.

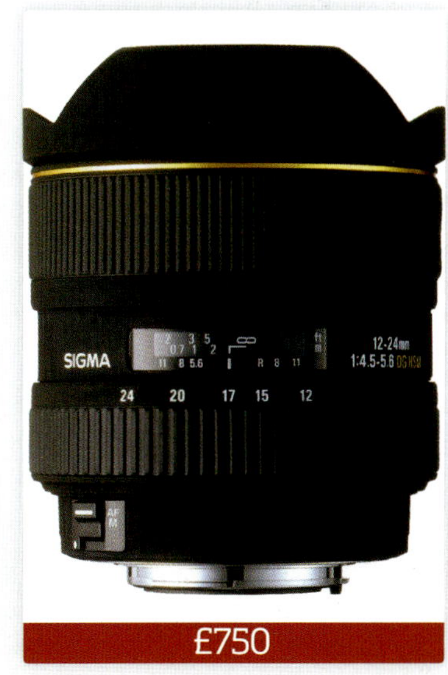

£750

Voigtlander 20mm f/3.5 Color Skopar SL II

LENS CONSTRUCTION: Nine elements in six groups
APERTURE RANGE: f/3.5 to f/22
FILTER THREAD: 52mm
DIMENSIONS: 63x28.8mm
WEIGHT: 205g
FITTINGS: Nikon and Pentax
WEBSITE: www.robertwhite.co.uk

This is one of the most affordable prime lenses on the market and also one of the smallest and lightest, as well as being manual focus only. This last point generally isn't an issue for landscape photographers. The manual focus action is smooth and the barrel boasts a clear hyperfocal scale that makes achieving a good depth-of-field a breeze, as well as an aperture ring. Optically, this lens is a very good performer with excellent sharpness once stopped down. A great budget prime lens.

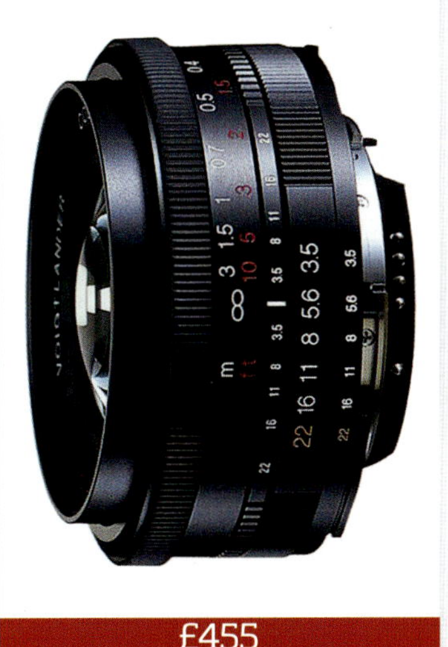

£455

Tamron 10-24mm f/3.5-4.5 Di II LD

LENS CONSTRUCTION: 12 elements in nine groups
APERTURE: f/3.5-4.5 to f/22
FILTER THREAD: 77mm
DIMENSIONS: 83.2 x 86.5mm
WEIGHT: 406g
FITTINGS: Canon, Nikon, Pentax and Sony
WEBSITE: www.intro2020.co.uk

Tamron's 11-18mm zoom has been a popular choice for years but this recent addition, with its extremely wide focal length range, brings even more versatility to wide-angle fans. It's a compact and lightweight option with good handling and an internal focusing system that will please filter users. Optical quality is very good, thanks to the inclusion of aspherical and LD (Low Dispersion) elements and enhanced multi-coatings.

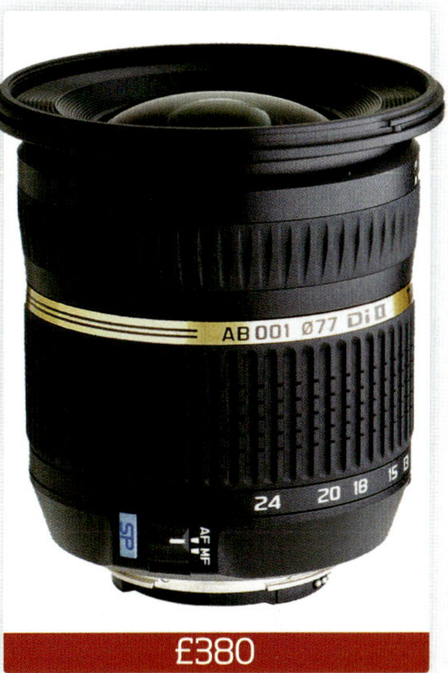

£380

EXPERT TUTORIAL

Make the most of your wide-angle lens

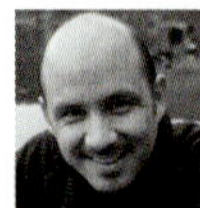

WITH ADAM BURTON Wide-angles are the lens of choice for the vast majority of landscape photographers and for very good reason. These lenses allow you to squeeze as much of a location into your viewfinder as is possible and capture a scene absolutely brimming with details and interest.

This can work to the advantage of the landscape photographer, particularly when using wide-angles to include foreground subject matter. Interesting foreground subjects will spring to life when captured with a wide-angle lens, quite literally grabbing the viewer's attention and pulling them in to explore the rest of the picture.

Using wide-angle zooms can be so addictive that you automatically zoom out to the widest setting at every opportunity. But this can have its problems too. Such lenses can be set so wide as to sometimes show up the corners of your equipment (lenses, filters and holders) in the frame; this is known as vignetting. Another problem with using extreme wide-angle lenses is barrel distortion, which shows up in the form of bendy horizons and buildings leaning over.

All this can be avoided by training yourself to set your wide-angle according to your subject matter. If shooting over water, then setting the focal length a few mm's up from the widest setting will reduce the chances of a bendy horizon. But when shooting mountainous terrain with an already uneven horizon, you can get away with shooting as wide as possible.

As well as focal length, pay attention to the height and the angle from vertical at which you have the camera set up. Trees will lean over when composed from low to the ground, so try setting the camera at head height and you may notice a big difference.

The benefits of a wide-angle lens far outweigh these issues. The impact a wide-angle can bring to your photographs is astounding and is the reason why most landscape photographers couldn't shoot without them.

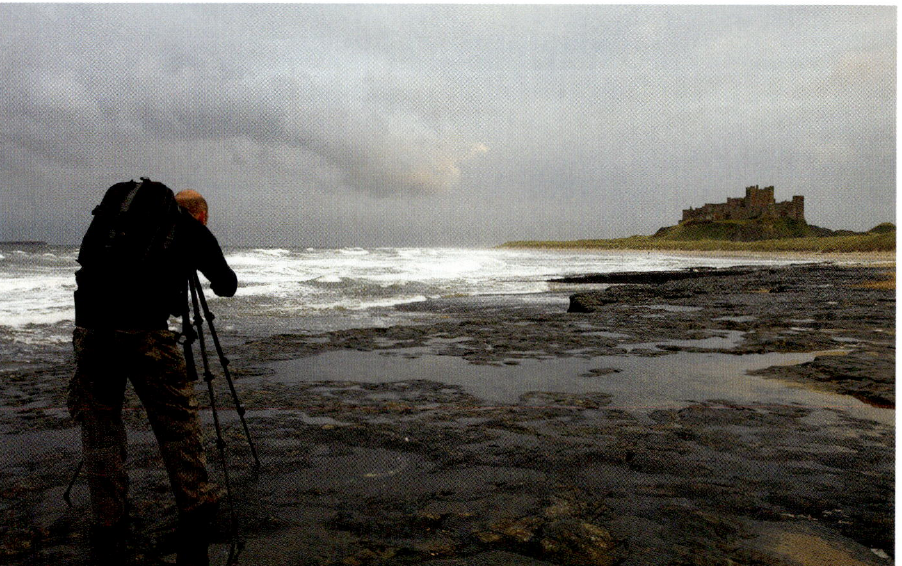

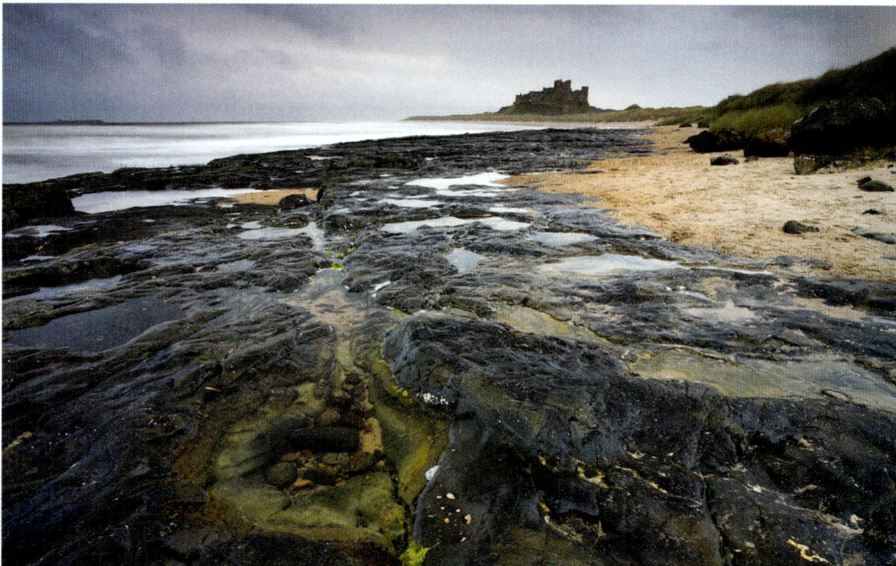

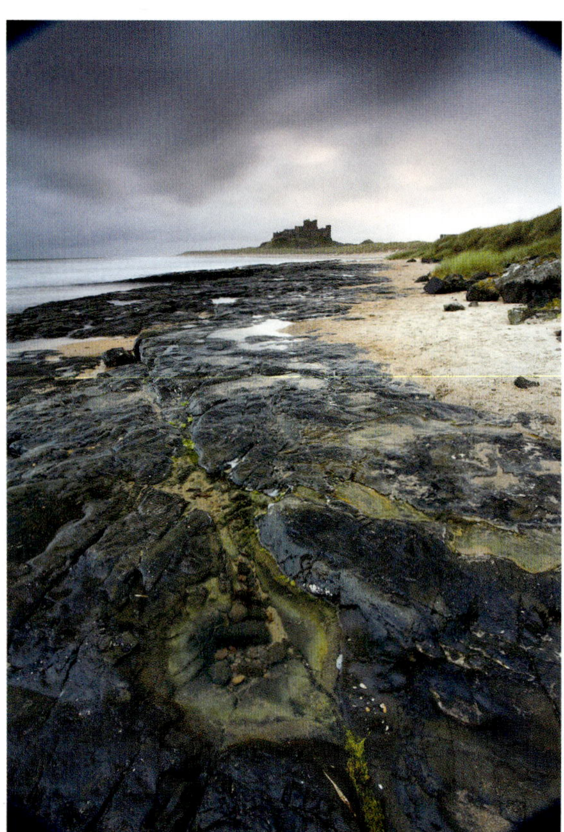

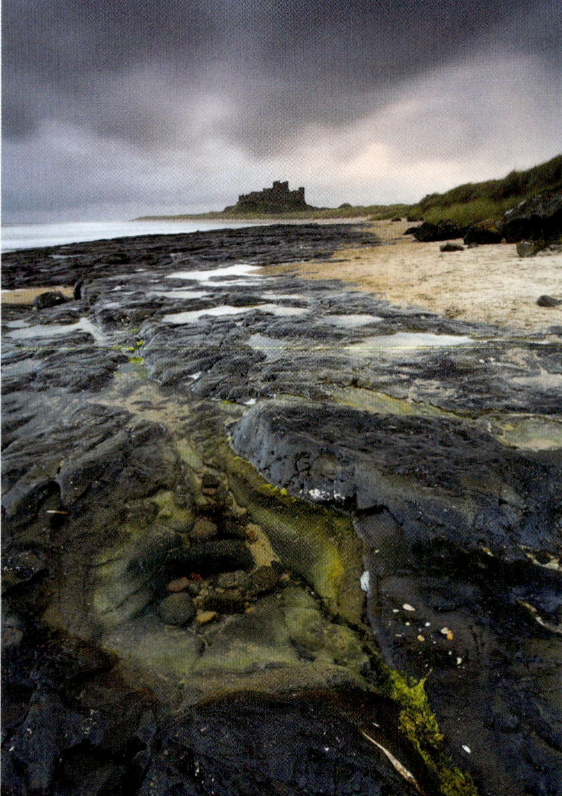

ABOVE: CHOOSE YOUR FORMAT My first image was taken in a horizontal format. It may seem natural to shoot landscapes in this orientation, but wide-angle shots can work better when composed vertically. This allows more room for large foreground details while still including lots of sky.

FAR LEFT: DON'T GO TOO WIDE If you go to the widest end of your zoom, you can suffer not only from barrel distortion, but also vignetting. Barrel distortion will mean that a horizon in the top half of the frame will curve downwards, especially noticeable if you are shooting seascapes. When you notice dark areas appear in the corners of your frame, you are suffering from a spot of vignetting! The wider your focal length the greater chance that the camera will include parts of your kit (e.g. filter holders). Both these problems can be avoided by not taking your lens to its absolute widest setting.

LEFT: GO LOW The scene could do with something to focus attention on the rockpool. It's common for many photographers to shoot with the tripod legs fully extended. But a viewpoint closer to the ground dramatically increases the impact of the foreground subject matter and can provide for a more dynamic composition.

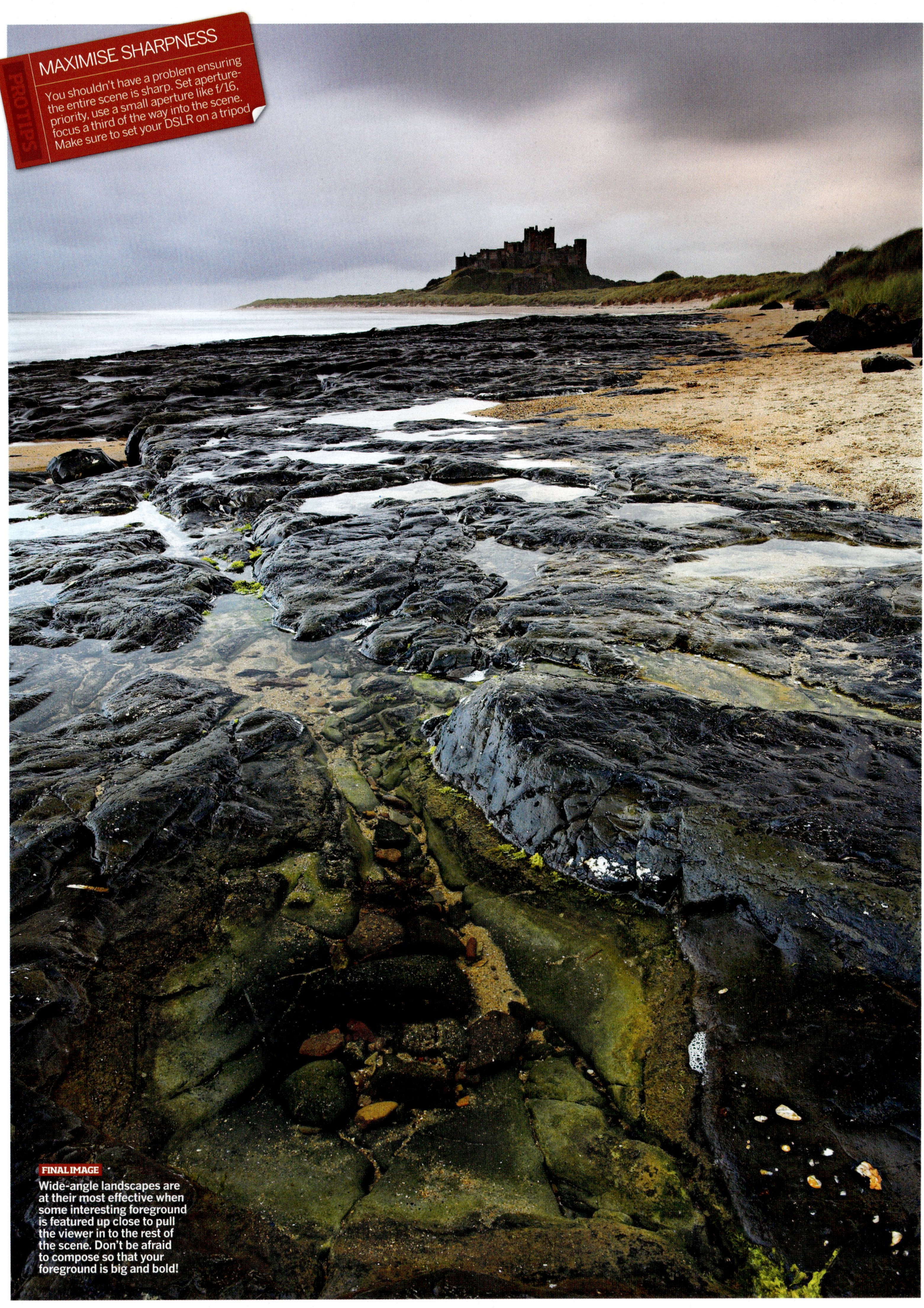

PRO TIPS

MAXIMISE SHARPNESS

You shouldn't have a problem ensuring the entire scene is sharp. Set aperture-priority, use a small aperture like f/16, focus a third of the way into the scene. Make sure to set your DSLR on a tripod

FINAL IMAGE

Wide-angle landscapes are at their most effective when some interesting foreground is featured up close to pull the viewer in to the rest of the scene. Don't be afraid to compose so that your foreground is big and bold!

Telephoto zooms

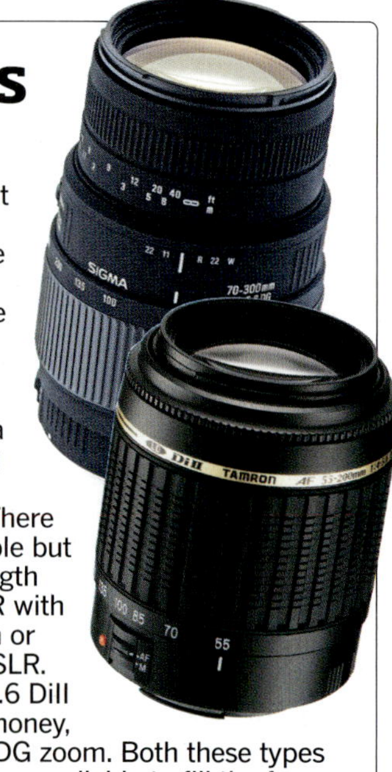

There is no argument that landscape photographers should place a decent wide-angle lens (be it prime or zoom) at the top of their wishlist. However, that's not to say that there shouldn't be a little room allocated in the gadget bag for a telezoom. While you'll predominantly be filling the frame with wide-angle vistas, you'll also find times when a telephoto can prove useful. This will usually be when you want to isolate a specific area or feature within the scene or when you want to create a layering effect through perspective compression (see below). There are a variety of telephoto zooms available but we'd recommend you opt for a focal length of around 55-200mm if you use a DSLR with an APS-C-sized sensor, or a 70-300mm or similar zoom if you have a full-frame DSLR. You'll find the Tamron 55-200mm f/4-5.6 DiII in particular to be very good value for money, along with Sigma's 70-300mm f/4-5.6 DG zoom. Both these types of telezooms are also great lenses to have available to fill the frame with any wildlife you may encounter as you roam the countryside.

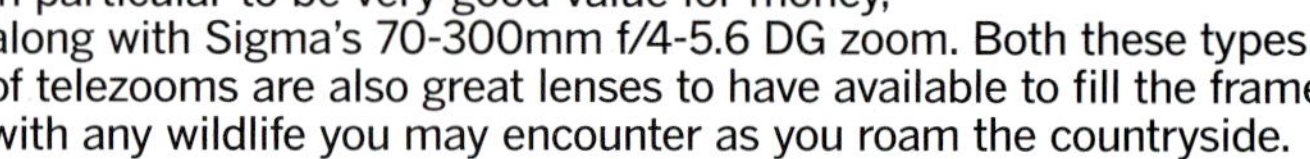

EXPERT TUTORIAL

Perspective compression

Photographers often talk about using a telephoto to compress perspective, but what does it mean?

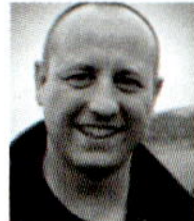

WITH MARK BAUER Technically speaking, telephoto lenses don't 'compress perspective', but practically speaking, you do get a different feeling of perspective from a telephoto shot than from a scene captured with a wide-angle lens. Wide-angle lenses seem to open up perspective and create a sense of depth, because nearby objects appear big, and further objects appear to be very small, suggesting distance. Added to this is the fact that wide-angle lenses create strong diagonals, which enhance the sense of depth (if arranged carefully within the frame). On the other hand, telephotos make distant objects appear larger, apparently compressing the planes of the image and therefore reducing the impression of depth. Lines tend not to stretch into diagonals, and parallels remain parallel, which increases the two-dimensional feel. Compared to a wide-angle view, this all adds up to an image that has a more static feel. And of course, the longer the lens, the greater the effect. So what kind of images benefit from the compression effects of longer lenses? The static character of telephoto images suits tranquil scenes, so hilly landscapes are ideal, especially where there are several planes or 'layers' that can be visually pulled together, so that they appear to be almost stacked on top of each other. The feeling of tranquillity can be enhanced by early morning mist, with the tops of the hills rising above a sea of mist. More dramatic images can be created in the right lighting conditions – look for alternating bands of light and dark, creating a 'layering of light'. Urban landscapes also work well, as you can use compression to juxtapose elements or to suggest a crowded environment.

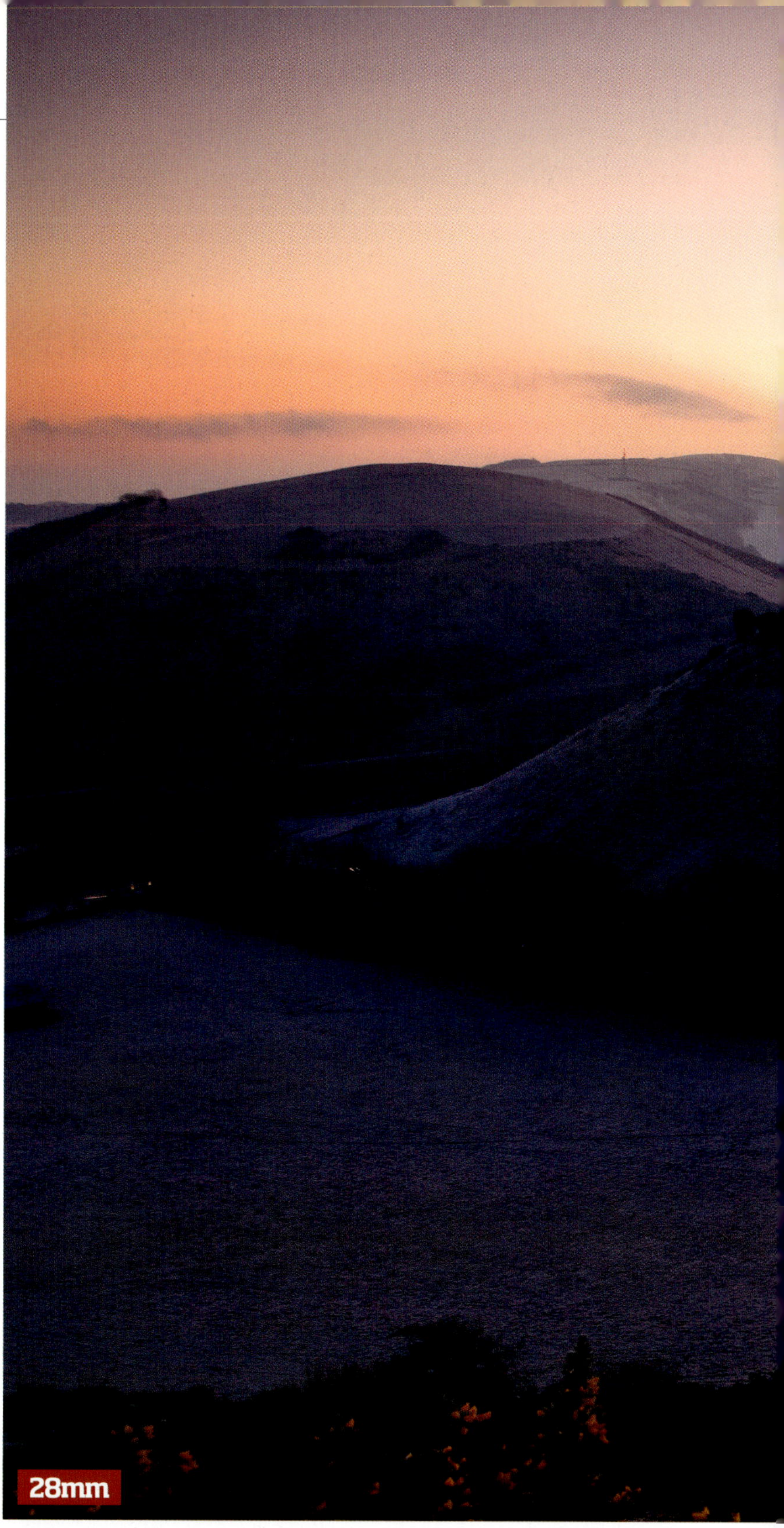

28mm

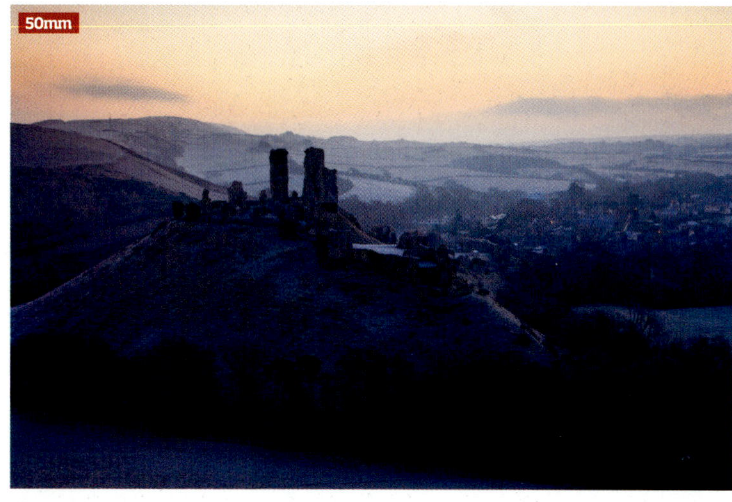

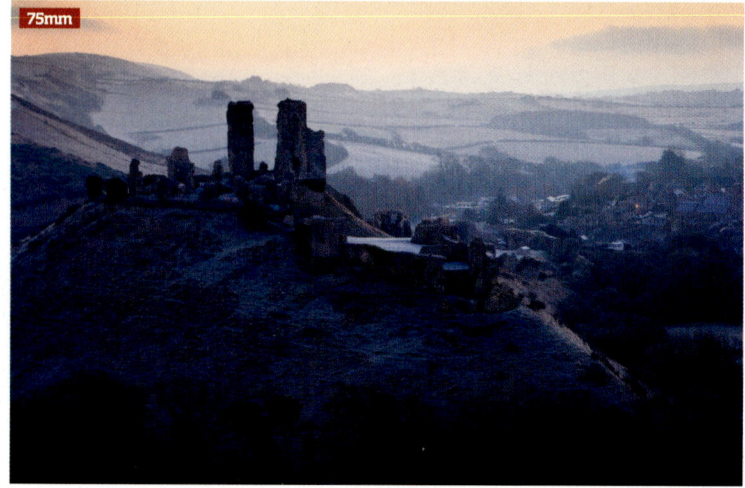

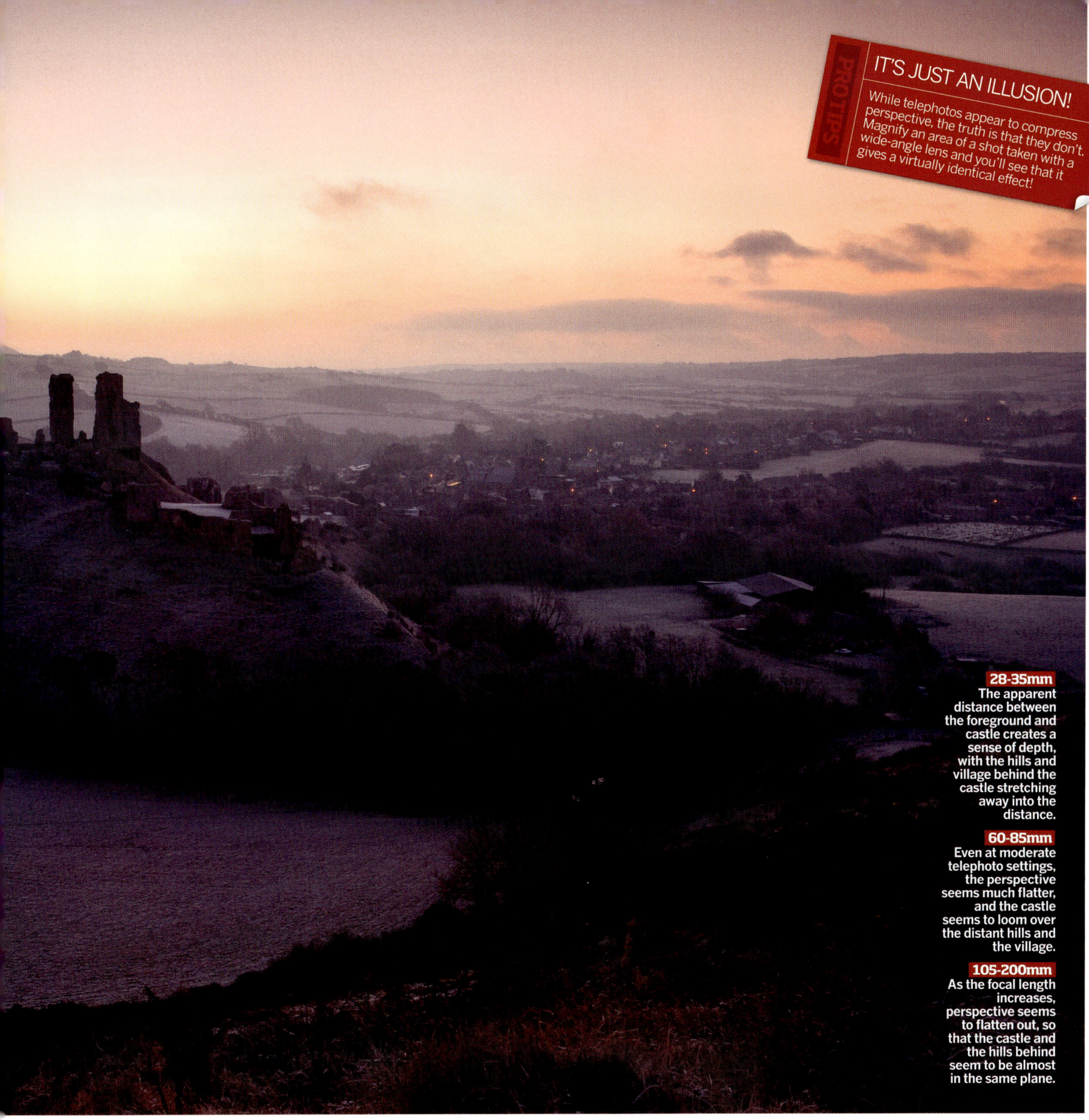

PRO TIPS

IT'S JUST AN ILLUSION!

While telephotos appear to compress perspective, the truth is that they don't. Magnify an area of a shot taken with a wide-angle lens and you'll see that it gives a virtually identical effect!

28-35mm The apparent distance between the foreground and castle creates a sense of depth, with the hills and village behind the castle stretching away into the distance.

60-85mm Even at moderate telephoto settings, the perspective seems much flatter, and the castle seems to loom over the distant hills and the village.

105-200mm As the focal length increases, perspective seems to flatten out, so that the castle and the hills behind seem to be almost in the same plane.

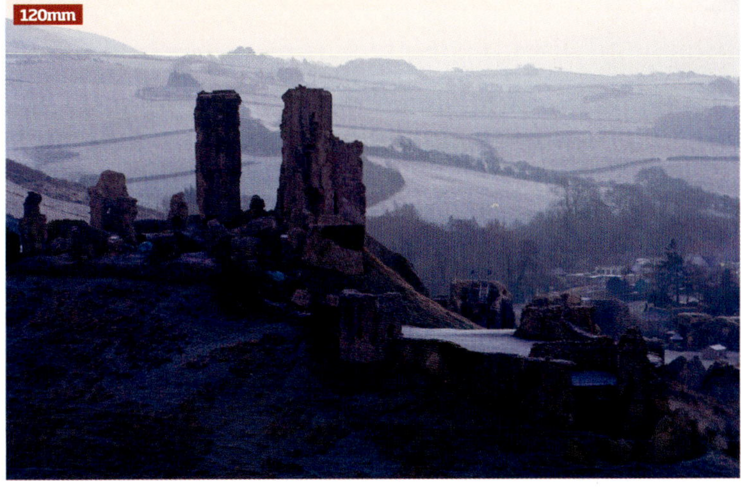
120mm

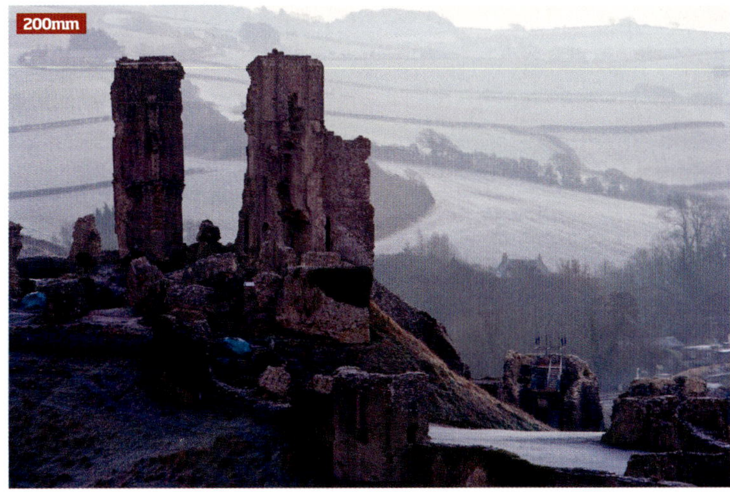
200mm

Choosing the right tripod

FOR LANDSCAPES, A TRIPOD should be viewed as an essential part of your outfit. You'll usually be using a small aperture setting to maximise depth-of-field, along with a low ISO rating to give the highest quality results, which will result in long shutter speeds. Hand-holding might be feasible with some shots but with a tripod you never need to worry about the shakes. You'll also find that by placing the camera on a support, you can spend more time and attention on fine-tuning the framing of the scene to get the best possible composition.

You'll find a huge variety of tripods on offer, so choosing one isn't straightforward, but there are two key factors to consider. The first is stability – while cheaper models may be tempting, the fact is if a tripod doesn't provide a stable platform, it fails. So ensure you pick a model that is sturdy enough to keep your camera kit totally still when shooting. The second factor to think about is how much a tripod weighs, which is important as you'll be carrying it, along with the rest of your gear, for considerable distances. Most tripods are made from aluminium, which is very sturdy and fairly lightweight, although you're looking at tripods weighing around 2kg or more for decent models. If you want a tripod that's just as sturdy but far lighter, you'll want to check out tripods made from carbon-fibre, although you'll have to be prepared to pay a premium for one.

The selection of tripods recommended here have all received the highest ratings in *Digital SLR Photography* magazine. We've chosen examples that cover various price ranges to ensure you find a model that suits your budget. Bear in mind that with the more expensive models, you buy the tripod and the head separately, so you can mix and match to suit your needs. We've stated average street prices at time of publication.

Interchangeable tripod heads

Most high-end tripods aren't supplied with a head. This allows users to choose their preferred legs and a specialist or general-purpose head. The two most common types of heads are as follows:

BALL AND SOCKET: These range from very simple heads with one control to complex units with panoramic locks and gauges, grip-locks, and hydraulic ball-locking systems. Usually stronger and quicker to adjust than pan and tilt heads, they allow free movement in all directions. 'Slipping' used to be a problem, not so much now, though.

THREE-WAY HEADS: Commonly available as pan and tilt heads, these are good for precision work like macro photography, but are great for all types of photography. Panning gauges, showing the shooting angle, are useful for panoramic shots, although there are specialised heads made for this too. Fluid heads have the smoothest panning motion, making them ideal for sports photographers.

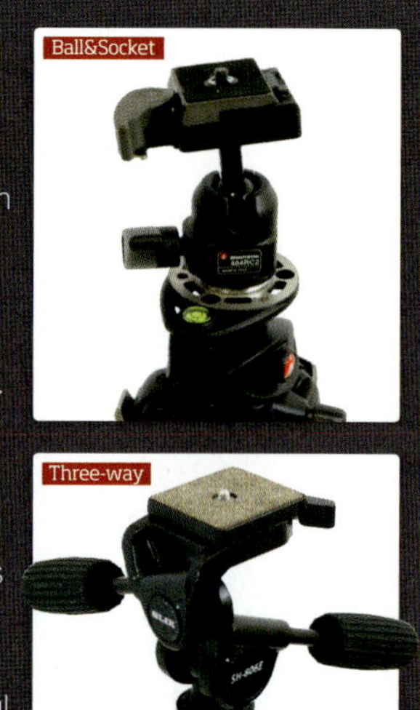

Features

1) HEAD There are various types of tripod head available, from ball and socket to three-way pan and tilt. Some have interchangeable heads. We have tested all the tripods here with three-way pan and tilt heads, which are the most popular for general use. When choosing a tripod, attach your DSLR securely and ensure the head is free from movement.

2) QUICK RELEASE PLATE These allow you to quickly attach and detach your DSLR to/from the tripod. All of the tripods in this review have one.

3) LEG LOCKS Most of the tripods in this test feature 'clip' locks, which are easy to use and provide a firm lock.

4) LEG SECTIONS Tripods with three leg sections or less tend to be the most sturdy, as the more sections you have, the less stable they can become.

5) SPIRIT LEVELS Useful for landscape photography in particular, many tripods feature built-in spirit levels, but if not, you your local photo store should sell one that slots on to your hotshoe.

6) BAG HOOK Some tripods have hooks on the central column, from which a bag can be hung, using its weight to add stability to the tripod in windy conditions.

7) TRIPOD FEET Spikes are good for grip outdoors but will scratch flooring. Rubber feet offer good grip indoors and outside and are the best choice for general use.

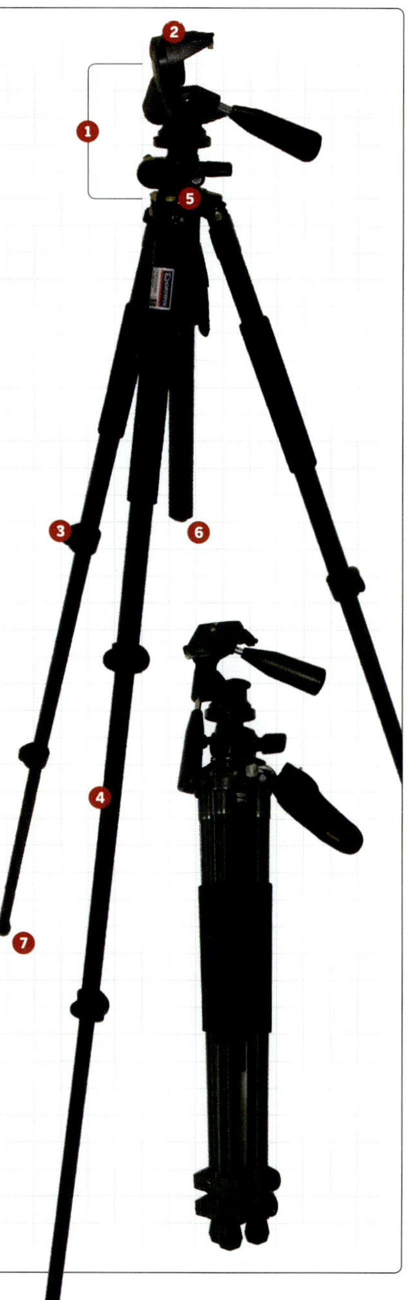

Giottos MTL9351B + MH5011 head

LENGTH (CLOSED): 64cm
NUMBER OF LEG SECTIONS: 3
HEIGHT (LEGS EXTENDED): 159cm
TYPE OF HEAD: Three-way pan and tilt
WEIGHT: 2.1kg
WEBSITE: www.daymen.co.uk

The Giottos has very solid aluminium legs with foam insulators, to keep' hands from freezing to them on cold days. The nuts and locks are a combination of plastic and die-cast aluminium, and are as solid as could be hoped for at this price. The three-way head is easily controllable and features three spirit levels in addition to the one on the legs, so there's no excuse for wonky horizons! It has a lockable rotational central column, which can be removed and re-inserted horizontally or inverted for macro or copy work. The tripod is very sturdy for the price, and comes with its own tool kit in case you need to make any adjustments. There is also a hidden bag hook underneath the central column. The MTL9351B had absolutely no problems coping with our test camera (Nikon D80) and would provide a very suitable platform on which the amateur landscaper could mount his DSLR.

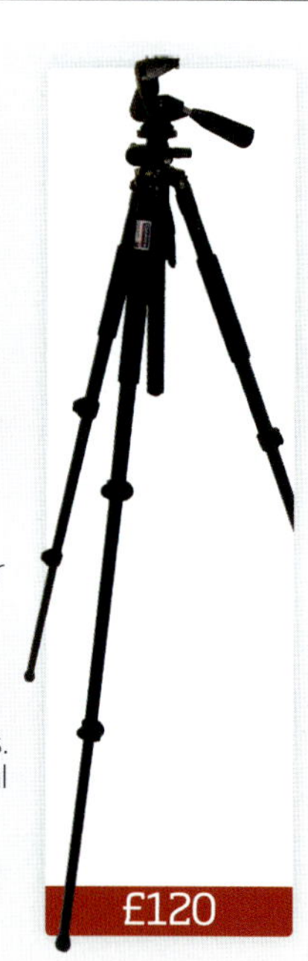

Giottos MTL3361B + MH5001 head

LENGTH (CLOSED): 68cm
HEIGHT (LEGS EXTENDED): 165cm
NUMBER OF LEG SECTIONS: 3
MAXIMUM LOAD: 8kg
WEIGHT: 3.3kg
WEBSITE: www.daymen.co.uk

The build quality of the Giottos is very good. It's heavy, but very solid. The thick aluminium legs offer good stability, even in strong winds. The joints and locks are built to a high quality, and come with a tool kit should they need adjusting. At its maximum height with the central column extended, it still feels stable, and kept our test camera very steady. The tripod has rubber feet, which are slightly pointy, making it perfect for beaches and fields, but it takes a bit longer to stabilise on tarmac or hard surfaces; although once it is set up, it is perfectly steady. The central column can be removed and replaced horizontally, which, when combined with the three-position lockable legs (and they open really wide), allows the camera to get down really low for macro work. With this head fitted, there are three spirit levels to keep your shots straight, and panning is a breeze. There is also a bag hook.

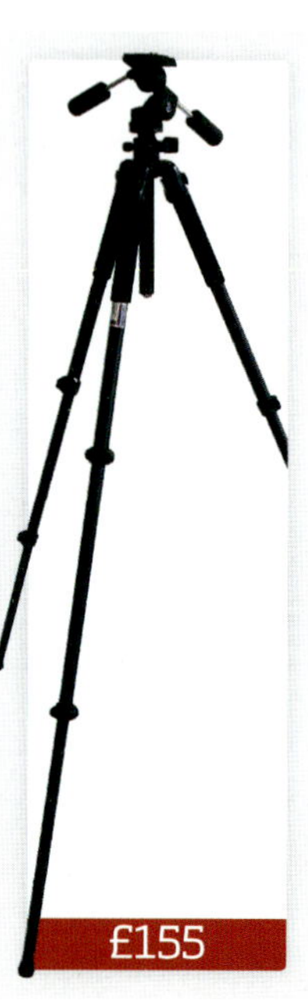

Giottos MT8246B + MH1302-652 head

LENGTH (CLOSED): 51cm
HEIGHT (LEGS EXTENDED): 148cm
NUMBER OF LEG SECTIONS: 4
MAXIMUM LOAD: 3kg
WEIGHT: 1.375kg
WEBSITE: www.daymen.co.uk

This tripod is exceptionally light, especially for its size, yet it is sturdy, although the maximum load may prove restrictive for some. The rubberised twist locks are secure and comfortable to use and foam leg grips give a comfortable grip in cold weather. The three-position angle locks ensure that the legs don't slip, which is reassuring to those using expensive kit. The central column is reversible for low level and macro shots, and has a bag hook. The ball and socket head is also very secure, and it is easy to manoeuvre the head into just about any position. It has a variable friction control, allowing the user a great deal of control, which means that precision adjustments are quick and easy to implement. The three spirit levels help to ensure that horizontals and verticals are perfectly aligned, making this a great all round tripod for almost any type of photography, not least landscapes.

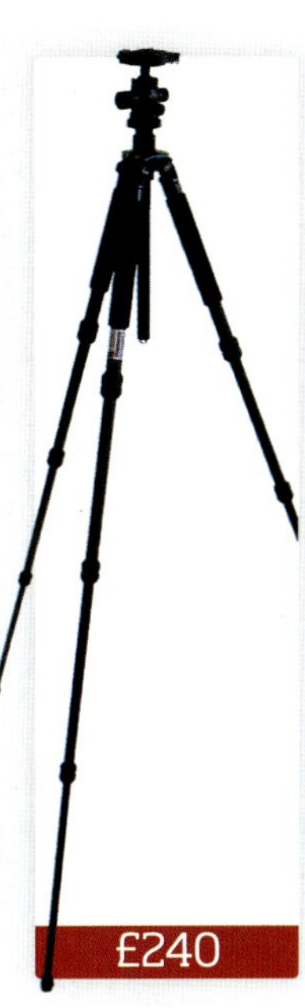

£240

Manfrotto 190CXPRO3 + 484 RC2 head

LENGTH (CLOSED): 58cm
HEIGHT (LEGS EXTENDED): 146cm
NUMBER OF LEG SECTIONS: 3
MAXIMUM LOAD: 5kg
WEIGHT: 1.62kg
WEBSITE: www.bogenimaging.co.uk

This Manfrotto is exceptionally light, and its sleek design looks fantastic. Despite its thin legs, it was sturdy and supported our test camera with ease. The twist locks are very strong and prove quick to use. The central column can be raised and moved into horizontal position without removing it from the legs, making the tripod perfect for macro and low level shots, and very easy to use. The multi-position leg locks have a depressable button, making them much easier and nicer to use than those that have clips that must be lifted. The ball and socket head is very smooth and easy to use, as one switch controls everything. This is ideal for quick positioning, but not as precise as some of the other heads in the test. There is a spirit level, to ensure that your tripod is level, and the centre column boasts a bag hook, allowing extra weight to be attached for stability in high winds.

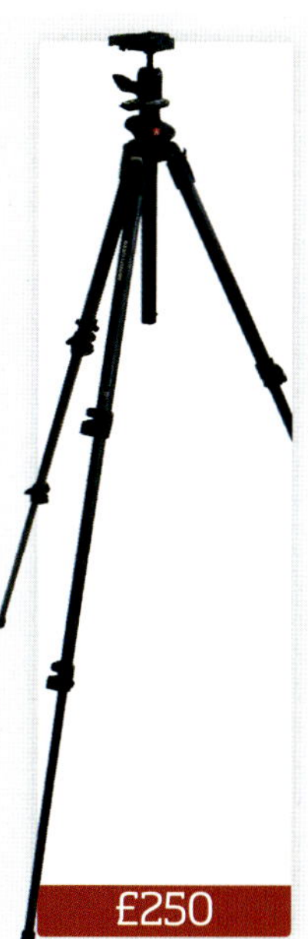

£250

Manfrotto 190XPROB + 460 MG head

LENGTH (CLOSED): 57cm
HEIGHT (LEGS EXTENDED): 146cm
NUMBER OF LEG SECTIONS: 3
MAXIMUM LOAD: 5kg
WEIGHT: 2.25kg
WEBSITE: www.bogenimaging.co.uk

This aluminium tripod from Manfrotto is one of the lightest in this price category. The legs are very sturdy and supports the camera perfectly well in all positions. The flip locks are easy to open and close and very secure, and there are vari-position locks to keep the legs secure at different settings. Perhaps the most interesting feature of the legs, is that the central column can be switched to horizontal position, for macro shots, without removing it from the legs. This is an excellent feature, as it makes the process very easy and fast to carry out. The head is very versatile, as it can pan, tilt and swivel in just about any direction, and is very easy to operate. The lack of panning handles may not be to everyone's taste, but the head is so versatile that it more than makes up for it. Spirit levels can be found on the head and central column brace, and a bag hook is located on the legs.

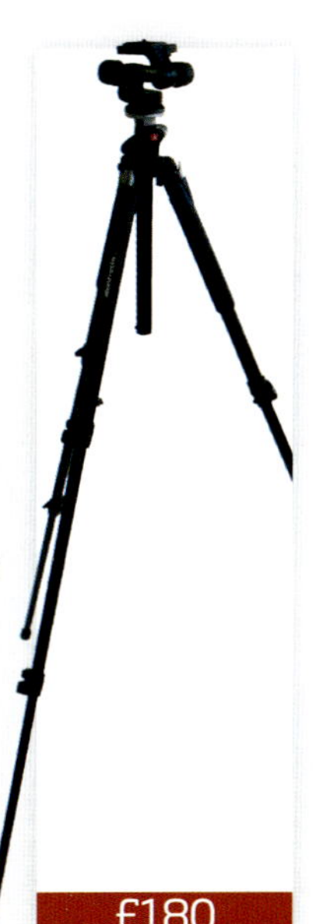

£180

Velbon Sherpa 435 With PHD-41Q head

LENGTH (CLOSED): 53cm
HEIGHT (OPEN): 161cm
NUMBER OF LEG SECTIONS: 3
WEIGHT: 1.49kg
MAX LOAD: 3kg
WEBSITE: www.intro2020.co.uk

At the more affordable end of the market is this combined head and legs set from Velbon. The tripod's black aluminium legs have three sections, locked in place with easy-to-open clip-style locks. The centre column is adjustable and reversible for low-angle shooting. For an entry-level model, the PHD-41Q head is a good buy too. It's bigger and more sturdy than others in this bracket and will take loads of up to 3kg with no problem. We like the head's relative simplicity: using it quickly becomes second nature. Two padded handles control movement, and one of these unscrews and fits inside the other when the tripod is stored. A well-designed quick-release plate completes the package. This is a cracking buy for the beginner or intermediate photographer who wants a general purpose tripod to improve their images and open more options.

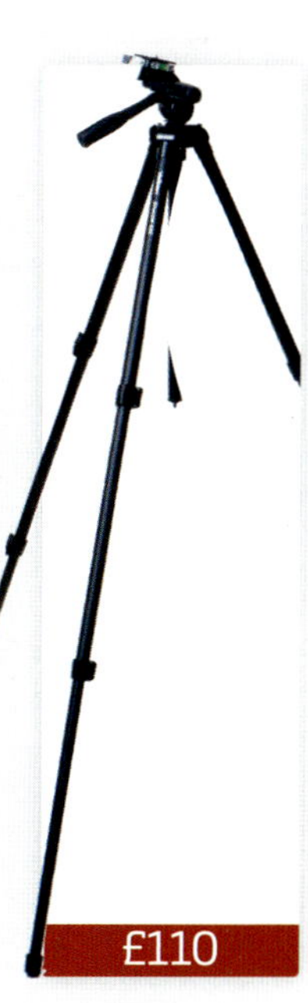

£110

Manfrotto 055XPROB + 322RC2 head

LENGTH (CLOSED): 65.5cm
HEIGHT (LEGS EXTENDED): 178.5cm
NUMBER OF LEG SECTIONS: 3
MAXIMUM LOAD: 7kg
WEIGHT: 3.15kg
WEBSITE: www.bogenimaging.co.uk

The build quality of this die-cast aluminium tripod is excellent. It is very sturdy, and very reassuring. The 055XPROB features the same dual positioning central column as the 190XPROB, as well as a spirit level, bag hook and foam leg grips, which help to protect the user's hands when using the tripod in cold weather. The legs each have a four-position lock, which makes it versatile and secure. You'll either love or hate the trigger-style grip head, but we found it incredibly quick and easy to adjust, getting your camera into just the right position with the minimum of fuss. Not having to tighten levers also saves time, and reduces the risk of knocking the head out of place. The head has its own spirit level, allowing you to make sure that your camera is level. This head is particularly useful when combined with the versatility of the central column of the tripod and when shooting macro.

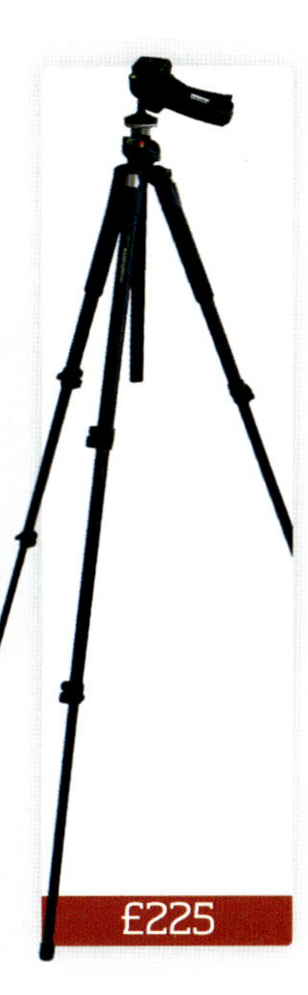

£225

Slik Pro 700DX with 700DX pan & tilt head

LENGTH (CLOSED): 76cm
HEIGHT (LEGS EXTENDED): 190cm
NUMBER OF LEG SECTIONS: 3
MAXIMUM LOAD: 6.8kg
WEIGHT: 3.2kg
WEBSITE: www.intro2020.co.uk

The largest tripod in this category is very sturdy and feels as though it could withstand any treatment. The design is simple but stylish, and it certainly looks like a tripod for serious use. Although it is quite heavy, it is still very portable for its size. The locks are strong and secure, yet easy to open, while the reversible central column allows users to take low level and macro shots with ease. This is particularly effective when used with the legs open wide, which can be done easily using the three-position locks, which hold them firmly in position. The pan and tilt head features a panning lock, and has a very smooth panning motion. The quick release plate is circular, which makes it very easy to attach and detach the camera. There are two spirit levels, which help to keep horizontals and verticals straight. Although there is no bag hook, the tripod is so sturdy you are unlikely to miss it.

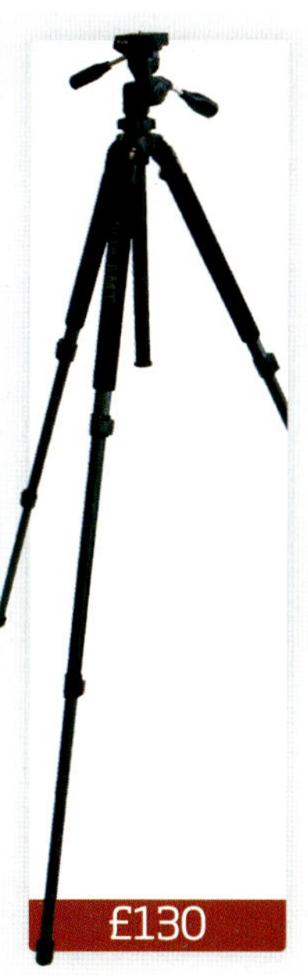

£130

Gadget bags and backpacks

YOUR MAIN CONSIDERATIONS should be how much kit can it hold and whether to go for a bag that hangs over the shoulder or a backpack. Most outdoor photographers prefer backpacks as they distribute weight over your shoulders and back, making it far easier to carry gear over long distances. The daypack holds photo gear in the bottom section and general items in the top compartment, while dedicated photo backpacks are designed with larger kits in mind. Consider the following:

Comfort: As you carry more kit, the weight increases, so shoulder straps are important. The wider and more padded they are, the less they dig into your shoulders. Waist straps are useful, as they relieve tension from the lumbar region and help keep your back straight. Another important factor is the bag's frame. Some are sturdier than others, which may seem uncomfortable at first, but can help keep your back straight on long treks.

Capacity: Think about how much kit you plan to carry. This will ultimately determine the size of bag you need. All the bags in this test have adjustable compartments, so they are quite versatile. We also list internal dimensions, so you can see exactly how much space they offer.

Features (see panel below): Some photographers just want a bag with lots of space, others are more demanding over specific features. Most have have front pockets, designed to help you organise your memory cards and batteries into used and unused. Many of the bags have water bottle holders, tripod clips or pouches and rain covers.

Build Quality: How well the backpack is put together, including the stitching, zippers and weatherproofing, determines how long it ought to last, how strong it is and how well it protects your equipment.

Price: We've stated average street prices at time of publication.

Fitting and wearing a bag properly

If you're carrying a lot of heavy kit, it's important that your bag sits correctly on your back or at your side. This advice can prevent all kinds of back and posture problems. With a backpack, ensure that both straps are over your shoulders and tightened so that the bag sits in the centre of your back. If it has waist and chest straps, make sure you use them to distribute the weight evenly across your back, rather than just your shoulders. For shoulder bags, pull the strap over your head to the opposite shoulder. This will distribute the weight better than if it were on the closest shoulder and stops it from slipping off your shoulder, or being easily snatched.

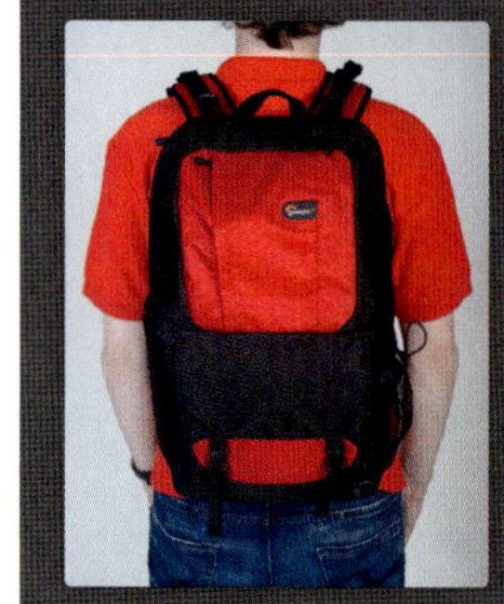

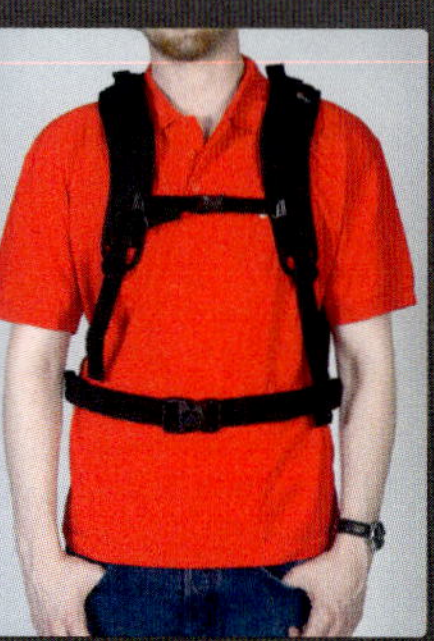

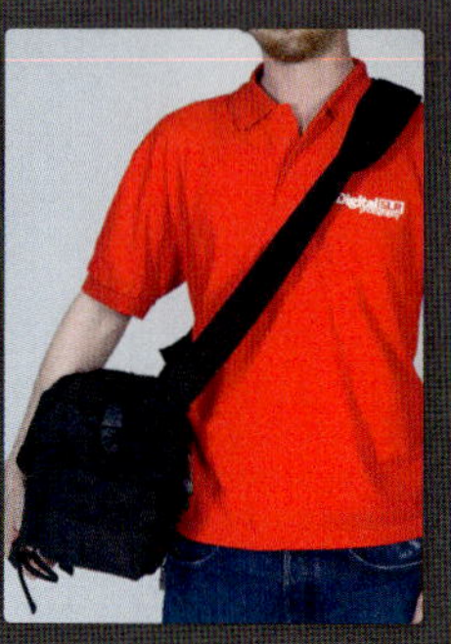

Features

1) STRAPS Check to see if the straps are adjustable, padded and wide, to stop them from cutting into your shoulders on long journeys. Also look for waist straps.

2) PADDING Some bags have pressure pads on the back, which will take a lot of the strain out of long journeys and spread the weight of the gear over a larger area.

3) STORAGE/CAPACITY Does the bag hold all the equipment you will need for your photography? If there is too much empty space, the bag will be unbalanced, which can be bad for your back. All the bags in this test feature adjustable dividers and offer quite a bit of versatility.

4) WEATHERPROOFING/ RAIN COVER Most bags are weather resistant. Some are weather proof, and others have all-weather covers that can be pulled out from a hidden compartment, usually on the base.

5) LAPTOP COMPARTMENT Make sure that the laptop compartment is big enough for your computer, as they vary in size. The padding is also important here.

6) ACCESSORY CLIPS Some bags allow you to attach further bags, tripods and monopods, but some are only compatible with the manufacturer's own clip systems.

7) ZIPS If you go out a lot in bad weather or near water, make sure that the zips are up to it. Wildlife photographers should also consider the noise made by the zips, as animals can be easily frightened off.

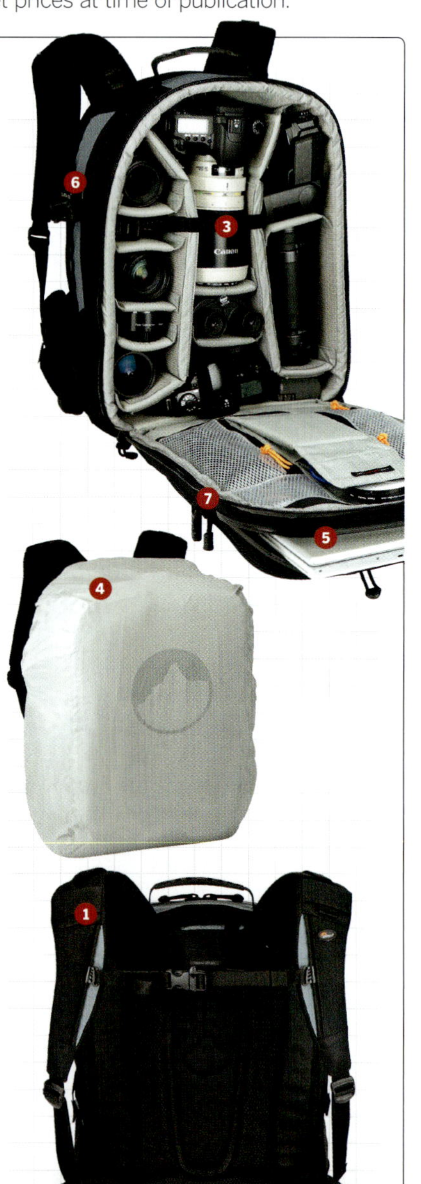

Camera Armor Seattle Sling

WEIGHT: 1.2kg
DIMENSIONS (OUTER): 370x240x215mm
DIMENSIONS (INNER): 279x114x203mm
WEBSITE: www.daymen.co.uk

The Seattle Sling strap is placed over the head to hang the bag on the back, which means weight is better distributed. It has no zippers – the main flap features a large Velcro-type fastener. Inside is the bright orange nylon inner dry bag, which provides protection against water, dust and sand. The seal has magnetic strips and is rolled over three times before being secured by clips (outside the bag) to keep it firmly sealed. The interior compartment has padded, movable dividers. It's a bag designed to hold a small to medium-sized outfit – a central area is large enough to hold a standard DSLR with kit lens. Four smaller compartments hold lenses or accessories. There aren't any pockets on the outside, so small accessories will need to be stored in this area too.

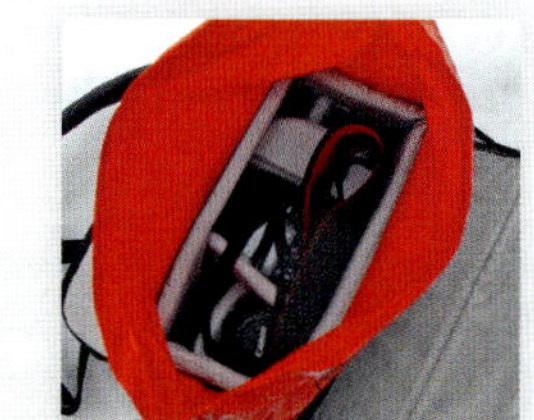

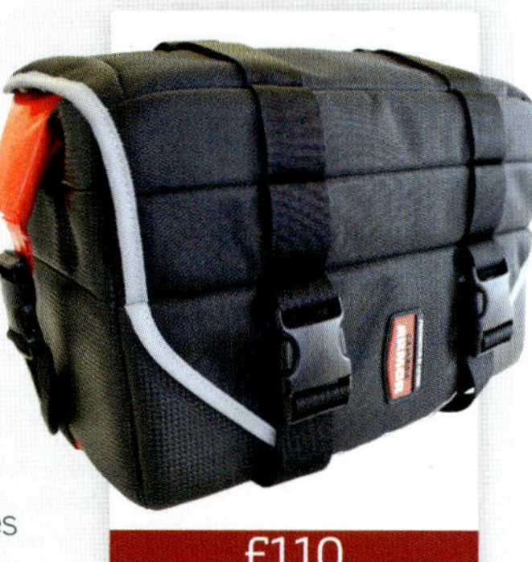

£110

Lowepro Classified 250 AW

WEIGHT: 1.9kg
DIMENSIONS (OUTER): 465x280x355mm
DIMENSIONS (INNER): 380x160x280mm
WEBSITE: www.daymen.com

A discreet camera bag with room for lots of camera gear as well as a laptop. The interior of the bag is very deep, so you can double-up on storage by stacking items on top of each other. The bag's depth also makes it very suitable for cameras with long lenses. A padded section provides storage for a 15in laptop. Leather is used to good effect throughout the bag and the grab handles and shoulder strap are very well designed. Entry into the main section of the bag is through a clever roof zip set-up that is easy to access on the move and is protected by the handle buckling over it. Realistically, you'll be able to fit at least two DSLRs with an additional two or three lenses in the spacious main section. A luggage sleeve means that you can attach the Classified 250AW to the handles of a wheelie case. The bag is hand-luggage friendly too.

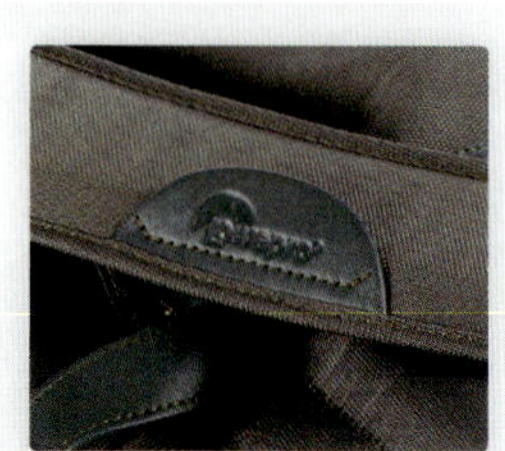

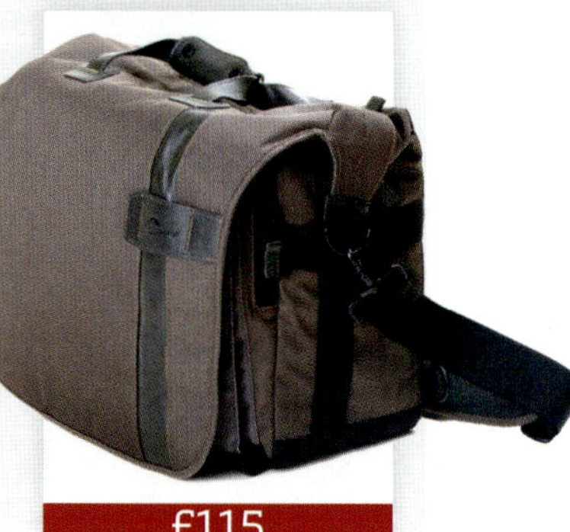

£115

Tamrac Expedition 8

WEIGHT: 3.3kg
DIMENSIONS (OUTER): 330x560x340mm
DIMENSIONS (INNER): 280x520x160mm
WEBSITE: www.intro2020.co.uk

Despite its large size, this impeccably-made bag is comfortable, even when fully laden. The soft pads disperse pressure across the back and the straps are secure and easily adjustable. The Expedition 8 has space for a pro DSLR body with a large telephoto zoom, as well as seven other lenses, two spare camera bodies and two flashguns. There is also copious space for accessories with spent batteries and full memory cards down one side, full batteries and new cards down the other. Red 'flags' indicate used or fresh. There is a wide range of accessories that can be clipped on either to the straps of the bag or the bag itself, using Tamrac's Modular and Strap Accessory Systems (M.A.S and S.A.S). There is also a handy tripod foot pocket which, combined with the straps, makes carrying a tripod much easier and comfortable.

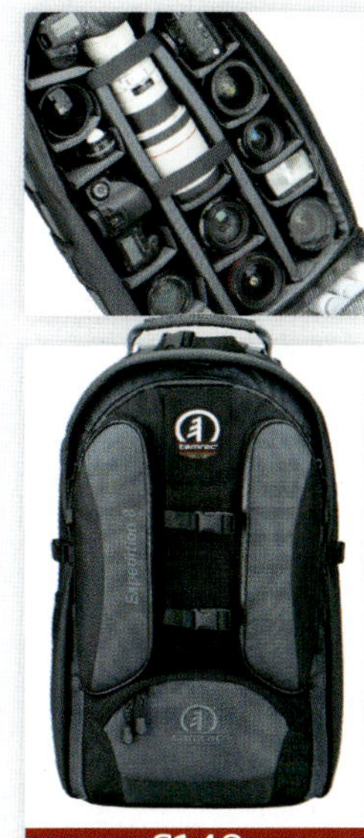

£140

Tamrac Adventure 6

WEIGHT: 0.89kg
DIMENSIONS (OUTER): 290x220x390mm
DIMENSIONS (INNER): 240x130x140mm
WEBSITE: www.intro2020.co.uk

As a day or travel bag, this is a nice size for the amateur snapper and, priced at just £50, it's cheap too. Like most day sacks, it is divided into two main sections: the top compartment is like a normal bag, for storing maps, a packed lunch or a cagoule, though you'd struggle to squeeze a thicker jacket. The bottom part is set up for photo gear, and divided by removable pads. It's quite a tight fit for a DSLR and three lenses, though it is big enough for a camera with a standard lens and one compact zoom lens – ideal light travel kit. If you needed to carry more, you could always store chargers and a flashgun in the main compartment. The front pocket is also large enough for memory cards and batteries. The straps include the full waist and chest support but lack any padding around the waist, while the shoulder straps are quite thin; though the back of the bag has decent padding.

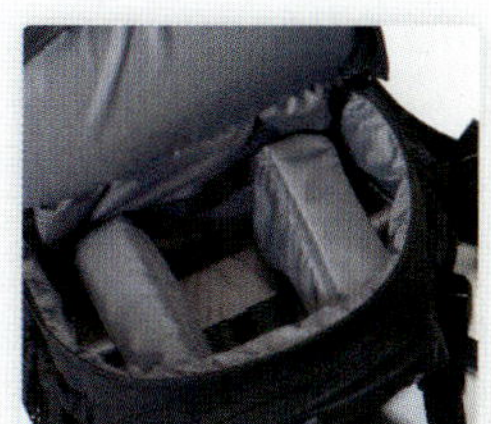

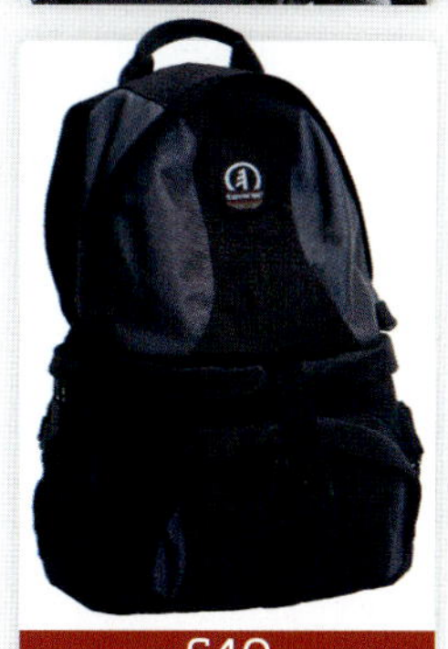

£40

Lowepro Fastpack 350

WEIGHT: 1.85kg
DIMENSIONS (OUTER): 315x245x490mm
DIMENSIONS (INNER): 280x155x270mm
WEBSITE: www.lowepro.com

Fastpack is designed for the multimedia snapper. The lower storage section is a 'Slingshot' design that allows you to quickly access your camera without fully opening the bag. There's room for three or four lenses plus accessories and even a pro DSLR. The dividers are all moveable too, so you can arrange them to suit your kit. The top section is designed as a normal day sack, with plenty of space for clothing or equipment. The longer body of this bag also allows it to house a 17in laptop in a padded zipped section. There are additional pockets on the front for storing smaller items, while inside the bottom section are pockets for memory cards. The shoulder straps and back support are well padded and there are chest and waist straps for extra support. The bag is made from a tough, water-resistant fabric, though there's no weatherproofing on the zips.

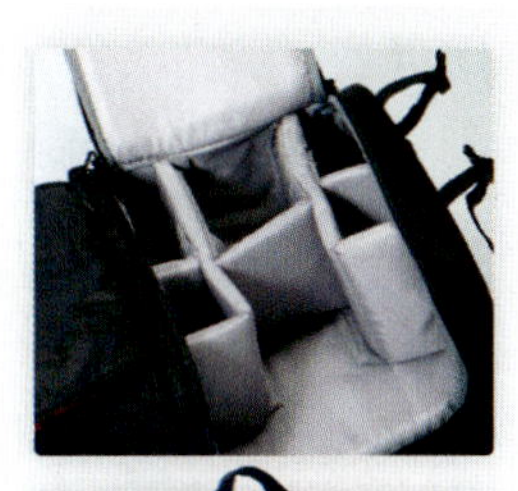

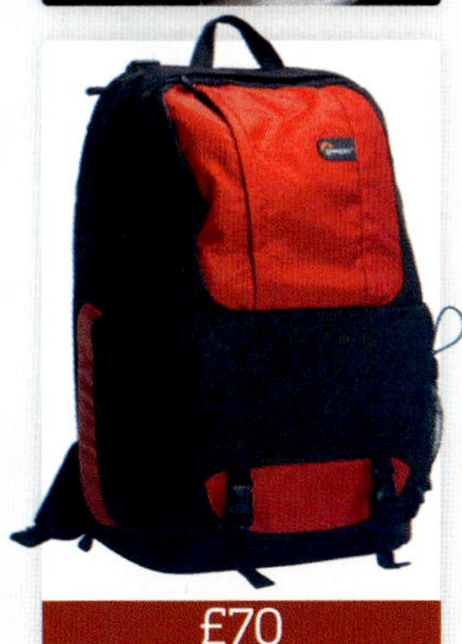

£70

Lowepro Vertex 200 AW

WEIGHT: 3.3kg
DIMENSIONS (OUTER): 320x260x470mm
DIMENSIONS (INNER): 300x165x440mm
WEBSITE: www.lowepro.com

The Vertex can withstand rough handling and serious conditions. The main section is very spacious, with over a dozen compartments separated by adjustable, padded walls. There is plenty of room to fit a couple of cameras, six lenses and still have space for a flashgun and accessories. On the inner side of the front compartment are five small pockets to hold smaller accessories like filters, batteries, lens cloths etc. The main area of this front section is padded out to hold a laptop computer. On the outer front of this section are two more compartments that run the length of the bag with space for a tripod between them. Within both are smaller pockets for holding memory cards and small accessories that you may need fast access to. Other features worth mentioning are the carry strap at the top, two side pockets and the all weather cover.

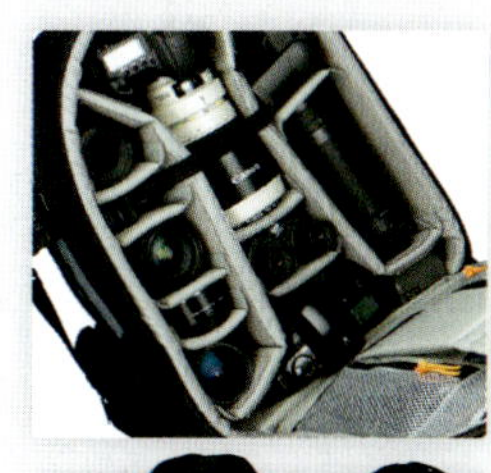

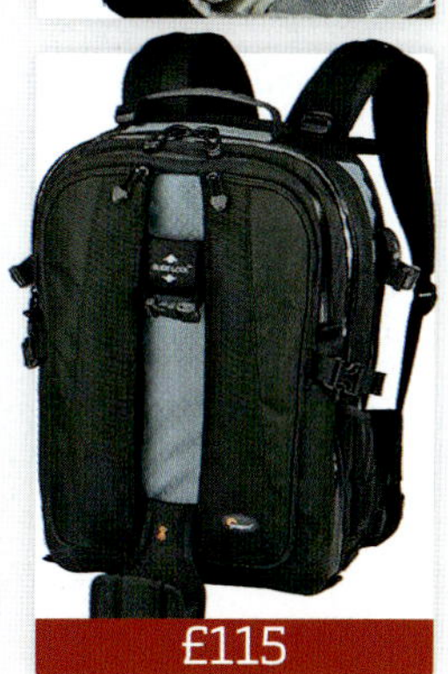

£115

Crumpler Pretty Boy backpack

WEIGHT: 0.9kg
DIMENSIONS (OUTER): 370x480x220mm
DIMENSIONS (INNER): 290x180x180mm
WEBSITE: www.intro2020.co.uk

The Pretty Boy's shell-like construction has the fresh look that Crumpler is famous for and is available in a variety of colours. Inside, it follows the normal day sack set up – the top section is fairly large and with a bit of effort, you could probably get a fleece and a raincoat tucked away. The bottom photo section is nicely padded with, in this case, bright orange removable pads. Because this section of the bag is rounded, it isn't as spacious as it might have been, but it's still large enough to house a DSLR, a couple of extra lenses and accessories. Also, as the zip opens straight across, the bag levers right open, allowing easy access. The shoulder straps are wide, while the back support is well padded, but it lacks the waist and chest straps. While the fabric is thick and water-resistant, there's no waterproofing on the zips or fold out cover.

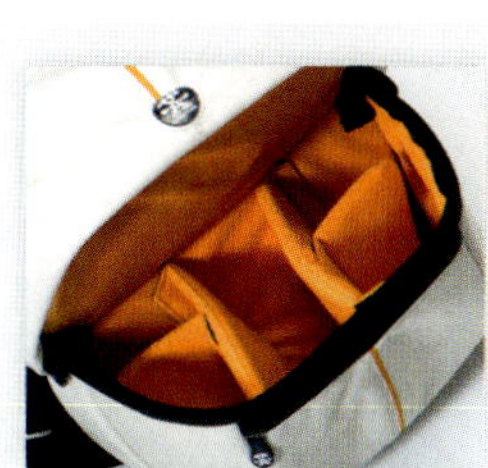

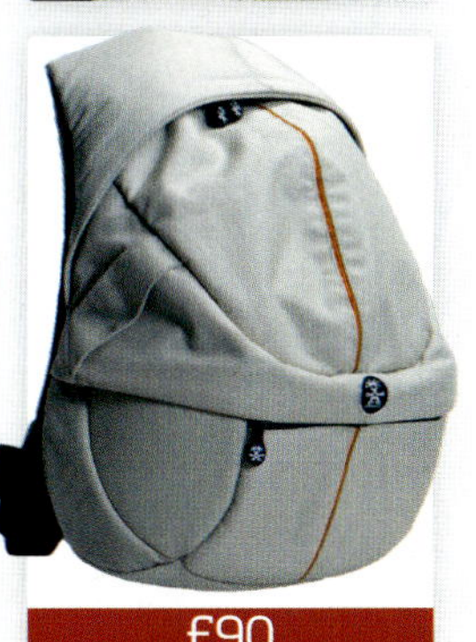

£90

Lowepro Pro Runner 350 AW

WEIGHT: 2.1kg
DIMENSIONS (OUTER): 330x265x455mm
DIMENSIONS (INNER): 285x115x385mm
WEBSITE: www.daymen.com

If you're planning a lengthy trip and need to carry a large photo outfit as well as a laptop and other accessories, then the Pro Runner, a recent replacement for the popular CompuTrekker is definitely one that you should consider. Capable of holding two to three DSLRs, plus several lenses, the Pro Runner is a big bag that has been designed to offer a high level of protection to your kit. It's one of the toughest and most rugged bags in this price bracket. In fact, the Lowepro's standout feature is not only the level of padding it offers to your equipment but also how it's designed to sit on your back. When fully laden backpacks of this size are heavy and an ill-fitting backpack can cause strain on your back, but the Lowepro's enhanced lumbar padding will ensure your vertebra remain ache-free. If you need a spacious bag, then make sure to check out this new backpack.

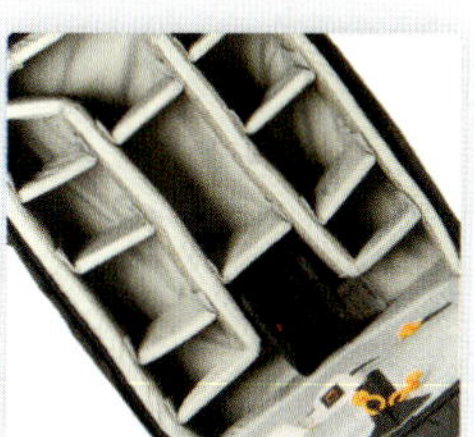

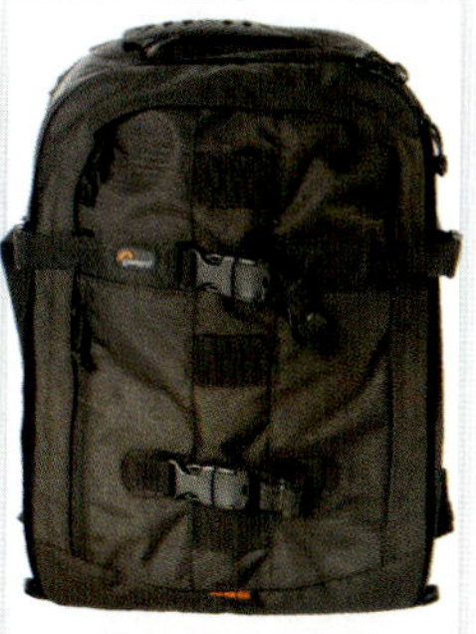

£140

Essential accessories

CHOOSING WHAT YOU NEED to take with you or leave behind isn't easy. You have to balance the fact that you don't want to be walking around with a heavy load with that of not wanting to discover miles from your base that you're missing a vital piece of kit. Here we run through the items that make up a shortlist of accessories to consider.

1) NAVIGATIONAL AIDS There are a number of useful tools available to make sure you head in the right direction. A simple compass and an Ordnance Survey map are the basic requirements – both are available from high street camping shops. If you use a map, we'd recommend a waterproof casing, such as the Aquamap case from Outdoor Designs (www.outdoordesigns.co.uk). Handheld GPS units have become far more commonplace and if you're serious about your outdoor photography, one that we've found to deliver a superb performance is the Active 10 by SatMap (www.satmap.com). It's expensive at around £295 but is incredibly accurate and is preloaded with maps for the whole of the UK, with additional maps available on SD cards. If you're keen on shooting sunrises and sunsets, there are a number of sun compasses that do a great job, from the credit-card sized £3 Depssi card by Blue Pond (www.bluepondimages.com) to the £20 Flight Logistics (www.flight-logistics.com).

2) MEMORY CARDS The price of memory cards has fallen to such a low that there is little excuse for not having a small collection of them in your kit bag. In terms of capacity, we recommend going for a set of two to six 4GB cards, depending on the length of your trip. Choose from a reputable brand like Lexar or SanDisk to minimise the risk of a card developing a fault and losing any images stored on it.

3) LENS HOOD As well as preventing flare from the sun, which can ruin picture quality, a lens hood also provides suitable protection for your lens in the rain, so leave it fitted at all times. Watch out for vignetting on ultra wide-angle lenses.

4) REMOTE RELEASES Long exposures mean camera shake is a real problem. Using an electronic remote release helps minimise camera movement when firing the shutter. The type you'll need depends on the DSLR you own, so check your instruction book or the manufacturer's website. Prices start at around £20 for a basic remote.

5) PERSONAL STORAGE DEVICE If you plan a trip running any longer than a weekend, you'll most likely need some form of image back-up. A laptop's the ideal choice if you want to Photoshop your images while away, but for most, a personal storage device is a better option. Choose a model with a large LCD monitor so that you can review and edit images. The Jobo Giga Vu Evolution and Extreme models are excellent, but our favourite is the 80Gb Epson P-6000, which has slots for SD and CompactFlash cards and a bright, sharp 4in screen.

6) CLEANING KIT Keep one or even two lens cloths in your gadget bag. As well as being perfect for cleaning dirt marks and dust from your lens surfaces, they're also ideal to wipe away raindrops. Two cloths allow you to use one just for moisture and heavy soiling.

7) HOTSHOE SPIRIT LEVEL Avoiding uneven horizons is relatively easy. Use a tripod with an integral spirit level or slip a cheap and cheerful spirit level onto your hotshoe. Alternatively, buy a Seculine Action Level (www.intro2020.co.uk) and use its colour LEDs and audible beeps to help you straighten up your camera.

8) LIGHT METER For perfect exposures, you can't beat the precision of a handheld meter. While your camera's integral meter is very accurate, many pros still swear by the extra versatility and precision given by a handheld meter. For those looking for absolute reassurance, we'd recommend the Sekonic L-308s, which is the latest version of the landscaper's favourite. Small, accurate and easy to use, this tidy little number represents excellent value for money at £130.

9) SPARE BATTERIES Make sure you take your charger away with you and charge your batteres the night before. If you can, carry a spare set with you. If your DSLR uses a lithium-ion cell, as well as the branded battery, there are various third party options too. Ask your dealer or check the classified and dealer ads in *Digital SLR Photography* magazine for details. If your DSLR uses AA batteries, you'll find rechargeables from the likes of Energizer are superb, as is the new range of Eneloop batteries from Sanyo ((www.intro2020.co.uk).

10) SAFETY PACK It's worth keeping a small selection of high-energy snack bars in your kitbag to keep you going beyond meal times or in an emergency. You should also pack a whistle and a torch just in case you get lost or have an accident while on your own. If you're heading to isolated areas, make sure you take your mobile phone and ensure it's fully charged before you leave. Always tell someone your plans.

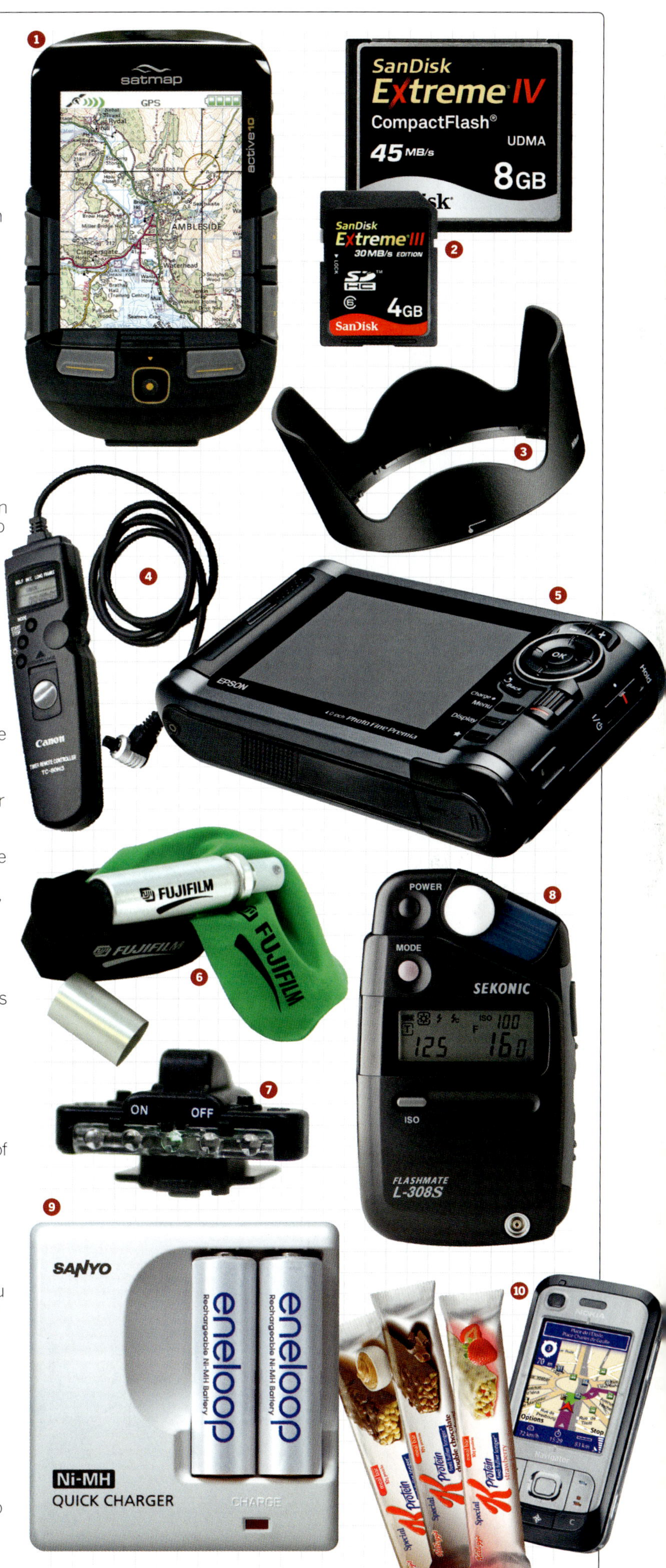

Clothing accessories

DEDICATED OUTDOOR PHOTOGRAPHERS are often shooting from before dawn until after dusk and you'll find them dressed accordingly. As well as thick clothing to deal with cold temperatures and high winds, you should also consider breathable garments to allow perspiration to evaporate in the heat and comfortable footwear that can handle hours of trudging along green countryside, rocky mountains and wet bogs. Ensure you're protected from the elements by following our guide to the best.

1) KEEP YOUR HEAD WARM WITH A BEANIE HAT! You lose close to a third of your body heat through your head and so it's important to wear a hat or cap in cold conditions. While baseball caps are OK, their peak will get in the way when you hold the camera to your eye. You can always spin it round but maybe opt for a beanie hat instead, which will help keep your head warm and won't take up much space when you take it off. You'll find them available in plain or patterned designs to suit your fashion sense (or lack of it!).

2) KEEP YOUR FINGERS NIMBLE! Cold winds can really freeze up your fingers and make it more difficult to press buttons and tweak controls on your DSLR. The easiest solution is to wear gloves, although standard types are quite thick and still make it difficult to operate your camera. Our favourites are both made by Outdoor Designs (www.outdoordesigns.co.uk) and are well worth trying out. The Takustretch has a grip palm and is made from wind-resistant materials to keep your hands warm. Better still is the Konagrip convertible, a windproof fleece glove with leather grip palm and flip-over finger mitt.

3) WEAR GOOD FOOTWEAR! You're more than likely going to cover miles in pursuit of stunning landscapes, so your average trainers aren't the best choice. Depending on how far you plan to walk, the type of terrain and time of year, you should look to wear shoes that are comfortable, hard-wearing and practical. Walking boots are best for serious treks and the likes of the £90 Berghaus Explorer (www.berghaus.com) are ideal, offering comfort, durability and support. You'll find them available for men and women in various colours. Another great option is Patagonia's Thatcher hiking shoes (www.patagonia.com), which are extremely comfortable and lightweight and incredibly durable. They're fashionable too and very well priced at around £60.

4) DON'T FORGET YOUR SOCKS! Cold or wet feet make walking around a real misery, as can wearing too thick a sock in warmer conditions. It's worth buying a couple of pairs of decent socks to suit the season and type of shoe you wear. Bridgedale (www.bridgedale.com) are leaders in this department, offering socks to suit cold weather, light treks or longer walks where comfort is essential. They've a bewildering choice on offer, but we'd recommend the Endurance Trekker and Comfort Trekker for longer walks, and the lightweight Bamboo Crew in warmer weather.

5) KEEP YOUR BODY WARM AND DRY! The humble fleece is an unsung hero in outdoor clothing, proving relatively lightweight, incredibly warm and very hard-wearing. They're also available in various designs and colours too, so are as fashionable as they are practical. You'll find all high street fashion stores stock their own brands, but we'd really recommend you check out those from outdoor specialists like Patagonia, Paramo and Berghaus as they're generally made from better quality materials. In cold weather the general rule is wear one or two thinner layers as opposed to one thick layer as the air between each layer is warmed up. So a fleece top with an outer fleece is a good option to consider. If it's especially cold or windy, a windproof jacket adds an extra layer of protection. For this guide, we tried out a number of fleeces and found the Patagonia R1 Pullover and Berghaus Arana to be excellent choices as a fleece top. The Berghaus Aura is a decent choice as an outer layer, while we found when shooting by the coast that Paramo's Pajaro and Cascada offered superb protection from the wind and sea-spray and are well worth investing in. Incidentally, when choosing colours, bear in mind right reds are great for visibility, so perfect when heading to remote locations, but not such a good choice if you ever plan on stalking wildlife!

6) PROTECT YOUR LEGS! In truth, few amateur photographers head outdoors in anything other than a pair of jeans and while they're comfortable, they're not ideal when the going gets wet. If the weather is unpredictable or you know you'll be shooting near the coast, consider a pair of waterproof trousers. Again, outdoor specialists are best, with Paramo's Cascada trousers generally considered to be one of the best.

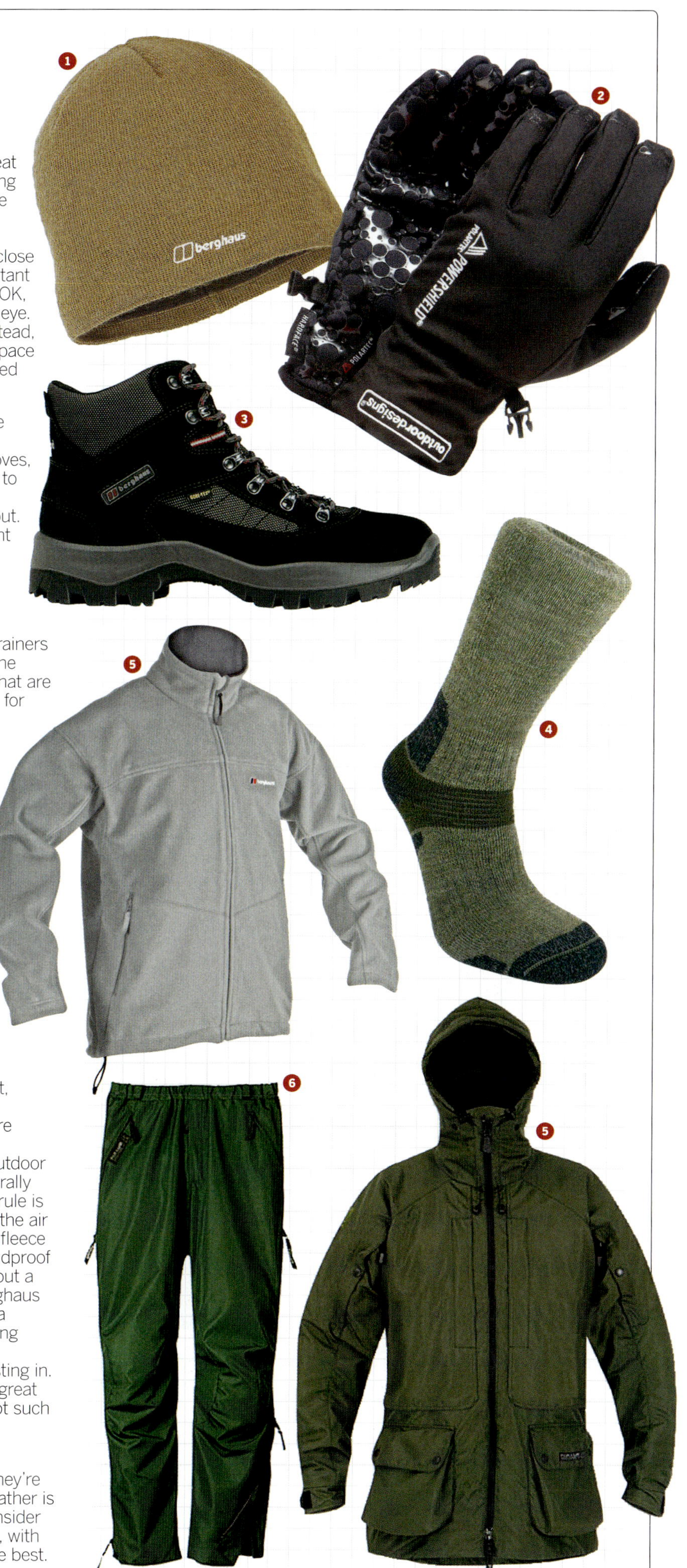

LOCATION GUIDE

REVISED & UPDATED
FANTASTIC NEW UK LOCATIONS ADDED!

YOUR EXPERT GUIDE TO 40 OF THE UK'S MOST STUNNING LOCATIONS

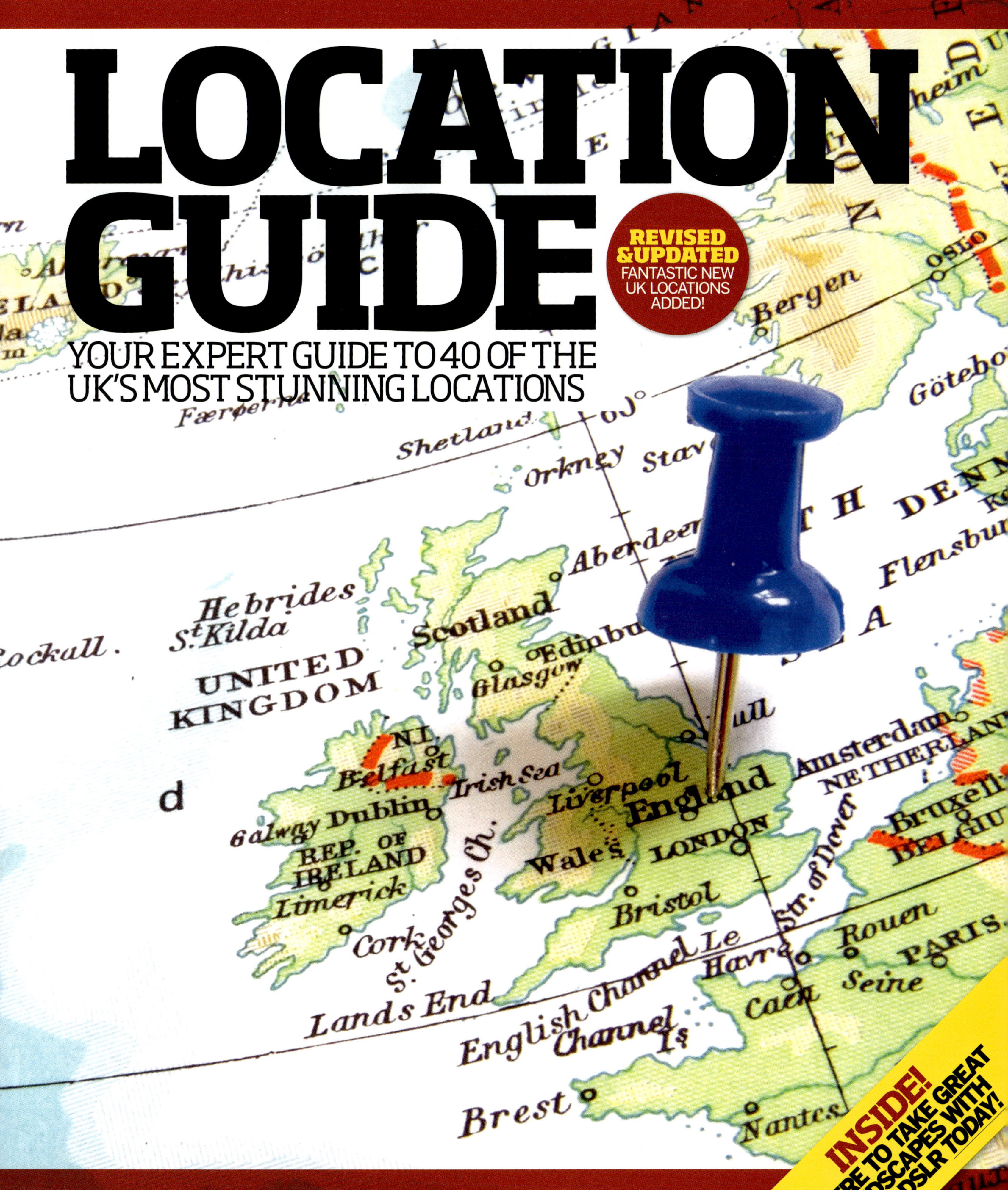

INSIDE! WHERE TO TAKE GREAT LANDSCAPES WITH YOUR DSLR TODAY!

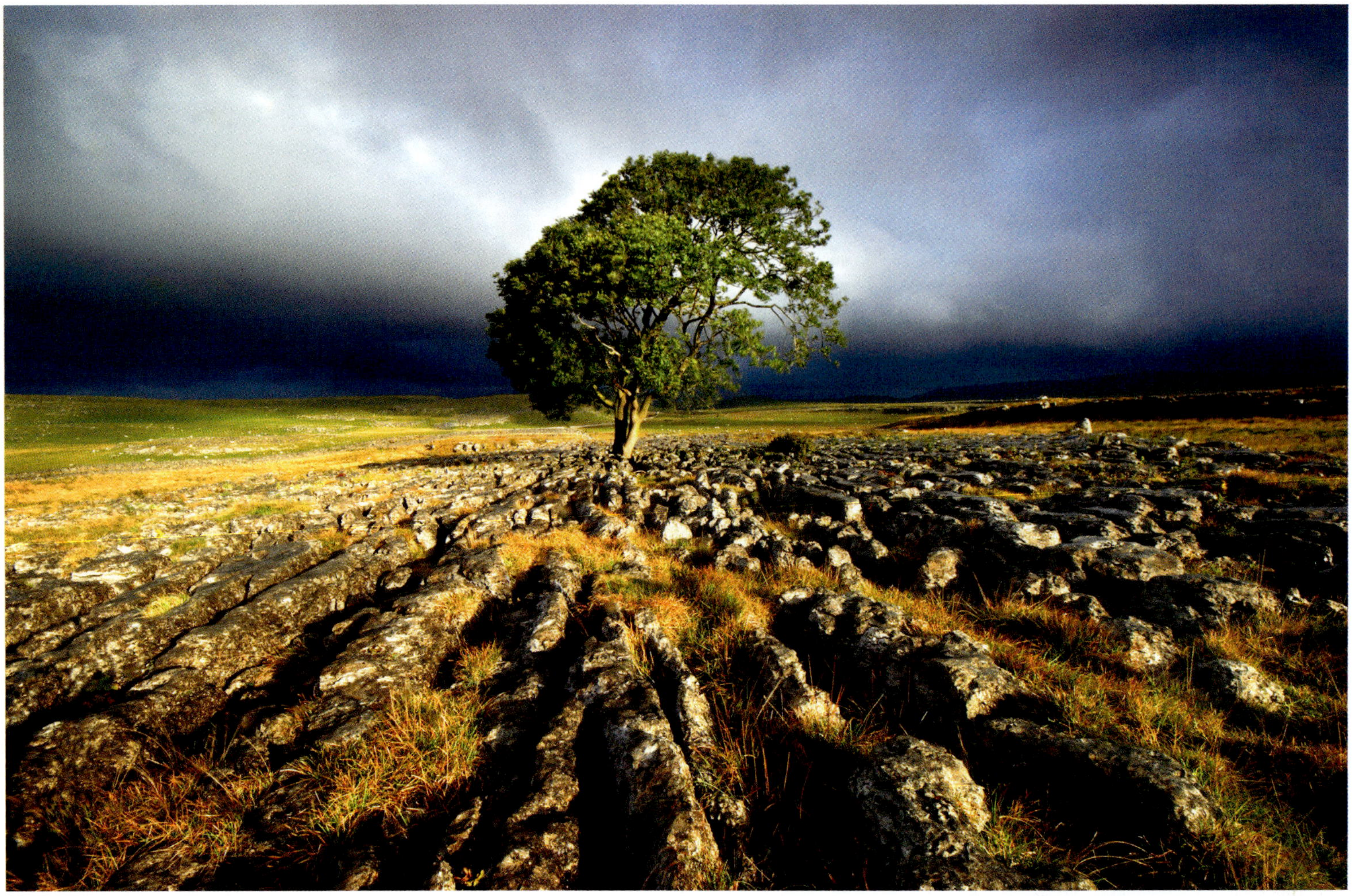

ED RHODES

Northern England

Yorkshire Dales
North Yorkshire

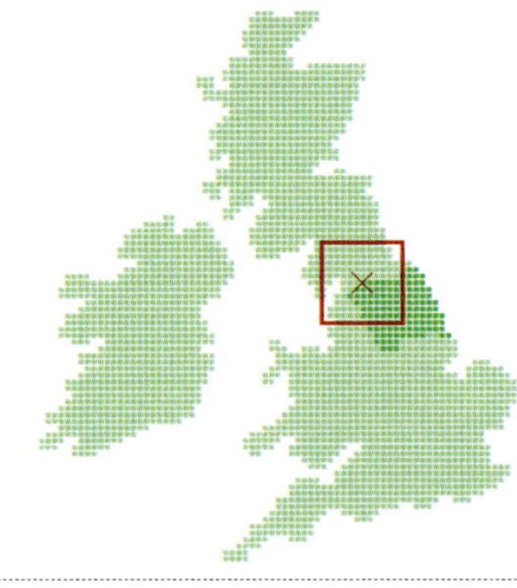

Above: Sunburst on a lone tree at Malham, an area providing incredible photo potential.
Right: Bolton Abbey in Wharfedale, Yorkshire Dales National Park, is open every day.

LOCATED: North Yorkshire and Cumbria
GETTING THERE: The Yorkshire Dales are bordered by major trunk roads and easily accessed by car; with the M6 skirting the west, the A66 to the north, the A1 to the east, and the M65, A65 and A59 to the south.
O/S REF: SD875899 **WEB:** www.yorkshiredales.org

COVERING AN AREA OF 680 square miles, this National Park is located in the north of England, and straddles the central Pennines in the counties of North Yorkshire and Cumbria.

The Dales landscape is one of great variety. In the valleys, the network of dry stone walls and hay meadows show the impact centuries of farming have had on this landscape.

The limestone is famous for its stunning 'pavements' or scars – plateaux of bare and weathered rock that provide perfect foreground interest and lead-in lines. Deep crevasses have developed in the rock to create a mosaic of interlocking 'clints' and 'grykes'. Illuminated by low, warm sunlight, they create stunning scenic images. Visit places like Malham Cove, White Scars near Ingleton, the plateau of Moughton near Austwick and waterfalls such as High Force at Teesdale in the north.

Photographers shouldn't overlook the Dales' popular riverside beauty spots, such as Bolton Abbey in Wharfedale and Aysgarth Falls in Wensleydale. Try some cheese, Gromit!

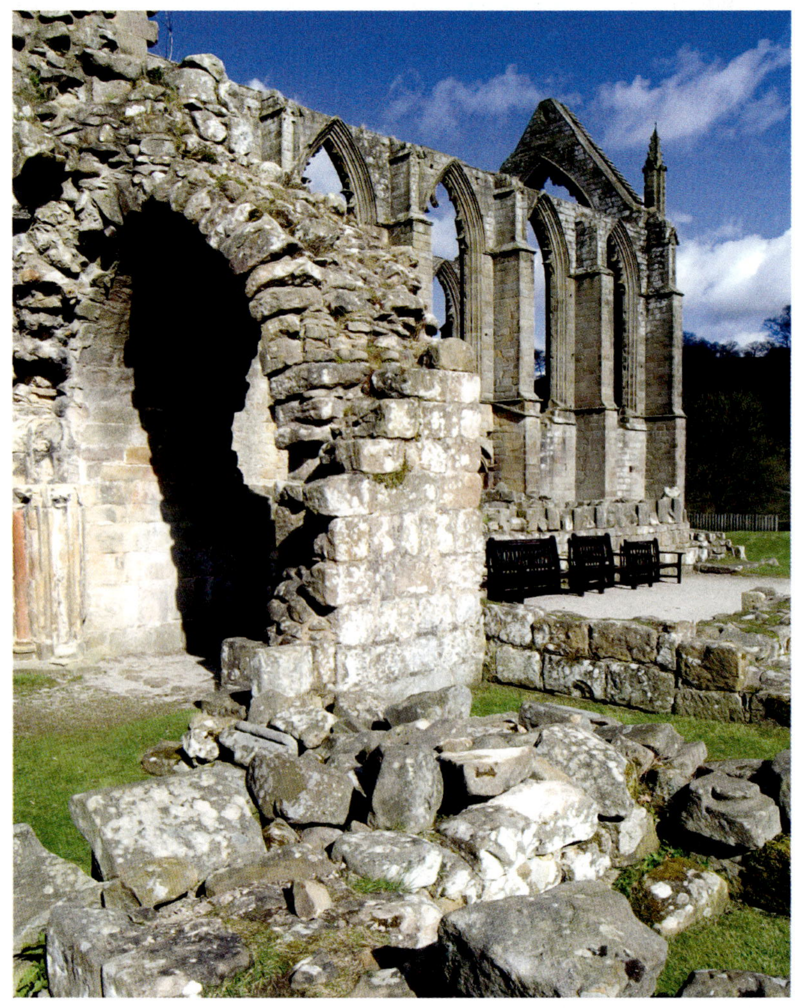

ISTOCK-PHOTO

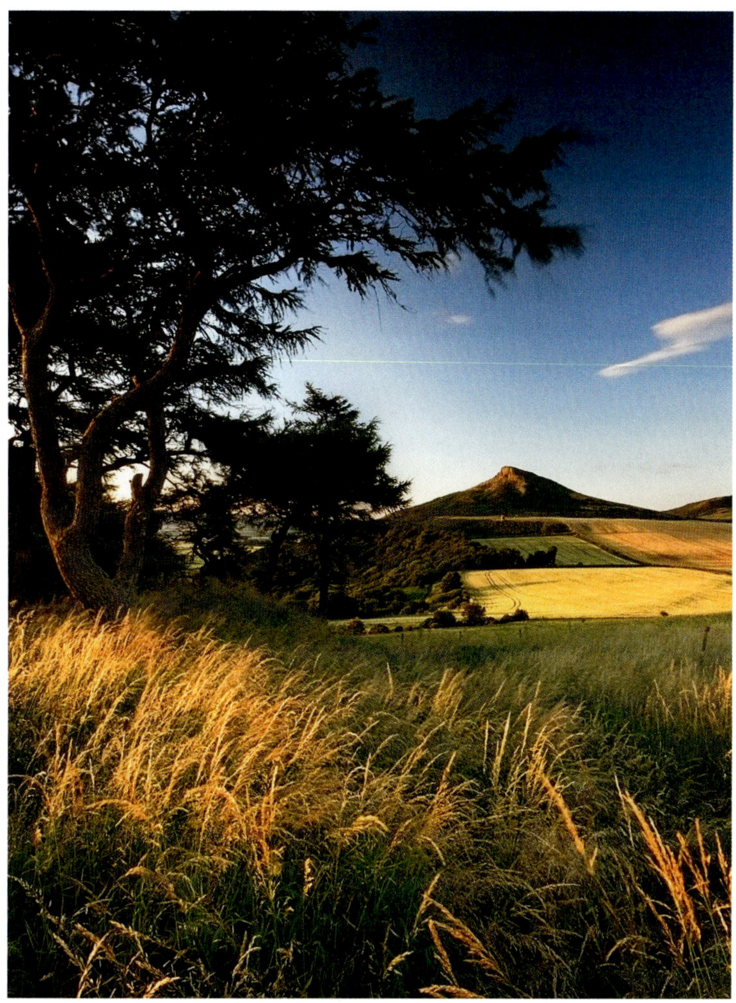
LEIGH REBECCA

Northern England

Embleton Bay Northumberland

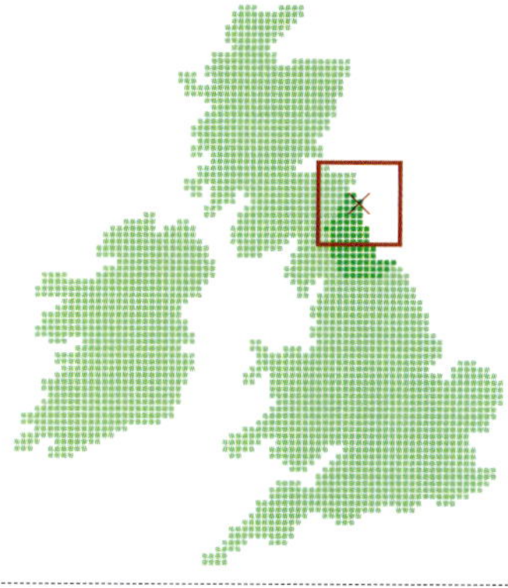

Below: Sunset doesn't have to be over the sea at Embleton Bay. Here it lights the castle.

LOCATED: Northumberland **GETTING THERE:** From the A1, between Newcastle and Berwick upon Tweed, take the B1340 from Alnwick or the B6347 – both towards Christon Bank. The B1339 then runs parallel to the coast, with minor roads leading to the sea at Newton and Embleton.
O/S REF: NU243231 **WEB:** www.visitnorthumberland.com

EMBLETON BAY IS ONE OF Northumberland's finest bays. The iconic Dunstanburgh Castle stands on the cliffs at the south end of the bay and dominates this stretch of coastline. It is one of the UK's most photographed castles, being particularly photogenic at sunrise – so set your alarm early and get there with time to spare. At low tide, a great sweep of golden sands is exposed, along with rockpools and wavy patterns that – if included within your composition – will add interest and depth to your pictures.

With the dramatic castle ruins beyond forming a key focal point, it's easy to understand why this is such a good location for landscape photography. It's a popular beach among tourists, who reach it from Embleton Village or Low Newton, so visit early to photograph clean sands, free of messy footprints.

When you visit Embleton Bay, don't forget to explore the adjoining coastline and surrounding area for more photo options. Places like Alnmouth, Bamburgh and Holy Island are only a short drive away and are equally photogenic.

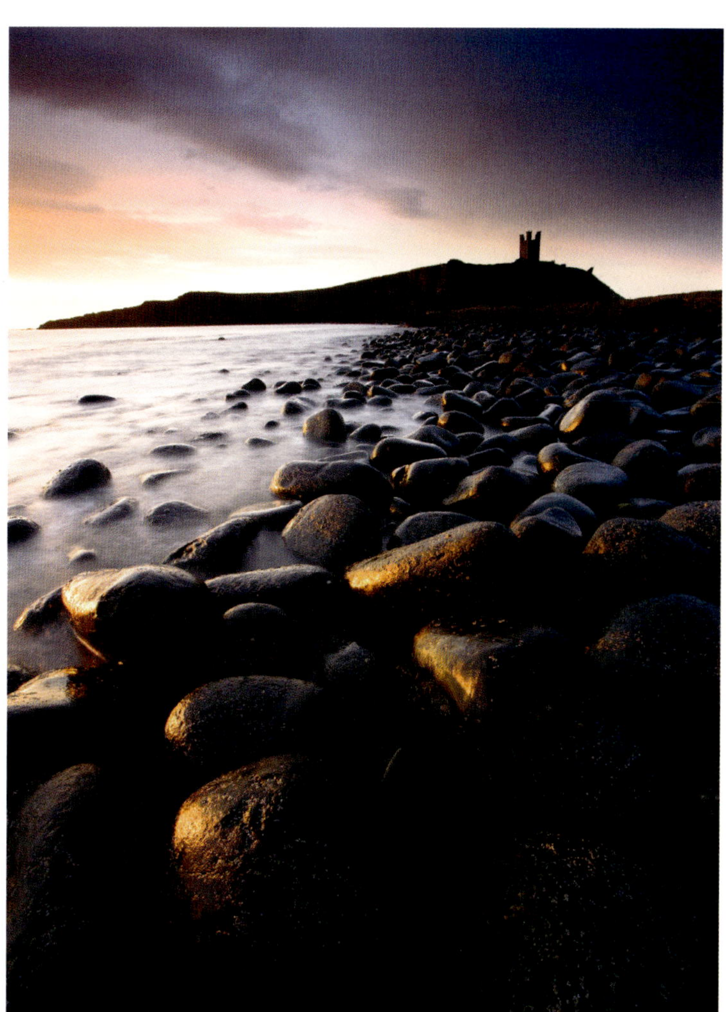
LEE FROST

Northern England

Roseberry Topping North Yorkshire

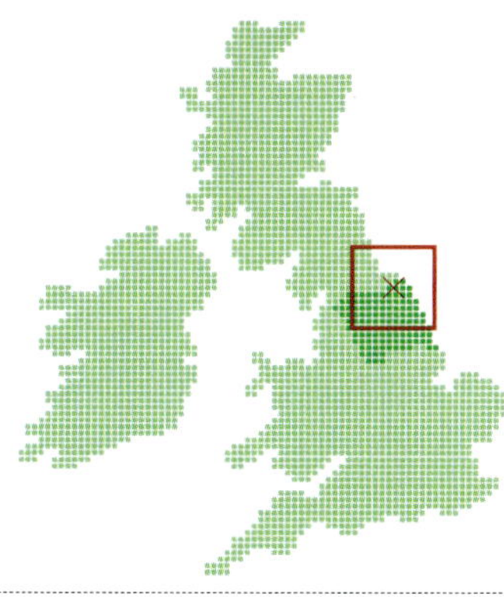

Above: Like a mini Matterhorn, Roseberry thrusts up from Cleveland. The approach to the hill has many features to give the peak context.

LOCATED: Newton-under-Roseberry, North Yorkshire
GETTING THERE: It is located one mile from Great Ayton next to Newton-under-Roseberry on the A173 Great Ayton–Guisborough road.
O/S REF: NZ579126 **WEB:** www.nationaltrust.org.uk

ROSEBERRY TOPPING IS A DISTINCTIVE HILL on the border between North Yorkshire and the borough of Redcar and Cleveland.

Its summit is half-cone-shaped with a jagged cliff. From the top, you can enjoy a magnificent 360° panorama stretching as far as Teeside in one direction and the Yorkshire Dales the other.

The area is rich in wildlife – particularly moorland birds – but most photographers visit to capture wider views of this iconic location. The 'Cleveland Matterhorn', to give it its ironic local nickname, is traditionally best photographed in context with its surroundings. An array of footpaths wind through this beautiful landscape – including the Cleveland Way – so it is easy to explore the area in order to find good viewpoints.

Visit in advance and earmark potential compositions; by doing so, you can ensure that you are in position and ready when the light is at its best. Being located on the northern edge of the North Yorkshire Moors, and not far from the coast, the whole region is bound to appeal to scenic photographers.

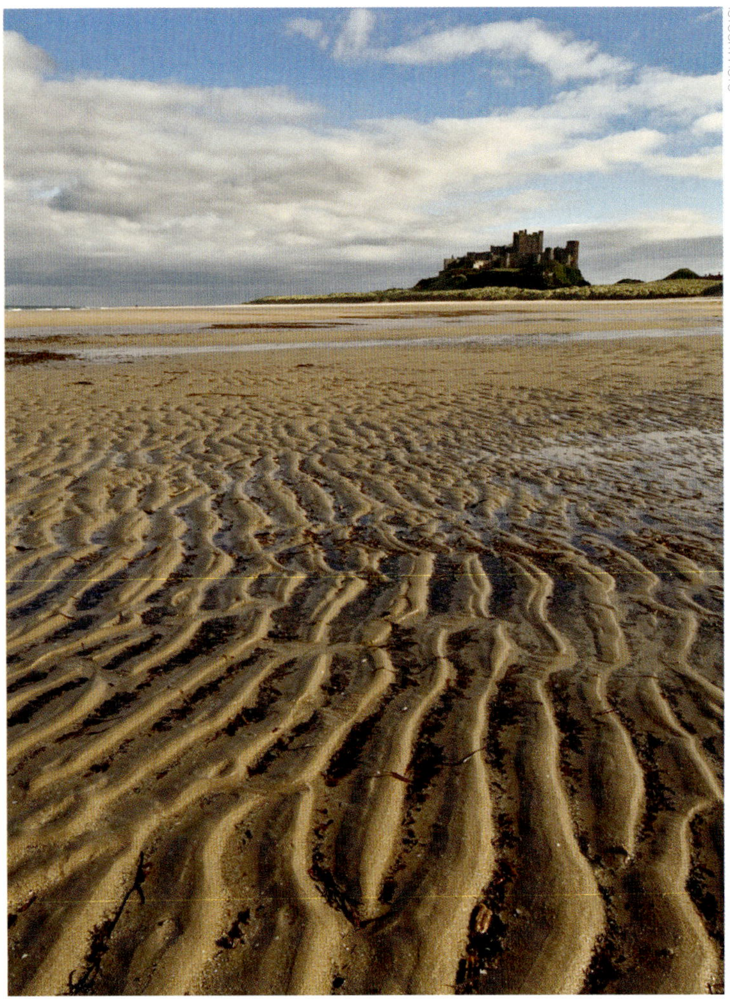
ISTOCKPHOTO

Northern England

Bamburgh Castle
Northumberland

Above: Sand patterns provide perfect lead-in lines towards the distant castle.

LOCATED: Near Belford, Northumberland
GETTING THERE: The castle is situated 42 miles north of Newcastle and 20 miles south of Berwick-upon-Tweed. From the A1, take either the B1342 or B1341 and follow the signs to Bamburgh, where there is parking.
O/S REF: NU184351 **WEB:** www.bamburghcastle.com

THIS IS ONE OF THE MOST imposing and photogenic castles in England. Some photographers seem to live there! It's certainly worth arriving early and staying until after the sun has set.

Positioned on a basalt outcrop, it dominates this stretch of the beautiful Northumberland coastline. The stunning sandy bay here stretches for miles – starting three miles south of Bamburgh, at Seahouses, and extending virtually uninterrupted all the way to Cheswick Sands, 15 miles to the north. That's a good hike in a day, so get your comfy socks on.

This is a location not short of foreground interest. North-west of the castle is interesting, deeply-scarred dolerite rock, which can be utilised to add interest and drama to views of the castle.

Alternatively, photograph the castle from the beach at low-tide, or from the sand dunes when the tide is high. Second World War defences, a ship wreck and a nearby lighthouse provide yet more picture potential. For the best light, visit at dawn or dusk, when you'll also find the location will also be less populated.

Northern England

Holy Island of Lindisfarne
Northumberland

Below: The ruins are best photographed in the evening light with the rough North Sea crashing into the shoreline.

LOCATED: Near Berwick-upon-Tweed, Northumberland
GETTING THERE: Take the A1 North of Alnwick or South of Berwick and head for Beal. Holy Island is signposted off the A1. Ensure you abide by the safe causeway crossing times.
OS REF: NU136417 **WEB:** www.lindisfarne.org.uk

LINDISFARNE IS A TIDAL ISLAND off the north-east coast of England, also known as Holy Island. It can only be reached via car by driving over a causeway at low tide. This is a truly photogenic place. Large parts of the island, and all of the adjacent intertidal area, are protected as Lindisfarne National Nature Reserve to help safeguard the internationally-important wintering bird populations. Its best known and well photographed landmark is Lindisfarne Castle – a 16th century fortification, which has been under the care of the National Trust since 1944. Sited on top of a volcanic mound, the castle is distinct and picturesque. It can be seen for miles around and best shot from the beach, where the rocky shore creates ideal foreground interest. This is a great location for shooting close-ups of interesting and colourful texture of subjects like old fishing boats and rock detail. Therefore, in addition to a wide-angle, carry a medium telephoto or macro lens for isolating details when you visit. The light is best at first and last light. The castle can also look striking silhouetted against a colourful sky.

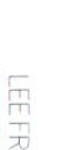
LEE FROST

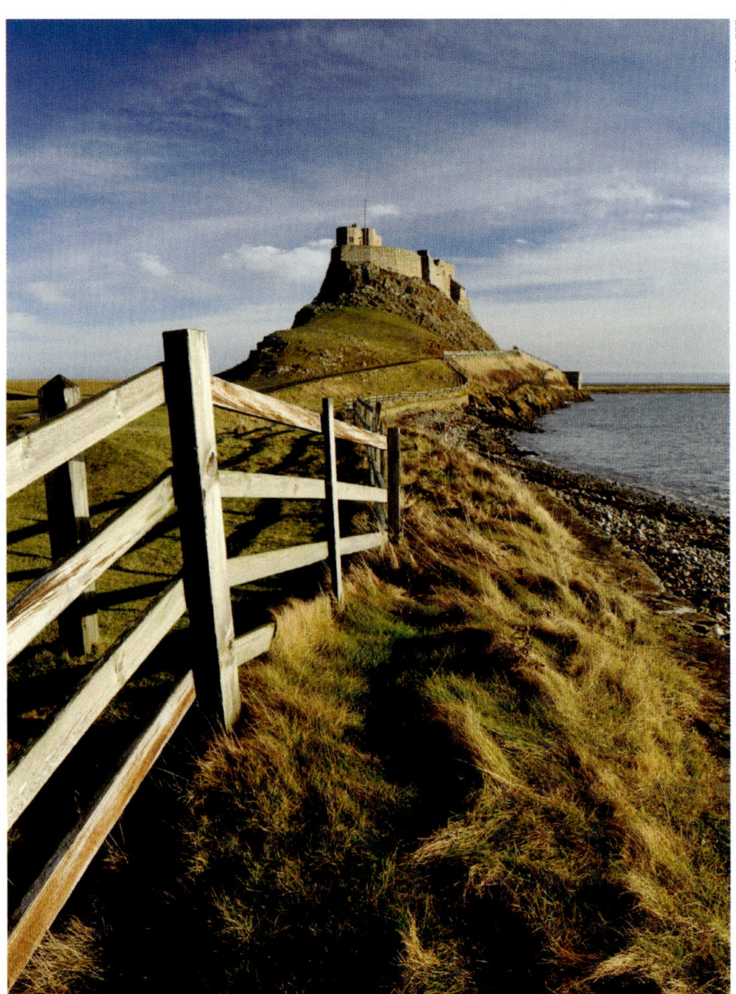

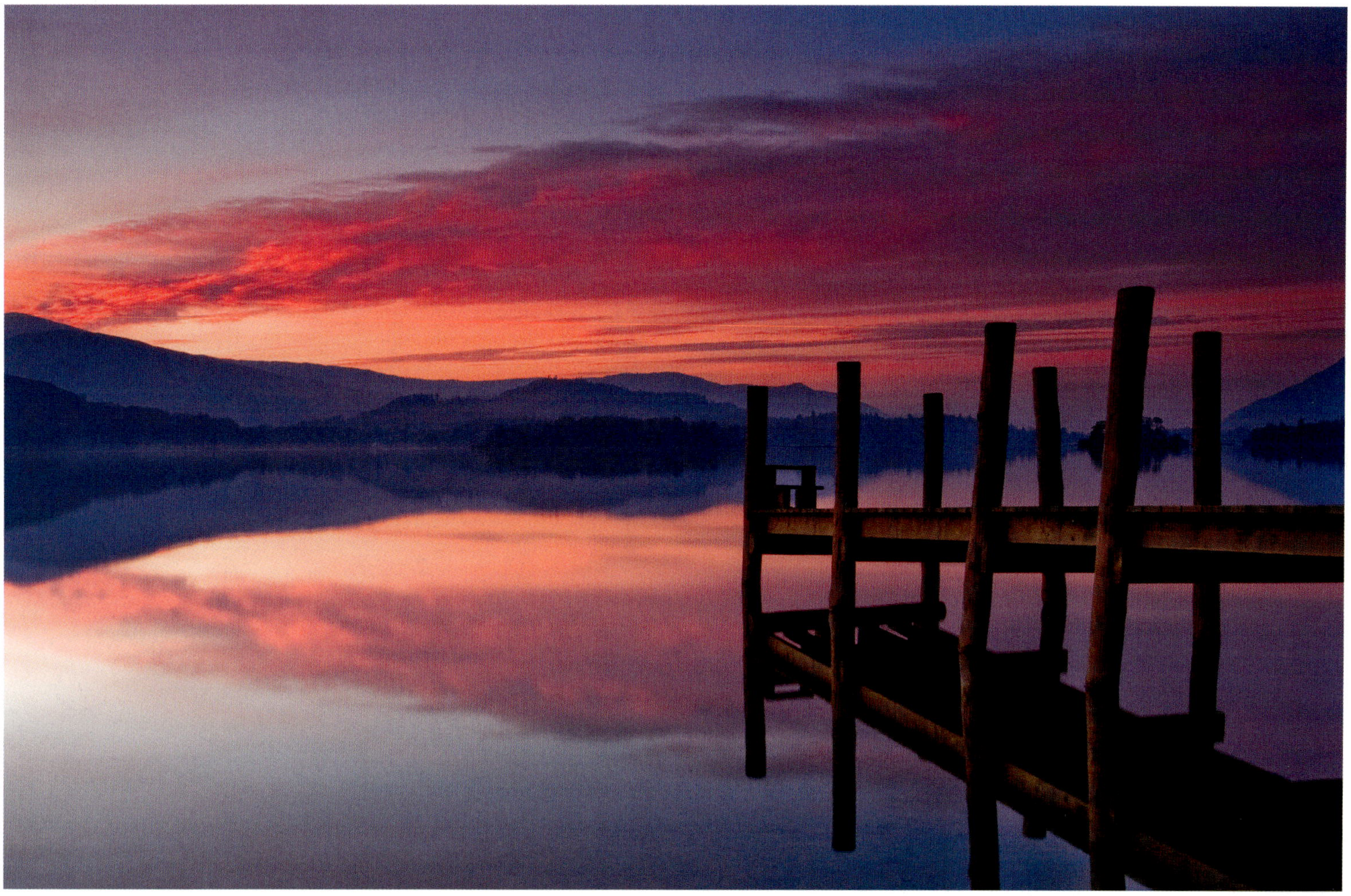

NEIL HIGGINS

Northern England

The Lake District
Cumbria

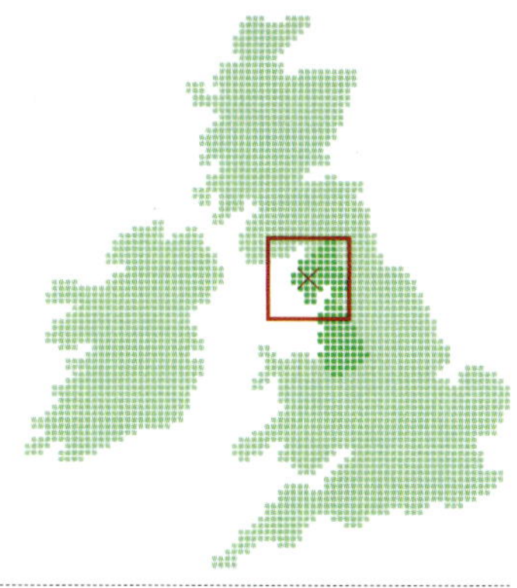

Above: Not a caravan, nor another living soul in sight. Early morning in the Lakes.
Right: Mountains and clouds reflected in lakes, everywhere you look.

LOCATED: Kendal and Keswick in Cumbria
GETTING THERE: The M6 runs to the east of the Lake District National Park. Take junction 36 and then A590 for the southern end of the Lake District or junction 40 and the A66 or A592 for the northern end.
O/S REF: SD419976 **WEB:** www.cumbria-the-lake-district.co.uk

THE LAKE DISTRICT – or 'The Lakes' – is renowned for its stunning beauty and as a result it gets very busy all year round.

Undulating hills are decorated with every shade of green, whilst moorland and peat bogs add their own charm, colours and textures to the fabric of the fells. Woods and forests nestle in hillsides and, along the Cumbrian coast, sandstone cliffs meet sandy dunes.

However, it's the lakes that landscape photographers will be most drawn to. All are photogenic, but Buttermere, Ullswater and Windermere are particularly well suited to scenic photography.

Visit on still, windless days for the best reflections. Derwentwater, the widest of the lakes, is overlooked by the mighty Skiddaw and, with the bustling market town of Keswick on its northern shore, it is a popular beauty spot. Photographers will adore this location. With its photogenic jetty and rowing boats, stunning landscape images are possible. Whilst the Lake District is worthy of a visit throughout the seasons, it is best during autumn, when the landscape is golden and colourful and the crowds have dwindled a bit.

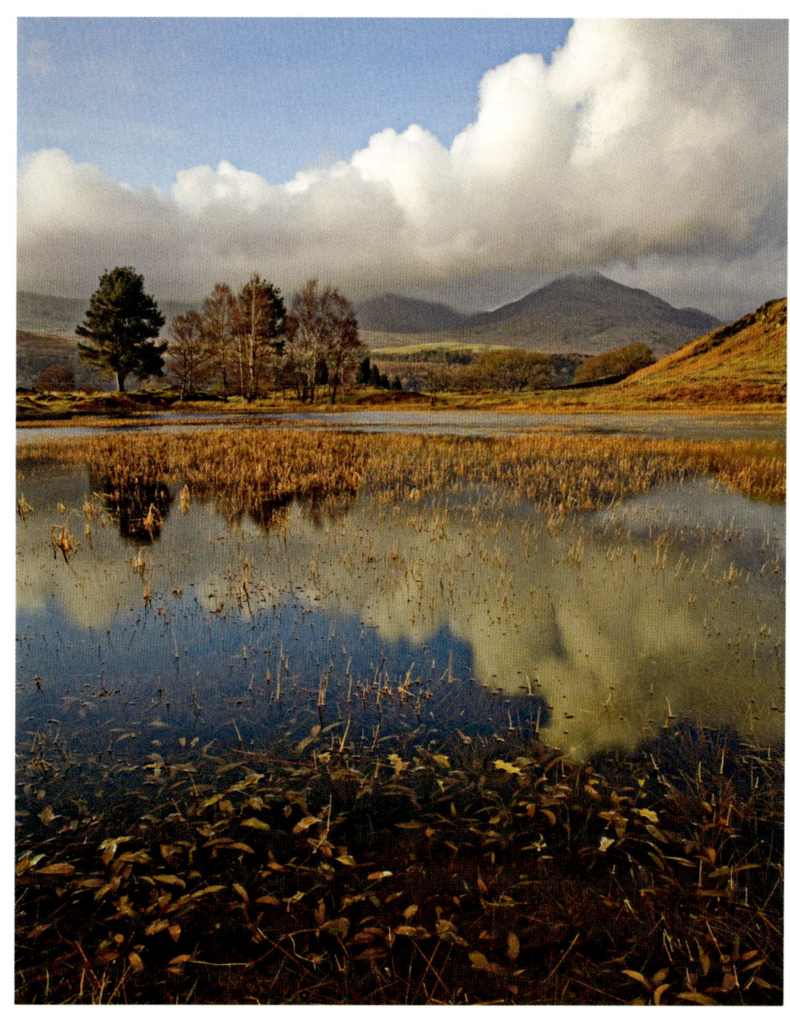

NEIL HIGGINS

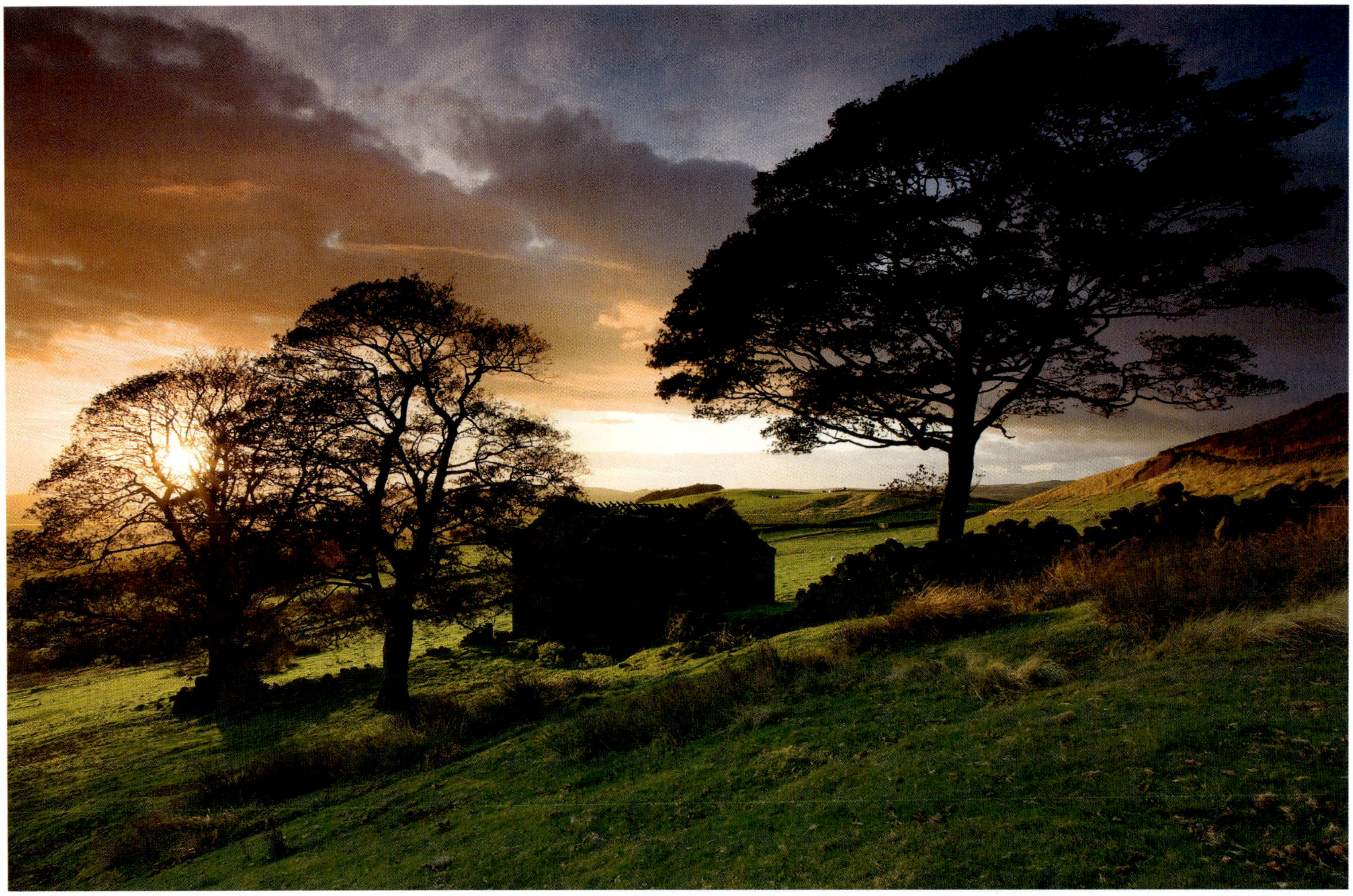

RICHARD WHEELER

Central England

Peak District
Derbyshire

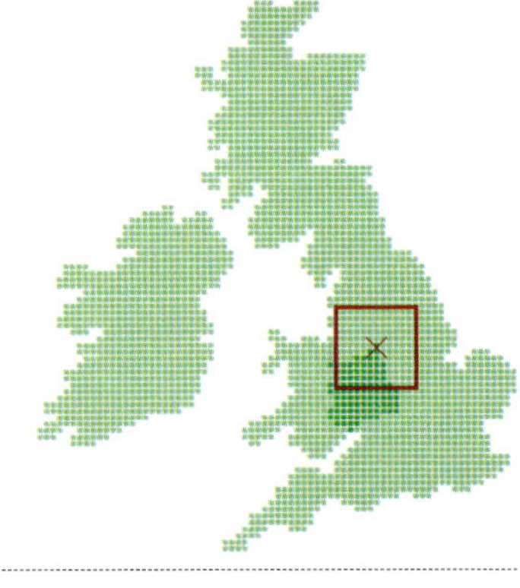

Above: An ND graduated filter will help to balance the light levels of sky and land.
Right: Grindstones hewn from the rock then abandoned provide foreground interest.

LOCATED: Peak District, Derbyshire **GETTING THERE:** From SE: M1 to junction 25, A52 to Derby, then A6 north through Duffield, Belper, or stay on A52 to Ashbourne. From NE: take the M1 to junction 33, through Sheffield take either A57 or A625. From SW: M5, M42, A42, M1 then as from SE.
O/S REF: SK141769 **WEB:** www.visitpeakdistrict.com

THE PEAK DISTRICT IS home to Britain's first National Park. 126,000 acres of gritstone edges, limestone dales and peat moorland combine to create a diverse and photogenic landscape. From the 'Dambusters' practice reservoirs near Bamford, across the hills to Castleton and Chapel-en-le-Frith, the High Peak is very popular among visitors to the park.

At the eastern edges, the park is punctuated with gritstone cliffs, from Stanage Edge in the north to Harland Edge in the south, which used to be quarried to produce grindstones. Some can still be seen abandoned on the hillside adding interest to images.

The southern area is littered with deep limestone dales carved from the soft rock during the last Ice Age. Locations like Lathkill Dale, Tissington and the beautiful Dove Dale are well worth visiting with your camera. The moors to the west of the park are bleak but atmospheric. Take the high road to Macclesfield. When skies are dark and stormy and the light becomes more dramatic, great landscapes are there just waiting to be captured.

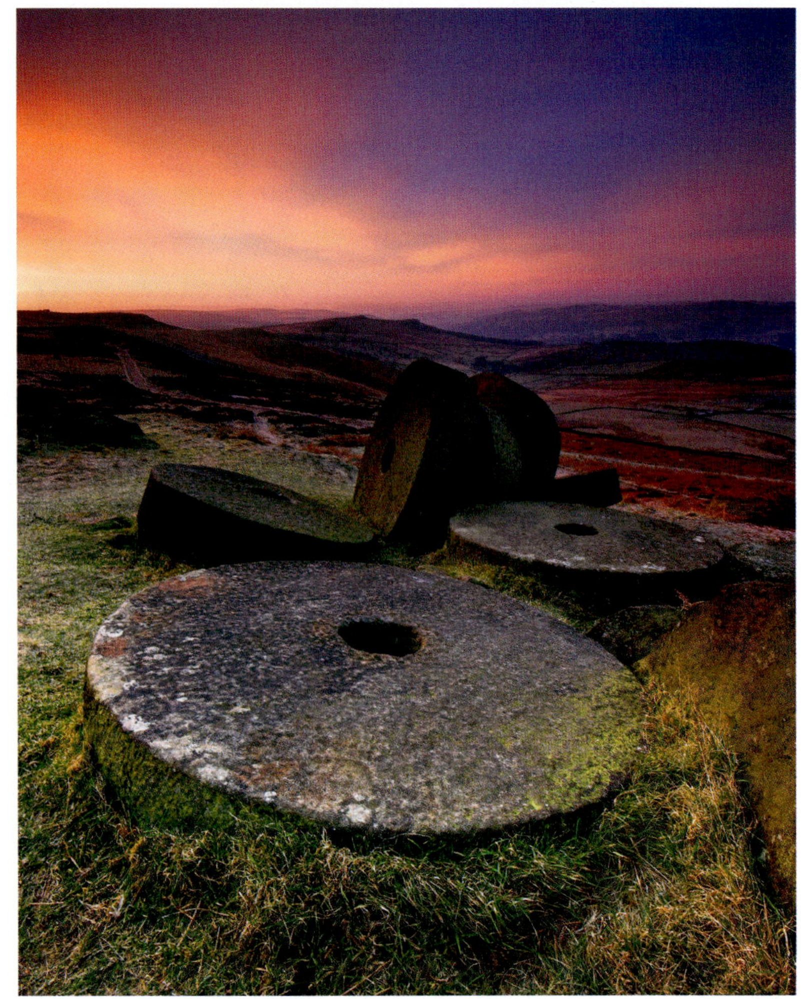

PAUL SUTTON

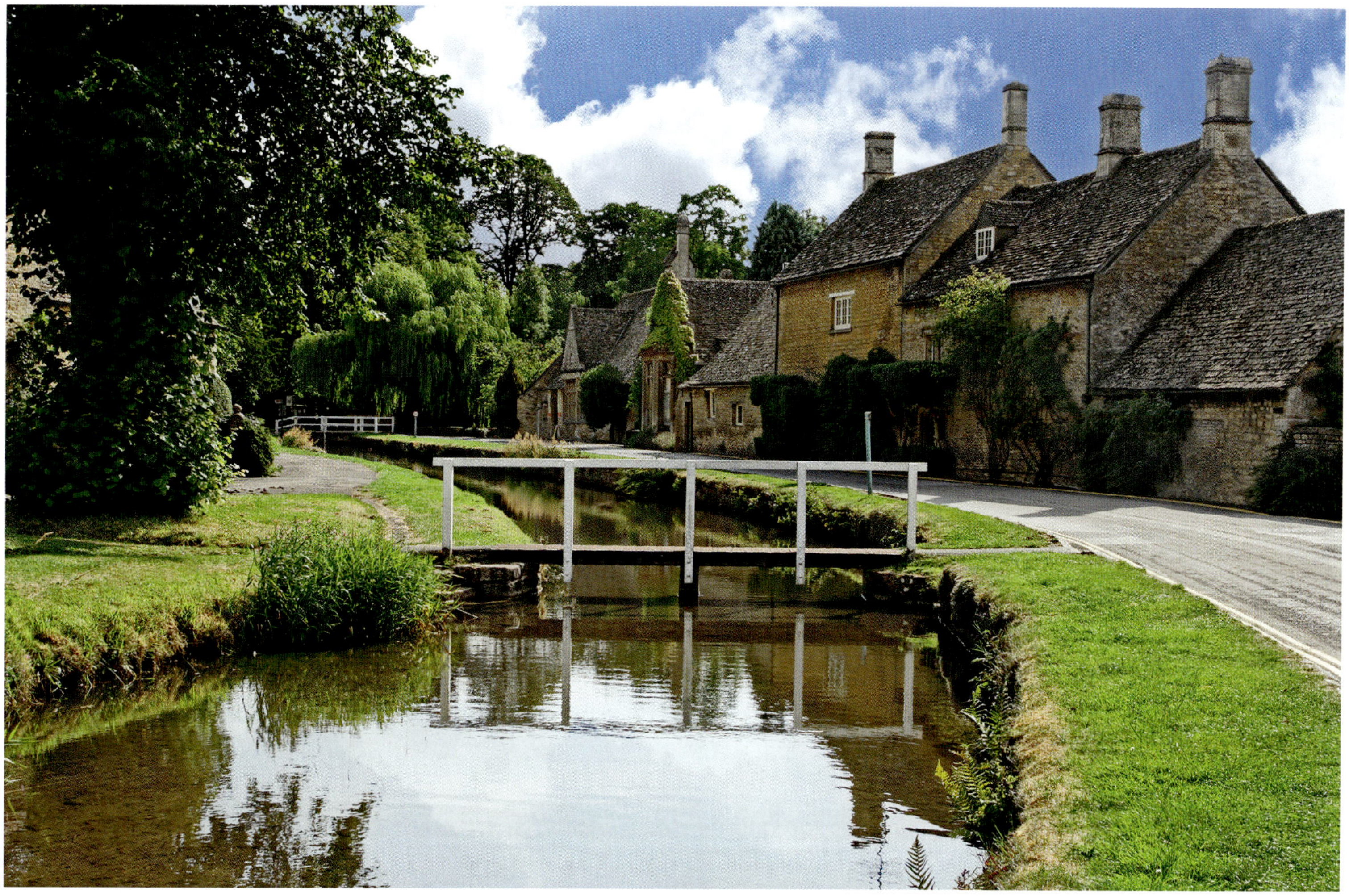

Central England

The Cotswolds
Central England

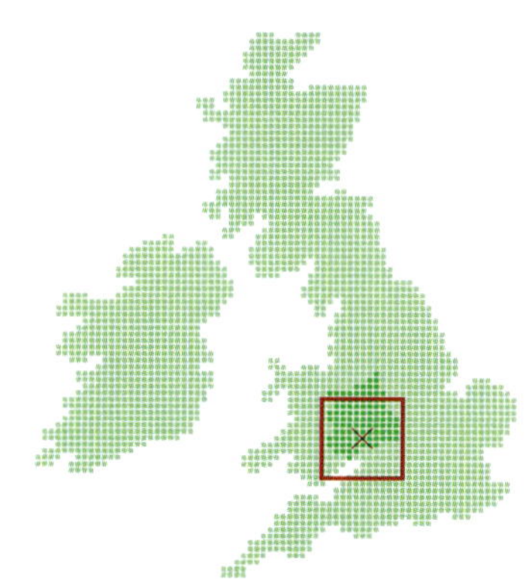

Above: As well as landscapes, also look to shoot quaint village scenes too.

Right: Broadway Tower is a folly located on Broadway Hill, Worcestershire.

LOCATED: Six counties including Gloucestershire, west Oxfordshire, south-west Warwickshire **GETTING THERE:** The Motorway network provides easy access via the M4 or M40 from London and the south-east; the M4 from Wales; and the M5 from the north, Midlands and the south-west. **O/S REF:** SP188239 **WEB:** www.visitcotswolds.co.uk

THE COTSWOLDS ARE A RANGE of limestone hills. To the west they have a scarp slope rising out of the Severn Vale to the highest point at Cleeve Common. From here they slope gently eastwards towards the upper Thames Valley – drained by picturesque rivers such as the Coln and the Windrush.

The underlying stone, with its thin soils, is responsible for the now scarce limestone grasslands that support a wonderful range of flora. The stone is also responsible for the famous Cotswold architecture – 'chocolate box' cottages, hamlets and villages of outstanding beauty. Chipping Campden, Stow-on-the-Wold, Moreton-in-Marsh and Bourton-on-the-Water are among the best known and picturesque, but you should also explore the less touristy areas.

Spring is a wonderful time to visit, when the rolling countryside is green and foliage is fresh and vibrant. The Cotswolds are also well known for their many miles of drystone walls – marking the borders of fields and farmland. They will appeal to scenic photographers, who will use them to aid composition and add interest and depth.

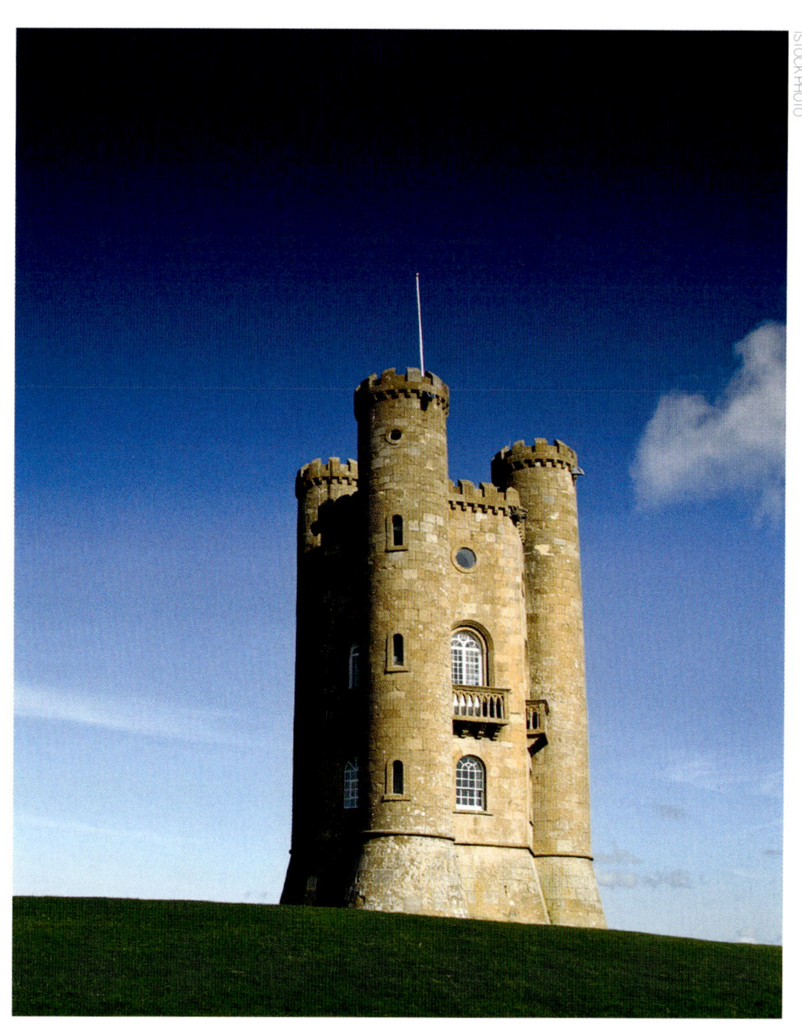

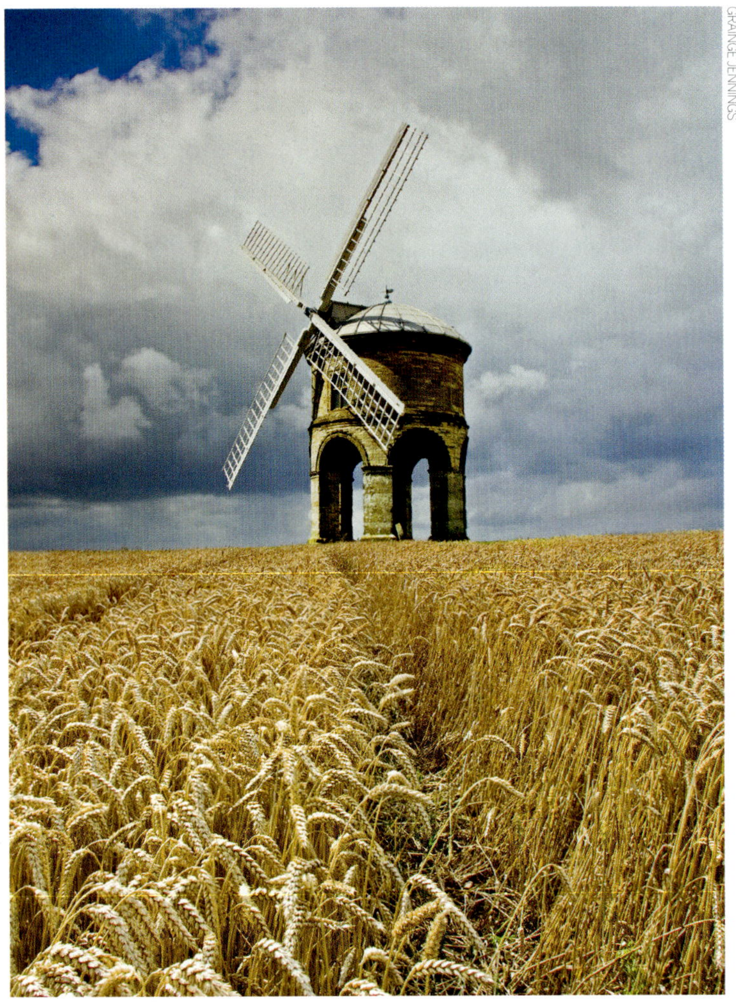

GRAINGE JENNINGS

Central England

Chesterton Mill
Warwickshire

Above: Clever use of this furrow as a lead-in line draws the eye towards the mill.

LOCATED: Near Leamington Spa
GETTING THERE: From the M40, Chesterton Windmill is located just off the B4455 (Fosse Way), approx five miles to the south of Leamington Spa, near the village of Harbury.
O/S REF: SP348594 **WEB:** www.shakespeare-country.co.uk

STANDING HIGH ON A HILLTOP overlooking the Roman Fosse Way, this unique windmill is an eye-catcher for miles around.

The mill is domed, circular and raised high on six stone pillars, creating beautiful arches. These support two raised floors. It is like no other building in the country. Landscape photographers should quickly recognise its picture potential.

In summer, crops like barley and wheat are grown nearby and on sunny evenings, the soft, evening light illuminates the mill, its white sails and the gently swaying crops. Attractive cloud will add interest to landscape images and, if you are fortunate, the setting sun will add colour and vibrancy to the sky.

A wide-angle lens will help you create images bursting with depth and life, and a deep depth-of-field will enable you to achieve back-to-front sharpness. This unique viewpoint is worth visiting at any time of the year. The mill can look as striking and dramatic in black & white as it does in colour, so don't overlook the possibility of converting your colour images during post-processing.

Eastern England

Southwold Pier
Suffolk

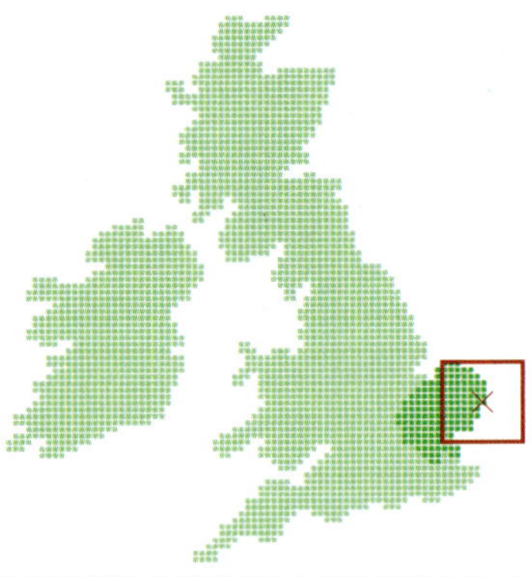

Below: Suffolk boasts of the most photogenic piers in the UK.

LOCATED: Southwold, Suffolk
GETTING THERE: From the A12, take the A1095 toward Reydon and follow signs for Southwold. There are several car parks in the town.
O/S REF: TM512766 **WEB:** www.visit-suffolkcoast.co.uk

SOUTHWOLD PIER IS ONE of the finest examples of a pier to be found anywhere in the UK. Following extensive renovation, it is now complete with a pavilion, restaurant, bar, amusements and the well-known water clock.

It's a pier that has proven highly photogenic, particularly at sunrise. Also, make sure to try photographing it in silhouette, as its instantly recognisable shape is perfectly suited to being captured as an outline. The clean, sandy beach is punctuated by photogenic wooden groynes to the south of the pier and riprap rocks to the north, creating an interesting choice of foreground options.

Consider using an ND filter when photographing views of the beach and pier – the longer exposure time this creates will blur the movement of the water and enhance the sense of movement.

Don't overlook Southwold's row of impeccable, brightly-coloured beach huts lining the shore when you visit the attractive beach and seafront with your digital SLR.

There's also a famous brewery. What more could you want?

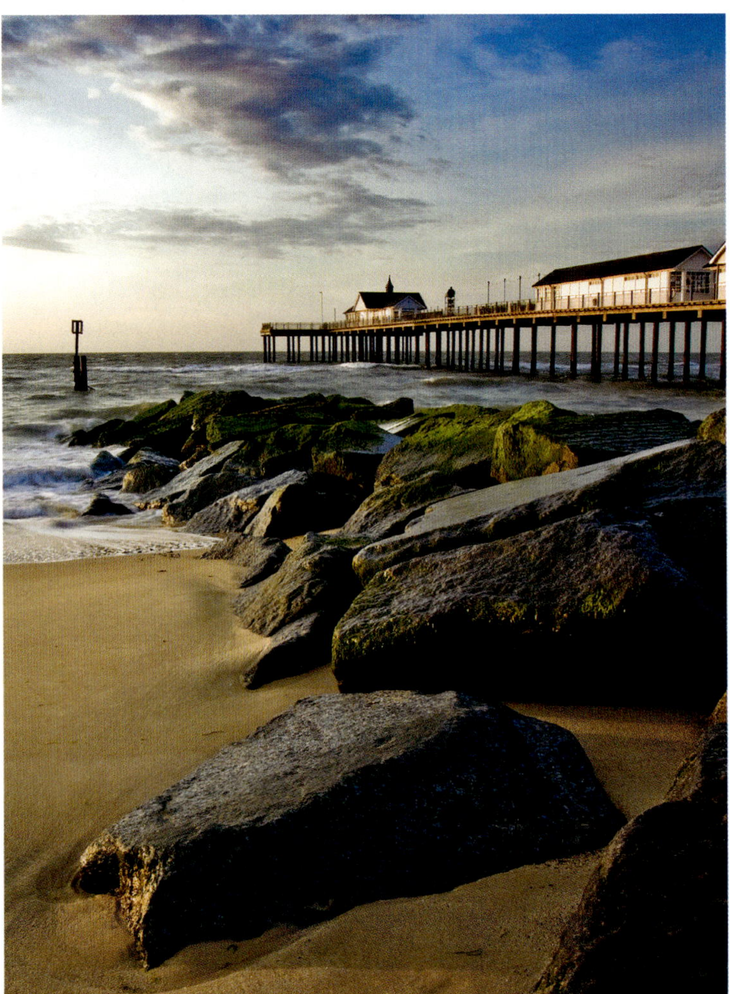

ISTOCKPHOTO

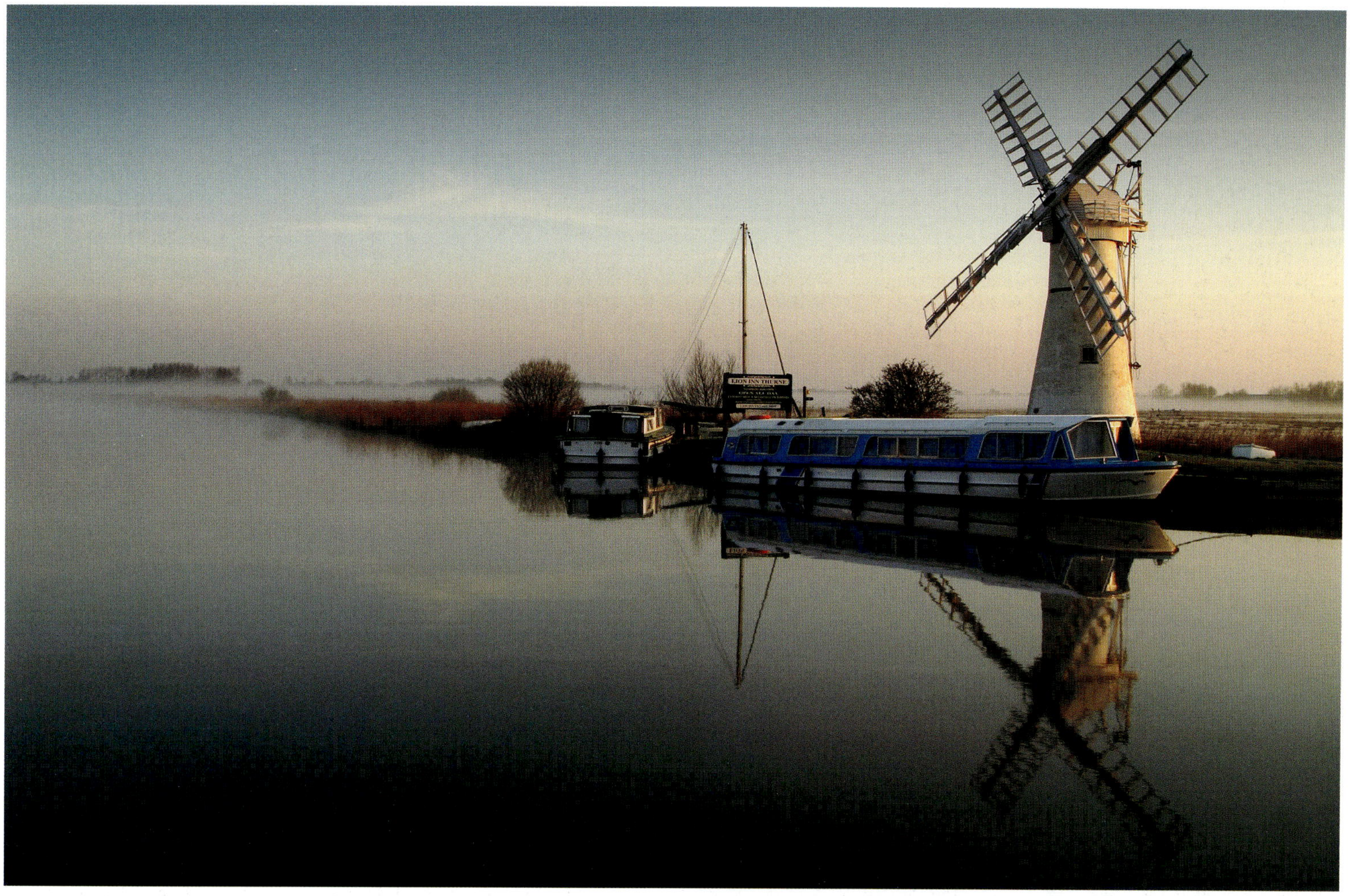

GARY HORNER

Eastern England

Thurne Mill
Norfolk

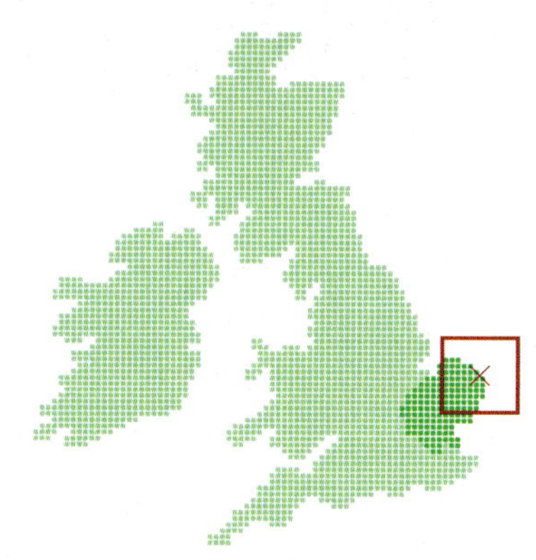

Above: The light colours of the mill cnstrast with the dark stormy clouds behind it. Try out various compositions, including using the river as foreground.

LOCATED: Norfolk Broads
GETTING THERE: From Norwich, take the A47 to Acle, then the A1064 to Billockby. Take the B1152 and follow the signs to the village of Thurne.
O/S REF: TG401159 **WEB:** www.visitnorfolk.co.uk

THURNE IS A SMALL riverside Broadland village that either gives or takes its name from the River Thurne, which flows directly by.

Thurne Mill, which presumably takes its name from the village or the river, since they were there first, is owned by the Norfolk Windmills Trust and is a major local landmark. The mill is also known as Morse's Mill (we don't know who Morse was or where he got his name). This white painted structure, and its large sails, can be seen from miles away. The view of the mill and its surroundings epitomise the Broads – huge skies and low, distant horizons.

A wide-angle lens is essential in order to capture dramatic images of this stunning structure in context with its surroundings. The white mill looks stunning in contrast with a deep blue, polarised sky. It is equally dramatic when set against a dark, menacing stormy sky.

Unsettled weather often produces the most photogenic light and conditions for landscape photography and out here you can see the weather rolling in from miles away. So don't be a fair weather photographer – visit whatever the conditions.

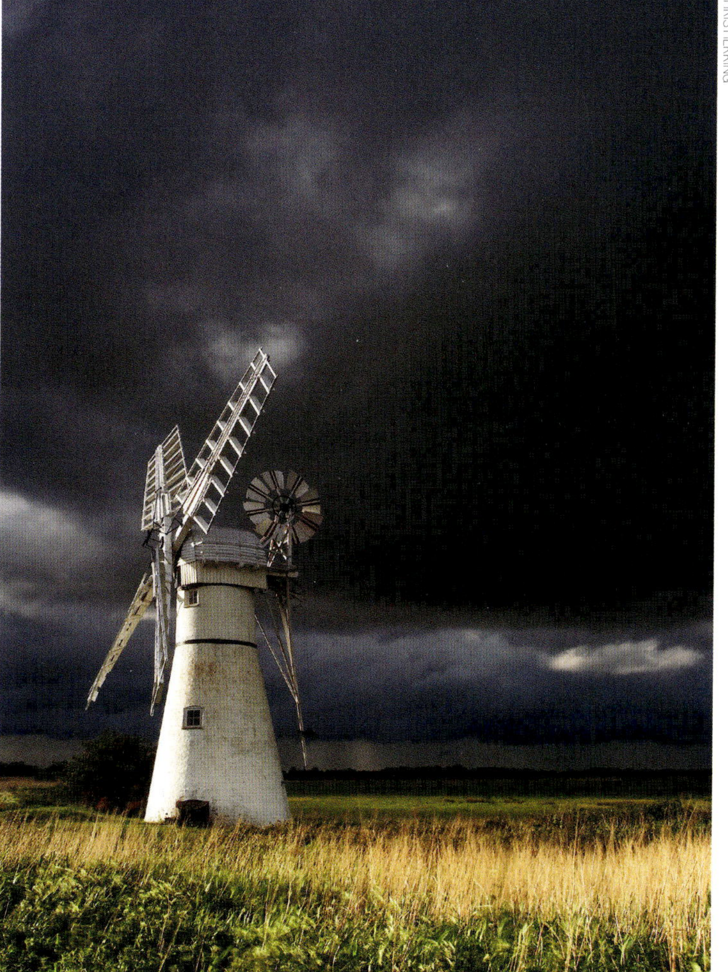

CHRIS HERRING

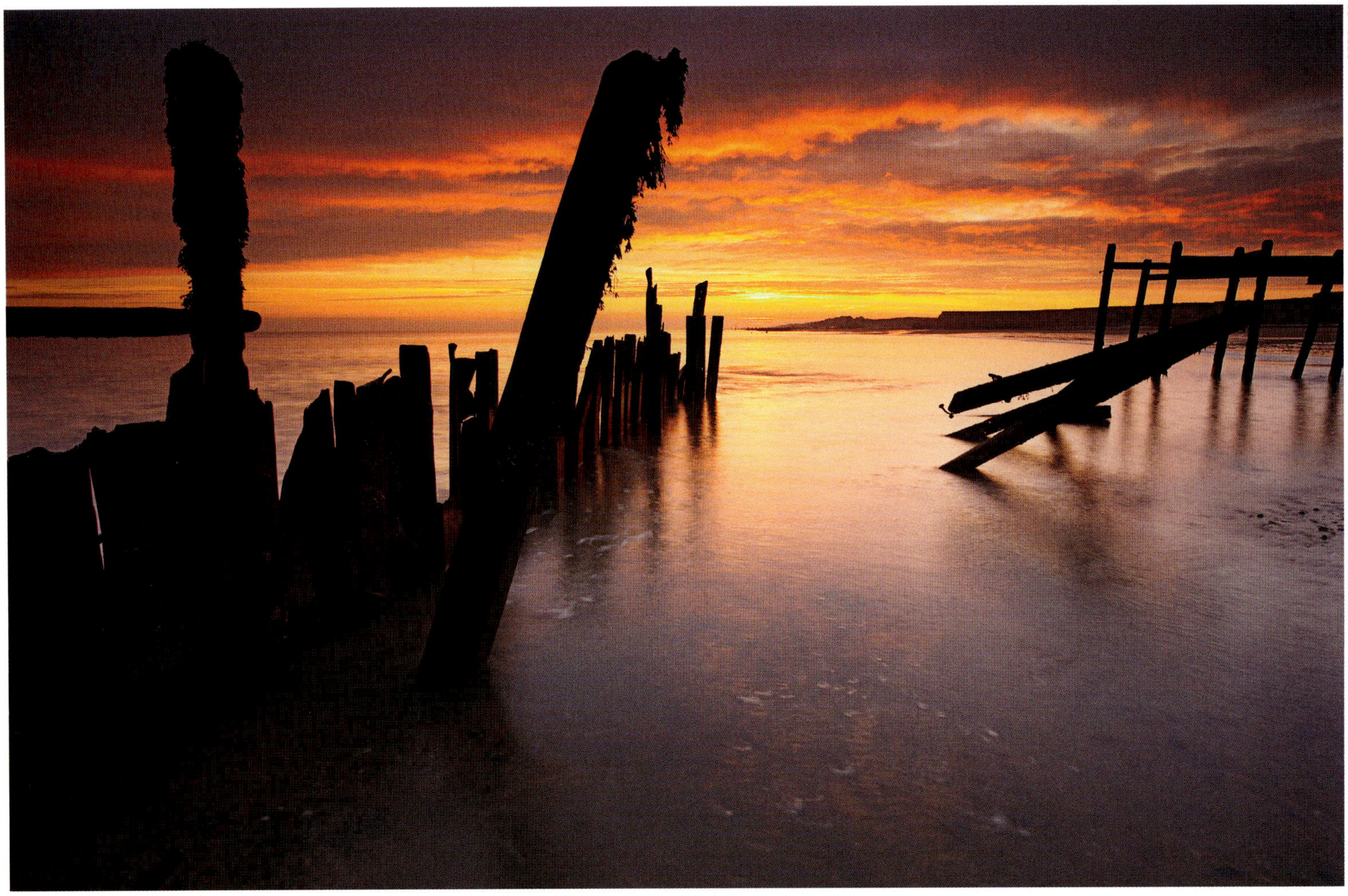

JON GIBBS

Eastern England

Happisburgh Norfolk

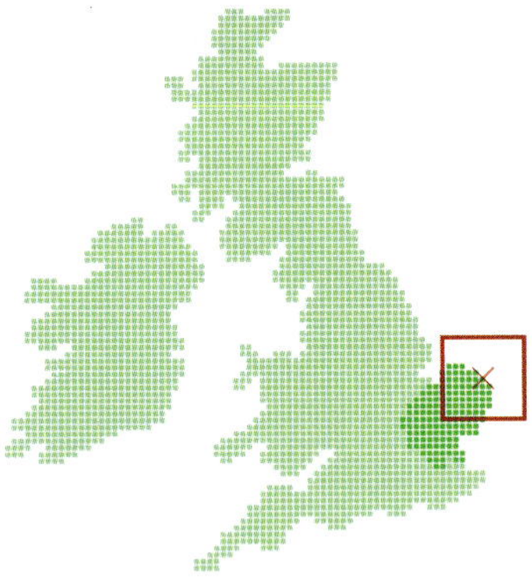

Above: These worn sea defences are perfect subjects for good foreground interest.

Right: The strong contrast of colour and dark clouds add impact to the composition.

LOCATED: North Norfolk coast
GETTING THERE: From the A149 to North Walsham, take the B1145 and then the B1159 signposted to Happisburgh.
O/S REF: TG384311 **WEB:** www.norfolktouristinformation.com

HAPPISBURGH IS A SMALL VILLAGE on the coast of north Norfolk. This is a truly exposed location, battered by the sea. Wooden sea defences were built to protect the village more than 50 years ago, but they have been unable to stop the erosion. Of course, this is tragic for the people living here, but it helps make Happisburgh a wonderful location for landscape photographers.

The decaying and broken sea defences offer huge amounts of foreground interest, particularly at sunrise, when this spot is arguably at its most photogenic. Outdoor photographers can easily spend hours on the beach, experimenting with compositions and blurring the tide using long exposures.

There are also opportunities to shoot close-ups of texture and detail, as stones and shells have been driven into the battered wood and rock defences so swap your wide-angle lens for a macro.

When you have finished taking pictures on the beach turn your attention to the famous red-and-white striped lighthouse, which is perched on the cliffs above the beach.

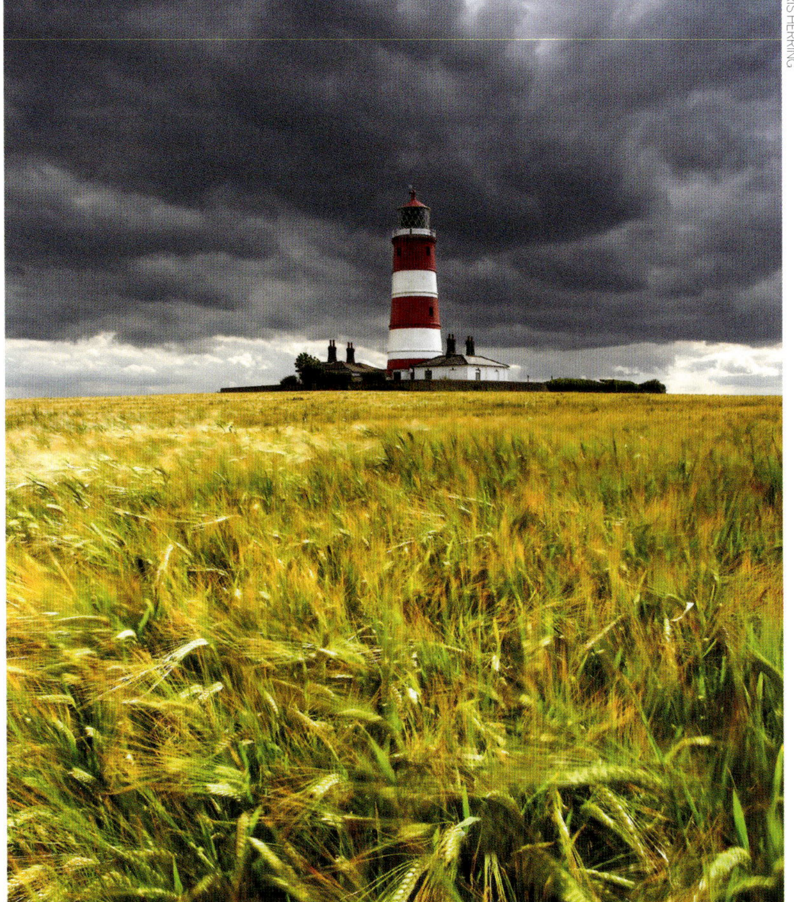

CHRIS HERRING

HELEN DIXON

Southern England

Richmond Park London

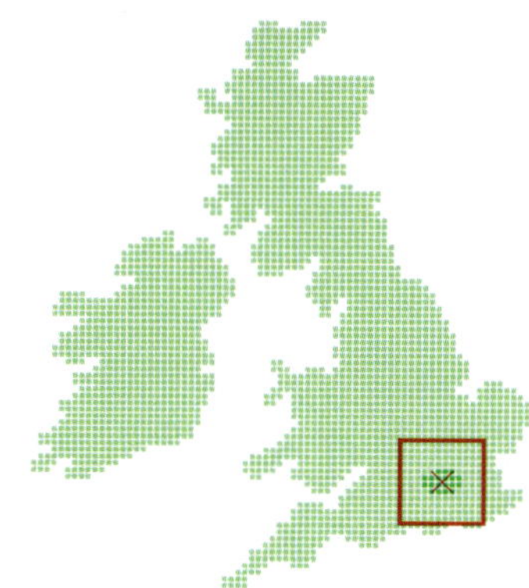

Above: Get up early and combine morning mist with the stunning colours of sunrise. It's hard to believe that this incredible scene was taken inside the M25.

LOCATED: London **GETTING THERE:** By tube/rail go to Richmond Station (British Rail or District Line) and then catch the 371 or 65 buses to the pedestrian gate at Petersham. If driving, there are six car parks within the park.
O/S REF: TQ194739 **WEB:** www.royalparks.org.uk/parks/richmond_park

AT ALMOST 1,000 hectares, Richmond Park is the largest Royal Park in London. Yes that's right, these stunning scenes were shot in the suburbs of our nation's metropolis. This attractive landscape of hills, woodland, ponds, gardens and grasslands, set amongst ancient trees, is a haven for outdoor photographers, yet it's so close to the heart of the capital. Get up early to beat the joggers and the most dedicated dog-walkers and make the most of sunrise.

You can visit at any time of year and return with stunning images, but Richmond Park is arguably at its best during autumn – when foliage is red and golden and mist hangs over the parkland after a clear, still night. The park is designated as a National Nature Reserve (NNR), a Site of Special Scientific Interest (SSSI) and a Special Area of Conservation (SAC) and is home to a wealth of flora and fauna, including over 600 free roaming deer. They can sometimes be caught with a good telephoto or long zoom and included within the landscape to add scale and interest.

Visit at dawn or dusk to enjoy the best light of the day.

Southern England

New Forest Hampshire

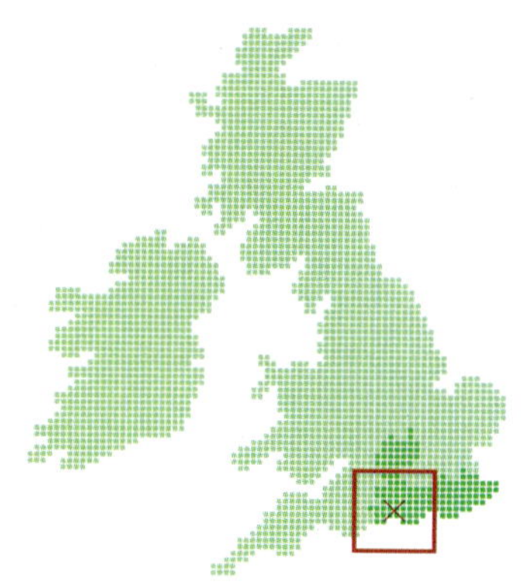

Below: As well as general scenics, head into the forest for dramatic compositions. An ND grad filter darkens the sky and evens out the exposure of the scene.

LOCATED: Hampshire
GETTING THERE: The New Forest is easily accessed, regardless of the direction you approach it from. From Basingstoke, take the M3, M27 and then the A31 – which cuts across the National Park – or the A337 to Lyndhurst.
O/S REF: SU299075 **WEB:** www.thenewforest.co.uk

THE NEW FOREST IS ENGLAND'S smallest National Park and is an area of outstanding natural beauty.

Located in the south-west of Hampshire, it consists mainly of lowland heath and woodland. This is a location bursting with potential for outdoor photographers. It is renowned for its wildlife and natural history, but its landscape is equally photogenic and that's the bit we're interested in, after all.

The heathlands are at their best in August, when the heather is flowering. Among good locations to visit are Isbley Common, Backley Plain and Rockford Common. Early risers may be rewarded with mists hanging in the bottom of the valleys after still, clear nights, adding atmosphere and mood to your scenic shots.

However, the New Forest is undoubtedly at its best in late October and early November – when the autumn colours are at their peak. Soft morning or evening light will add even more warmth to your shots. A polarising filter will remove glare from foliage and help further saturate the stunning autumnal colours.

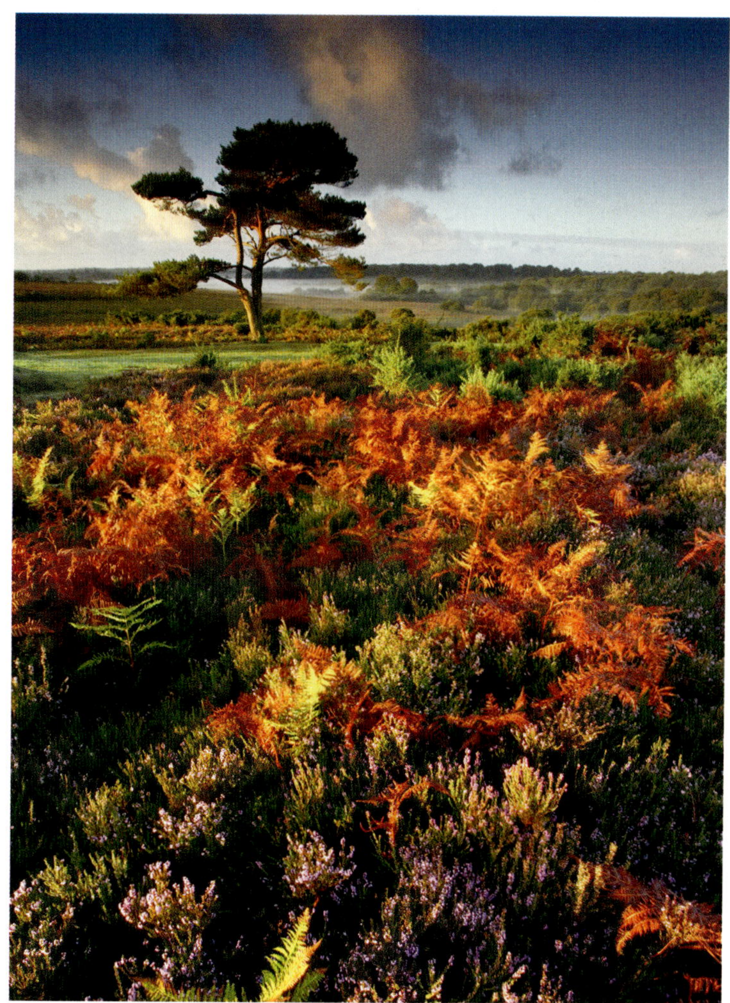

HELEN DIXON

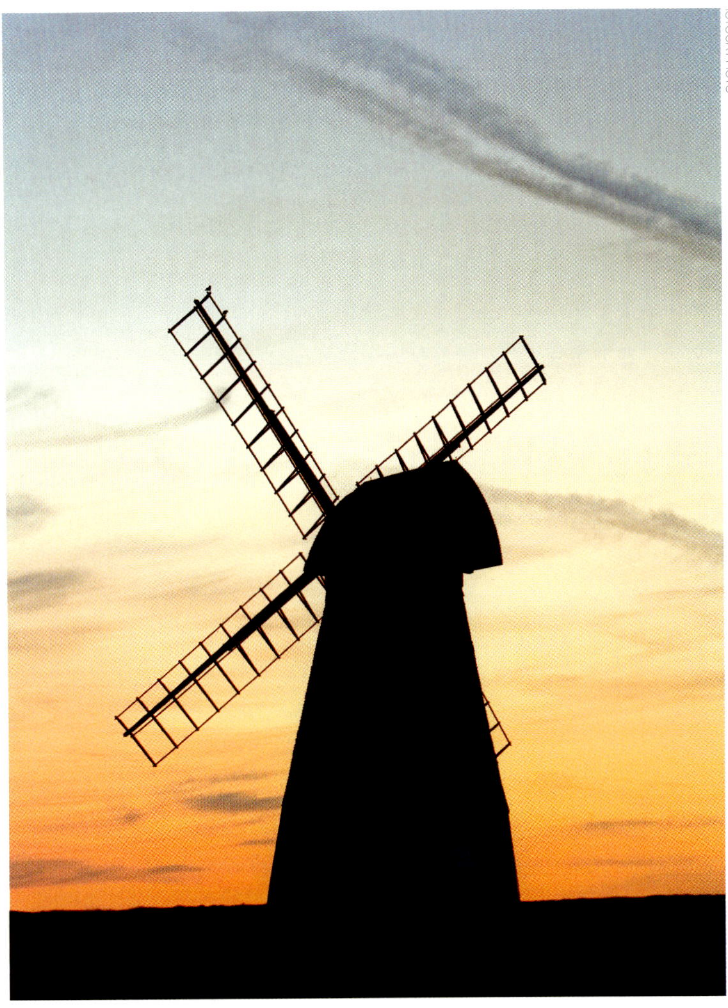
ISTOCK PHOTO

Southern England

Rottingdean
Sussex Downs

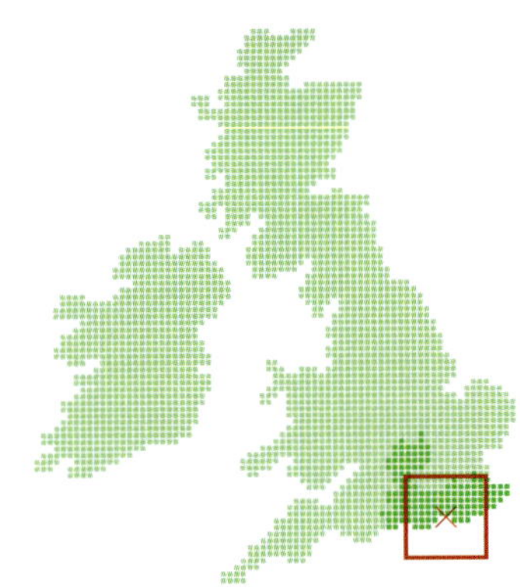

Above: The old wooden windmill is an iconic symbol for the Rottingdean area. With such a recognisable shape, silhouettes are the order of the day.

LOCATED: Near Brighton, Sussex
GETTING THERE: From the M25, take the M23 and then the A23 towards Brighton. Take the A27 toward Lewes, before turning right on to the B2123 signposted to Rottingdean.
O/S REF: TQ366025 **WEB:** www.visitsussex.org

THIS UNUSUAL, BLACK SMOCK windmill is an instantly recognisable local landmark, which acts as a beacon, pointing visitors towards the coastal village of Rottingdean.

The windmill, which was built in 1802, stands to the west of the village on Beacon Hill, which is why it is also known as Beacon Mill. This location boasts sweeping views towards the Sussex coast, but it is the often restored mill itself that will get digital SLR photographers reaching for their memory cards.

As always, light is the key ingredient. Morning and evening light create contrasting results – so visit at different times of the day. In spring and summer, the surrounding meadowland is punctuated with colourful wild flowers that generate good foreground interest.

Using a wide-angle lens, get close to the vegetation in order to stretch perspective – this will increase the three-dimensional feel of your landscapes. The bold outline of the mill is perfectly suited to being shot as a silhouette. A colourful sunset or sunrise will allow you to contrast its inky, black outline against a warm orange sky.

South-west England

Swanage Bay
Dorset

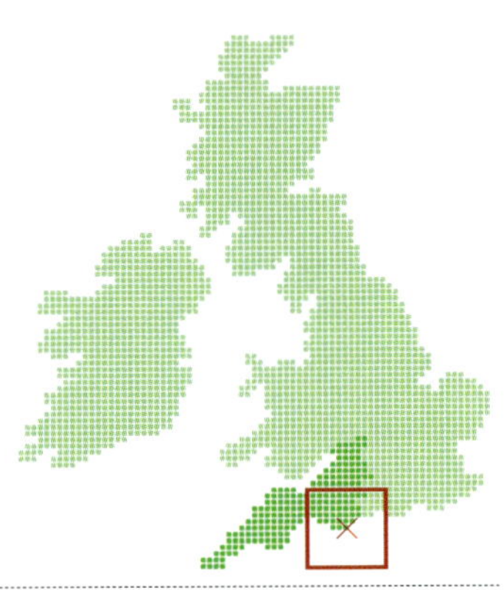

Above: The wooden groynes at Swanage bay create perfect lead-in lines in landscape images.

LOCATED: Swanage is South of Poole and East of Dorchester
GETTING THERE: From Poole, take the A35and then the A351 signposted to Corfe and Swanage. From Dorchester, take the A352 and then join the A351. There is ample parking within the town and seafront.
O/S REF: SZ0278 **WEB:** www.visitingpurbeck.co.uk

SWANAGE IS A SMALL COASTAL TOWN in the south-east of Dorset, situated at the eastern end of the Isle of Purbeck, approximately eight miles south of Poole. Originally a small port and fishing village, Swanage flourished in the Victorian era as a seaside resort. This is a place bursting with picture potential, including an attractive pier, jetty, sandy bay, colourful beach huts and photogenic groynes, jutting out to sea. An early start will be rewarded with a quiet beach, mostly free of people, and good early light on fine days. Nearby are a number of other good locations for landscape photography, including Studland Bay, Poole harbour, Durlston Bay and the magical ruins of Corfe Castle. Swanage is busy with tourists during summer, so photographers are best visiting at quieter times of the year outside of the school holidays. A wide assortment of focal lengths is required to realise the full picture potential of this attractive town. Wellies are also useful if you wish to walk to Peveril Point Road along the seafront, the southern-most tip of Swanage Bay, which boasts sweeping views to Old Harry Rocks.

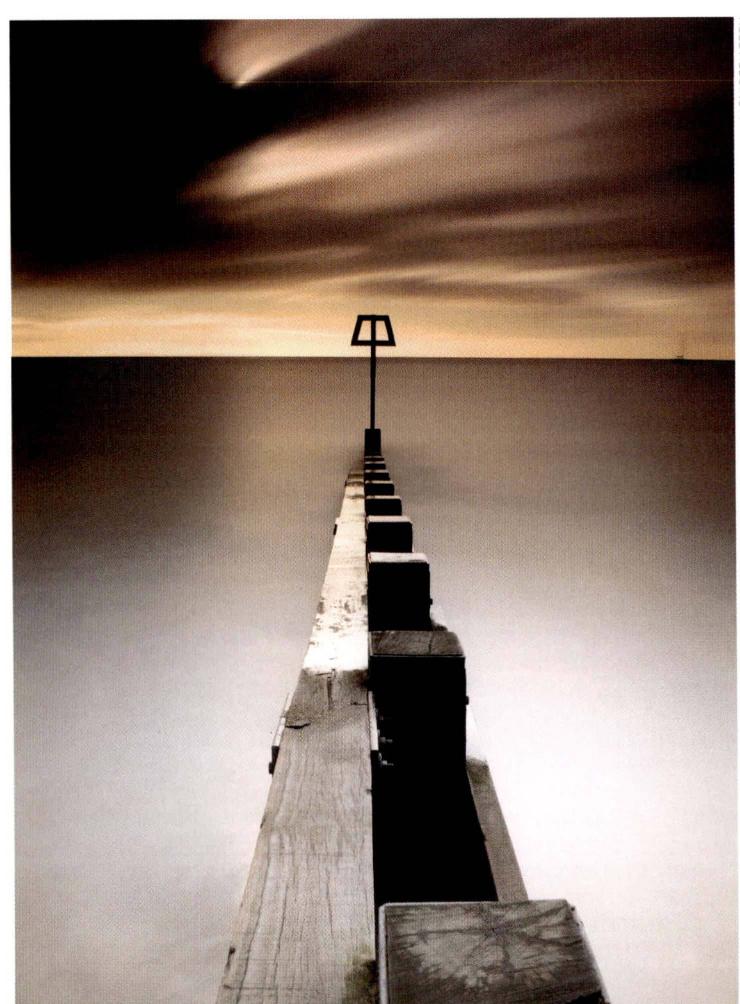
ROSS HODDINOTT

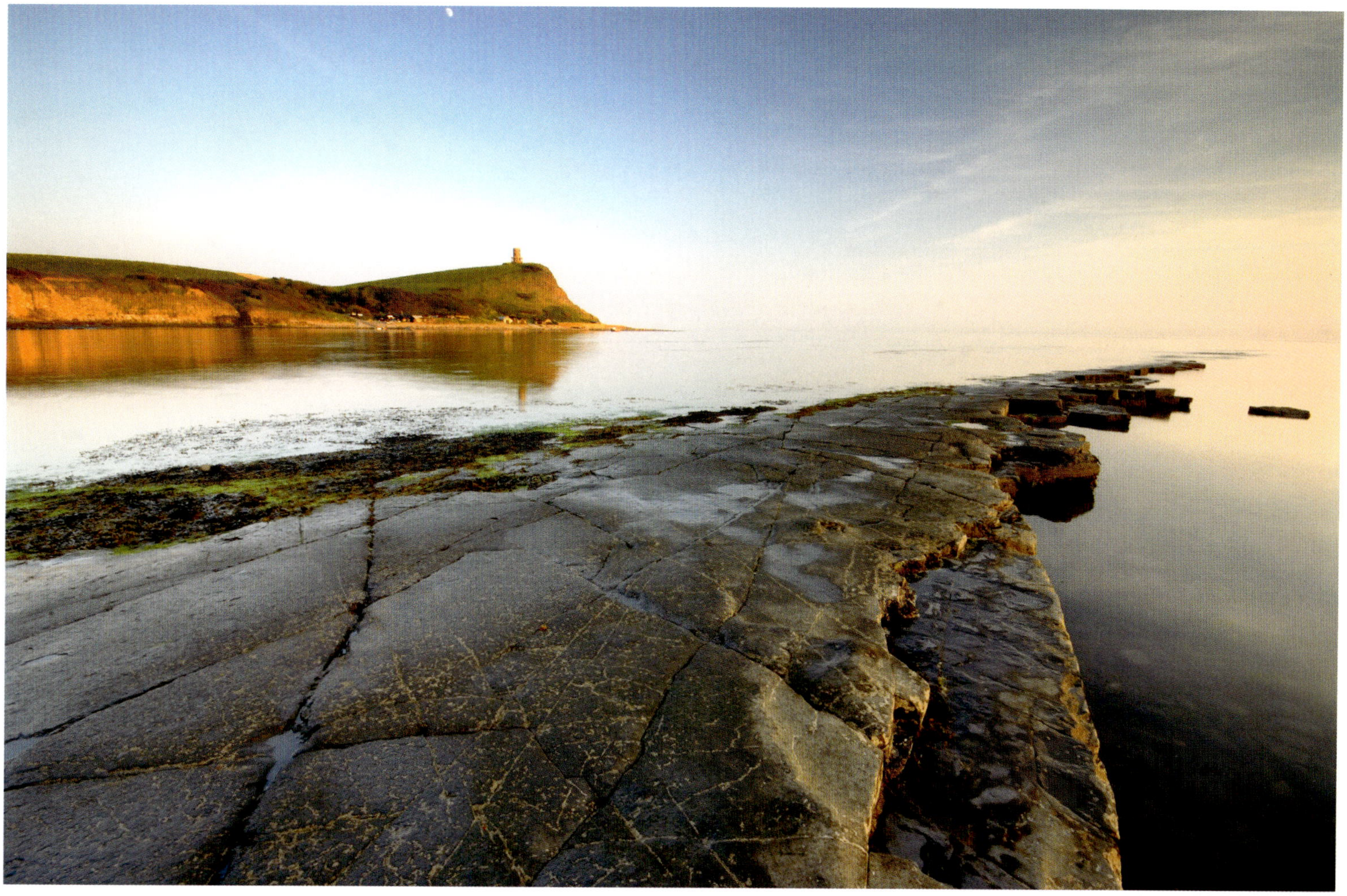

ROSS HODDINOTT

South-west of England

Kimmeridge Bay
Dorset

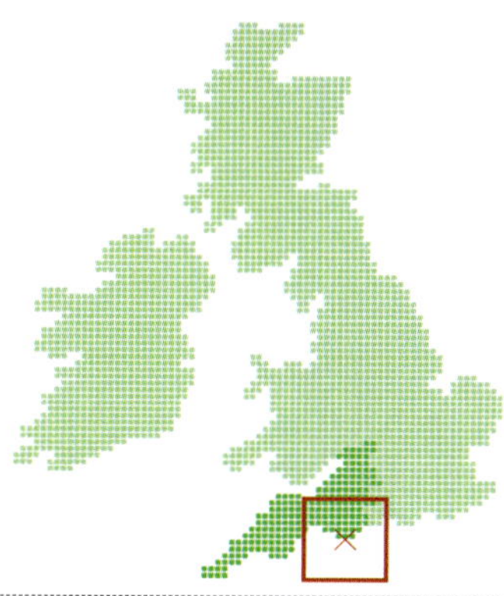

Above: Another good case for knowing tide times. Evening light bathes the bay.
Right: Night creeps in as a long exposure catches the last light of the dying day.

LOCATED: Near Lulworth **GETTING THERE:** Via the A351 through Wareham, heading towards Swanage. At the base of Corfe Castle turn right towards Church Knowle. Taking the second turning on the left to Kimmeridge. Toll road to the bay during the season.
O/S REF: SY906789 **WEB:** www.purbeck.gov.uk

KIMMERIDGE BAY FORMS PART of Dorset's famous Jurassic coastline. This location is not only renowned for its geology, rockpools and marine wildlife, but for its photographic potential. Parking is free and the walk down to the rocky beach is short, although there is a charge to drive the toll road from the village to the bay during the holiday season.

This location is best visited later in the day with the best light at sunset. At low tides, photogenic rock ledges are exposed and the Clavell Tower, a 19th century folly built by a vicar, perched on the adjacent cliff top, adds interest to the distance view. The tower was moved 25 metres away from the crumbling cliff between 2006 and 2008 by the Landmark Trust and can be rented for a holiday!

Other than the wider views, consider taking more abstract looking images of the rock ledges – maybe with the tide gently lapping over them – using a short telephoto lens. Also look for detail, rock formations, marine life and even fossils whilst visiting this stunning part of the Purbeck coast.

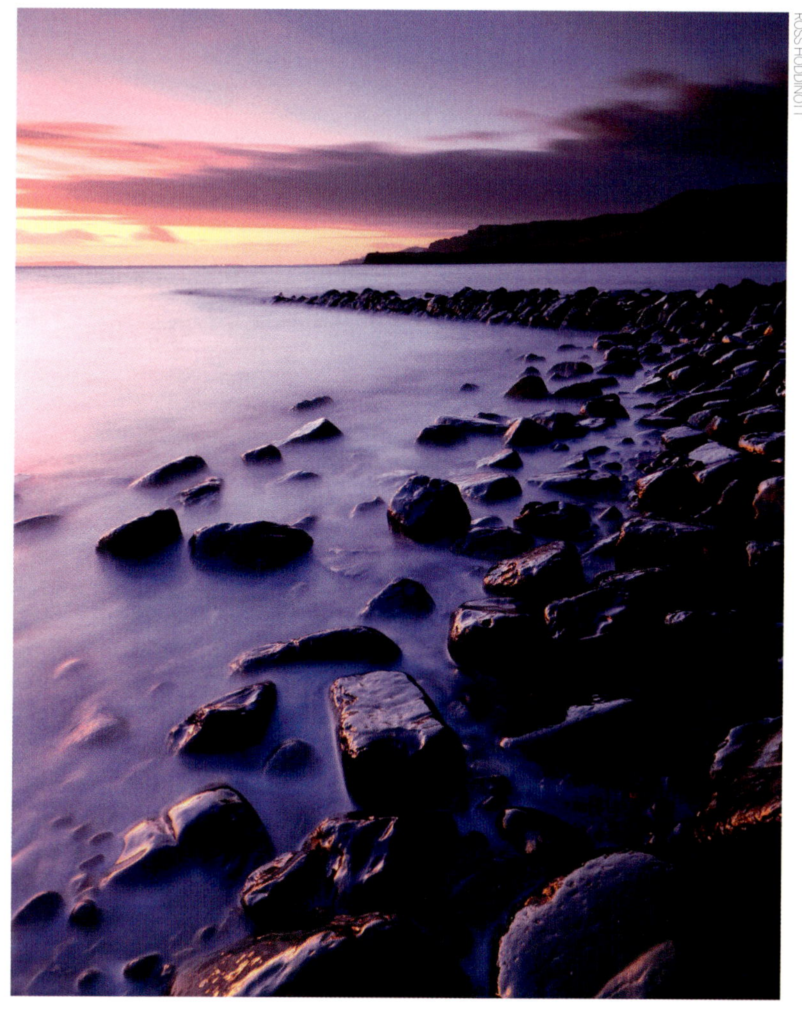

ROSS HODDINOTT

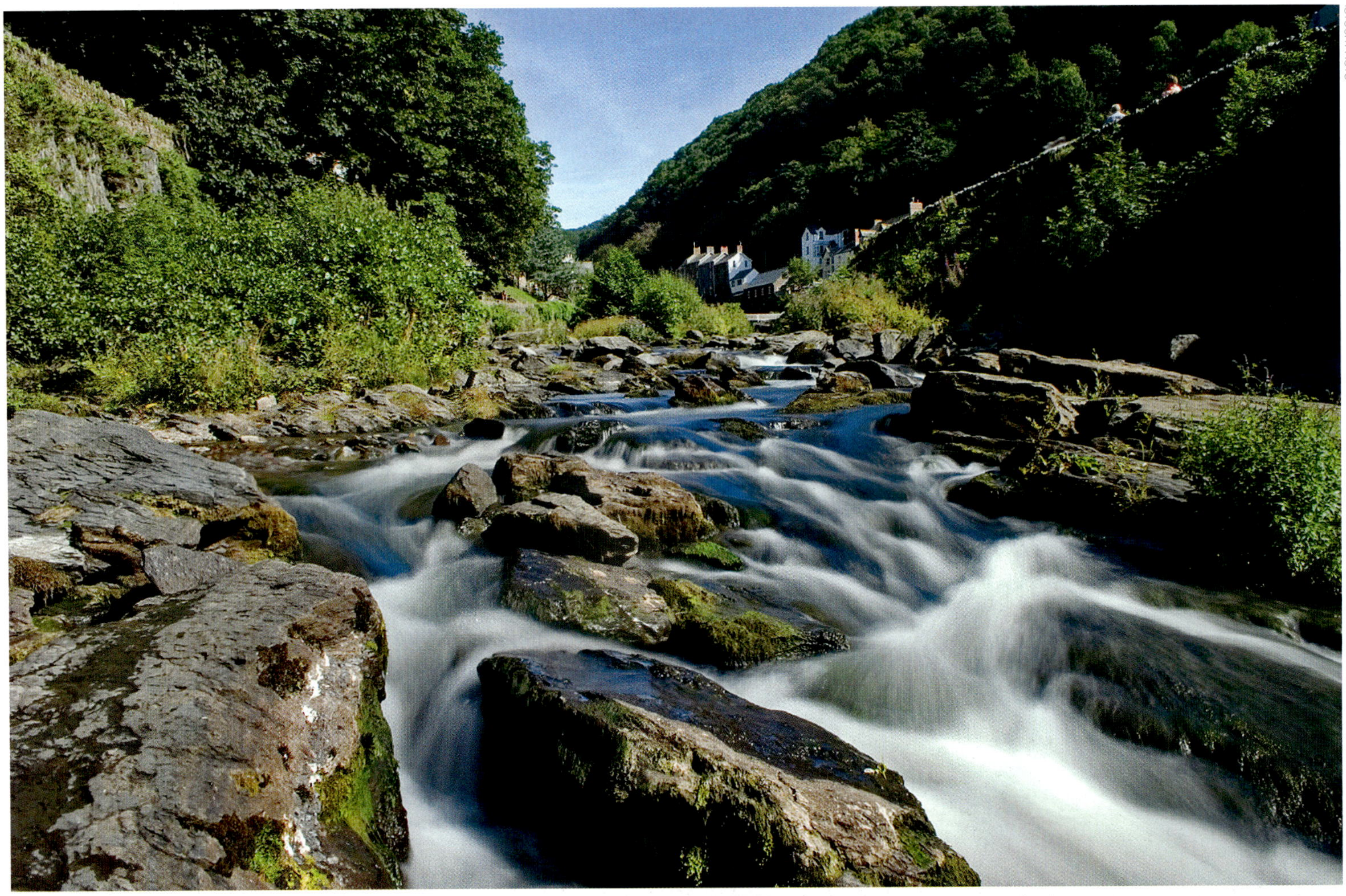

ISTOCK PHOTO

South-west England

Exmoor National Park Devon/Somerset

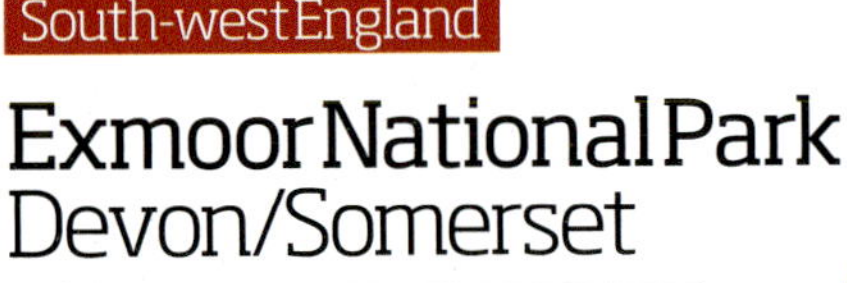

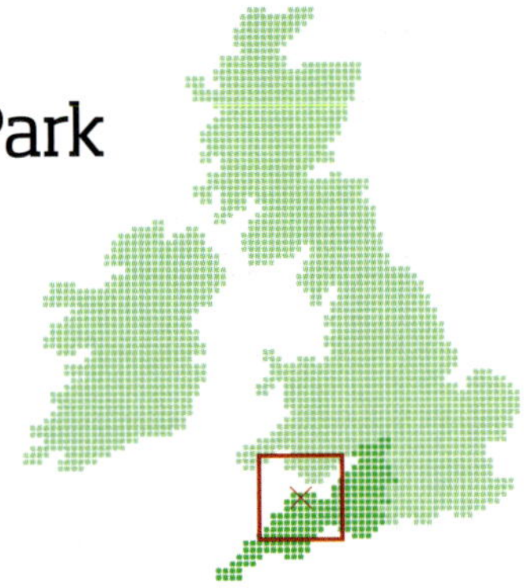

Above: The River Lyn is rushing in the foreground with houses of Lynmouth.

Right: Head to the coast late in the day and capture stunning coastal scenes like this.

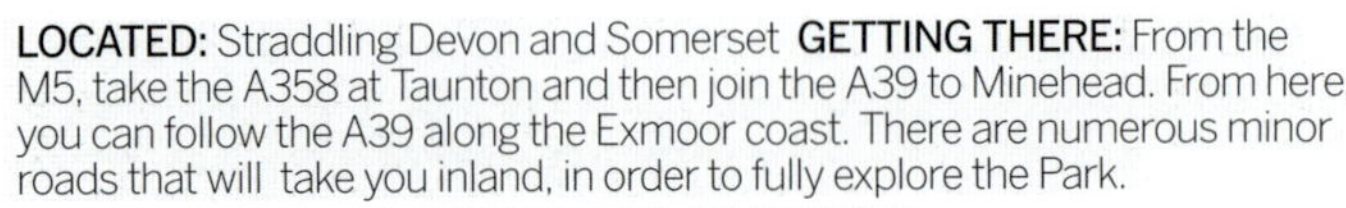

LOCATED: Straddling Devon and Somerset **GETTING THERE:** From the M5, take the A358 at Taunton and then join the A39 to Minehead. From here, you can follow the A39 along the Exmoor coast. There are numerous minor roads that will take you inland, in order to fully explore the Park.
O/S REF: SS891415 **WEB:** www.visit-exmoor.co.uk

EXMOOR NATIONAL PARK covers 267 square miles of the beautiful rolling Devon and Somerset countryside. Boasting both wonderful coastline and lush countryside, this is a rich landscape.

The Park has 34 miles of coastline, including the highest cliffs in England – which reach a height of 1,350ft at Culbone Hill. The coast varies greatly, from the sandy bay at Combe Martin to the pebbly shores of Porlock and Bossington. Near Lynmouth is the Valley of the Rocks – a remarkable stetch of coastline. The rocky outcrops look striking bathed in soft, warm evening sunlight.

Exmoor is best known for its wooded valleys and moorland. On a clear day, the view from the summit of Dunkery Beacon, or Quantock Hills, is thrilling. In late summer, the moors are carpeted in pink and purple heather. Windswept trees add interest and a focal point to wide-angle views. Exmoor is home to photogenic rural towns and hamlets, like Bampton, Dunster and Selworthy. Don't forget to visit Tarr Steps – a prehistoric clapper bridge crossing the River Barle – one of the Park's most recognisable landmarks.

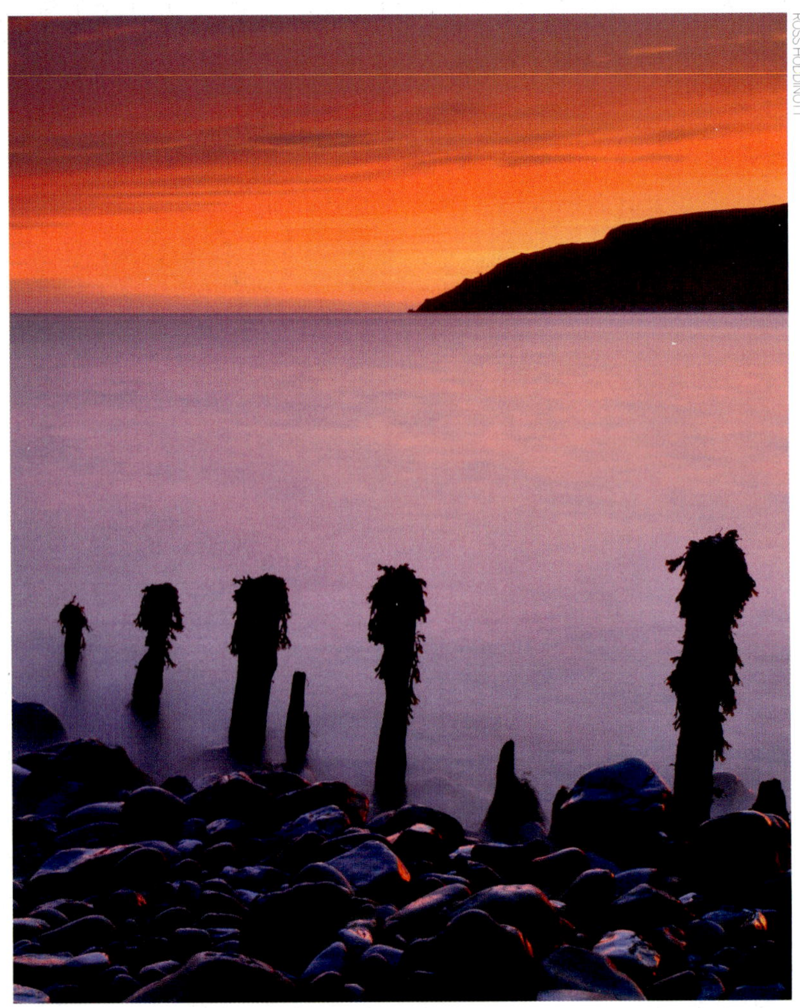

ROSS HODDINOTT

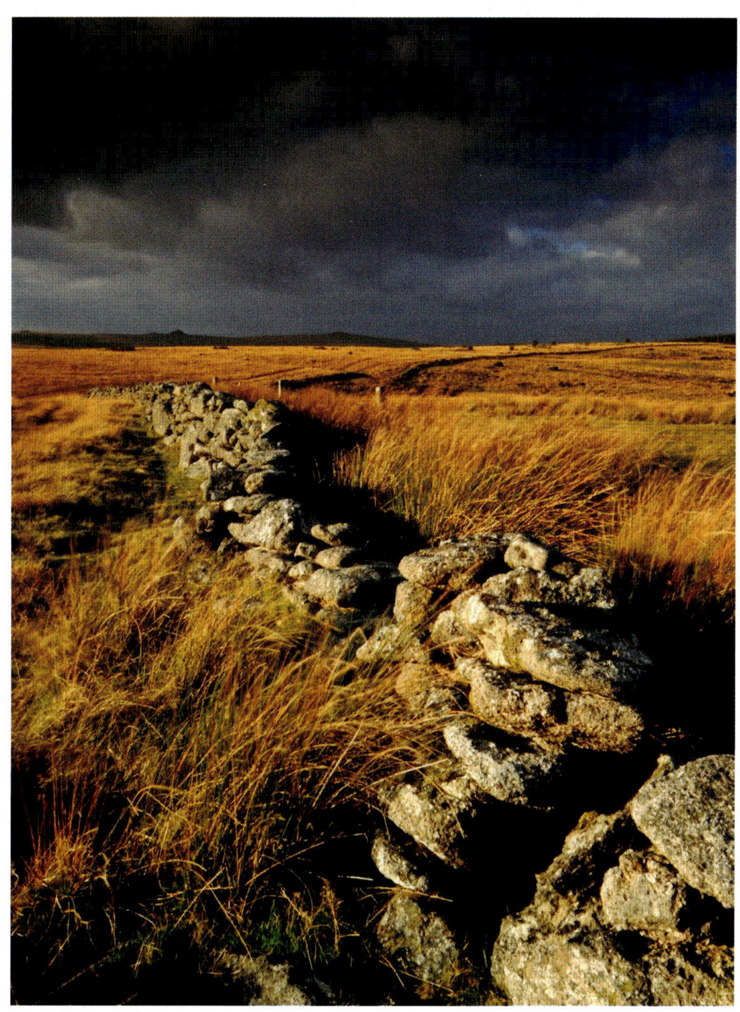
ROSS HODDINOTT

South-west of England

Porth Nanven
Cornwall

Below: A small aperture on a wide lens gives 'dinosaur egg'-to-'Brisons' sharpness. Set up a tripod at the water's edge for a motion blurred foreground.

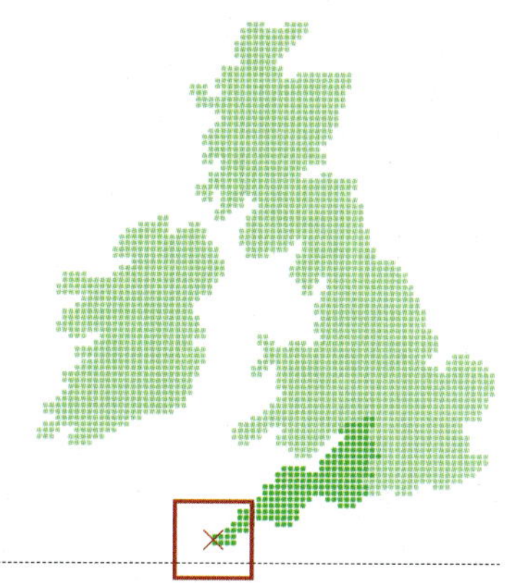

LOCATED: Near St Just, west Cornwall
GETTING THERE: From Penzance, take the A3071 to St Just. From the town centre, follow the signs to the Cot Valley. At the end of this narrow, minor road is a small parking area.
O/S REF: SW355307 **WEB:** www.visitcornwall.com

PORTH NANVEN (also known as Cot Valley Beach) is a secluded little beach at the seaward end of the Cot Valley in Cornwall. It has been designated a Site of Special Scientific Interest and is a location just bursting with photogenic landscape potential.

The beach is referred to locally as 'dinosaur egg beach' due to the remarkable number of ovoid boulders – ranging greatly in size and covering the beach and foreshore. They can be photographed in context – as part of a bigger beach scene and seascape – or isolated, using a longer focal length lens in order to emphasize their fascinating colour and shape.

A mile or so out to sea is a pair of big rocks called the 'v'. They are perfectly positioned for landscape photography, as they can be utilised to harness the horizon in wide-angle views of the beach. They can also look good photographed alone, particularly in the evening when there is a colourful sunset behind them.

Porth Nanven is best photographed in the evening, when the beach and coast are bathed in soft, warm light.

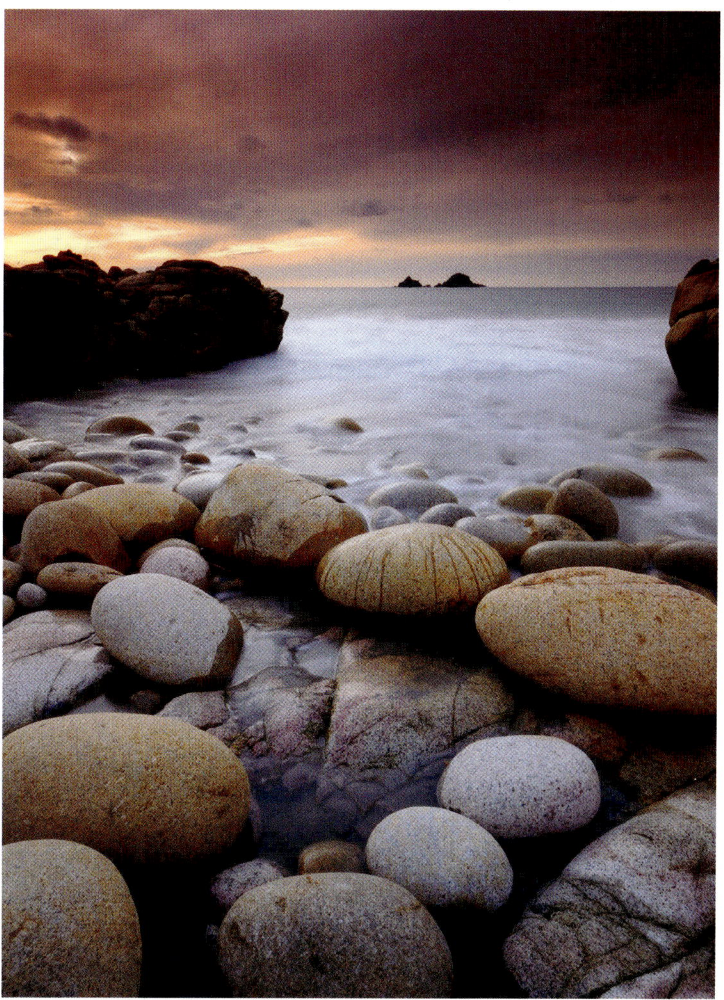
ROSS HODDINOTT

South-west of England

Dartmoor
Devon

Above: Early morning is a good time for clear skies before cloud blows in from the west but when it's this dark and brooding, conditions are perfect for moody shots.

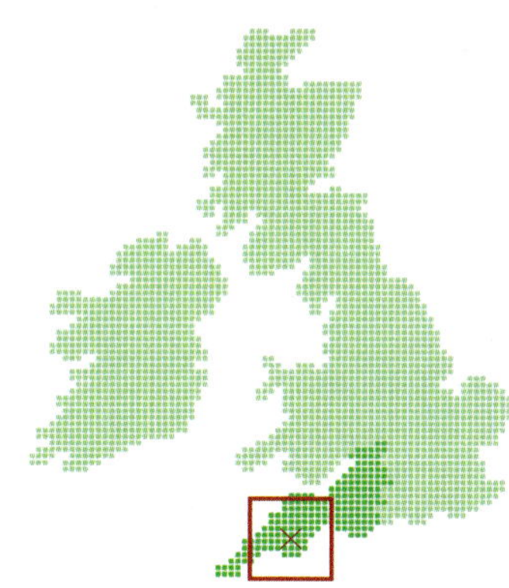

LOCATED: Between Exeter and Plymouth
GETTING THERE: Dartmoor is reached by both the A30 and A38, which offer rapid journey times from the M5 straight to the fringes of the National Park.
O/S REF: SX657758 **WEB:** www.dartmoor-npa.gov.uk

DARTMOOR IS GREAT BRITAIN'S LAST remaining wilderness. The designated National Park covers an area of 368 square miles making it is the largest region of open country in southern England.

Its rugged, windswept appearance makes it is a landscape photographer's paradise. In late summer, the bracken, heathers and gorse combine to carpet large areas with colour.

The best views of its outstanding scenery are enjoyed from one of 160 or so granite tors that dominate the landscape. Houndtor and Haytor are among the most spectacular and popular.

The unusual rock formation of Bowerman's Nose, near Manaton, will also appeal to photographers, as will the picturesque villages of Widecombe and Buckland-in-the-Moor. The ancient clapper bridge at Postbridge is also worth visiting, as is Brentor – a tiny church perched on the top of a rocky outcrop near Tavistock, with wonderful sweeping moorland views. With Dartmoor boasting moorland streams, steep wooded valleys, ancient archeology and curious granite crosses, landscape photographers are spoilt rotten.

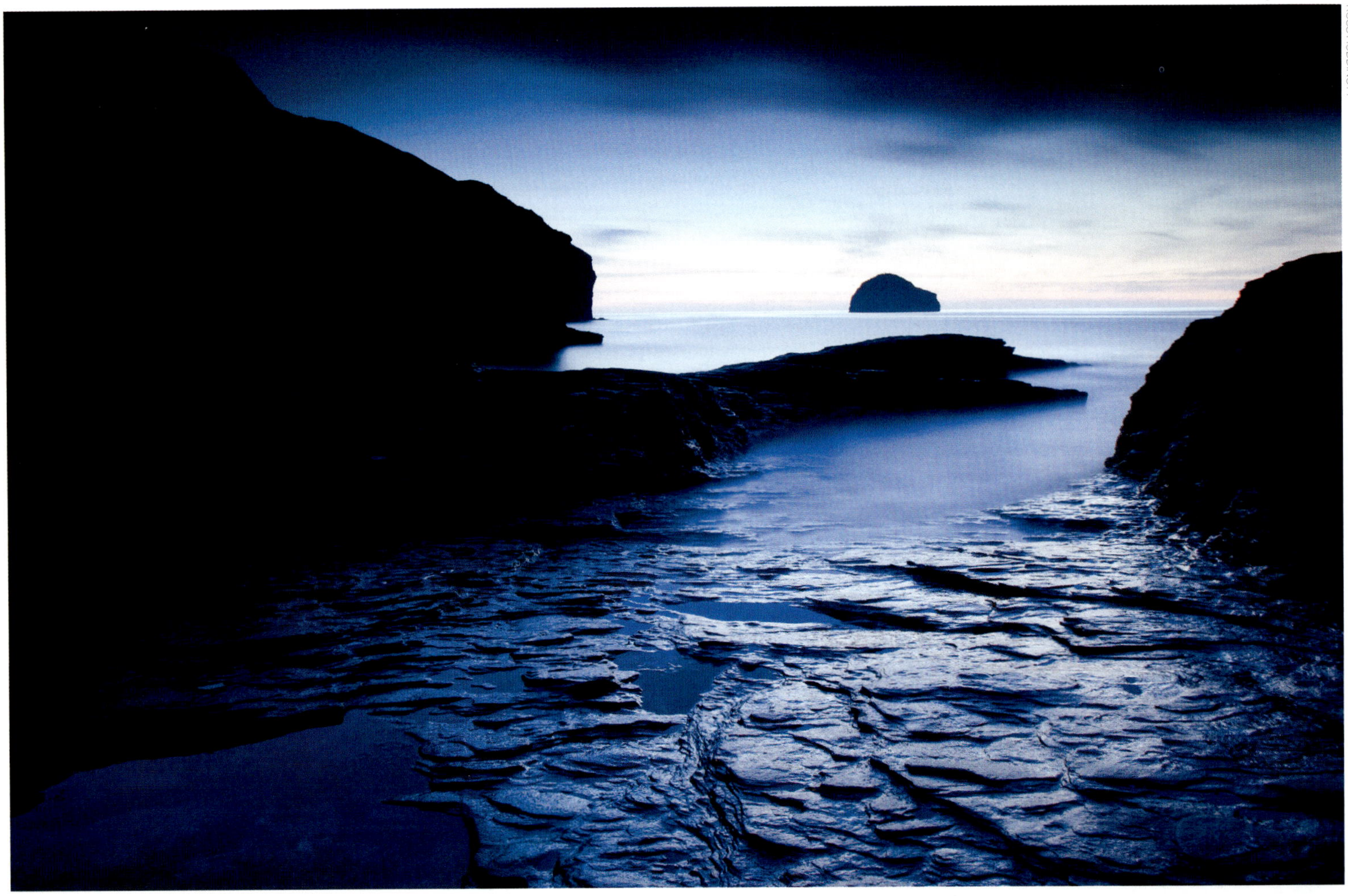

ROSS HODDINOTT

South-west England

Trebarwith Strand
Cornwall

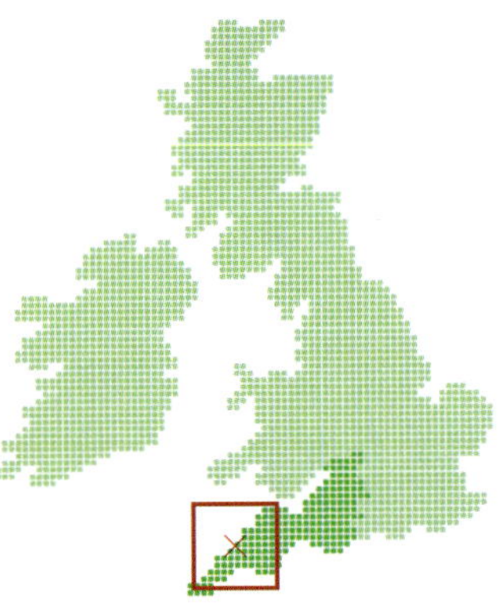

Above: A lengthy exposure creates ethereal, atmospheric looking seascapes.

LOCATED: Near Tintagel, north Cornwall **GETTING THERE:** Follow the A39 from Wadebridge north to Camelford. At Camelford take the B3266, then the B3263 to Tintagel. About a mile before Tintagel, turn left and follow signs to Trebarwith Strand. There is a car park near the beach. **O/S REF:** SX 05056 86408 **WEB:** www.north-cornwall.com

TREBARWITH STRAND HAS TO BE one of the most photogenic locations along the north Cornish coast. It is approximately two and a half miles south of Tintagel and a great location to visit with your DSLR – at either high or low tide. The beach is at the bottom of a deep valley with many attractive views along the Heritage Coastline. You can either photograph the rugged coastline from the coastpath above, or shoot from the beach itself. Low tides reveal a wonderful sandy bay with jagged outcrops. Over centuries, the tide has carved interesting shapes into the rock, so there is no shortage of picture potential or foreground interest here. Rough seas can prove particularly dramatic and Gull Rock, positioned around 500 metres offshore, further enhances the picturesque setting.

A wide-angle lens is essential when you visit and a moderate zoom will also be useful for isolating detail and photographing crashing waves. The rocks can be slippery, so watch your footing and wear appropriate footwear. Also, the tide can rise quickly and catch you unaware, so check tide times before your visit.

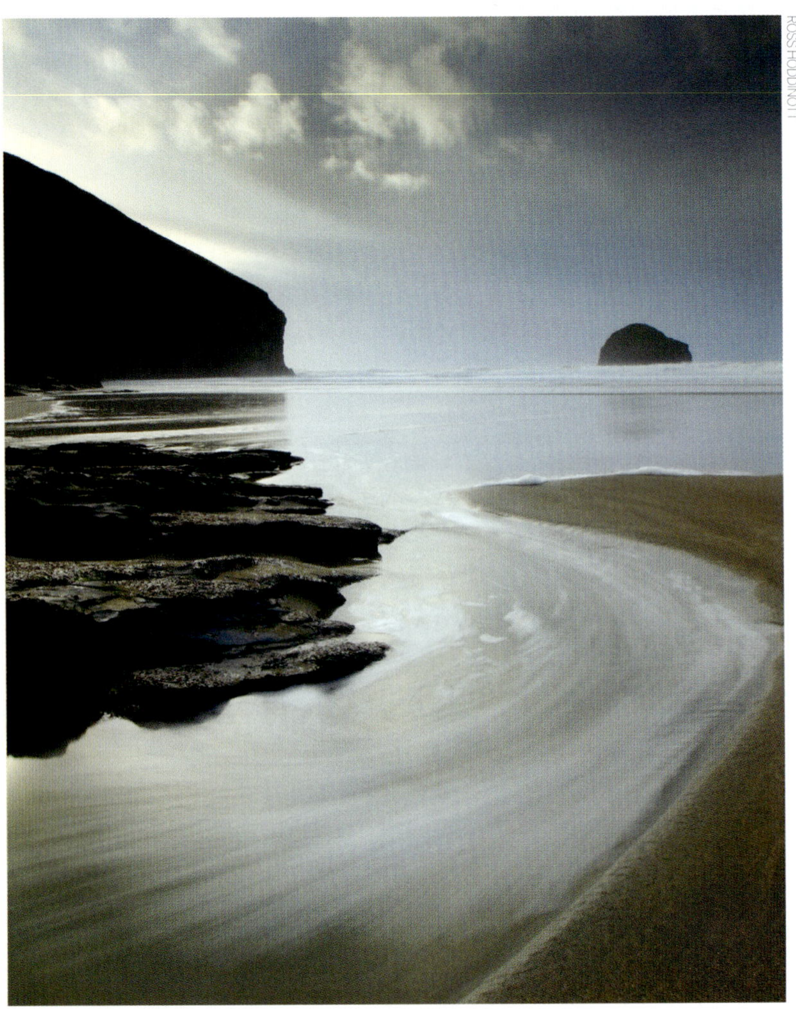

ROSS HODDINOTT

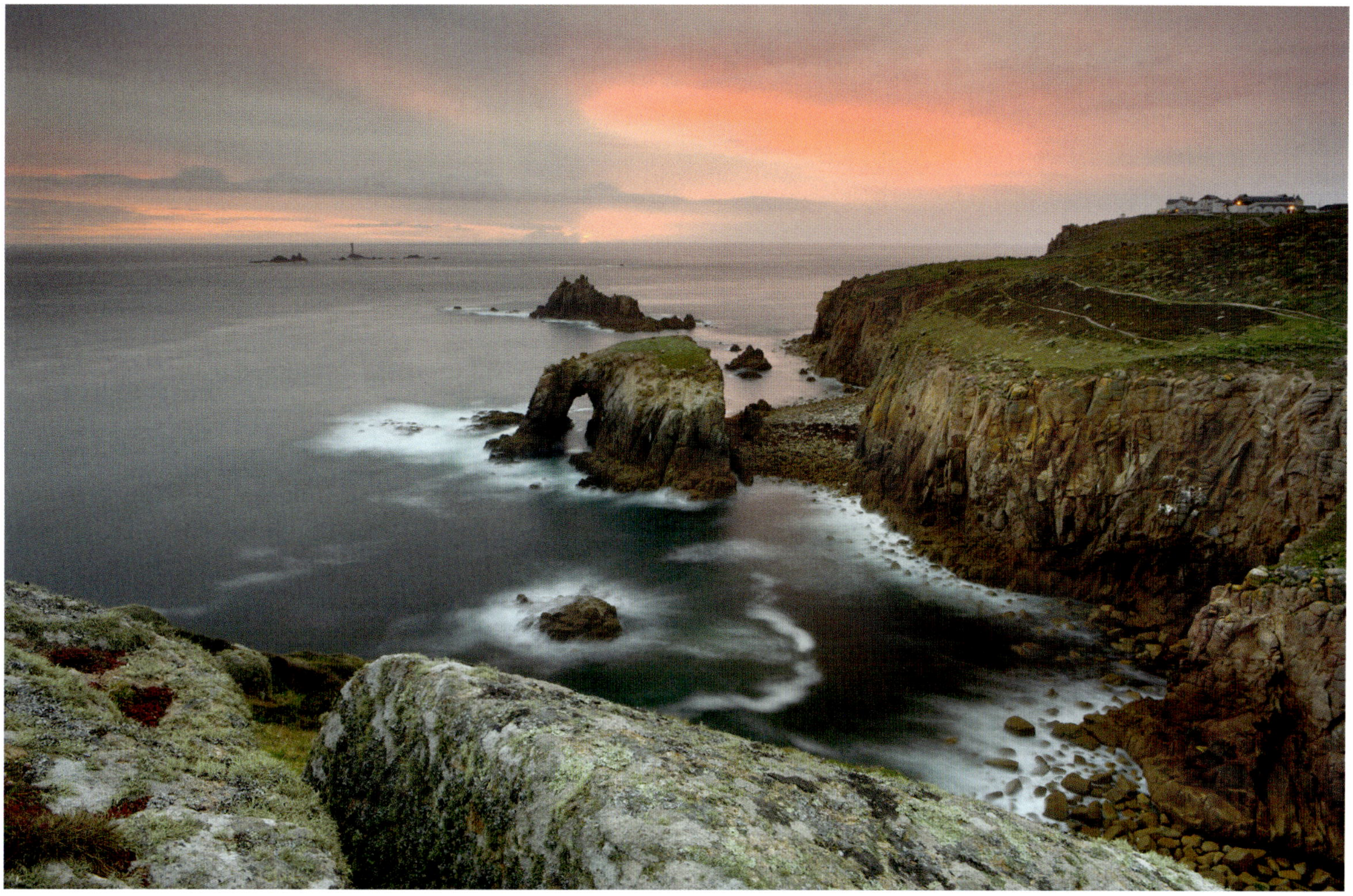

ADAM BURTON

South-west of England

Land's End
Cornwall

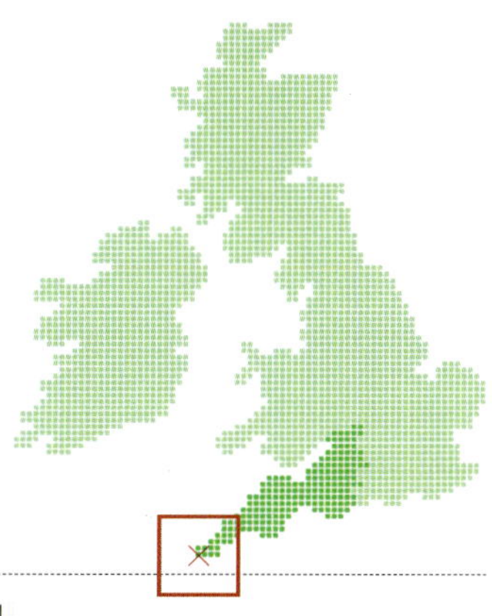

Above: Enys Dodman arched rock is one of Cornwall's most famous and photogenic landmarks.

LOCATED: Near Sennen, West Cornwall
GETTING THERE: From Penzance, follow the A30 signposted to Sennen and Land's End. The visitor centre and attractions at Land's End are well signed. There is ample parking here, but you have to pay to park.
O/S REF: SW342254 **WEB:** www.visitcornwall.com

FAMOUSLY, LAND'S END is the UK's most westerly point. It might be a major tourist attraction today, complete with a shopping centre, but the main attraction remains its unique location and amazing coastline. A short walk in either direction along the coastal path from the main complex provides fantastic ocean views as far as the eye can see. There are many interesting and unusual rock formations just off shore, which are perfect for wild landscape images. These include the famous Enys Dodman arched rock, which is situated just off Pordennack Point above Greeb Farm. Also visible is the scenic Longships Lighthouse, a couple of miles out to sea. Although photogenic in the morning light, it is often best in the evening when the sun is setting out to sea. This is a wonderful location from which to photograph winter storms and large waves crashing against the Cornish headland. It is a great place to visit throughout the seasons and whatever the weather. As it's at the very tip of the country, it's worth taking some time to explore the coastline as you're unlikely to visit too often!

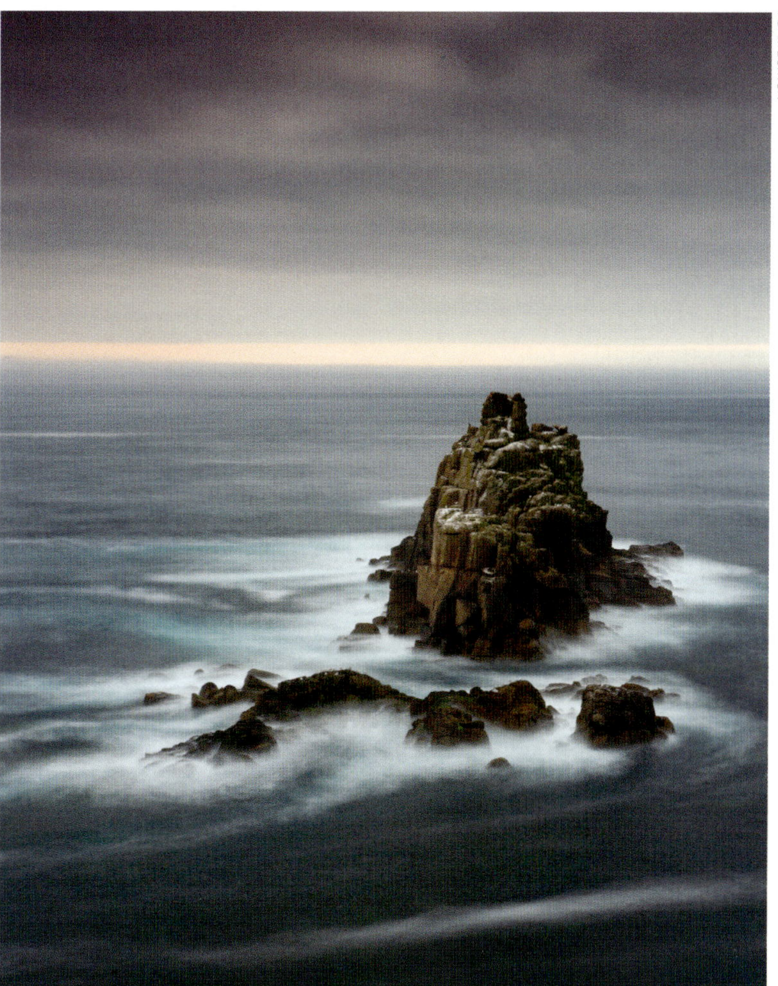

ADAM BURTON

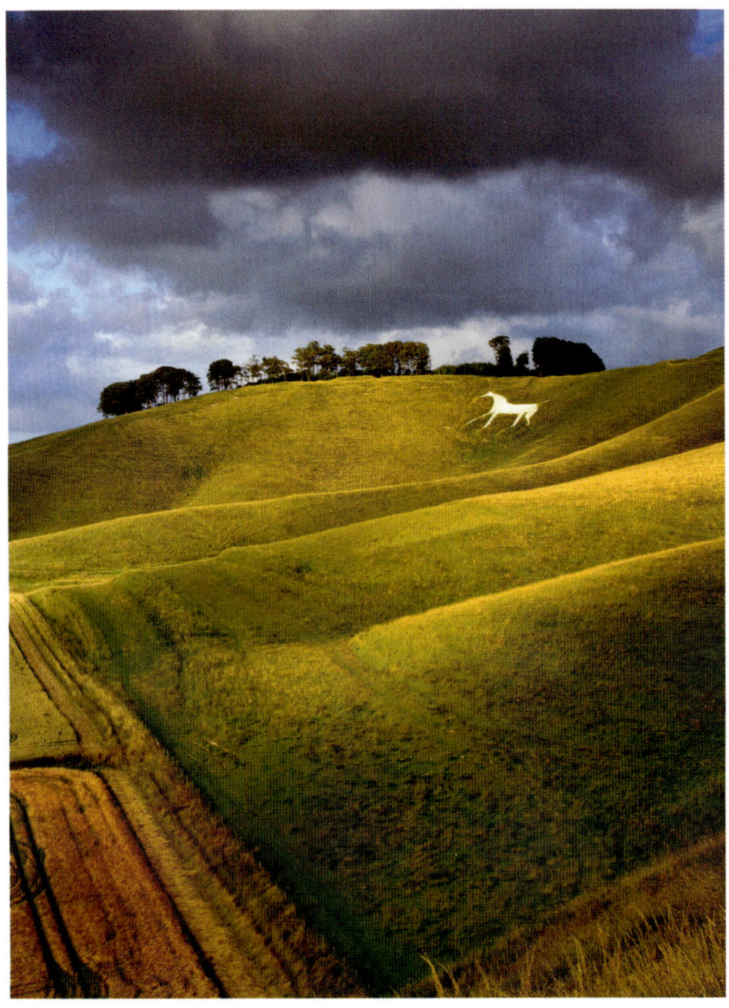

MARK BAUER

South-west of England

Cherhill
Wiltshire

Above: Cherhill white horse looks particularly photogenic placed in context with the surrounding countryside.

LOCATED: East of Calne, Wiltshire
GETTING THERE: It is situated on the edge of Cherhill Down, off the A4 Calne to Marlborough road just east of the village of Cherhill.
OS REF: SU 049 696 **WEB:** www.visitwiltshire.co.uk

THE CHERHILL WHITE HORSE is a 38-metre stone structure, erected in 1845, and is the second oldest of the Wiltshire horses. Situated on the edge of Cherhill Down, it is located just below earthworks known as Oldbury Castle and also found nearby is the . The horse is wonderfully placed, being high on a steep slope, and is easily visible from below and from a distance. Facing north-east, the horse is best photographed in the warm, evening light and particularly suits dappled light or when there is dramatic sky overhead. A good viewpoint is from a lay-by alongside the westbound carriageway of the A4, which passes below the horse. From near here, a footpath climbs the hill towards the horse itself. Although it can be tempting to photograph it so that it fills the frame – either by getting close to it, or by shooting it using a telephoto lens – often the best approach is to photograph it in context with its surroundings. In late spring and summer, the nearby farmland is usually vibrant with grasses or crops, adding interest and colour to wide-angle shots.

South-west England

Botallack tin mines
Cornwall

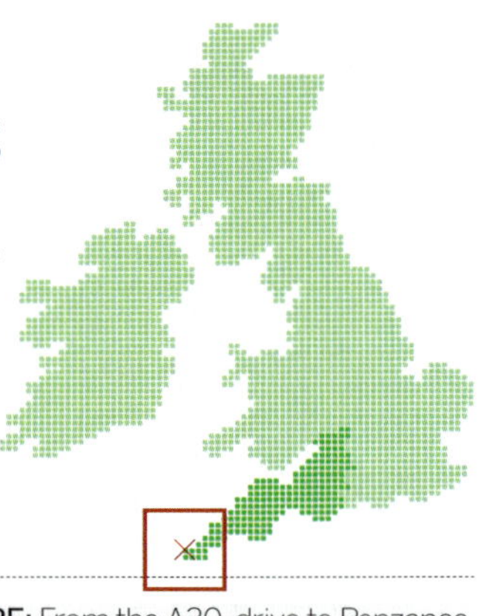

Below: You can photograph the twin mine shafts from adjacent cliffs in order to achieve a natural, parallel viewpoint.

LOCATED: Near St Just **GETTING THERE:** From the A30, drive to Penzance. Take the A3071 to St Just, then the B3306 toward Pendeen. When you reach Botallack, turn left just before righthand bend. Follow this track for 300m before parking adjacent to The Count House, a National Trust property.
O/S REF: SW362335 **WEB:** www.cornish-mining.org.uk

PERCHED PRECARIOUSLY on the cliffs at Botallack are the Crowns engine houses. Located between St Just and Pendeen in west Cornwall, this area is littered with the remains of Cornwall's once great mining industry. The twin remains of the Crown's engine houses are one of Cornwall's most recognisable landmarks. Built around 1815, today they are protected as part of the Cornwall and West Devon Mining Landscape World Heritage Site. They are best photographed at high tide, when the sea is crashing over the jagged rocks below. A short to medium telephoto lens is a good lens choice, allowing you to isolate the mine shafts. A lengthy exposure can create ethereal, atmospheric results, so an ND filter is a useful attachment. Wear good, supportive footwear, as the coastpath is steep in places. Our advice is to visit in early evening, when the light is best suited to the location. Pictures of the mines often suit black & white conversion, so don't overlook this possibility when processing your images, or you could try taking a series of exposures and generate a dynamic HDR landscape.

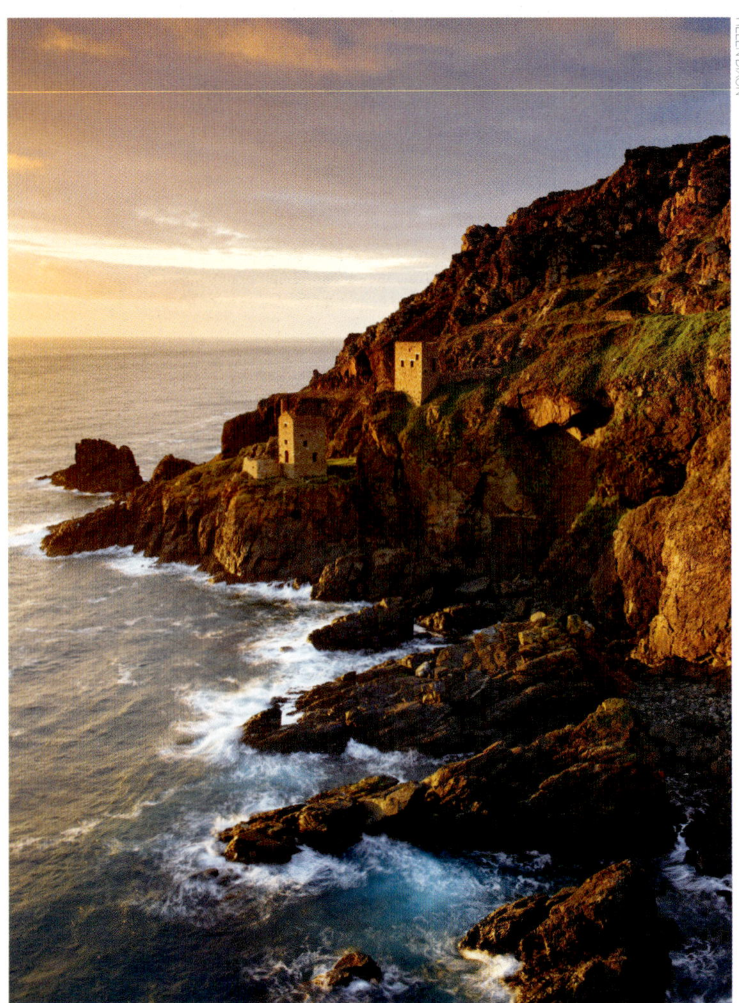

HELEN DIXON

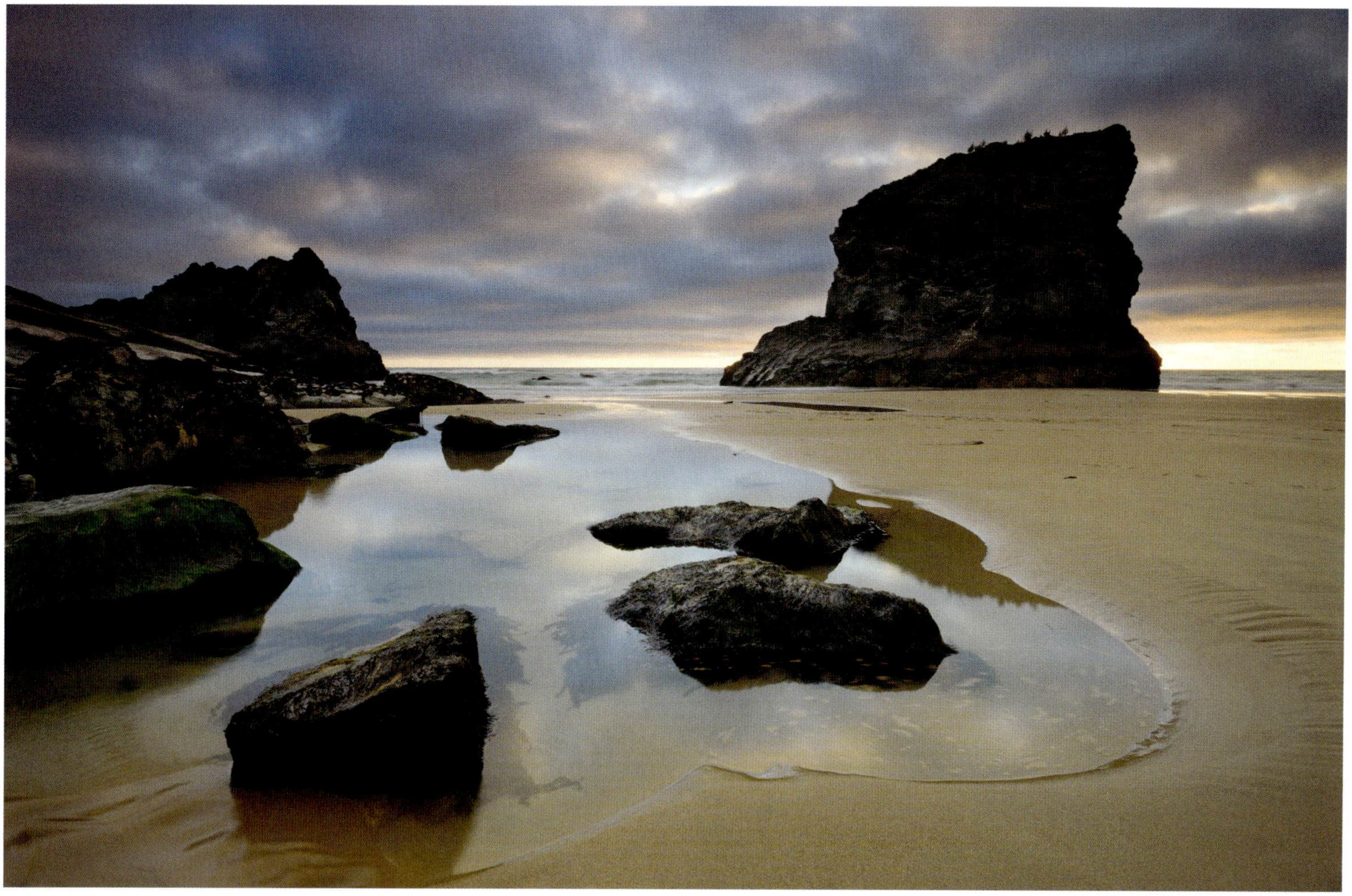

ADAM BURTON

South-west England

Bedruthan Steps
Cornwall

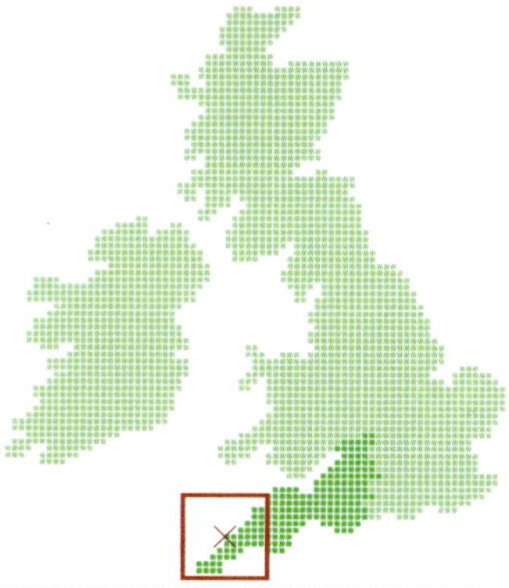

Above: In late spring, the cliff tops are carpeted with wild flowers – perfect foreground interest.

LOCATED: Near Newquay
GETTING THERE: Just off B3276 from Newquay to Padstow, six miles south west of Padstow. Park at the National Trust car park at Carnewas and Bedruthan Steps.
O/S REF: SW849692 **WEB:** www.cornwallbeachguide.co.uk

BEDRUTHAN STEPS is one of the most spectacular stretches of coastline in the UK. Coastal erosion has worn back the cliff face, leaving huge outcrops of volcanic rock scattered along the length of the beach. These towering monoliths are surrounded by water at high tide and are best photographed from the coastal path above. In spring, the cliff tops are carpeted in colourful thrift and the rugged cliffs glow in the warm, late evening light. At low tide the beach is accessible via a steep staircase. The descent and climb back up is steep, but it is well worth the effort, as this sandy bay is a spectacular site when the tide is low and sunset bathes the view in golden light. However, due to safety, the gate providing access to the steps is locked between November and February. Bedruthan Steps is photogenic throughout the seasons, but particularly in spring with the emerging foliage and during the winter months when stormy clouds create images with intense drama. A wide-angle lens is essential, together with a tripod for stability. An ND filter will be useful if you wish to blur the water's motion.

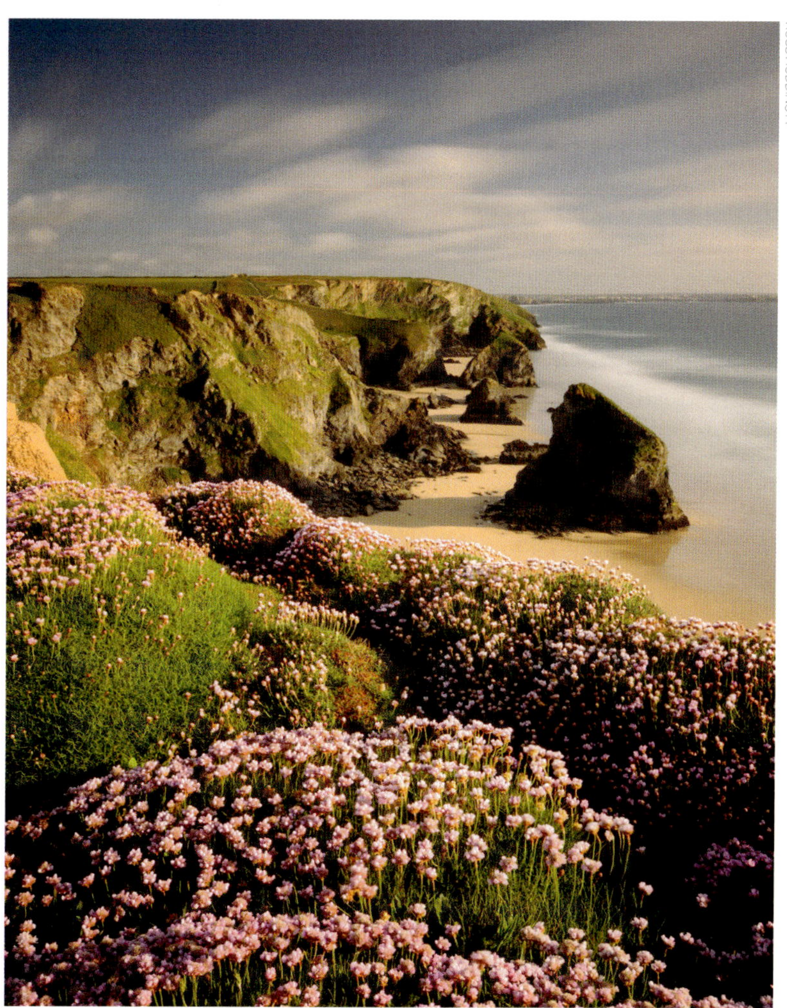

ROSS HODDINOTT

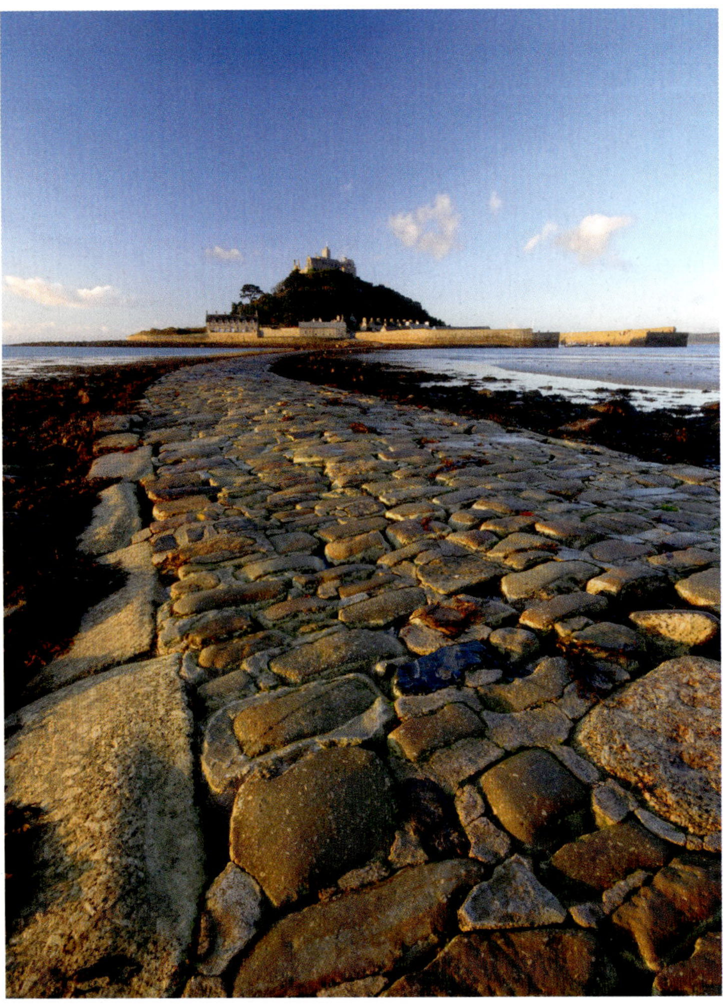
ROSS HODDINOTT

Scotland

Plockton Ross-Shire

Below: On calm mornings, photograph the picturesque reflections in the attractive harbour of Plockton.

LOCATED: Ross-Shire, West Highlands
GETTING THERE: Take the A87 toward the Kyle of Lochalsh. It is approximately six miles from here and Plockton village is clearly signed.
OS REF: NG803334 **WEB:** www.plockton.com

NEAR THE SEAWARD END of Loch Carron lies the picturesque village of Plockton – on the coastal route from Stromeferry to Kyle of Lochalsh. This delightful, small lochside village is one of the most attractive in Scotland – it is an idyllic place in an idyllic setting, and thanks to the warm Gulf Stream even boasts a number of palm trees! A row of neatly painted cottages hugs the shoreline, following the curve of the modest harbour. Across the harbour are views of whitewashed cottages standing on a craggy point with the mountains of Western Ross forming a dramatic backdrop. On calm, still mornings the boats moored in the harbour, together with their perfect reflections, create a picturesque scene waiting to be exploited by photographers. This is a place where it appears time has stood still. Within an hour's drive are similarly photogenic locations, like Eilean Donan Castle, Glenelg and the Brochs, the Isle of Skye and Applecross Bay. You will take countless pictures when you visit, so carry plenty of memory cards and a portable storage device to keep your images safely backed-up.

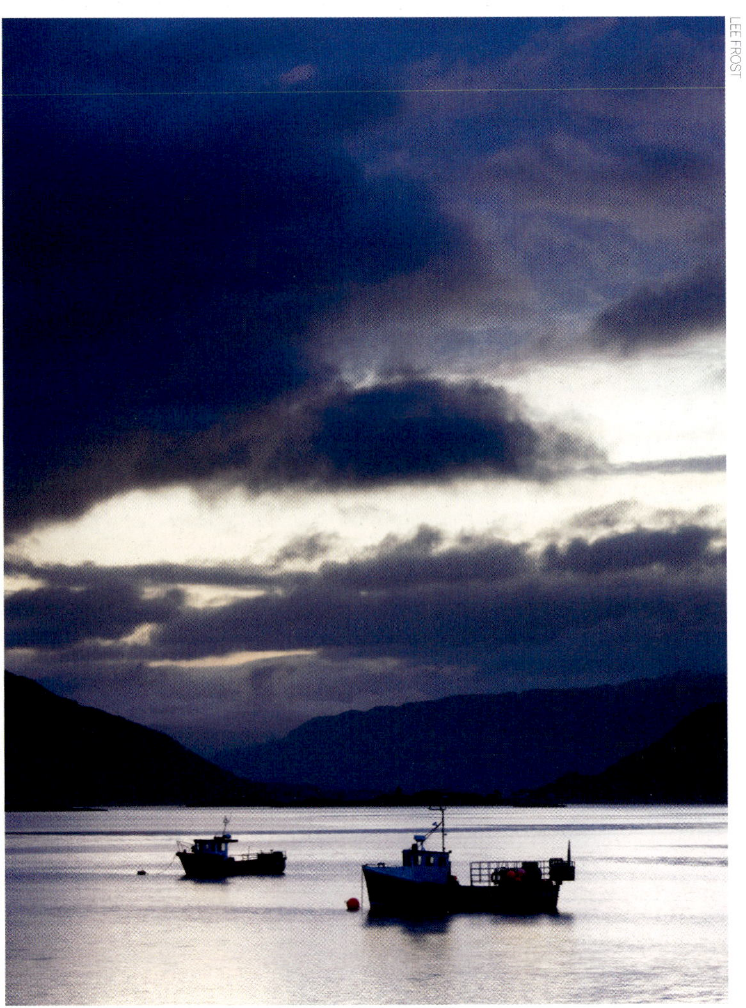
LEE FROST

South-west of England

St Michael's Mount Cornwall

Above: Knowing tide times is critical when photographing this location.

LOCATED: Marazion, near Penzance
GETTING THERE: Follow the A30 past Hayle. Drive through the village of Crowlas, before coming to a roundabout. Take the 2nd exit, signposted to Marazion. Follow the signs to Marazion, where there is ample parking.
O/S REF: SW514298 **WEB:** www.stmichaelsmount.co.uk

THIS IS ONE OF THE SOUTH-west's most recognisable and dramatic landmarks and a favorite with landscape photographers. Perched upon this craggy little island is an enchanting medieval castle and church. St Michael's Mount, which is cared for by the National Trust, can be reached via a causeway at low tide, or by boat at high tide. However, photographers will prefer to take pictures from the beautiful sandy bay at Marazion.

This is a location that is good at both sunrise and sunset, at both high and low tide, and throughout the seasons. However, it is best at low-tide, as you can utilise the brick causeway – leading to the mount – as foreground interest to help lead the viewer's eye towards the island. Don't just visit when the conditions are sunny – this is a location well suited to stormy, dramatic skies, rough seas and crashing waves. A wide-angle lens will help you to include lots of interest in your foreground to help you create image bursting with depth. Don't forget your wellies when you visit and make sure to check tide times in advance.

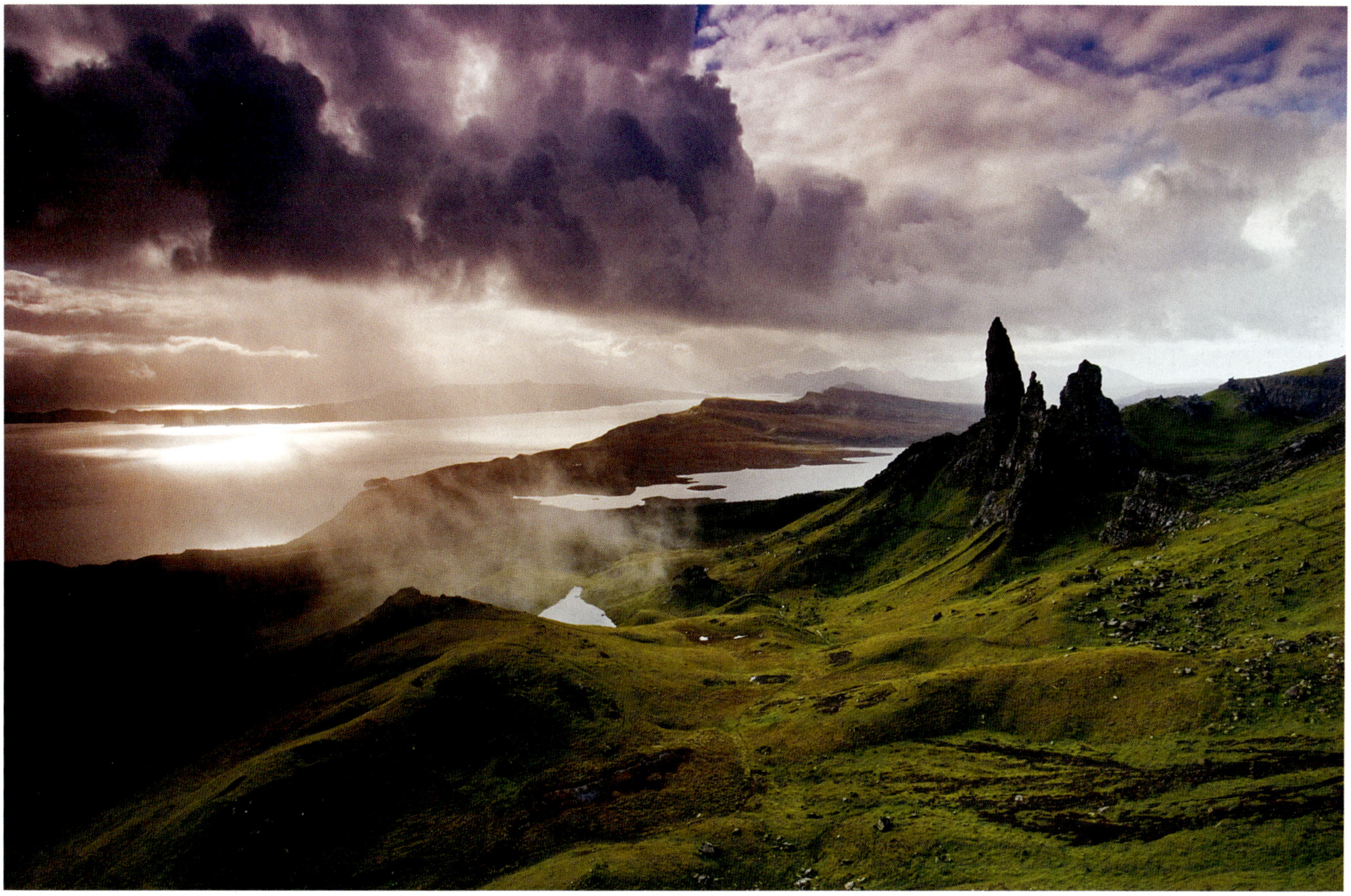

ADAM BURTON

Scotland

Isle of Skye West Scotland

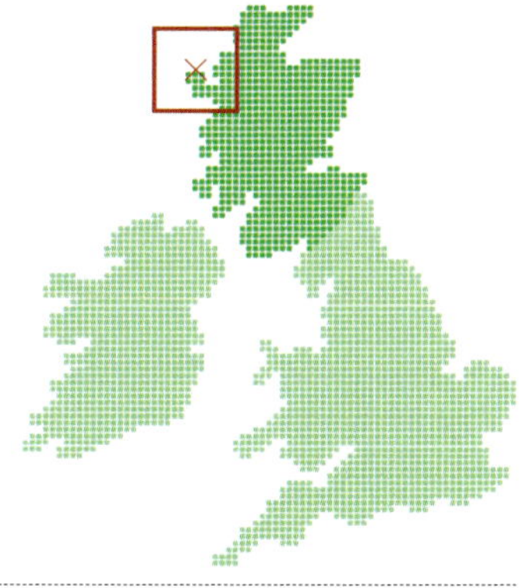

Above: Old Man of Storr basalt columns creates a scene of prehistoric beauty.
Right: The Quiraing offers incredible scenes and is easily accessible by road.

LOCATED: Off the west coast of Scotland
GETTING THERE: Skye can be reached via road and also ferry. From Glasgow, take the A82 and then the A87 to the Kyle of Lochalsh. From here, travel over the toll bridge and onto Skye itself.
O/S REF: NG531297 **WEB:** www.skye.co.uk

EVERY LANDSCAPE PHOTOGRAPHER should make a resolution to visit and photograph the incredible Isle of Skye at some point.

Found on the west coast of mainland Scotland, it is the largest and best known of the Inner Hebrides. Skye is renowned for its stunning natural beauty. This is simply a magnificent location for photography – a wonderful variety of landscapes awaits.

Rising straight out of the sea to a height of over three thousand feet – and often shrouded in mist – the Cuillin mountains are regarded by many as the finest in Britain. The fantastic pinnacles of the Storr and the Quiraing are among the natural wonders of Scotland. In addition to its natural beauty, Skye also has many man-made features with picture appeal. These include standing stones, brochs (small drystone roundhouses) and many ruined buildings and deserted settlements. And, of course, the fairly new and controversial road bridge.

However, it is the magical light, created by ever-changing weather, which makes Skye such a special place for scenic photographers.

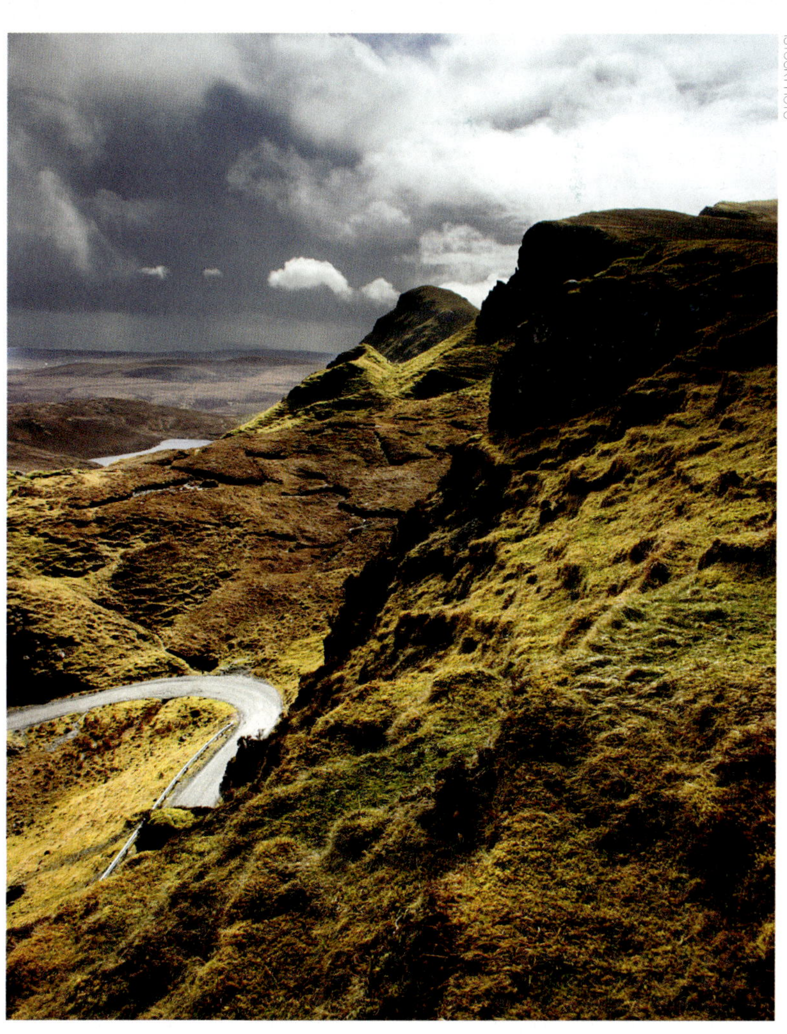

ISTOCKPHOTO

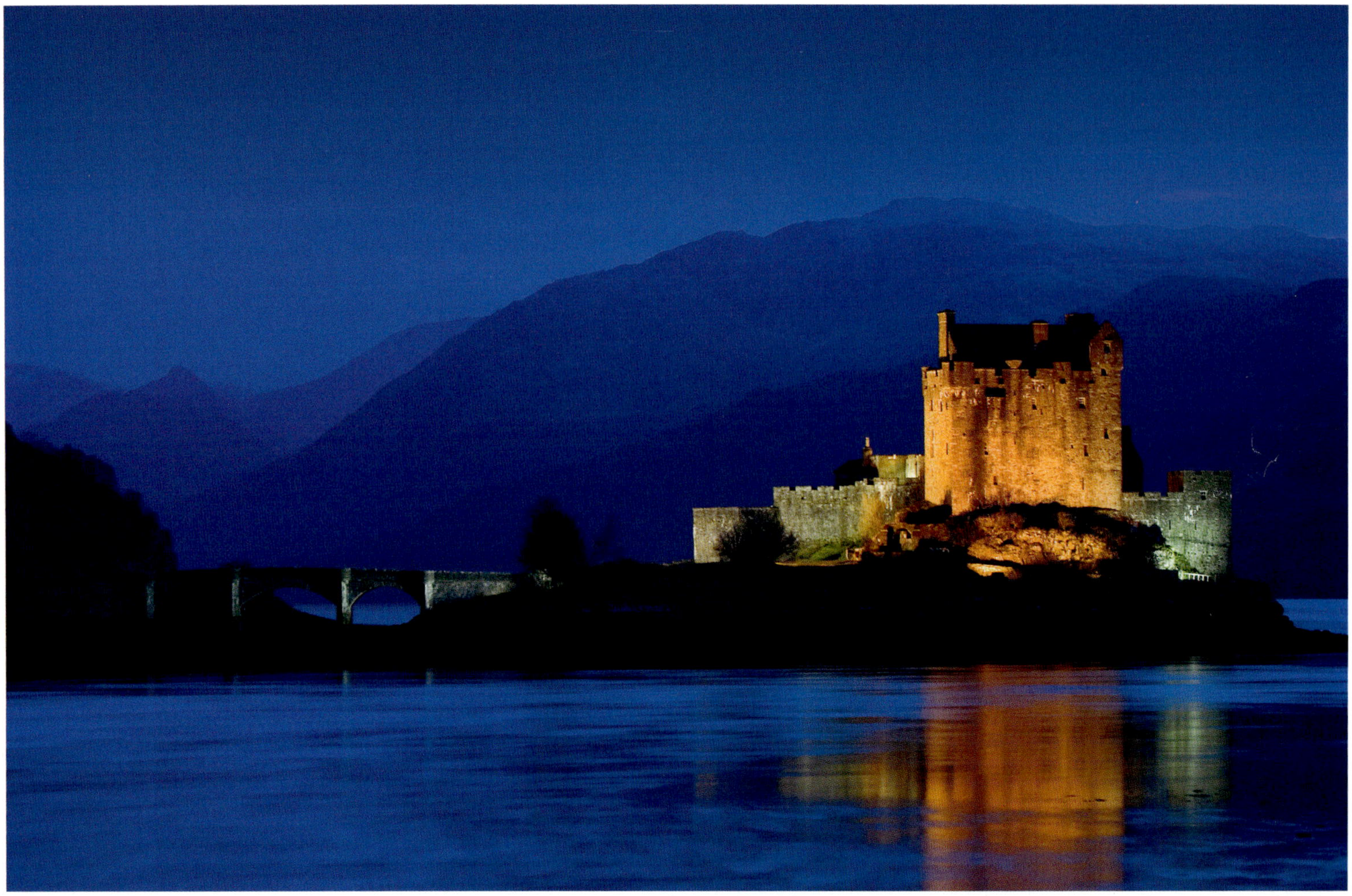

JOHN CARROLL

Scotland

Eilean Donan Castle
Inverness-shire

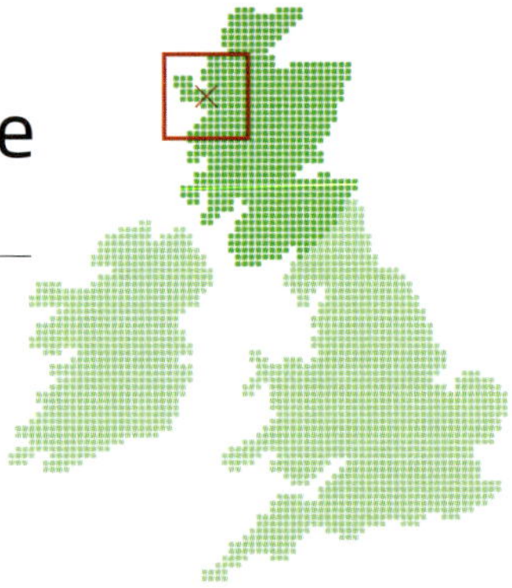

Above: As well as capturing the castle during daylight, make sure to return at night. Right: The bridge provides a perfect lead-in to this telephoto shot of the castle.

LOCATED: Near Dornie, Inverness-shire.
GETTING THERE: The castle and visitor centre are found on the A87 – eight miles before Skye. Follow signs for the castle.
O/S REF: NG880260 **WEB:** www.eileandonancastle.com

SITUATED ON ITS OWN island at the meeting point of three great sea-lochs and surrounded by magnificent mountain scenery, Eilean Donan Castle is one of Scotland's most stunning locations. It's also very close to Skye, so drop in on the way.

It is possibly the most photographed castle in the UK and, when the light and conditions are right, you will return from this viewpoint with wonderfully dramatic and atmospheric images. When the water is still, you will capture mirror-like reflections of the castle and highland scenery, adding yet more interest to your photos.

Don't pack your DSLR away and return home too soon – the castle is photogenic at dusk when the castle is often illuminated by floodlighting. A long exposure of several seconds will be required, so don't forget to pack a sturdy tripod!

Being such a dramatic, atmospheric location, images of the castle can suit black & white photography too, so shoot colour with possible conversion later in mind. Revisit your images during post-processing and make some moody mono prints.

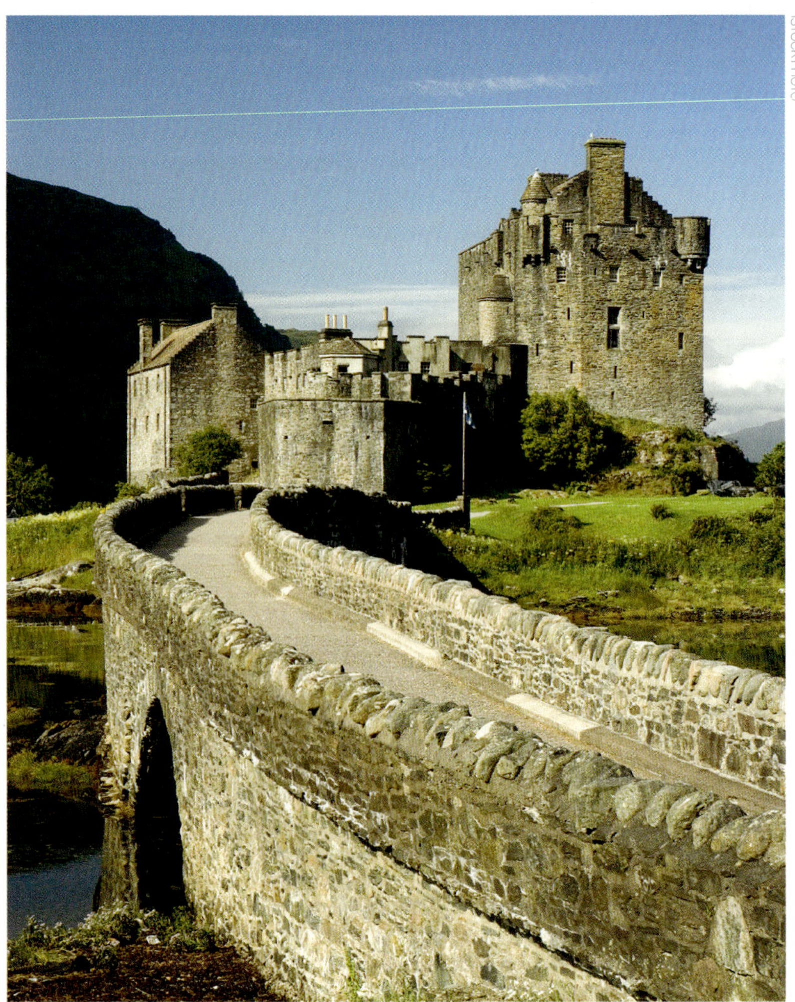
ISTOCK PHOTO

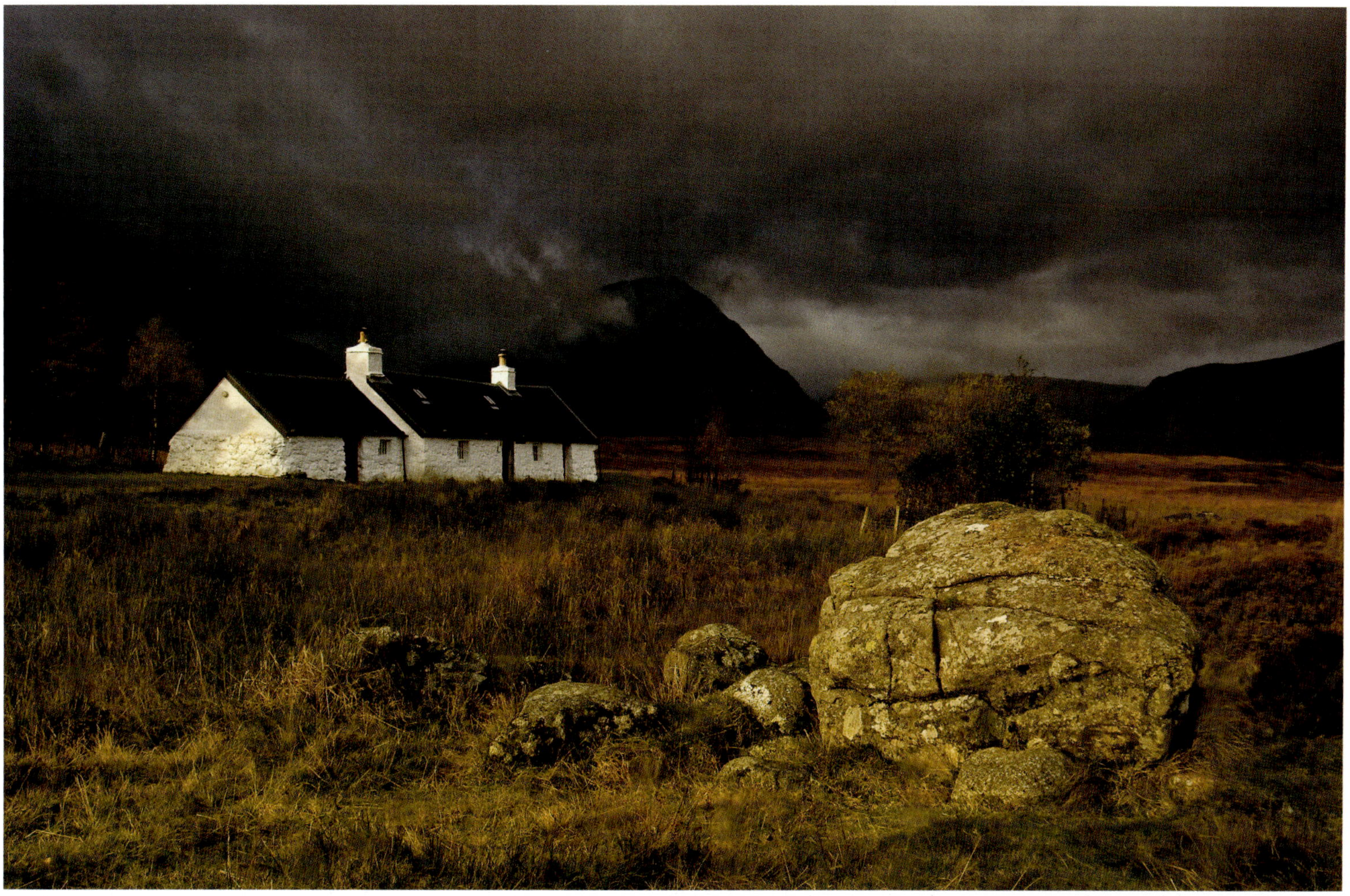

COLIN MILL

Scotland

Rannoch Moor & Glencoe, Scotland

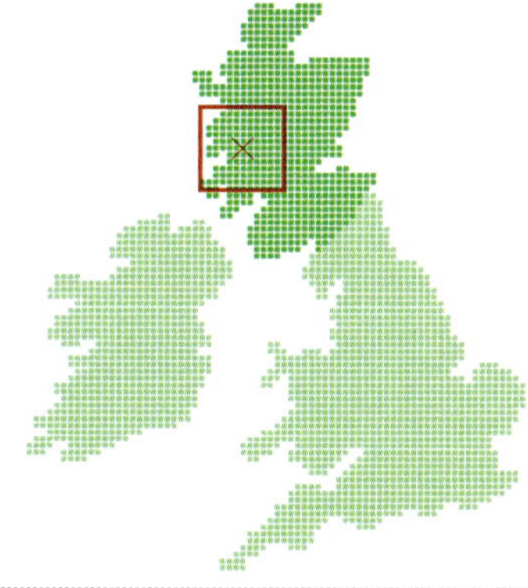

Above: No visit to Glencoe is complete without a shot of Black Rock Cottage.
Right: This foreground lighting will last for just seconds, but you can wait for hours.

LOCATED: Scotland
GETTING THERE: From Glasgow, follow the M8 and cross the Erskine wBridge. Join the A82 to Dumbarton and Loch Lomond. Take the A82 over Rannoch Moor and to Glencoe.
O/S REF: NN168567 **WEB:** www.visitscotland.com

THE GLENCOE REGION contains some of the most magnificent and spectacular scenery anywhere in the UK. The glen lies east to west, with the steep hillsides of The Three Sisters to the south, and the Aonach Eagach to the north.

Guarding the entrance to the glen, from Rannoch Moor, is the mighty Buachaille Etive Mor. It is everything a mountain should be – an almost perfect pyramid that is often snow-capped during the winter months. The classic view of the mountain is from Black Rock Cottage. This iconic dwelling can be found on the A82 before you enter into Glencoe fully. It is on a small single track road that ends at the Glencoe Ski Centre.

The vast expanse of Rannoch Moor stretches across Argyll to Glencoe and is crossed if approaching the glen from the east. The moor is wild and sombre and well worth visiting throughout the year, but autumn and winter are normally best. Unsettled weather suits this wild landscape, so wear warm, waterproof clothing and always take care when walking in mountainous regions.

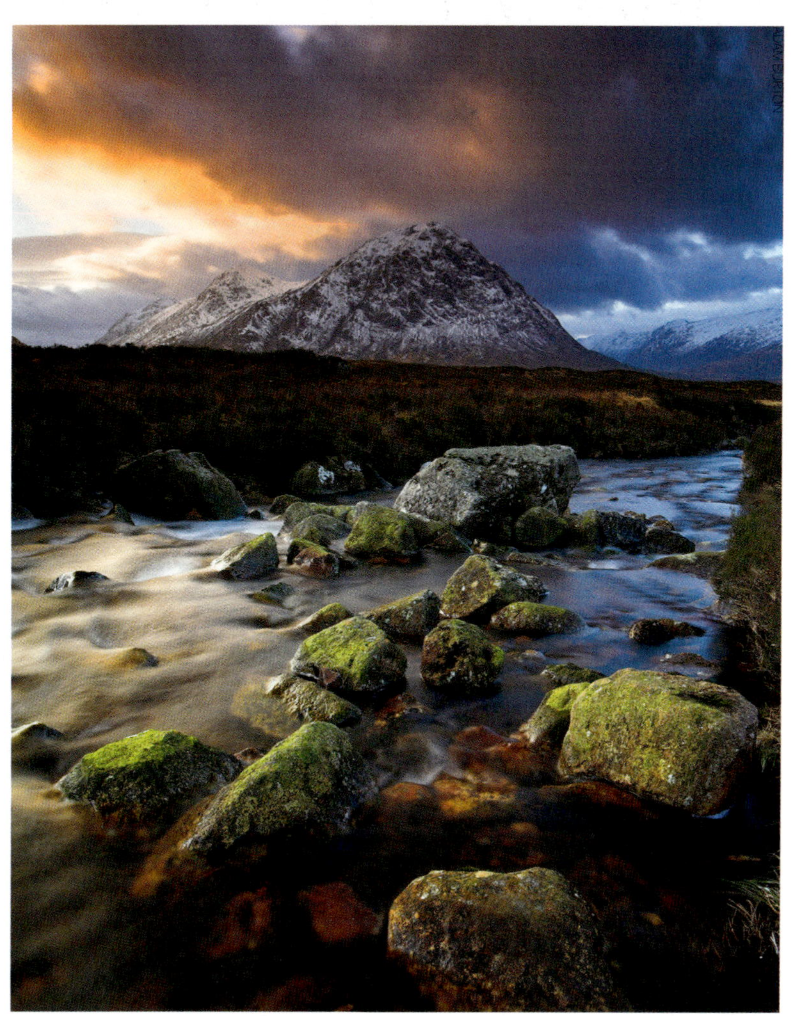

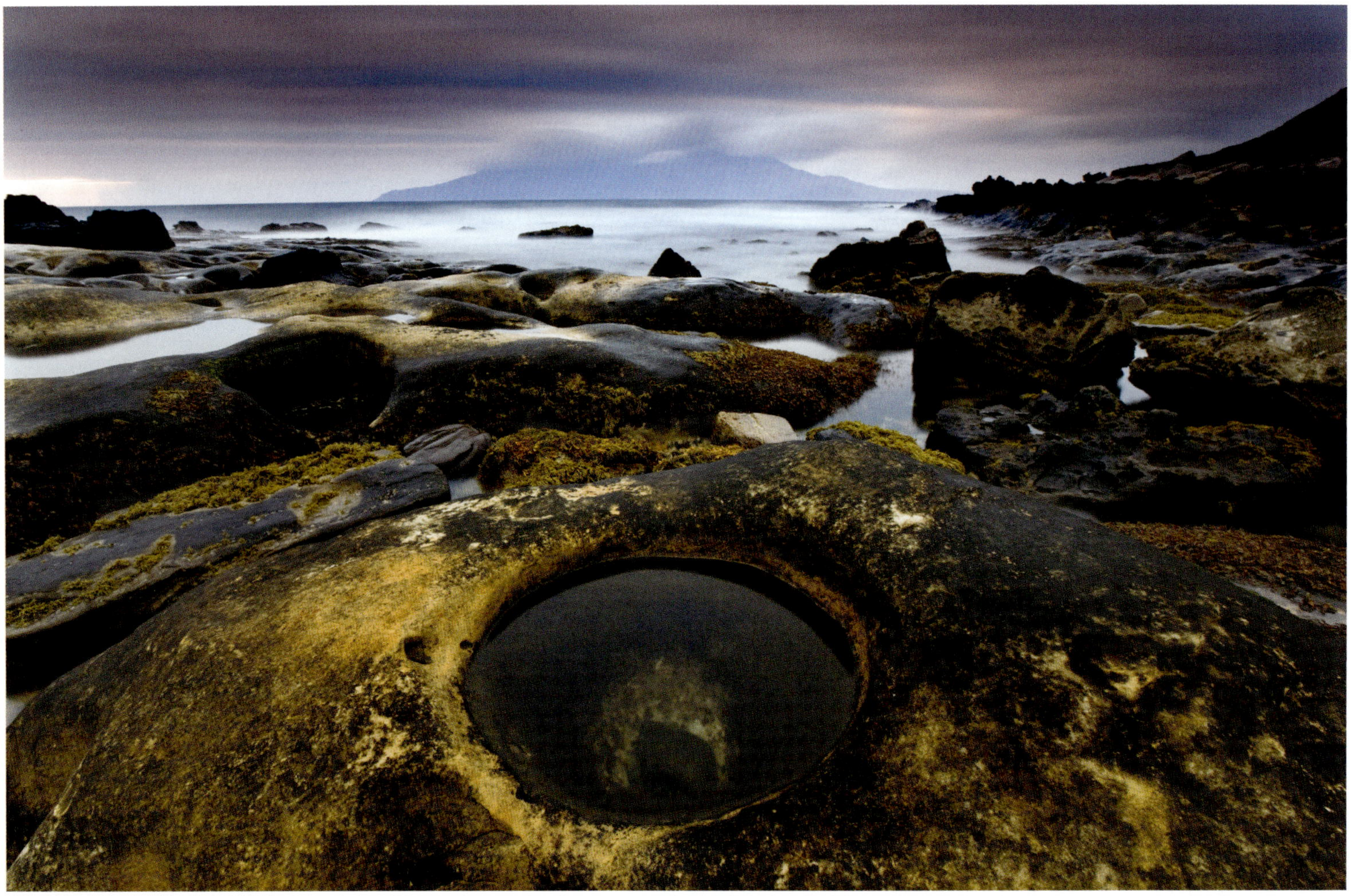

LEE FROST

Scotland

Isle of Eigg Scotland

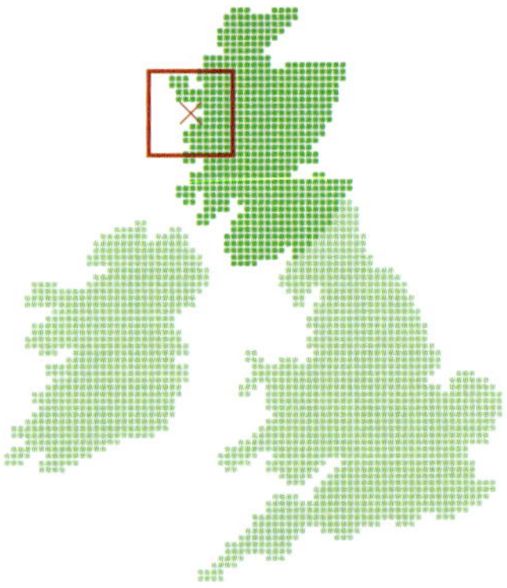

Above: Dramatic views towards Rum are possible from Eigg.

LOCATED: Near Mallaig, Inverness-shire
GETTING THERE: There are daily sailings to Eigg on the Caledonian Macbrayne ferry service from Mallaig, located around an hour's drive from Fort William on the A830. For more information, visit: www.arisaig.co.uk
OS REF: NM4884 **WEB:** www.isleofeigg.net

LYING TEN MILES off the Scottish west coast, the Isle of Eigg is one of the most beautiful Hebridean Islands. The island has a fascinating history, superb wildlife and birdlife and a temperate maritime climate. Although only a small Island, this is a haven for photographers. The spectacular beach at Laig Bay is a favourite among landscape photographers. The rugged shore is full of interest, detail and colour and, together with the spectacular backdrop of Rum in the distance and the cliffs of Cleadale behind, great scenic images are almost guaranteed. Also worth visiting is the sandy beach of Singing Sands Bay. This is slightly further up the coast, but shares the dramatic view of Rum, which is often shrouded in low hanging cloud. Graduated Neutral Density filters can be used to enhance stormy, menacing skies – both hard and soft transition filters are worth having in your camera bag. Eigg is also home to lush woodland and an old colonial style mansion. Photographers should be prepared to walk reasonable distances to reach the best viewpoints so remember to pack some suitable footwear and warm, waterproof clothing.

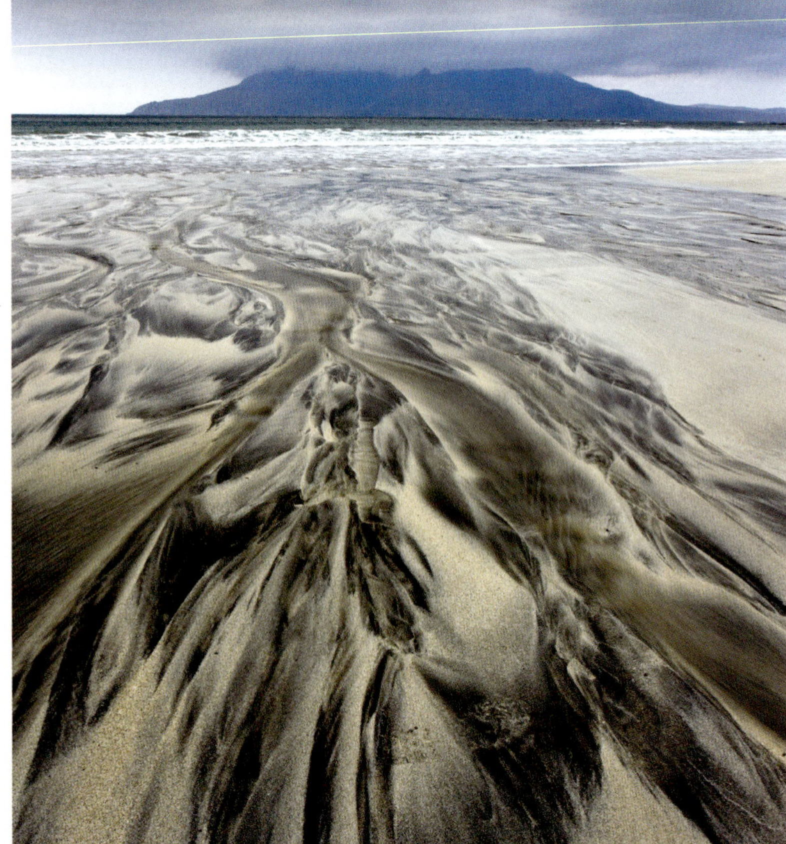

LEE FROST

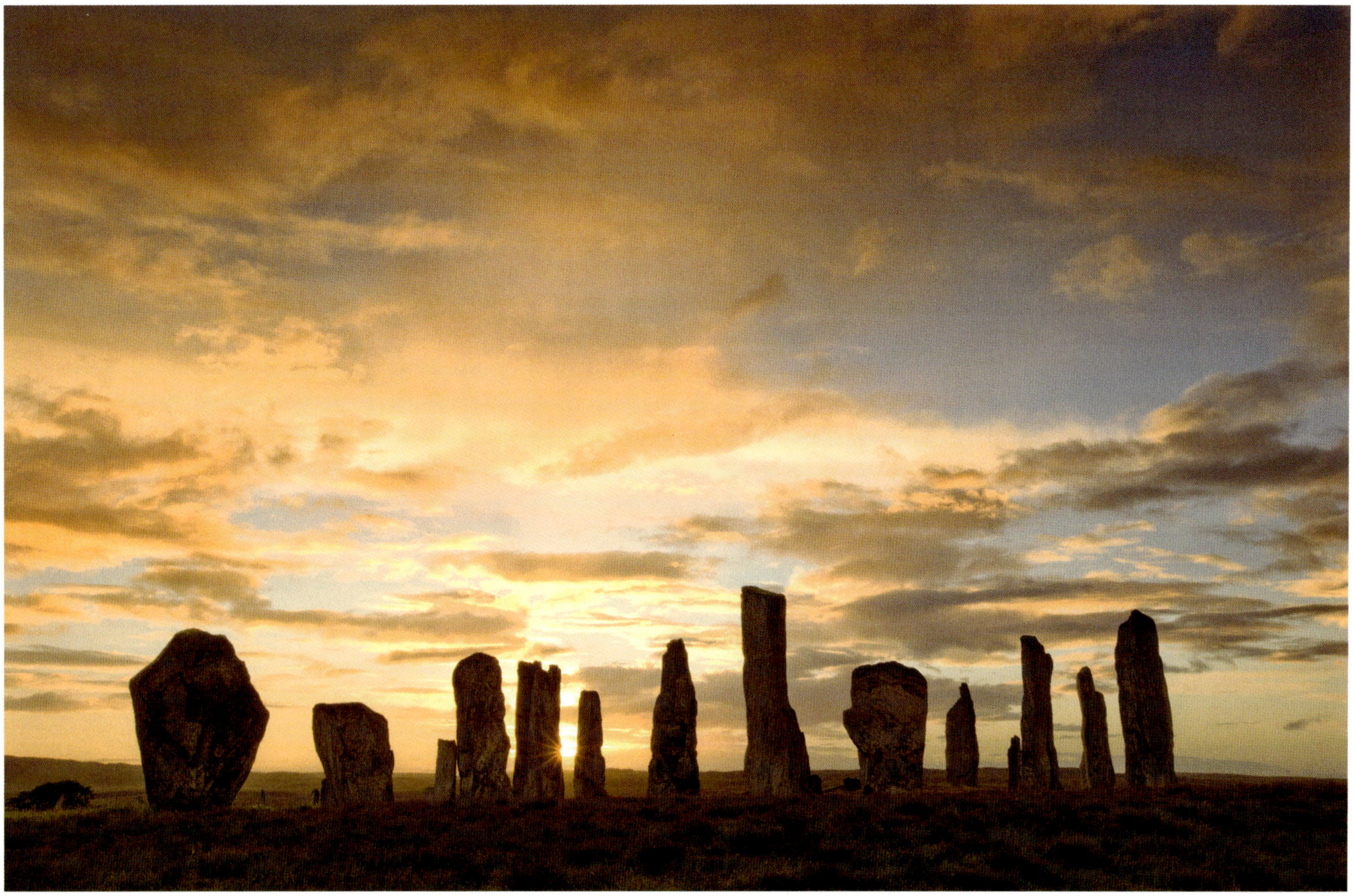

LEE FROST

Scotland

Isle of Lewis Scotland

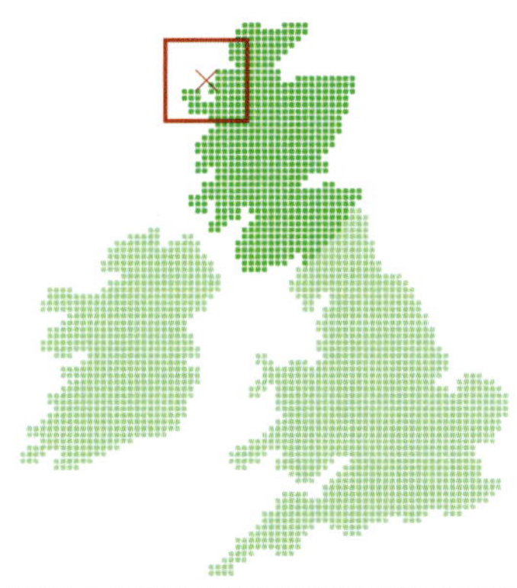

The Isle of Lewis is a very remote location but offers plenty of photographic potential for those willing to make the journey to reach it!

LOCATED: North West of the Hebrides **GETTING THERE:** Caledonian MacBrayne run ferries to two ports in Lewis and Harris. Stornoway Airport, is the main airport for flights to the Western Isles. Flights run direct from Edinburgh, Glasgow, Aberdeen and Inverness.
OS REF: NB426340 **WEB:** www.isle-of-lewis.com

THE ISLES OF LEWIS and Harris are at the north west corner of the Hebrides, a group of Islands known as the 'long islands' as they stretch for 100 miles. Both the east and west coasts of the Island have rugged stretches of cliffs often giving way to huge beaches of clean white sand. Inland, the terrain is principally level moorland dotted with fresh water lochs. Quite simply, this is a location busting with picture potential. The Butt of Lewis, in the extreme north, is home to high, steep cliffs. The highest point is 142ft high, and crowned with a spectacular lighthouse – its light is visible for 19 miles. Tolsta is a crofting village, notable for its long, white sandy beaches. The tranquil and beautiful beach of nearby Traigh Mhor is about two miles in length and its wonderful white sands are full of beautiful patterns and texture. Lewis is also steeped in history. Callanish Standing Stones is one of the most important megalithic complexes in Europe. The circle is particularly photogenic set against a dramatic or colourful sky. Take along a ten-stop ND filter to capture motion in the clouds.

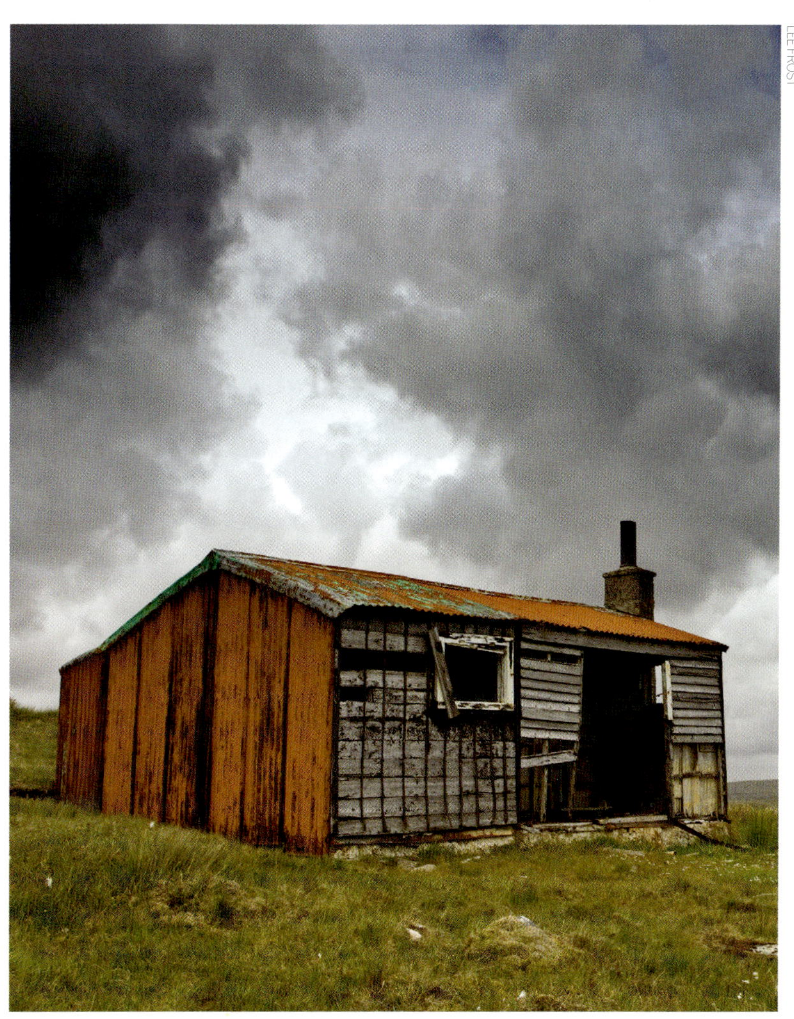

LEE FROST

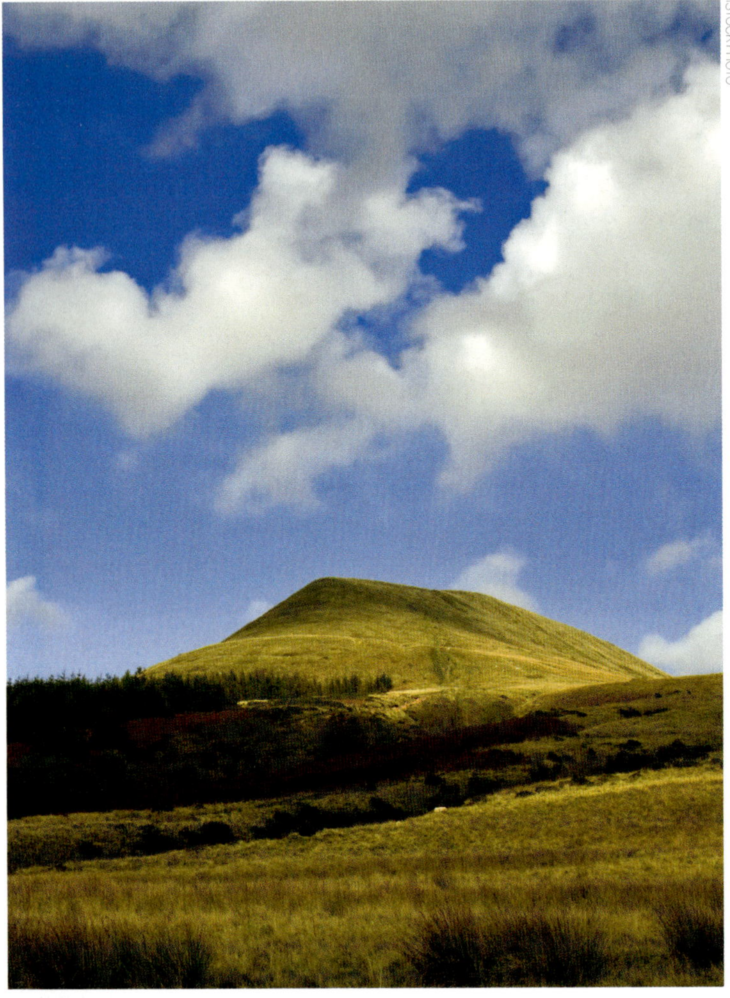

Wales

Elegug Stacks Pembrokeshire

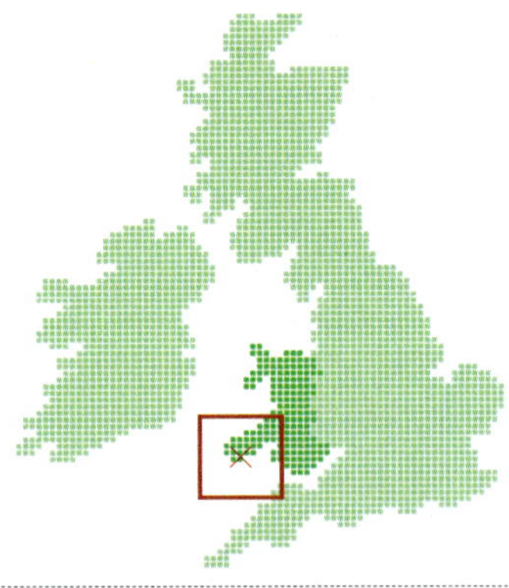

Below: A menacing, stormy sky will help landscape photographers realise the full drama of this unique location.

LOCATED: Nr Merrion on the Castlemartin Peninsula **GETTING THERE:** From Cardiff, follow the M4 and then the A48 to Carmarthen. Join the A40, A77 and then the A4075 to Pembroke and then to Merrion. Follow the sign for 'Stack Rocks' just past the army base in Merrion on the B4319.
O/S REF: SR926944 **WEB:** www.visitpembrokeshire.com

ELEGUG STACKS are two limestone pillars standing freely a short distance from the cliffs on the coastline of Pembrokeshire in south-west Wales. The stacks are found on the Castlemartin peninsula, where colonies of guillemots, razorbills and kittiwakes can be found – Elegug is actually Welsh for Guillemot. This is one of the most dramatic coastal viewpoints in Wales and is particularly photogenic when there is a stormy sky overhead. A wide-angle lens is essential in order to capture the full drama of this unique viewpoint, while photographers who also enjoy shooting nature may want to carry a powerful telezoom for photographing sea birds. The rock stacks lie just to the east of the Green Bridge of Wales, another fascinating and photogenic rock formation, worth visiting while you are in the area. Stack Rocks car park is approached through the Castlemartin military zone. Because the Ministry of Defence train in this area, there is only access to Elegug Stacks on certain days, when the shooting ranges are closed. We advise you ring before you visit on 01646 662367 to avoid making a wasteful trip.

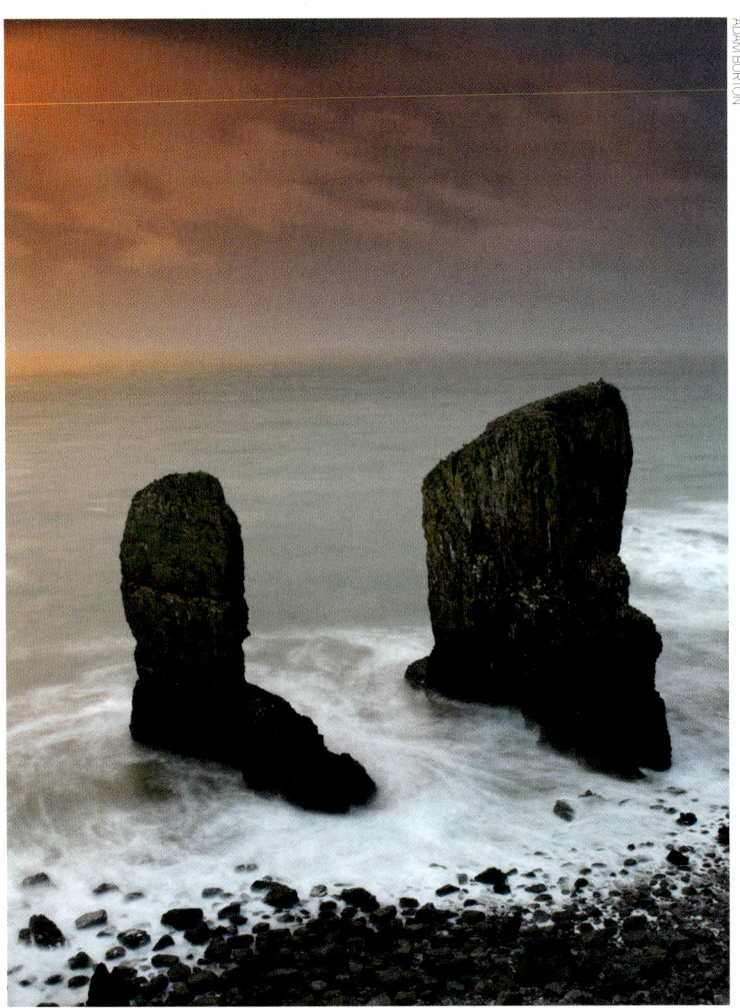

Wales

Brecon Beacons South Wales

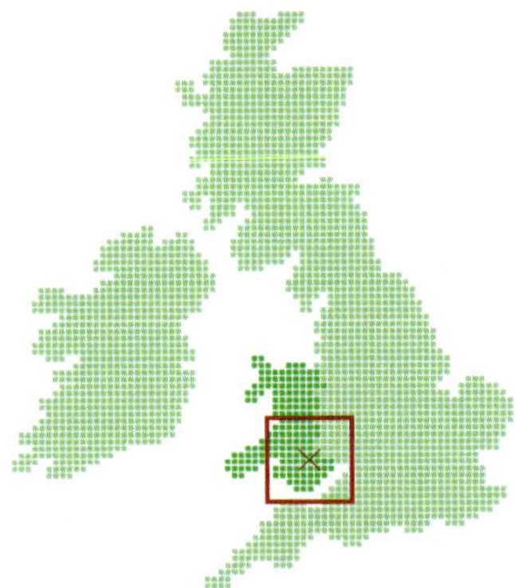

Above: The green peaks of the Brecon Beacons are easily reached by foot.

LOCATED: South Wales **GETTING THERE:** The Park is well served by good trunk roads from the motorway network. From the M4, take the A449 to Raglan and then the A40. From Cardiff, simply take the A470. From the M5, take the M50 to Monmouth and join the A40 into the area.
O/S REF: SO034198 **WEB:** www.breconbeaconstourism.co.uk

THE BRECON BEACONS National Park contains some of the most spectacular and distinctive upland formations in southern Britain.

The park stretches from Hay on Wye in the east to Llandeilo in the west. Its photogenic and diverse landscape boasts moorland, forests, steep valleys, impressive waterfalls, lakes, caves and gorges.

Arguably, autumn and winter are the best times to plan your visit, with the snow-capped Beacons providing a dramatic backdrop. Changeable weather conditions, when sun and rain alternate rapidly, suit this rugged landscape well.

The mountains are mostly gentle and grassy on the southern side, with steep escarpments on the north. The summits are easily accessed – good news for photographers wishing to shoot impressive, far reaching panoramas. On a clear day, the view from Pen y Fan (the highest summit) is awe-inspiring. This is also 'waterfall country', being home to some of the UK's most magnificent falls – like Henrhyd Falls, the highest in south Wales. The curtain waterfall of Sgwd yr Eira is among the most photogenic.

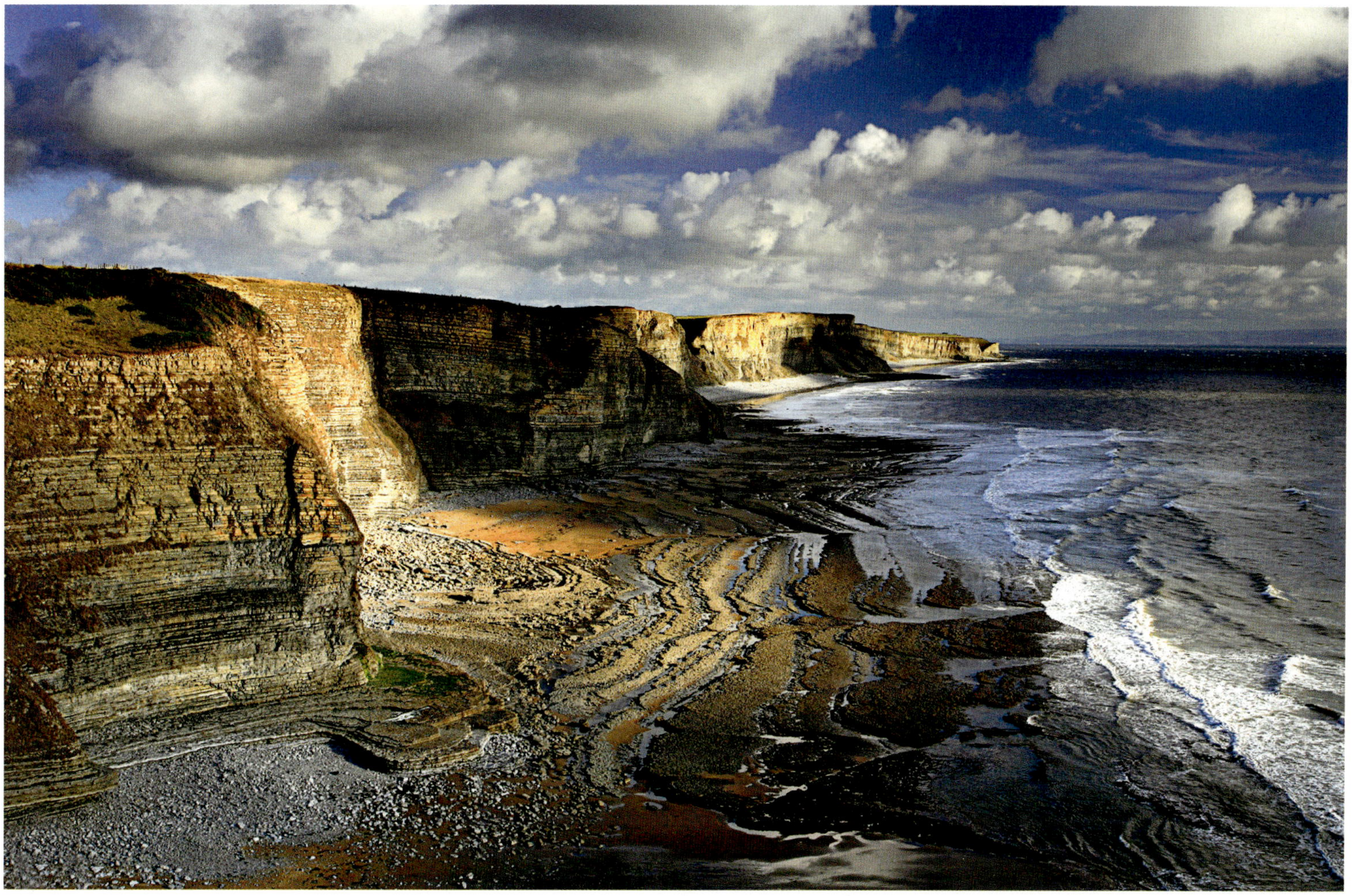

MARI STERLING

Wales

Dunraven Bay South Wales

Above: Constantly moving clouds and water provide a new shot every minute.
Right: Southerndown, Dunraven Bay offers potential at both low and high tide.

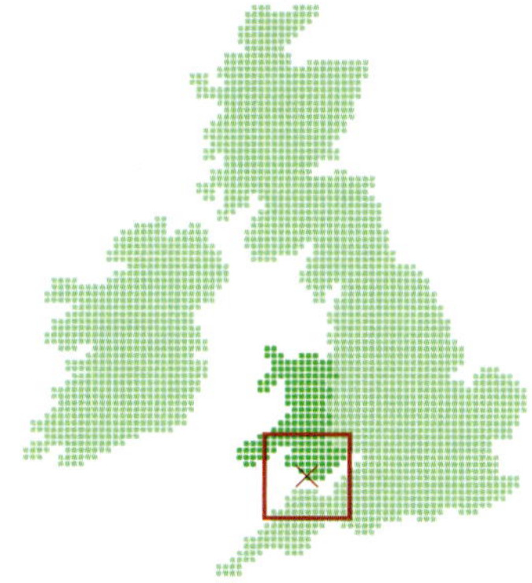

LOCATED: Glamorgan Heritage Coast, South Wales **GETTING THERE:** From the M4, take the A473 from junction 35 at Pencoed. At Hermstone, take the left sign-posted Ogmore. Turn right at St Brides Major (sign-posted Southerndown) and just after the Three Golden Cups pub turn left to the car park.
O/S REF: SS885735 **WEB:** www.visitwales.com

FORMING PART OF THE stunning Glamorgan Heritage Coast, Dunraven Bay is one of the most photogenic beaches in Wales.

At low tide, its wide sandy bay is often wet and reflective, enabling photographers to shoot a mirror image of the scenery and sky. The rugged cliffs boast fascinating geology, with wonderful shapes and texture carved into the rock. Rockpools and patterns in the sand create interesting foregrounds and, even at high tide – a time to avoid at many coastal locations – the wide pebble ridge is photogenic as the waves lap over it. You may prefer to take pictures from the cliff tops. If so, the best place to catch the evening light is around Trwyn Y Witch (Witch's Nose Point). As this coastline mostly faces south-west, winter is the best time of year for photographers to visit, when the low sun is further south in the sky. However, as Dunraven Bay is oriented in a more westerly direction, this mitigates the seasons to a degree – Trwyn Y Witch looks great in low summer sun. Book a B&B and spend a couple of days here to ensure you make the most of this location's potential.

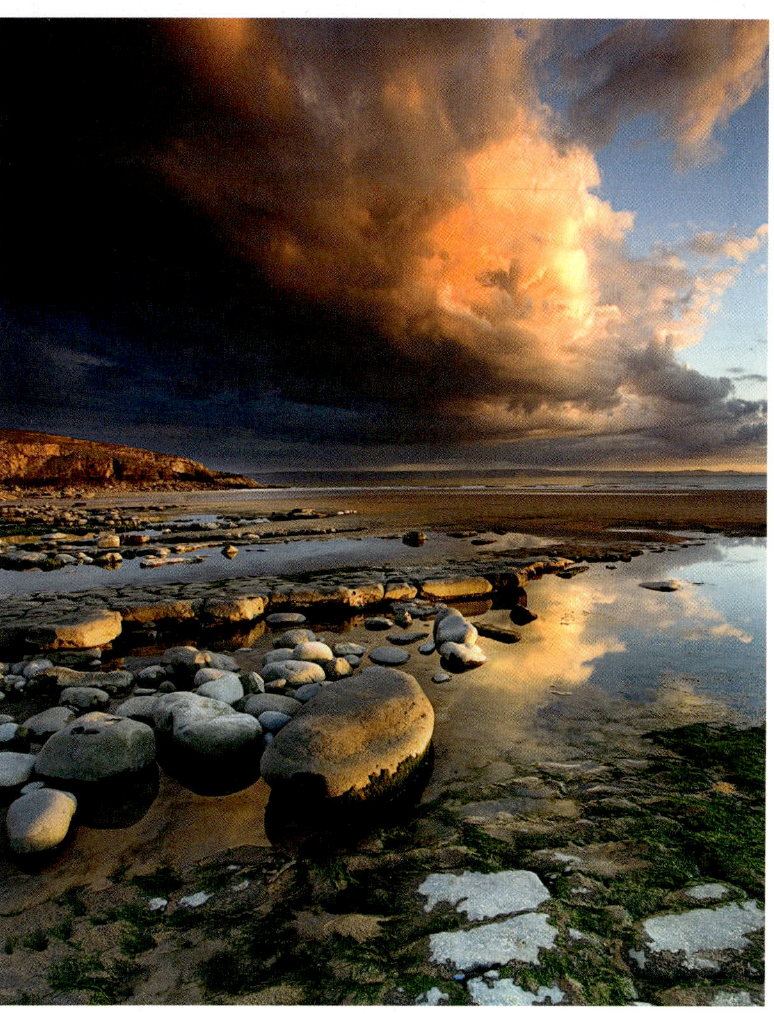

MARI STERLING

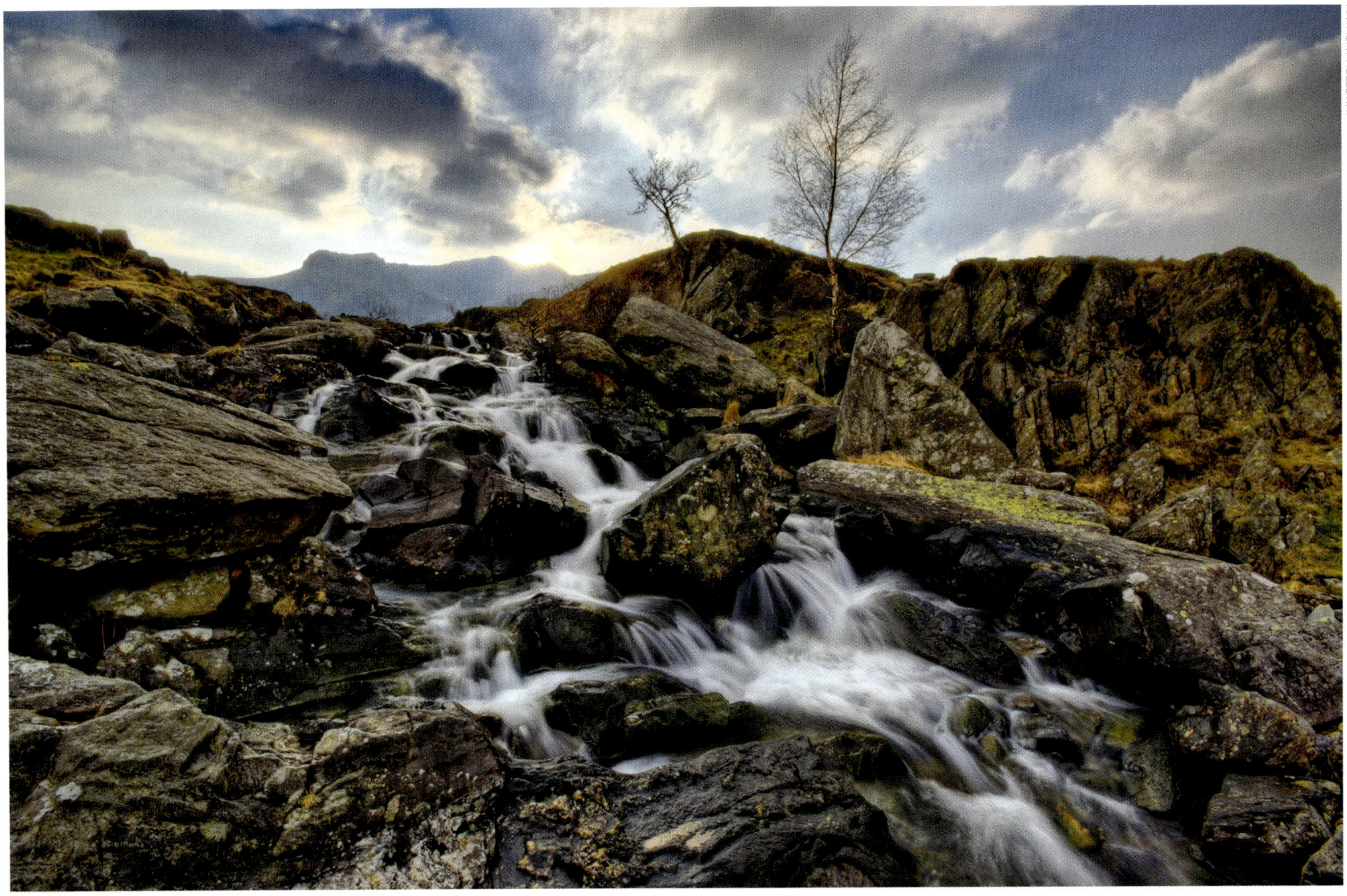

ANTHONY HOLLOWAY

Wales

Snowdonia North Wales

Above: Spend a couple of hours shooting Idwal overflow, near Llyn Idwal overflow.

Right: A stile on Mount Snowdon, lit by sunset light, provides foreground interest.

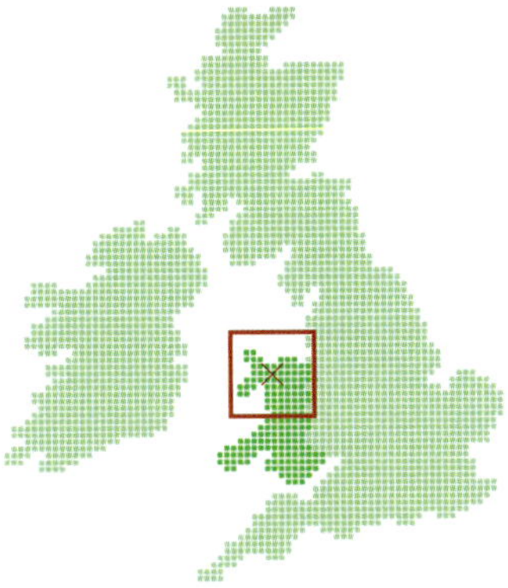

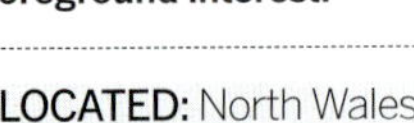

LOCATED: North Wales
GETTING THERE: From Birmingham, take the M6 north and then the M54 for north and mid Wales. Join the A5 to Snowdonia. The A5, along with the A470, are the Parks main roads.
O/S REF: SH782562 **WEB:** www.visitsnowdonia.info

SNOWDONIA NATIONAL PARK is an area of outstanding natural beauty. Covering 838 square miles, it is home to some of the most magnificent scenery in Wales. And while some locations look best in good weather, the rugged beauty of Snowdonia suits stormier conditions. Snowdon – at 1,085meters, the highest mountain in Wales – is an impressive sight and will provide a focal point for many successful images. During winter, the mountain peaks are usually capped with snow and stormy, while dramatic skies help photographers capture the wild beauty of this landscape. Aside from its impressive mountain ranges, there is much to entice landscape photographers. The region is renowned for its beautiful forests, reflective lakes and large waterfalls. Check out the vast slate quarries, too. The area around Capel Curig is particularly photogenic, but with so much picture potential everywhere, this really is an area that you need to spend time exploring. Much can be reached by car but we'd recommend you explore the mountains on foot to really feel in touch with the scenery you're shooting.

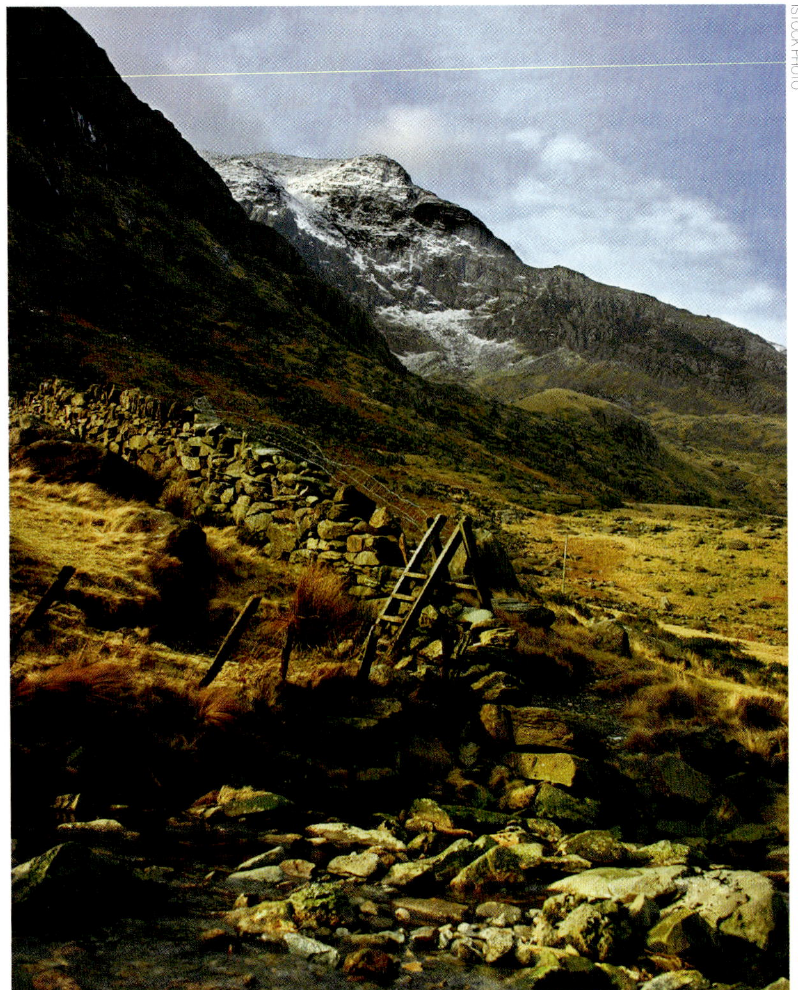

ISTOCKPHOTO

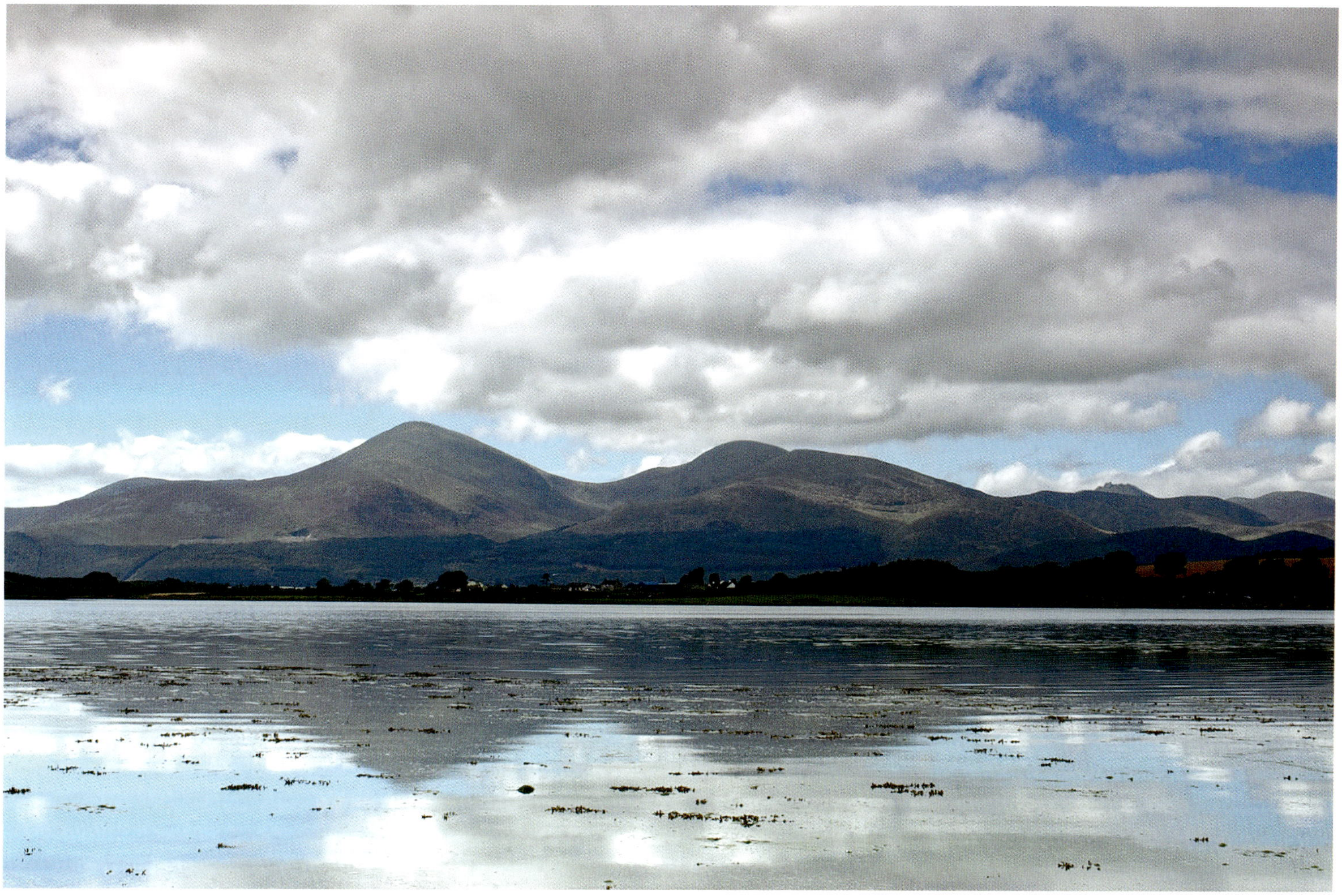

Ireland

Carlingford Bay County Louth, Eire

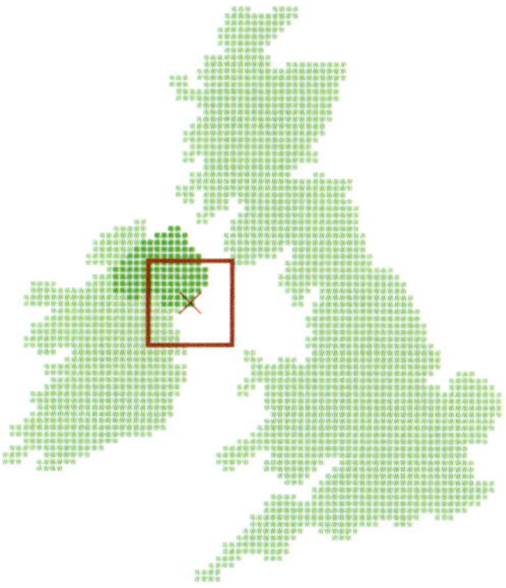

Above: The Mourne mountains are the most picturesque mountain district in Ireland.

Right: Make sure to visit the beautiful Glen River in the Mourne mountains.

LOCATED: Near both Belfast and Dublin

GETTING THERE: It is just over an hour's drive from Dublin and Belfast airports. From the M1, take the R173 and follow the signs to Carlingford.

O/S REF: J186116 **WEB:** www.carlingford.ie

LESS THAN AN HOUR'S drive from Dublin or Belfast, Carlingford nestles between Slieve Foy, Carlingford Lough and the Mourne mountains. This is an area of spectacular panoramas, unspoiled natural beauty and historic landmarks.

Carlingford Lough is a sheltered inlet of the Irish Sea, over ten miles long and flanked by mountains. Its sheltered sands, rocky islands and boulder shores will appeal to scenic photographers.

The shapes and textures of the pebbles on the beach are very photogenic. Still weather creates attractive reflections, while unsettled conditions produce stormy views, with dramatic lighting.

Fishing remains an important industry on the Lough, and stone quays pepper the shoreline. The region offers a rich heritage of ancient and not so ancient monuments – prehistoric stone formations and earth works, Norman castles and medieval abbeys all add further picture potential.

Also worth visiting with your camera are the nearby Victorian seaside resorts of Warrenpoint, Rostrevor and Omeath.

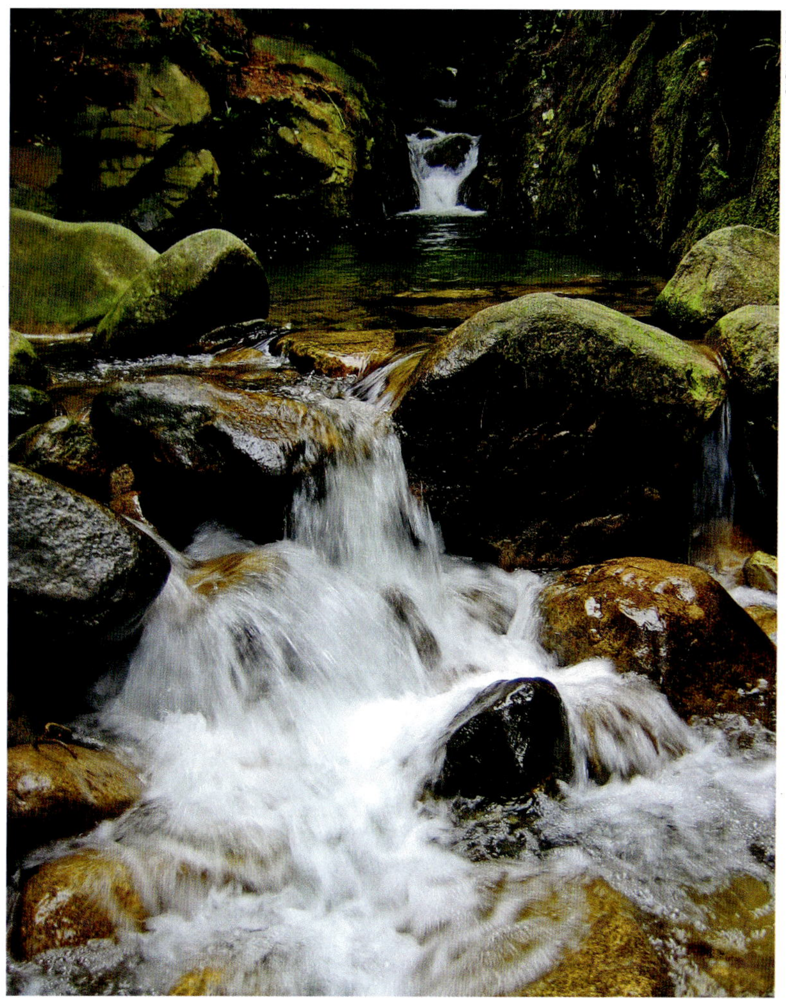

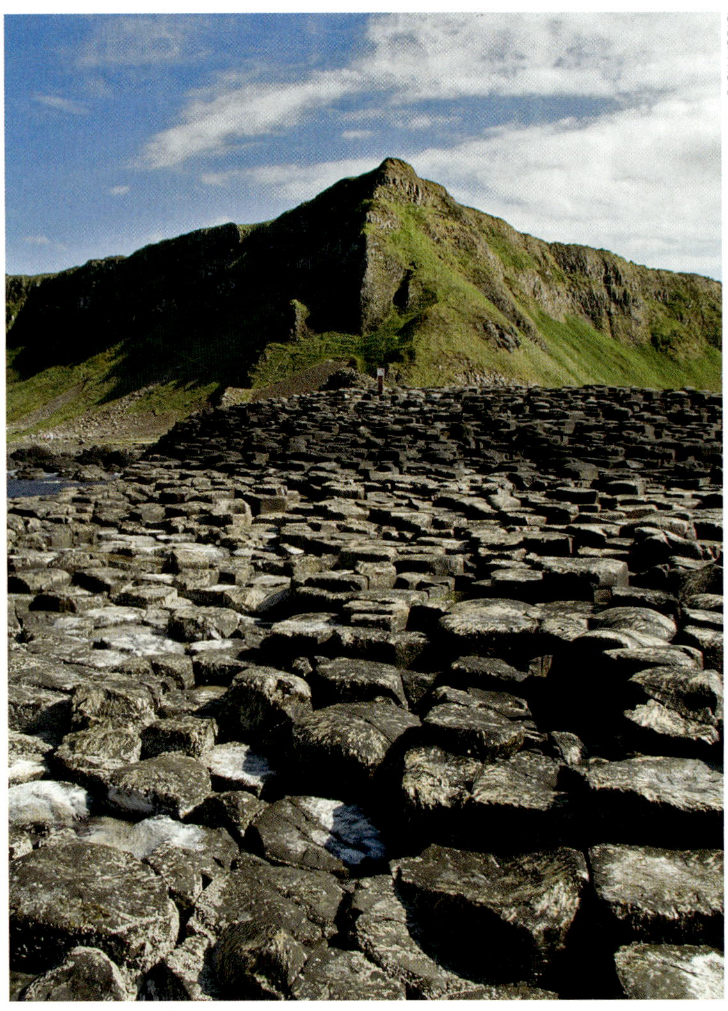

ISTOCK PHOTO

Northern Ireland

Giant's Causeway Northern Ireland

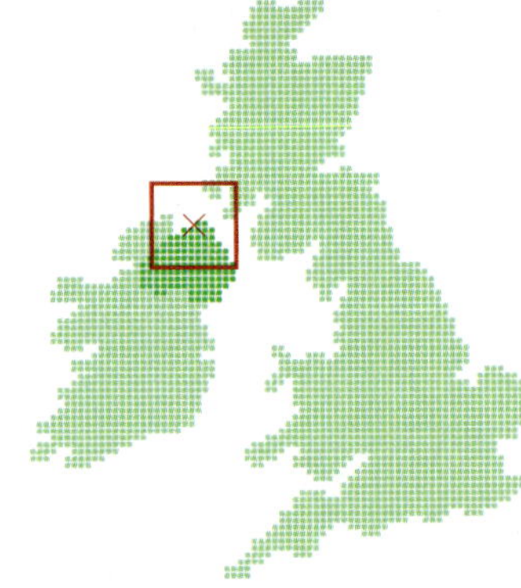

Above: Balanced composition creates journey through the fore-, mid- and background. Shoot with the camera upright and use the Causeway to lead the eye into the scene.

LOCATED: North coast of County Antrim, Northern Ireland
GETTING THERE: From the A2, take the B146 Causeway to Dunseverick road two miles east of Bushmills and follow signs for the Causeway.
O/S REF: C952452 **WEB:** www.giantscausewaycentre.com

GIANT'S CAUSEWAY IS steeped in history and legend, most relating to Irish warrior Finn McCool's feud with Scottish rival Benandonner. McCool was said to have built the 'causeway' to walk across the sea to Scotland.

It is a World Heritage site and is Northern Ireland's most iconic and best known viewpoint. It is renowned for its striking, polygonal columns of layered basalt – actually a geological phenomenon caused by the cooling of lava after an ancient volcanic eruption.

The stunning coastal scenery here is quite simply among the most awe-inspiring you will find anywhere – this is a location that landscape photographers must visit whilst in Northern Ireland.

A wide-angle lens is essential to capture sweeping views of the Causeway. Explore this location and search for the distinctive stone formations that are found here, like the fancifully named 'wishing chair', 'camel', 'harp' and 'organ'. This is a hugely popular tourist attraction, so try to avoid visiting during peak times when other people can inhibit good landscape photography.

Northern Ireland

Waterfoot Co Antrim, Northern Ireland

Below: With over a mile of stony beach, there is no shortage of photo opportunities.

LOCATED: Co Antrim, Northern Ireland
GETTING THERE: From the M2, take the A43 toward Cushendall. Join the A2 and follow the signs to Waterfoot.
O/S REF: D242248 **WEB:** www.discovernorthernireland.com

WATERFOOT IS A PRETTY HAMLET in County Antrim, situated between the towns of Carnlough and Cushendall on the north-west coast of Northern Ireland.

It is situated at the foot of Glenariff – one of the Glens of Antrim – and has a beautiful mile-long beach. The village lies by Red Bay, named due to the reddish sand that washes from the exposed sandstone on the cliffs down to the shore. Landscape photographers will be drawn to Waterfoot's photogenic beach, but there is much more in this area to shoot, aside from the bay.

The harbour is one of the most sheltered and picturesque on the Antrim coast and, a short distance away, stands the White Lady, a chalk figure carved by the sea washing against the cliffs.

Nearby Glenariff Forest Park boasts outstanding scenery. It is a designated 'Area of Outstanding Natural Beauty'. Bisecting the Park are two small but beautiful rivers – the Inver and the Glenariff. Here you will find spectacular waterfalls, tranquil pools and stretches of fast flowing water tumbling through rocky steep-sided gorges.

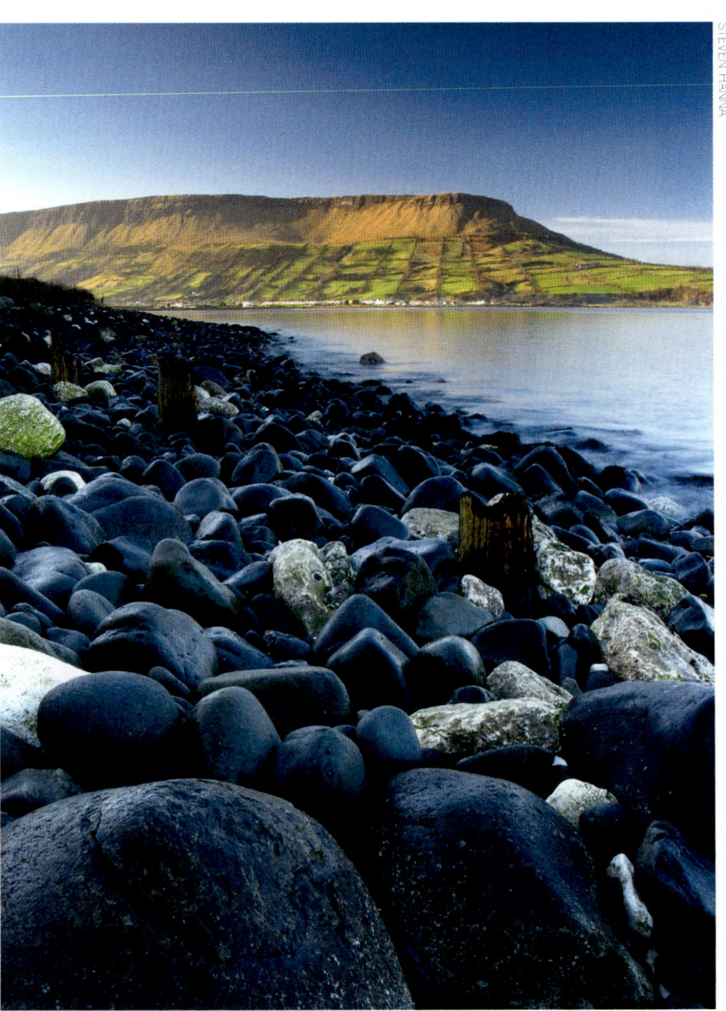

STEVEN HANNA

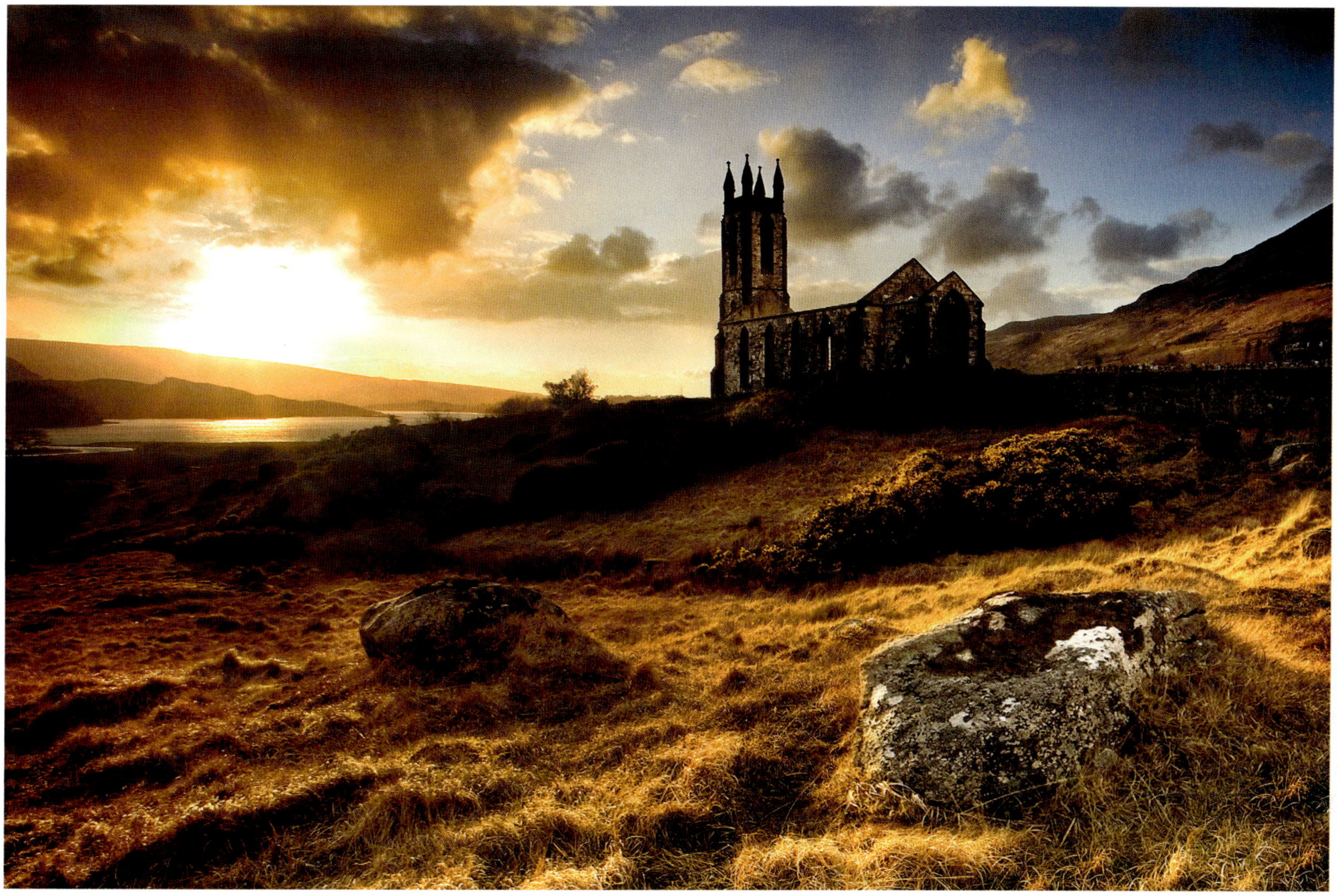

GARY McPARLAND

North-west Ireland

Donegal Ireland

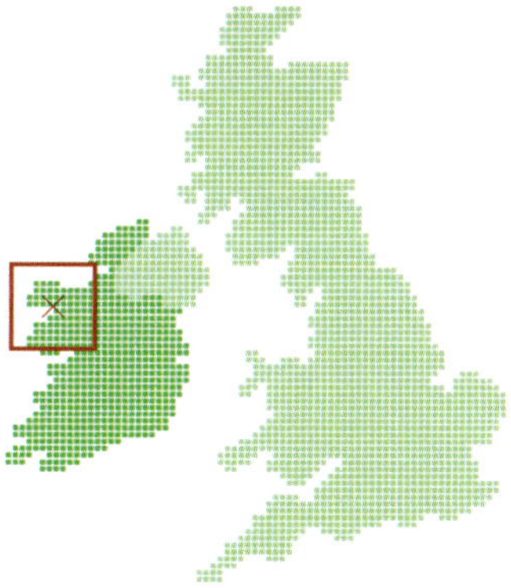

Above: Dunlewy Church is located in Derryveagh, Poisoned Glen.

Right: Fanad Head lighthouse warns shipping away from the dangers near Fannet Point.

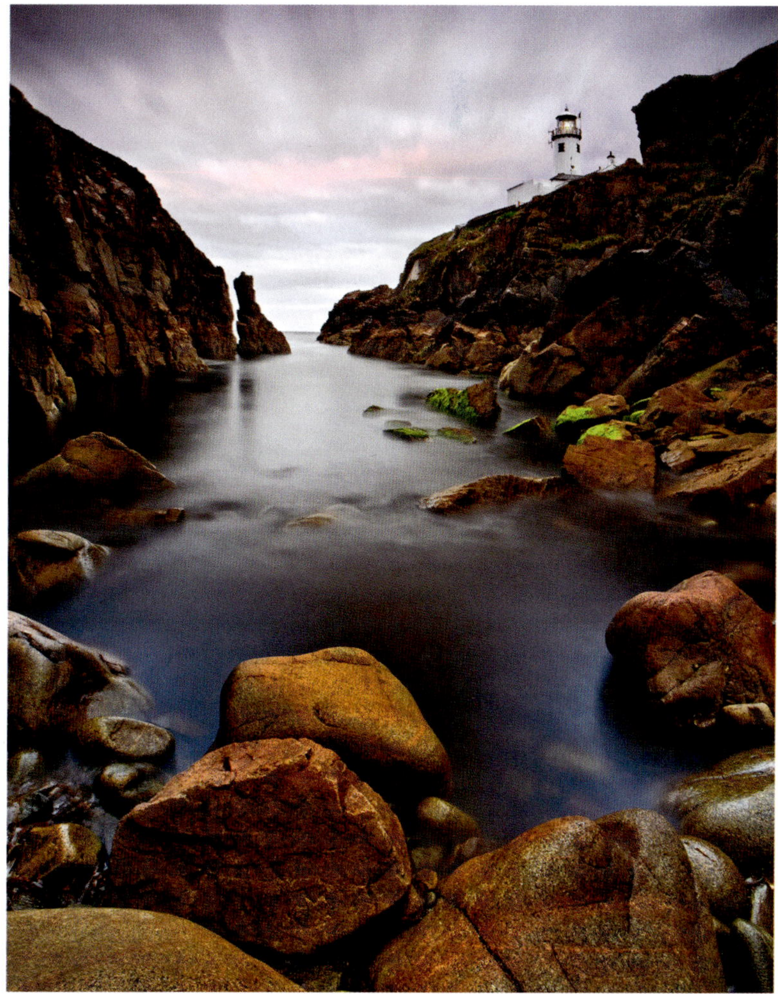

GARY McPARLAND

LOCATED: North West Ireland
GETTING THERE: County Donegal is serviced by the main N15 and N56 roads, from which you can explore the region.
O/S REF: G931787 **WEB:** www.discoverireland.com

WITH ITS SOARING SEA CLIFFS, which plummet up to 300 metres, deserted white sandy beaches and rugged landscape, Donegal is a spectacular county in Ireland's north west corner. The county consists chiefly of low mountains with a deeply indented and photogenic coastline, forming natural loughs of which Lough Swilly and Lough Foyle are notable. The famous Hills of Donegal consist of two major ranges, the Derryveagh mountains in the north and the Bluestack mountains in the south. The Slieve League cliffs are the second highest sea cliffs in Europe. Malin Head is the most northerly point in the island of Ireland. It lies at the top of the Inishowen Peninsula, jutting out into the wild North Atlantic, and is a great location for coastal photography. Landscape photographers should allow themselves plenty of time to explore this beautiful region. The coast here is a typical of an ocean coastline – rocky coves interspersed with sandy beaches and numerous small settlements, which are just begging to be explored and photographed. This is a wild place, full of atmosphere.

ADAM BURTON

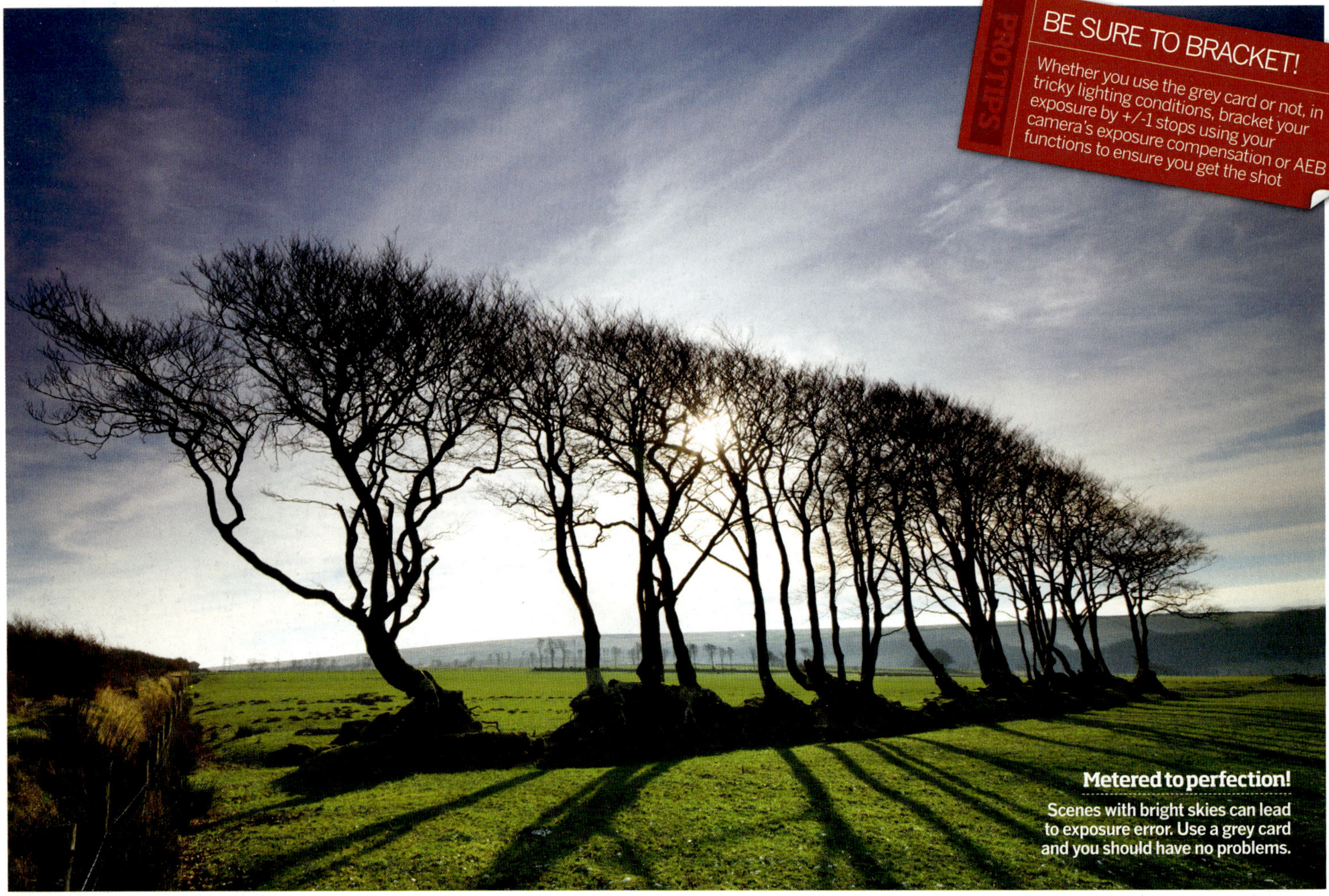

PRO TIPS

BE SURE TO BRACKET!

Whether you use the grey card or not, in tricky lighting conditions, bracket your exposure by +/-1 stops using your camera's exposure compensation or AEB functions to ensure you get the shot

Metered to perfection!

Scenes with bright skies can lead to exposure error. Use a grey card and you should have no problems.

How to use your free exposure metering and WB cards

The 18% grey card can be used to ensure perfect exposures when shooting in tricky lighting conditions (see below). Both reference cards can also be used to set a custom White Balance. Depending on the camera you use, you need to take a White Balance reading off the grey or the white card (your camera's instructions will show you how)

DIGITAL SLRS USE sophisticated exposure systems and all work using the same assumption that the average of the scene that is being metered from is a mid-tone, or 18% grey to be exact; i.e. the average of all dark, light and mid-tones mixed together is 18% grey. It's the basis of all metering patterns and works surprisingly well but while it's fine for the majority of shooting situations, it can lead to incorrect exposures when the scene or subject is considerably lighter or darker in tone than 18% grey. For example, very dark areas can fool the metering system into overexposing the image. Similarly, very light subjects, such as a snow scene, can fool the camera into underexposing them – making them appear darker than they are – as the light meter will take a reading designed to render them as a mid-tone. As a camera is trying to render an image 'grey', it's your job to ensure you compensate to keep the tones true to life. You can do this by either using one of your camera's exposure override facilities, such as exposure compensation or the AE-Lock button, or by metering from an area of the scene that has a mid-tone. And that's where our grey card comes in. Using it is very simple as our step by step guide below illustrates. The key thing to remember is that you need to place the grey card in similar lighting to your scene, for instance, don't place it in a shaded area if your scene is bathed in sunlight. Also, make sure that the card fills the metering area – we'd recommend you use spot or partial metering as the card won't need to fill the entire image area – but any is suitable. You can either lock the exposure using your camera's AE-Lock facility or note the aperture and shutter speed and then switch to Manual mode and set these, although this method isn't suitable to days here lighting is variable. The card has AF reference lines to help your camera's autofocus lock on to it. However, you don't necessarily need it to be in focus to work correctly. The grey card (as well as the white card) can also be used to take a custom White Balance reading from too.

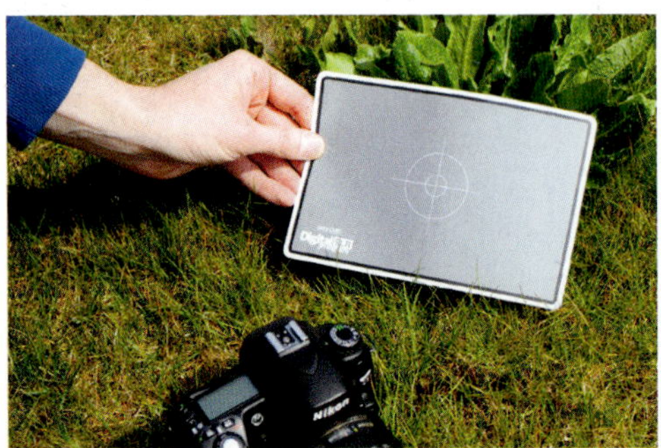

1 GETTING STARTED Place your grey card on the ground angled towards you and ensure it's located in a spot that is bathed in the same light as the majority of your scene you plan to shoot.

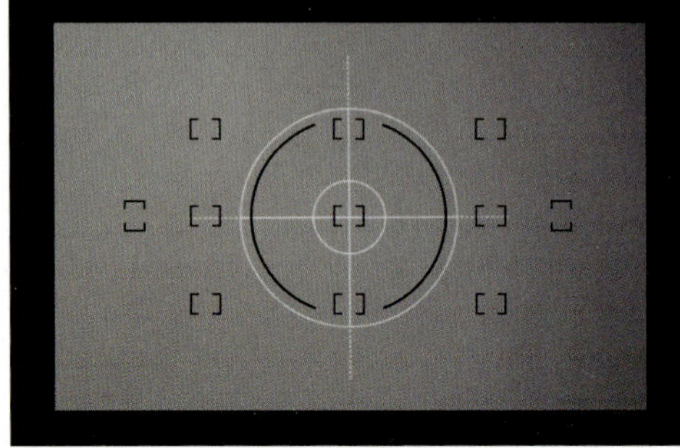

2 TAKE A METER READING Ensure that the entire metering area is filled by the grey card (in this instance we're using multi-zone metering) and lock the exposure with the AE-Lock button.

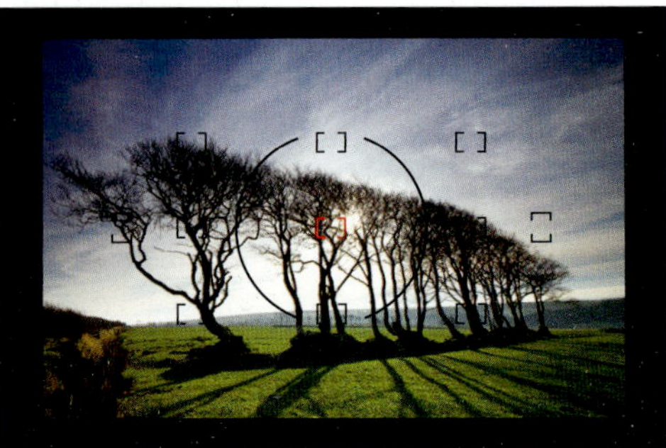

3 COMPOSE & SHOOT With this exposure locked, you can compose your scene and take your shots. When you check it on your LCD monitor, the exposure should be perfect.

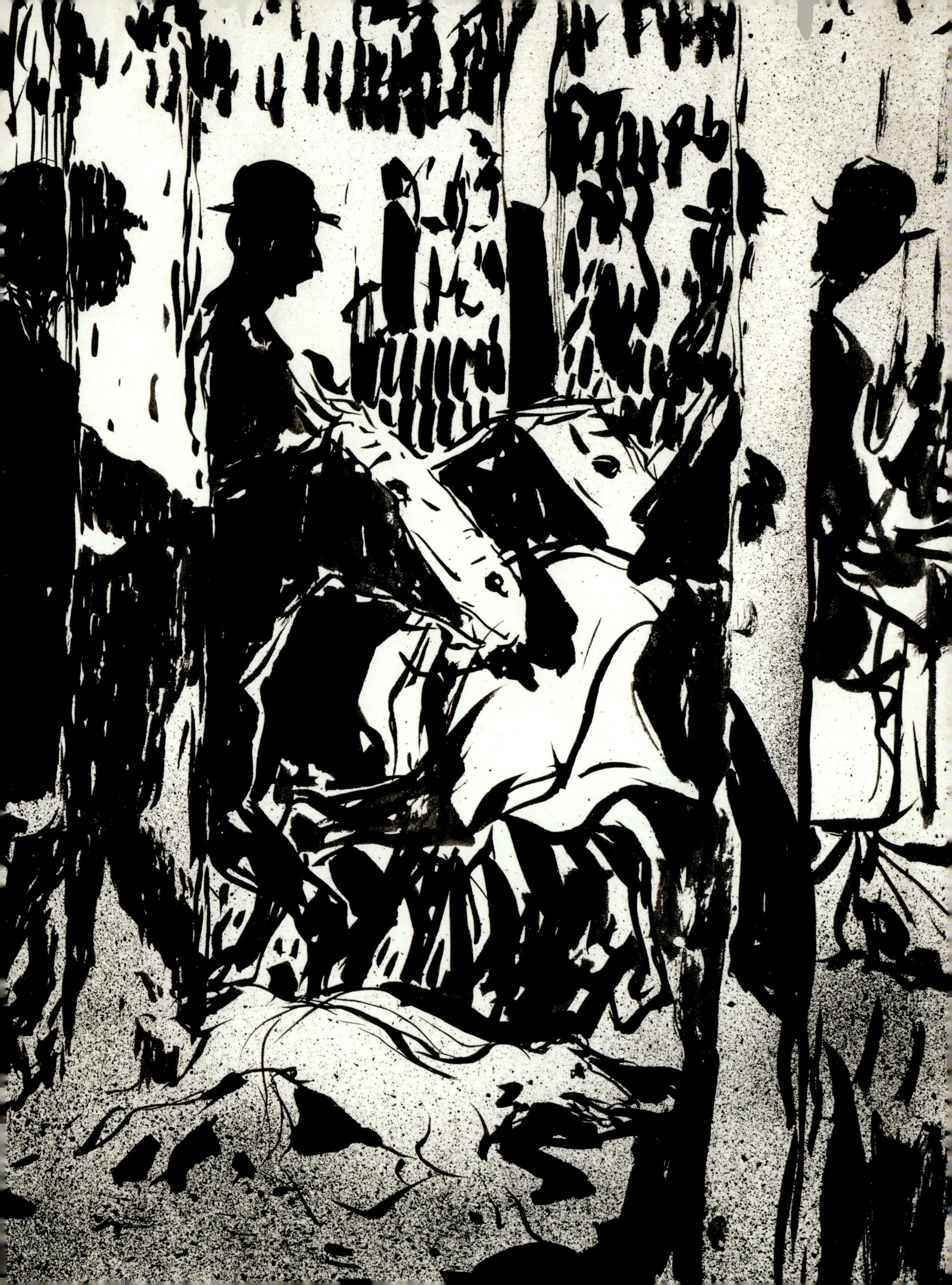

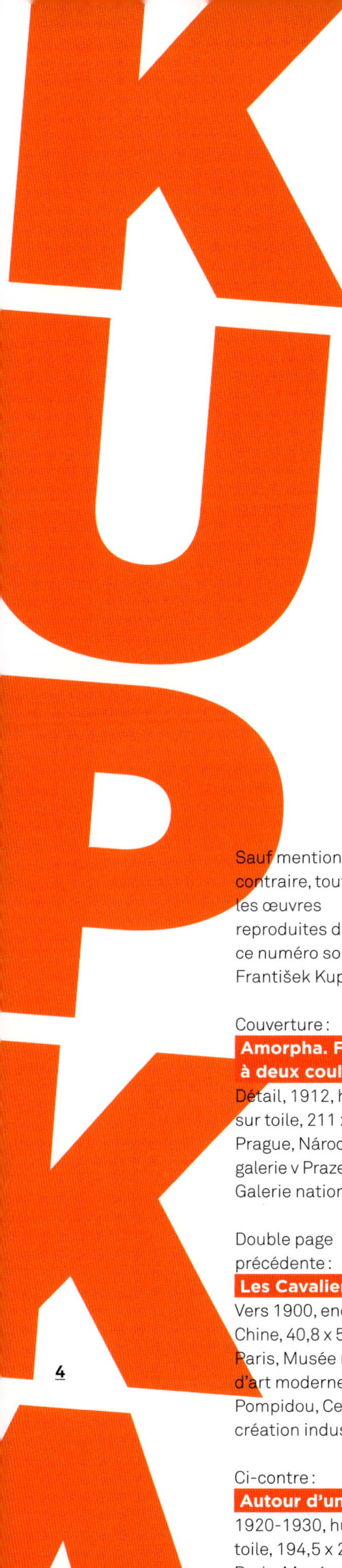

SOMMAIRE

6

Le mouvement du monde
Entretien avec Brigitte Leal

12

Prague-Vienne-Paris
Par jérôme Coignard

22

Chronologie
Par Charlotte Petitjean

24

Une plume au vitriol
Par Annick Colonna-Césari

30

Explorer l'invisible
Par Magda Chansel

38

Les couleurs et les sons
Par Annick Colonna-Césari

44

Commentaires d'œuvres
Par Guitemie Maldonado

64

Guide pratique

Sauf mention contraire, toutes les œuvres reproduites dans ce numéro sont de František Kupka.

Couverture : **Amorpha. Fugue à deux couleurs** Détail, 1912, huile sur toile, 211 x 220 cm, Prague, Národní galerie v Praze, Galerie nationale.

Double page précédente : **Les Cavaliers** Vers 1900, encre de Chine, 40,8 x 54,1 cm, Paris, Musée national d'art moderne, Centre Pompidou, Centre de création industrielle.

Ci-contre : **Autour d'un point** 1920-1930, huile sur toile, 194,5 x 200 cm, Paris, Musée national d'art moderne, Centre Pompidou.

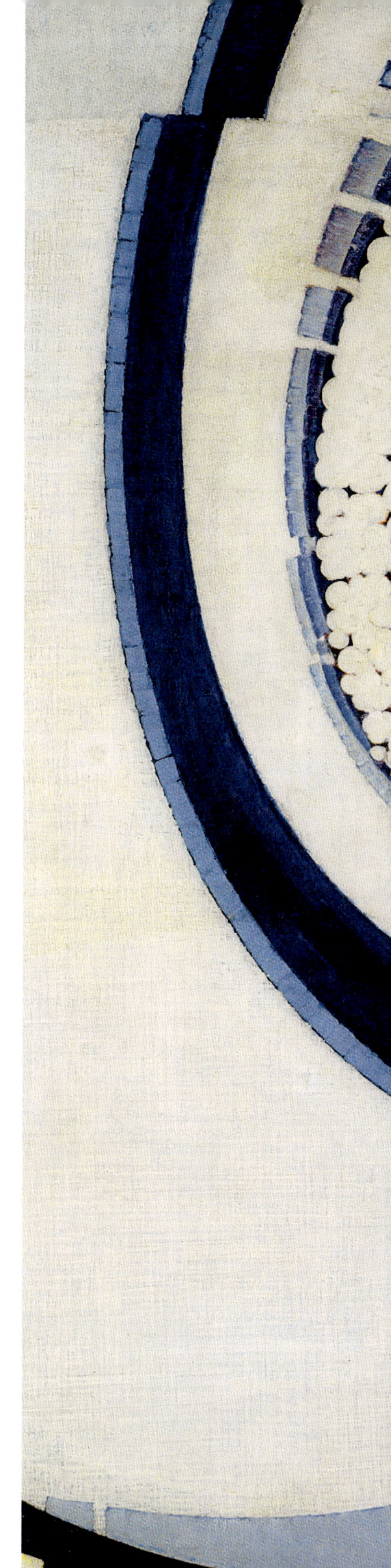

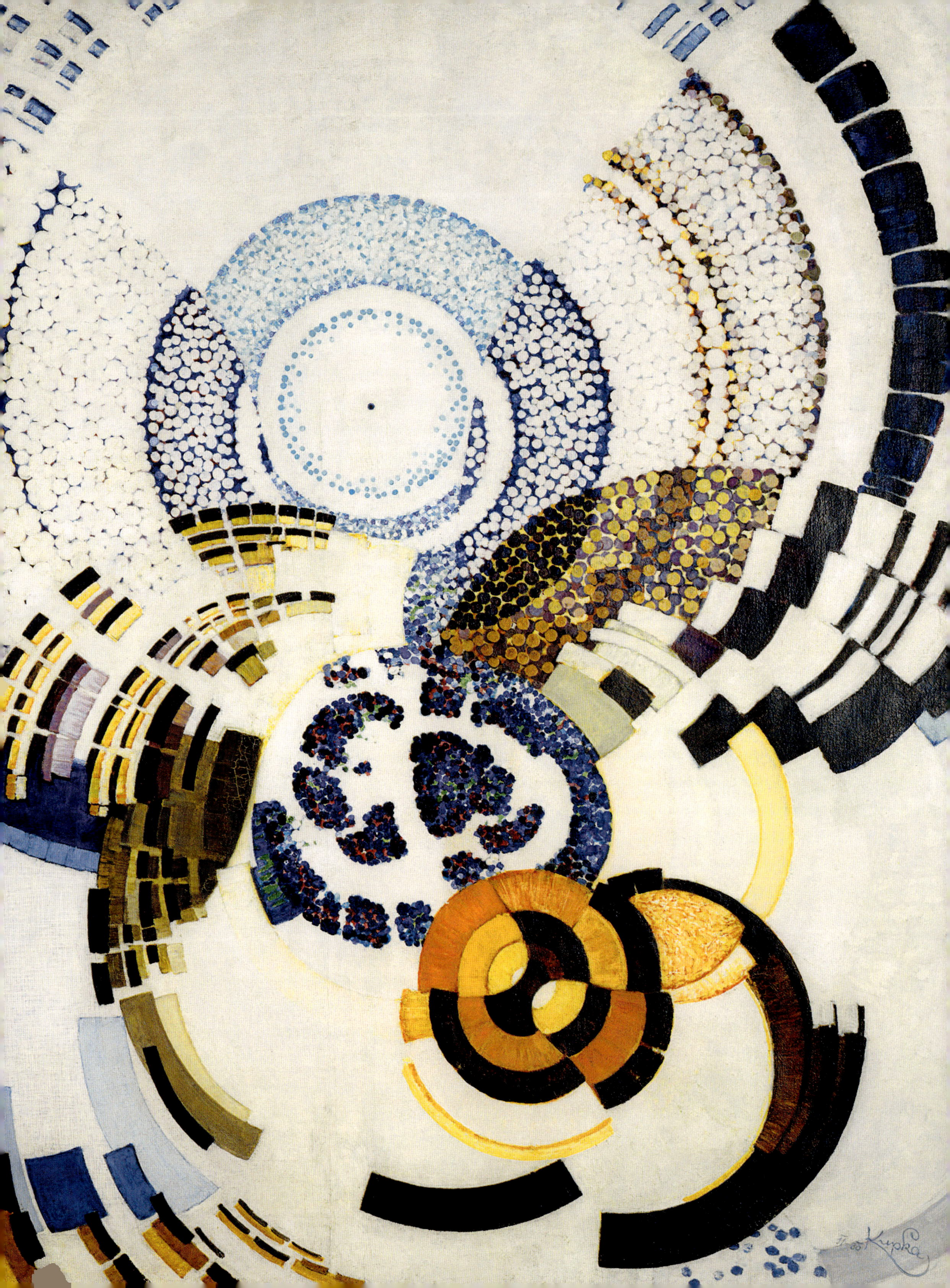
Kupka

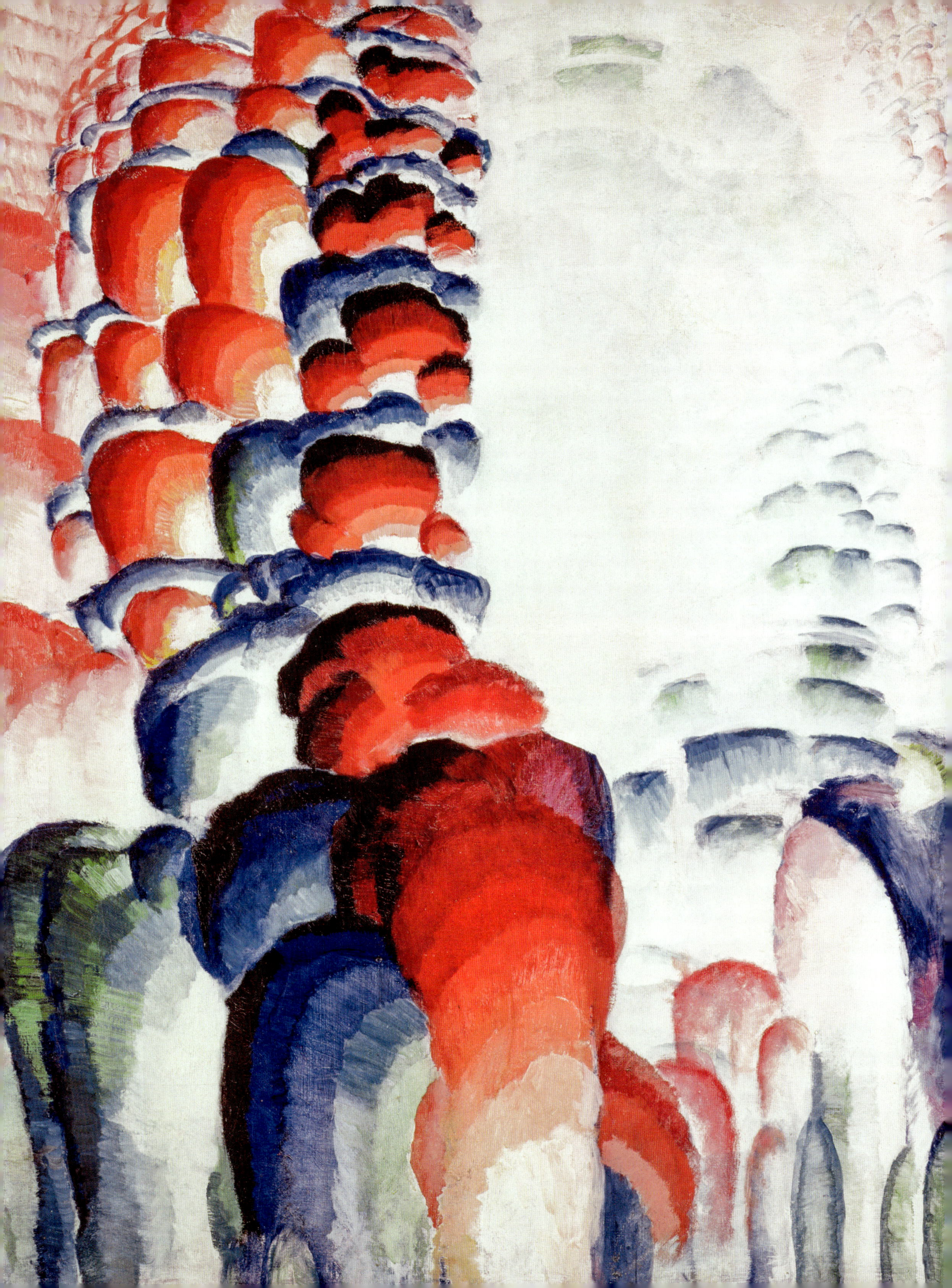

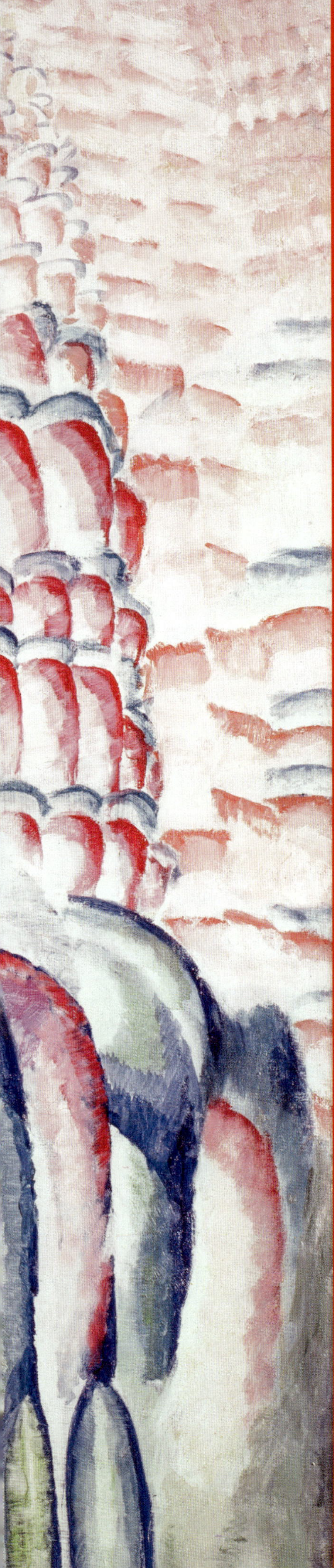

ENTRETIEN

LE MOUVEMENT DU MONDE

KUPKA

Tableaux symbolistes, dessins satiriques et passage à l'abstraction… les quelque trois cents œuvres réunies au Grand Palais offrent un panorama très complet de la carrière de l'artiste tchèque. Entretien avec Brigitte Leal, directrice adjointe du Musée national d'art moderne au Centre Georges Pompidou et commissaire de l'exposition.

PROPOS RECUEILLIS PAR GUILLAUME MOREL

Cette rétrospective est la première grande exposition consacrée à František Kupka (1871-1957) en France depuis celle du musée d'Art moderne de la Ville de Paris, en 1989. Quelle vision nouvelle offre-t-elle de l'œuvre de l'artiste ?

En trente ans, le regard sur Kupka a changé. L'exposition de 1989, passionnante, proposait un parcours très formaliste, en étudiant l'œuvre de façon thématique. À l'époque, les écrits de l'artiste étaient peu accessibles et encore rarement étudiés. En 2003, l'exposition « Aux origines de l'abstraction », organisée au musée d'Orsay, a ouvert de nouveaux chantiers de recherche en s'intéressant à l'influence des sciences de la vision sur la naissance de l'abstraction. Kupka a traversé l'histoire, connu deux guerres, et son travail se nourrit de son intérêt pour la science, la photographie, la philosophie… Des apports

Ci-contre :
Motif hindou ou Dégradés rouges
1919-1923, huile sur toile, 124,5 x 122 cm,
Paris, Musée national d'Art moderne, Centre Pompidou.

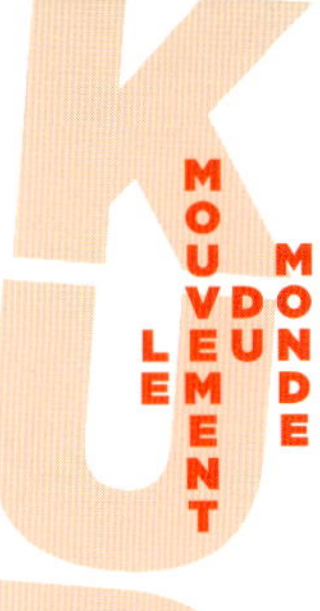

Page de droite, de haut en bas

Femme cueillant des fleurs
1909, pastel sur papier, 42,3 x 39 cm, Paris, Musée national d'art moderne, Centre Pompidou, Centre de création industrielle.

Femme cueillant des fleurs
1910-1911, aquarelle, graphite et pastel sur papier, 45 x 47,5 cm, Paris, Musée national d'art moderne, Centre Pompidou, Centre de création industrielle.

extérieurs à l'histoire de l'art, qui renouvellent notre vision de sa peinture. Kupka aspire à une spiritualité, à une harmonie, avec un sens très nordique, germanique, du rapport de l'homme à la nature. Cela transparaît dans son œuvre. Le tableau *La Petite fille au ballon,* représentant sa belle-fille, est ainsi lié à son goût pour le naturisme, qui n'est pas anecdotique, mais révélateur d'une façon d'être et de penser.

Comment rendre compte de la complexité de cette œuvre dans une exposition destinée à être vue et comprise par un très large public ?

Notre rétrospective est chronologique, avec quelques encarts thématiques, et tient compte de ces nouvelles lectures qui ont pu être faites de l'œuvre de l'artiste. Elle réunit trois cents peintures, dessins, gravures, manuscrits, journaux, livres illustrés... qui offrent un panorama très complet de sa carrière. Ce déploiement doit rendre le cheminement perceptible, de l'académisme de ses débuts – aux couleurs déjà expressionnistes – à ses compositions des années 1940-1950, en passant par les chefs-d'œuvre symbolistes, les dessins satiriques et, bien sûr, le basculement vers l'abstraction. Le parcours se construit autour de deux éléments fondamentaux, la grille analytique de décomposition du mouvement et le travail sur la couleur, qui rend son art immédiatement séduisant.

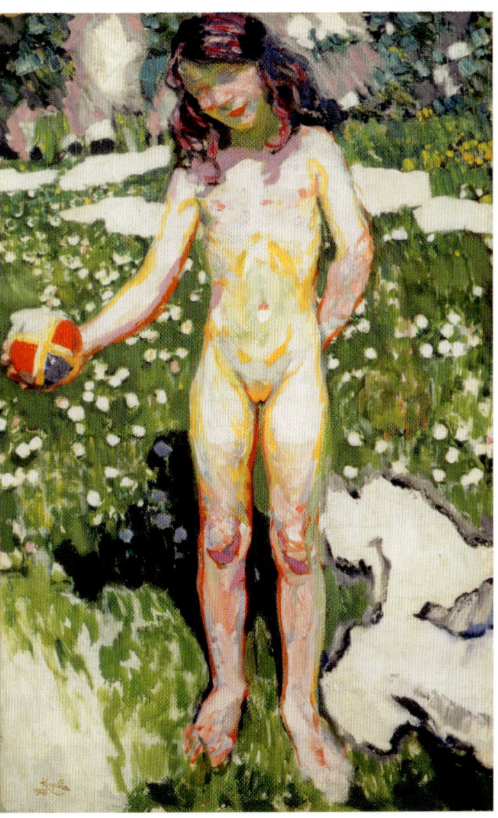

La Petite fille au ballon
1908, huile sur toile, 114 x 70 cm, Paris, Musée national d'art moderne, Centre Pompidou, Centre de création industrielle.

Quel rôle Kupka joue-t-il véritablement dans la naissance de l'abstraction ?

L'image non figurative apparaît dans les années 1910-1912, mais il est impossible de désigner l'auteur de la première œuvre abstraite. Souvent considérée comme telle, l'aquarelle de Vassily Kandinsky de 1910 date-t-elle bien de cette année-là ? L'abstraction émerge simultanément en plusieurs pays d'Europe et de façons différentes. Kandinsky, formé à Munich, a développé une abstraction lyrique de la nécessité intérieure. Mondrian suit la voie du cubisme et de la théosophie. Kupka s'intéresse à la décomposition de l'image, à la structure du mouvement. En ce sens, il est plus proche de Francis Picabia et de Marcel Duchamp. Pour Kupka, vouloir imiter la nature est vain et dépassé. Son abstraction trouve sa source dans l'époque symboliste. En 1880, il part du lotus qui, à force de décomposition, va le mener jusqu'au cercle parfait, représentation du cosmos. Le passage à l'abstraction se fait en 1912, après une phase futuriste fondée sur la captation du mouvement comme force vitale. L'invention des *Plans verticaux* marque son basculement définitif. Il n'y aura jamais de retour à la figure.

Pour Kupka, la couleur, essentielle, prime-t-elle sur la forme ?

Kupka est un coloriste extraordinaire. Sa palette, ses déclinaisons, cette beauté de la

peinture, très décorative, sont héritées de son passé viennois. Un artiste français n'aurait pas pu peindre ainsi. Cette puissance de la couleur est présente dès ses débuts, aux tonalités fauves. À l'heure du cubisme, Georges Braque et Pablo Picasso refusaient de construire leurs compositions par la couleur. Kupka, lui, en a toujours fait un élément fondamental. À cette même période, ses *Plans verticaux* éblouissent par leurs bleus, leurs violets, leurs rouges, qui font vibrer les compositions. Kupka s'est nourri des théories sur la couleur de la fin du XIXe siècle et de l'époque du symbolisme. Mais la couleur témoigne surtout de sa sensibilité au monde. Elle renvoie à l'idée de spiritualité et de correspondance entre les arts, notamment entre la peinture et la musique.

L'exposition met en lumière des épisodes moins connus de sa carrière, notamment la période « machiniste » des années 1920. De quoi s'agit-il ?

Cette phase a souvent été écartée des expositions. Ces œuvres, qu'il n'a jamais montrées, témoignent de son intérêt pour le cinéma. Les questions du montage et du collage ont passionné les cubistes. Ainsi de Fernand Léger, et de son *Ballet mécanique,* en 1924. Kupka, comme Duchamp, s'intéresse davantage au dynamisme. Après la photographie et le cinéma, l'homme voit le monde autrement, et l'art permet de montrer le mouvement du monde. C'est ce qui intéresse Kupka, au-delà de l'imagerie industrielle.

Kupka se forme dans la Vienne fin de siècle, avant d'évoluer dans le Paris des avant-gardes. Conservera-t-il des liens avec la Tchécoslovaquie ?

Oui, il multiplie les allers-retours. À Prague, Kupka est considéré en tant qu'artiste comme un héros national, la figure majeure de la

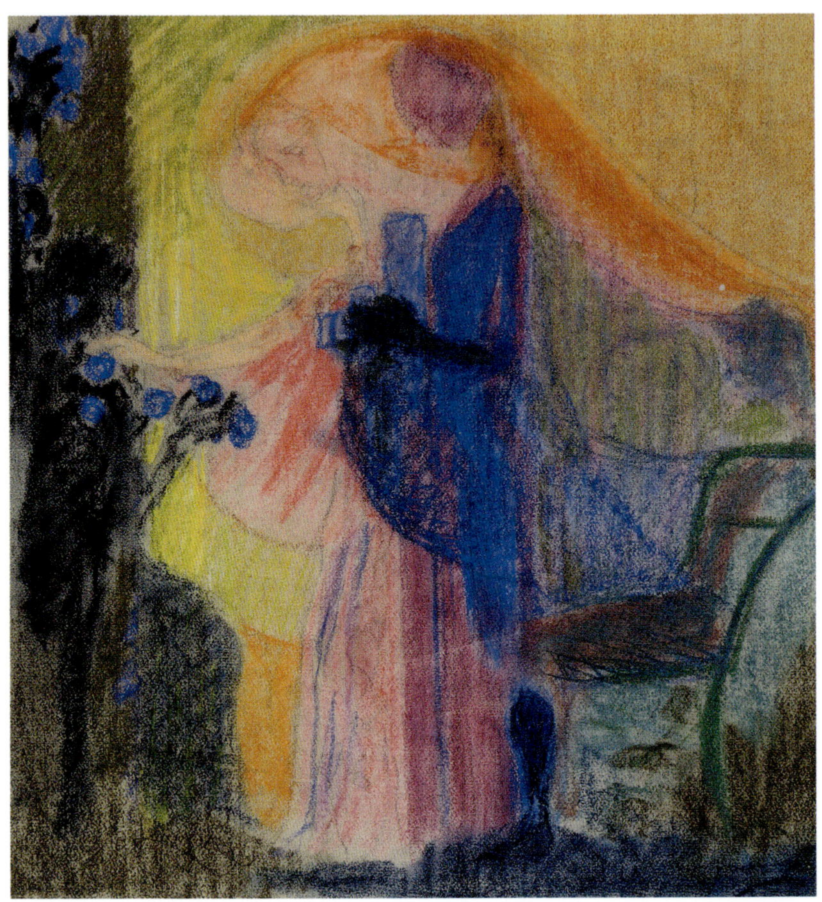

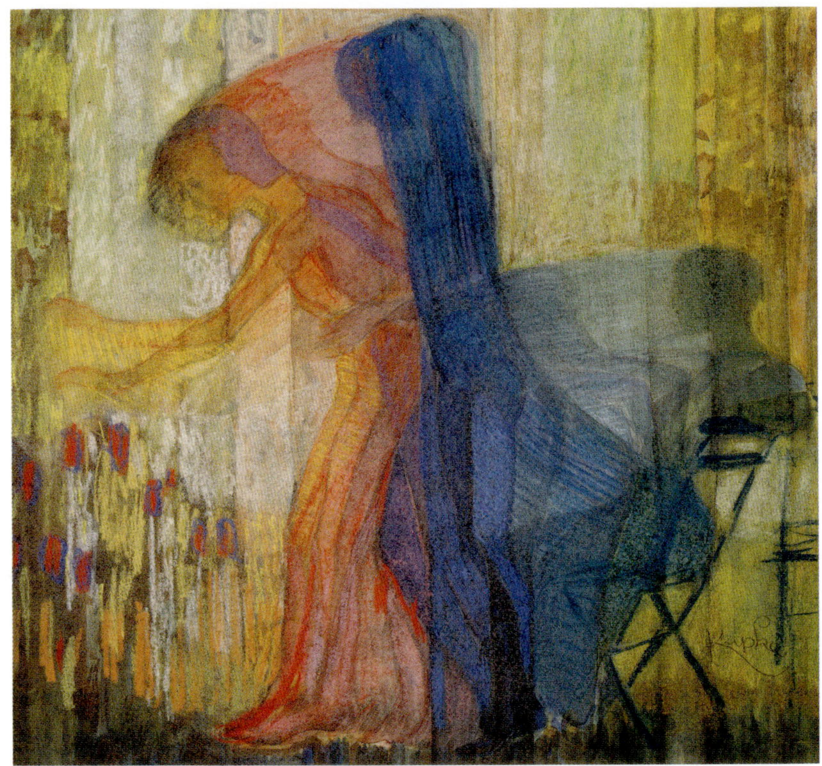

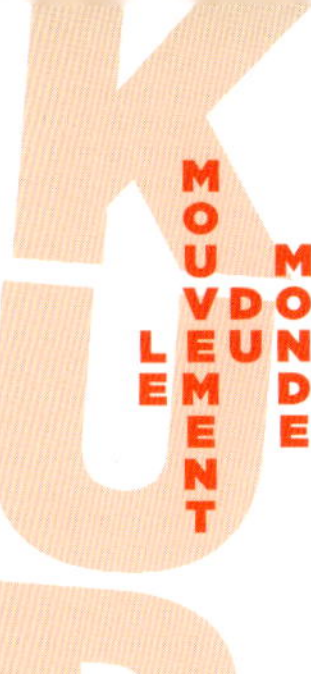

Page de droite :
Traits, plans, espace III
1921-1927, huile sur toile, 180 x 128 cm, Paris, Musée national d'art moderne, Centre Pompidou, Centre de création industrielle.

modernité. Il gardera toujours un contact serré avec la Tchécoslovaquie. Il participe à de nombreuses expositions dans son pays d'origine, en parallèle à celles qui s'ouvrent à Vienne ou à Paris, dans les années 1920. Il est très présent sur la scène artistique européenne, et même internationale. Car dès les années 1930, et par l'intermédiaire de Marcel Duchamp, il est reconnu aux États-Unis. Le MoMA, qui ouvre ses portes en 1929, achètera ainsi plusieurs de ses œuvres.

Cette ouverture sur le monde contredit l'image de l'artiste solitaire, hermétique à ce qui l'entoure, qu'il s'appliquait à cultiver. Quel homme était-il ?
Kupka avait un caractère ombrageux, mélancolique. Il a vécu des moments de profonde dépression. Mais il ne cessera de nouer des liens avec les acteurs de la vie culturelle et intellectuelle de son temps. À Vienne, il connaît les artistes, les écrivains, les philosophes. À Paris, il fréquente assidûment Marcel Duchamp – voisin de son atelier à Clichy – et ses frères, le sculpteur Raymond Duchamp-Villon et le peintre Jacques Villon. Ils formeront une sorte de phalanstère artistique. Ils partagent un même intérêt pour la philosophie de Bergson et la photographie d'Étienne-Jules Marey. Kupka aura également des affinités avec Francis Picabia, et connaît les écrits de Vassily Kandinsky, qu'il retrouve dans le groupe Abstraction-Création, dans les années 1930.

Abstraction Noir et Blanc
vers 1928-1930, gouache sur papier, 28 x 27,9 cm, Paris, Musée national d'art moderne, Centre Pompidou, Centre de création industrielle.

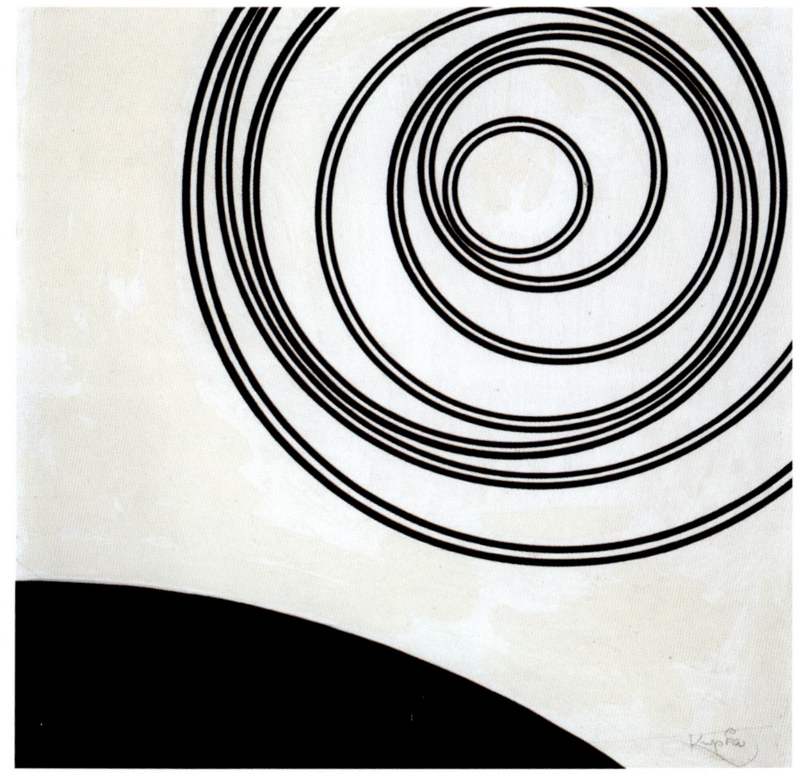

Ses relations avec les sciences, la philosophie, la musique, les cultures orientales, la poésie, la religion… ont accompagné Kupka dans sa quête d'une peinture nouvelle qui s'éloignerait de l'imitation de la Nature. Peut-on le considérer, au-delà de l'abstraction, comme un pionnier de l'art conceptuel ?
Il produit une œuvre intellectuelle, théorique. Nous avons les écrits de Kandinsky, de Malevitch, de Mondrian et de Kupka, quatre piliers de l'abstraction. Tous s'appuient sur leurs théories, et chacun mène son propre combat, défend sa vision du monde. Ils s'expriment dans des revues. Kupka écrit dans *Abstraction/Création* vers 1930-1932. C'est un vrai manifeste. Il participe à ce brassage intellectuel, mais il n'envisage pas le monde de façon conceptuelle. Sa vision est autre. Le plan, le cercle, la couleur sont à ses yeux des êtres vivants. Il y a une dimension presque organique dans sa peinture. Il croit véritablement à l'idée d'une rédemption par l'art et par la couleur. L'abstraction n'est pas un art mathématique. Elle résulte d'un cheminement intérieur. Kupka est un artiste d'une culture encyclopédique, qui invente un univers à sa mesure. ■

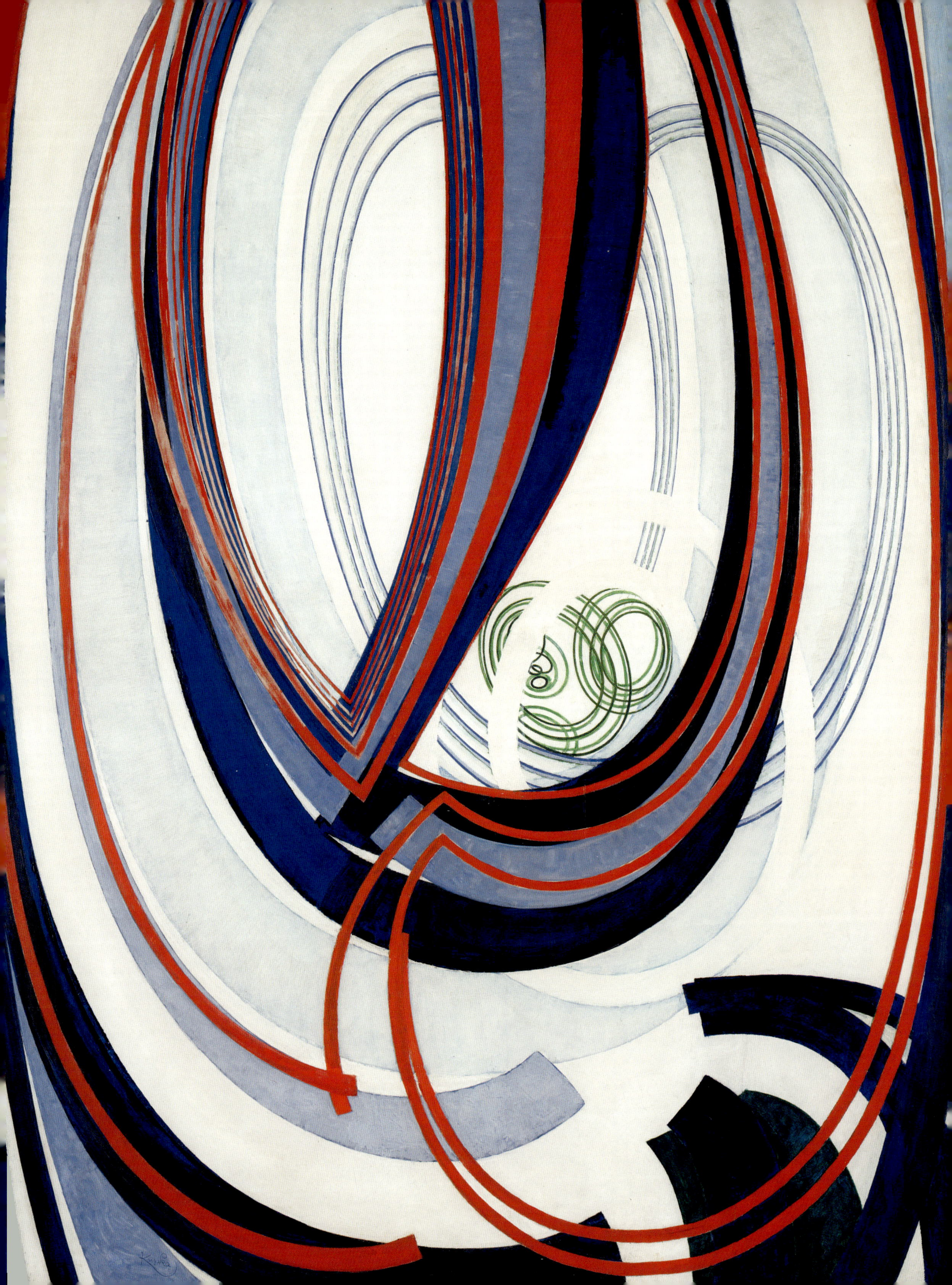

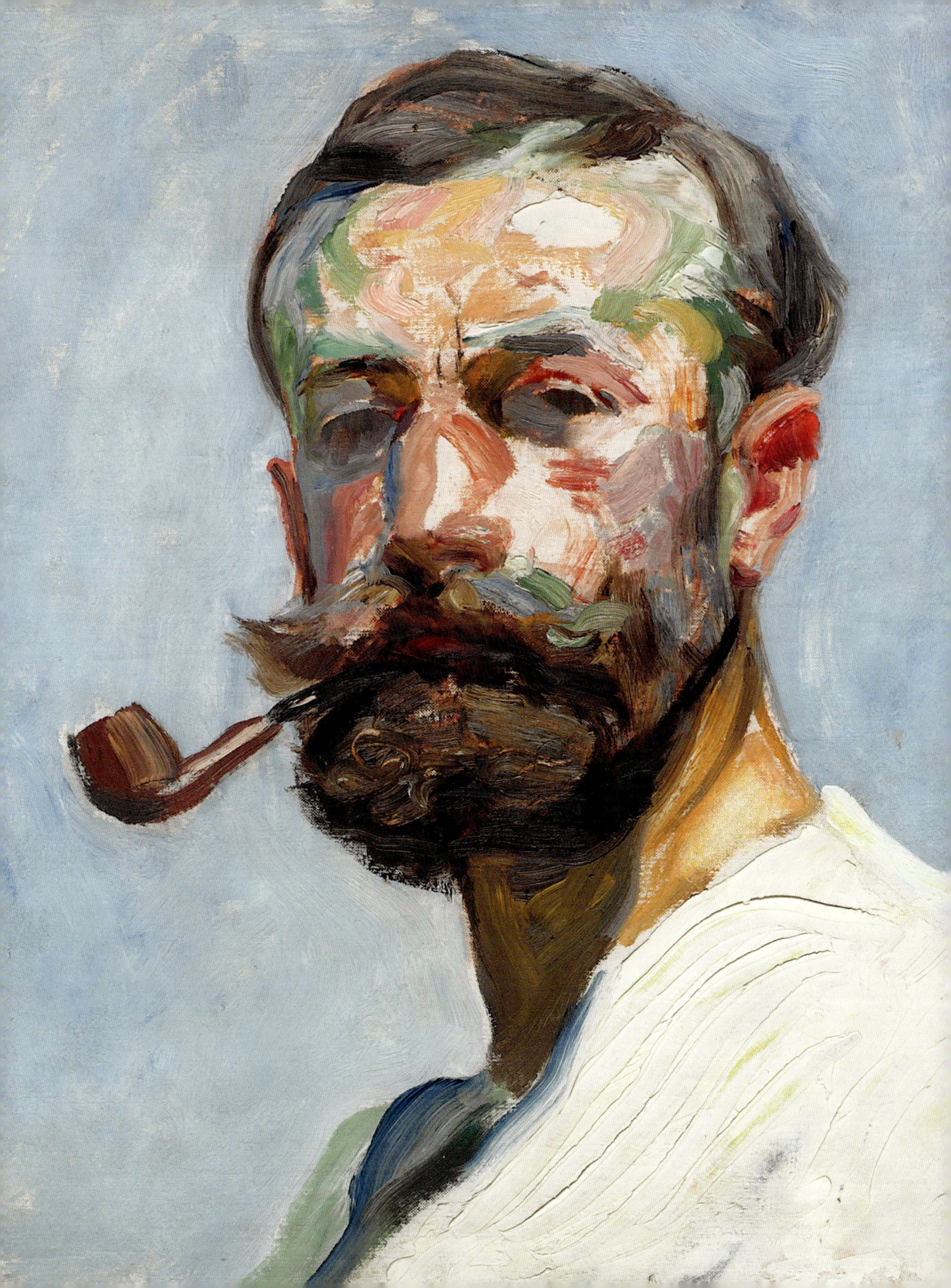

Page de gauche :
Autoportrait
Détail, 1910, huile sur toile, 46 x 55 cm, Prague, Národní galerie v Praze, Galerie nationale.

PRAGUE-VIENNE-PARIS PAR KUPKA

Tout se joue entre ces trois villes. L'effervescence culturelle de la capitale austro-hongroise attire František Kupka (1871-1957) qui y nourrit sa passion pour la philosophie, le spiritisme, les sciences et la littérature. Installé en France dès 1896, il y mène une intense activité d'illustrateur avant de reprendre ses recherches picturales.

PAR JÉRÔME COIGNARD

Ci-dessous :
Soleil d'automne
1905-1906, huile sur toile, 103 x 111 cm, Prague, Národní galerie v Praze, Galerie nationale.

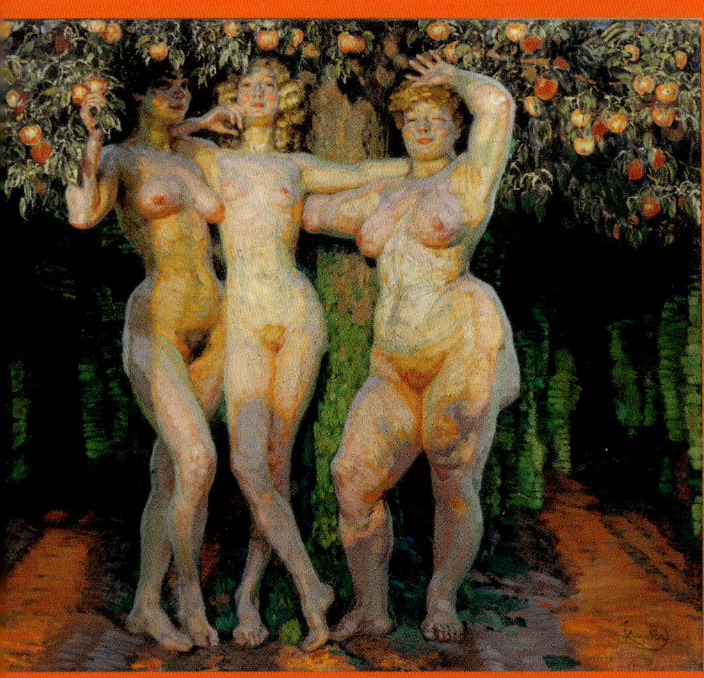

Né en Bohême orientale, dans une famille modeste, marqué par la mort prématurée de sa mère, František Kupka (1871-1957) révèle dès sa petite enfance un don exceptionnel pour le dessin. Un sellier qui le prend comme apprenti l'initie au spiritisme. Fort de ses succès à l'école d'art de Jaromer, Kupka entre à l'Académie des beaux-arts de Prague en 1889 et suit les cours de l'artiste nazaréen František Sequens dans la classe de peinture historique et religieuse. Paradoxalement, l'art des Nazaréens [Ndlr : peintres allemands influencés par le catholicisme et le romantisme] déjà passé de mode aura une grande influence sur son œuvre comme sur l'art tchèque du xxe siècle. Pour subvenir à ses besoins, Kupka exerce l'activité de médium. Diplômé en 1891, il décide de poursuivre sa formation à la prestigieuse Académie de Vienne. Il peint d'ambitieuses allégories, comme *Le dernier rêve de Heine mourant* qui attire l'attention de l'impératrice Élisabeth et lui vaut de peindre quelques portraits pour l'aristocratie autrichienne. Attiré par l'effervescence de la capitale de l'Empire austro-hongrois, il y parfait sa

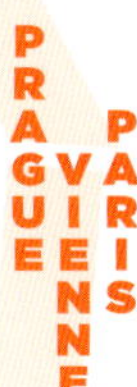

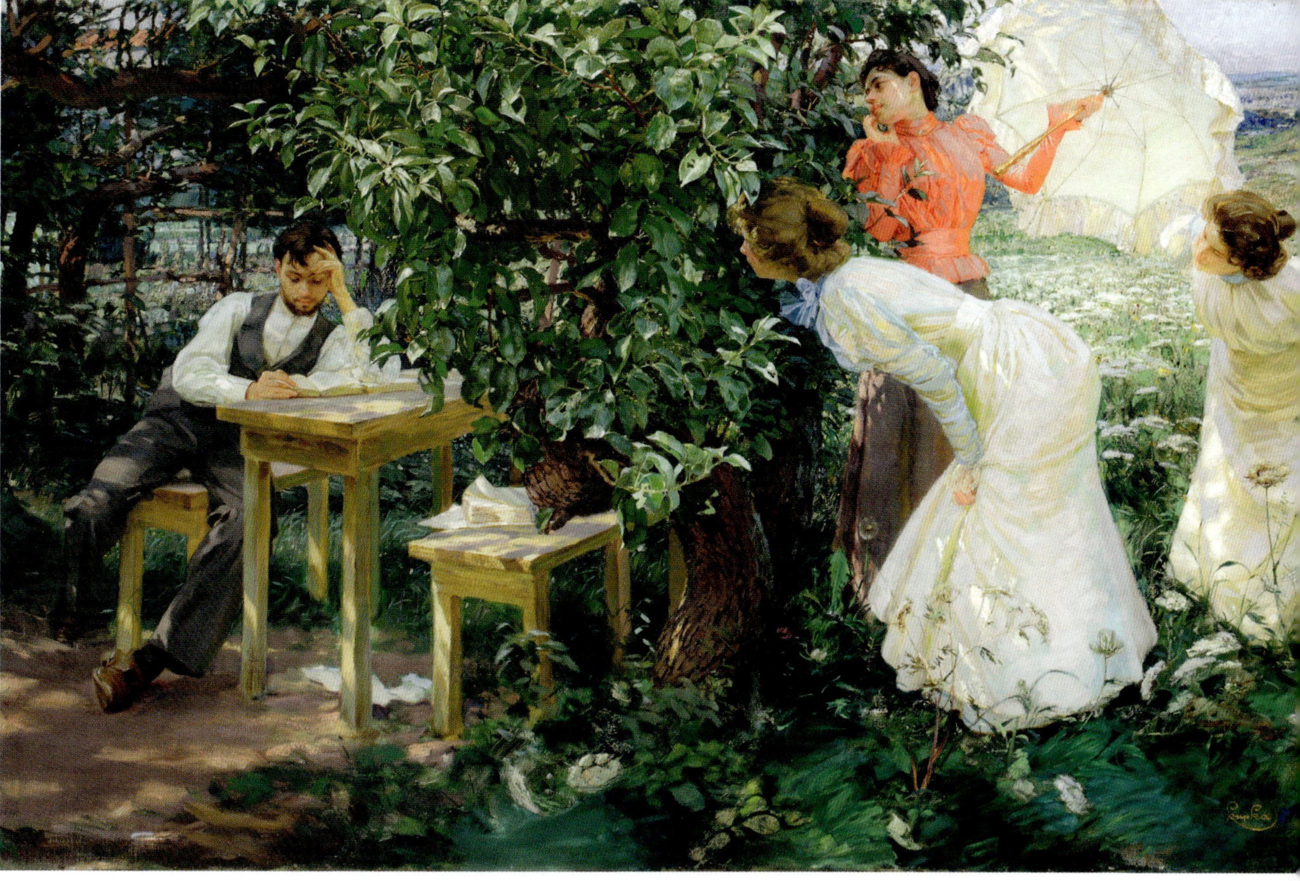

Le Bibliomane
1899, huile sur toile, 94 x 151 cm, Prague, château de Prague.

culture philosophique, scientifique et littéraire avec ses amis Arthur Rössler, futur critique d'art proche de Schiele, et Milos Maixner, un ancien condisciple praguois, tous deux dotés d'une bonne culture philosophique. C'est le temps des lectures et des conversations enflammées.

Au plus près de la nature

Kupka se passionne toujours pour le spiritisme et les sciences occultes. L'appartement qu'il partage avec Maixner devient le lieu de rencontre d'un groupe de théosophes. Grâce à son ami, il fait la connaissance de l'artiste Karl Diefenbach et s'installe dans sa maison d'Hüttelsdorf en 1894. Entouré de sa famille et de ses disciples, le maître y a adopté une hygiène de vie basée sur un régime végétarien, des bains de soleil et la gymnastique pratiquée nu dans la nature. Kupka en conservera l'habitude jusqu'à la fin de sa vie, été comme hiver. Chez Diefenbach, qui invite volontiers ses amis pianistes ou violonistes à jouer pendant qu'il peint avec ses disciples, il approfondit l'étude des relations entre peinture et musique. Des quelques mois passés au sein de cette communauté, Kupka dira plus tard que ce fut l'une des expériences les plus enrichissantes de sa vie. C'est lors de cette même année 1894 que naît sa liaison intense et douloureuse avec une fem me plus âgée : Maria Bruhn, styliste danoise, dirige à Vienne une maison de couture pour laquelle il réalise des dessins. En 1895, l'exposition de son tableau *Quam ad causam sumus* au Kunstverein de Vienne est remarquée par la critique. Mais un compte rendu assassin, qui lui reproche de vouloir *« chanter un duo en solo »,* le plonge dans le désespoir. En compagnie de Maria, Kupka voyage au Danemark et en Norvège. Cependant, le retour à la peinture s'avère difficile. Mécontent d'une ambitieuse composition allégorique, *Hymne à l'Univers,* l'artiste la détruit. Dépité, il décide de quitter Vienne et s'installe à Paris au printemps 1896. S'ensuit une rupture importante : rupture avec Diefenbach, avec le mysticisme, avec l'ascétisme, rupture (éphémère) avec les sciences occultes et avec Maria qu'il suspecte de le vampiriser… La vie parisienne chasse les miasmes

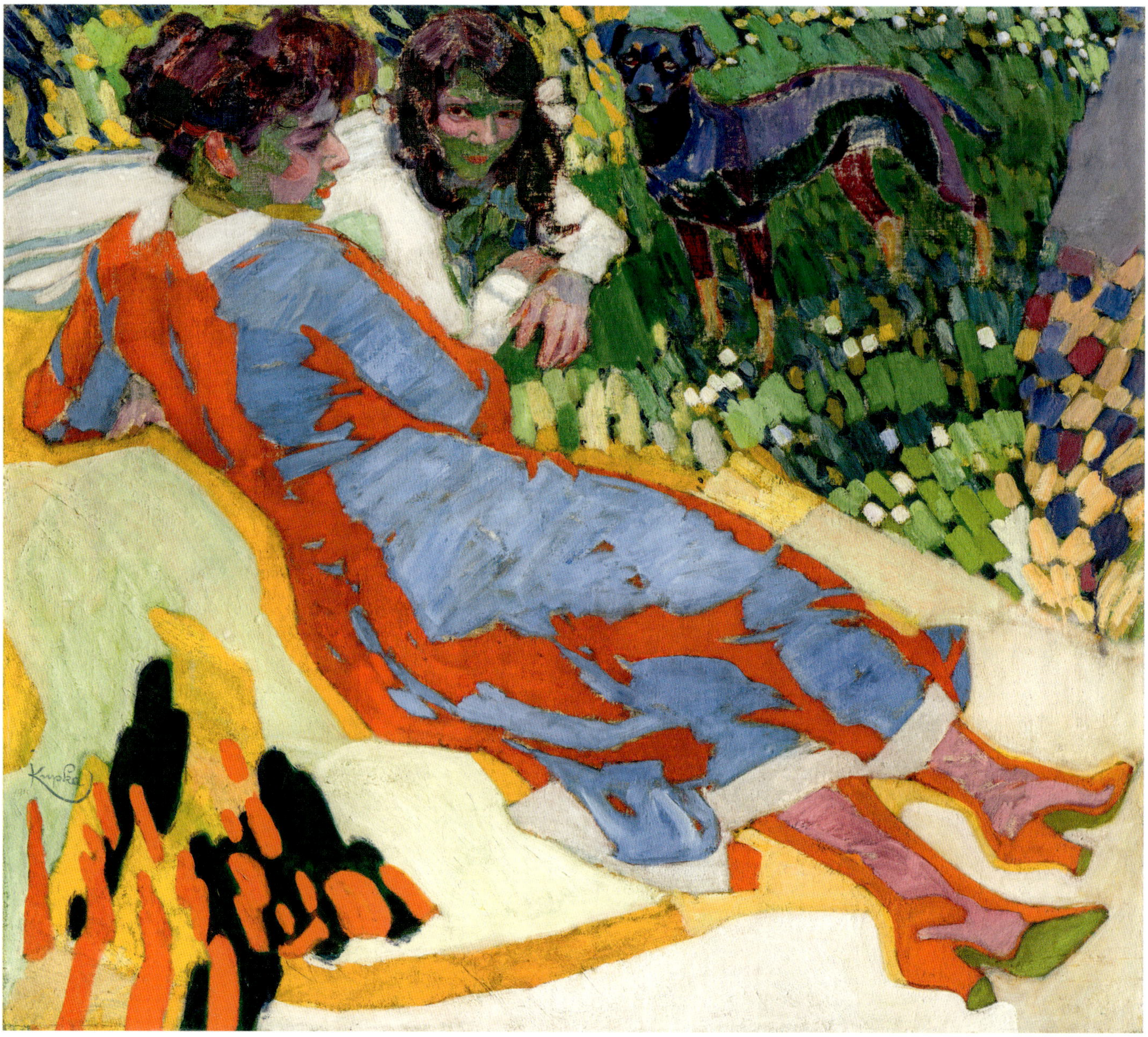

Portrait de famille
1910, huile sur toile,
103 x 112 cm, Prague,
Národní galerie v Praze,
Galerie nationale.

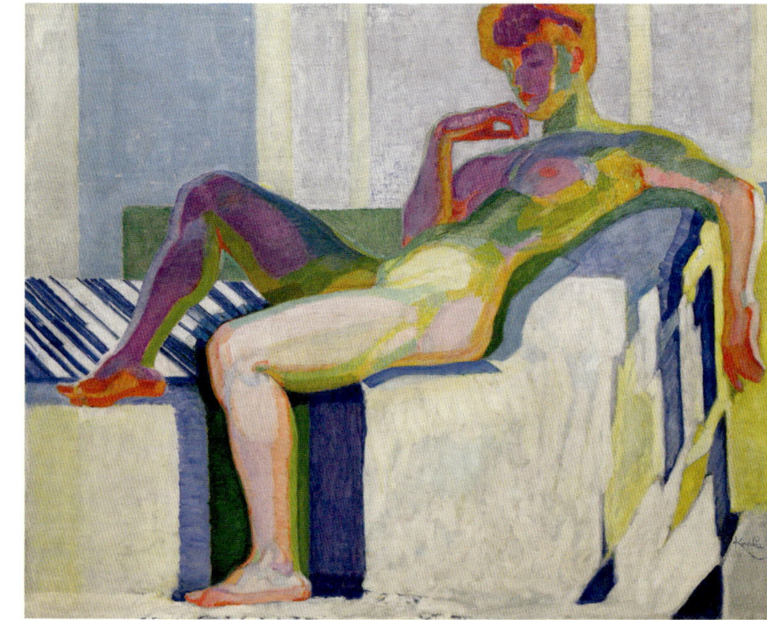

Grand nu,
Plans par couleurs
1909-1910, huile sur toile,
150,2 x 180,7 cm,
New York, The Solomon R.
Guggenheim Museum.

Le Rouge à lèvres
1908, huile sur toile, 63,5 x 63,5 cm, Paris, Musée national d'art moderne, Centre Pompidou, Centre de création industrielle.

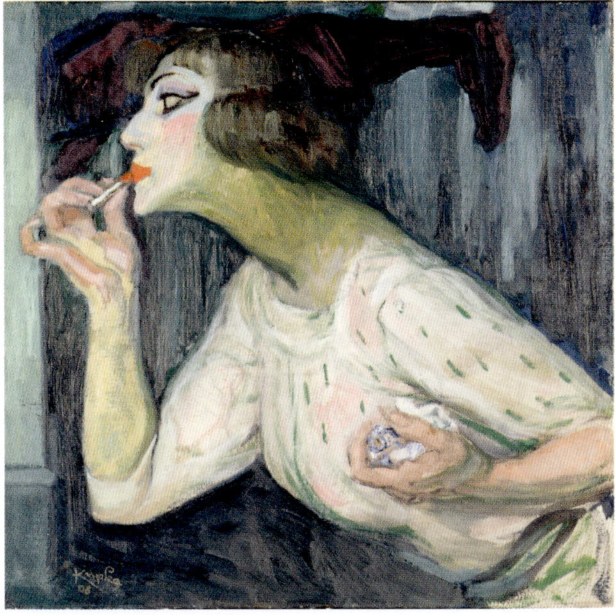

L'Archaïque
1910, huile sur toile, 110 x 90 cm, Paris, Musée national d'art moderne, Centre Pompidou, Centre de création industrielle.

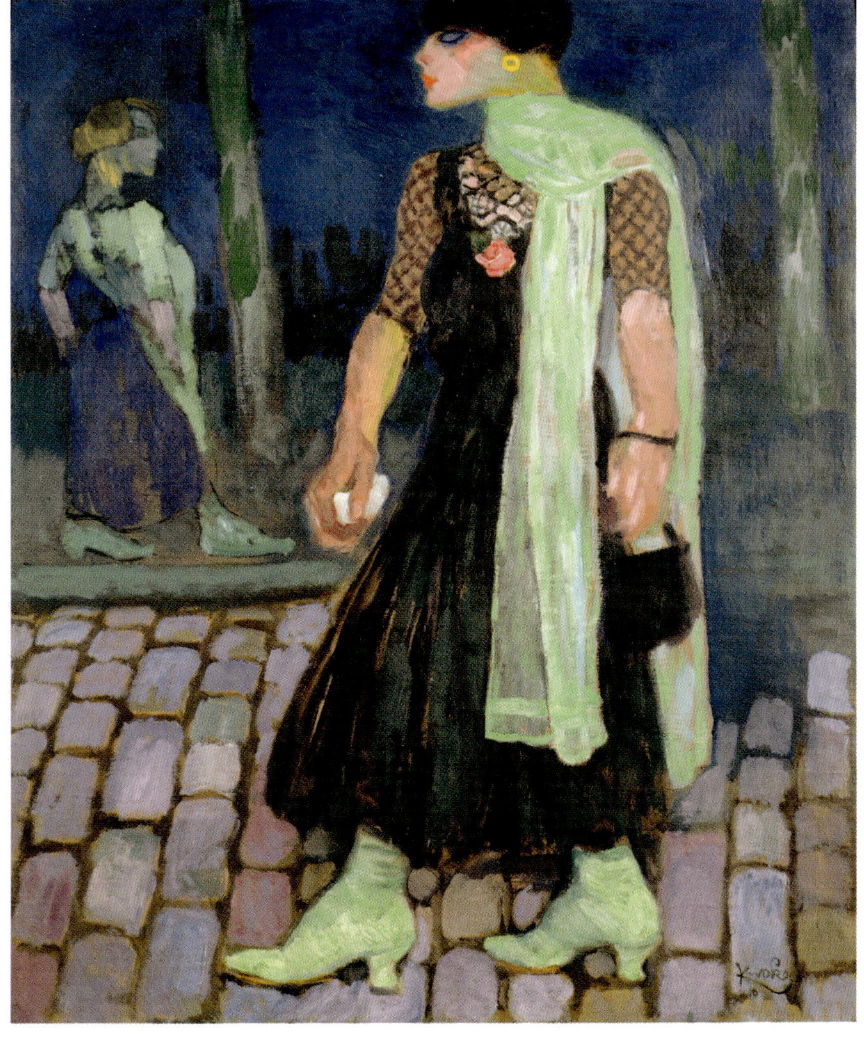

de la Vienne décadente. *«À Vienne, j'étais malade, comme quand on se laisse aller physiquement […]. J'ai fini par en avoir l'âme détraquée»,* écrit-il à son ami Rössler, le 10 mars 1896. Il conclut : *«Je veux retourner parfaire ma formation à la seule bonne source – auprès de la nature.»* Kupka fait la connaissance de son illustre compatriote Alfons Mucha auquel il rend visite régulièrement à partir de 1896. Insatisfait de sa peinture, il fréquente brièvement l'Académie Jullian et l'École des beaux-arts où il travaille dans l'atelier de Jean-Paul Laurens. Parallèlement, il se consacre à des études scientifiques. La redoutable Maria, qui l'a rejoint à Paris, lui procure aide financière et commandes de dessins de mode. Après une escapade à Londres pour tenter de lui échapper, il s'installe avec elle dans une maison à La Bretèche, près de Paris. C'est là qu'il peindra *Le Bibliomane,* témoin de son retour au travail d'après nature (p. 14). Opérée à Vienne d'un cancer, Maria meurt en 1898. Avec elle disparaît la menace que Kupka sentait peser sur lui. Il peut désormais sublimer leur relation dans sa peinture.

Une vie de bohème

À son retour à Paris, il mène la vie de la bohème montmartroise. Il se met en ménage avec la Goulue, fréquente Aristide Bruant et les chansonniers de la Butte, crée des affiches, commence à dessiner pour la presse humoristique. Il rencontre Gabrielle, modèle qui devient sa compagne pour quelques années. En 1899, il fait sa première apparition dans une exposition parisienne, envoyant *Le Bibliomane* et deux autres œuvres au Salon de la Société nationale des beaux-arts. L'année suivante, ses œuvres présentées à l'Exposition universelle, dans le pavillon autrichien, lui valent une médaille d'argent. Il débute une importante correspondance avec le poète et homme politique tchèque Josef Machar dont il fait le portrait à Vienne en 1901

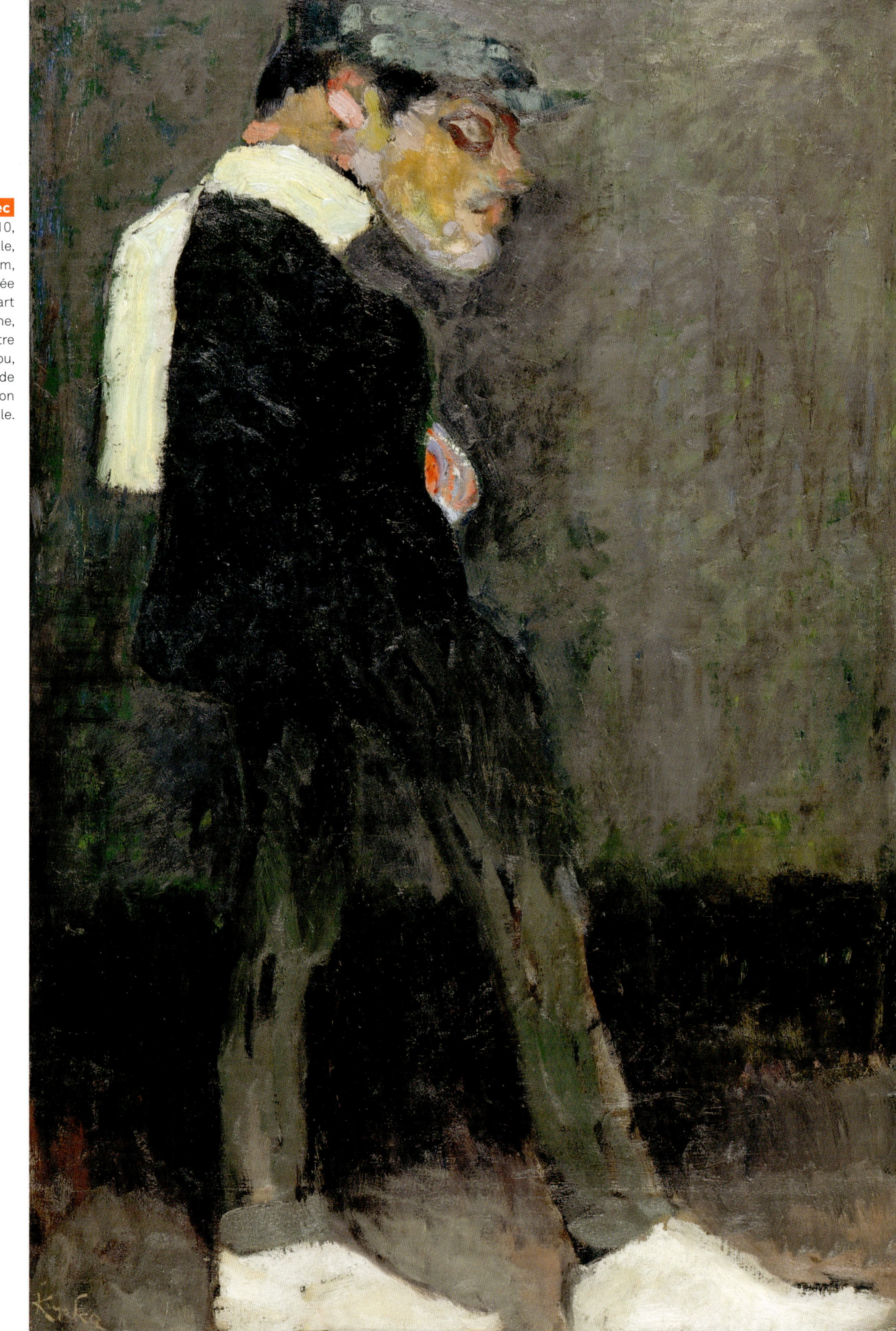

Le Mec
1910,
huile sur toile,
104 x 68 cm,
Paris, Musée
national d'art
moderne,
Centre
Pompidou,
Centre de
création
industrielle.

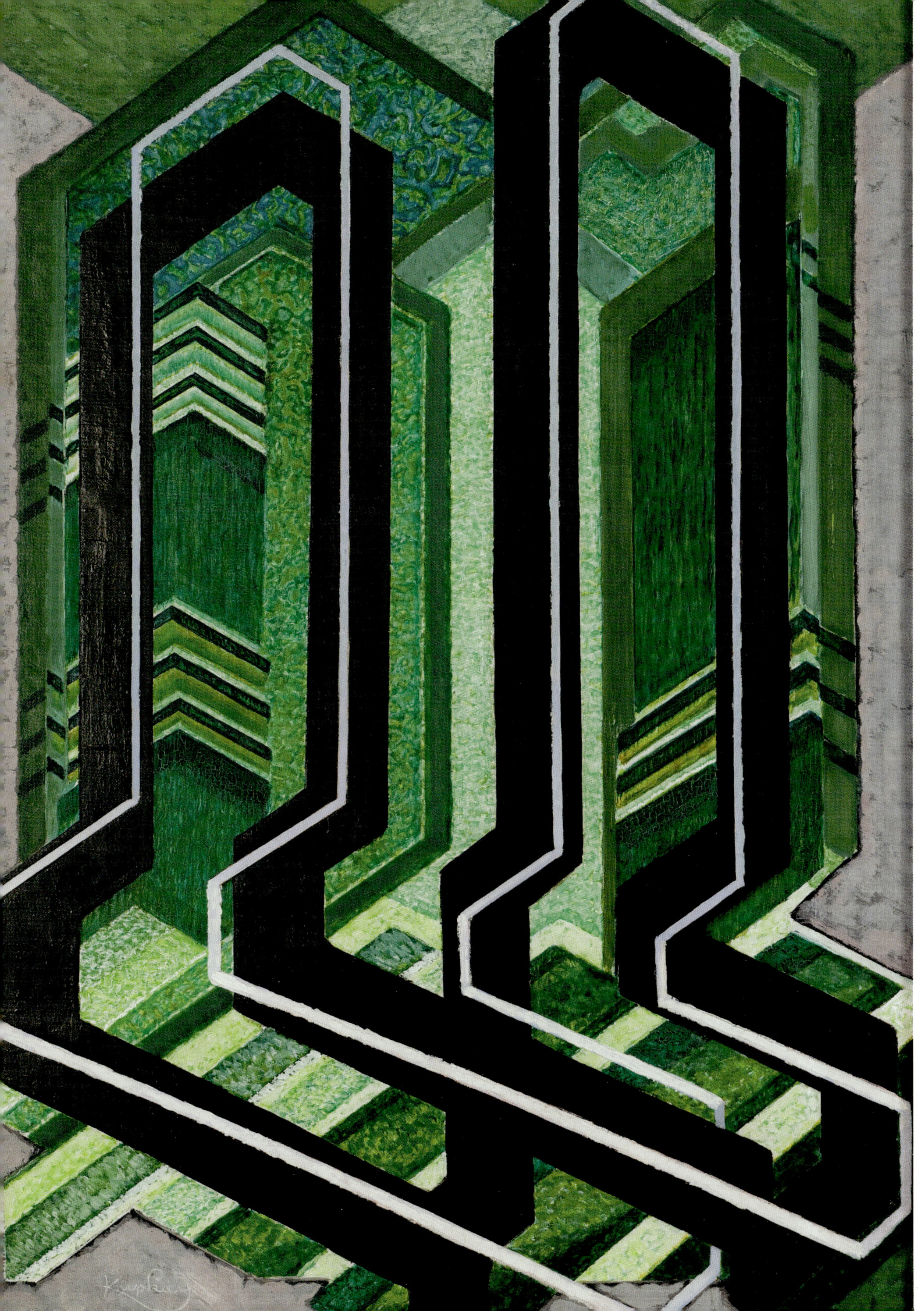

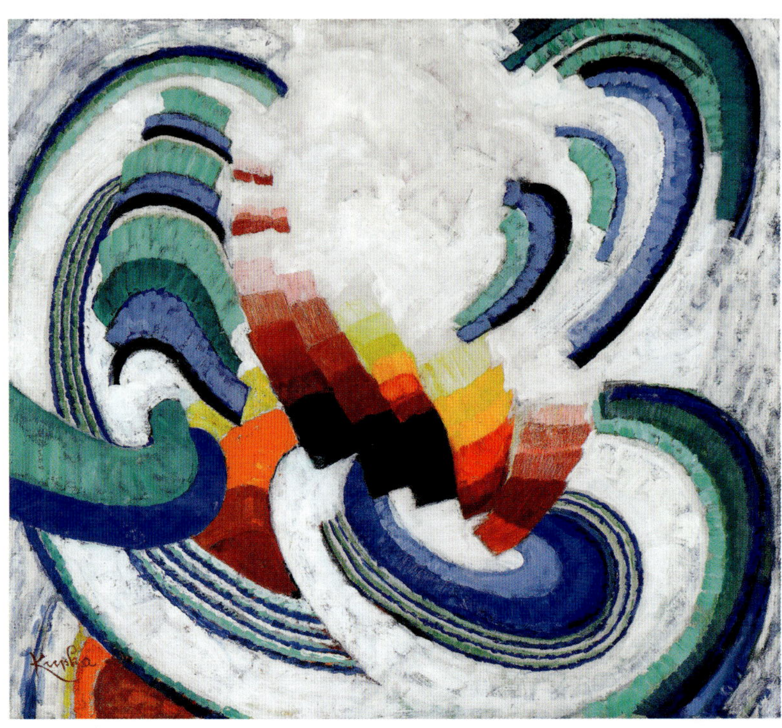

Tourbillon
1923-1924, huile sur toile, 72,5 x 79 cm, Paris, Musée national d'art moderne, Centre Pompidou, Centre de création industrielle.

et qui, de son côté, publiera une biographie du peintre dans une revue tchèque. À Prague, Machar demeure son principal contact avec les milieux anarchisants et anticléricaux.

Dans les années 1900, Kupka se consacre presque exclusivement au dessin de presse, suscitant l'intérêt des cercles radicaux tchèques. Il présente une sélection de dessins et lithographies à la Première Exposition ouvrière de Prague en 1902. Organisée par des cercles progressistes pour promouvoir leurs idées, l'exposition itinérante de ses dessins satiriques en Bohême et en Moravie (1904-1905) suscitera polémique et scandale, dans un contexte politique très tendu. Réalisées à la même époque, ses illustrations pour des ouvrages de bibliophilie restent marquées par le symbolisme et la Sécession viennoise. Il reçoit la commande des illustrations de *L'Homme et la Terre,* l'ouvrage monumental du géographe anarchiste Élisée Reclus (p. 28). La publication sera posthume : l'auteur meurt en juillet 1905 après avoir rencontré l'artiste et admiré les premiers dessins.

Nouvelles recherches picturales

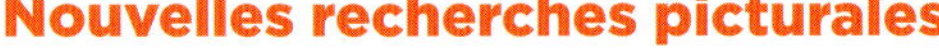

En 1906, Kupka s'installe à Puteaux dans une maison atelier, avec sa compagne Eugénie Straub (il l'épouse en 1910) et la fille de celle-ci, en même temps que Jacques Villon et Raymond Duchamp-Villon. Le jardin est contigu à celui de Jacques Villon auquel le lie une solide amitié. Il y habitera jusqu'à sa mort. Cette installation marque la reprise effective de ses recherches picturales, mises en veilleuse pendant son intense activité journalistique. Sa participation au Salon d'Automne et au Salon des Indépendants permet de suivre sa trajectoire artistique. Ses envois au Salon d'Automne de 1911 (dont *Plan par couleurs, grand nu)* effarouchent la critique qui dénonce, dans un climat de plus en plus xénophobe, une atteinte au *« goût français ».* Il fait à nouveau scandale en 1912 avec *Amorpha. Fugue à deux couleurs* et *Amorpha. Chromatique chaude.* Selon le poète et critique d'art Alexandre Mercereau, c'est à propos de ces tableaux-manifestes, premières œuvres non figuratives exposées au public, qu'Apollinaire parle pour la première fois d'orphisme. Cependant, le nom de Kupka est étrangement absent des écrits sur l'art du poète. Sa défiance à l'égard des « ismes » permet peut-être de l'expliquer.

Kupka assiste épisodiquement aux réunions du groupe de Puteaux (Villon, Duchamp-Villon, Gleizes, Metzinger, Picabia, Léger...). Si on sait aujourd'hui qu'il participe au Salon de la Section d'Or de 1912, Kupka, dans ses écrits, ne dit mot de ses échanges avec les Duchamp-Villon et avec le groupe de Puteaux, qui associe également Apollinaire, et des critiques comme André Salmon, Maurice Raynal ou Mercereau. D'ailleurs, il reste muet sur ses relations avec le milieu artistique. Il dit vivre en ermite, n'a ni galerie ni mécène, ce qui ne l'empêche pas d'être au fait de l'actualité artistique. Il achève en 1913 la rédaction de ses notes, base de son

Page de gauche :
Le Trait austère
1925, huile sur toile, 116,5 x 81 cm, Paris, musée d'Art moderne de la Ville de Paris.

principal ouvrage théorique, *La Création dans les arts plastiques,* qui ne paraîtra (en tchèque) que dix ans plus tard.

Engagé volontaire en 1914 dans le 3e régiment de Marche de la Légion étrangère, Kupka participe aux premiers combats de la Grande Guerre. Son camarade Blaise Cendrars évoquera dans *La Main coupée* (1946) la témérité de Mme Kupka le rejoignant sur le front. Évacué pour raisons de santé en 1915 et réformé, il finira la guerre avec le grade de capitaine. En 1917, il participe activement à la constitution de l'armée tchèque en France, reconnue comme armée régulière l'année suivante. Devenu président de la colonie tchécoslovaque de Paris, Kupka rencontre en 1919 l'industriel Jindrich Waldes qui devient son ami et son mécène. Lié aux fondateurs de la toute jeune République tchèque, l'artiste séjourne souvent à Prague en 1919 et 1920. En 1922, il est rémunéré comme professeur chargé d'initier à la culture française les étudiants tchèques de l'Académie de Prague. Son enseignement traduit sa vaste culture, mêlant considérations esthétiques, philosophiques, musicales, poétiques ou scientifiques.

Le temps de l'Abstraction-Création

Le début des années 1920 est marqué par deux expositions personnelles dans des galeries parisiennes et par la parution d'une première monographie que lui consacre Louis Arnould-Grémilly. Kupka illustre son recueil *Quatre Histoires de blanc et noir, « explication orphique de la terre »,* de nombreuses gravures sur bois d'après ses peintures. Il assiste aux « vendredis » de Mercereau, avec qui il partage le goût de l'occultisme, se lie avec Félix Del Marle, disciple français de Mondrian. Ami de Theo van Doesburg, qui a salué en lui l'inventeur de l'abstraction géométrique dans la revue *De Stijl,* Kupka devient membre du mouvement Abstraction-Création dès sa fondation en 1931. Dans une lettre à Waldes, il se déclare *« grandement stimulé »* par ces artistes qui prêchent, *« de façon parfaitement fanatique, qu'il ne faut rien peindre ni imaginer d'après la nature ».* Tandis qu'à New York, le MoMA présente trois de ses œuvres à l'exposition « Cubism and Abstract Art », à Paris ses peintures, certaines figuratives, sont montrées avec celles de Mucha au Jeu de Paume, musée des Écoles étrangères contemporaines. Recherché par les Allemands, Kupka passera la Seconde Guerre mondiale réfugié à Beaugency, dans la famille de son épouse. En 1946, une grande rétrospective est organisée à Prague. À Paris, il expose au Salon des Réalités nouvelles dont il deviendra président d'honneur en 1956. Il meurt l'année suivante. Malgré une rétrospective au Musée national d'art moderne en 1958 et l'importante donation de sa veuve au musée, c'est le début d'un long purgatoire. ■

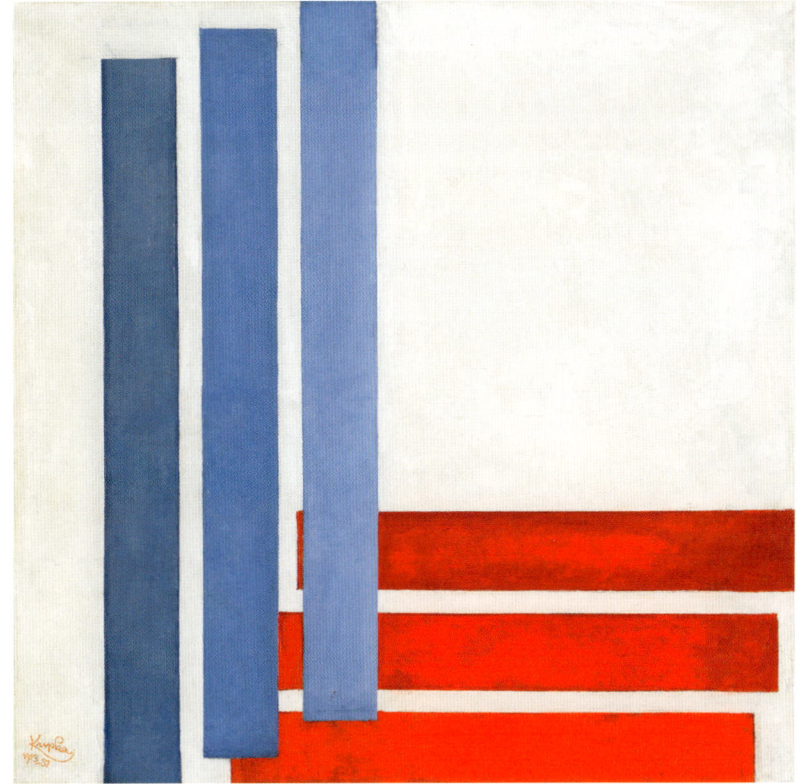

Ci-dessus : **Trois bleus et trois rouges** 1957, huile sur toile, 64 x 64 cm, Paris, Musée national d'art moderne, Centre Pompidou, Centre de création industrielle.

Page de droite : **Série C VI** 1935-1946, huile sur toile, 70 x 70 cm, Prague, Národní galerie v Praze, Galerie nationale.

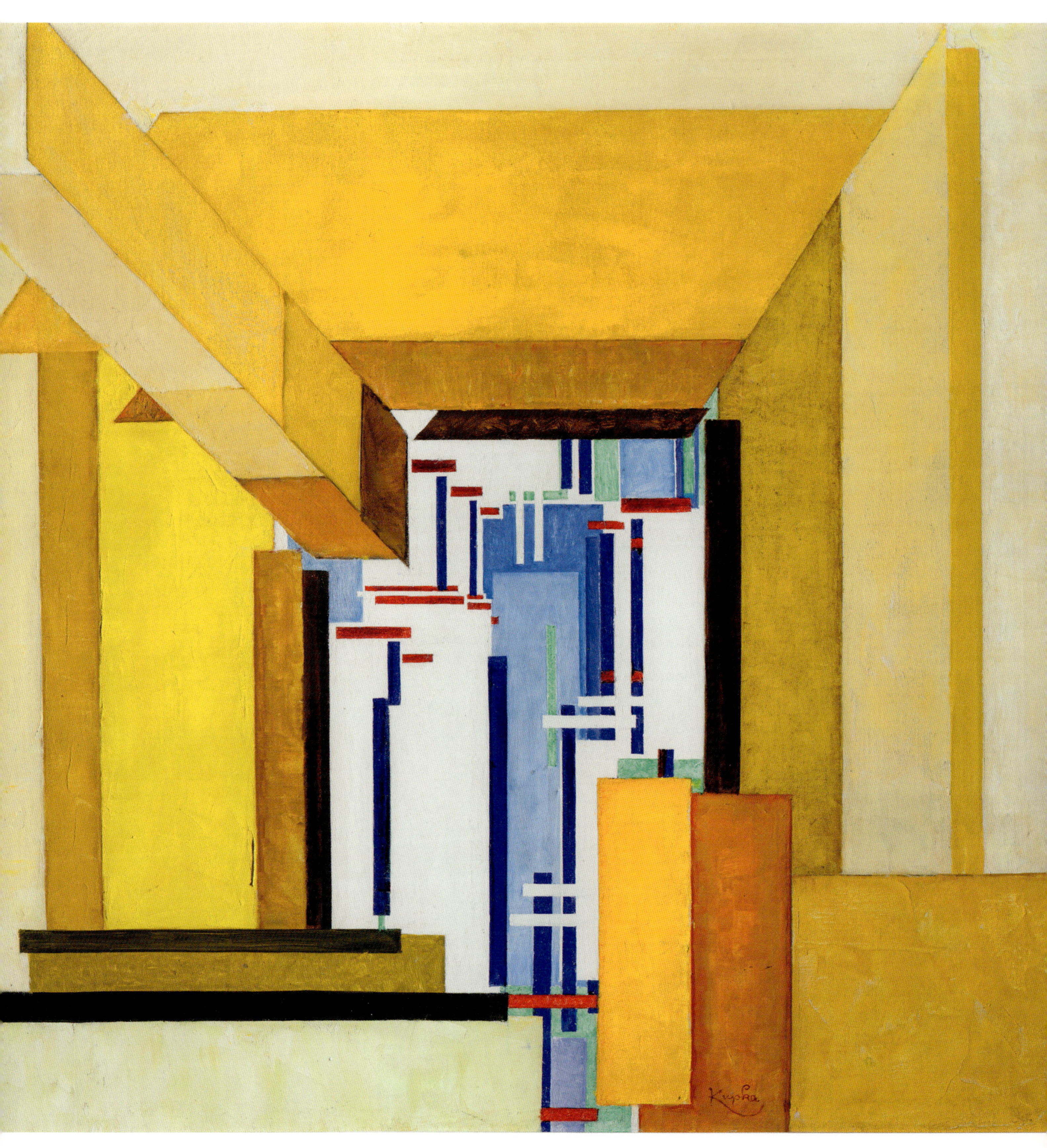
Kupka

CHRONOLGIE KUPKA

PAR CHARLOTTE PETITJEAN

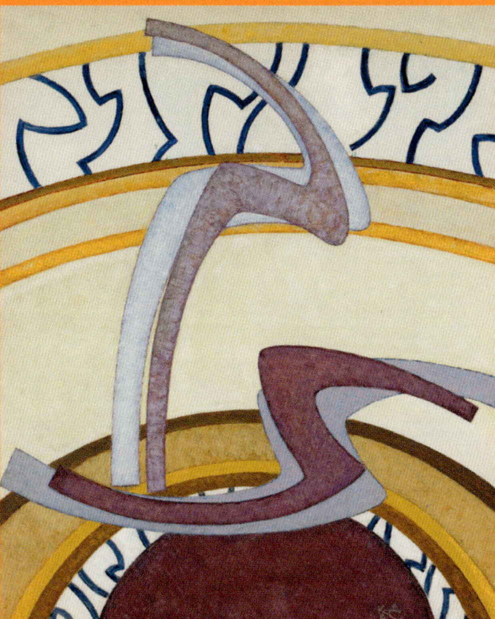

Construction n°II
1952-1953, 99 x 80 cm, New York, The Solomon R. Guggenheim Museum.

1871-1872

František Kupka naît le 22 septembre dans la ville d'Opočno, en République Tchèque (Bohême orientale). Il est l'aîné d'une fratrie de cinq enfants. La famille déménage à Dobruška en 1872. Kupka apprend à dessiner grâce à son père, clerc de notaire. Le jeune František a une santé fragile, il est souvent malade et gardera toute sa vie les séquelles de la petite vérole qu'il contracte à l'âge de trois ans.

1887-1889

Il quitte son foyer et voyage en Bohême du sud. On l'emploie comme broyeur de couleurs dans un atelier de Domažlice. En 1888, il intègre la classe préparatoire de l'École des beaux-arts de Prague et s'inscrit l'année suivante dans le cours de peinture historique et religieuse de František Sequens. Il donne des cours de dessin et devient médium pour gagner sa vie.

1891

Il obtient le diplôme de l'Académie de Prague.

1892

Il s'inscrit à l'École des beaux-arts de Vienne. Lectures d'ouvrages scientifiques, de traités de théosophies et d'occultisme.

1896

Il s'installe à Paris, au 83, boulevard de Clichy.

1899-1901

En mai, ses œuvres sont exposées pour la première fois à Paris par la Société nationale des beaux-arts. *Le Bibliomane* et deux dessins au fusain *(Les Copistes* et *La Pompe)* sont présentés. La même année, Kupka devient illustrateur pour plusieurs revues : *Der Tag* (Berlin), *Cocorico, La Plume.* Il réalise aussi des affiches pour les cabarets de Montmartre. En 1900, il participe à l'Exposition universelle, au Grand Palais, et expose dans la section réservée aux artistes autrichiens. Il reçoit une médaille d'argent pour *Les Fous.* En 1901, il s'installe au 57, rue Caulaincourt, où il aura comme voisin Jacques Villon, et réalise ses premiers dessins satiriques pour *L'Assiette au beurre.*

1904

Kupka participe à l'Exposition Universelle de Saint-Louis, aux États-Unis, avec l'envoi d'*Épona-ballade. Les joies,* qui lui vaut une médaille d'or. La même année, Élisée Reclus lui demande d'illustrer son encyclopédie historico-géographique *L'Homme et la Terre.*

1906

Jacques Villon et Kupka s'installent dans des maisons-ateliers à Puteaux, au 7, rue Lemaître. Raymond Duchamp-Villon les rejoindra l'année suivante. Le 7 décembre, Kukpa est nommé « membre correspondant » de l'Académie tchèque des arts et des sciences. Cette même année, il participe au Salon d'automne pour la première fois et y présente *Soleil d'automne*.

1909-1910

Le 20 févier, le *Manifeste du Futurisme* de Filippo Marinetti est publié à la une du *Figaro.* Cela influence Kupka qui entreprend alors des recherches picturales sur le mouvement. Il commence donc la série « Femme cueillant des fleurs ». En 1910, il épouse Eugénie Straub, rencontrée six ans auparavant.

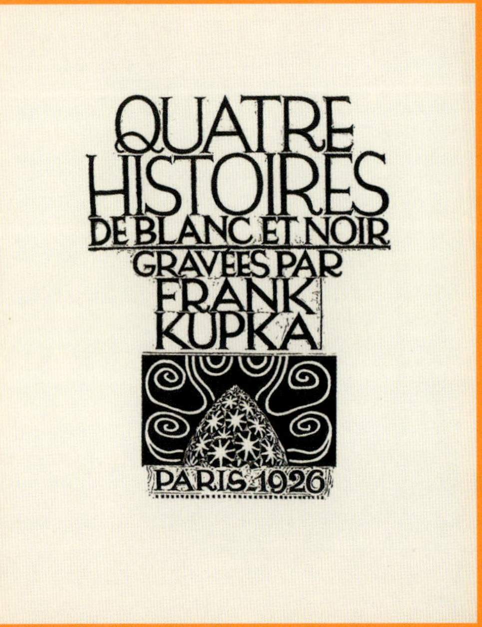

QUATRE HISTOIRES DE BLANC ET NOIR GRAVÉES PAR FRANK KUPKA

PARIS 1926

Quatre histoires de blanc et noir: Page de titre
Novembre 1926, 33 x 25,4 cm, Paris, Musée national d'art moderne, Centre Pompidou, Centre de création industrielle.

1914-1918

Il s'engage dans la Légion étrangère et part sur le front de la Somme aux côtés de Blaise Cendrars. Évacué pour des raisons de santé en 1915, il entreprend ensuite une activité de propagande visant à former une armée tchécoslovaque en France.

1922-1923

Kupka devient professeur aux Beaux-Arts de Paris. Il y enseigne la culture française aux étudiants boursiers d'origine tchèque. En 1923, il publie *La Création dans les arts plastiques.*

1926

Il publie à compte d'auteur *Quatre histoires de blanc et noir* et est nommé Officier de la Légion d'honneur en qualité de « professeur à l'École supérieure des beaux-arts de Prague ».

1932

Parution du premier numéro de la revue *Abstraction-Création art non figuratif* dans lequel Kupka publie un dessin géométrique.

1934

Il se sépare d'Abstraction-Création mais reste en contact avec ses membres.

1939-1944

Durant la Seconde Guerre mondiale, Kupka se réfugie dans le Loiret, à Beaugency, où sa femme a une maison.

1946

Il expose au premier Salon des Réalités nouvelles auquel il participera régulièrement par la suite. Une rétrospective est organisée à Prague et la République tchèque achète une quarantaine d'œuvres.

1951-1953

Kupka signe un accord avec le marchand d'art Louis Carré qui l'expose dans sa galerie new-yorkaise. Deux ans plus tard, le Salon des Réalités nouvelles lui rend hommage.

1957

Kupka meurt le 24 juin, à Puteaux, d'un cancer du poumon. Le Musée national d'art moderne organise l'année suivante une grande rétrospective en son honneur et acquiert plusieurs de ses tableaux.

Pithécanthropes
1902, gouache sur carton, 59,5 x 62 cm, Prague, galerie Zdeněk Sklenář.

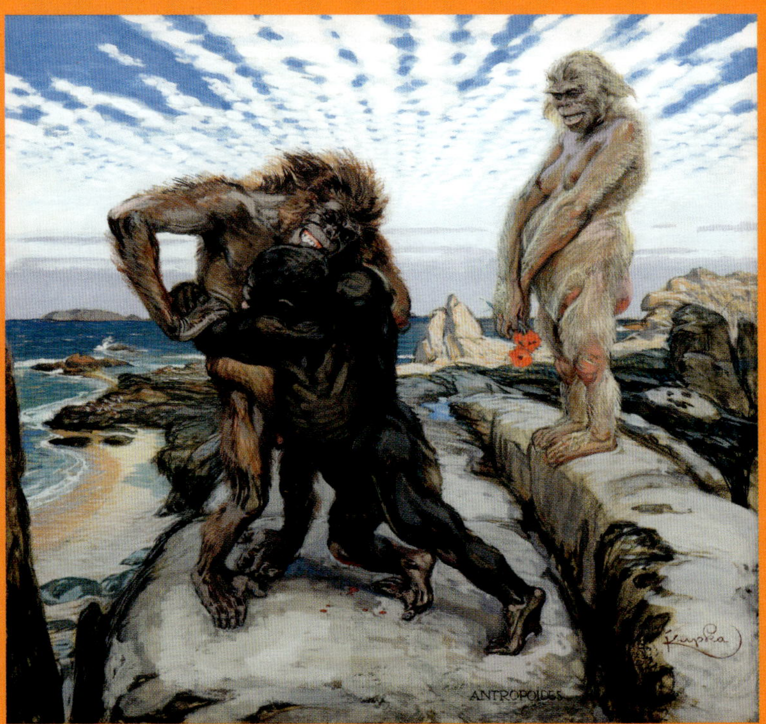

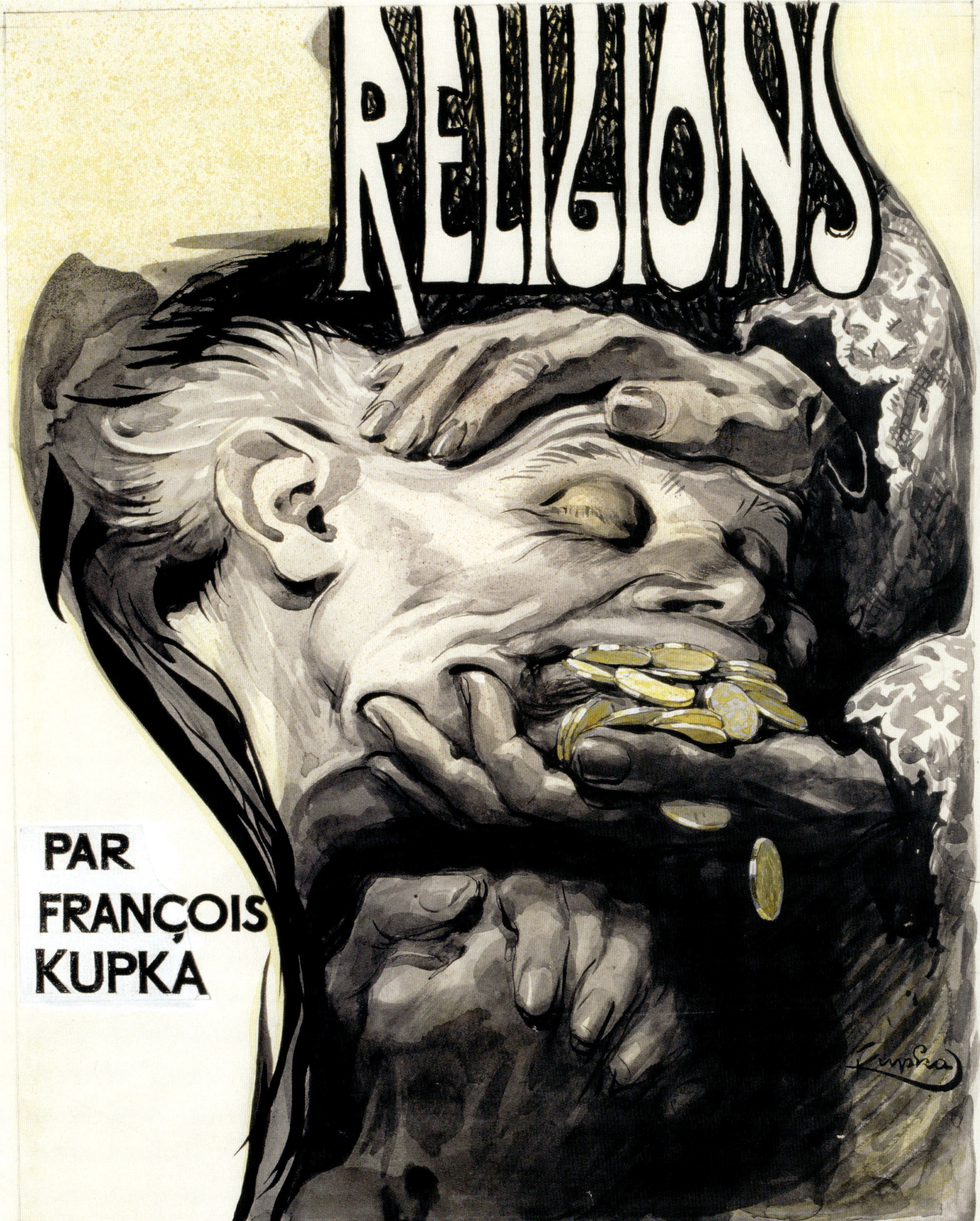
RELIGIONS
PAR
FRANÇOIS
KUPKA
Kupka

UNE PLUME AU VITRIOL

KUPKA

Installé à Paris, sans clients ni marchands, Kupka accepte les commandes de journaux et d'éditeurs. Ses convictions libertaires s'expriment dans des revues satiriques ou d'obédience anarchiste. De 1901 à 1907, il fustige notamment avec brio la rapacité du capitalisme dans *L'Assiette au beurre.*

PAR ANNICK COLONNA-CÉSARI

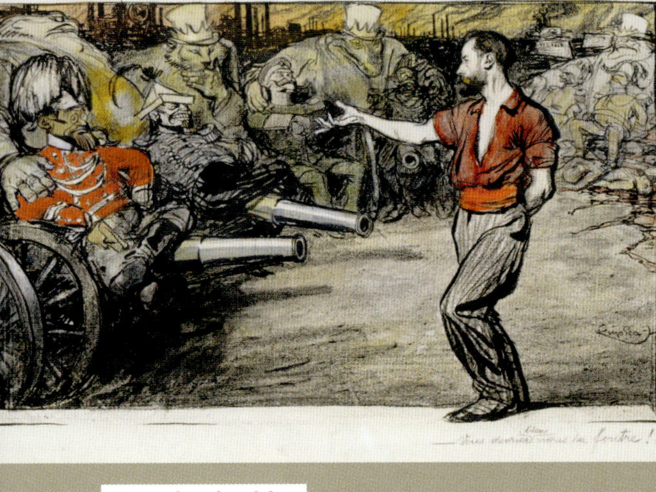

Vous devriez bien nous la foutre...
1904, encre de chine et aquarelle sur papier, 44,5 x 59,5 cm, Paris, musée d'Orsay.

On connaît le peintre, beaucoup moins le dessinateur. Peut-être parce que František Kupka a lui-même rétrospectivement déprécié son travail d'illustrateur de presse, le jugeant antinomique par rapport à sa mission d'artiste, sa véritable ambition. L'expression graphique a pourtant joué un rôle primordial au tournant du siècle, alors que, après ses études aux Beaux-Arts de Prague et de Vienne, il s'installe définitivement à Paris. À l'époque, ses tableaux n'ont pas encore basculé dans l'abstraction et restent empreints de symbolisme. Mais n'ayant *« ni clients ni marchands »*, comme le décrit Brigitte Leal, commissaire de l'exposition, il n'a d'autres moyens, pour subvenir à ses besoins et continuer à peindre, que d'accepter les commandes provenant de journaux, et plus tard, d'éditeurs de livres. C'est ainsi qu'il va exécuter jusqu'au début des années 1910 des centaines de dessins figuratifs, à l'encre, à la gouache ou à l'aquarelle, des gravures et des lithographies, dévoilant une facette inattendue de sa personnalité.

Page de gauche :
Religions
Couverture de *L'Assiette au Beurre*, n°162, 7 mai 1904, aquarelle, plume, crayon noir, encre, gouache, vélin, 57,2 x 42,8 cm, Paris, musée d'Orsay, conservé au musée du Louvre.

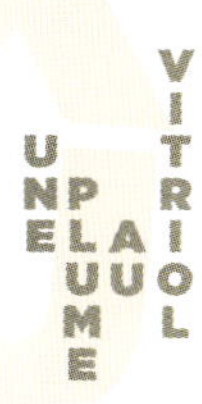

Balançoire que tout ça
1901, encre de Chine et aquarelle sur papier, 44,5 x 39,2 cm, Paris, musée d'Orsay.

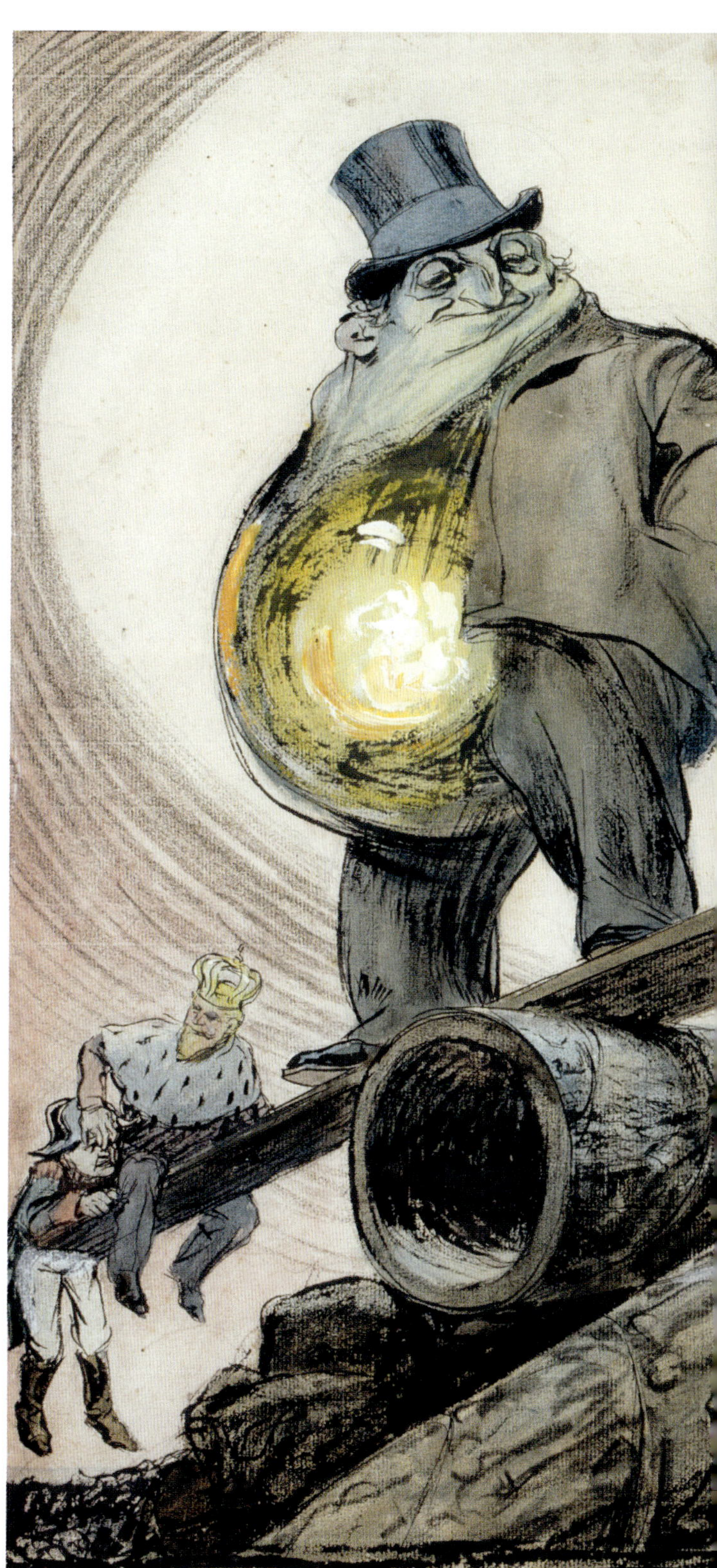

Est-ce son compatriote Alfons Mucha qui lui en a soufflé l'idée ? Sans doute. Quand ils se rencontrent, ce dernier réalise déjà des affiches pour les pièces de Sarah Bernhardt. Et Kupka, excellent dessinateur depuis l'enfance, suivra son exemple pour le compte des cabarets Le Chat noir et L'Âne Rouge. Il se prend d'autant plus au jeu que la fréquentation du cercle anarchiste montmartrois ravive ses convictions libertaires. Ce qui lui importe alors avant tout, c'est de témoigner de la réalité. Car *« Kupka est un artiste militant »,* affirme Brigitte Leal.

Satire et engagement

Alors que règne l'effervescence politique, les revues satiriques auxquelles il collabore lui offrent l'opportunité d'ausculter le monde moderne, se faisant l'écho de ses dérives, de ses vices et de ses folies. Et ceci sur tous les tons. Dans une veine satirique, humoristique, voire graveleuse, pour des publications telles que *Frou Frou, La Vie en rose, Cocorico, Le Cri de Paris, La Plume* ou *Le Rire,* mises en caricatures des travers bourgeois. De manière bien plus engagée, lorsqu'il s'agit de revues d'obédience anarchiste. Tout particulièrement *L'Assiette au beurre,* qui recevra également les contributions d'artistes tels que Félix Vallotton, Kees van Dongen, Juan Gris ou Jacques Villon. Kupka, lui, collabore à l'hebdomadaire dès sa création. De 1901 à 1907, il participe à treize de ses publications, dont trois lui sont entièrement confiées, ayant pour thème, « L'Argent », « Les Religions » et « La Paix ».

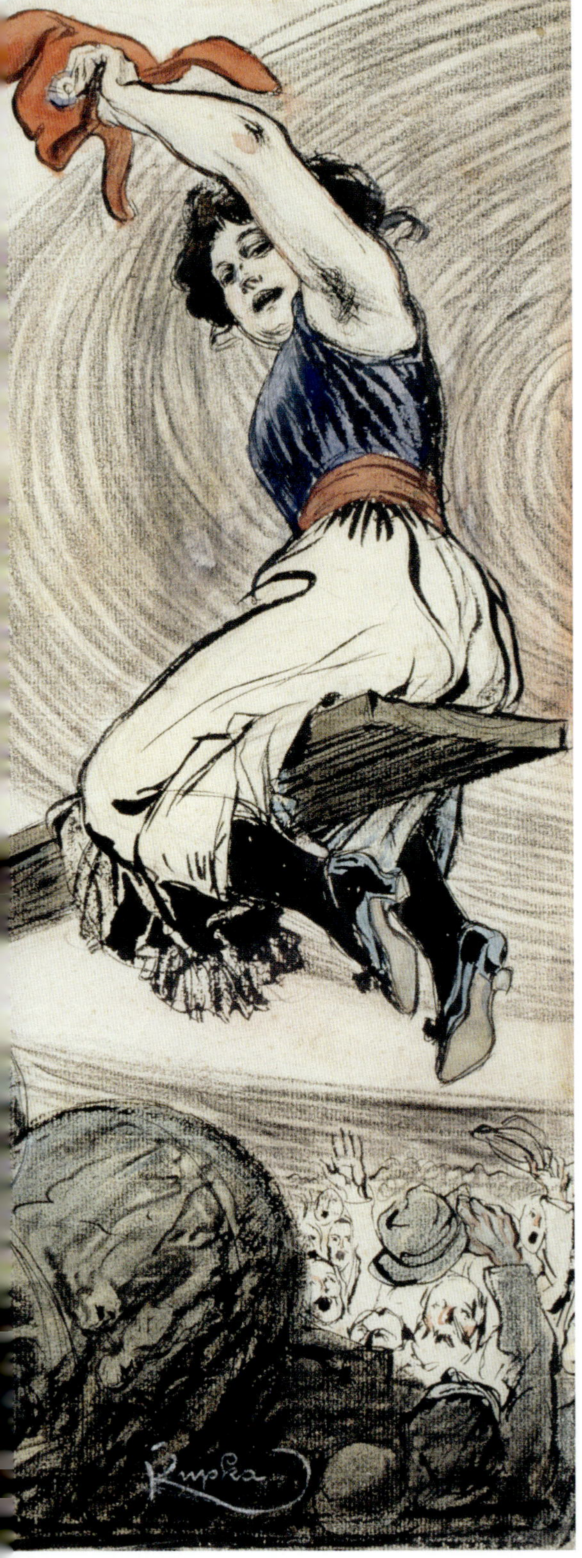

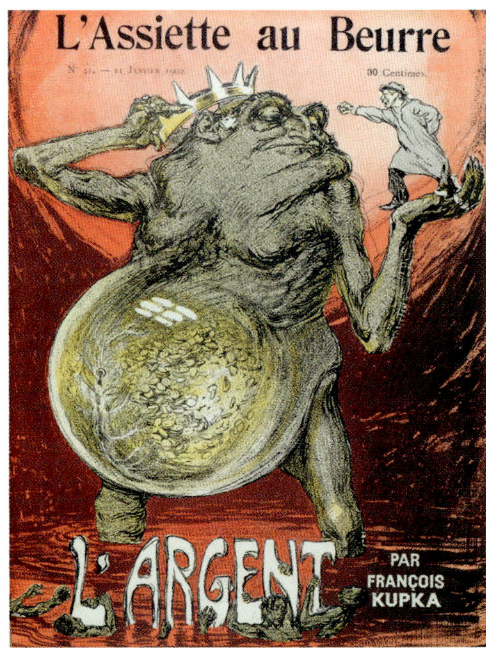

L'Argent
Couverture de *L'Assiette au Beurre,* 11 janvier 1902, lithographie, Paris, Bibliothèque historique de la Ville de Paris.

Ci-dessous :
L'Argent
1899, huile sur toile, 81 x 81 cm, Prague, Národní galerie v Praze, Galerie nationale.

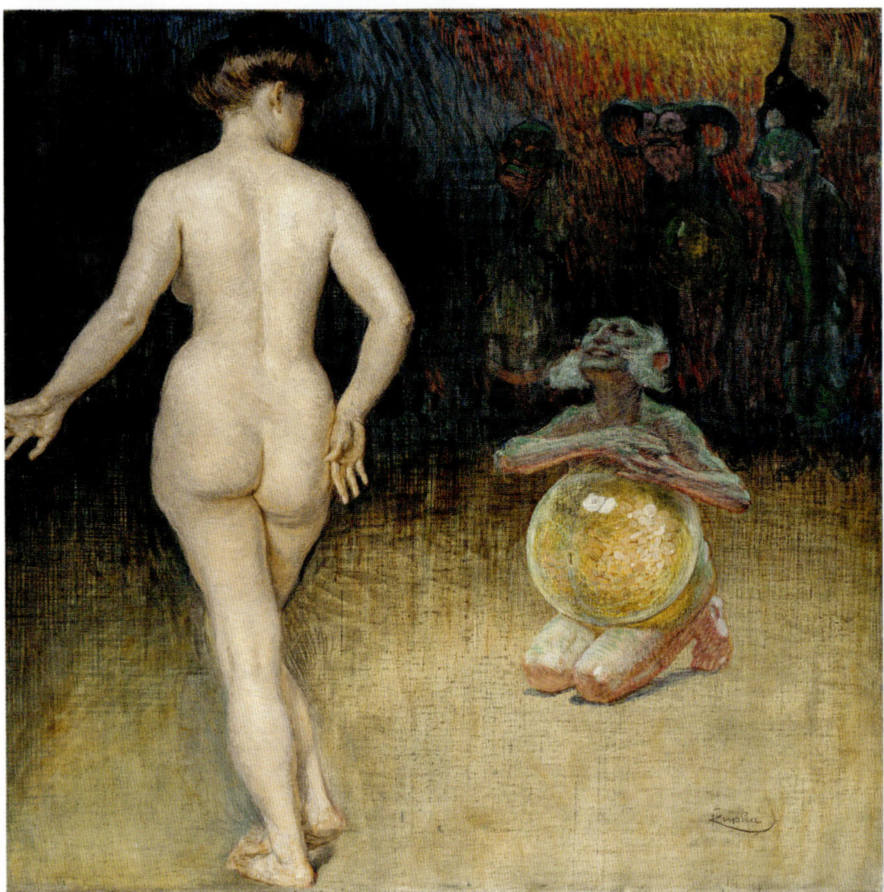

Plume et pinceau plongés dans le vitriol, le peintre tchèque, apparemment éloigné du mysticisme de ses débuts, fustige guerres coloniales, fureurs nationalistes et fanatismes religieux. Et s'insurge contre la corruption des pouvoirs, la rapacité du capitalisme exploiteur. À l'image de la couverture du numéro consacré à l'argent, sur laquelle s'étale un immonde bonhomme, au ventre explosant de pièces d'or (p. 27). C'est dans cet environnement qu'il tisse des liens avec le géographe-historien Élisée Reclus, figure du mouvement anarchiste. En 1904, ce dernier lui demande de travailler à sa monumentale entreprise : son encyclopédie, baptisée *L'Homme et la Terre*.

Féru de sciences, Kupka accepte le défi mais, bien que changeant de registre, il y déploie une vision de l'humanité dépourvue de complaisance, tout en sauvagerie et cruauté barbare. Il confirme d'ailleurs ses opinions en donnant en 1905 quelques dessins au journal anarchiste *Les Temps nouveaux*. L'un des plus percutants montre un ouvrier crucifié sur un engrenage géant. Cette même année, le nouveau propriétaire de *L'Assiette au beurre* met un terme à leur contrat, tout en continuant à publier ses caricatures jusqu'en 1907, date à laquelle Kupka, visiblement dépité, déclare à son propos : il *« ne veut que des dessins qui ne troublent pas les lecteurs. Je suis trop révolutionnaire »*. Sa réputation de dessinateur grandissant, il reçoit alors des commandes d'éditeurs, pour l'illustration de textes littéraires. Édulcorant son fiel, il s'attellera au *Cantique des Cantiques*, aux *Erynnies* de Leconte de Lisle, à la *Lysistrata* d'Aristophane ou encore au *Prométhée enchaîné* d'Eschyle.

Affiche publicitaire pour l'encyclopédie géohistorique *L'Homme et la Terre* d'Élisée Reclus
1905, lithographie, 135 x 95 cm, Paris, bibliothèque Forney.

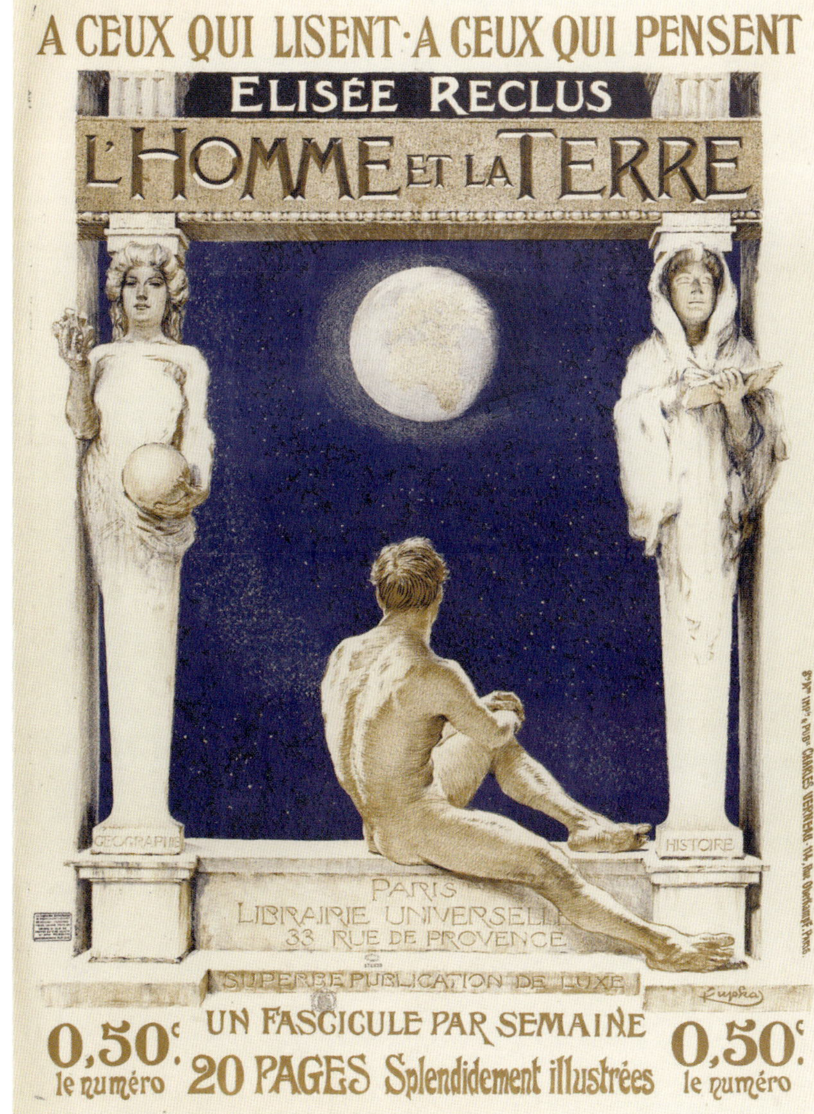

Désillusions

C'est à partir des années 1910 que le libertaire abandonne le dessin au profit de ses recherches picturales. *« Alors que le mouvement anarchiste s'essouffle, il se recentre sur son art, sans doute désillusionné »*, avance Pascal Rousseau, auteur de *Kukpa en 15 questions*, publié chez Hazan. Au cours de l'été 1912, il est amené à expliquer son choix à un journaliste tchèque. *« À cette occasion,* écrit dans le catalogue l'historienne d'art Markéta Theinhardt, *Kupka qualifie d'"antédiluviens" ses premiers travaux pour la presse, assurant qu'il ne compte pas revenir dessus, car ce serait déshonorant, tout en*

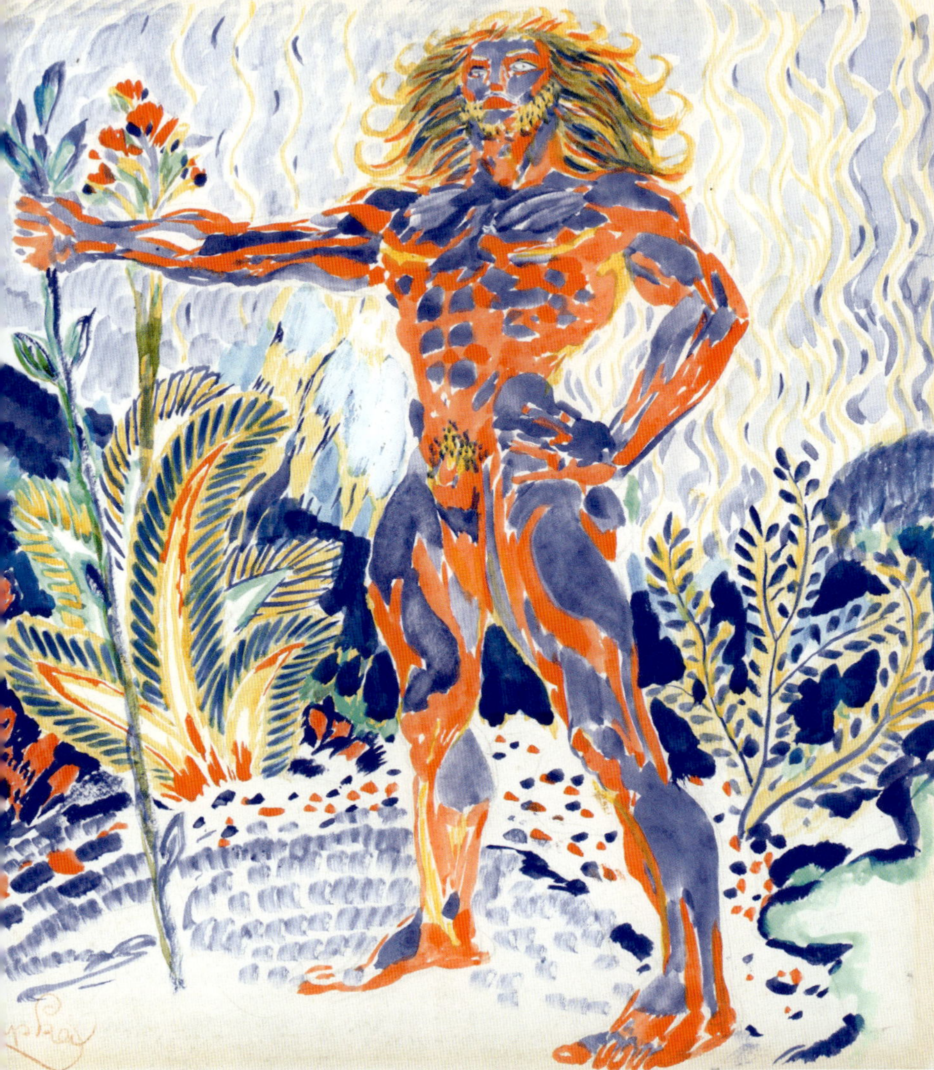

Prométhée bleu et rouge
1909-1910, dessin, 32,1 x 29,3 cm, Prague, Národní galerie v Praze, Galerie nationale.

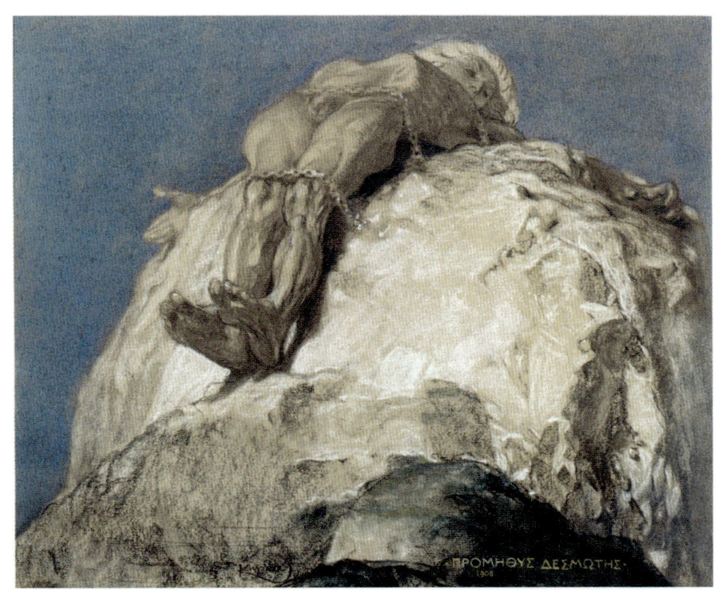

Prométhée enchaîné
1908, craie, fusain, pastel, 48 x 59 cm, Paris, Musée national d'art moderne, Centre Pompidou, Centre de création industrielle.

admettant reconnaître dans les œuvres du "nouveau" František Kupka, certains traits déjà présents dans ceux-ci.» «*Souvenez-vous,* déclare ce dernier à son interlocuteur, *de ses lignes de couleur et de lumière apparaissant si étrangement dans ses caricatures et dessins, fortuitement, comme amenées par le vent. C'est ici que se situent les débuts du Kupka d'aujourd'hui.*» Dans un texte manuscrit datant de la même époque, le peintre durcit son propos. Invoquant Pallas Athéna, déesse de la Sagesse et de l'Art, il lui demande de lui pardonner son «*méfait*», ajoutant: «*J'espérais pouvoir aider à aplanir les maux dont souffre la société et dont j'étais moi-même victime, par des dessins forcément tendancieux.*»

Selon Brigitte Leal, l'artiste tchèque n'a cependant pas renié ses convictions de jeunesse. En témoigne, assure-t-elle, son engagement dans la guerre de 1914: «*Bien qu'antimilitariste, il part comme volontaire sur le front de la Somme avec Blaise Cendrars, pour défendre le territoire français.*» Pendant la Seconde Guerre mondiale, il soutiendra par des bulletins et des manifestes la cause de la Tchécoslovaquie, occupée par les nazis. Kupka le peintre a sans doute voulu oublier le dessinateur, mais pas ses idéaux. ■

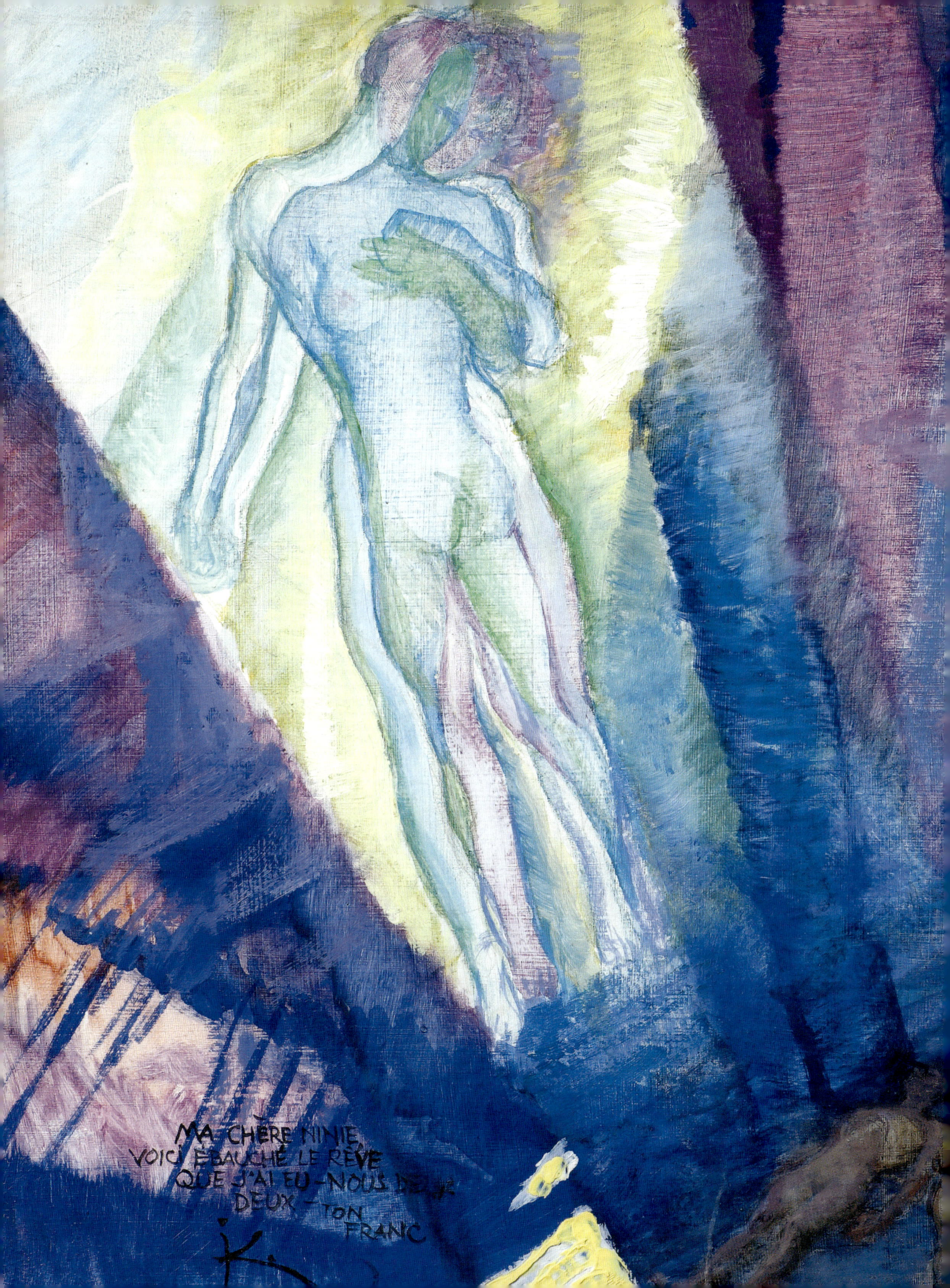
MA CHÈRE NINIE,
VOICI ÉBAUCHÉ LE RÊVE
QUE J'AI EU - NOUS
DEUX - TON
FRANC
K.

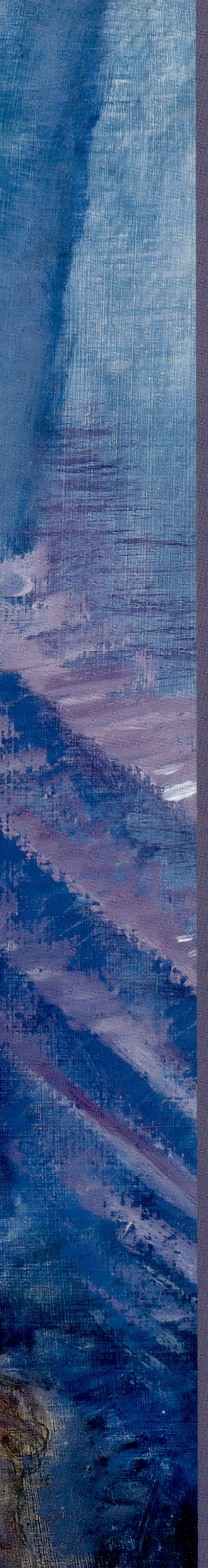

Le Rêve
Vers 1906, huile sur carton, 31,5 x 32 cm, Bochum, Kunstmuseum Bochum.

EXPLORER L'INVISIBLE

KUPKA

Rayons X, ondes électromagnétiques, radiotélégraphie, théories de la perception… nombre de découvertes et d'hypothèses scientifiques de la fin du XIXe siècle confortent Kupka dans son rejet de la peinture « rétinienne », fondée sur l'imitation du réel. Sa conception de l'œuvre d'art et du rôle de l'artiste-visionnaire doit aussi beaucoup au courant occultiste.

PAR MAGDA CHANSEL

L'œuvre abstraite de František Kupka résulte tout d'abord d'un constat, exposé de façon péremptoire dans *La Création dans les arts plastiques,* ouvrage théorique publié par le peintre en 1923. À l'instar de Duchamp, qu'il fréquente au sein du groupe de Puteaux à partir de 1911, Kupka y considère la peinture *« rétinienne »* comme révolue. Ce constat est nourri de multiples références. Féru d'occultisme et pratiquant le spiritisme, Kupka est convaincu de l'existence d'un monde au-delà du visible. La théosophie, notamment, lui fournit une conception de la création comme un tout pénétré d'une force vitale d'ordre spirituel dont l'homme, au travers de ses processus intellectuels et de ses état affectifs, n'est qu'une des manifestations. Il est également au fait des théories de la perception (physiologie des sensations, psychologie des formes et des couleurs, physique de la lumière et du son) qui ont bouleversé la compréhension du phénomène de la vision depuis 1800, en démontrant les limites de l'organe visuel dans la perception de la réalité, ainsi que le caractère éminemment subjectif du phénomène optique.

Plans par couleurs (Femme dans les triangles)
1910-1911, huile sur toile, 109 x 99,5 cm, Paris, Musée national d'art moderne, Centre Pompidou, Centre de création industrielle.

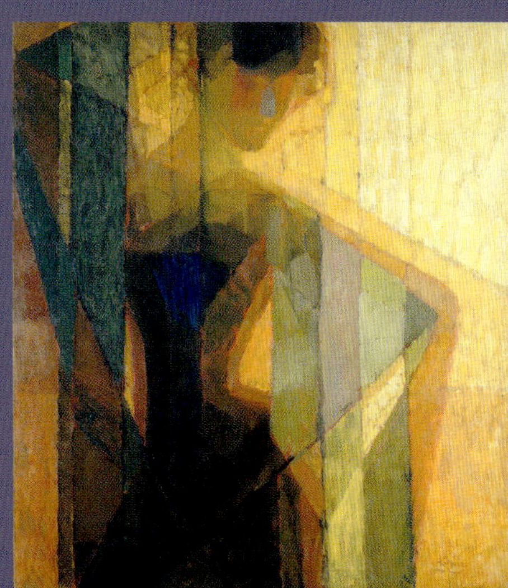

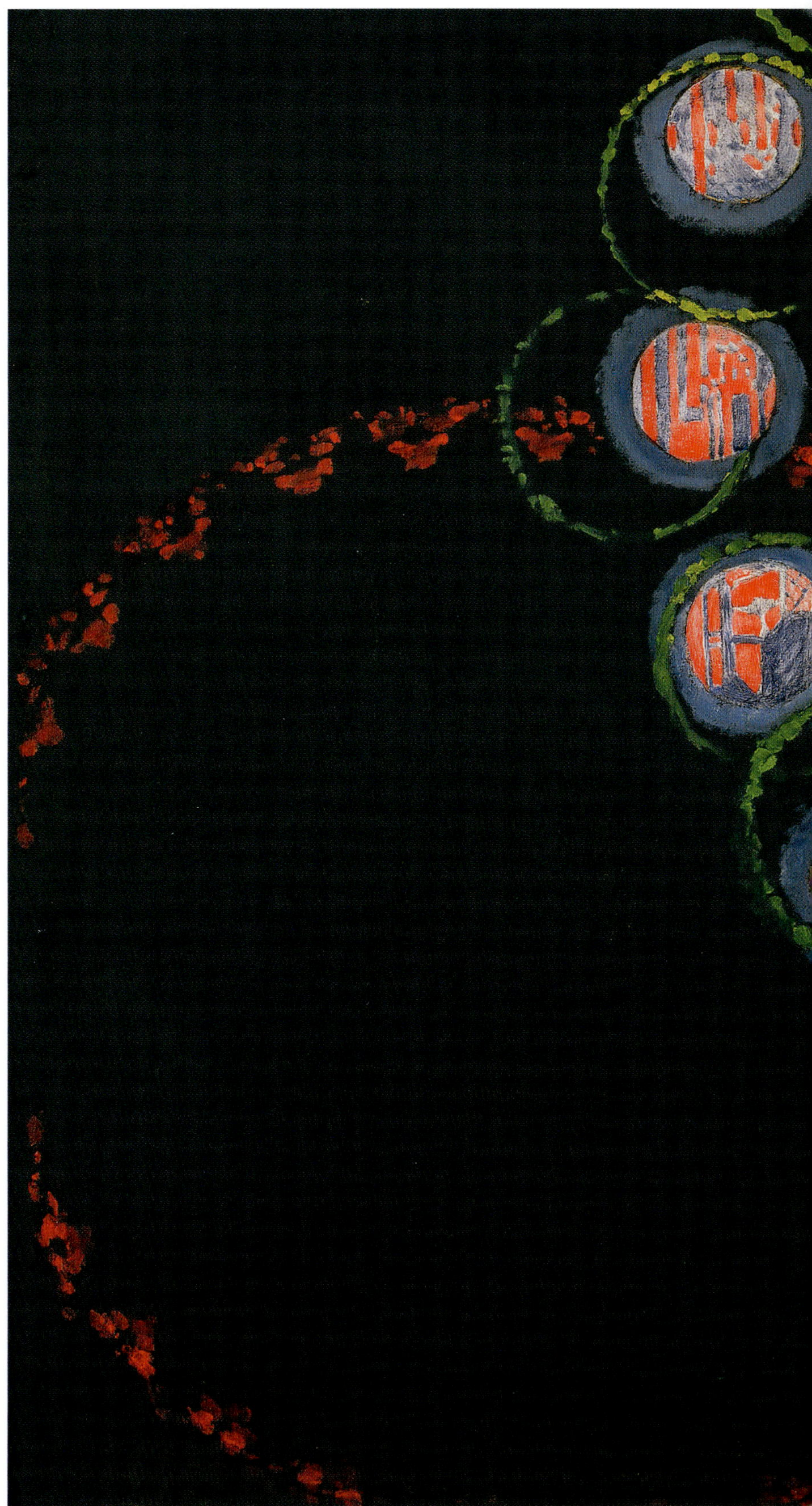

Le Premier pas
1910-1913,
huile sur toile,
83,2 x 129,6 cm,
New York, Museum of
Modern Art, MoMA.

Réfutant en bloc les esthétiques impressionniste, fauve, et même l'avant-garde de son temps – le cubisme, dans lequel il décèle *« l'espoir de sauver l'objet »* (Philippe Dagen, *F. Kupka, La Création dans les arts plastiques,* édition du Cercle d'art, 1989), Kupka se déclare un antiréaliste et entreprend de repenser la peinture en mettant d'abord en question son fondement depuis l'Antiquité : la *mimesis.* Il est conforté dans sa méfiance à l'égard de l'imitation par les découvertes et les hypothèses scientifiques majeures de la fin du XIXe siècle : rayons X, ondes électromagnétiques, radiotélégraphie, théories ondulatoires de manière générale, qui modifieront profondément la perception de la réalité et, surtout, feront de l'univers l'expression d'une grande vibration, dont son nouvel art s'efforcera de refléter les principes.

L'étude des sciences

À l'instar d'un Baudelaire, qui en 1863 incitait les peintres à trouver la part transitoire de la beauté dans la modernité, Kupka, au début des années 1910, exhorte les artistes à chercher dans l'étude des sciences un principe de validité pour la représentation de la réalité. Savoir manipuler des instruments modernes comme le microscope ou le télescope devient, selon lui, une condition *sine qua non* du métier de peintre. Abreuver la vision subjective de l'artiste aux sources de l'objectivité scientifique, faire se marier l'esprit analytique des temps modernes aux sciences occultes, voici l'objectif de cet artiste paradoxal qui *« refusera avec une assurance inébranlable toute distinction entre les perceptions des sens et les visions de*

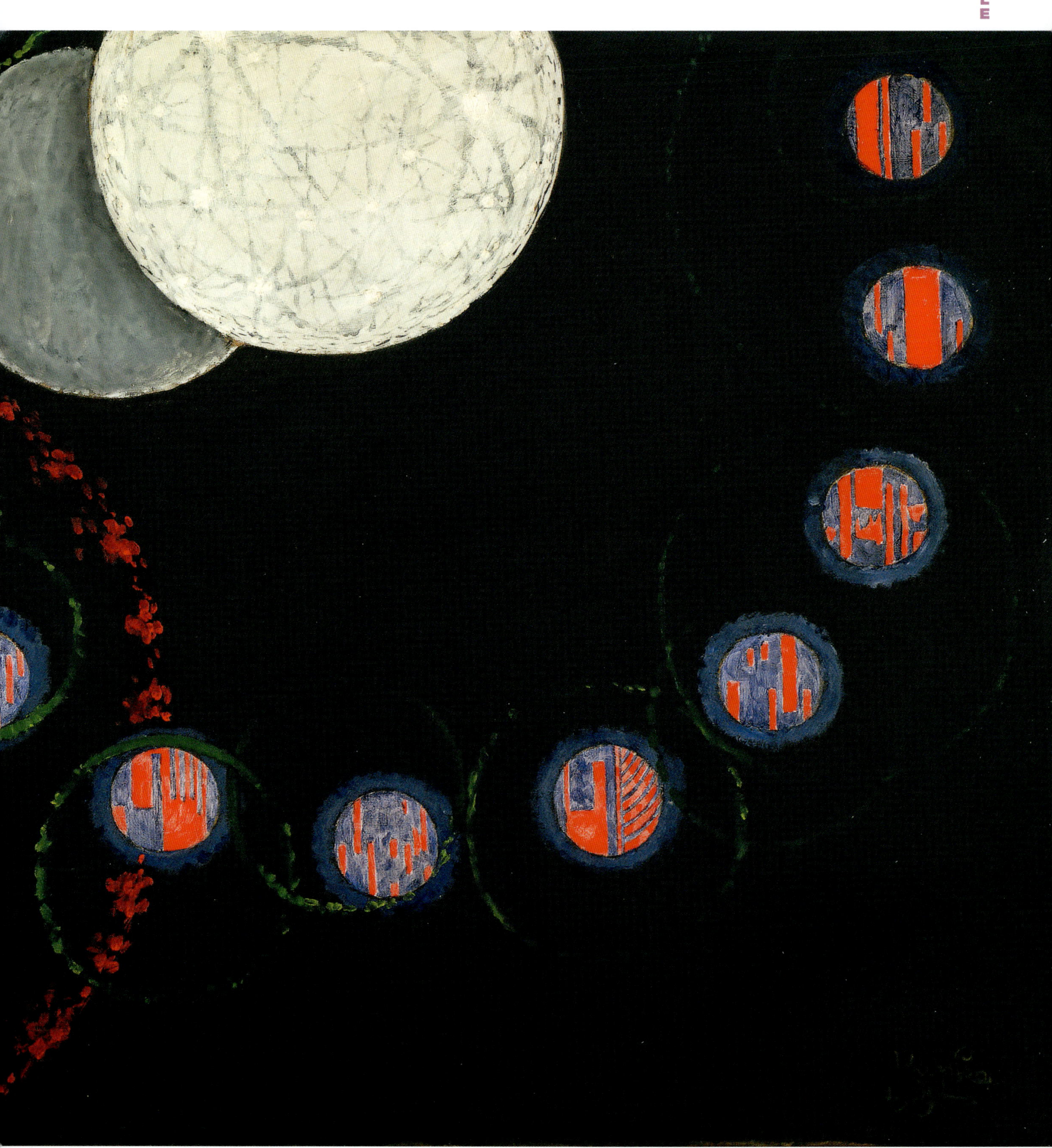

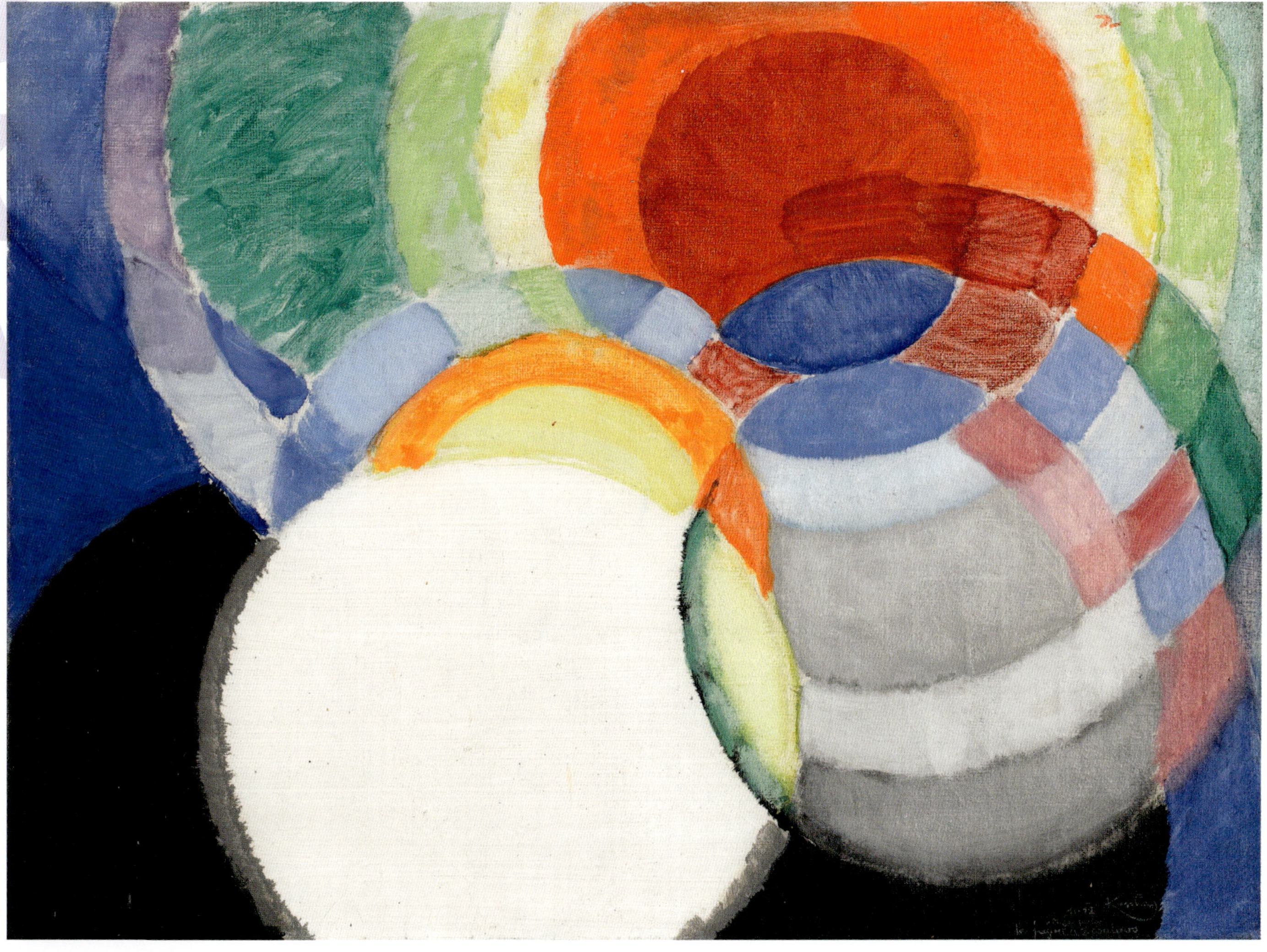

Disques de Newton Étude pour Fugue à deux couleurs
1911-1912, huile sur toile, 49,5 x 65 cm, Paris, Musée national d'art moderne, Centre Pompidou, Centre de création industrielle.

l'esprit » (M. Lamac, in catalogue de l'exposition « František Kupka, 1871-1957 », musée d'Art moderne de la Ville de Paris, 1989).

La conception du *Rêve,* tableau de petites dimensions que Kupka dédie à sa femme (p. 30), renvoie précisément à une vision onirique, mais son traitement formel rappelle incontestablement les clichés radiographiques. *« Ma chère Ninie, voici ébauché le rêve que j'ai eu – nous deux – deux / ton Franc »,* inscrit le peintre directement sur la toile, la répétition du mot *« deux »* évoquant déjà l'idée de dédoublement qui se joue dans la représentation. Une silhouette double donc, transparente – fusion des corps astraux des deux époux – flotte en apesanteur, au dessus des corps matériels dont elle s'est détachée. Elle semble avoir parcouru un grand espace, suggéré par l'étagement des trappes horizontales visibles à droite du tableau. La surface entière de cette toile est conçue com me une grande réverbération, tant par ses couleurs – des bleus, violets et jaunes qui varient en intensité et en tonalité –, que par ses formes – aplats verticaux ou horizontaux qui semblent se démultiplier à l'infini, reflétant le dédoublement initial des corps des deux époux.

Ce dédoublement, Kupka en parle encore dans une lettre adressée à son ami Arthur Roessler en 1897. *Le Premier pas,* œuvre de 1910, pourrait être la transcription visuelle de cette cor-

respondance (p. 32). *« Hier j'ai vécu un moment de dédoublement de conscience au cours duquel j'ai eu l'impression d'observer le globe terrestre de l'extérieur. J'étais dans l'immensité vide de l'espace et je voyais les planètes tourner tranquillement. »* Dédoublement de la conscience de l'artiste d'abord, du corps céleste blanc qui apparaît au centre de la peinture, des mouvements rotatifs mêmes des planètes qui tournent autour de cet astre blanc silencieux, autant de répétitions qui impriment à cette représentation un rythme inexorable, inscrit dans la durée, que Kupka arrive à capter de façon remarquable.

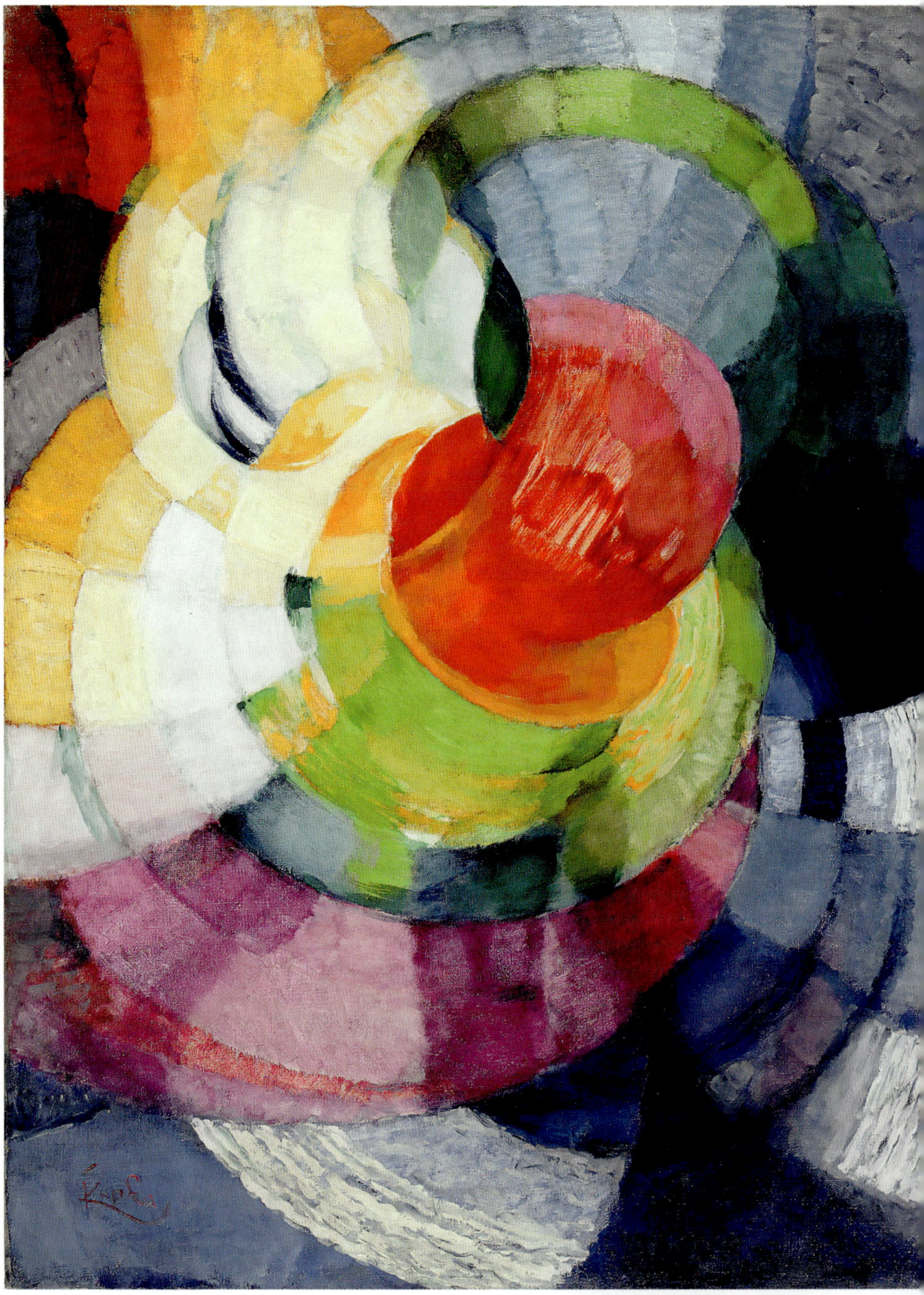

De l'importance des rayons X

Dans *Le Rêve,* le traitement en transparence de la silhouette fusionnée des deux époux évoque par ailleurs l'imagerie radiographique et la découverte des rayons X par Wilhelm Conrad Röntgen, en 1895. Cette découverte, suivie à la fin des années 1890 par celle de la télégraphie sans fil, *« contribue à généraliser la conscience d'une redéfinition radicale de la réalité, conçue désormais comme un espace empli d'ondes et d'oscillations électromagnétiques. »* (L. Henderson, in catalogue de l'exposition « František Kupka, 1871-1957 », op. cit.).
Les spiritualistes y trouvent leur compte, car ils y voient des ressemblances avec la photographie des esprits qui confortent leur doctrine. De même, la télégraphie sans fil stimule les expériences pseudo-scientifiques d'enregistrement et de transmission télépathique de la pensée.
Tout en se disant *« guéri de la transcendance »* après son arrivée à Paris en 1896, Kupka suit des cours de physique, physiologie et biologie à la Sorbonne qui l'amènent à se penser en véritable matérialiste. Mais il trouve paradoxalement dans les ouvrages ésotériques, notamment *Dans l'Invisible,* publié par Léon Denis en 1904, un vocabulaire et des images qui affinent sa propre conception de l'œuvre d'art et du rôle de l'artiste. Assimilant les photographies des esprits aux radiographies, Denis conçoit en effet la plaque photographique comme un *« regard ouvert sur l'invisible ».* Kupka compare l'esprit de l'artiste à *« un film ultrasensible,*

Disques de Newton
1912, huile sur toile,
100,3 x 73,7 cm, Philadelphie,
Philadelphia Museum of Art

capable de sentir (voir) les mondes inconnus dont les rythmes nous apparaitraient incompréhensibles. » Dans cette perspective, *Plans par couleur* (1909-1911, p. 31), construit également sur le principe d'un cliché radiographique, devient *« le film psychique »* sur lequel l'artiste-visionnaire dépose sa vision de l'invisible. La figure translucide, éclairée à contre-jour (notons le détail du nez nettement contrasté par rapport au reste du visage, trait typique des radiographies crâniennes), est inscrite dans un réseau vertical de larges aplats colorés, qui dictent la structure rythmique de la composition. Au-delà de la saisie transparente d'une forme matérielle, il s'agit là encore pour Kupka de capter sur la toile le mouvement, suggéré ici par la rotation subtile du buste féminin. La dématérialisation de la figure, obtenue par son

Printemps cosmique II
1911-1923,
huile sur toile,
115 x 125 cm,
Prague, Národní galerie v Praze,
Galerie nationale.

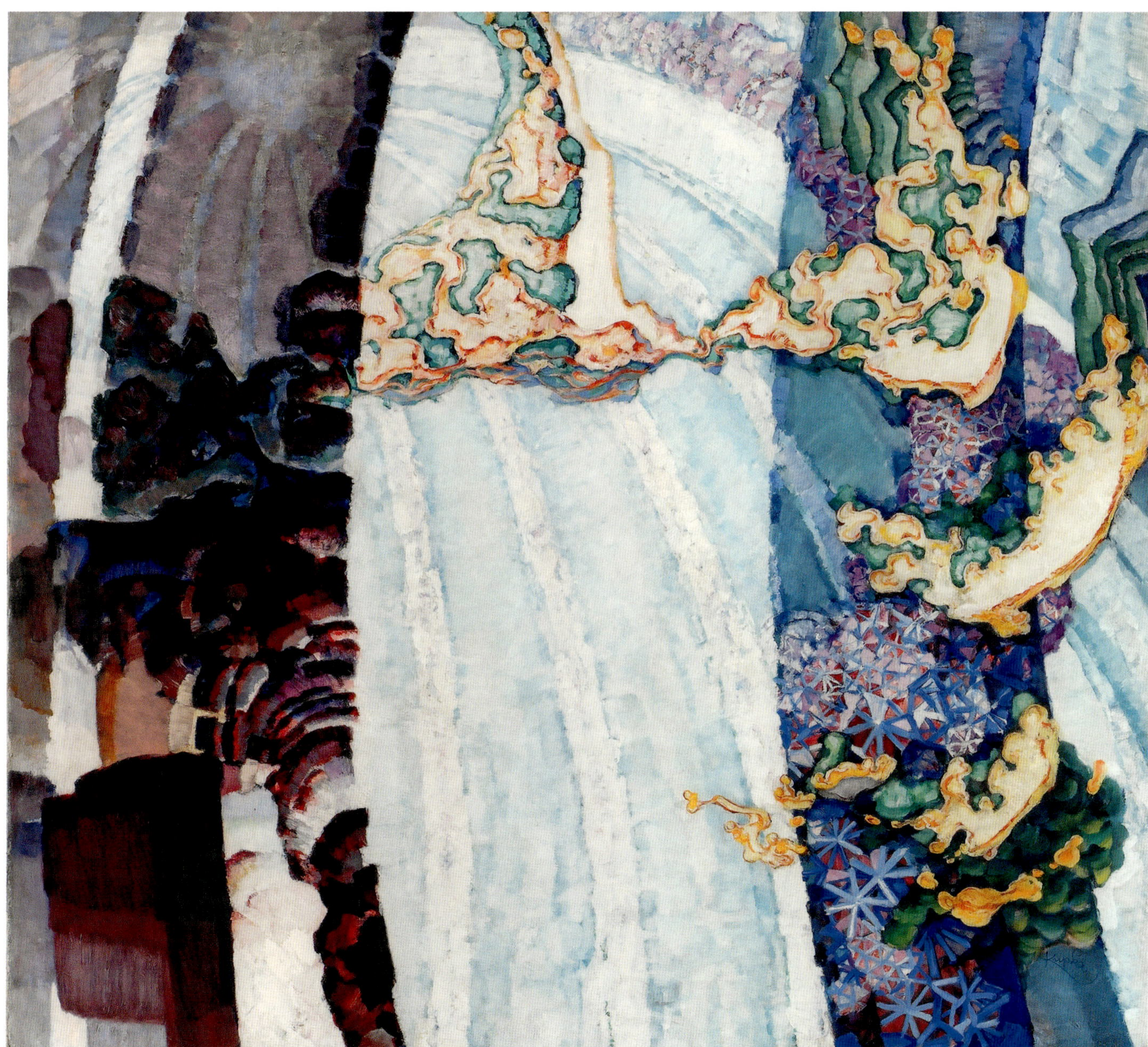

découpage en séquences, emprunte de façon explicite à la chronophotographie d'Étienne Jules Marey. C'est dans les clichés de ce physiologiste français que l'on parvient à capter l'invisible : en l'occurrence les étapes transitoires des mouvements, imperceptibles pour l'œil humain.

L'artiste télépathe

Mais si dans *Plans par couleurs,* la conception de l'artiste clairvoyant prévaut encore, dans les œuvres réalisées à partir de 1912, notamment dans les *Disques de Newton*, ce paradigme évolue. En se détournant du règne immatériel et transparent de la radiographie, Kupka s'oriente vers d'autres aspects de l'électromagnétisme. L'accent porte désormais sur la notion de télépathie, entendue à l'époque comme un phénomène électromagnétique. Selon Kupka, l'artiste émet des ondes télépathiques qu'il transmet directement à l'esprit du spectateur par l'intermédiaire de l'œuvre d'art. (L. Henderson, in catalogue de l'exposition « František Kupka, 1871-1957 », op. cit.) Celle ci devient alors le lieu d'une abstraction chromatique pure, génératrice d'ondes de lumière colorée, censées se réverbérer directement dans l'esprit du public. Désormais, c'est l'œuvre d'art qui, loin de se contenter de rendre visible l'invisible, se conçoit elle-même sur le modèle de la nature, en retranscrivant la pulsation du monde au moyen des propriétés électromagnétiques de la couleur. En fait, les *Disques de Newton* illustrent fidèlement le spectre coloré et le mouvement généré par la vitesse de vibration de chaque couleur.

Poussant encore plus loin l'analogie entre nature et création artistique, avec des œuvres comme *Printemps cosmique I* et *II,* Kupka déploie la vibration du monde à l'échelle de la toile. Dans cette vibration s'inscrit l'origine de la matière vivante, du règne minéral aux formes organiques et à la conscience de l'homme, dont le rythme et les formes deviennent ceux de l'œuvre. L'artiste télépathe serait doté d'une forme de superconscience qui le rend apte à percevoir cette vibration et à la répercuter.

Fantaisie physiologique, une gravure sur bois présente dans l'édition tchèque de *La Création dans les arts plastiques,* en est l'illustration : pinceau à la main, le peintre se définit moins par son instrument traditionnel que par un système nerveux qui produit des étincelles se propageant en ondes électromagnétiques, à travers l'éther, vers d'autres consciences. Kupka pousse ici le principe de l'exploration de l'invisible à ses limites. L'artiste télépathe peut se passer du support matériel de son art et communiquer directement à son public sa vision de la création. Il devient alors un médium, paradoxe ultime pour un peintre nourri au positivisme du tournant du XXe siècle. ■

Localisations de mobiles graphiques I, 1912-1913, huile sur toile, 300 x 194 cm, Madrid, musée Thyssen-Bornemisza.

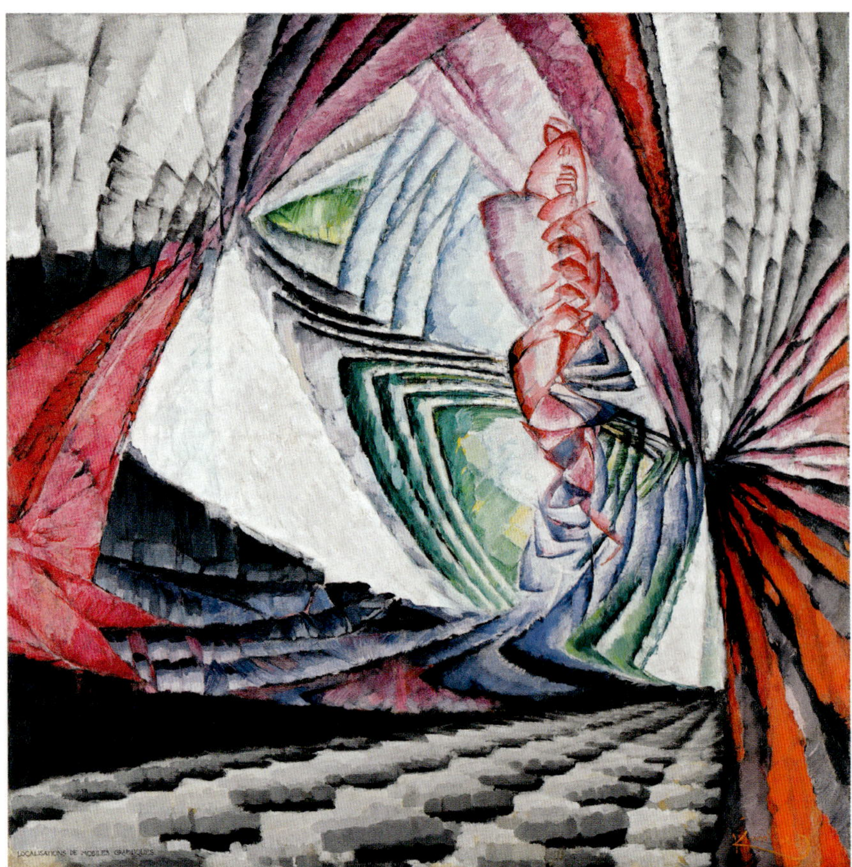

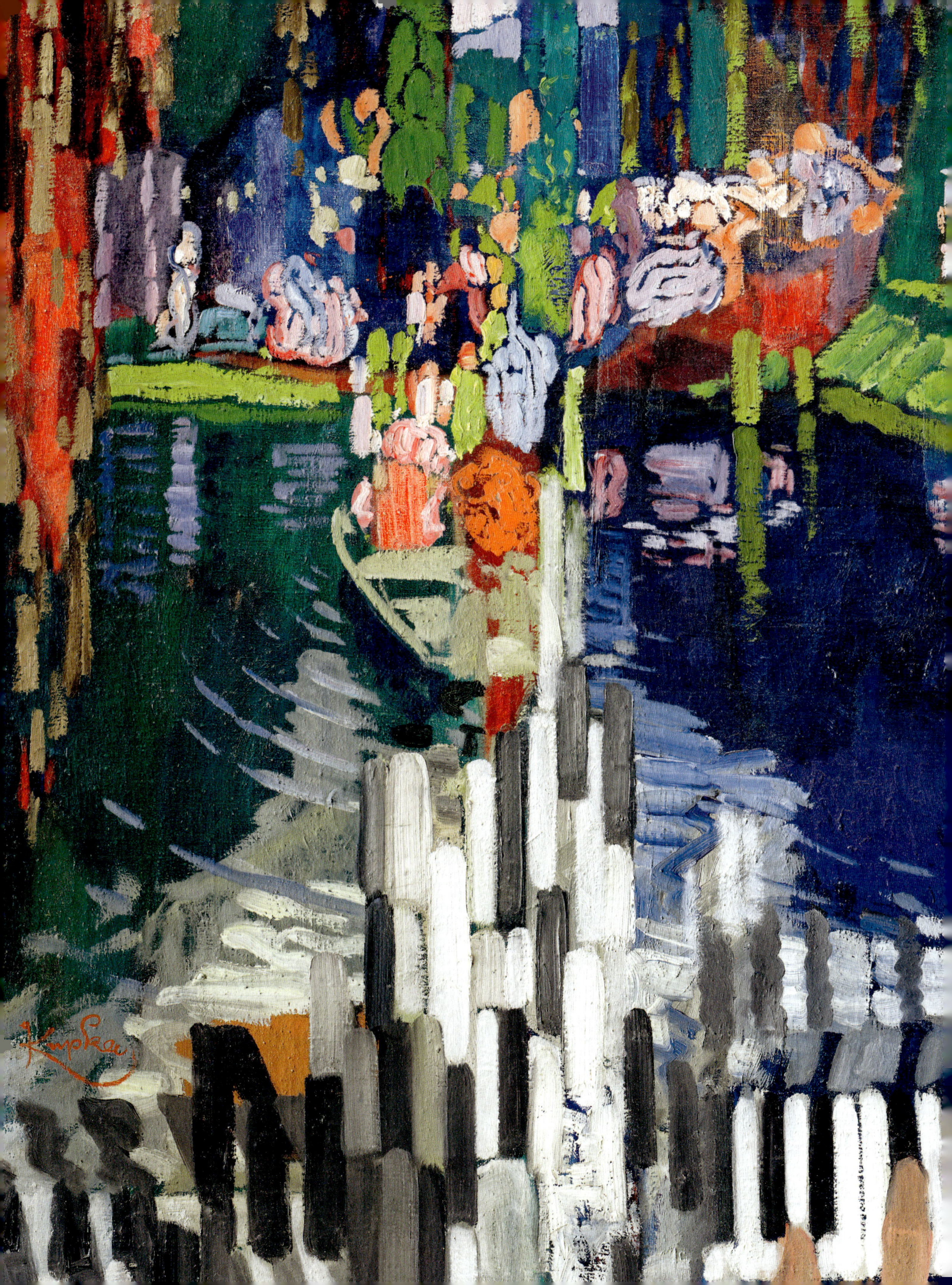

Les Touches de piano. Le Lac
1909, huile sur toile, 79 x 72 cm, Prague, Národní galerie v Praze, Galerie nationale.

LES COULEURS ET LES SONS

KUPKA

À l'instar d'autres pionniers de l'avant-garde, voulant s'affranchir du mimétisme pictural, Kupka se tourne vers la musique, art immatériel par excellence. Il conçoit ses toiles à la manière de symphonies chromatiques, y transposant parfois le modèle structurel de la fugue ou y transmettant le tempo du jazz.

PAR ANNICK COLONNA-CÉSARI

Interviewé à Paris par un envoyé spécial du *New York Times*, František Kupka déclarait en 1913 : « *Je tâtonne toujours dans l'obscurité, mais je crois pouvoir trouver quelque chose entre la vue et l'ouïe et je peux créer une figure en couleurs comme Bach l'a fait en musique. À ces conditions, je ne saurais plus me contenter d'une copie servile.* »
Un an plus tôt, l'artiste tchèque avait exposé, au Salon d'Automne, des œuvres pour la première fois résolument abstraites, composées d'entrelacs de formes circulaires, *Amorpha. Fugue en deux couleurs* et *Amorpha. Chromatique chaude,* inspirées des fugues du Cantor de Leipzig (p. 40-41). Si leurs anneaux concentriques dépourvus de sujet déclenchent l'ironie de la critique, elles s'inscrivent dans la sensibilité de l'époque. Au moment où la peinture se libère du joug de la représentation, certains pionniers de l'avant-garde, tels Vassily Kandinsky, Paul Klee ou Piet Mondrian, se tournent, à l'instar de Kupka, vers la musique, art immatériel par excellence, qui leur fournit de nouveaux principes de composition. Cette tendance s'ancre dans le vague synesthésiste

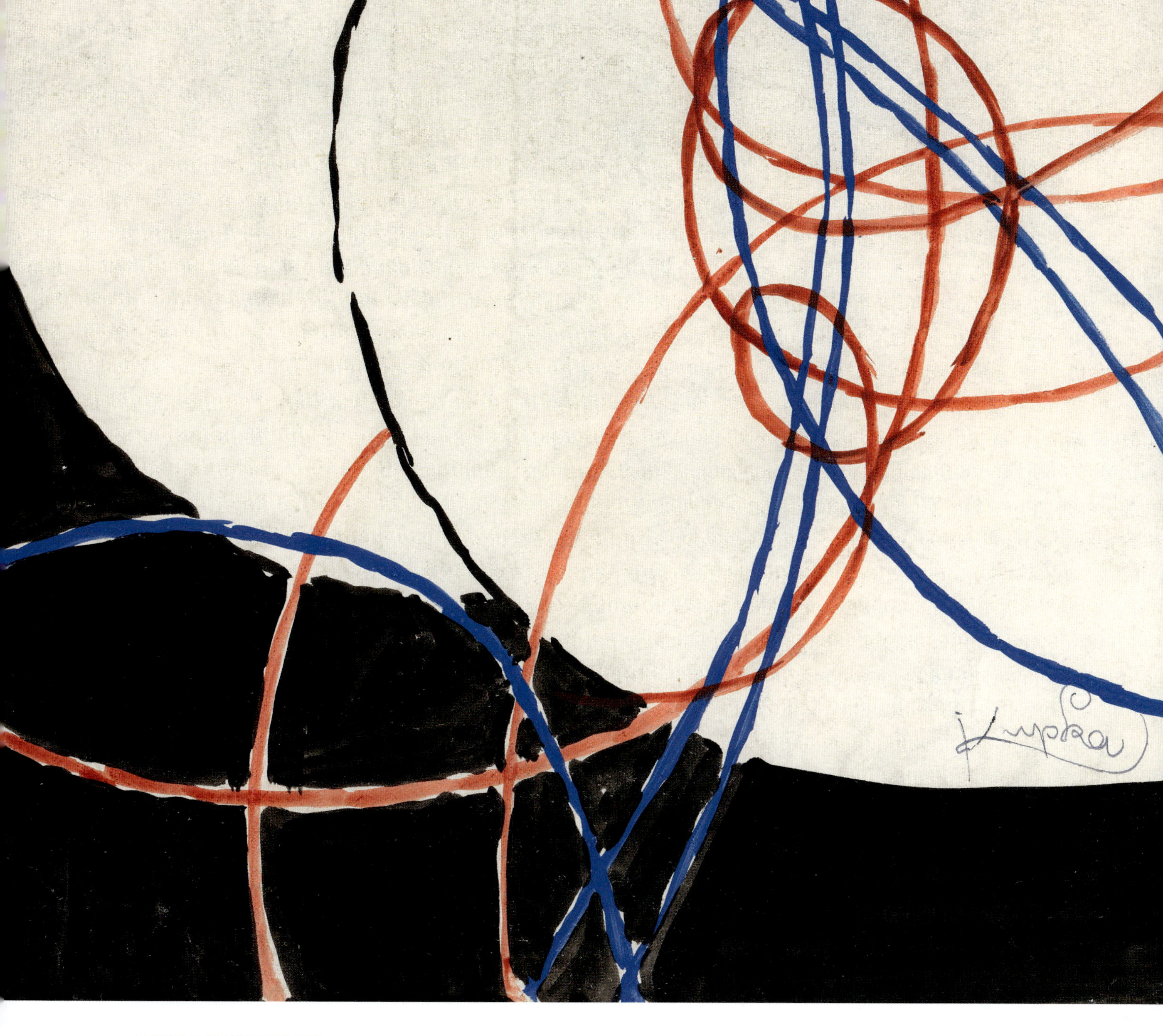

Étude pour Amorpha. Fugue à deux couleurs
1912, gouache et encre sur papier, 21 x 22,4 cm, New York, Museum of Modern Art, MoMA.

lancée au siècle précédent par les Romantiques. *« Les parfums, les couleurs et les sons se répondent »,* avait énoncé Baudelaire dans son célèbre poème *Correspondances.* La perspective de ces analogies sensorielles enthousiasme la génération symboliste et incite les peintres abstraits à concevoir leurs toiles à la manière de symphonies chromatiques. Dès 1909, elles avaient soufflé à Kupka un étrange tableau, intitulé *Les Touches de piano. Le lac* (p. 38) Au premier plan, on distingue les doigts d'un pianiste, posés sur des touches noires et blanches, d'où s'élèvent des sortes de sons colorés, qui prennent la forme de petits personnages se promenant en barque sur le lac. À moitié figurative, l'œuvre, constituée pour partie de plans verticaux, annonçait en fait le glissement de l'artiste vers l'abstraction. Dans *Nocturne,* réalisé dès l'année suivante, les sujets ont disparu. Ne restent que des touches verticales, évoquant un clavier, l'ensemble flottant dans l'obscurité bleutée de la nuit. Dorénavant, par ses titres, ses sujets, ses formes et ses couleurs, sa peinture renverra à la musique, *« et ceci toute sa carrière durant »,* affirme Brigitte Leal,

commissaire de l'exposition. *« Ce goût lui vient de son éducation viennoise »,* poursuit cette dernière. Contrairement à Kandinsky et à Klee qui pratiquaient le piano (et même le violon, pour le premier), lui ne joue pas d'un instrument, pas plus qu'il ne cherchera à réaliser des décors d'opéra ou à collaborer avec les Ballets russes, comme le feront Robert et Sonia Delaunay.

Des expériences multisensorielles

Hostile aux embrigadements, il n'adhère pas non plus totalement aux concepts synesthésistes, trop subjectifs à ses yeux, allant jusqu'à les qualifier d'*« illusion »* dans son traité esthétique, *La Création dans les arts plastiques. « Ce sont surtout les sciences qui l'ont amené à la musique »,* analyse Pascal Rousseau, auteur de l'ouvrage *František Kupka en 15 questions,* publié chez Hazan. De la même façon que le peintre, dans sa quête de compréhension du monde, s'intéressait aux rayons X ou à la chronophotographie, il se délecte des expériences multisensorielles d'Isaac Newton, se passionne autant pour les théories ondulatoires qui rapprochent le son et la lumière que pour les théories de la musique. En particulier celles de son professeur et compatriote, Eduard Hanslick, qu'il côtoie durant son séjour à Vienne. *« Une rencontre cruciale »,* d'après Pascal Rousseau.

En effet, explique l'historien d'art, *« Hanslick défend l'idée d'une "musique pure" se construisant, en dehors du réel, à partir de ses propres constituantes que sont les notes ».* Suivant un cheminement identique, Kupka expérimentera une peinture résultant de l'unique jeu des lignes et des couleurs, affranchi de tout mimétisme. C'est grâce à son ami, le compositeur et pianiste allemand Walter Morse Rummell, installé à Paris, qu'il découvre les compositions de Bach. *« À la fois scandées, répétitives et sophistiquées, elles l'ont profondément influencé »,* poursuit Brigitte Leal. Aux sons, Kupka cherche des équivalents

Au-dessus :
Étude pour Amorpha. Fugue à deux couleurs
1912, gouache et encre sur papier, 21,6 x 22,9 cm, New York, Museum of Modern Art, MoMA.

Au-dessous :
Étude pour Amorpha. Fugue à deux couleurs
1912, gouache et encre sur papier, 21,3 x 22,8 cm, New York, Museum of Modern Art, MoMA.

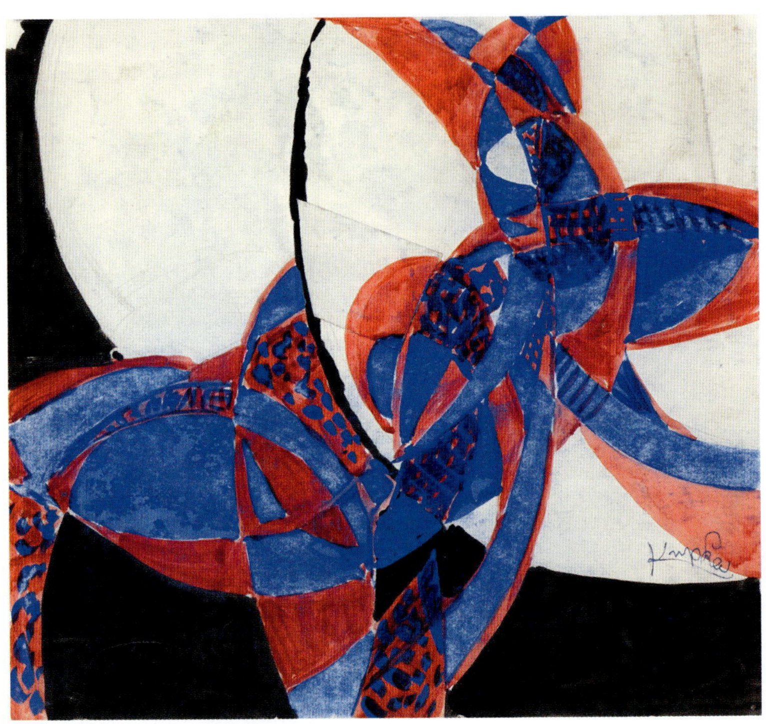

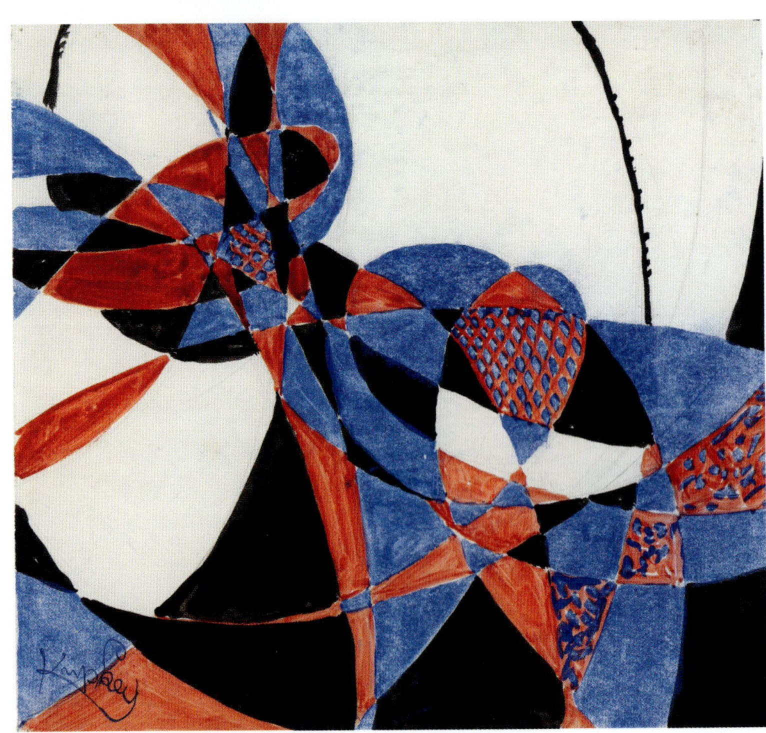

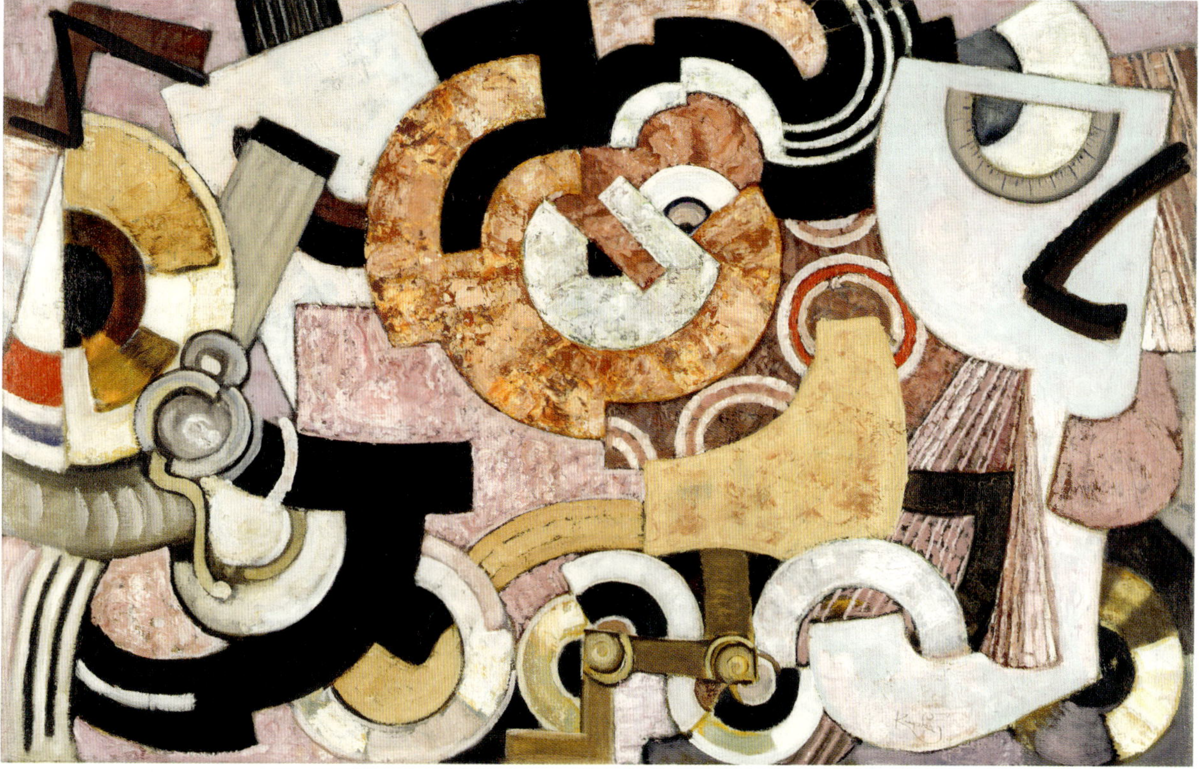

Jazz-Hot n°I
1935, huile sur toile, 60 x 92 cm, Paris, Musée national d'art moderne, Centre Pompidou, Centre de création industrielle.

Page de droite :
Musique
Détail, 1930-1932, huile sur toile, 85 x 93 cm, Paris, Musée national d'art moderne, Centre Pompidou, Centre de création industrielle.

plastiques, les rythmes colorés faisant écho à ceux de la musique. Et transpose sur la toile le modèle structurel de la fugue, véritable absolu artistique, selon lui, au même titre qu'une *« colonne dorique ».*

Au rythme du jazz et des moteurs

Son évolution esthétique prend une tournure inattendue dans la décennie 1920. Kupka délaisse alors le modèle de la peinture pure, qui avait présidé à la création d'*Amorpha.* Et, porté par le souffle de la modernité, entame un travail inspiré des machines industrielles. *« La rupture stylistique ne remet pas en cause ses préoccupations initiales »,* estime pourtant Arnaud Pierre, dans le catalogue de l'exposition. Car Kupka n'en reconduit pas moins le parallèle entre peinture et musique, entre phénomène visuels et acoustiques, comme l'illustre *Musique,* tableau qui sous forme d'un enchevêtrement d'organes métalliques, évoque le *« concert des forces mécaniques en mouvement ».* Dans ces mêmes années, Kupka découvre le jazz, dont il transmet le tempo à travers ses toiles *Jazz-Hot* et *Bock syncopé.* La rupture, là encore, n'est pas aussi flagrante qu'il y paraît, ainsi que l'expliquait déjà en 1925 le critique Hugues Panassié : *« Le jazz ressemble surtout au Bach des fugues, des concertos brandebourgeois. Ici et là, nous avons une ligne mélodique qui se développe sur un rythme immuable. »* Dans l'entre-deux-guerres, l'artiste en viendra à fusionner les deux univers, associant les rythmes du jazz à ceux des moteurs, *« transmission des aspects sonores et visuels propres à la modernité technique et industrielle »,* résume Arnaud Pierre. Et la musique continuera de l'accompagner, jusque dans ses œuvres ultimes. Certaines, constituées de plans colorés, semblent réactiver, sur un mode minimaliste, le souvenir des touches de piano des premières années. *« De la musique avant toute chose »,* écrivait Verlaine... ■

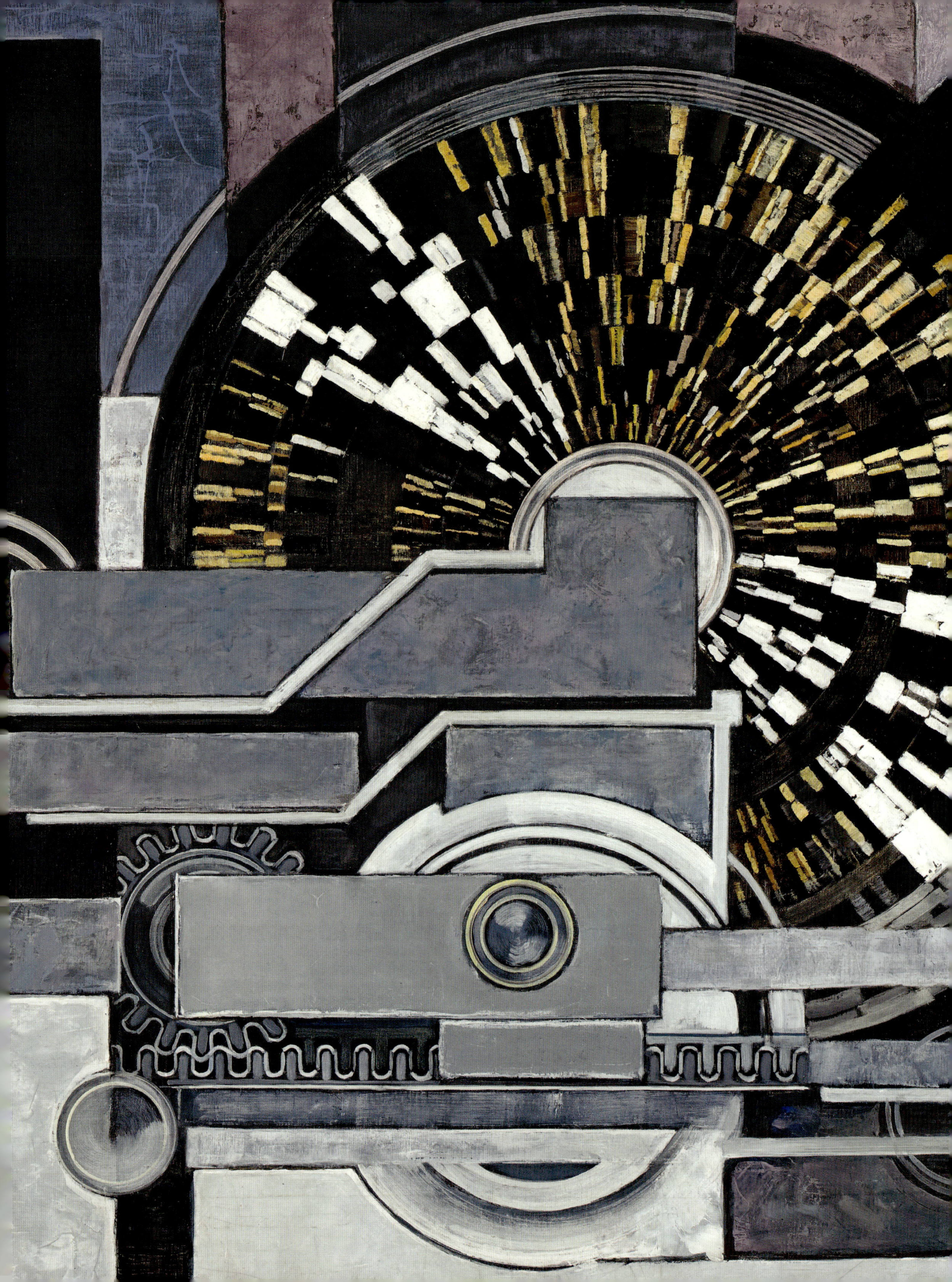

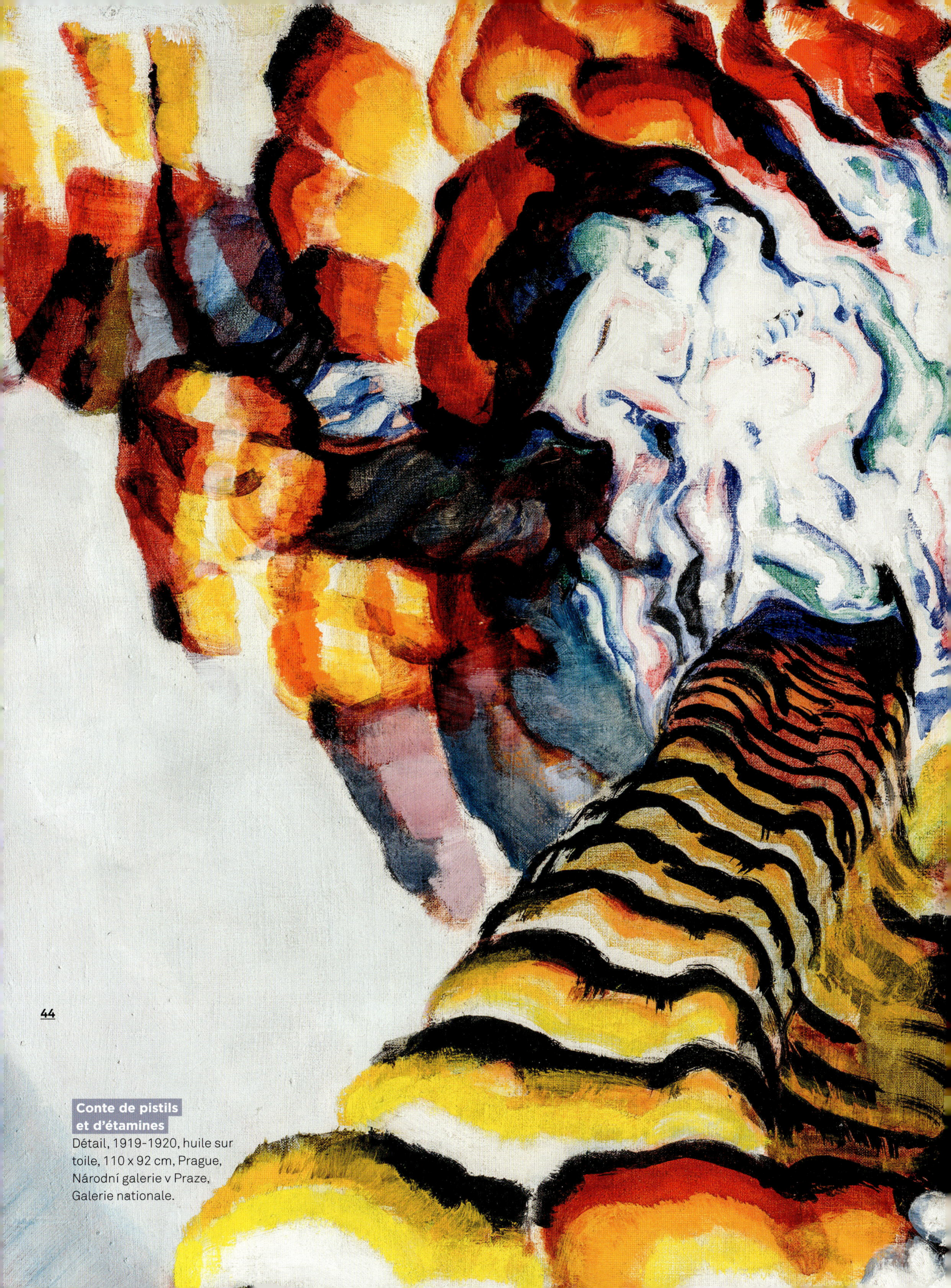

Conte de pistils et d'étamines
Détail, 1919-1920, huile sur toile, 110 x 92 cm, Prague, Národní galerie v Praze, Galerie nationale.

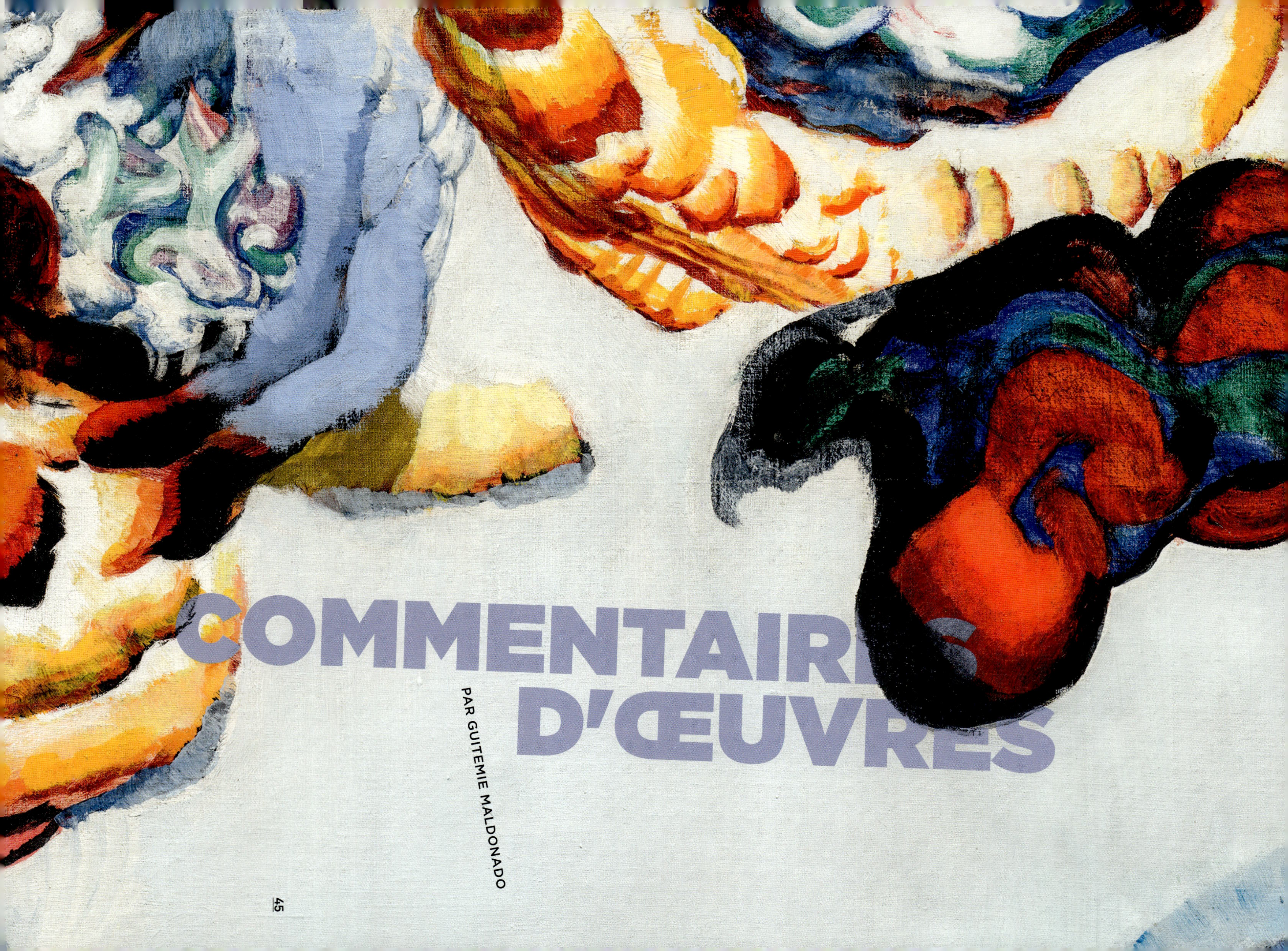

COMMENTAIRES D'ŒUVRES

PAR GUITEMIE MALDONADO

ORIGINES

Les Nénuphars
1900, estampe, aquatinte en couleurs sur papier, 34,5 x 34,7 cm, Paris, Musée national d'art moderne, Centre Pompidou, Centre de création industrielle.

Formé à Prague puis à Vienne et installé à Paris en 1896, František Kupka infuse dans ses premières œuvres l'esprit du symbolisme qui domine l'Europe au tournant du xxe siècle. Le triptyque *L'Âme de lotus* en témoigne. Élaborée autour d'un motif indien, l'œuvre est construite sur une nette opposition : à droite, les séductions de la chair, traitées avec force détails, sont incarnées par une ronde de danseuses lascives qu'écarte le prince Siddhartha (futur Bouddha) ; à gauche, des arabesques évoquant l'Art nouveau traduisent l'élévation de la conscience à laquelle aspire le sage. La fleur de lotus d'où émane une forme lumineuse place l'œuvre sous le signe du mysticisme théosophique à la source duquel l'artiste, comme nombre de ses contemporains, a puisé des moyens d'interpréter le monde. Dans la *Doctrine secrète* d'Helena Blavatsky (1888), le lotus est présenté comme une fleur sacrée, symbolisant les pouvoirs créatifs de la nature physique et spirituelle. C'est d'après un autre de ses ouvrages, *La Voix du silence,* que Kupka a intitulé l'ensemble des quatre gravures auquel appartient *Le Commencement de la vie* (ou *Les Nénuphars).* Ici deux cercles surgissent de la fleur de lotus. L'un enferme une efflorescence lumineuse, l'autre un embryon humain ; les larges feuilles circulaires de nénuphars géants (baptisés *Victoria amazonica* ou *Victoria regia* par les botanistes) qui ponctuent la surface de l'eau leur font écho. Et par la déclinaison de cette forme, simple et unitaire, c'est une formulation plastique qui s'élabore, de l'idée non seulement de l'origine, mais aussi de la plénitude, voire de cette perfection qui ne peut s'atteindre qu'en esprit.

L'Âme de lotus
1898, aquarelle sur papier, 38,5 x 57,7 cm, Prague, Národní galerie v Praze, Galerie nationale.

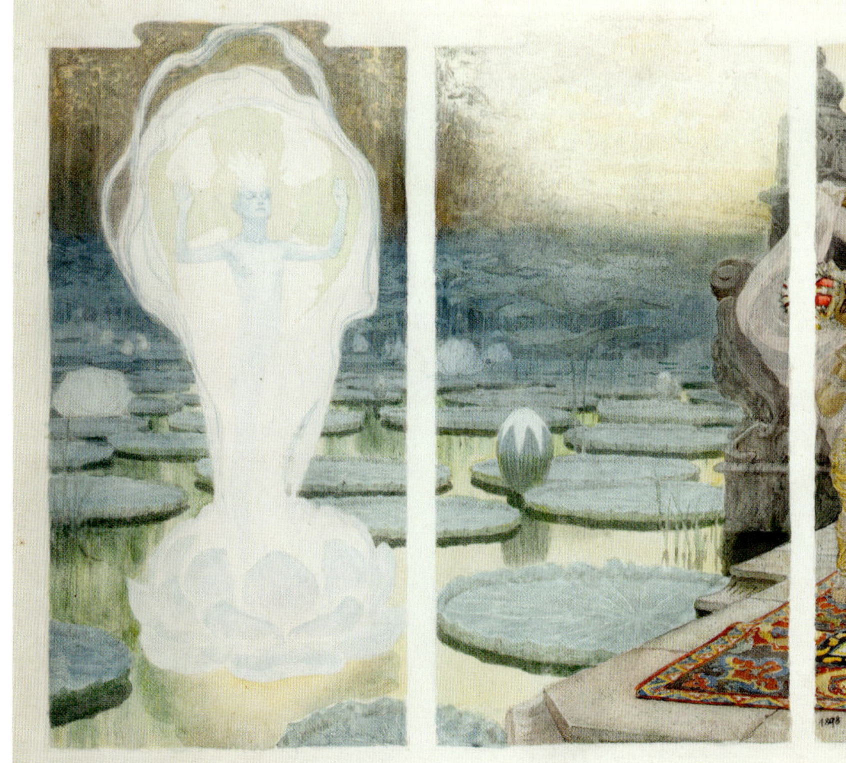

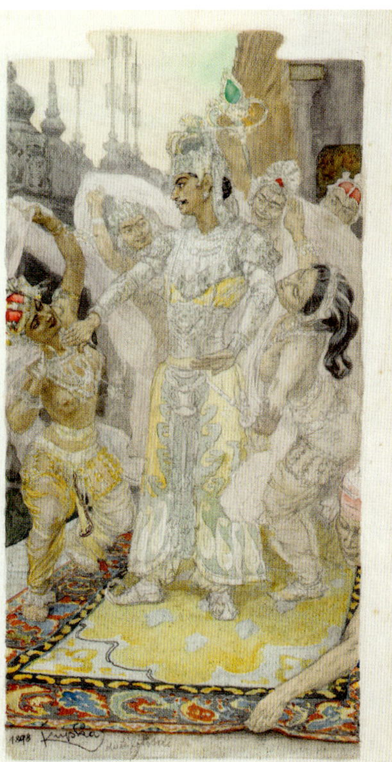

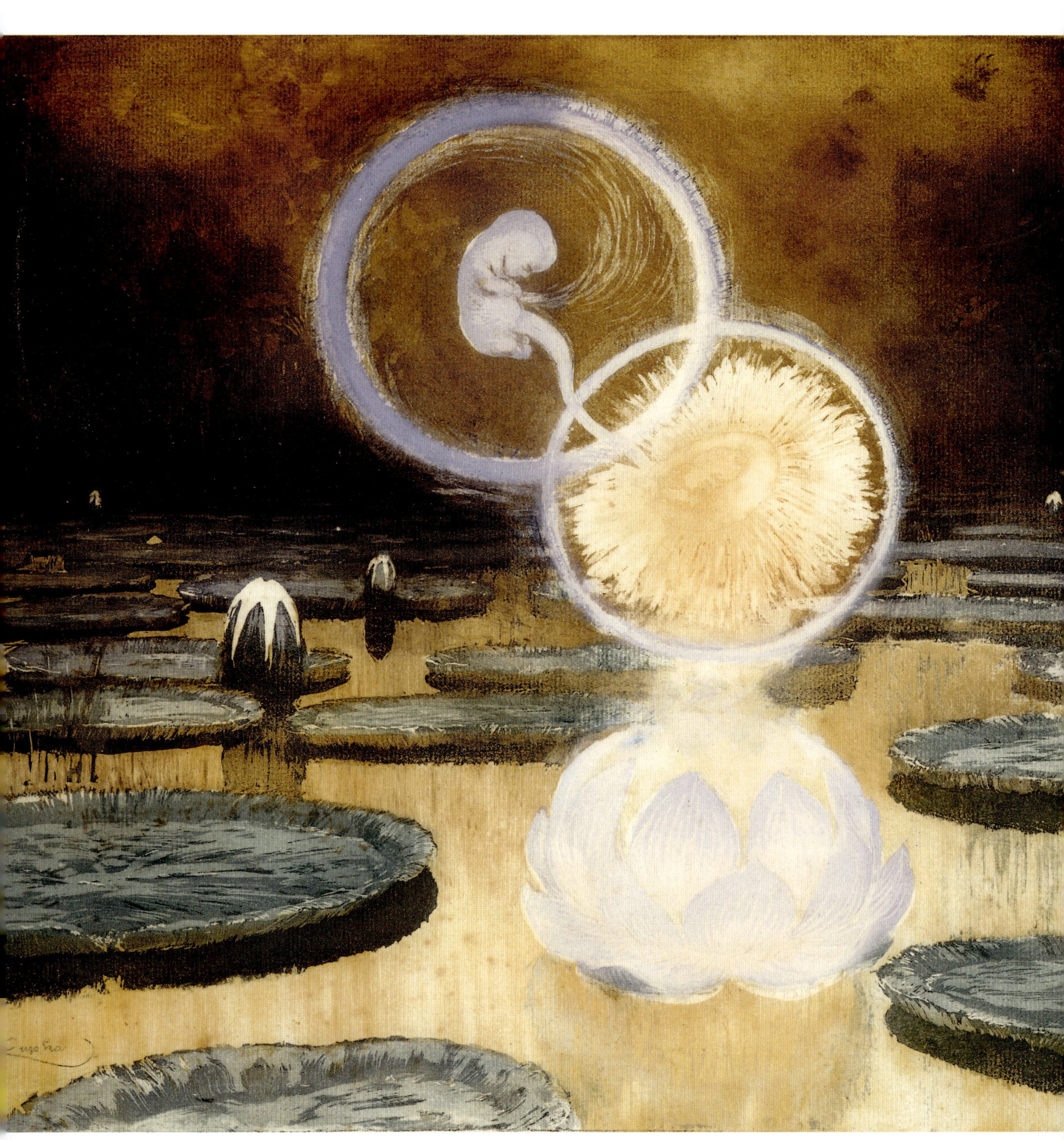

L'Eau. (La baigneuse).
1906-1909, huile sur toile, 63 x 80 cm, Paris, Musée national d'art moderne, Centre Pompidou, Centre de création industrielle.

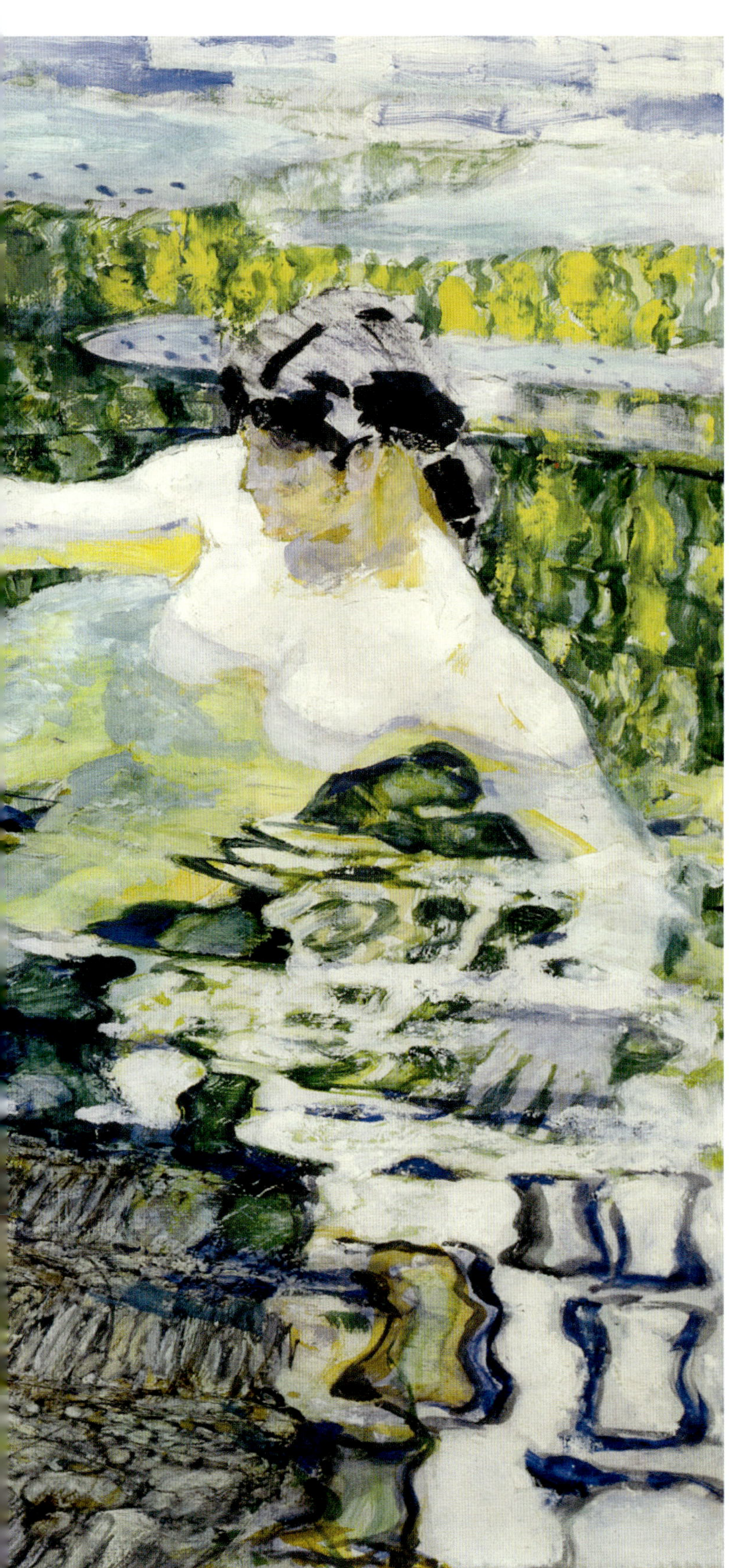

L'EAU

Autour de 1906, les baigneuses fournissent à Kupka le thème de plusieurs peintures et études. 1906, c'est l'année de la mort de Paul Cézanne qui, dans ses dernières œuvres, représenta des groupes de nus en pleine nature et contribua à nourrir l'inspiration arcadienne qui imprègne les débuts du fauvisme et du cubisme. Si le genre n'est ni nouveau ni rare à l'époque, Kupka en livre une vision toute personnelle. En témoigne le titre qui éclipse la figure féminine au profit de l'élément liquide dans lequel elle est presque entièrement immergée; ce seul fait est d'ailleurs en soi remarquable, puisque les baigneuses «peintes» évoluent traditionnellement sur la terre ferme. Kupka a d'ailleurs éliminé une seconde figure, représentée debout sur le bord dans les études préparatoires, pour centrer sa composition sur la nageuse et plus encore sur les ondes en cercles concentriques marquant la surface de l'eau autour et à partir de son corps. Le peintre saisit ainsi les mouvements propres à l'eau, imprime à l'espace une dynamique d'expansion à la fois lente et puissante. Il produit un effet de rimes plastiques par la répétition du cercle, une forme à laquelle il a ensuite consacré certaines de ses compositions abstraites. La gamme chromatique obéit à cette même logique duelle: dominée par les verts et les jaunes, elle évoque la végétation ainsi que les jeux de la lumière sur et à travers l'eau, tout en participant à l'élaboration de rimes plastiques au sein d'une surface à la fois plane et profonde, unifiée et morcelée.

Ci-contre :
La Gamme jaune
1907, huile sur toile, 79 x 79 cm, Paris, Musée national d'art moderne, Centre Pompidou, Centre de création industrielle.

Page de droite :
Le Rouge à lèvres n°II
1908, huile sur toile, 73 x 54 cm, Paris, Musée national d'art moderne, Centre Pompidou, Centre de création industrielle.

FARDS

Dans les temps qui suivent son installation définitive à Paris, Kupka vend des illustrations à la presse satirique et engagée. L'efficacité expressive du trait qu'il a développée pour ces productions alimentaires se retrouve dans *Le Rouge à lèvres :* tant la pose de la figure que le cadrage dénotent une précision acérée et une capacité de synthèse frôlant parfois la caricature. Quant au lecteur mis en scène dans *La Gamme jaune,* Margit Rowell, dans le catalogue de la rétrospective du musée Guggenheim (New York, 1975), l'a rapproché d'un portrait photographique de Baudelaire par Nadar. Avec ces deux sujets, l'artiste s'inscrit dans le monde trivial de la rue qui acquiert grâce à la peinture des allures hiératiques et dans celui de la littérature symboliste et de ses aspirations spirituelles. Les titres orientent cependant l'attention dans une autre direction, sur les expérimentations chromatiques qui confèrent leur puissance aux deux tableaux : le rouge mis sur les lèvres se diffuse au reste de la figure, en des jeux de dégradés que souligne la dominante bleue ; quant aux jaunes et orangés, ils saturent la composition jusqu'à générer des verts, suivant les mécanismes de la perception étudiés par Michel-Eugène Chevreul. Tel est en définitive l'objet de la peinture : les résonances psychologiques de la couleur, ses capacités d'amplification. *« Percevoir les couleurs,* écrit Kupka, *jouir des attraits dont elles ornent notre vie, c'est en effet un véritable bonheur. Leur diversité ajoute à l'arsenal de nos sensations une donnée nouvelle, la possibilité d'enrichir pensées et sentiments d'un nouveau registre chromatique. »*

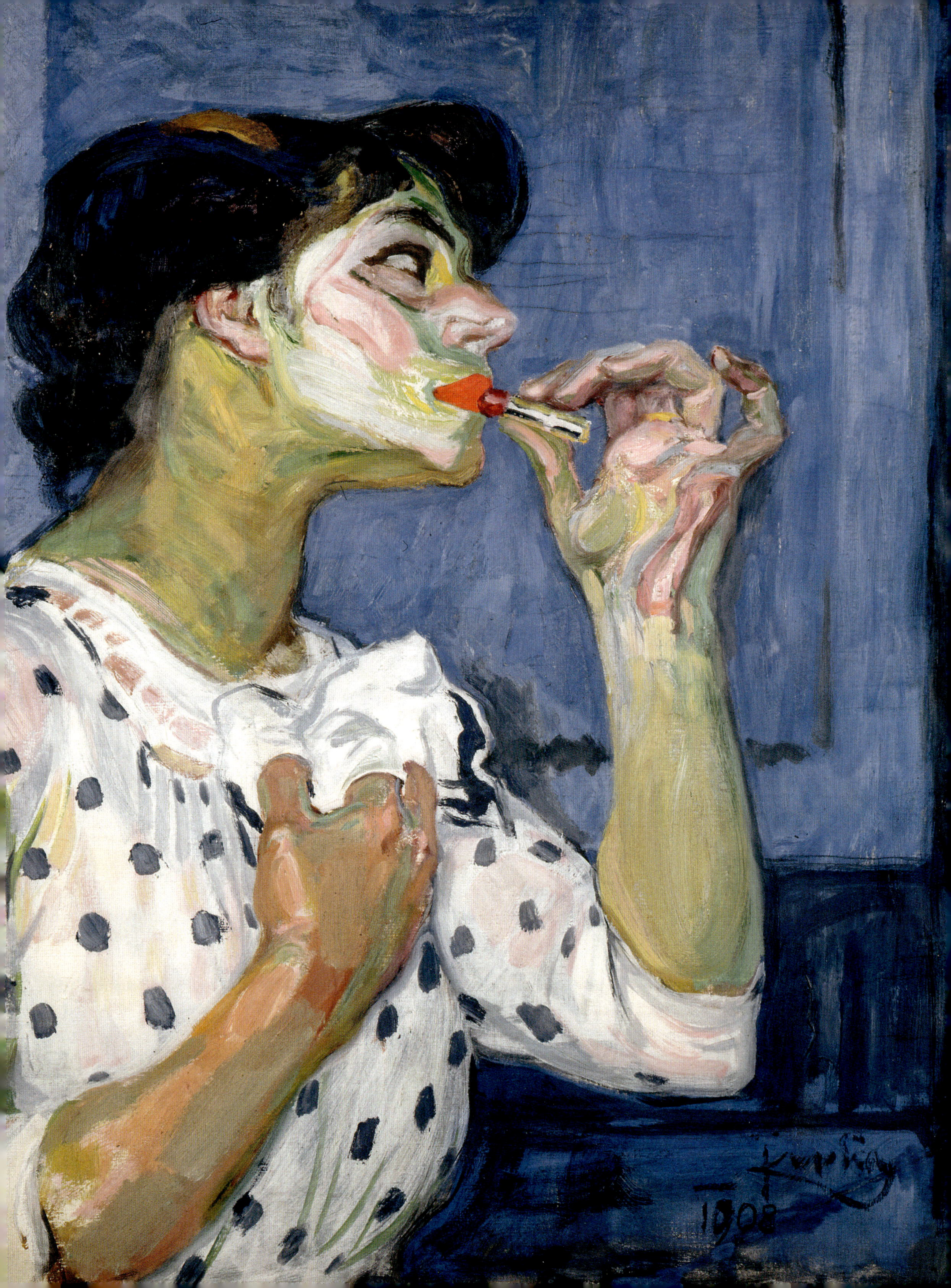

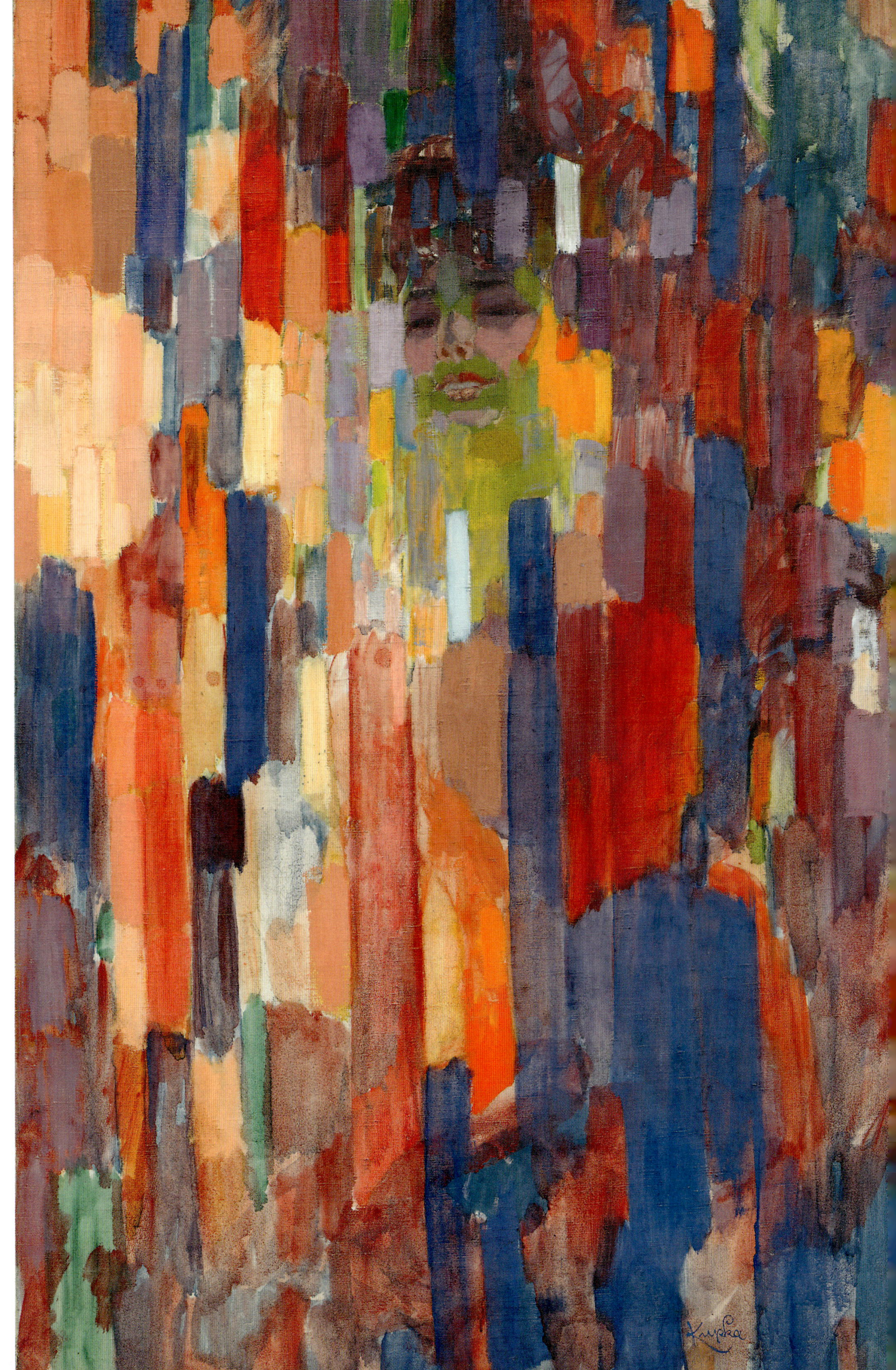

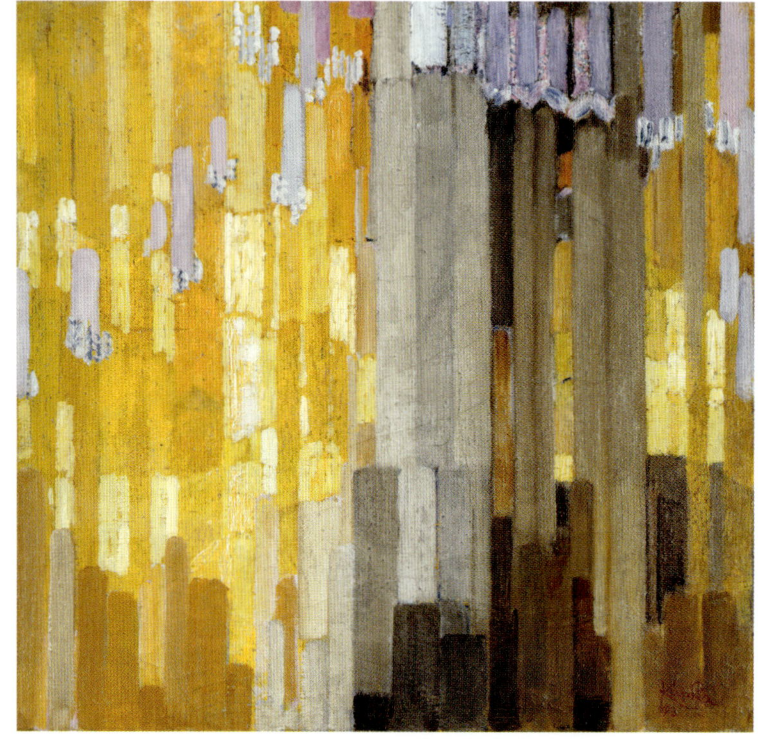

Page de gauche :
Madame Kupka dans les verticales
1910, huile sur toile, 135,5 x 85,3 cm, New York, Museum of Modern Art, MoMA.

Ci-contre :
Ordonnance sur verticales en jaune
1913, huile sur toile, 70 x 70 cm, Paris, Musée national d'art moderne, Centre Pompidou, Centre de création industrielle.

VERTICALES

À partir de *Touches de piano. Le lac* (1909), les bandes verticales deviennent chez Kupka des éléments plastiques en soi, induisant au sein de ses compositions des mouvements ascendants ou descendants, des rythmes et des tensions. Seul le visage de Madame Kupka échappe au découpage qui, via les segments de diverses tailles et les contrastes chromatiques, restitue le corps en voie de disparition, comme une silhouette, une concentration de matière, un noyau d'énergie, voire des mouvements d'air. Ces traces de figuration s'estompent progressivement au profit d'un *Arrangement de verticales,* du *Langage des verticales* et enfin de l'ensemble des *Plans verticaux* (1912-13) qualifiés en 1936 par Alfred Barr, conservateur du MoMA de New York, de *« premières abstractions géométriques pures de l'art moderne ». L'Ordonnance sur verticales en jaune* repose ainsi sur un dégradé de couleurs traduisant, suivant leurs densités et tonalités, la lumière ou la profondeur, la légèreté ou le poids. La peinture reflète les réflexions de l'artiste sur les propriétés spécifiques de la verticale qui, écrit-il dans *La Création dans les arts plastiques, « est l'échine de la vie dans l'espace, l'axe de toute construction »* et possède *« toute la majesté de la statique » : « Elle contient à la fois le haut et le bas, les réunit, mais divise l'espace horizontalement. Reproduite en une série de parallèles, la verticale devient une attente angoissante et muette qui se répand à l'horizontale. »* Par contraste, régularité et stabilité sont renforcées par des segments bleus formant dans la partie haute une ligne ondulante et s'achevant en pluie, comme en suspension.

« Solennelle, la verticale est l'échine de la vie dans l'espace, l'axe de toute construction ; elle monumentalise le moindre croquis mis au carreau. Ne vous est-il jamais arrivé de sentir une verticale s'insinuer, contre votre gré, dans votre champ de vision ? C'est l'ombre d'un cil, tombant sur la paroi externe de l'œil »

Kupka, *La Création dans les arts plastiques*

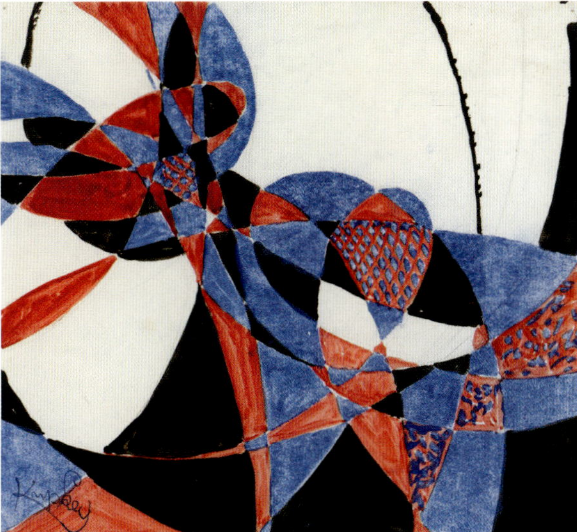

Ci-contre :
Étude pour Amorpha. Fugue à deux couleurs
1912, gouache et encre sur papier,
21,3 x 22,8 cm,
New-York, Museum of Modern Art, MoMA.

Page de droite :
Étude pour Amorpha. Fugue à deux couleurs
1912, gouache et encre sur papier,
28,4 x 29,4 cm,
New-York, Museum of Modern Art, MoMA.

CIRCULAIRES

L'histoire a tardivement accordé à Kupka la place qui lui revenait au sein des pionniers de l'art abstrait. Les deux peintures de la série des *Amorpha* exposées à Paris, au Salon d'Automne de 1912, comptent pourtant parmi les premières œuvres non figuratives présentées au public, non sans rencontrer de fortes réticences : incomprises par la commission d'organisation, elles furent associées au cubisme et l'une des toiles accrochée dans l'escalier du Grand Palais, au grand dam de l'artiste ; la critique déconcertée associa les courbes déployées par l'artiste à des *« arabesques futuristes échevelées »* (Louis Vauxcelles). Plus sévères, certains n'y virent que des compositions décoratives. Les recherches de Kupka excèdent de beaucoup cette orientation, comme en témoignent les nombreuses études et variations sur ce motif d'enroulements, de chevauchements et d'intersections, de même que la réduction chromatique à deux couples d'opposés qui, loin de toute séduction, vise à accroître le dynamisme de l'ensemble. Le titre, *Amorpha,* consomme certes la rupture avec la représentation des apparences, mais c'est pour mieux pointer ce qui est ici en jeu, dans l'agencement de ces arcs de cercle, de ces « formes arrondies » que la rotation *« imprime au monde astral »* : à savoir la traduction plastique du mouvement et, plus insaisissable encore, l'expression de la dimension du temps par les contrastes de couleurs et l'usage des courbes, *« allusion visuelle au successif ».*

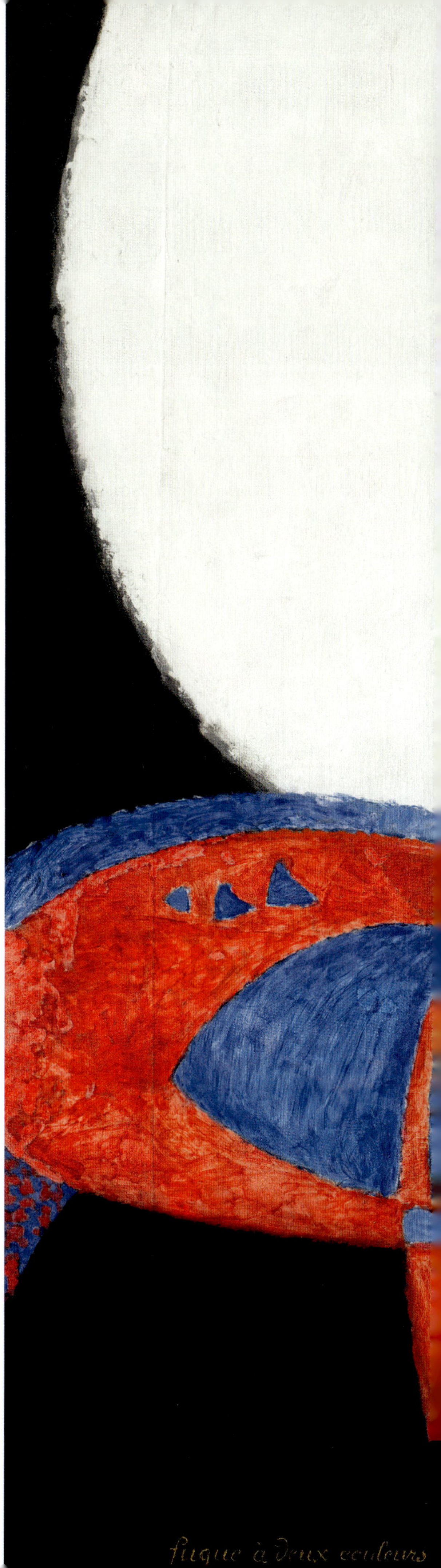

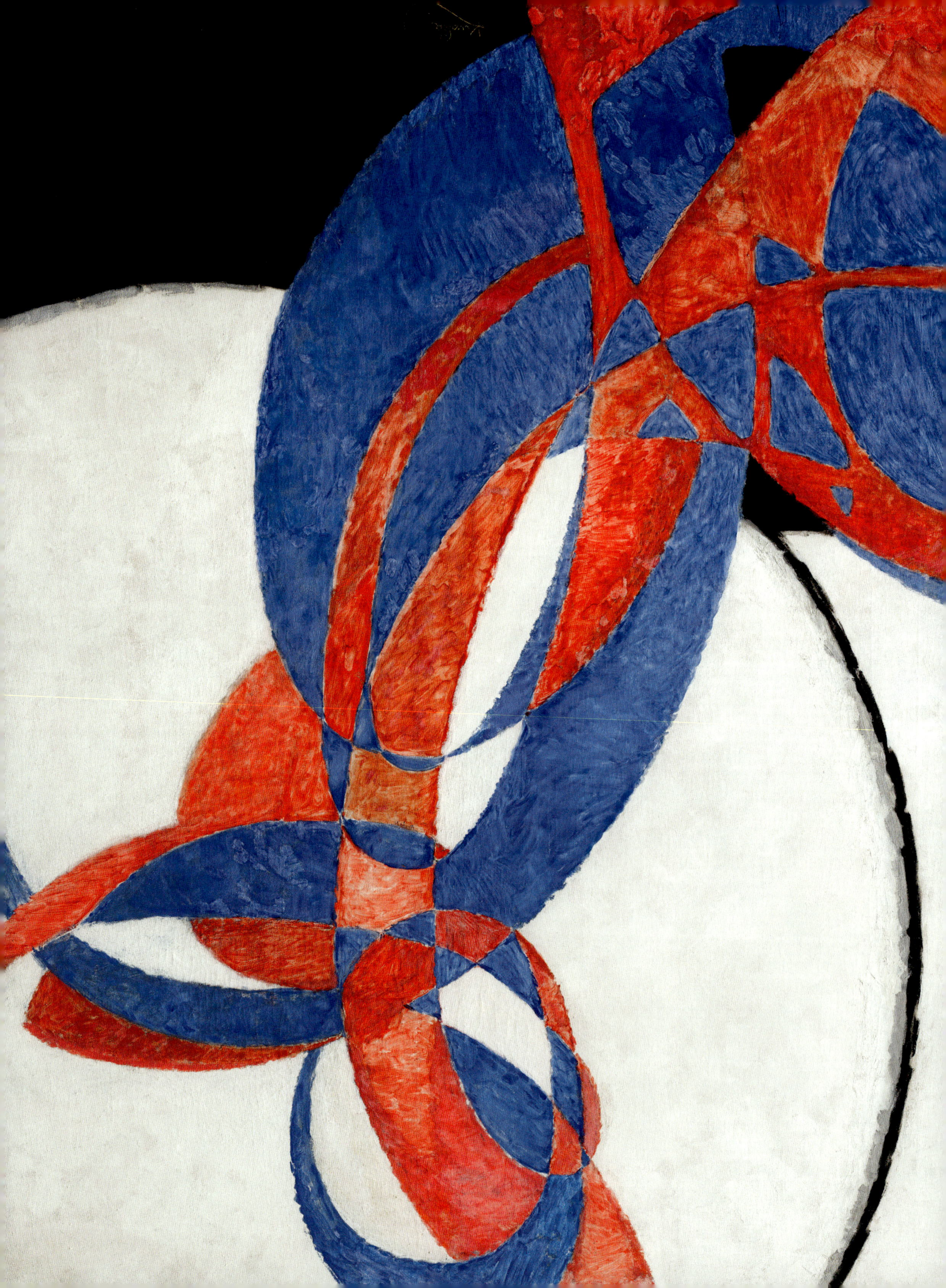

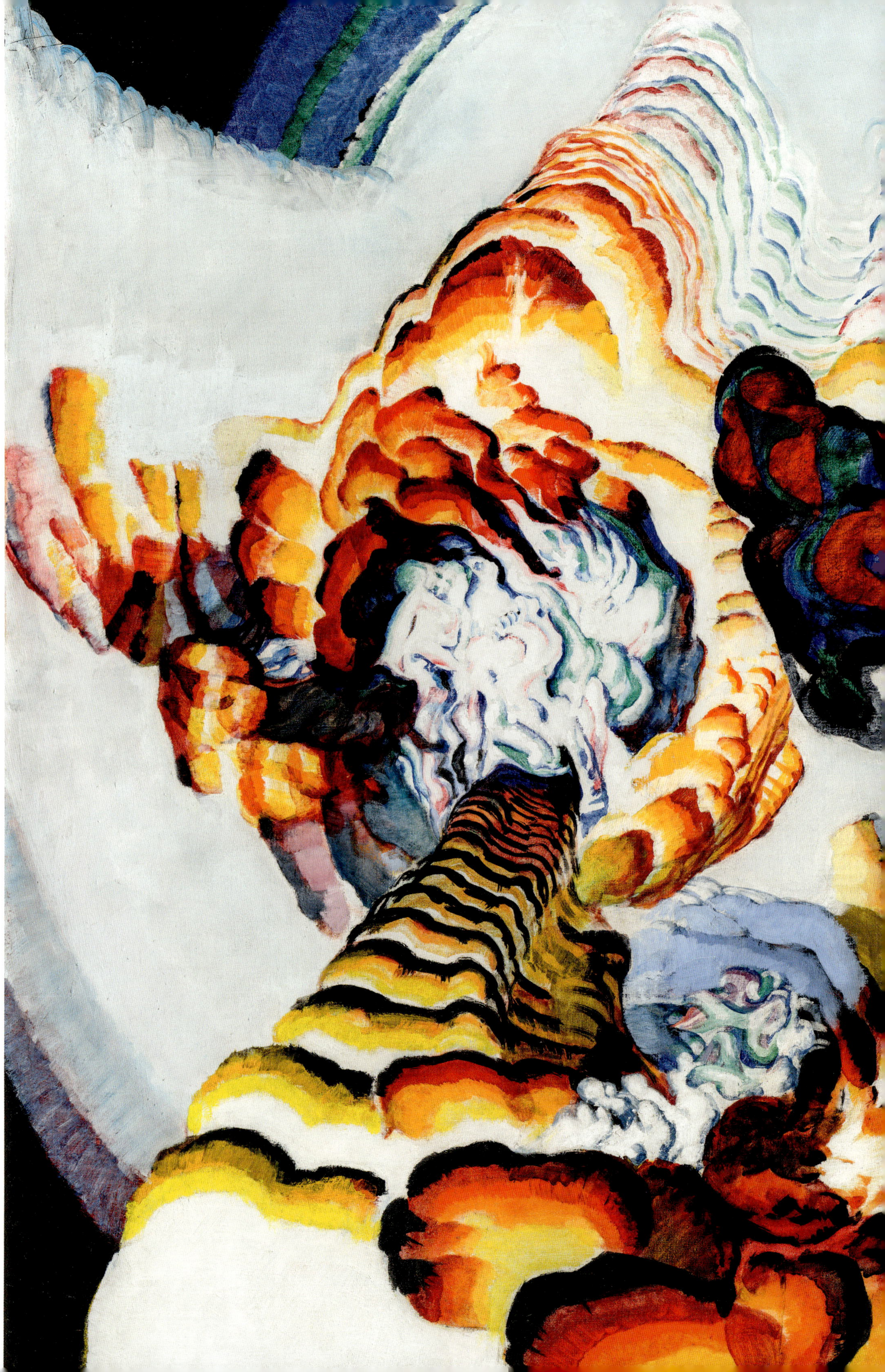

Conte de pistils et d'étamines
1919-1920, huile sur toile, 110 x 92 cm, Prague, Národní galerie v Praze, Galerie nationale.

FÉCONDATION

D'une œuvre à l'autre, Kupka varie les motifs, tantôt géométriques, tantôt organiques, comme pour cette composition bourgeonnante dont il a donné différentes versions. Dans celle conservée à Prague, les formes occupant la zone centrale évoquent plus explicitement des corps enlacés ; ainsi est établi le registre du conte où les pistils et étamines figurent pour les principes masculins et féminins et la reproduction en général. Les textes rédigés par l'artiste, *La Création dans les arts plastiques* tout particulièrement, résonnent de son intérêt pour la science et la profonde compréhension qu'elle permet du monde des phénomènes, là où microcosme et macrocosme s'avèrent reliés par des mécanismes et des forces communes. Avec cette profusion de formes et de couleurs, c'est bien la nature qui est évoquée : *« Les étamines aux exubérantes formes phalliques fécondent les gracieux pistils. Fête du pollen dans un gynécée baigné de soleil, enveloppé de pétales dont l'éclosion protège l'événement de la conception. »* Mais plus encore, *« le drame de la constitution de la matière organisée »*, dont l'*Action chimique* et le *Mouvement* sont les protagonistes que traduit ce long cortège de formes, com me un enchaînement sans fin : *« Aux cellules reproductrices viennent s'ajouter d'autres cellules et à celles-ci d'autres encore,* écrit Kupka. *C'est ainsi que chaque organisme se lance à la conquête de son environnement, se déploie, grandit, pour prendre finalement la forme ostensible de la lutte qui oppose son organisme propre à celui du monde ambiant. »*

« Chaque plante se couronne de fleurs qu'elle élève au-devant de la lumière du jour. Les étamines aux exubérantes formes phalliques fécondent les gracieux pistils. Fête du pollen dans un gynécée baigné de soleil, enveloppé de pétales dont l'éclosion protège l'événement de la conception. »

Kupka, *La Création dans les arts plastiques*

« Chez le peintre, c'est tout l'ensemble nerveux, tout le psychisme qui concourt à la formation d'images visuelles dont toutes sont loin d'être statiques. Souvent c'est, là aussi, une danse dont chaque figure n'est exécutée qu'une fois, ou encore une poussée dynamique, une explosion chaotique, un tohu-bohu où tout change de place. »

Kupka, *La Création dans les arts plastiques*

La Foire (Contredanse)
1921-1922,
huile sur toile,
73 x 298 x 5 cm,
Prague, musée Kampa.

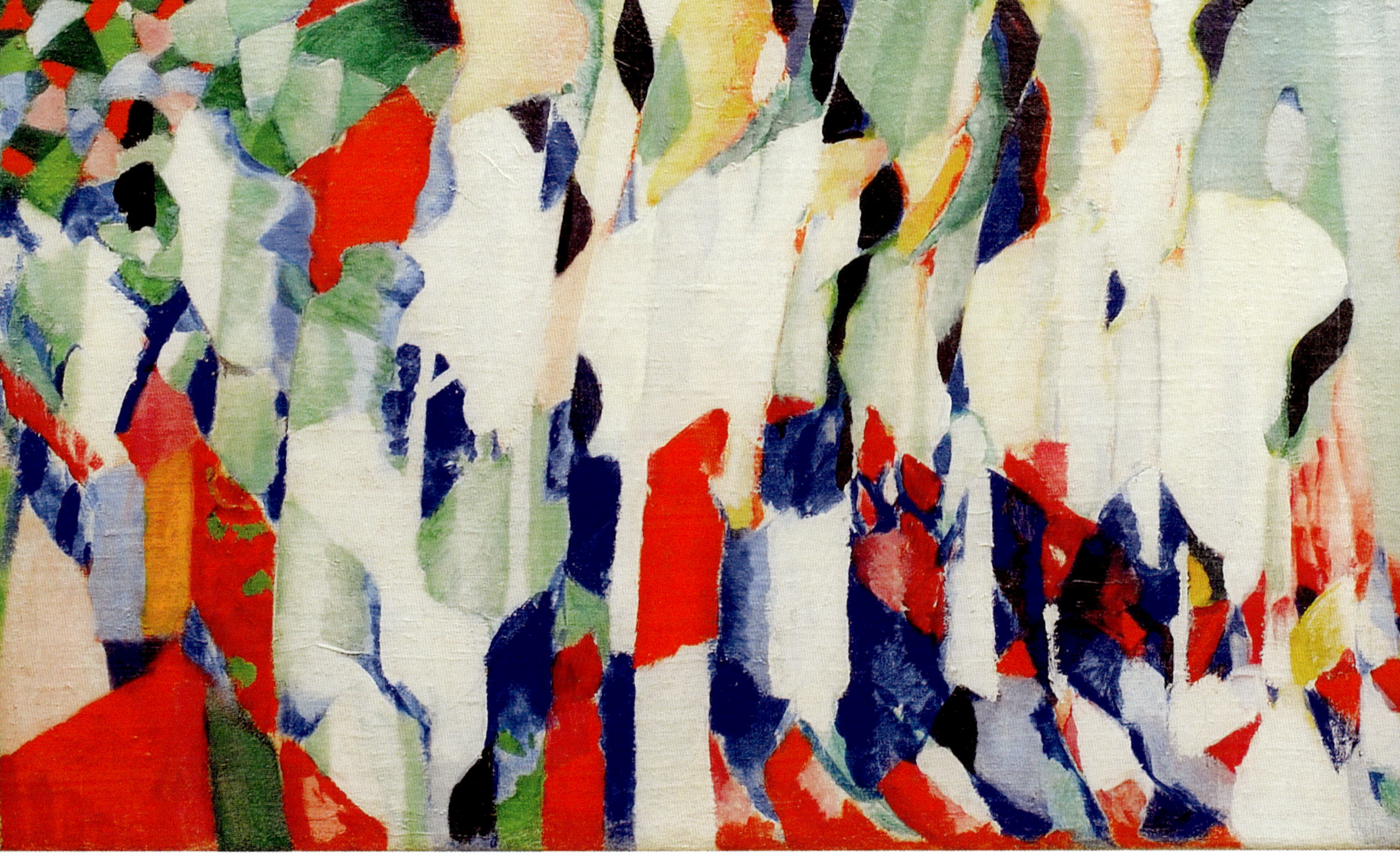

MOUVEMENTS

Parmi les œuvres qui ont précédé le passage de Kupka à l'abstraction, on compte plusieurs études de mouvement, dont les séries de *Femme cueillant une fleur* et de *La Petite fille au ballon,* mais aussi un pastel représentant deux femmes dansant le tango *(Le Tango,* 1909), lequel témoigne de son intérêt pour la musique. Dans tous les cas, c'est par la décomposition des formes et des couleurs qu'est transcrite la dynamique des corps ; ainsi se communique-t-elle à l'espace bidimensionnel, immobile et limité du tableau. Une décennie plus tard, le motif du divertissement populaire et de la danse réapparaît dans cette composition qui s'étire amplement dans le sens de la longueur. La division de l'espace, voire son morcellement, n'en est que plus sensible, accentuée par la succession rapide imprimée à l'œil dans son déplacement latéral. Les verticales déployées parallèlement dans la longueur se courbent vers le haut et dessinent comme des ondes, qui ne sont pas sans évoquer la propagation du son ; si l'on croit parfois y reconnaître les silhouettes des danseurs (en particulier dans la partie droite), elles traduisent l'impression d'une foule bigarrée ainsi que les différentes étapes du mouvement dont elles établissent le rythme dominant. S'y adjoignent – sur le mode du contrepoint ou de l'accompagnement – des rythmes secondaires, arabesques et ondulations, engendrés par les contrastes et échos chromatiques qui insufflent à l'ensemble la pulsation de la vie.

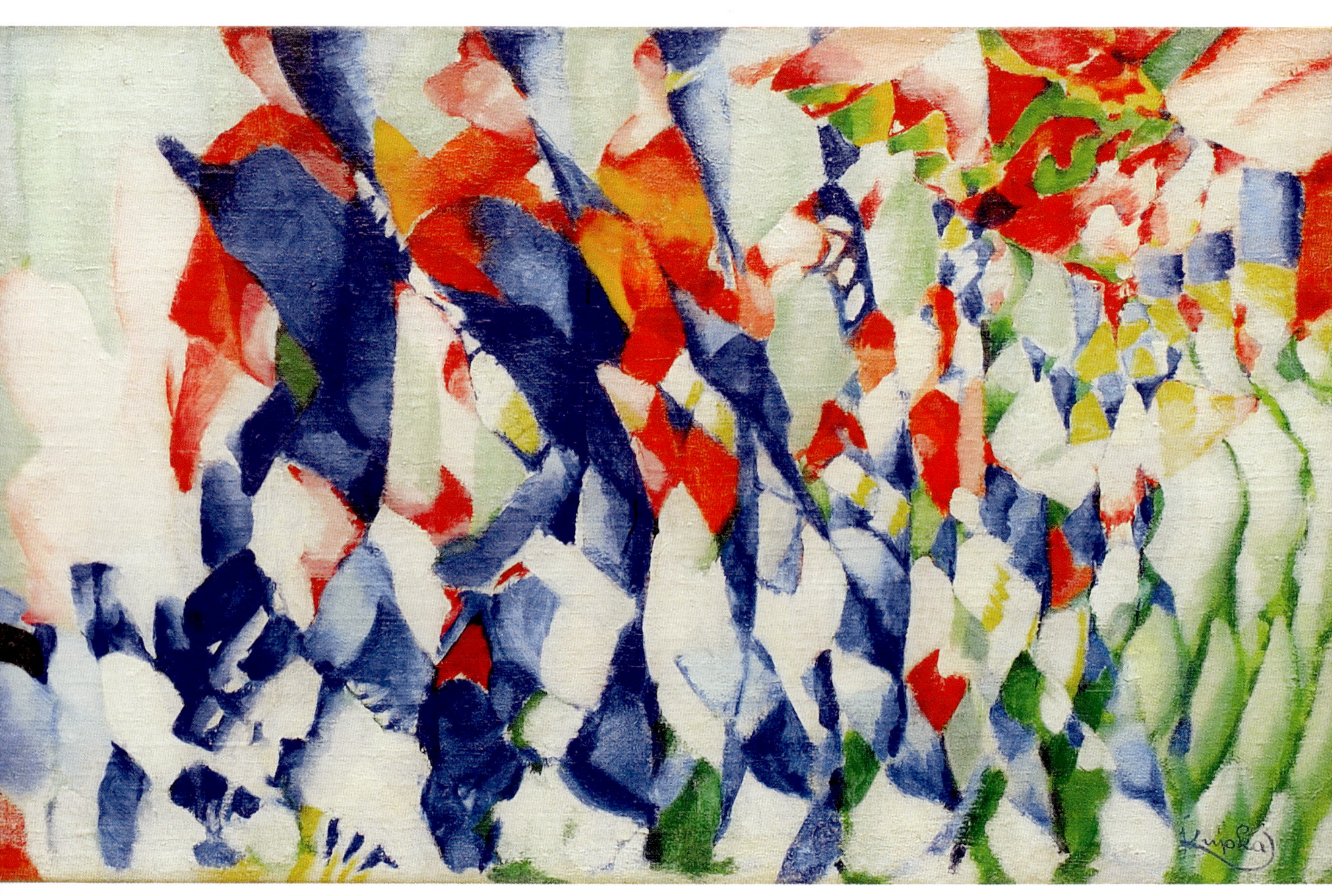

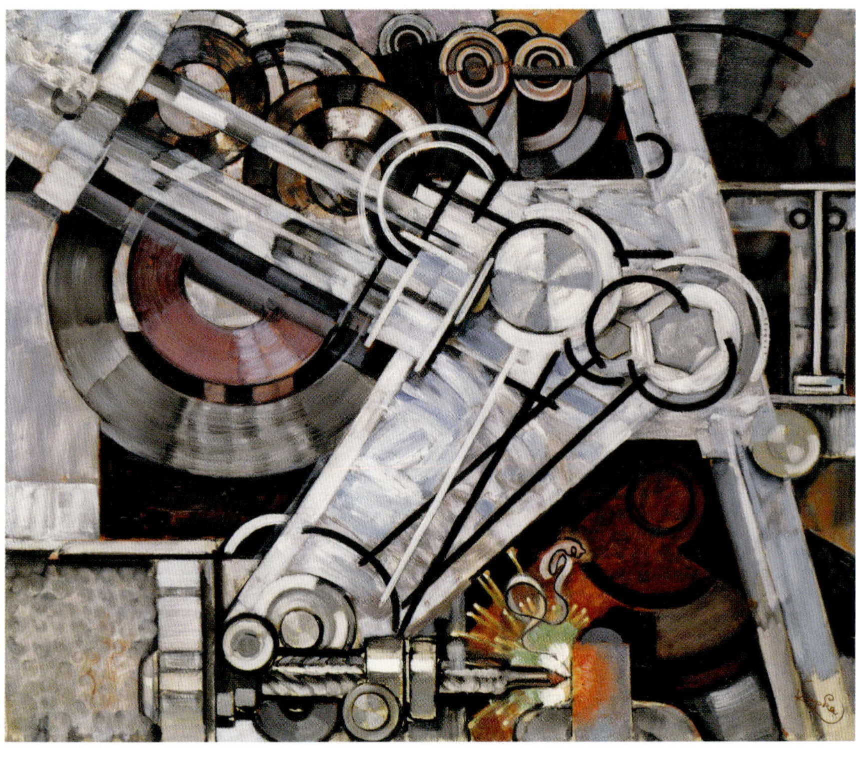

Ci-contre:
Machinisme
1927-1929, huile sur toile, 73 x 85 cm, Madrid, musée Thyssen-Bornemisza.

Page de droite :
Synthèse
1927-1929, huile sur toile, 180 x 125 cm, Prague, Národní galerie v Praze, Galerie nationale.

MACHINES

Les années 1920 ont été pour Kupka une période fort contrastée. Si sa situation financière reste difficile, son œuvre commence à trouver plus d'écho sur la scène artistique parisienne : en 1921, la galerie Povolozky organise sa première exposition personnelle, en 1922, paraît la première monographie consacrée à son œuvre en français et son entourage s'enrichit de soutiens fidèles, le collectionneur Jindřich Waldes, les artistes Pierre-Antoine Gallien et Felix Del Marle. Dans ce contexte, l'artiste cherche à renouveler son iconographie en explorant de nouveaux thèmes, dont l'univers de la machine auquel il consacre alors une trentaine de peintures, plus ou moins explicitement figuratives. Ainsi dans *Machinisme,* échauffement, étincelles et fumée indiquent l'action très concrète de l'imposant système de bielles et pistons qui constitue, signe de la puissance engagée, la majeure partie de la composition. Signe aussi de l'extrême précision d'un tel mécanisme visant à la transmission de forces pour servir un but donné : « *Les choses,* écrit Kupka, *émergent d'une sorte de chaos pour rentrer dans des organismes plus logiques.* » Sans se départir de cette rigueur, *Synthèse* déploie dans le plan une variation sur le motif du cercle et les mouvements d'entraînement, qui n'est pas sans rappeler les *Disques* de Fernand Léger, en plus complexe et moins coloré. Car la gamme choisie ici est une évocation du métal, minéral, gris froid ou doré, luisant et l'ensemble s'impose comme une image de l'énergie maîtrisée.

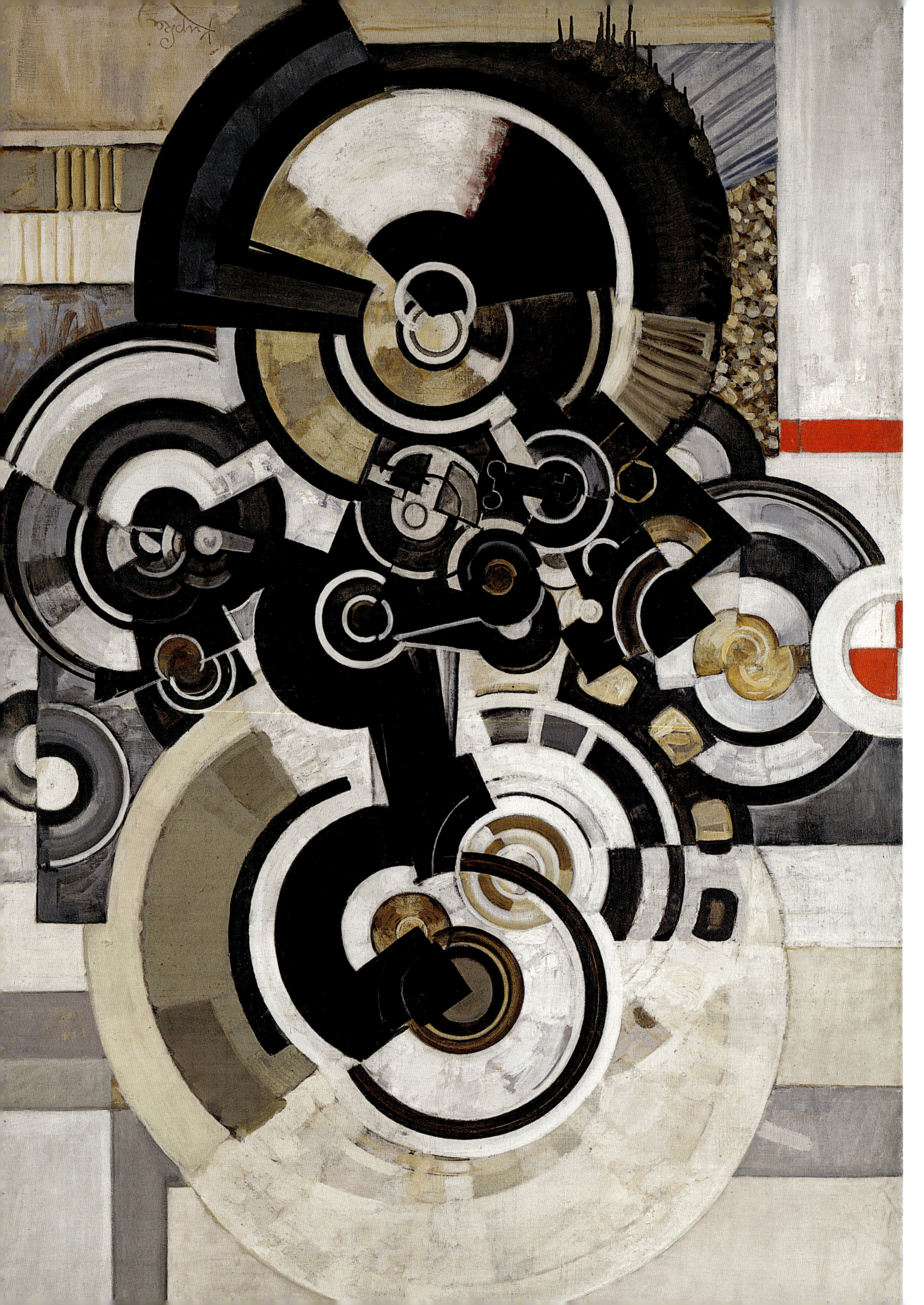

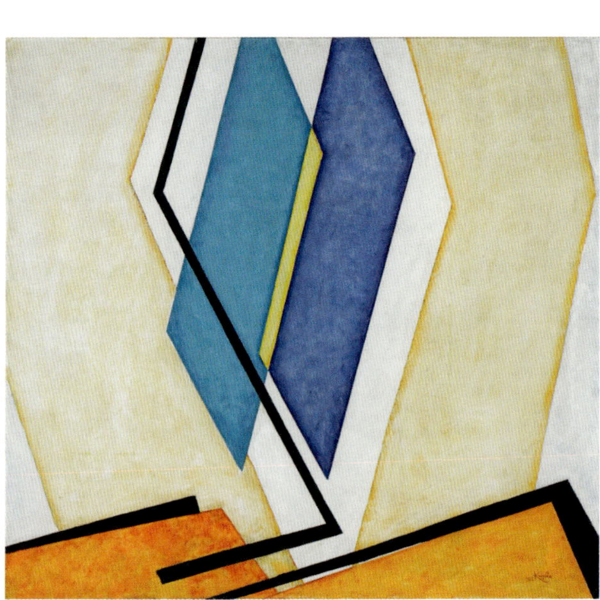

Deux bleus n°I
1955, huile sur toile, 100 x 105 cm, Cholet, musée d'Art et d'Histoire, dépôt du Centre Pompidou.

Page de droite :
Blanc automne
1952, huile sur toile, 70 x 70 cm, Paris, Musée national d'art moderne, Centre Pompidou, Centre de création industrielle.

ANNÉES 1950

Les œuvres réalisées par Kupka après la Seconde Guerre mondiale tranchent par leur simplification, voire leur réduction. Les titres en distinguent des composantes formelles, types de structure *(Contrastes, Plans verticaux et diagonaux, Traits animés)* ou couleur isolée *(Trois bleus et trois rouges),* dont la peinture déploie les spécificités plastiques : tout en se démarquant nettement de l'ensemble, les trois rectangles blancs instaurent une tension verticale qui contrebalance les lignes horizontales et assure l'équilibre parfait de la composition ; quant aux deux parallélogrammes bleus, entourés par le jaune qui perce également entre eux, ils sont comme le cœur d'une combustion irradiant dans l'espace entier, au-delà des limites du tableau. Dans les deux œuvres, l'élément principal est le plan de couleur, dont l'artiste affirme, dans *La Création dans les arts plastiques,* qu'il est le moyen propre de la peinture où *« toutes les étendues - et, avec elles, les lumières et les obscurités - se présentent de face »,* ce qui suffit à garantir au peintre *« une liberté absolue »,* la possibilité de *« définir à son gré, arbitrairement, la raison d'être de ses étendues ».* La conquête de cette autonomie, amorcée plusieurs décennies plus tôt et consolidée depuis les années 1930, trouve là son ultime réalisation, alors même que s'ouvre pour l'art abstrait une nouvelle étape de son histoire, celle de l'organisation (avec, entre autres le Salon des Réalités nouvelles auquel Kupka prend part), de la formalisation et de la radicalité.

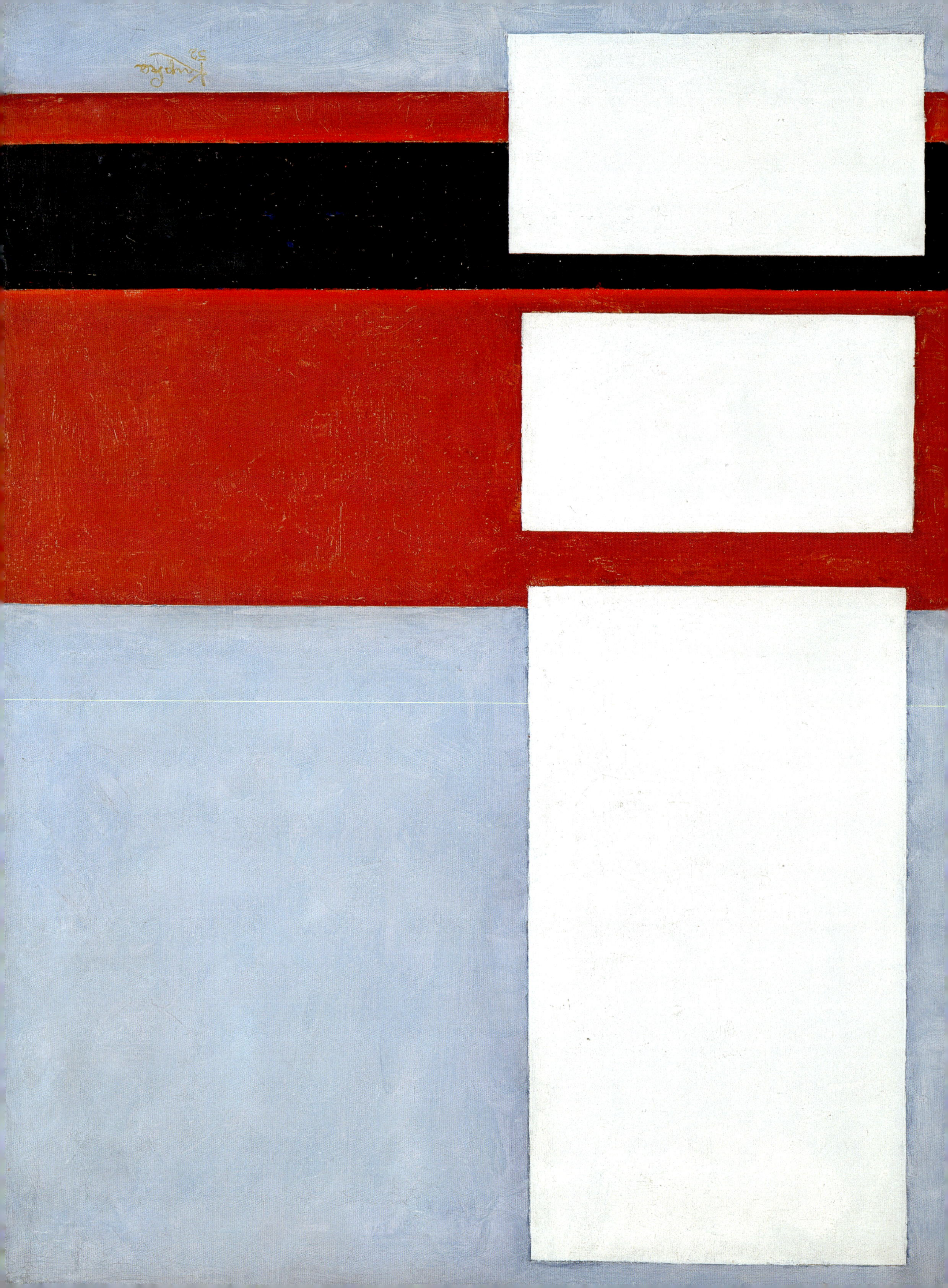

GUIDE PRATIQUE

La rétrospective « **Kupka, pionnier de l'abstraction** » est présentée du 21 mars au 30 juillet 2018 au Grand Palais, Galeries nationales, entrée square Jean Perrin, avenue du Général Eisenhower, 75008 Paris. Tél. : 01 44 13 17 17 – www.grandpalais.fr

Horaires

– Ouverture du jeudi au lundi de 10 h à 20 h, le mercredi de 10 h à 22 h.
– Fermeture hebdomadaire le mardi.
– Fermeture le mardi 1er mai et le samedi 14 juillet 2018.

Accès

– Métro : lignes 1 et 13 (arrêt Champs-Élysées-Clemenceau) ou ligne 9 (Franklin D. Roosevelt).
– Bus : lignes 28, 42, 52, 63, 72, 73, 80, 83, 93.

Commissariat

– Commissaires : Brigitte Leal, conservateur général, directrice adjointe en charge des collections du Musée national d'art moderne, Centre Pompidou, Markéta Theinhardt et Pierre Brullé, historiens de l'art.
– Scénographe : Véronique Dollfus.

À lire

- *Quatre histoires de blanc et noir gravées par Frank Kupka,* fac similé, tirage limité à 300 exemplaires numérotés, relié, coffret toilé, éditions de la Rmn-Grand Palais, 2018.
- *Kupka, pionnier de l'abstraction,* carnet d'expo de Pierre Brullé, coédition Découvertes Gallimard-Rmn-Grand Palais, 64 p., 2018.
- Pascal Rousseau, *František Kupka en 15 questions,* 96 p., Hazan, 2018.
- Arnauld Pierre, *Maternités cosmiques. La recherche des origines de Kupka à Kubrick,* Hazan, 2010.
- *František Kupka. La collection du Centre Georges Pompidou, Musée national d'art moderne,* éditions du Centre Pompidou, 2003.
– *František Kupka, 1871-1957 ou l'invention d'une abstraction,* catalogue de l'exposition du musée d'Art moderne de la Ville de Paris, Paris-Musées, 1990.
– *Kupka, La Création dans les arts plastiques,* éditions Cercle d'Art, 1989.

À voir

– *Kupka, pionnier de l'abstraction,* film réalisé par Jacques Loeuille, 52 min, coproduction Zadig productions, Česká televize, Arte France, Rmn-Grand Palais.

Difficile d'aborder l'œuvre si complexe de Kupka sans multiplier les approches. Conservateurs ou universitaires, les auteurs du catalogue s'y emploient, explorant parfois des chemins peu balisés. Mentionnons *Les civilisations antiques, sources d'inspiration et de réflexion* par Pierre Brullé ; *František Kupka et Emmanuel Swedenborg* par Linda Dalrymple Henderson ; *Une « pharmacie spirituelle ». Les cours de Kupka auprès des jeunes artistes tchécoslovaques à Paris* par Anna Pravdova.

■ *Kupka, pionnier de l'abstraction,* collectif, 320 p., 321 ill., éditions de la Réunion des musées nationaux-Grand Palais, Paris 2017, 49 €.

Nous remercions Florence Le Moing et Sandrine Mahaut, de la RMN-Grand Palais, ainsi que Tereza Ježková et Karolina Pláničková, de la Národni Galerie de Prague, pour l'aide apportée à l'élaboration de ce numéro.

©ADAGP, Paris, 2018
Crédits photographiques: ©Prague, Národní galerie v Praze, Galerie nationale: couverture, p. 12, 13, 15h, 21, 27bd, 29h, 36, 38, 39, 44, 45 ,56, 57, 46, 61, 65 ; ©Centre Pompidou, Musée national d'art moderne-MNAM/CCI, Dist. RMN-Grand Palais/J. Faujour: p. 2, 3, 31; ©Centre Pompidou, MNAM/CCI, Dist. RMN-Grand Palais/J.C Planchet: p. 4, 5, 11, 16h, 17, 42; ©Peter Willi/Bridgeman Images: p. 6, 7; ©Centre Pompidou, Musée national d'art moderne-MNAM/CCI, Dist. RMN-Grand Palais/DR: p. 8, 48, 49 ; ©Centre Pompidou, MNAM-CCI, Dist. RMN-Grand Palais/image Centre Pompidou, MNAM-CCI: p. 9h, 10, 29b, 62, 63; ©Centre Pompidou, MNAM-CCI, Dist. RMN-Grand Palais/P. Migeat: p. 9b, 47, 53; ©Prague, Castle Administration/Jan Gloc: p. 14; ©The Solomon R. Guggenheim Foundation/Art Resource, NY, Dist. RMN-Grand Palais: p. 15b; ©The Solomon R. Guggenheim Foundation: p. 22; ©Centre Pompidou, MNAM-CCI, Dist. RMN-Grand Palais/C. Bahier/P. Migeat: p. 16b; ©Musée d'Art moderne de la Ville de Paris/Roger-Viollet: p. 18; ©Centre Pompidou, MNAM-CCI, Dist. RMN-Grand Palais/B. Prévost: p. 19, 20, 34, 43, 50, 62, 66, 67; ©Centre Pompidou, MNAM-CCI, Dist. RMN-Grand Palais/A. Laurans: 23h; ©Galerie Zdeněk Sklenář, Prague, CZ: p. 23b ; ©RMN-Grand Palais (musée d'Orsay)/T. Le Mage: p. 24, 25, 26, 27g; ©Bibliothèque Historique de la Ville de Paris/Archives Charmet/Bridgeman Images: p. 27h; ©Roger-Viollet: p. 28; ©Bochum, Kunstmuseum Bochum; p. 30, 31g; ©Digital image, The Museum of Modern Art, New York/Scala, Florence: p. 32, 33, 40, 41, 54, 55; ©Philadelphia, Philadelphia Museum of Art: p. 35; ©Museo Thyssen-Bornemisza, Madrid: p. 37, 60; ©Musées de Strasbourg/N.Fussier: p. 51 ; ©New York, The Museum of Modern Art, MoMA: 52; ©Prague, musée Kampa: p.58, 59.

Hors-série de Connaissance des Arts
Directeur de la publication-Gérant de SFPA : Francis Morel
Directeur de la rédaction : Guy Boyer @
Directeur du développement : Philippe Thomas @
Rédactrice en chef adjointe des hors-série et des développements numériques : Lucie Agache @
Rédactrice-iconographe : Diane de Contades @
Chefs de fabrication : Sandrine Lebreton @, Anaïs Barbet @ assistée de Marine Milac

Pour ce numéro :
Rédacteur en chef adjoint :Jean-Michel Charbonnier
Maquette : Laëtitia Loas-Orsel @
Secrétariat de rédaction : Danielle Marti @
Rédactrice-iconographe : Charlotte Petitjean @

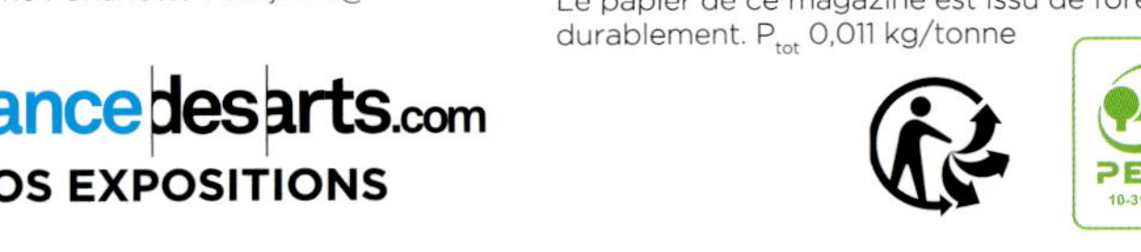

LE SITE DE VOS EXPOSITIONS

Diffusion des hors-série :
Jérôme Duteil @ : 01 87 39 82 35
Abonnements et vente au numéro : 01 55 56 71 08.
Les personnes dont le nom est suivi du signe @ disposent d'une adresse e-mail, à composer comme suit : initialeduprénomnom@cdesarts.com

Connaissance des Arts est édité par SFPA (Société Française de Promotion Artistique), Sarl au capital de 150 000 €.
Connaissance des Arts est une publication du Groupe Les Échos.
Président-directeur général : Francis Morel
Directeur général délégué : Christophe Victor
Directeur délégué : Bernard Villeneuve
Directrice du pôle Arts et Classique : Claire Lénart Turpin
10 boulevard de Grenelle CS 10817 75738 Paris Cedex 15
Tél. : 01 87 39 73 00 – Fax : 01 44 88 51 88
e-mail : cda@cdesarts.com – 304 951 460 RCS. Paris
Commission paritaire : 1020 K 79964 – ISSN 1242-9198
H. S. n° 799 – Dépôt légal : 1er trimestre 2018
Photogravure : Key Graphic (Paris)
Impression : Deux-Ponts (Bresson)
Origine du papier : France. Taux de fibres recyclées : 0%
Le papier de ce magazine est issu de forêts gérées durablement. P_{tot} 0,011 kg/tonne

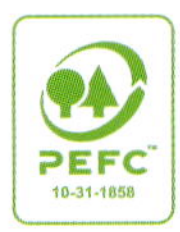

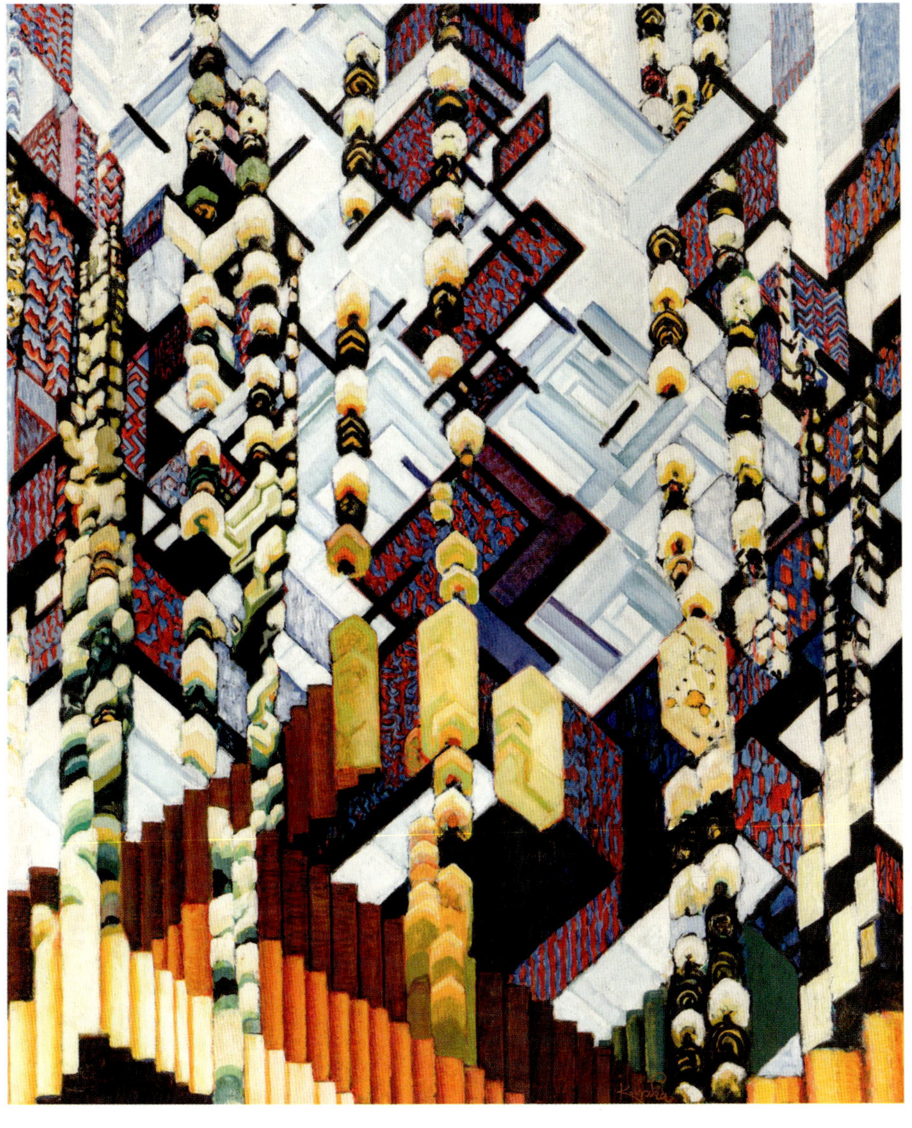

Réminiscence hivernale
1915-1923,
huile sur toile,
180 x 150 cm,
Prague, Národní
galerie v Praze,
Galerie nationale.

Double page
suivante :
Ordonnance sur verticales
1911-1920,
huile sur toile,
58 x 72 cm,
Strasbourg,
musée d'Art moderne
et contemporain,
dépôt du Centre
Pompidou.

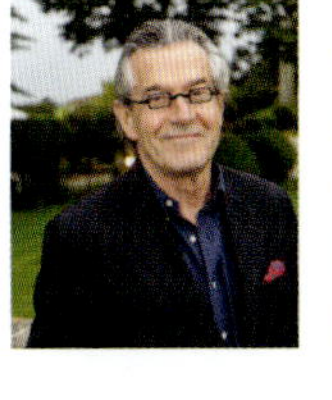

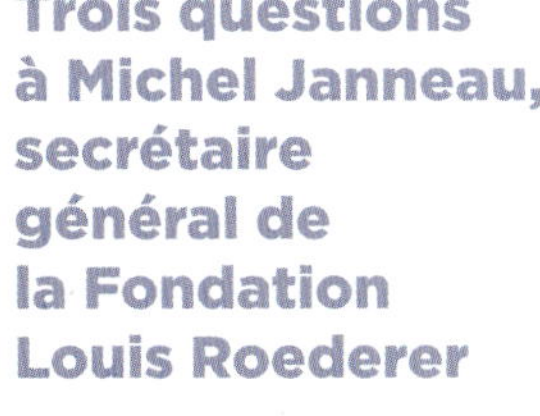

Trois questions à Michel Janneau, secrétaire général de la Fondation Louis Roederer

À quel type de manifestations artistiques la Fondation Louis Roederer a-t-elle apporté son soutien ?

Depuis la création de la Fondation Louis Roederer, fin 2011, nous avons soutenu plus de 60 projets. Les plus marquants à mes yeux ont été : « 100 chefs-d'œuvre » à la BnF (2012/2013), « Imaginez l'imaginaire » de Julio Le Parc au Palais de Tokyo (2013), « Un moment si doux » de Raymond Depardon au Grand Palais (2013/2014), où nous avons également accompagné Bill Viola (2014). En 2015, je conserve un grand souvenir de Takis et Sugimoto au Palais de Tokyo et de Clergue au Grand Palais. La BnF revient très fort, fin 2015, avec Anselm Kiefer. Je ne peux pas ne pas citer Alberola au Palais de Tokyo (début 2016) et Seydou Keïta au Grand Palais (printemps 2016). Plus récemment, 2017 aura été l'année d'Avedon à la BnF et d'Irving Penn au Grand Palais. Je voudrais aussi rappeler tout ce que nous avons fait au cours des années 2003 à 2011, dans le cadre d'un mécénat direct par le Champagne Louis Roederer, maison mère de la Fondation. Ce furent de grandes années à la BnF, avec Nachtway (nos débuts !), Capa , Couturier, Salgado, « La Photographie Humaniste », déjà Alberola, Sophie Calle et « Controverses »... Je m'en voudrais aussi de ne pas évoquer des « amitiés » tellement constitutives de la trame de notre action : Planche (s) Contact à Deauville jusqu'en 2017, le Festival d'Aix-en-Provence, la Bourse Louis Roederer à la BnF et notre escapade annuelle au Café de Flore pour son prix littéraire si différent des autres !

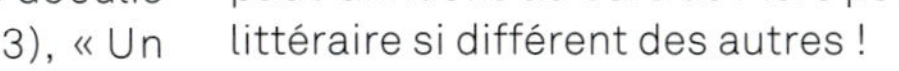

Quels sont vos axes d'investigation ?

La photographie fait partie de nos domaines de prédilection. Nous avons véritablement découvert la grandeur de cet art à la BnF en 2003 et ce fut un coup de foudre. Nous l'entretenons désormais par une soigneuse fréquentation des Rencontres d'Arles ! Nous n'avons pas vraiment d'axes d'investigation car tout est affaire de passion. Nous ne mécénons pas directement des artistes. Nous faisons un choix dans la programmation des institutions dont nous sommes partenaires en nous efforçant de maintenir un équilibre. Ceci dit, comme en Champagne, les millésimes varient. Il y a de grandes années du Palais de Tokyo. Jean de Loisy, son président, est un remarquable chef de caves. Le Grand Palais est vraiment le spécialiste des moments intenses et notre marraine, la BnF, revient régulièrement sur scène avec un don inné de la scénographie et une intelligence qui nous ont tant séduits à Richelieu en 2003.

Pourquoi avez-vous sélectionné l'exposition du Grand Palais sur Kupka ?

Parce que c'est un peu la magie du Grand Palais. Parce que l'artiste est magnifique de générosité, de modestie, de singularité. C'est un étudiant à vie qui nourrit son œuvre de tout ce qui provoque son universelle curiosité. C'est également un grand pionnier de l'abstraction, encore méconnu, et nous aimons, face à un si grand talent, à des œuvres si « craquantes », contribuer à rétablir la justice que mérite la beauté !

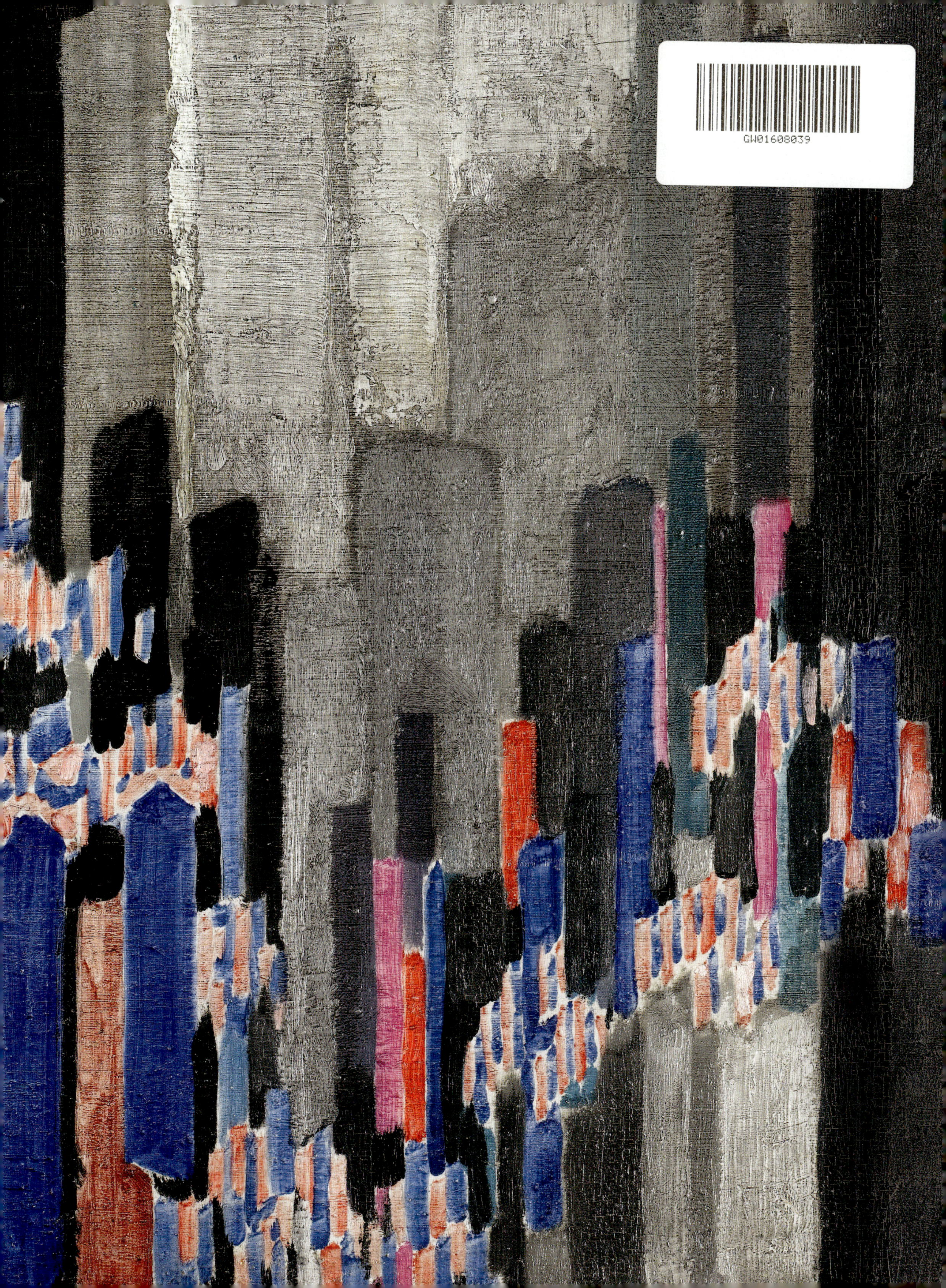